DEFENDING LIFE 2010

Proven Strategies for a Pro-Life America

A State-by-State Legal Guide to
Abortion, Bioethics, and the End of Life

Americans United for Life, Washington, DC 20005 & Chicago, IL 60607

First edition published 2006

Published in the United States of America

978-0-9777204-6-0

Cover & book design by Erin Cox

AMERICANS UNITED FOR LIFE

President & CEO: Charmaine Yoest, Ph.D.

Americans United for Life
655 15th Street NW, Suite 410, Washington, DC 20005; 202-289-1478
310 South Peoria Street, Suite 500, Chicago, IL 60607-3534; 312-568-4700

"This year's AUL legal guide, *Defending Life 2010*, provides a valuable resource for pro-life leaders. This state-by-state scorecard of progress in the effort to defend life lets elected officials, grassroots activists, and citizens know exactly where we are on our shared priority. I am proud that the report reflects the sweeping reforms we have enacted in Texas, saving thousands of lives in the process. This is not a book you leave on the shelf to collect dust. This information is ammunition in a fight that is far from over. I know you will find this guide informative and useful as you continue to promote and protect life in your state."

Rick Perry, Governor, Texas

"*Defending Life* is a valuable resource for anyone dedicated to protecting human life through our legal system. I encourage you to use this resource in your efforts to build a pro-life community across the nation."

Cathy McMorris Rodgers, Member of Congress, Washington

"I really value the rock-solid legal advice in each year's edition of *Defending Life*. From the beginning of life to the end of life, AUL's legal guide has more concrete usable information on pro-life law than any other resource. It is a must-have tool for every state legislator."

Lance Kinzer, State Representative, Kansas

"AUL's *Defending Life* is the best legal resource for state legislators in the country. If you are looking to pass meaningful laws that protect human life from beginning to end, this is the book you need."

Todd Lamb, State Senator, Oklahoma

"*Defending Life 2010* provides a comprehensive resource for state legislators. Not only is the analysis of the legislative and judicial work methodical, but it is also educational in communicating the rights of the unborn."

Linda L. Upmeyer, State Representative, Iowa

"For the past several years, AUL's annual *Defending Life* books have been the go-to source for up to the moment, accurate information of the pro-life pulse in the United States. AUL has earned the reputation as a trusted partner for pro-life legislators across America. May God continue to bless your excellent efforts in leading the pro-life movement."

Delbert Scott, State Senator, Missouri

DEFENDING LIFE 2010

Proven Strategies for a Pro-Life America

A State-by-State Legal Guide to
Abortion, Bioethics, and the End of Life

An Educational Publication of
Americans United for Life
655 15th Street NW, Suite 410
Washington, DC 20005
(202) 289-1478

310 South Peoria Street, Suite 500
Chicago, IL 60607-3534
(312) 568-4700

(800) 626-6149 • www.AUL.org

DEFENDING LIFE 2010 OVERVIEW

FORWARD

BY DAVID J. SHAFER
State Senator, Georgia

As early as I can remember, my parents explained to me that I was a special gift to them. I was adopted.

As I grew older, they explained more. My biological mother was a college student. She was not married to my biological father, although they thought they might one day get married. They had decided that it would be best for me to be raised by a mother and father who were married.

My parents learned about me months before I was born, when their application to adopt a baby was approved and matched to me.

They got a call on the day I was born, and eleven days later they picked me up from the orphanage.

The day before, coincidentally, was Mother's Day.

My mother told me once that it took an hour for them to drive home, and that she held me in her arms the whole way. She said at the end of that car ride, it was as if I had not been hers for just an hour, but for all eleven days and the many months before that.

Many years later, at the urging of the parents who raised me, I visited the place where I was born. The building still stood, but it was no a longer a home for unwed mothers. Instead, it sheltered homeless men.

Also at their urging, I searched for and found my biological mother. In that very first conversation, she brought up abortion, saying I probably wondered if she had considered it. No, she quickly said, she not considered it, because in 1965, it was not something that was considered.

The world has changed, of course. Eight years after I was born, the U.S. Supreme Court declared that unborn babies were not persons. Unwed mothers were suddenly confronted with new and frightening choices. In the years that followed, over 50 million unborn babies have been aborted. Over a million babies are aborted each year, far surpassing deaths from any other cause. Thanks to the Supreme Court, there is no more dangerous place for a baby than the womb.

As you might expect from the circumstances of my birth, the fight to save the lives of the unborn is very personal to me. In my time in the Georgia State Senate, I have done my best to promote legislation protecting life, working to pass bills guaranteeing that mothers faced with an unplanned pregnancy would have access to ultrasound photographs and medical information before being forced to make a decision about abortion.

Americans United for Life (AUL) has been at my side every step of the way. Founded in 1971, more than a year before the decision in *Roe v. Wade*, AUL is the oldest pro-life organization in the country. Long known as "the legal arm of the pro-life movement," AUL has helped legislators like me craft laws to foster a culture where human life is understood, respected, and cherished.

You hold in your hands one of the best resources available in the legislative effort to defend human life. *Defending Life 2010* is a vital tool to help develop and promote new pro-life laws that will save lives and promote a culture of life.

Although we have lost control of the White House and Congress to those who do not share our values on this important issue, I am heartened by the great progress that is nonetheless being made. The number of surgical abortions is on the decline, and the number of Americans who identify themselves as pro-life is on the rise.

Thanks in no small measure to the work of organizations like AUL, we are getting closer to the day that every baby will have the same opportunity I had—to take a first breath in this world, welcomed in love and protected by law.

FROM THE PRESIDENT

Dear Friends of Life:

Welcome to *Defending Life 2010*, our fifth edition of this annual compendium of resources for building a culture of life through the American legal system.

As this year's edition goes to print, we are working strenuously to educate Capitol Hill and the American public about the numerous threats to life and rights of conscience in the healthcare reform bills currently making their way through Congress. Whatever the outcome of this push for healthcare reform legislation, the maneuverings of pro-abortion U.S. senators and representatives—who, at this writing, are consistently defeating efforts to add pro-life correctives to the healthcare bills—reveal their ultimate objective. They will not be satisfied until the nation's laws enshrine the complete moral equivalence of abortion with health care.

Witness the cavalier assertion that California Democratic Rep. Lynn Woolsey made during a congressional debate: "Abortion is a legal medical practice. Why are we even having to talk about it? We're not talking about whether you can or can't have your tonsils out … ."

Imagine a world in which we cannot differentiate between an abortion and a tonsillectomy. This is precisely the situation we now face. The first link on Planned Parenthood's Web site under the organization's name is "health," and the first category under health is "abortion." The abortion lobby wants to win by definition. They know that if they succeed at defining abortion as part of health care, they will have shifted the entire debate.

Yet, as I write this, poll after poll is showing that American public opinion is shifting dramatically against abortion. What is preventing abortion advocates from claiming victory in the fight for the hearts, minds, and wallets of U.S. taxpayers? In no small measure, one reason is the tremendous amount of effort expended by committed pro-life people on the state level.

The majority of states continue to successfully pursue and implement a life-affirming legislative agenda. This year, as the most radically pro-abortion administration in history took shape in Washington, the number of requests AUL received from state legislators and pro-life activists increased exponentially. During the 2009 state legislative sessions, AUL has provided more than 2,400 policy guides and model legislation to more than 325 requestors—more than four times the assistance we provided in 2008. We also actively consulted in 30 states on legislation and potential ballot initiatives.

We are working hard to grow our resources to meet that demand. As I write this, we are preparing a new major initiative for states: a comprehensive, three-tiered plan to achieve the protection of life sought by our movement for so many years.

I feel so fortunate to work with a remarkable team of committed attorneys. And we are deeply grateful we have been able to significantly expand both our legal team and our presence in Washington this year with a move into new office space in Metropolitan Square, across the street from the Treasury Department.

And lastly, we appreciate you. It's a great honor to stand together with men and women across this great country, who share our commitment to working together, "Defending Life."

For Life,

Charmaine Yoest

Charmaine Yoest, Ph.D.
President & CEO

FROM THE EDITOR

Welcome to *Defending Life 2010*! AUL is enormously encouraged by the progress we made in 2009 toward restoring a culture of life, and we are confident that 2010 will be even better!

Importantly, the majority of states have continued their pursuit of life-affirming laws and policies, despite Congress and the Obama Administration's relentless pursuit of a strategy to implement a regime of unregulated and unrestricted abortion-on-demand, to fund unethical and destructive biotechnologies, to coerce and undermine the consciences of healthcare providers, and to marginalize the elderly, the vulnerable, and those facing the end of life.

In 2009, more than 60 pro-life measures were enacted in the states, a marked increase from 2008. This accomplishment is especially notable given that there was a nearly one-third decline in the number of pro-life measures introduced in the states in 2009 (as compared to 2008 activity levels). Several notable and promising developments and trends also emerged in 2009:

- The states considered approximately 300 abortion-related measures, the vast majority of them life-affirming, and virtually every state considered at least one pro-life measure.

- Several states introduced resolutions opposing the federal "Freedom of Choice Act" (FOCA), a radical piece of legislation that would enshrine abortion-on-demand into American law and override all federal and state laws regulating or restricting abortion. Meanwhile, attempts in five states to enact state versions of FOCA were handily defeated.

- States continued to seek to protect the unborn in contexts other than abortion by enacting protections for unborn victims of violence, encouraging substance-abuse treatment for pregnant woman, and providing legal recourse for families whose unborn children are killed through the criminal acts or neglect of others.

- Measures to regulate biotechnologies and to prohibit or restrict technologies that destroy nascent life increased by nearly 20 percent—the first increase in such legislation in 3 years.

- While legislation to protect healthcare providers' freedom of conscience declined by 50 percent, for the first time in three years, measures to protect conscience outpaced measures to violate or compel conscience by a margin of 2 to 1.

- State legislation on end of life issues doubled from 2008 activity levels.

These life-affirming trends—especially during an economic crisis—bode well for the 2010 state legislative sessions and the continuing pursuit of a renewed culture of life.

Many of the necessary building blocks for a culture that respects and protects life and for laws that reflect that desired cultural imperative are contained in this volume. By design, *Defending Life* emphasizes the importance of life-affirming legislation and seeks to educate legislators, the media, and the American public on the full spectrum of life issues and the many opportunities and challenges we face. We also hope it will encourage everyone to stay active and informed not just at the federal level, but also at the state and local levels. As this one-of-a-kind legal guide shows, in the states we are making significant progress—state by state, law by law, and person by person—toward the day when everyone is welcomed in life and protected in law.

Defending Life 2010 has several key components:

- In-depth discussions of key legislative and policy issues related to abortion, protection of the unborn, bioethics, the end of life, and healthcare rights of conscience.

- Review and analysis of the 2009 state legislative sessions, overviews of the important gains and key defeats in the ongoing fight to preserve and defend the sanctity of all human life, and strategic recommendations for each of the 50 states.

- Thirty-two pieces of model legislation developed by AUL experts to assist legislators and policymakers in drafting, debating, and passing life-affirming laws.

- Specific information on each of the states, including an overall ranking of the states and a thorough analysis of each state's successes, opportunities, and challenges.

Thank you for your support of AUL and for *Defending Life*!

Denise M Burke

Denise M. Burke
Vice President of Legal Affairs
Editor-in-Chief

TABLE OF CONTENTS

LEGAL RECOGNITION OF UNBORN & NEWLY BORN 289

BIOETHICS & BIOTECHNOLOGY 341

END OF LIFE 411

HEALTHCARE RIGHTS OF CONSCIENCE 463

STATE OF THE STATES 505

APPENDIX 823

ABORTION

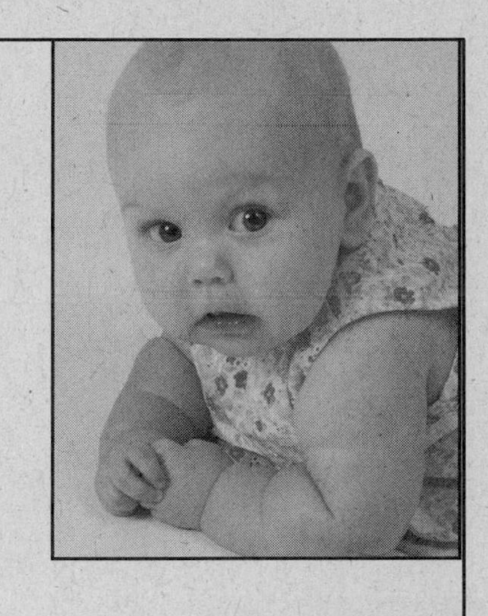

Abortion

Today we find ourselves at a critical juncture in our efforts to protect women and the unborn from the scourge of abortion. More pro-life laws are in effect than ever before, and there is increasing public recognition of the negative impact of abortion on women. However, the current political environment in Washington, D.C. and in some states present new challenges.

Chief among these challenges is the federal "Freedom of Choice Act" (FOCA), a radical attempt to enshrine abortion-on-demand into American law, sweep aside existing laws supported by the majority of Americans (such as requirements that licensed physicians perform abortions, fully-informed consent, and parental involvement), and prevent states from enacting similar protective measures in the future. It is also a cynical attempt by pro-abortion forces to prematurely end the debate over abortion and declare victory in the face of mounting evidence that the American public does not support the vast majority of abortions being performed in the U.S. each year and that abortion has a substantial negative impact on women. Moreover, the aims of FOCA can be realized through either one comprehensive piece of legislation or by the current piecemeal approach being pursued by Congress and the Obama Administration.

Clearly, FOCA's reach is intentionally broad. It would immediately wipe away many of the pro-life gains achieved over the past 20 years.

These gains have been realized, in large part, through a systematic and strategic effort in the states to select tactical steps that provide real gains today while laying the groundwork for much larger gains in the future. We often think of momentous U.S. Supreme Court rulings such as *Roe v. Wade* as arriving suddenly on the scene. For the general public, these landmark cases sometimes come as a surprise, radically changing our law, social policy, and culture. However, for those working for the change, the landmark case often represents not a sudden break with the past, but the culmination of decades of persistent legal work to build precedent through small victories.

Mississippi provides an excellent example of the effectiveness of a systematic legal strategy to combat the evil of abortion. Over the past 15 years,

Mississippi has adopted more than 15 pro-life laws. As a result, abortions in the state have decreased by nearly 60% and six out of seven abortion clinics have closed—leaving only one embattled abortion clinic in the entire state.

AUL actively advocates the systematic adoption and implementation of life-affirming laws in the states. In this section, we provide state lawmakers, state Attorneys General, public policy groups, lobbyists, the media, and others involved in the cause for life with proven legal strategies and tools that will, step by step and state by state, lead to a more pro-life America and help set the stage of the state-by-state battle that will follow *Roe*'s ultimate reversal.

This Section includes topical overviews on a range of important legislative strategies and initiatives, along with AUL's model legislation. These resources are specifically designed to implement effectively a systematic pro-life strategy proven to reduce abortions and to protect women from the negative consequences of abortion.

The Road Map To Overturning *Roe v. Wade*

What can the states do now?

By Clarke D. Forsythe
Senior Counsel, Americans United for Life

"*What we call abortion today will be looked back on as barbarism and one of the reasons is that [future generations] will be able to better control fertility...This notion of surgical abortion is going to be looked back on as barbaric.*"
- William Saletan, Contributor, *Slate*[1]

Efforts to overturn *Roe v. Wade* began immediately after the decision was handed down. Although the overturning of *Roe* will not happen during the Obama Presidency and may seem to be a long-term prospect, there are progressive steps the states need to take to be ready for that opportunity. Those steps will, in turn, result in the states becoming more pro-life socially, politically, and legally.[2]

State legislators and state policy organizations need to have an articulated vision for a culture of life in their state, a clear understanding of the opportunities and obstacles before them, a comprehensive plan that they are actively working toward year by year, and a track record of success.

It is a tall order, especially when considering judicially-imposed abortion-on-demand in every state and the aggressive push for abortion by the Obama Administration and by the 111th Congress. And it helps explain why comprehensive protection for human life has so far eluded our grasp.

Because the President and Congress will aggressively push abortion as much as possible over the next three years, the states—and state organizations—are key. What the states accomplish, or don't, in the next several years—in terms of legislative protection for life, medical regulations to protect women, and reducing the number of abortions—will largely determine the future of *Roe*: whether, how, and on what timeframe it will be overturned. The states are the constitutional forum in American politics best positioned to reflect public opinion on abortion and to take positive action to protect human life and protect women from the negative impact of abortion. And just as abortions dropped approximately 19 percent during the Clinton years because of life-affirming state legislation and other factors, new political, legislative, educational, and cultural initiatives can have an impact in undermining *Roe* and reducing abortion even while the Obama Administration is in power.

What follows outlines five essential elements to help a state effectively plan for the overturning of *Roe*:

(1) Strategic assessment;
(2) Comprehensive plan;
(3) Task force on status of abortion law when *Roe* is overturned;
(4) Legislative building blocks for success; and
(5) Raising public awareness of the nega-

tive impact of abortion on women.

(1) Start With a Strategic Assessment

States need to thoroughly and frankly assess the strengths and weaknesses of their organizations and accomplishments and thoroughly understand the cultural, political, legislative, and constitutional obstacles that impede their success before they can identify solutions to those obstacles. What has been the track record in the state legislature over the past decade? Is the legislature improving in pro-life strength? Legislative victories, even small ones, build important political momentum.

Despite *Roe*, states have enacted legislation over the past three decades that has limited the abortion license, reduced abortions, increased legal protection for the unborn, and increased protection for women from the physical and psychological risks of abortion. For example, 36 states have unborn victims of violence laws which virtually did not exist in 1973, and 26 of those establish legal protection at conception. Likewise, 32 states have informed consent laws that didn't exist in 1973.

Looking forward, there are strategies the states can pursue that can improve the situation, prepare the ground for future progress, and work toward a culture of life. A spectrum of political and legislative success is outlined in the 50-state ranking in *Defending Life 2006-2010*. Different states are on different points of the spectrum in their ability to limit abortion and protect life in the law. Louisiana and Mississippi are very different from California and New York. But all states need a vision of a culture of life in their state and a strategy to get there from where they are in 2010.

A few states have devised a plan to prepare their state for the overturning of *Roe* and are making periodic assessments. Criteria for such an assessment can be found in the State Rankings in *Defending Life 2006-2010*. A comprehensive strategy will necessarily include constitutional, political, legislative, educational, and cultural initiatives because the national policy of abortion-on-demand—imposed by the federal courts in every state—has become a broadly-based problem, ingrained in our culture over the past 37 years.

(2) A Long-Term Comprehensive Plan

Roe v. Wade is a tremendous obstacle to a culture of life in America. By distorting the U.S. Constitution, the Supreme Court imposed a law of abortion-on-demand in every state and county across the country and empowered federal courts in every state to eliminate abortion prohibitions or regulations that arguably conflict with *Roe*. No matter how strongly public opinion may support abortion prohibitions or regulations, the federal courts are empowered by *Roe* to invalidate and sweep away that popular support, and they have done so in hundreds of instances over the past 37 years.

A direct assault on *Roe*—by constitutional amendment or through the courts—is not feasible in the next three years because of obstacles currently beyond our control. Those obstacles include the Obama Administration (which is aggressively pro-abortion), the current political make-up of the U.S. Senate (which is aggressively pro-abortion and responsible for confirming new justices), the current makeup of the U.S. Supreme Court, and the state of public opinion.

For example, we do not have five votes on the

Supreme Court to overturn *Roe*, let alone the six that would be realistically necessary for a stable overruling. The makeup of the Supreme Court is unlikely to improve during the Obama Administration, and it may become even more pro-abortion.[3]

For these reasons, a long-term plan is necessary. The five primary elements of such a comprehensive plan include:

- A constitutional strategy which (1) corrects state activist court decisions creating a state version of *Roe,* or (2) prevents state judges from taking policy and legal determinations inherent in the abortion issue away from the people;
- A legislative strategy that (1) restricts abortion as much as possible in light of federal court obstruction, and (2) makes abortion an anomaly by affirmatively protecting a developing human being outside the context of abortion as much as possible;
- An educational strategy that (1) increases public awareness that abortion is bad for women socially, physically, and psychologically, (2) denigrates Supreme Court control of the abortion issue, and (3) helps voters understand both the practical implications of *Roe* and of overturning *Roe*;
- A political strategy that establishes the protection of human life as a key political value for voters and elects public leaders who oppose legal abortion and other assaults on human life and dignity; and
- A cultural strategy that (1) reduces out-of-wedlock pregnancy, (2) strengthens marriage, (3) builds an ever-widening network of services to women with unplanned pregnancies, and (4) informs women and citizens generally of those services.

(3) Task Force on Status of Abortion Law When Roe is Overturned

Abortion prohibitions were effectively enforced before *Roe* to protect women and unborn children from abortion. But abortion prohibitions no longer exist in more than 40 states—either because they have been repealed or because a state judicial version of *Roe* makes them unenforceable. Contrary to public assumption, there will be no immediate change in the states when *Roe* is overturned. Abortion will remain legal in most states until the legislature affirmatively acts.

Thus, a task force within each state—made up of doctors, lawyers, legislators, law enforcement experts, and others—should be recruited to evaluate the legal status of abortion in that state when *Roe* is overturned.[4]

That task force should also anticipate legislative and judicial moves by abortion advocates to block the enforcement of any current or new laws, and create a media and legislative plan to pass the strongest possible limits on abortion and to enforce them effectively.

(4) Legislative Building Blocks for Success

Given the severe constraints of the Supreme Court's decisions in *Roe v. Wade*, *Doe v. Bolton*, and *Planned Parenthood v. Casey*, AUL's model legislation regarding abortion is designed to do several things:

- Affirmatively protect the unborn child within the context of abortion;
- Affirmatively protect the unborn child outside the context of abortion;
- Reduce abortions as much as possible;
- Limit the scope of the abortion license in law;
- Protect women from the dangers and risks of abortion;
- Educate women, legislators and the public about the risks of abortion; and
- Create test court cases with various objectives, such as improving medical regulations, limiting the sweep of *Roe,* demonstrating the contradictions of *Roe*, and educating the public.

This requires a close examination of current obstacles and opportunities, especially of what the Supreme Court and the justices have said in previous cases.

Every issue of *Defending Life* includes model legislation to further these objectives. These models are also available on AUL's website (www.AUL.org).

(5) Public Awareness of the Negative Impact of Abortion on Women

Progress will depend on raising public awareness of the negative impact of abortion on women through education and legislation.

James Hunter's analysis of the 1991 Gallup Poll on "Abortion and Moral Beliefs" in his book, *Before the Shooting Begins,* shows that the American public and women see abortion as two sides of a coin: the impact (from abortion or restricting it) on the unborn, and the impact (from abortion or restricting it) on women. His analysis also shows that the public adheres to a series of myths about abortion (its benefit to women) and about *Roe* (the impact of overturning it). The public sees legal abortion as a "necessary evil," bad for the unborn child but good for women (keeping them out of the "back alley" by providing safe abortions).

For this reason, public education that emphasizes the impact on the unborn alone is insufficient because it fails to account for this paradigm. The public is concerned about both the impact on women and the impact on the unborn from abortion or from abortion prohibitions.

The Supreme Court, along with the public, assumes that legal abortion is, on balance, good for women. Justice Blackmun, in the Court's opinion in *Roe,* relied on the assumption that "abortion is safer than childbirth." The data the Court relied upon was thin and flawed, and no attention was given to the long-term risks of abortion. Critically, the public is still not aware of the true risks.

Legislation that focuses on short-term and long-term risks to women can educate legislators, the public, and the media. Public awareness can and must be made through both education and legislation.

Further Considerations

Political Obstacles and Solutions

There is an obvious dynamic between legislation and elections. States should have a plan to use each election cycle as a means of increasing pro-life representation in the legislature and educate voters to view a candidate's position on abortion as a key qualifying criterion.

Political obstacles can tie up pro-life legislation for years, and it requires persistence and a carefully tailored strategy to circumvent such obstacles. For example, Tennessee recently finished an eight-year battle over legislation. It began in 2000 when the Tennessee Supreme Court manufactured a right to abortion in the state constitution in *Planned Parenthood v. Sundquist.*[5]

A constitutional amendment to overturn the decision was introduced in 2001, but it was stymied by the Speaker of the House every year until 2009. With a new speaker, the Tennessee House and Senate finally passed SJR 127 in 2009, a state constitutional amendment intended to overturn *Sundquist*. When the vote finally came, all Republicans and more than half of the Democrats voted for the amendment.[6]

Examples such as this demonstrate that pro-life citizens in each state need to be organized and focused on supporting pro-life public officials and candidates for public office. Educational and legislative campaigns are necessary building blocks to political reform because they shape the political climate and the issues that make up the next election campaign.

For example, each state needs one or more effective political action committees (PACs) to help pro-life public officials and provide an opportunity for pro-life citizens to identify and financially assist pro-life officials and candidates. Pro-life governors, attorneys general, legislators, and state and county prosecutors are key, because they are the state legal officials who will vote for pro-life laws, sign them, defend them in court, or effectively enforce them.

Educational Obstacles & Solutions

Legislative initiatives are limited or supported by public opinion and how legislators read public opinion. Therefore, public and media education is key to shaping public understanding that will in turn support legislation.

Effective public education on abortion must effectively address the paradigm that the public views the abortion issue as two sides of a coin (balancing the impact on the unborn and the impact on women) and sees legal abortion as a "necessary evil." In general, the American public is in ignorance regarding the risks of abortion. Therefore, the answer to the myth of abortion as a necessary evil is to raise public awareness of the negative impact on women.

Because there are so many myths about abortion and *Roe*, public education to prepare a state needs to emphasize seven themes:

1) Abortion is bad for women.
2) The people should decide the abortion issue, not the Supreme Court.
3) The Supreme Court causes abortion to be uniquely controversial because it imposes a nationwide policy of abortion—for any reason, at any time of pregnancy—that is supported by only seven percent of Americans.
4) Overturning *Roe* means the people will decide the issue.
5) Overturning *Roe* will leave abortion legal in most states until the legislature affirmatively acts.
6) The law can protect women and the unborn through abortion laws just as it has through unborn victims of violence laws, wrongful death laws, and

other laws that confer legal recognition and protection on the unborn.

7) There are resources/services available to enable a woman to carry to term and to raise a child or to formulate an adoption plan.

No state educational strategy can be effective without a vibrant and coordinated media strategy which employs press releases, media interviews, op-ed articles, comprehensive website/online content, and blogging to spotlight legislative issues, the positions and decisions of public officials and candidates, and the conflict between pro-life policies and pro-abortion policies. In addition, the power of social media (*e.g.* Facebook, Twitter, and YouTube) is in going "viral." For example, within a few months after the 2008 elections, www.FightFOCA.com's online anti-Freedom of Choice Act (FOCA) petition hit over 700,000 signatures.

Constitutional Obstacles & Solutions

State constitutions may be shaped by legislatures and ratified by the people, but they are often distorted by judges. Constitutional provisions, state supreme court decisions, or constitutional changes by ballot initiatives may block positive judicial or legislative changes.

Currently, 16 states need to overturn state versions of *Roe*—state appellate decisions creating a right to abortion under the auspices of the state constitution.[7] Even when *Roe* is overturned, these state court decisions will block enforcement of abortion prohibitions and perhaps abortion regulations as well.

Generally, the evidence suggests that appointed state supreme courts, which are less responsive to the people, have been more pro-abortion than elected judiciaries.[8] Thus, pro-life leaders must monitor and oppose efforts in their states to move state appellate judiciaries, especially the state supreme or highest court, toward an appointed system.

Effectively Protecting Persons

Protecting the unborn as human persons is important. But the most important question is: What are the most effective means? How can developing human beings be effectively protected in the context of current opportunities and obstacles?

Unborn victims of violence laws and wrongful death laws have progressively done this, state by state, for the past quarter century. States should work for unborn victims of violence, wrongful death laws, and other laws[9] that protect the unborn from conception. These are essential building blocks to more comprehensive protection. But, if states have these in force, what more can be done?

"Personhood" organizations have sprouted in various states to sponsor state human life amendments (HLAs) or constitutional personhood amendments. States must thoroughly explore the pros and cons of abstract state human life (personhood) amendments. These have been proposed in several states without a track record of success, sufficient deliberation, or any effective plan to succeed.

Certain questions need to be answered. What is the purpose of such an amendment? Is it intended to overturn *Roe v. Wade*? Or is it intended to fix a legal or constitutional problem in the particular state?

Realistically, a personhood amendment cannot and will not overturn *Roe* because it does not create a direct conflict with *Roe* and because the U.S. Supreme Court can easily refuse to hear any case. The Court has rejected similar cases on numerous occasions over the past three decades. The most likely result is either the Supreme Court will refuse to hear the case or the courts will follow the result in the case of Arkansas Amendment 68 (1988), where Amendment 68 did not create a direct conflict with *Roe* and the Amendment was invalidated only insofar as it conflicted with the federal Hyde Amendment.[10]

The real question is whether an amendment, or which version of an amendment, can fix a particular constitutional problem in the state. This requires a state-by-state—not a one-size-fits-all—evaluation.

If a state has already enacted unborn victims of violence laws, wrongful death laws, and other protective laws that provide legal recognition and protection from conception, the state might consider (1) a constitutional amendment specifically drafted to address the state version of *Roe*, as Tennessee did in 2009; (2) a constitutional amendment like that in the Rhode Island constitution, which neutralizes the state constitution as an independent source of abortion rights,[11] or the Arkansas constitution which relates to the public funding of abortion;[12] or (3) statutory preambles like the Missouri preamble, which includes wording that human life begins at conception and unborn children have protectable interests in life and well-being, and which was permitted to go into effect (without a specific ruling as to constitutionality) by the U.S. Supreme Court.[13] The "State Constitutional Amendment" in this volume is one option.

At the very least, before any such amendment is considered, legislative and political building blocks for success should be in place.

Conclusion

Clearly, state organizations cannot do all of this at once. They need to constantly strive to improve and consistently look to and learn from those who are doing it better. The most challenging aspect is deciding what priorities need to be addressed in an ordered manner to build success, public awareness, and political momentum. In that regard, AUL has developed a powerful tool—*Defending Life*—to help states prioritize their strategy and take steps to best implement a lasting culture of life.

Endnotes

[1] Tocqueville Forum Roundtable on Bioethics, *Technology and the Human Person: Prospects for the Future of American Democracy* at 53:04 (Georgetown University October 11, 2008), available at https://mediapilot.georgetown.edu/sharestream2gui/getMedia.do?action=streamMedia&mediaPath=0d21b6201e2c11dd011e3aa64cb90020&cid=0d21b6201df9d7e6011e20cfb5eb0052&userFrom=deeplinking (last visited September 8, 2009).

[2] *See The Road Map to Reversing* Roe v. Wade, Defending Life 2009 63 (2009) (framed in the wake of the U.S. Supreme Court's 2007 decision in *Gonzales v. Carhart* and the 2008 elections).

[3] Justice Sotomayor will not tip the balance on the Court, but she will solidify and extend into the future the pro-*Roe* majority on the Court. There is still a majority—Roberts, Kennedy, Scalia, Thomas, Alito—who will uphold virtually any regulation of abortion that makes medical sense.

[4] A good place to start would be a careful reading of Paul Benjamin Linton, *The Legal Status of Abortion in the States if* Roe v. Wade *is Overruled*, 23 Issues in Law & Medicine 3 (2007).

[5] 38 S.W.3d 1 (Tenn. 2000).

[6] By law, both chambers of the legislature must again adopt SJR 127 in the 2011-12 legislative session before it is placed on the ballot in 2014.

[7] *See Judicial Activism Also Plagues the States: State Constitutional Rights to Abortion*, Defending Life 2009 127 (2009).

[8] *See* AUL's State Supreme Court Project, available at http://www.aul.org/State_Supreme_Courts (last visited September 9,

2009).

[9] *See Primer on Legal Recognition and Protection of the Unborn and Newly Born, supra.*

[10] *See Little Rock Family Planning Services v. Dalton*, 860 F.Supp. 609 (E.D. Ark. 1994), *aff'd*, 60 F.3d 497 (8th Cir. 1995), *cert. denied in part, rev'd in part*, 516 U.S. 474, 475-76 (1996) ("We grant certiorari as to the second of these questions. Accepting (without deciding) that the District Court's interpretation of the Hyde Amendment is correct, we reverse the decision below insofar as it affirms blanket invalidation of Amendment 68.").

[11] *See* Art. I, § 2 of the constitution of Rhode Island.

[12] *See* Amendment 68, § 1 of the constitution of Arkansas.

[13] *Webster v. Reprod. Health Servs.*, 492 U.S. 490 (1989).

Beware of FOCA-by-Stealth:
How a radical abortion-on-demand agenda is being implemented piecemeal, and how it could impact the states

By Denise M. Burke
Vice President of Legal Affairs, Americans United for Life

Beginning in the spring of 2009, abortion advocates and their allies began insisting in the media and in communications with their supporters that the "Freedom of Choice Act" (FOCA), while important, was not an immediate priority and concerned Americans had overreacted to a piece of legislation that had not even been introduced in the current Congress. And despite having control of Congress and the Executive Branch, some even appeared to confess they do not have the votes needed for passage.

What are the reasons for this sudden and very public change of tune? Why—when they have President Obama's promise to finally enact FOCA, 20 years after it was first proposed—do they appear to be quickly conceding defeat?

The apparent back-pedaling on a long-established priority is a testament to the ferocious opposition engendered by this radical federal power-grab masquerading as common legislation. However, as history has repeatedly shown, abortion advocates' apparent concessions should be viewed with a great deal of skepticism. Now more than ever, we need to beware of FOCA-by-Stealth: attempts by the Administration, Congress, and abortion advocates to enact FOCA piecemeal while purposefully attempting to deflect—or at least neutralize—public opposition to their far-reaching abortion-on-demand agenda.

Clearly, the Administration, Congress, and abortion advocates have stolen a page from the successful pro-life playbook of progressive strategy. However, instead of targeted laws designed to fence in the abortion license and to protect women from the negative impact of abortion, they are using a variety of executive, budgetary, and legislative means to realize their "full vision of reproductive freedom"—code words for unrestricted, unregulated, unapologetic, and taxpayer-funded abortion-on-demand.

Recognizing an Ally, Abortion Advocates Waste No Time Making Demands

In December 2008 (just one month after the election), a coalition of pro-abortion groups—including Planned Parenthood, NARAL Pro-Choice America, and the American Civil Liberties Union (ACLU)—gave an expansive set of "marching orders" to the Obama Administration. In a 55-page memorandum subsequently posted on the Obama Transition Team's website, the coalition urged the incoming Administration to, among other things:

- Rescind the "Mexico City Policy" first implemented by President Ronald Reagan in 1984 to prohibit federal taxpayer funding of programs and organizations that promote or perform abortions overseas.

- Restore federal taxpayer funding for the United Nations Population Fund (UNFPA), which actively promotes abortion worldwide and is arguably complicit in the continued enforcement of restrictive population control programs and forced abortions.
- Remove U.S. Food and Drug Administration (FDA) restrictions on minors' access to over-the-counter "emergency contraceptives" (also known as Plan B). Then-existing FDA protocols required girls under 18 years of age to have a valid prescription for this potentially-dangerous drug.
- Reverse the December 2008 decision by the U.S. Department of Health and Human Services (HHS) requiring recipients of certain federal funding to certify compliance with existing federal laws protecting healthcare professionals who are morally opposed to promoting or providing abortions or contraceptives.
- Appoint federal judges—including U.S. Supreme Court justices—who support abortion rights and would interpret that right in an increasingly expansive and radical manner.
- Increase Title X family planning funding, which provides funding to Planned Parenthood, from $300 million in fiscal year 2009 to at least $700 million in 2010.
- Repeal the Hyde Amendment, which limits federal taxpayer funding for abortions of Medicaid-eligible women.
- Provide federal taxpayer funding of abortions for federal employees and their dependents, members of the Armed Forces and their dependents, residents of the District of Columbia, Peace Corps volunteers, Native American women, and women in federal prisons.
- Increase federal funding of international family planning programs from $461 million in fiscal year 2009 to $1 billion for 2010.
- Ensure public funding for abortion is included in any healthcare reform legislation.

Finally and predictably, the document also specifically called on President Obama to take the lead in calling for Congress to pass the "Freedom of Choice Act" and—as he has already promised—sign it into law once it arrives at his desk.

Each of the demands listed above—and others contained in this controversial and extensive wish list—embody the "spirit of FOCA" and represent incremental but critical steps toward implementing its radical agenda. Sadly, the Obama Administration and its allies in Congress have acted quickly to meet and even exceed the demands of abortion activists.[1]

How Is FOCA's Expansive and Radical Agenda Being Implemented?

Despite the increasing backlash against both FOCA and the Administration's apparent desire to centralize power and authority in the federal government at the expense of the States and the people, abortion advocates within and outside the Administration have not been dissuaded from their goal of unfettered, federal government-controlled, and taxpayer-funded abortion-on-demand. Instead, they are clearly determined to pursue what they believe is the path of least resistance: FOCA-by-Stealth.

Rather than a direct and possibly losing battle and debate over FOCA as a single piece of legislation, they are resorting to a strategy of incremental and relentless implementation of the principles, spirit, and intent of FOCA. In pursuit of this strategy, they are already using a variety of tools including Executive Orders; Executive Branch appointments; federal budget appropriations; federal legislation; action on long-standing budgetary riders; efforts to overhaul the nation's healthcare system; and even potential Senate ratification of international conventions to advance and fund a radical pro-abortion agenda.[2]

How Will the FOCA-by-Stealth Agenda Impact the States?

FOCA—whether implemented as a single piece of legislation or piecemeal—creates a new and dangerously radical right. It establishes the right to abortion as a "fundamental right," elevating it to the same status as the right to vote and the right to free speech (which, unlike the abortion license, are specifically mentioned in the U.S. Constitution). Critically, in *Roe v. Wade*, the Supreme Court did not define abortion as a fundamental right. And, with the exception of a couple of minor attempts by specific justices in later opinions to distort the Court's jurisprudence and classify abortion as a fundamental right, the Court has not subsequently defined abortion as a fundamental right.[3] Thus, FOCA goes beyond any Supreme Court decision in enshrining unlimited abortion-on-demand into American law.

FOCA would also subject laws regulating or even touching on abortion to judicial review using a "strict scrutiny" framework of analysis. This is the highest standard American courts can apply and is typically reserved for laws impacting such fundamental rights as the right to free speech and the right to vote. Prior to the Supreme Court's 1992 decision in *Planned Parenthood v. Casey* (which substituted the "undue burden" standard for the more stringent strict scrutiny analysis), abortion-related laws (such parental involvement for minors and minimum health and safety standards for abortion clinics) were almost uniformly struck down under strict scrutiny analysis. If enacted, FOCA would be applied retroactively to all federal and state abortion-related laws and would result in their invalidation.

In elevating abortion to a fundamental right, FOCA poses an undeniable and irreparable danger to common-sense laws supported by a majority of Americans. Among the more than 550 federal and state laws that FOCA would nullify are:

- "Partial Birth Abortion Ban Act of 2003;"
- "Hyde Amendment" (restricting tax-

payer funding of abortions);

- Restrictions on abortions performed at military hospitals;
- Restrictions on insurance coverage for abortion for federal employees;
- Informed consent laws;
- Reflection periods;
- Parental consent and notification laws;
- Health and safety regulations for abortion clinics;
- Requirements that licensed physicians perform abortions;
- "Delayed enforcement" laws (banning abortion when *Roe v. Wade* is overturned and/or the authority to restrict abortion is returned to the states);
- Bans on partial-birth abortion;
- Bans on abortion after viability. FOCA's apparent attempt to limit post-viability abortions is illusory. Under FOCA, post-viability abortions are expressly permitted to protect the woman's "health." Within the context of abortion, "health" has been interpreted so broadly that FOCA would not actually proscribe any abortion before or after viability.
- Limits on public funding for elective abortions (thus, making American taxpayers fund a procedure that many find morally objectionable);
- Limits on the use of public facilities (such has public hospitals and medical schools at state universities) for abortions;
- State and federal legal protections for individual healthcare providers who decline to participate in abortions;
- Legal protections for Catholic and other religiously-affiliated hospitals who, while providing care to millions of poor and uninsured Americans, refuse to allow abortions within their facilities.

Notably, pro-abortion groups do not deny FOCA's draconian impact. For example, Planned Parenthood has explained, "FOCA will supercede anti-choice laws that restrict the right to choose, including laws that prohibit the public funding of abortions for poor women or counseling and referrals for abortions. Additionally, FOCA will prohibit onerous restrictions on a woman's right to choose, such as mandated delays and targeted and medically unnecessary regulations."[4]

What Has Been the Impact of State FOCA's?

To date, seven states have enacted versions of FOCA, further entrenching and protecting the right to abortion in those states: California, Connecticut, Hawaii, Maine, Maryland, Nevada, and Washington.

Notably, states that have enacted FOCAs have experienced increases in abortion rates despite the steady decrease in the national abortion rate over the past 15 years and/or have maintain abortion rates that are often significantly higher than the national rate. Supporting evidence for this conclusion is aptly provided by the experiences of Maryland and Nevada—both of which enacted state FOCAs in the early 1990s.

Maryland enacted a FOCA in 1991. According to the pro-abortion Alan Guttmacher Institute, Maryland's abortion rate[5] in 1991 was approximately 4.6 percent higher than the national

rate. However, from 1991 through 2005, Maryland's abortion rate increased each year while the national rate declined each year. Notably, in 2005 (14 years after enacting a FOCA), Maryland's abortion rate was 62 percent higher than the national rate.

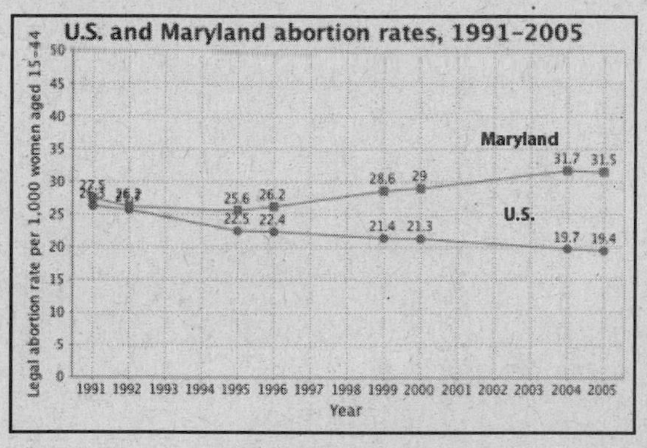

Source: Guttmacher Institute

Further, Nevada enacted a FOCA by ballot initiative in 1990. From 1991 through 2000, the Nevada abortion rate remained consistently higher (and, at times, significantly higher) than the national abortion rate.

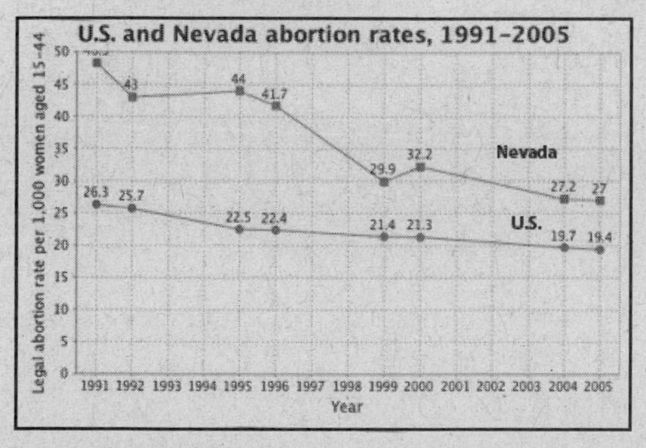

Source: Guttmacher Institute

The experience of these states aptly demonstrates that the enactment of a federal FOCA will not reduce abortion rates, but will likely result in an increase in abortions nationwide. This would reverse the trend of the last 15 years, during which we have experienced a notable decrease in the abortion rate—a decrease directly attributable to the enactment of protective state laws like informed consent and parental involvement. However, it is these protective and effective laws and others that FOCA targets for elimination.

What Can the States Do to Oppose FOCA?

It is critical the states continue to push and enact protective and life-affirming legislation, demonstrating a continuing commitment to women and the unborn. Specific recommendations for each of the 50 states are available in the State Report Cards section of this volume. Moreover, states should consider collectively voicing their opposition to FOCA through legislative resolutions and other measures. AUL has prepared a model state resolution opposing the "Freedom of Choice Act." In 2009, this resolution was adopted in Georgia, Missouri, and Oklahoma.[6]

Conclusion

Clearly, FOCA will not make abortion safe or rare; on the contrary, it will actively promote abortion and do nothing to ensure its safety. Thus, abortion advocates' unrelenting campaign to enact FOCA is a wake-up call to all Americans. If implemented, FOCA would invalidate common-sense, protective state laws the majority of Americans support. It would not protect or empower women. Instead, it would protect and promote the abortion industry, sacrifice women and their health to a radical political ideology, and silence the voices of everyday Americans who want to engage in a meaningful public discussion over the availability, safety, and even desirability of abortion.

Endnotes

[1] For a timeline of actions taken by Congress and the Obama Administration that are furthering FOCA-by-Stealth, see http://www.aul.org/FOCAbyStealthTimelin (last visited August 26, 2009).

[2] For more analysis of FOCA-by-Stealth, *see* http://www.aul.org/FOCA_by_stealth (last visited August 26, 2009).

[3] *See City of Akron v. Akron Ctr for Reproductive Health*, 462 U.S. 416, 420 n.1 (1983) (majority opinion authored by Justice Powell) and *Thornburgh v. ACOG*, 476 U.S. 747, 772 (1986) ("A woman's right to make that choice freely is fundamental.").

[4] *See e.g.* http://www.nrlc.org/FOCA/PPFAfoca-questions-12445.mht (a January 2004 factsheet published by the Planned Parenthood Federation of America) (last visited August 26, 2009).

[5] The "abortion rate" is defined as the number of women per 1,000 in the state who underwent an abortion in any given year.

[6] More information about the "Freedom of Choice Act" is available at www.fightfoca.com (a project of AUL Action).

Abortion:
A survey of federal and state laws

By Mailee R. Smith
Staff Counsel, Americans United for Life

In *Roe v. Wade*,[1] the U.S. Supreme Court held that the right of privacy secured by the Due Process Clause of the Fourteenth Amendment includes a woman's "fundamental right" to determine whether or not to terminate her pregnancy. Since that time, legislatures have attempted to dampen the blow of abortion-on-demand by regulating the practice of abortion through legislation aimed at protecting both women and the unborn. The following is a general survey of federal and state laws regarding the most prominent of these regulations and issues.

Informed Consent

Generally, informed consent laws (also known as women's "right-to-know" laws) require certain information to be provided to a woman before her consent to an abortion is truly informed. The U.S. Supreme Court not only upheld Pennsylvania's informed consent law in *Planned Parenthood v. Casey*,[2] but it also refused to review a lower court ruling which found Mississippi's informed consent law constitutional.[3] The Court stated that the "right to choose" does not prohibit a state from taking steps to ensure that a woman's choice is informed and thoughtful.[4] The Court held, "In attempting to ensure that a woman apprehends the full consequences of her decision, the State furthers the legitimate purpose of reducing the risk that a woman may elect an abortion, only to discover later, with devastating psychological consequences, that her decision was not fully informed."[5]

Further, the Court also upheld Pennsylvania's 24-hour reflection period. The Court stated, "The idea that important decisions will be more informed and deliberate if they follow some period of reflection does not strike us as unreasonable, particularly where the statute directs that important information become part of the background of the decision."[6] While Planned Parenthood argued that such reflection periods create an undue burden on women, the Court disagreed. Instead, the Court held that a 24-hour reflection period is not an undue burden, even if such a law has the effect of increasing the cost and risk of delay of abortions.[7] The Court concluded that such information requirements are rationally related to a state's legitimate interest in ensuring that a woman's consent to abortion be fully informed. Furthermore, the Court held that it is not unconstitutional to require the physician to be the person providing the mandated information.[8]

In 2007, the Court reaffirmed the states' substantial interests in providing women with accurate medical information. In *Gonzales v. Carhart*, the Court stated that "it seems unexceptionable to conclude some women come to regret their choice to abort the infant life they once created and sustained," noting "[s]evere depression and loss of esteem can follow."[9] The Court went on to conclude "[t]he State has an interest in ensuring so grave a choice is well informed."[10] These acknowledgements pave the way for states to promulgate more protective informed consent laws.

Currently, 32 state informed consent laws are in effect, 24 of which require one-day (usually 24-hour) reflection periods before the performance of an abortion.[11] States have also begun requiring information be given to women regarding fetal pain, the availability of ultrasounds, and the existence of a link between abortion and breast cancer.

Parental Involvement

Parental involvement laws[12] are also constitutional under the U.S. Supreme Court's decision in *Casey*. Specifically, the Court stated, "Our cases establish, and we reaffirm today, that a State may require a minor seeking an abortion to obtain the consent of a parent or guardian, provided that there is an adequate judicial bypass procedure."[13] The Court also stated certain provisions have "*particular force* with respect to minors."[14] For example, a reflection period provides parents with an opportunity to consult with the minor and "discuss the consequences of her decision in the context of the values and moral or religious principles of their family."[15]

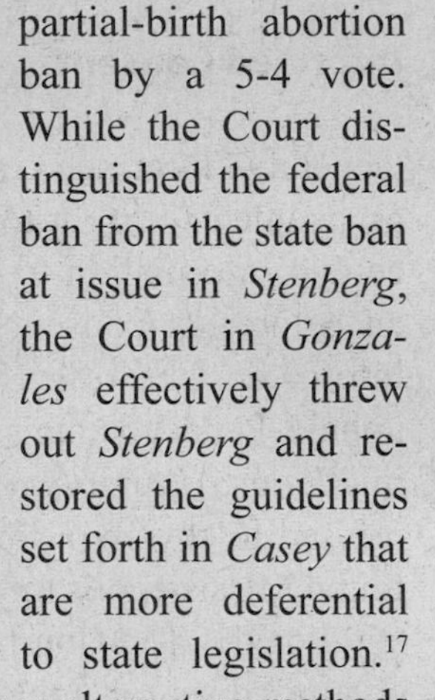

Thirty-seven state parental involvement laws are currently in effect. Twenty-five states require parental consent for minors seeking abortion, and twelve states require parental notice for minors seeking abortion.[16]

Partial-Birth Abortion

The seminal case on partial-birth abortion is *Gonzales v. Carhart*, decided in April 2007. Reacting to the Court's earlier (2000) decision in *Stenberg v. Carhart* (invalidating 30 state bans on partial-birth abortion), Congress enacted the "Partial Birth Abortion Ban Act," which President George W. Bush signed into law in November 2003. While the Act sought to prohibit the performance of partial-birth abortions across the nation, it immediately met a firestorm of litigation, culminating in the *Gonzales* decision.

In *Gonzales*, the Court upheld the federal partial-birth abortion ban by a 5-4 vote. While the Court distinguished the federal ban from the state ban at issue in *Stenberg*, the Court in *Gonzales* effectively threw out *Stenberg* and restored the guidelines set forth in *Casey* that are more deferential to state legislation.[17] Because there were other alternative methods for late-term abortions, the Court ruled the federal ban did not require a health exception.[18] The Court also narrowed the unlimited health exception laid out in *Doe v. Bolton* to a focus on "significant health risks"—effectively rejecting the contention that an unlimited emotional health exception is required for every

abortion regulation.[19]

The federal ban is now the gold standard for state partial-birth abortion bans. Currently, 18 states maintain enforceable partial-birth abortion bans.[20]

Public Funding of Abortion

Congress passed the Hyde Amendment in 1976, which restricts federal funding of Medicaid abortions to cases of life endangerment, rape, and incest. In *Harris v. McRae*, a case championed by AUL, the U.S. Supreme Court upheld the Hyde Amendment and also held that states participating in the Medicaid program are not required under Title XIX of the Social Security Act to fund medically-necessary abortions for which there is no federal reimbursement.[21] The Court also concluded the government may rationally distinguish between abortion and other medical procedures, because "no other procedure involves the purposeful termination of a potential life."[22]

Seventeen states fund abortions for low-income women similar to the way in which they fund other pregnancy and general health services. Thirty-two states and the District of Columbia fund abortions similar to the funding under the Hyde Amendment; in other words, abortions are publicly funded for low-income women only in the case of life endangerment, rape, or incest. One state provides coverage for abortions only in life-saving situations (in apparent violation of the Hyde Amendment).

Abortion Clinic Regulations and Provider Requirements

In the late 1960s and early 1970s, proponents of abortion argued the legalization of abortion would ensure proper surgical and follow-up care for women seeking abortion. Yet as story after story of botched abortions surfaces, nothing has proven to be further from the truth. In an attempt to remedy the substandard conditions found in abortion clinics across the nation, states have begun promulgating regulations aimed at the abortion industry. The U.S. Supreme Court has not yet spoken on the constitutionality of state abortion clinic regulations. However, clinic regulations have been consistently upheld in the lower courts under *Planned Parenthood v. Casey*. For example, in *Greenville Women's Clinic v. Bryant*, the Fourth Circuit held that South Carolina's statute regulating abortion clinics did not place an undue burden on women seeking abortion or violate the Equal Protection Clause by distinguishing between clinics on the basis of the number of abortions performed.[23] The plaintiff-abortion clinics appealed, but the U.S. Supreme Court denied review.[24] In 2002, following a second legal challenge, the Fourth Circuit again upheld South Carolina's regulations, and the Supreme Court again denied review.[25]

In 2007, Missouri enacted a law regulating facilities that perform abortion as "ambulatory surgical centers," mandating that such clinics meet stringent health and safety requirements. Twenty-one other states have enacted abortion clinic regulations (of varying strength) that apply to all abortions, and five states regulate the provision of abortions only after the first trimester.[26] Eight states have enacted regulations that are either in litigation, enjoined, or not enforced.

Forty-three states and the District of Columbia limit the performance of surgical abortions to licensed physicians. Moreover, in all but a small number of these states, the physician-only laws can appropriately be interpreted to apply to the provision of non-surgical abortions (*i.e.* RU-486). Also, in the interest of patient health and safety, 11 states, as part of their clinic regulations or other law, require that abortion providers maintain hospital admitting privileges.

State Constitutional Rights to Abortion

Importantly, since 1973 courts in an increasing number of states have manipulated their state constitutions to find abortion rights that have no basis in the history of the state or its constitution. These court decisions currently block important regulations of abortion in those states. And these decisions threaten to restrict the right of the people to self-government when *Roe v. Wade* is overturned.

The U.S. Constitution contains a "supremacy clause" which declares that the federal constitution and laws, including U.S. Supreme Court decisions interpreting those laws, are supreme over state law. However, court decisions by state courts may create more expansive rights under the state constitution than exist under the U.S. Constitution.[27] Thus, the U.S. Supreme Court allows state courts to create broader rights to abortion than exist under *Roe v. Wade*, *Planned Parenthood v. Casey,* and *Gonzales v. Carhart*. In many of these state cases, courts have manipulated privacy clauses in the state constitutions to create an unprecedented right to abortion.

There are at least 16 states[28] with state constitutional rights to abortion, which would block prohibitions—and also probably some regulations—in those states. In effect, this means that state courts have invalidated under the state constitution state laws like parental consent and informed consent that the U.S. Supreme Court has allowed under *Roe v. Wade* and its progeny. Only an amendment to the state constitution or an overruling decision by the state supreme court can change such state court decisions.

RU-486 and Emergency Contraception

There is currently much debate surrounding the safety and efficacy of both RU-486 ("the abortion pill") and "emergency contraception," or Plan B.

On September 28, 2000, the Food and Drug Administration (FDA) approved RU-486 under Subpart H, the agency's accelerated approval regulations. Despite multiple citizen petitions warning against approval of RU-486 or requesting a stay of its approval, RU-486 is currently available throughout the United States and any person with a medical license can prescribe the RU-486 regimen. However, Ohio has taken steps toward ensuring the drug is used as safely as possible. In 2004, the state legislature passed a law demanding clinics abide by the specific regimen laid out by the FDA when it first approved RU-486.

The battle surrounding the "emergency contraception drug," Plan B, involves its status as a prescription drug. In 2001, several pro-abortion organizations petitioned the FDA to make Plan B available over the counter. The FDA originally denied the application, but its decision was left open for further consideration. On August 24, 2006, the FDA approved over-the-counter sales of Plan B to women 18 years of age and over. However, on March 23, 2009, a federal district court in New York ruled that

Plan B must be made available to 17-year-olds and directed the FDA to reconsider its policies regarding access by minors. The Obama administration did not appeal this decision and the FDA intends to comply with the ruling.

In at least nine states, pharmacists can dispense Plan B without a prescription simply by entering into an agreement with a physician. There has also been a push in many states to require that Plan B be readily available in hospital emergency rooms, and now at least 15 states require sexual assault victims be given information about and/or access to "emergency contraception."

Endnotes

[1] 410 U.S. 113 (1973).
[2] 505 U.S. 833 (1992).
[3] *Barnes v. Moore*, 970 F.2d 12 (5th Cir. 1992), *cert. denied*, 506 U.S. 1013 (1992)
[4] *Casey*, 505 U.S. at 872.
[5] *Id.* at 882.
[6] *Id.* at 885.
[7] *See id.* at 886-87.
[8] *Id.* at 884.
[9] 550 U.S. 124, 159 (2007).
[10] *Id.*
[11] Four states have enacted informed consent laws that are either in litigation or enjoined.
[12] Generally, parental involvement laws require either *notification* to a parent or guardian or a parent's or guardian's *consent* before a minor may undergo an abortion.
[13] *Casey*, 505 U.S. at 899.
[14] *Id.* (emphasis added).
[15] *Id.* at 899-00.
[16] Parental involvement laws are in litigation or enjoined in six states.
[17] *See generally*, *Gonzales*, 550 U.S. 124.
[18] *Id.* at 164.
[19] *Id.* at 161.
[20] Laws banning partial-birth abortion are enjoined or in litigation in 15 states.
[21] 448 U.S. 297 (1980).
[22] *Id.* at 325.
[23] 222 F.3d 157 (2000).
[24] *See Greenville Women's Clinic v. Bryant*, 531 U.S. 1191 (2001).
[25] *See Greenville Women's Clinic v. Comm'r, S.C. Dep't of Health & Envtl. Control*, 317 F.3d 357 (4th Cir. 2002), *cert. denied*, 538 U.S. 1008 (2003).
[26] Note that the breadth and degree of these regulations differ vastly from state to state.
[27] *Jankovich v. Ind. Toll Road Comm'n*, 379 U.S. 487 (1965); *Lynch v. New York*, 293 U.S. 52 (1934).
[28] *See e.g.*, C. Forsythe, "Judicial Activism Also Plagues the States: State constitutional rights to abortion," *Defending Life 2009*, pp. 127-129. The state constitutions that have been interpreted as having a broader constitutional right to abortion than the U.S. Constitution are Alaska, Arizona, California, Connecticut, Florida, Idaho, Massachusetts, Minnesota, Mississippi, Montana, New Jersey, New Mexico, New York, Tennessee, Vermont and West Virginia.

2009 State Legislative Sessions in Review:
Abortion & contraception

By Denise M. Burke
Vice President of Legal Affairs, Americans United for Life

In April 2007, the public debate over abortion was irrevocably altered. In the landmark *Gonzales v. Carhart* decision, the U.S. Supreme Court upheld the federal ban on partial-birth abortion and abdicated, at least in part, its role as the unofficial "National Abortion Control Board."

In its decision, the Court signaled an increasing willingness to blunt attempts by abortion extremists to use the courts to unilaterally impose their radical agenda on the American public, as well as an increasing willingness to let the people decide abortion policy. The recent actions of state legislators, pro-life activists, and policy groups confirm this critical shift. While abortion extremists have recycled the hyperbolic rhetoric of the 1970s, legislators and the public are increasingly considering prudent responses to the mounting evidence of the negative impact of abortion.

Overall Trends and Analysis

The majority of states continue their pursuit of life-affirming laws and policies, despite the incremental strategy of Congress and the Obama Administration to implement a regime of unregulated and unrestricted abortion-on-demand. Several notable and promising developments and trends emerged in 2009:

- The states considered approximately 300 abortion-related measures, the vast majority of them life-affirming, and virtually every state considered at least one pro-life measure.
- Several states introduced resolutions opposing the federal "Freedom of Choice Act" (FOCA), a radical piece of legislation that would enshrine abortion-on-demand into American law and override all federal and state laws regulating or restricting abortion. Meanwhile, attempts in five states to enact state versions of FOCA were handily defeated.
- Informed consent, ultrasound requirements, enhanced parental involvement requirements, and comprehensive health and safety regulations for abortion clinics continued to receive significant attention in the states.

These life-affirming trends—especially during an economic crisis—bode well for the 2010 state legislative sessions and the continuing pursuit of a renewed culture of life.

ABORTION

In 2009, the states considered approximately 300 measures related to abortion, a decrease of 33% from 2008 levels. However, this decrease was less than expected, given state legislatures' understandable focus on economic and budgetary issues.

Constitutional Amendments

A small number of states, including Missouri, New Jersey, Tennessee, and West Virginia, considered measures declaring that their state constitutions do not encompass a right to abortion and/or a right to state taxpayer funding of abortion. Tennessee's measure carries over to 2010.

Legislative Resolutions

At least nine states—Alabama, Georgia, Illinois, Missouri, Montana, Nebraska, North Dakota, Ohio, and Oklahoma—considered resolutions opposing the federal "Freedom of Choice Act." An AUL-drafted resolution was passed by the Missouri House of Representatives and by both chambers in Georgia and Oklahoma.

Statutory Redefinitions—
Medical Emergency Exceptions

A few states, including Alaska and Arizona, considered legislation to modify – and in most cases limit – their definition of "medical emergency" in abortion-related laws.

Abortion Bans

Comprehensive Abortion Bans
At least two states—Alabama and Georgia—considered sweeping bans on abortion.

Partial-Birth Abortion Bans
At least eight states—including Arizona, Arkansas, Hawaii, Kansas, Kentucky, and Michigan—considered measures to ban partial-birth abortion.
Arizona and Arkansas enacted bans on the procedure, while Kansas Governor Kathleen Sebelius vetoed a similar measure in April 2009.

Post-Viability Abortions
At least four states, including Kansas and Utah, considered measures related to post-viability abortion.

Utah enacted a measure prohibiting post-viability abortions except in cases of life endangerment, "serious risk of substantial and irreversible impairment of a major bodily function," severe fetal abnormality as certified by two physicians, or rape or incest reported to the police. Under the measure, performing a prohibited abortion is a felony.

Conversely, Kansas Governor Sebelius vetoed a measure modifying the state's definition of "viability" to the point at which a child can survive with or without medical intervention (as opposed to the current law which provides that viability is attained when the child can survive without the application of "extraordinary measures").

Saline Abortions
Minnesota considered a ban on saline abortions.

Sex-Selective Abortions
At least five states—including Michigan, Minnesota, Mississippi, Oklahoma, and West Virginia—considered measures to ban abortions performed for sex selection. Oklahoma became the third state to enact such a ban.

"Personhood" Legislation
A small number of states—including Georgia, Maryland, Montana, North Dakota, and Virginia—considered constitutional amendments or other measures to define unborn chil-

dren from the moment of conception as "persons" under state laws or to provide the unborn "equal rights and protections" under the state's constitution and laws. A primary intent of such legislation is to ban abortion.

Abortion Alternatives

Despite budgetary shortfalls, a number of states considered measures to fund the life-affirming work of pregnancy care centers (PCCs).

Direct Funding of PCCs
At least 13 states—including Kansas, Louisiana, Missouri, North Dakota, Oklahoma, Pennsylvania, Texas, and Wisconsin—considered measures providing direct taxpayer subsidies to PCCs.

The Louisiana legislature allocated $1.5 million to PCCs.

Missouri's budget allocates $2 million to provide "alternatives-to-abortion services" for any pregnant woman at or below 200% of the federal poverty level. The program will offer a range of services to a woman during her pregnancy and for one year following birth.

North Dakota, Oklahoma, and Texas also allocated state funds to PCCs, and Wisconsin's annual budget provides $154,000 to organizations providing "alternatives-to-abortion."

Meanwhile, Kansas Governor Mark Patterson eliminated $355,000 in appropriated funding to PCCs.

Funding Through "Choose Life" License Plates
At least seven states—including Louisiana, Missouri, North Carolina, Texas, and Virginia—considered measures to approve "Choose Life" license plate programs that provide earned revenue to PCCs. In March 2009, Virginia approved its "Choose Life" program.

Pro-PCC Resolution
Kentucky considered a resolution commending the work of PCCs.

Regulation of PCCs
At least four states—Michigan, New York, Texas, and West Virginia—considered measures to regulate PCCs.

Abortion Funding

In 2009, legislation and issues related to the use of state taxpayer funding for abortion were debated in a number of states.

State Funding for Abortions
At least eight states—including Iowa, Maryland, Minnesota, Tennessee, Virginia, and West Virginia—considered measures related to the use of state funding (including Medicaid funding) for abortions.

Iowa, Maryland, and Minnesota reauthorized their existing permissive funding policies.

Prohibition on the Use of State Funding for Abortion Counseling or Referrals
A few states, including Minnesota and West Virginia, considered measures to prohibit the use of state funding for abortion counseling or referrals.

Prohibition of the Use of State Facilities and Employees for Abortions
A small number of states, including Rhode Island and West Virginia, considered measures

to prohibit the use of state facilities (such as state-run hospitals) or state employees for the provision of abortions.

Prohibition on Use of State Education Funding for Abortions
A few states, including Virginia and West Virginia, considered measures to prohibit or limit the use of funding slated for education (including funding for state universities) for abortions.

Prohibitions on Use of State Family Planning Funding for Abortions
At least nine states—including Colorado, Kansas, Michigan, Tennessee, Texas, and Virginia—considered measures prohibiting the use of state family planning funding to provide or promote abortion.

Colorado reenacted a long-standing restriction prohibiting those who perform abortions from receiving state family planning funding.

Texas again approved a state budget measure requiring that recipients of state family planning funding segregate their family planning services from abortion services, maintaining separate incorporation, governing structure, facilities, and funding sources.

Meanwhile in Kansas, Governor Sebelius vetoed language in the state's budget bill that would have required family planning funds be dispersed on a priority-based system. The system would have effectively excluded abortion providers like Planned Parenthood.

Insurance Coverage
At least four states—including California, New York, and Oklahoma—introduced measures related to private insurance coverage of abortion. Similarly, at least two states, North Carolina and West Virginia, considered limits on the use of taxpayer funding to purchase insurance (that includes coverage for abortions) for state employees.

Informed Consent

At least 16 states—including Arizona, California, Connecticut, Indiana, Iowa, Kansas, Kentucky, Massachusetts, Mississippi, Missouri, Nebraska, New York, North Dakota, Rhode Island, Tennessee, and Texas—considered measures requiring informed consent for abortion or modifying existing requirements.

Arizona enacted legislation requiring informed consent and a 24-hour reflection period before an abortion. Under the new law, a woman must receive information about the nature of the procedure, the immediate and long-term risks of abortion, the risks of childbirth, alternatives to the procedure, and the probable gestational age and anatomical and physiological characteristics of the unborn child. A woman must also receive information about medical assistance benefits, the father's liability for child support, and public and private agencies available to assist her.

Kansas enacted a measure expanding the requirements for the written materials abortion providers give to women considering abortion. The materials must now include contact information for perinatal hospices and a list of organizations that provide free ultrasound examinations. Abortion providers must also inform women that the state-mandated written materials are also available online.

North Dakota enacted a measure requiring abortion providers to inform women that abortion ends the life of a "whole, separate, unique human being," Kansas Governor Sebelius vetoed a similar measure.

Notably, a number of states considered informed-consent enhancements, such as coerced abortion prevention, counseling on fetal pain, and ultrasound requirements.

Coerced Abortion Prevention
At least 12 states—including Arizona, Kansas, Michigan, Minnesota, Missouri, North Dakota, Ohio, Rhode Island, and Texas—considered measures to prevent women from being coerced into having an abortion. Typically, these bills required abortion providers to inform or counsel women on coercion and the protective services available to them. Some also criminalized coercive behavior.

Arizona enacted an omnibus measure including a requirement that abortion providers personally inform women they may not be coerced into an abortion.

Kansas enacted a measure requiring abortion providers to post signs indicating that no one may coerce a woman into an abortion, that an abortion requires a woman's voluntary consent, and that a woman may report coercive behavior to law enforcement.

North Dakota enacted a measure requiring abortion clinics to prominently display signs with the following statement: "No one can force you to have an abortion. It is against the law for a spouse, a boyfriend, a parent, a friend, a medical care provider, or any other person to in any way force you to have an abortion."

Similarly, Ohio enacted a measure requiring abortion clinics to post signs stating that no one may coerce a woman into having an abortion and encouraging any woman who feels that she is being coerced to discuss it with the clinic staff.

Fetal Pain
At least seven states—including Alaska, Indiana, Missouri, New York, and Utah—considered measures to require medical personnel to counsel women on the pain an unborn child may feel during an abortion.

Utah enacted a measure requiring abortion providers to offer a woman seeking an abortion at 20 weeks' gestation or later anesthesia for the unborn child.

Ultrasound Requirements
At least 22 states—including Alabama, Connecticut, Florida, Illinois, Kansas, Kentucky, Maryland, Nebraska, New Jersey, North Carolina, North Dakota, Rhode Island, South Carolina, Texas, Utah, Virginia, West Virginia, and Wyoming—considered ultrasound requirements.

Kansas and North Dakota enacted measures requiring the abortion provider must offer a woman the opportunity to undergo an ultrasound and to hear the fetal heartbeat before an abortion.

Nebraska enacted a law requiring abortion providers, when they perform an ultrasound prior to an abortion, to display the image so the woman can see it and to answer any questions the woman has about the ultrasound. The provider must also offer the woman a list of organizations that perform ultrasound examinations as part of abortion counseling.

Further, at least three states introduced measures to restrict the non-medical use of ultrasounds. Connecticut enacted a measure requiring that all ultrasounds be ordered by a physician and performed for a "medical purpose."

Paternal Consent/Spousal Involvement
Ohio considered a measure requiring "paternal consent" for an abortion, while West Virginia again considered a measure requiring spousal consent.

Parental Involvement

In 2009, parental involvement for abortion—either parental consent or notice—continued to be actively debated in a number of state legislatures.

Parental Consent
At least ten states—including Alaska, Arizona, Massachusetts, New York, North Carolina, Rhode Island, Virginia, and West Virginia—considered measures to require parental consent for abortion or to modify existing consent requirements.

Arizona amended its law to require notarization of a parent's written informed consent. The legislature also established evidentiary standards for judicial bypass hearings when a minor is seeking to have the consent requirement waived. Finally, it also prohibited a parent from refusing financial support as a means to coerce a daughter into having an abortion.

Parental Notice
At least 11 states—including Connecticut, Delaware, Florida, Hawaii, Iowa, Montana, New Hampshire, New Mexico, and New York—introduced measures to require parental notice for abortion or to amend existing notification requirements.

Provider Requirements

Abortion Clinic Regulations
At least eight states—including Minnesota, Montana, Tennessee, Texas, Virginia, and West Virginia—considered health and safety regulations for abortion clinics. Some of these measures included abortion-specific regulatory schemes, while others sought to regulate abortion clinics as "ambulatory surgical centers."

Admitting Privileges and Licensing Requirements
At least three states—Indiana, Virginia, and West Virginia—considered measures to require abortion providers to have hospital admitting privileges.

Physician-Only Requirements for Abortion
At least four states—including Arizona, Nevada, Minnesota, and West Virginia—considered measures to limit the performance of abortions to licensed physicians or to certain categories of physicians. Arizona enacted a measure limiting the performance of surgical abortions to physicians, and Nevada enacted measures prohibiting "osteopathic medical professionals" and chiropractic physicians from performing abortions.

West Virginia considered a measure precluding any one "who has admitted to committing or has been adjudicated as having committed medical malpractice" from performing abortions.

Reporting Requirements
At least 12 states—including Iowa, Kansas, Michigan, Mississippi, Missouri, Oklahoma, West Virginia, and Wyoming—considered measures mandating the reporting of demographic and other information related to abortion to state agencies (typically, the state Department of Health).

Oklahoma enacted a measure expanding the requirements of its existing reporting law. Meanwhile, the Kansas legislature failed to override Governor Sebelius' veto of specific reporting requirements for post-viability abortions. The measure would have required specific information on the diagnosis necessitating the late-term abortion and a certification that the abortion was, in fact, medically necessary.

Sexual Abuse Reporting Requirements
At least five states, including Mississippi and Pennsylvania, introduced measures to strengthen or clarify existing sexual abuse reporting requirements. For example, Mississippi considered the AUL-developed "Child Protection Act," a comprehensive measure requiring the reporting of all suspicions of sexual abuse by designated individuals, including all employees of and volunteers in abortion clinics; mandating the retention of evidentiary samples; and creating a civil cause of action against anyone who takes a minor across state lines to circumvent the home state's parental involvement law.

Abortion Litigation Fund

Utah enacted a measure providing for a litigation fund to be used to pay for the legal defense of the state's abortion-related restrictions, if needed.

State "Freedom of Choice Acts"

At least five states—including Illinois, Minnesota, New Mexico, New York, and Rhode Island—considered state versions of the federal "Freedom of Choice Act," providing for an unrestricted state right to abortion and abolishing any existing regulations of or restrictions on abortion.

Ensuring Access to Abortion Clinics

At least four states—including Delaware, Montana, New York, and Rhode Island—considered measures to create so-called bubble zones around abortion clinics (areas where clinic demonstrators may not enter) and to criminalize actions that inhibit access to clinics.

Training Abortion Providers

New York considered a measure to require medical residency training in obstetrics, gynecology, internal medicine, women's health, and osteopathy to include training in induced abortions and complications.

CONTRACEPTION AND EMERGENCY CONTRACEPTION

In 2009, 25 states considered more than 60 measures related to contraception. The vast majority of the measures sought to expand access to both contraceptives and "emergency contraception" or Plan B.

Definition of Contraception

A small number of states—including Alabama, Arizona, Colorado, and Virginia—considered measures classifying or defining "contraception." Alabama and Arizona considered measures to exempt FDA-approved contraception from the state's "abortion" definition and from compliance with the abortion-related laws, such as informed consent and parental involvement.

Colorado enacted a measure defining "contraception" as "a medically acceptable drug, device, or procedure used to prevent pregnancy" and "emergency contraception" as "a drug approved by the Federal Food and Drug Administration that prevents pregnancy after intercourse, including but not limited to oral contraceptive pills." The measure exempts "mifepristone (RU-486) and any other drug or device that induces a medical abortion" from its definition.

Contraceptive Coverage

Insurance Mandates
At least nine states—including Illinois, Kentucky, Michigan, New York, Oklahoma, Pennsylvania, South Dakota, and Wisconsin—considered measures to require insurance coverage of contraceptives. Wisconsin enacted a coverage mandate.

Minors' Access
At least four states—Mississippi, Montana, Texas, and West Virginia—considered measures expanding insurance coverage for contraception for minors. Conversely, at least three states—Georgia, Pennsylvania, and Texas—considered measures requiring parental involvement for minors seeking contraception.

Contraception Information in Schools
North Carolina enacted a measure requiring "medically accurate information" about contraception and "reproductive health" in educational programs for middle school students.

Emergency Contraception

The most significant area of legislative activity related to contraceptives involved access to so-called "emergency contraception" or Plan B. At least 14 states considered such measures. This level of activity mirrored what we have seen over the past few years.

Informed Consent for Emergency Contraception
Texas considered a measure mandating informed consent for and the provision of certain medical and safety information to anyone receiving "emergency contraception."

Emergency Room Access
At least ten states—Arkansas, Hawaii, Michigan, Missouri, Oklahoma, Pennsylvania, Texas, Utah, Virginia, and West Virginia—considered measures to expand emergency room access to "emergency contraception" or Plan B.

Utah enacted a measure requiring emergency rooms to provide, at the request of a sexual assault victim, information about "emergency contraception."

Virginia enacted a measure permitting a sexual assault nurse (in the absence of a physician) to provide "emergency contraception" to a victim.

State "Prevention First" Legislation
Taking a cue from Congress, which has introduced the "Prevention First Act, an act that uses federal funds to expand access to contraceptives including "emergency contraception" and to promote its use, at least two states—Florida and Washington—considered similar measures at the state level, while Georgia considered a resolution urging the enactment of the federal measure.

Collaborative Practice Agreements
A small number of states, including New York, considered measures permitting nurses, pharmacists, and other health care providers to dispense "emergency contraception" under a collaborative practice agreement with a physician.

Access at State Universities
New York again considered a measure, "The Public University Emergency Contraception Act," requiring every college and university of the State University of New York (SUNY) and the City University of New York to provide "emergency contraception" to any student requesting it and requiring the widespread provision of information at such colleges and universities on the safety and availability of "emergency contraception" on campus.

Emergency Contraception Education Programs
At least two states—Michigan and West Virginia—considered legislation creating state-funded educational programs for "emergency contraception."

A Winning Strategy:
Approaching abortion bans with prudence

By Clarke D. Forsythe, *Senior Counsel, Americans United for Life*
& Mailee R. Smith, *Staff Counsel, Americans United for Life*

In *Roe v. Wade*,[1] the U.S. Supreme Court held that the states may not prohibit any abortions before viability, a holding expressly reaffirmed by the Court in the 1992 case *Planned Parenthood v. Casey*.[2] Since *Roe*, several attempts have been made to enact abortion prohibitions—by Rhode Island in 1973, Utah in 1991, Louisiana in 1991, and Guam in 1991—and all failed.[3] Other attempts have been made to induce the Court to reconsider *Roe*, and, so far, they too have failed. For example, in 2005 a motion by the original "Jane Roe," Norma McCorvey, requested the Court revisit *Roe*; it failed, with the Court refusing to even hear the case.[4]

Over the last few years, however, a number of states have debated and considered a variety of abortion prohibitions (or bans), including the following: prohibitions after viability, prohibitions on partial-birth abortions, delayed enforcement laws, and prohibitions on sex-selective abortions.

ISSUES

Prohibitions after Viability

Despite ill-informed claims to the contrary, a careful examination of *Roe* and its companion case, *Doe v. Bolton*,[5] shows that abortions may be performed for virtually any reason after viability. In *Roe*, the Court held that after viability "the State, in promoting its interest in the potentiality of human life, may, if it chooses, regulate, and even proscribe, abortion except where it is necessary, in appropriate medical judgment, for the preservation of the life or health of the mother."[6] In *Doe*, the Court defined the health exception in an unlimited fashion:

> [T]he medical judgment may be exercised in the light of all factors—physical, emotional, psychological, familial, and the woman's age—relevant to the well-being of the patient. All these factors may relate to health.[7]

Given this broad definition of "health," which includes psychological and familial factors as well as physical ones, it is clear that under *Roe* and *Doe* virtually any woman who wants to have an abortion after viability may obtain one. Thus, it is accurate to say that, unless and until the Supreme Court reviews and upholds a post-viability prohibition, abortions are legal throughout all nine months of pregnancy.

In *Casey*, Pennsylvania's post-viability provision was not challenged, but the Court did uphold the validity of the narrow medical emergency exception in the Pennsylvania law. This may suggest that similar language in a post-viability prohibition would pass constitutional muster.

The Court did note that it is only in "rare circumstances in which the pregnancy is itself a danger to [a woman's] own life or health," and stated that "a woman who fails to act before viability has consented to the State's intervention on behalf of the developing child."[8] Whether this language means that states may prohibit abortions after viability remains to be seen. The lower courts are divided on this question.

Finally, in *Gonzales v. Carhart*, the Court indicated that laws attempting to limit post-viability abortions by restricting the health exception can be valid (*e.g.*, limiting such abortions to significant threats to the mother's physical health).[9] The impact of this decision also remains to be seen.

To summarize, under *Roe* and *Doe*, abortions may be performed for any reason before viability and for virtually any reason after viability. States are not encouraged, at this time, to pursue post-viability prohibitions.[10]

Prohibitions on Partial-Birth Abortion

In 2000, the U.S. Supreme Court reaffirmed *Roe* and *Casey* and struck down the partial-birth abortion prohibitions of Nebraska and 29 other states.[11] Seeing the procedure as gruesome, dangerous to women, and medically unnecessary, the U.S. Congress thereafter passed the "Partial Birth Abortion Ban Act of 2003." The Act was immediately challenged in multiple federal courts, culminating in the Supreme Court's 2007 holding in *Gonzales* that the Act is entirely constitutional.

Significant for states considering partial-birth abortion bans are 1) the Court's restoration of the guidelines set forth in *Casey* that are more deferential to state legislation; 2) the Court's effective rejection of the claim that an unlimited emotional health exception is required in every abortion regulation; and 3) the conclusion that a health exception was not required in order for the federal ban to be constitutional.

The Court noted there is documented medical disagreement about whether the Act's prohibition of partial-birth abortion would ever cause significant health risks to women.[12] Thus, the question became whether the Act could stand when medical uncertainty persists. The Court answered this question in the affirmative, noting that the Court itself has given state and federal legislatures wide discretion to pass legislation in areas where there is medical and scientific uncertainty.[13] Further, the Court expressly stated that medical uncertainty does not foreclose the exercise of this discretion in the abortion context "any more than it does in other contexts."[14] In concluding that the Act does not impose an undue burden on a woman's right to choose abortion, the Court noted its holding was supported by the fact that alternatives are available to the prohibited procedure.[15]

Now that the Court has explicitly upheld the

federal ban, the time is ripe for state legislatures to enact state partial-birth abortion bans. While much of the general public believes state bans are unnecessary because the federal government has already banned partial-birth abortion, that assertion is incorrect for three basic reasons.

First, the penalties for violating the ban could be more stringent. For example, under the federal ban, violators can be fined or imprisoned for no more than two years, or both.[16] Contrast that to the ban in Louisiana, passed after the *Gonzales* decision, which states that a person violating the law "shall be imprisoned at hard labor for not less than one nor more than ten years, fined not less than ten thousand nor more than one hundred thousand dollars, or both."[17] Thus, there is room for states to pass laws with stricter penalties.

Second, a state ban ensures timely and effective enforcement. If for some reason—such as a change in administrations—the U.S. Attorney General decides not to enforce the federal ban, a state attorney general, along with local prosecutors, could step in and enforce a state ban.

Third, the federal ban may not reach the actions of all abortion providers. In order for the federal ban to be triggered, the abortion provider must either be on federal property (or a federal employee) or engaged in interstate commerce. While this is an area of law confusing even to most attorneys, the gist of the interstate commerce rule is that a private individual or business must be engaged in the flow of business across state lines in order for an offense to be considered federal in nature. It is hard to imagine an abortion provider that does not in some way engage in business across state lines. Women may come from across state lines; the abortion provider himself/herself may fly in from out of state; and the clinic surely purchases items or instruments from businesses in other states. However, to best ensure the eradication of partial-birth abortion in a state, the state must pass its own ban.

For states interested in introducing such a bill, AUL has drafted the "Partial-Birth Abortion Ban Act."

Delayed Enforcement Laws

In recent legislative sessions, states have begun considering and enacting "delayed enforcement laws." States interested in considering such laws must take into account several important legal and practical considerations.

As a standard text on statutory construction provides, "the power to enact laws includes the power to fix a future effective date. . . . A statute may take effect upon the happening of a contingency, such as the passage of a law in another jurisdiction, a vote of the people, or the passage of a constitutional amendment."[18] There are two caveats to this general rule. First, this power is determined by state law and must be verified in each state. Second, while the legislative authority to postpone an effective date to a future contingency seems fairly well established, the "abortion distortion factor" of federal constitutional law should never be taken for granted. In other words, a federal court might hold that even the threat of a future effective date has an unconstitutionally chilling effect on abortion today.

Assuming the legislature has the authority to postpone an effective date, a number of factors must be considered. First, vagueness in the statement of the future contingency should be avoided. If a future effective date is conditioned upon the Supreme Court overturning *Roe v. Wade*, does the Supreme Court have to specifically or uncategorically overrule *Roe* for the delayed enforcement provision to become effective? Second, consideration should be given to the relative expenditure of political resources to enact an abortion prohibition now or sometime in the future. Third, consideration should be given to what other laws might be enacted during the legislative session that will be enforceable now and have a positive impact in reducing abortion rates in the state by, for example, protecting women from the negative health consequences of abortions, protecting minors and parental rights through parental involvement laws, and protecting unborn victims of violence. All these factors should be weighed in the balance in considering an abortion prohibition with a delayed enforcement date.

Prohibitions on Sex-Selective Abortions

In recent years, the practice of sex-selective abortions has drawn increasing attention worldwide. The problem is so severe in some countries that, in 2005, the United Nations Population Fund termed the practice "female infanticide." The practice is common in some Asian countries, including China and India, but it is also being practiced in the United States, often by people who trace their ancestry to countries that commonly practice sex-selective abortions.

Lawmakers have begun focusing more attention on the problem of sex-selective abortions, but so far few states prohibit such inherently discriminatory procedures. It is, however, an area where pro-abortion advocates have little ammunition to challenge such bills from a public policy standpoint.

On this issue, AUL has drafted a "Ban on Abortions Performed for Reasons of Sex Selection, Potential Genetic Deformity, or Potential Disability."

KEY TERMS

- **Delayed enforcement law**s are abortion prohibitions which delay enforcement until, for example, *Roe v. Wade* is overturned by the U.S. Supreme Court or the authority to prohibit abortion is returned to the States.

- **Dilation & extraction (D&E)** is an abortion procedure that involves dilation of the cervix, the insertion of forceps to dismember the unborn child in the uterus, and the removal of body parts one at a time. The intention is not to remove the child intact.

- **Partial-birth abortion** is, according to the language of the federal ban, "an abortion in which the person performing the abortion—(A) deliberately and intentionally vaginally delivers a living fetus until, in the case of a head-first presentation, the entire fetal head is outside the body of the mother, or, in the case of breech presentation, any part of the fetal trunk past the navel is outside the body of the mother, for the purpose of performing an overt act that the person knows will kill the partially delivered living fetus; and (B) performs the overt act, other than completion of delivery, that kills the partially delivered living fetus. . . ."[19] The intention is to remove the child intact. Partial-birth abortion is also referred to as "**intact D&E**" and "**D&X**."

- **Sex-selective abortions** are abortions undertaken to eliminate a child of an undesired sex. The targeted victims of such abortions are overwhelmingly female.

- **Viability** is the state of fetal development when there is a reasonable likelihood of sustained survival of the unborn child outside the body of his or her mother, with or without artificial support.

MYTHS & FACTS

Myth: In order to challenge *Roe*, a state must pass an abortion prohibition.
Fact: Legislators should know it is not possible to force the Supreme Court to take any particular case, and it is not necessary to pass a prohibition bill to spark a test case and reexamination of *Roe v. Wade*; the issue is not the right bill but the right justices. The Court reexamined *Roe* in *Akron*, *Webster*, and *Casey*, though none of those cases involved an abortion prohibition. It would be advisable to seek a reexamination of *Roe* (when a sympathetic majority exists) with any statute that arguably conflicts with *Roe*, asking the Court to broadly return the issue to the people without having to ask the Court to specifically approve the constitutionality of specific prohibitions.

Myth: The partial-birth abortion procedure is entirely safe.
Fact: Medical evidence demonstrates that partial-birth abortions pose drastic short- and long-term risks for women undergoing the procedure.[20] Short-term risks include bleeding, infection, uterine perforation, lacerations, perforation of the uterine artery, traumatic uterine rupture, and harm caused by dilation.[21] Long-term risks include cervical incompetence and preterm birth in subsequent pregnancies.[22]

Myth: Partial-birth abortion bans endanger women's lives by prohibiting a sometimes necessary procedure.
Fact: Well-established alternatives to partial-birth abortion exist.[23] The Supreme Court agreed, ruling that safe alternatives to partial-birth abortion exist.[24] Furthermore, the partial-birth abortion procedure is never medically necessary. It has been clearly established that partial-birth abortion is not medically necessary for any maternal medical conditions, nor is it medically necessary for any fetal abnormalities.[25]

Even if the procedure was medically necessary in some circumstances, the federal ban contains an exception stating that the procedure may be used if "necessary to save the life of a mother whose life is endangered by a physical disorder, physical illness, or physical injury, including a life-endangering physical condition caused by or arising from the pregnancy itself."[26] Simply put, no woman's life is in danger because of a partial-birth abortion ban.

Myth: The "Partial Birth Abortion Ban Act" prohibits other forms of abortion, such as the D&E procedure.
Fact: The Supreme Court specifically rejected

this argument, concluding that the federal ban did not in any way infringe on the practice of D&E.[27]

Myth: Even without a ban, partial-birth abortions are performed only to save the life of the mother.

Fact: Abortion provider Martin Haskell, who developed the partial-birth abortion procedure, has admitted that 80 percent of partial-birth abortions in his own practice are done for "purely elective" reasons, with the remaining 20 percent performed for "genetic reasons" such as fetal anomalies or cleft palates.[28] Based on the fact the procedure is never medically necessary for fetal anomalies, Dr. Haskell has effectively admitted he never performs the procedure in order to save the life of the mother.[29]

Endnotes

[1] 410 U.S. 113, 164-65 (1973).
[2] 505 U.S. 833, 846, 879 (1992).
[3] *Doe v. Israel*, 358 F.Supp. 1193 (D. R.I. 1973), *aff'd*, 482 F.2d 156 (1st Cir. 1973), *cert. denied*, 416 U.S. 993 (1973); *Ada v. Guam Soc. of Obstetricians & Gynecologists*, *cert. denied*, 506 U.S. 1011 (1992); *Edwards v. Sojourner T.*, *cert. denied*, 507 U.S. 972 (1993).
[4] *McCorvey v. Hill*, 385 F.3d 846 (5th Cir. 2004), *cert. denied*, 543 U.S. 1154 (2005).
[5] 410 U.S. 179 (1973).
[6] *Roe*, 410 U.S. at 164-65.
[7] *Doe*, 410 U.S. at 179, 192 (citing *United States v. Vuitch*, 402 U.S. 62 (1971)).
[8] *Casey*, 505 U.S. at 851, 870.
[9] *Gonzales*, 127 S. Ct. 1610 (2007).
[10] In addition, consideration should be given to the prudential question of whether a post-viability prohibition will serve to reinforce an artificial biological demarcation (viability) that has no relation to the humanity of the unborn child without significantly reducing abortions, and whether any gain from a post-viability prohibition is better served by a prohibition on partial-birth abortion.
[11] *See Stenberg v. Carhart*, 530 U.S. 914 (2000).
[12] *Gonzales*, 127 S. Ct. at 1636.
[13] *Id.*
[14] *Id.* at 1637.
[15] *Id.*
[16] 18 U.S.C. § 1531(a).
[17] La. Rev. Stat. § 14:32.10(E).
[18] Sands, Sutherland Statutory Construction sec. 33.07, at 17 (5th Ed.).
[19] 18 U.S.C. § 1531(b).
[20] *See Amicus Curiae* Brief of American Association of Pro Life Obstetricians and Gynecologists (AAPLOG) et al. at 12-15, *Gonzales v. Planned Parenthood Federation of America* (SCOTUS Case No. 05-1382), available at http://www.aul.org/xm_client/client_documents/briefs/GonzalesvPP.pdf (last visited June 9, 2009) [hereinafter AUL *Gonzales v. Planned Parenthood* Brief]. The briefs authored by AUL and cited herein contain in-depth analyses of the expert testimonies presented by both sides in each of the three cases challenging the federal ban.
[21] *See id.* at 12-14.
[22] *See id.* at 14-15.
[23] *See Amicus Curiae* Brief of American Association of Pro Life Obstetricians and Gynecologists (AAPLOG) et al. at 26-27, *Gonzales v. Carhart* (SCOTUS Case No. 05-380), available at http://www.aul.org/xm_client/client_documents/briefs/GonzalesvCarhart.pdf (last visited June 9, 2009) [hereinafter AUL *Gonzales v. Carhart* Brief]; AUL *Gonzales v. Planned Parenthood* Brief, *supra*, at 15-17.
[24] *Gonzales,* 127 S. Ct. at 1637.
[25] *See* AUL *Gonzales v. Carhart* Brief, *supra*, at 7-15; AUL *Gonzales v. Planned Parenthood* Brief, *supra*, at 18-27.
[26] 18 U.S.C. § 1531(a).
[27] *Gonzales,* 127 S. Ct. at 1629.
[28] *See* Diane M. Gianelli, *Shock-Tactic Ads Target Late-Term Abortion Procedure*, Am. Med. News (July 5, 1993).
[29] For more information on the topics discussed in this article, please visit AUL's website at http://www.AUL.org.

Partial-Birth Abortion Talking Points

- Partial-birth abortions are not only deadly for the unborn child, but are also dangerous for women. Medical evidence demonstrates that partial-birth abortions pose drastic short- and long-term risks.[1] Short-term risks include bleeding, infection, uterine perforation, lacerations, perforation of the uterine artery, traumatic uterine rupture, and harm caused by dilation.[2] Long-term risks include cervical incompetence and preterm birth in subsequent pregnancies.[3]

- State partial-birth abortion bans are a necessary step in furthering the state's interests in both the protection of women and the prevention of infanticide. These significant state interests have been affirmed time and time again by the U.S. Supreme Court.[4]

- State laws are also necessary to ensure enforcement of the ban, even when the federal government is unwilling or unable to enforce the federal ban. Further, state legislatures may enact laws with stricter penalties.

- Partial-birth abortion bans do not endanger women's lives. The Supreme Court has specifically noted that other late-term abortion procedures are available to and safe for women.[5] Further, state bans on partial-birth abortion include an exception for circumstances when the life of the mother is endangered.

- Evidence demonstrates that the partial-birth abortion procedure is never medically necessary for maternal health conditions.[6] In the challenges to the federal ban, witnesses on neither side could recall real-life conditions, in their own practices or otherwise, where partial-birth abortion was necessary for a maternal medical condition.[7] Furthermore, there are no valid medical studies supporting the claim that partial-birth abortion is ever medically necessary. Neither an American Medical Association task force nor an American College of Obstetricians & Gynecologists panel could "find any medical conditions" or "come up with any situations that would require [a partial-birth abortion]."[8]

- Evidence further demonstrates that the partial-birth abortion procedure is never medically necessary for fetal anomalies.[9] In the challenges to the federal ban, not a single witness could identify a fetal anomaly that required the procedure.[10] Likewise, partial-birth abortion is not necessary for a subsequent diagnosis of a fetal anomaly, and in fact the procedure makes it more difficult to diagnose brain abnormalities.[11]

- Like the federal ban, a state partial-birth abortion ban should make an exception when the life of the mother is at stake;[12] on the other hand, state bans should not contain the all-inclusive "health exception," which would allow a mother to obtain a partial-birth abortion for any reason.[13]

Endnotes

[1] *See* Amicus Curiae Brief of American Association of Pro Life Obstetricians and Gynecologists (AAPLOG) et al. at 12-15, *Gonzales v. Planned Parenthood Federation of America* (SCOTUS Case No. 05-1382), available at http://www.aul.org/xm_client/client_documents/briefs/GonzalesvPP.pdf (last visited September 8, 2008) [hereinafter AUL *Gonzales v. Planned Parenthood* Brief].

[2] *See id.* at 12-14.

[3] *See id* at 14-15.

[4] *See* generally *Gonzales v. Carhart*, 127 S. Ct. 1610 (2007); *Planned Parenthood of Southeastern Penn. v. Casey*, 505 U.S. 833 (1992).

[5] *Gonzales*, 127 S. Ct. at 1637.

[6] *See* Amicus Curiae Brief of American Association of Pro Life Obstetricians and Gynecologists (AAPLOG) et al. at 7-15, *Gonzales v. Carhart* (SCOTUS Case No. 05-380), available at http://www.aul.org/xm_client/client_documents/briefs/GonzalesvCarhart.pdf (last visited September 8, 2008) [hereinafter AUL *Gonzales v. Carhart* Brief]; AUL *Gonzales v. Planned Parenthood* Brief, *supra*, at 18-27.

[7] *See* AUL *Gonzales v. Carhart* Brief, *supra*, at 7-14; AUL *Gonzales v. Planned Parenthood* Brief, *supra*, at 18-25.

[8] *See* AUL *Gonzales v. Carhart* Brief, *supra*, at 7-14; AUL *Gonzales v. Planned Parenthood* Brief, *supra*, at 18-25.

[9] *See* AUL *Gonzales v. Carhart* Brief, *supra*, at 7-15; AUL *Gonzales v. Planned Parenthood* Brief, *supra*, at 18-27.

[10] *See* AUL *Gonzales v. Carhart* Brief, *supra*, at 14-15; AUL *Gonzales v. Planned Parenthood* Brief, *supra*, at 25-27.

[11] *See* AUL *Gonzales v. Carhart* Brief, *supra*, at 14-15; AUL *Gonzales v. Planned Parenthood* Brief, *supra*, at 25-27.

[12] *See* 18 U.S.C. § 1531(a).

[13] Under *Doe v. Bolton*, the companion case to *Roe v. Wade*, the definition of "health" includes anything that may affect a woman's mental or physical well-being. *See Doe*, 410 U.S. 179 (1973). This effectively allows abortion-on-demand at any time during pregnancy. Thus, including a "health" exception would gut any partial-birth abortion regulation, making the exception apply to any reason the mother has for terminating her pregnancy.

State Partial-Birth Abortion Bans

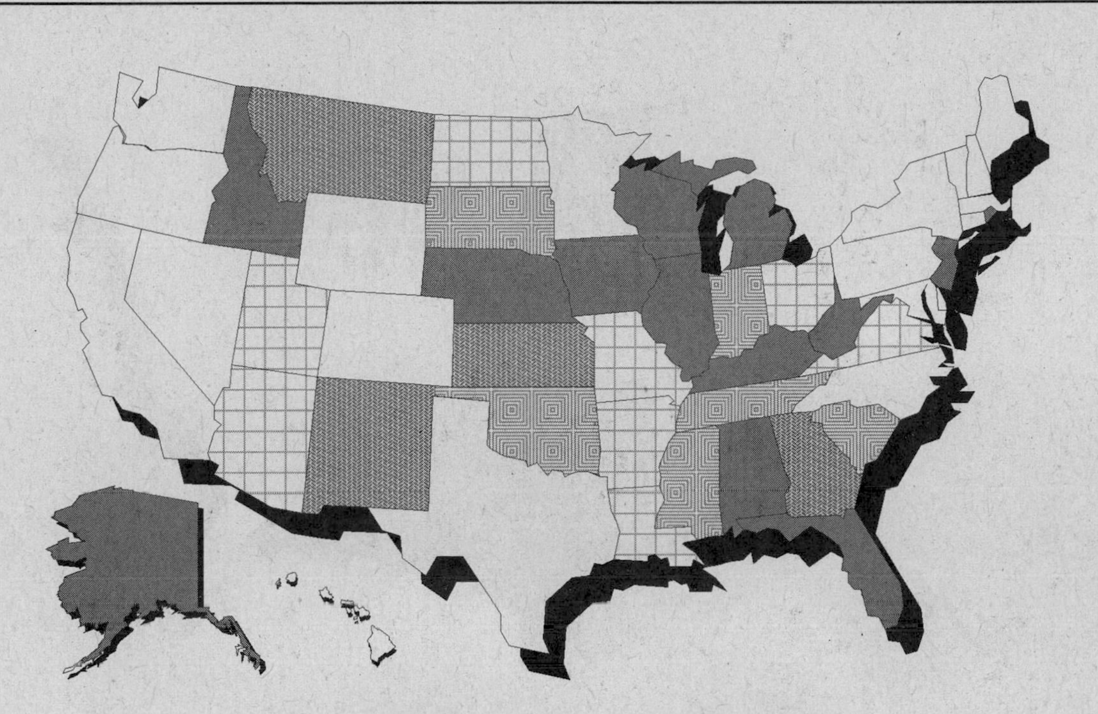

Eighteen state laws banning partial-birth abortion are in effect:

Eight state laws apply throughout pregnancy and have either been upheld in court or mirror the federal partial-birth abortion ban: AZ, AR, LA, MO, ND, OH, UT and VA.

Six state laws apply throughout pregnancy and have never been challenged in court: IN, MS, OK, SC, SD, and TN.

Four state laws apply only after viability: GA, KS, MT, and NM.

Thirteen state laws banning partial-birth abortion are enjoined or in litigation: AL, AK, FL, ID, IL, IA, KY, MI, NE, NJ, RI, WV, and WI.

Enforceable Abortion Prohibitions

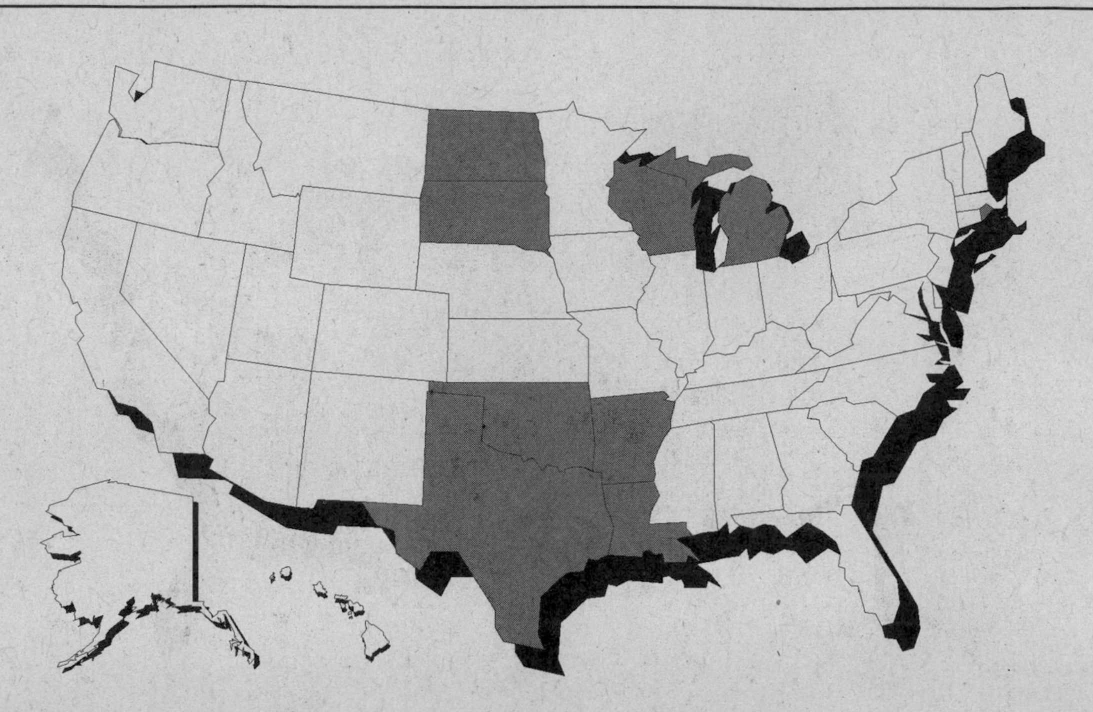

Nine states have enforceable abortion prohibitions (a pre-*Roe* ban and/or a recently-enacted "delayed enforcement" law): AR, LA, MI, ND, OK, RI, SD, TX, and WI.

Sex-Selective Abortion Bans

Three states ban abortions targeted toward the gender of the child: IL, OK, and PA.

Post-Viability Abortion Bans

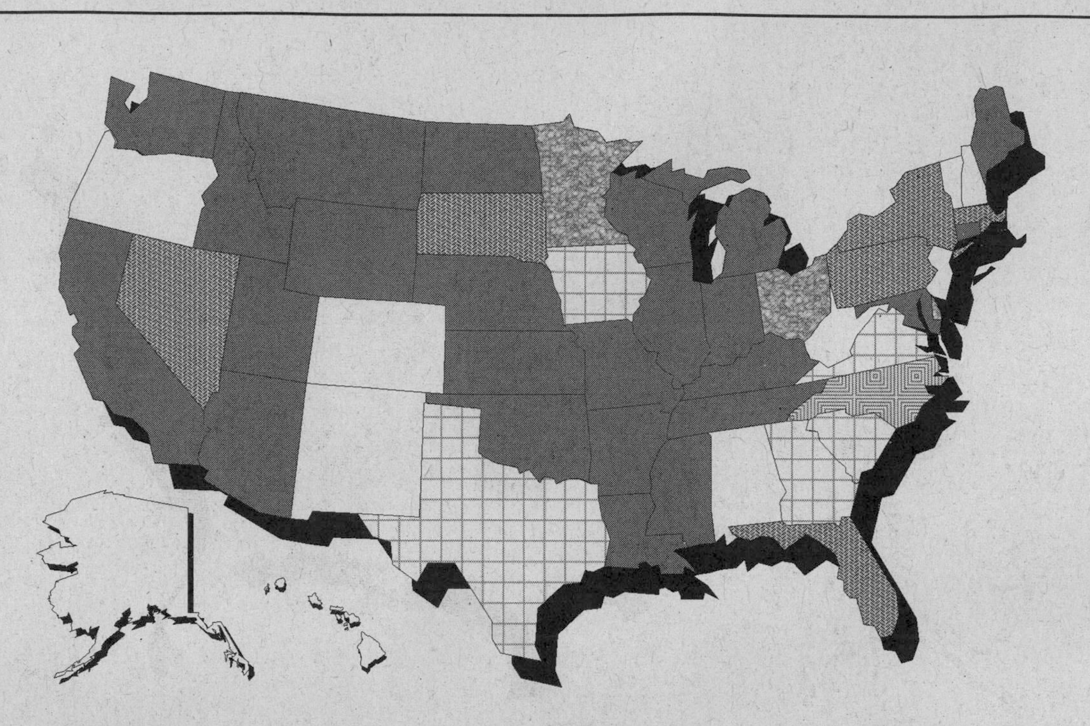

Thirty-seven states maintain enforceable post-viability bans:

Twenty-four states prohibit at viability: AL, AZ, AR, CA, CT, ID, IL, IN, KS, KY, LA, ME, MD, MI, MO, MT, NE, ND, OK, TN, UT, WA, WI, and WY.

Five states prohibit in the third trimester: GA, IA, SC, TX, and VA.

Seven states prohibit at 24 weeks: FL, MA, NV, NY, PA, RI, and SD.

One state prohibits at 20 weeks: NC.

Three states' laws have been permanently enjoined: DE, MN, and OH.

Informed Consent Laws:
Protecting a woman's right to know

By Mailee R. Smith
Staff Counsel, Americans United for Life

It has become all too clear that the unborn child is not the only victim of abortion—the woman is also victimized by the procedure. Studies have revealed that women suffer physically, emotionally and psychologically following abortion. Even the U.S. Supreme Court has recognized that severe depression and lack of esteem may follow.[1]

Thus, following *Roe v. Wade*, states began enacting informed consent laws, aiming to reduce "the risk that a woman may elect an abortion, only to discover later, with devastating psychological consequences, that her decision was not fully informed."[2] Over the last several legislative sessions, states have begun taking further steps to ensure that women fully understand the risks and implications of their decisions before choosing abortion. These steps, which AUL refers to as "informed consent enhancements," include providing women with information on fetal pain, the availability of ultrasound, and the link between abortion and breast cancer. States are also addressing the prevalence of instances when a woman is coerced against her will into having an abortion.

ISSUES

Informed Consent

Abortion clinics all too often fail to provide adequate and accurate information to women considering abortion. As a result, many women are physically and psychologically harmed by the abortion process. To better equip women with the knowledge they need before making an abortion decision and to ensure their consent is valid, informed consent laws should require the following information be provided to a woman at least 24 hours before an abortion:

- The name of the doctor who is to perform the abortion;
- A description of the procedure to be used;
- The risks of the abortion procedure as well as of childbirth;
- Scientifically accurate information about the unborn child;
- The possibility of medical benefits;
- The father's liability for support; and
- A brochure explaining risks of and alternatives to abortion and scientifically accurate information concerning the development of the unborn child.

In 1992, the U.S. Supreme Court ruled that informed consent laws are constitutional.[3] In 2007, the Court reaffirmed its approval of informed consent laws, holding that "[t]he state has an interest in ensuring so grave a choice is well-informed."[4]

AUL has drafted the "Women's Right to Know Act," which encompasses all of the above provisions and complies with the prevailing U.S. Supreme Court precedent.

Fetal Pain

In light of advances in modern medicine and in popular opinion, a few states have realized that traditional informed consent requirements can be enhanced to further ensure informed consent. For example, several states have already enacted legislation requiring women be informed that their unborn children can feel pain. In the medical community, the accepted consensus is that unborn children begin feeling pain as early as 20 weeks gestation.[5] This view is exemplified in the general practice of administering anesthesia during *in utero* procedures on unborn children who are 20 weeks gestation or more. And popular opinion accords with consensus in the medical community. In a 2004 Zogby poll, 77 percent of those surveyed said they favored laws requiring the provision of information about fetal pain to women who are 20 weeks gestation or more in their pregnancies.[6]

Unfortunately, general public concern over whether the unborn feel pain has, to a large extent, not translated into law. In fact, unborn children currently have less legal protection from pain than do commercial livestock in a slaughterhouse or animals in a laboratory.[7] It is therefore crucial that states work on implementing fetal pain information into their informed consent statutes. A fetal pain bill should include the following basic elements:

- A requirement that the abortion provider provide the pregnant woman information that unborn children at 20 weeks gestation and beyond are fully capable of feeling pain; and

- A requirement that the abortion provider provide the pregnant woman the option to administer anesthesia to alleviate or eliminate pain to the fetus.

AUL has drafted the "Fetal Pain Awareness and Prevention Act," which encompasses these provisions and ensures that women receive the necessary information about fetal pain.

Ultrasound

States have also begun enacting laws which require that a woman be given the option to see an ultrasound image of her unborn child and hear the heartbeat. Ultrasound requirements such as these serve an essential medical purpose in that they diagnose ectopic pregnancies, which if left undiagnosed can result in infertility or even fatal blood loss.

Further, ultrasound requirements ensure an truly informed choice because they allow a woman to see her unborn child as he or she really is, both by seeing his or her form and face on a screen and also by hearing the heartbeat. Medical evidence indicates that women feel bonded to their children after seeing them on the ultrasound screen.[8] Once that bond is established, researchers argue, a woman no longer feels ambivalent toward her pregnancy and actually begins to feel invested in her unborn child.[9]

Thus, ultrasound provisions both promote the woman's physical and psychological health and advance the states' important and legitimate interest in protecting life. To most effectively provide women with this opportunity, ultrasound laws should contain the following provisions:

- A requirement that the physician performing the abortion, the referring physician, or another qualified person assisting the physician either inform the woman that ultrasound and fetal heart tone monitoring services are available or, alternatively, provide a list of providers that perform the services free of charge;

- A requirement that the physician give the woman the option of viewing the ultrasound image; and

- A requirement that the physician adhere to standard medical practice within the community, which ensures that he or she accurately portrays the presence of external members and internal organs, if present and viewable, of the unborn child.

Each of these provisions is contained in AUL's "Woman's Ultrasound Right to Know Act."

The Link Between Abortion and Breast Cancer

While a link between abortion and breast cancer (the "abortion-breast cancer link," or "ABC link") is hotly disputed by pro-abortion activists, the majority of medical studies indicate there is a direct link between abortion and breast cancer. Currently, at least 29 out of 41 worldwide studies have independently linked induced abortion with breast cancer.[10]

Moreover, certain aspects of the relationship between pregnancy and breast cancer are undisputed. For example, it is scientifically undisputed that full-term pregnancy reduces a woman's lifetime risk of breast cancer.[11] It is also undisputed that the earlier a woman has a first full-term pregnancy, the lower her risk of breast cancer becomes, because—following a full-term pregnancy—the breast tissue exposed to estrogen through the menstrual cycle is more mature and cancer resistant.[12] In fact, for each year that a woman's first full-term pregnancy is delayed, her risk of breast cancer rises 3.5 percent.[13]

The theory that there is a direct link between abortion and breast cancer builds upon this undisputed foundation. During the first and second trimesters of pregnancy the breasts develop merely by duplicating immature tissues. Once a woman passes the thirty-second week of pregnancy (third trimester), the immature cells develop into mature cancer resistant cells.[14] This is where abortion fits into the complex scientific puzzle. When an abortion ends a normal pregnancy, the woman is left with more immature breast tissue than she had before she was pregnant.[15] In short, the amount of immature breast tissue is increased and this tissue is exposed to significantly greater amounts of estrogen—a known cause of breast cancer.

Women facing an abortion decision have a right to know that such medical data exists. At the very least, women must be informed that it is undisputed that pregnancy provides a protective effect against the later development of breast cancer.

Information on Hospice Care

For years, pro-abortion activists have spread the false idea that abortion is necessary for unborn children with fetal abnormalities. In many situations, what they deem a necessity is really the choice to abort a child that probably won't survive much longer than birth. For many families, however, aborting their unborn children is not an option, even when it is very likely the baby will die soon after birth. Information about the availability of hospice care for such children opens opportunities for women they might not otherwise have known about. For example, Minnesota requires abortion providers give women information on hospices that provide perinatal care for children born with fetal abnormalities. Essentially, women carrying a child with a lethal abnormality and considering giving birth (as opposed to undergoing an abortion) receive information about comprehensive care that runs from the diagnosis of the fetal abnormality to the child's death.

Coercion

Many women who arrive on the doorstep of an abortion clinic are not there of their own free will. They are there because someone else is forcing them to have an abortion. And we can only guess the lengths to which that other person went in order to get her (or take her) to the abortion clinic.

Pro-abortion advocates spend a great deal of time using the language of "freedom" and "choice." But for many women, abortion is anything but a free choice. A 2004 survey of American and Russian women found that 64 percent of American women who purportedly chose abortion reported they were pressured into their abortions.[16] For these women, abortion is a coerced nightmare justified by legalization and implicitly condoned by an abortion industry that puts profits ahead of women's health.

It is time to put women's health and right of conscience ahead of profits and ideology by enacting coercive abuse prevention (CAP) legislation. To effectively prevent coercive abuse, CAP legislation must address the coercion itself, the timely reporting of suspected coercion, and treatment for victims of coercive abuse.

First, coercive abuse must be clearly defined. Coercive abuse takes on many forms. Whether it is actual or threatened physical abuse, a denial of social assistance support, a threat to fire a pregnant woman, or blackmail, each form should be met with a penalty.

Second, facilities that provide abortion services should be required to report suspected coercive abuse to the proper authorities. Further, if a pregnant woman is being coerced into an abortion, she should know she has options. She should know that coercing an abortion is illegal and that there are counseling and protective services available.

Third, penalties must be capable of punishing and preventing the coercive abuse of pregnant women. This includes penalties for abortion providers who knowingly violate the requirements of these statutes.

AUL has drafted the comprehensive "Coercive Abuse Against Mothers Prevention Act," which encompasses these suggestions and also ensures states do not go too far and infringe on protected First and Fourteenth Amendment conduct.

KEY TERMS

- **Coercive abuse** in the abortion context is committed if a person knows of or suspects the pregnancy of a woman and engages or conspires with another to engage in certain conduct that is intentionally and purposely aimed at directing the woman to have an abortion and solely conditioned upon the pregnant female disregarding or refusing the person's demand that she seek an abortion.

- **Informed consent** is a legal phrase meaning a person must be fully informed of a medical procedure before giving true consent to that procedure. In the abortion context, it means that a woman is fully informed of the risks, alternatives, and other important medical information concerning the abortion. If a woman is not fully informed of what the procedure or its consequences will or could entail, her consent is not legally valid.

- A **medical emergency** occurs when a patient has a condition which, on the basis of the physician's good-faith medical judgment, complicates the medical condition of the patient as to necessitate an immediate abortion in order to avert the patient's death. A medical emergency also exists if a delay will create a serious risk of substantial or irreversible impairment of a major bodily function.

- **Reflection period** refers to the time between the woman's receipt of information and when the abortion is performed. This time period allows a woman to read the information and reflect upon her decision prior to the abortion.

MYTHS & FACTS

Myth: Informed consent laws intrude on the normal patient-physician relationship.
Fact: Most women never receive any consultation with the physician performing the abortion. There can be no intrusion on a relationship that does not exist in the first place.

Myth: Informed consent laws force women to receive biased and misleading information.
Fact: Such laws simply require a woman be informed of all medical risks and alternatives about which a reasonable patient would want to know.

Myth: Women already have access to all the information they need about abortion.
Fact: Researchers have found that 83 percent of women who seek abortion counseling have no prior knowledge about the abortion procedure or fetal development.[17] Furthermore, access to information is not the same as actually receiving information. A woman's health is placed in jeopardy when we begin presuming what she does and does not know.

Myth: Informed consent laws threaten a woman's right to choose.
Fact: Informed consent laws do not prevent a woman from choosing abortion. Rather, such laws ensure a woman makes an informed choice. Those who claim to be "pro-choice" should want to give women the objective information needed to make true choices.

Myth: A woman who might be denied informed consent already has the right to seek redress against the doctor by filing a malpractice action.
Fact: A woman will not be able to bring a successful malpractice action unless it can be shown the abortion provider violated the community standard of other abortion providers. If all or most abortion providers are failing to relay information—as is generally the case—a woman will be unable to recover damages. Moreover, women suffering post-abortion problems are, because of shame or embarrassment, less likely to bring such claims in the first place.

Myth: Abortion is 12 times safer than childbirth, thus informed consent laws do not improve the health of women.
Fact: Numerous medical studies now demonstrate the devastating health risks—both physical and psychological—of elective abortion, placing earlier claims that abortion is safer than childbirth in serious doubt.[18] Moreover, when research on the abortion-breast cancer risk is factored in, the risk of dying from an abortion is found to exceed the risk of dying from childbirth by orders of magnitude.[19]

Myth: Informed consent laws unconstitutionally interfere with a doctor's rights.
Fact: The joint opinion in *Casey* concluded that it was constitutional for a state to regulate physician speech as part of its regulation of the practice of medicine.[20] Moreover, informed consent laws are, in essence, consumer rights laws. Such laws require patients be informed about not only what the abortion provider believes is relevant, but also what a reasonable patient would believe is relevant. According to the American Civil Liberties Union (ACLU), patients should be informed of every risk in elective procedures, even those risks that are the most remote.[21] Because the abortion industry is a for-profit industry, its physicians have every financial reason to deceptively urge that very practical information is irrelevant.

Myth: Abortions will decrease simply because informed consent requirements are burdensome.
Fact: Statistics in Mississippi and Pennsylvania indicate the number of abortions decreases because women are informed, not because informed consent laws are burdensome.[22]

Myth: A new Harvard study unequivocally disproved the ABC link.
Fact: The study was so methodologically flawed that it hides the positive association between induced abortion and breast cancer.

Myth: We do not need to be so concerned about the link of one physical ailment (cancer) and abortion; it is just not that big of a deal.
Fact: Breast cancer is the second deadliest cancer for women (only behind lung cancer). In 2009, it is estimated that 192,370 new cases of invasive breast cancer will be diagnosed, with an additional 62,280 new cases of a more non-invasive form of breast cancer.[23] Approximately 40,610 women in the U.S. will die from breast cancer this year alone. Women are not being informed of the risks that surround their decision to procure an abortion. The amount of information that women receive should not be dependent on the political and social agenda of healthcare professionals.

Myth: Coercive abuse prevention (CAP) legislation is just another way to place a burden between a woman and her right to choose an abortion.

Fact: CAP legislation does not place a burden on a pregnant woman known or suspected to be a victim of coercive abuse. She is not legally required to report anything nor is she prohibited from obtaining an abortion whether or not she is a victim of coercive abuse. The reality is that CAP legislation removes burdens from women who want to proceed with their pregnancies and provides them with potentially vital information necessary to do so.

Myth: A 24-hour reflection period for those known or suspected to be victims of coercive abuse is a burden that will increase the likelihood that a woman will be abused.

Fact: A 24-hour reflection period allows a woman time to consider her treatment and protective options—options she may not have known about prior to their disclosure by the abortion provider. It also allows time for the proper agency to respond to the abortion provider's mandatory report. If she decides to pursue an abortion after the reflection period, she may do so. Moreover, seeking protective services will decrease the likelihood that she will be a victim of abuse because she may seek protective aid from the proper authorities. In emergency situations, the 24-hour reflection period can be waived to save a woman's life or to prevent substantial and irreversible bodily injury.

Myth: Most abused women will not pursue treatment or protective services because they are afraid of further reprisals from their abuser.

Fact: Even if this is true, it is irrelevant. Some women will choose to pursue treatment or protective services. Further, this is not a valid reason to prevent legislation from being enacted. Simply because some women will not take advantage of a law does not mean that all should be prevented from doing so.

Myth: CAP legislation proscribes constitutionally protected conduct.

Fact: CAP liability explicitly excludes constitutionally protected conduct, speech, and expressions of conscience. Emotional "heat of the moment" utterances are excluded, as are statements of belief concerning a woman's pregnancy or lifestyle and property rights concerning allocation of finances and assets.

Myth: CAP legislation is vague because "coercive abuse" could be inferred from conduct that is motivated by factors independent of the woman's pregnancy.

Fact: CAP legislation specifically targets conduct that is intentionally, willfully, and solely conditioned upon the pregnant female disregarding or refusing the person's demand that she seek an abortion. The conduct must also be purposely aimed at directing a woman to have an abortion. Like other crimes, the elements of coercive abuse must be proven beyond a reasonable doubt.

Myth: CAP legislation is unnecessary because the conduct it proscribes is already illegal.

Fact: It is true that CAP legislation encompasses conduct that is traditionally proscribed by a state's criminal code, but this observation is irrelevant. First, this fact is not unique among statutes that criminalize certain conduct. For example, kidnapping may involve crimes such as assault and battery, but this doesn't mean that someone cannot or should not be prosecuted for kidnapping. Second, CAP legislation is broader than the prohibition of coercive abuse. It includes penalty guidelines for those

convicted of coercive abuse and requirements for abortion providers, such as the mandatory reporting of suspected abuse and the disclosure of treatment and protection options to known or suspected victims. Many women will not pursue treatment or protection options on their own because they feel ashamed or simply do not know how. CAP legislation not only allows states to prosecute, but also provides an avenue of treatment and protection for women that otherwise would not have reported the abuse.[24]

Endnotes

[1] *Gonzales v. Carhart*, 127 S. Ct. 1610, 1634 (2007).
[2] *Planned Parenthood v. Casey,* 505 U.S. 833, 882 (1992).
[3] *See id.*
[4] *Gonzales*, 127 S. Ct. at 1634.
[5] Teresa Stanton Collett, *Fetal Pain Legislation: Is it Viable?* 30 Pepp. L. Rev. 161, 164 (2003).
[6] Zogby poll (April 15-17, 2004), surveying more than 1,200 people.
[7] *See, e.g.*, §2 of the Humane Slaughter Act, 7 U.S.C. 1902.
[8] Joseph C. Fletcher and Mark I. Evans, *Maternal Bonding in Early Fetal Ultrasound Examinations*, N.E. J. Med. 308, 392 (1983).
[9] *Id.*
[10] *See* American Association of Pro Life Obstetricians and Gynecologists, *Induced Abortion and the Subsequent Risk of Breast Cancer: An Overview* (2008), available at: http://www.aaplog.org/abortioncomplications.aspx (last visited June 10, 2009).
[11] The Coalition on Abortion Breast Cancer, *The ABC Summary*, available at http://www.abortionbreastcancer.com/abc.html (last visited June 11, 2009).
[12] *Id.*
[13] B. MacMahon et al., *Age of First Birth and Breast Cancer Risk*, 43 Bull. World Health Organization 209 (1970).
[14] Angela Lanfranchi, *The Breast Physiology and the Epidemiology of the Abortion Breast Cancer Link*, 12 Imago Hominis 228, 231 (2005).
[15] Angela Lanfranchi, *The Science, Studies and Sociology of the Abortion Breast Cancer Link*, 18 Research Bulletin 1, 4 (2005).
[16] Vincent Rue, et. al., *Induced Abortion and Traumatic Stress: A Preliminary Comparison of American and Russian Women,* Med. Sci. Monit. 10(10):SR5-16 (2004).
[17] R. Reardon, Aborted Women 101 (1987).
[18] *See, e.g.*, John M. Thorp et al., *Long-Term Physical and Psychological Health Consequences of Induced Abortion: Review of the Evidence*, 58[1] Obstet. & Gyn. Survey 67 (2003); David C. Reardon et al., *Deaths Associated with Abortion Compared to Childbirth: A Review of New and Old Data and the Medical and Legal Implications*, available at http://www.afterabortion.org/research/DeathsAssocWithAbortionJCHLP.pdf (last visited June 10, 2000) and originally published at 20[2] J. Contemp. Health Law & Pol'y 279 (2004); David C. Reardon et al., *Deaths Associated with Pregnancy Outcome: A Record Linkage Study of Low Income Women*, 95[8] S. Med. J. 834 (2002).
[19] See J. Brind et al., *Induced Abortion as an Independent Risk Factor for Breast Cancer: A Comprehensive Review and Meta-Analysis*, J. Epidemiol. Cmty. Health 50:481-96 (1996).
[20] *Casey*, 505 U.S. at 884.
[21] George Annas, The Rights of Hospital Patients: The Basic ACLU Guide to a Hospital Patient's Rights 68 (1992).
[22] Miss. Dept. Pub. Health, *Reported Induced Terminations of Pregnancy and Induced Termination Ratios, by Year and Race, Procedures Performed in Mississippi, 1976-2000*, 2000 Vital Statistics Mississippi (2001), available at http://www.msdh.state.ms.us/phs/statisti.htm (last visited June 10, 2009); Pa. Dept. of Health, *Pennsylvania Vital Statistics 1999*, Table D-1 (1999), available at http://www.health.state.pa.us/stats (last visited June 10, 2009).
[23] American Cancer Society, *What are the key statistics for breast cancer?*, available at http://www.cancer.org/docroot/CRI/content/CRI_2_4_1X_What_are_the_key_statistics_for_breast_cancer_5.asp (last visited June 11, 2009).
[24] For more information on the topics discussed in this article, please visit AUL's website at http://www.AUL.org.

Informed Consent Talking Points

- Informed consent laws—including 24-hour reflection periods—are constitutional as an expression of the state's interest in the health and safety of women.[1]

- Reflection periods do not increase health risks to women or place an undue burden on women who have to travel long distances, incur additional costs, etc. Not only has the U.S. Supreme Court rejected such arguments,[2] but most informed consent laws provide medical emergency exceptions and do not require that the information come personally from the abortionist himself—and thus women need not visit an abortion clinic twice.

- There is conclusive evidence that having an abortion can cause serious psychological problems and that women who experience post-abortion psychological problems would have benefited from informed consent laws.[3]

- Thousands of women have testified that they did not receive adequate counselling from abortion providers.[4]

- Recall bias[5] has never been shown to make a statistically significant effect in abortion-breast cancer link studies, even when explicitly tested.[6]

- Coerced abortion prevention (CAP) legislation advances a state's interest in preventing the abuse of pregnant women and decreasing the homicide rate among pregnant women. Prosecutions of abusers increase because more cases of coerced or attempts to coerce abortion are reported if women are informed of their rights and given information concerning treatment and protection options.

- CAP legislation increases the likelihood that victims of coercive abuse will receive treatment. Many women do not know about treatment options available for victims of coercive abuse. Abortion service provider regulations requiring the disclosure of treatment options to known or suspected victims of coercive abuse allow women to take advantage of such options.

Endnotes

[1] *See Planned Parenthood v. Casey*, 505 U.S. 833 (1992). The Court has also upheld a 48-hour reflection period for minors in the context of a parental notice law. *Hodgson v. Minn.*, 497 U.S. 417 (1990).

[2] *Casey*, 505 U.S. at 885-86; *see also id*. at 966-69 (Rehnquist, J., concurring in the judgment and dissenting in part); *Utah Women's Clinic v. Leavitt*, 844 F. Supp. 1482, 1490-91 (D. Utah 1994).

[3] *See* V. Rue, *Postabortion Syndrome: A Variant of Post Traumatic Stress Disorder*, in POSTABORTION SYNDROME: ITS WIDE RAMIFICATIONS 2-21 (E. Cosmi & P. Doherty, eds. 1995); *see also Lack of Individualized Counseling Regarding Risk Factors for Induced Abortion: A Violation of Informed Consent*, RESEARCH Bulletin Vol. 10, Nos. 1 & 2 (Ass'n for Interdisciplinary Research in Values

& Soc. Changes Sept./Oct. 1996); Franz & Reardon, *Differential Impact of Abortion on Adolescents and Adults*, 27 Adolescence 161-72 (Spring 1992); David et al., *Postpartum and Postabortion Psychotic Reactions*, 13 Family Planning Perspectives 2, 88-91 (Mar./Apr. 1981).

[4] *See, e.g.*, R. Reardon, Aborted Women 16-17, 335 (1987) (finding that 85 percent of women surveyed believed they were misinformed or denied relevant information during their pre-abortion counseling); *The Abortion Profiteers*, Chicago Sun-Times, Nov./Dec. 1978 (reporting that there is more high-pressure selling in abortion clinics than any real counseling).

[5] Recall bias is the suggestion that a woman with breast cancer is more likely to report prior abortions than a healthy woman who has had an abortion in the past.

[6] Angela Lanfranchi, *The Breast Physiology and the Epidemiology of the Abortion Breast Cancer Link*, 12 Imago Hominis 228, 235 (2005).

Informed Consent Laws

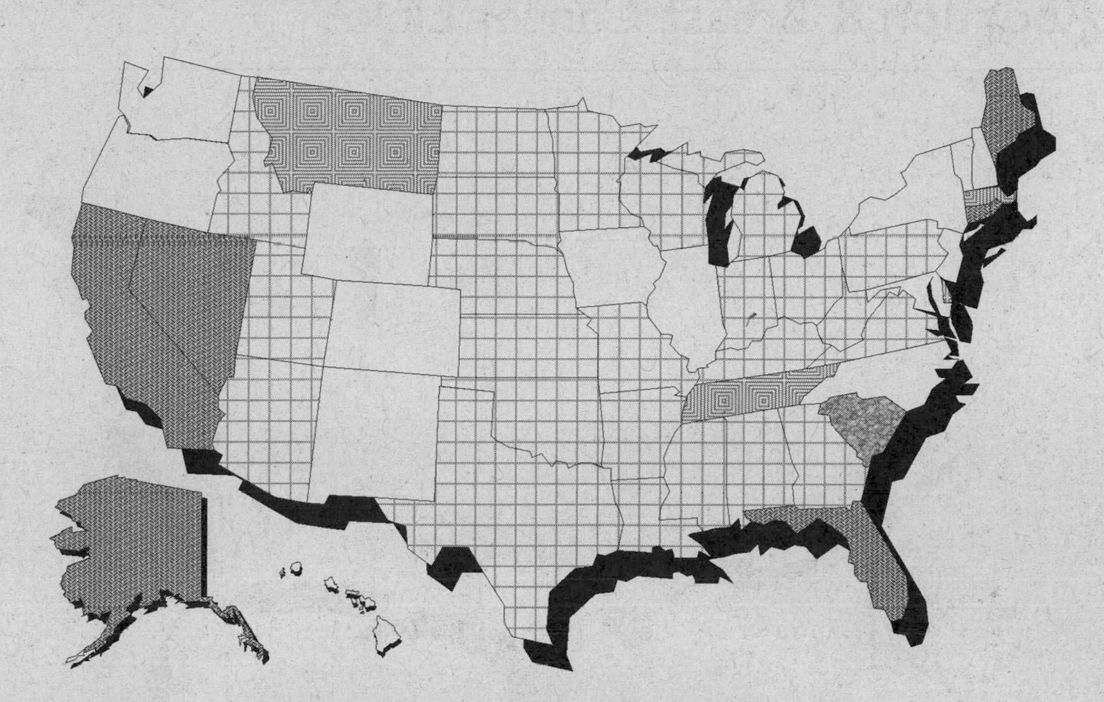

Thirty-two state laws are in effect:

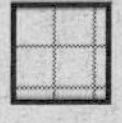

Twenty-four states require informed consent with a one-day reflection period (usually 24 hours): AL, AZ, AR, GA, ID, IN (18 hours), KS, KY, LA, MI, MN, MS, MO, NE, ND, OH, OK, PA, SD, TX, UT, VA, WV, and WI.

One state requires informed consent with a one-hour reflection period: SC.

Seven states require informed consent with no reflection period: AK, CA, CT, FL, ME, NV, and RI.

Four states have enacted informed consent laws that are in litigation or enjoined: DE, MA, MT, and TN.

Informed Consent Regarding Abortion & Breast Cancer Link

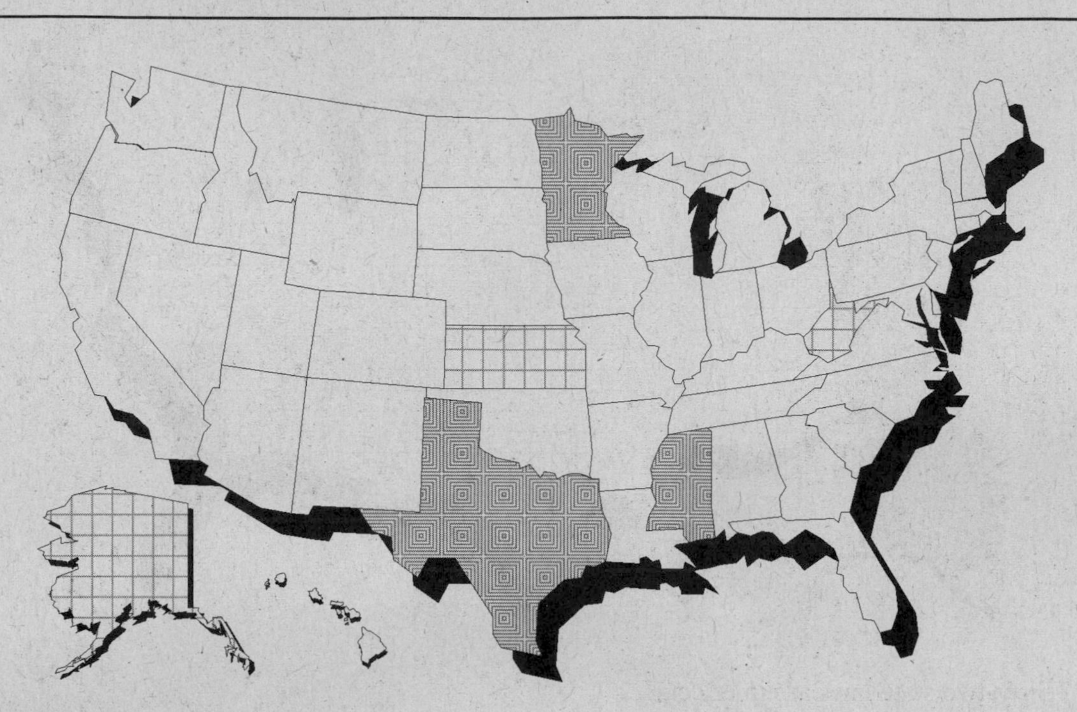

Three states explicitly require a physician to inform a woman seeking abortion of the link between abortion and breast cancer: MN, MS, and TX.

Three states include information about the link between abortion and breast cancer in the state-mandated educational materials that a woman must receive prior to abortion: AK, KS, and WV.

Informed Consent Regarding Fetal Pain

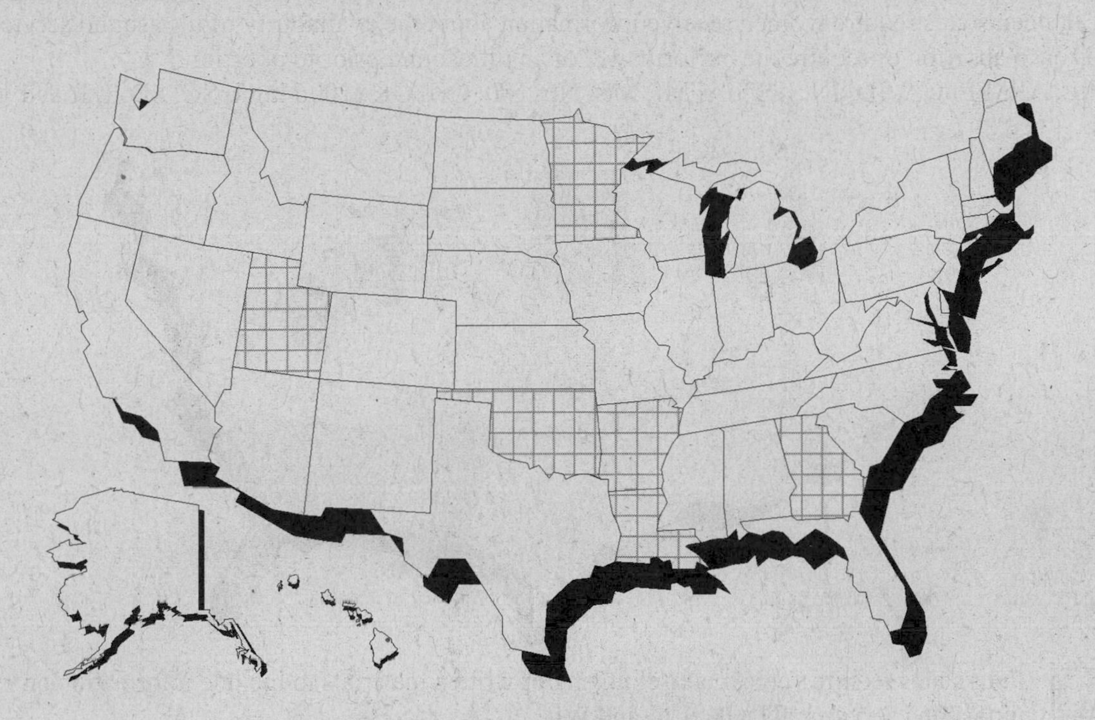

Six states require women receive information about fetal pain and/or the option of anesthesia for the unborn child: AR, GA, LA, MN, OK, and UT.

Informed Consent Regarding Ultrasound

Eighteen states require women receive information about the availability of ultrasound services prior to abortion or require the performance of an ultrasound prior to abortion: AL, AR, FL, GA, ID, IN, KS, LA, MI, MS, NE, ND, OH, OK (2006 law), SC, SD, UT, and WI.

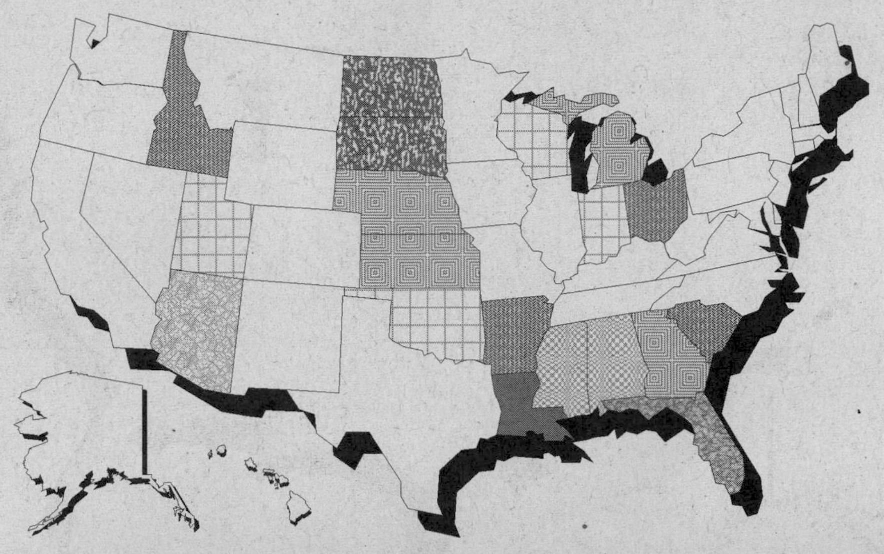

Four states require verbal counseling and/or written materials to include information on ultrasound services: IN, OK, UT, and WI.

Four states require verbal counseling and/or written materials to include information on ultrasound services and require the abortion provider to offer the opportunity to see an ultrasound image if ultrasound is used in preparation for the abortion: GA, KS, MI and NE.

Four states require the abortion provider to offer a woman the opportunity to see an ultrasound image if ultrasound is used in the preparation for the abortion: AR, ID, OH, and SC.

Two states require an ultrasound for each abortion and require the abortion provider to offer the opportunity to view the image: AL and MS.

One state requires an ultrasound after the first trimester and requires the abortion provider to offer the opportunity to view the image: FL.

One state requires an ultrasound at 20 weeks gestation and beyond to determine viability, and requires the abortion provider offer the opportunity to view the image: LA.

Two states require the abortion provider to offer the opportunity to view an ultrasound image: ND and SD.

One state's ultrasound requirement is enjoined: AZ (requires ultrasounds at and after 12 weeks gestation).

Coercive Abuse Prevention Laws

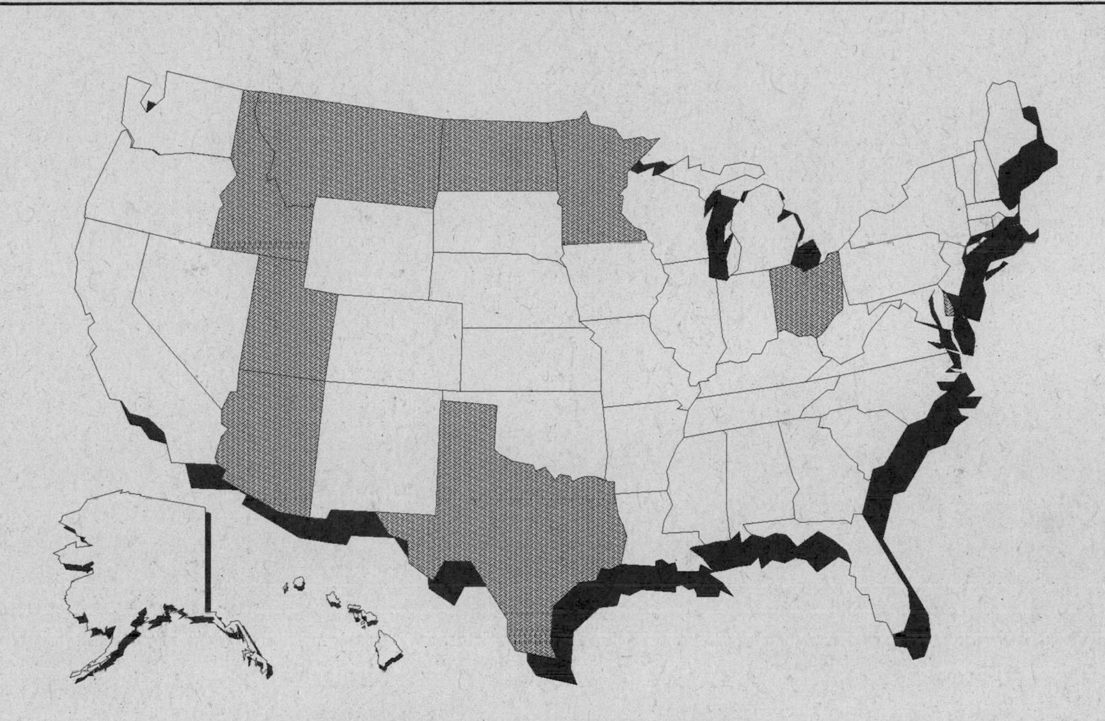

At least nine states have some form of coercive abuse prevention laws, with varying definitions and degrees of protection: AZ, DE, ID, MN, MT, ND, OH, TX, and UT.

Parental Involvement Laws:
Protecting minors and parental rights

By Mailee R. Smith
Staff Counsel, Americans United for Life

Thirteen-year-old "Jane Doe" was your everyday teen: She attended school and played on the school soccer team. But her normal life turned into a nightmare when her soccer coach initiated a sexual relationship with her, impregnated her, and took her to a local Ohio Planned Parenthood clinic for an abortion. The clinic never questioned the soccer coach, who posed over the phone as Jane's father and then personally paid for the girl's abortion. And where were her real parents? Their consent was never sought. In fact, they were never even informed.[1]

Sadly, Jane's story is not unique. Almost daily news stories reveal yet another teen that has been sexually abused by a person in authority— a coach, teacher, or other authority figure. Daily, teens are taken to abortion clinics without the consent or even the knowledge of their parents. The health and welfare of these minors is at risk, especially in states where parental involvement laws have not been enacted.

ISSUES

Parental Involvement

In 1992, a plurality of the U.S. Supreme Court ruled that a state may constitutionally require a minor seeking an abortion to obtain the consent of a parent or guardian.[2] Specifically, the Court held that certain provisions, such as a required reflection period and a chance for parents to privately discuss with their daughters the values and moral principles of the situation, carry particular force with respect to minors.[3] Based upon the Court's decision and subsequent lower federal court decisions, a parental involvement law is constitutional and does not place an undue burden on minors if it contains the following provisions:

- No physician may perform an abortion upon a minor or incompetent person unless the physician performing the abortion has obtained the consent of or has given 48 hours notice to a parent or legal guardian of the minor or incompetent person.

- An exception to the requirement exists when there is a medical emergency or when consent notice is waived by the entitled party.

- A minor may bypass the requirement through the courts (*i.e.*, judicial bypass).

The purpose behind parental involvement laws is clear. Immature minors often lack the ability to make fully informed choices that take into account both immediate and long-range consequences. Yet the medical, emotional, and psychological consequences of abortion are often serious and can be lasting, particularly when the patient is immature. Moreover, parents usually possess information essential to a physician's exercise of his or her best medical judgment concerning the minor. Parents who are aware that their minor has had an abortion may better ensure the best post-abortion medical attention. As such, parental consultation is usually desirable and in the best interest of the minor. For these reasons, parental involvement laws protect the health and welfare of minors, as well as foster family unity and protect the constitutional rights of parents to rear their children.

AUL has drafted both a "Parental Consent for Abortion Act" as well as a "Parental Notification of Abortion Act."

Parental Involvement Enhancements

The situation surrounding Jane Doe's abortion may have been different if the local Planned Parenthood affiliate had followed the law in Ohio. Unfortunately, it is often too easy for abortion clinics to sidestep the law by claiming they were duped into believing they had contacted the proper party. A simple way to combat such claims is to reinforce current parental involvement laws with identification or notarization requirements.

More specifically, states should require that parents present positive, government-issued identification before a minor obtains an abortion. A step further would require that parents' consent forms are notarized. Copies of the identification or notarized documents must then be kept by the abortion clinic in the minors' medical records. When such actions are required, ignorance of an adult's true identity is no excuse for failing to follow the law.

Another way to enhance existing parental involvement laws is to enact specific standards for judicial review in evaluating judicial bypass petitions. Currently, most consent and notice requirements contain very basic criteria, simply requiring that the minor be mature enough to make the decision, or requiring that the abortion would be in the minor's "best interest."

An Arizona appellate court case[4] has delineated the type of criteria a judge should use in evaluating the maturity of a minor petitioning for judicial bypass. It is an excellent example of how the more basic judicial bypass requirements can be enhanced. Looking to U.S. Supreme Court precedent stating that minors "often lack the experience, perspective, and judgment to recognize and avoid choices that could be detrimental to them," the court concluded that maturity may be measured by examining a minor's experience, perspective, and judgment.[5]

"Experience" refers to all that has happened to the minor during her lifetime, including the things she has seen or done. Examples include the minor's age and experiences working outside the home, living away from home, traveling on her own, handling her personal finances, and making other significant decisions.[6]

"Perspective" refers to the minor's ability to

appreciate and understand the relative gravity and possible detrimental impact of available options, as well as the potential consequences of each. Specific examples include the steps she took to explore her options and the extent to which she considered and weighed the potential consequences of abortion.[7]

"Judgment" refers to the minor's intellectual and emotional ability to make the abortion decision without the consent of her parents or guardian. This includes the minor's conduct since learning of her pregnancy and her intellectual ability to understand her options and make an informed decision. Consideration should be given to whether the minor's decision resulted from impulse rather than careful consideration.[8]

Such guidelines will give judges the foundation they need to more freely evaluate the true maturity level of those minors seeking an abortion without parental involvement.

KEY TERMS

- **Parental involvement** laws are those laws requiring parental notification or consent prior to the performance of an abortion on a minor. **Parental notification** laws simply require that a parent or legal guardian be notified that a minor will be having an abortion, while **parental consent** laws require a parent or legal guardian to consent to the abortion.

- A **medical emergency** occurs when a patient has a condition which, on the basis of the physician's good faith medical judgment, so complicates the medical condition of the patient as to necessitate an immediate abortion in order to avert the patient's death. A medical emergency also exists if a delay will create a serious risk of substantial or irreversible impairment of a major bodily function.

- **Judicial bypass** is the means by which a minor can petition a circuit court for waiver of the parental consent or notice requirements. Such court proceedings are confidential. If a court finds that the minor is sufficiently mature and well-informed to decide on her own whether to have an abortion, the court issues an order authorizing the minor to have the abortion without parental consent or notice. A court may also issue such an authorization if it finds that a pattern of physical, sexual, or emotional abuse by a parent necessitates a bypass of the parental consent or notice law.

MYTHS & FACTS

Myth: An estimated 12 percent of teens do not even live with their parents. Involving the parents of these teens will be impossible and totally unrelated to the teen's health.
Fact: Parental involvement legislation recognizes that many family situations are less than ideal. In most states, alternative procedures are available through judicial bypass, and some states allow notification or consent of another family member.

Myth: Mandatory parental involvement laws will force many teens to go out of state to obtain an abortion.

Fact: As more states enact and enforce parental involvement laws, the option to go out of state will cease to exist, and parental rights and minors' health protection will continue to expand. Migration to other states is a reason to pass parental involvement laws, not to avoid them.

Myth: Parental involvement laws simply delay teens from getting abortions until the second trimester, when abortion is more dangerous.
Fact: This myth is directly contrary to data from both Minnesota and Missouri.[9]

Myth: Parental involvement laws force teens to obtain dangerous illegal abortions.
Fact: The majority of states have enforceable parental involvement laws. Only one case—that of Becky Bell in Indiana—has been suggested to involve an unsafe abortion, and even that case is wholly undocumented. The autopsy report failed to show any induced abortion. It is terrible public policy to fail to enact a law on the basis of an isolated, unproven case.

Myth: Parental involvement laws expose teens to the anger of abusive parents.
Fact: Under the parental involvement laws in most states, a teen who states she has been abused or neglected will be exempted from the laws' requirements. In addition, the laws make it more likely that a minor who is being abused or neglected will get the help she needs; under most state laws, doctors who become aware of abuse claims must report the abuse allegation to public officials who conduct an anonymous investigation. Such teens also have the option of utilizing the judicial bypass procedure.

Myth: Most teens are mature enough to make their own decisions.
Fact: Young teens often have difficulty assessing long-term consequences and generally have narrow and egocentric views of their problems.[10] Parental involvement is needed to give teenagers some perspective. Moreover, the question is not simply of maturity, but of responsibility. As long as a teenager is not emancipated, a parent or guardian is responsible for her medical care and upbringing. When a teen is injured by an abortion, it is the parent or guardian—not the teen—who is responsible for the teen's care and health costs.[11]

Endnotes

[1] Facts related to this story can be found in court documents as well as in AUL's *amicus curiae* brief in the case, located at http://www.aul.org/xm_client/client_documents/briefs/Roe_v_PP_OH_05-2008.pdf (last visited June 19, 2009). The case is *Roe v. Planned Parenthood*, Supreme Court of Ohio (No. 07-1832).
[2] *Planned Parenthood v. Casey*, 505 U.S. 833, 899 (1992).
[3] *Id.*
[4] *In the Matter of B.S.*, 74 P.3d 285 (Ariz. Ct. App. 2003).
[5] *Id.* at 290.
[6] *Id.*
[0] *Id.* at 291.
[8] *Id.*
[9] J.L. Rogers et al., *Impact of the Minnesota Parental Notification Law on Abortion and Birth*, 81 AM. J.PUB. HEALTH 294, 296 (1991); Jacot et al., *A Five-Year Experience with Second-Trimester Induced Abortions: No Increases in Complication Rate as Compared to the First Trimester*, 168[2] AM. J. OBSTET. GYNECOL. 633 (Feb. 1993).
[10] *See generally* J. Piaget & B. Inhelder, THE PSYCHOLOGY OF THE CHILD (1969).
[11] For more information on the topics discussed in this article, please visit AUL's website at http://www.AUL.org.

Parental Involvement Talking Points

- Parental involvement laws advance key state interests: protecting the health and welfare of minors, and protecting the constitutional right of parents to rear their children.

- Parental involvement laws increase teenage sexual responsibility and reduce teenage demand for abortion. Parental involvement laws also result in lower birthrates among teens.

- Parental involvement laws are supported by the majority of Americans, regardless of their positions on abortion.

- Parental involvement laws ensure that parents have the opportunity to discuss their daughter's medical history with a physician and that they, in return, have their questions answered about the abortion procedure and follow-up care.

- Parental involvement laws recognize the traditional rights of parents to direct the rearing of their children. Ironically, notification is required before virtually all non-emergency procedures except abortion.

- Studies indicate less than half of teenagers inform their parents of their abortions, and many of those teenagers who do not inform their parents exaggerate their parents' reactions.

- There is evidence that abortion results in serious psychological problems for both minor and adult women.[1] Moreover, because of their immature developmental stage, adolescents are at a higher risk of suffering severe psychological problems from abortion, possess an elevated risk of suicide, and are even more likely to enter into a cycle of deliberately seeking replacement pregnancies.[2]

- Teens are even more at risk of developing breast cancer from having an abortion than are adult women.[3]

- Stories and litigation concerning the exploitation of young women by adult males is increasingly common. To combat the threat of these sexual predators abusing girls and then taking them for abortions, states should enact identification and notarization requirements to ensure that the person informed of or consenting to the abortion is truly the minor's parent or guardian.

- When judges have specific criteria to reference when evaluating the maturity of minors in judicial bypass proceedings, judges have more liberty in their decisions to truly act in the minors' best interests.

Endnotes

[1] CATHERINE BARNARD, THE LONG-TERM PSYCHOLOGICAL EFFECTS OF ABORTION (Inst. for Abortion Recovery & Research 1990). For more information on studies finding that abortion poses severe short- and long-term effects, and particularly for minors, *see* AUL's amicus brief in the case *Doe v. Arpaio*, available at http://www.aul.org/xm_client/client_documents/briefs/DoevArpaio.pdf (last visited June 19, 2009).

[2] Franz, *Differential Impact of Abortion on Adolescents and Adults*, ADOLESCENCE, 27(105):161-72 (1992); Campbell, *Abortion in Adolescence*, ADOLESCENCE, 23:813-24 (1988).

[3] Daling et al., *Risk of Breast Cancer Among Young Women: Relationship to Induced Abortion*, J. NAT'L CANCER INST., 86:505-14 (1994). Daling, an abortion supporter, found that teenagers with a family history of breast cancer who obtained an abortion before the age of 18 had an incalculably high risk of developing breast cancer. *Id.* *Every single female* under the age of 18 in the study who obtained an abortion and had a family history of breast cancer *developed breast cancer* by the age of 45. *Id.*

Parental Involvement Laws

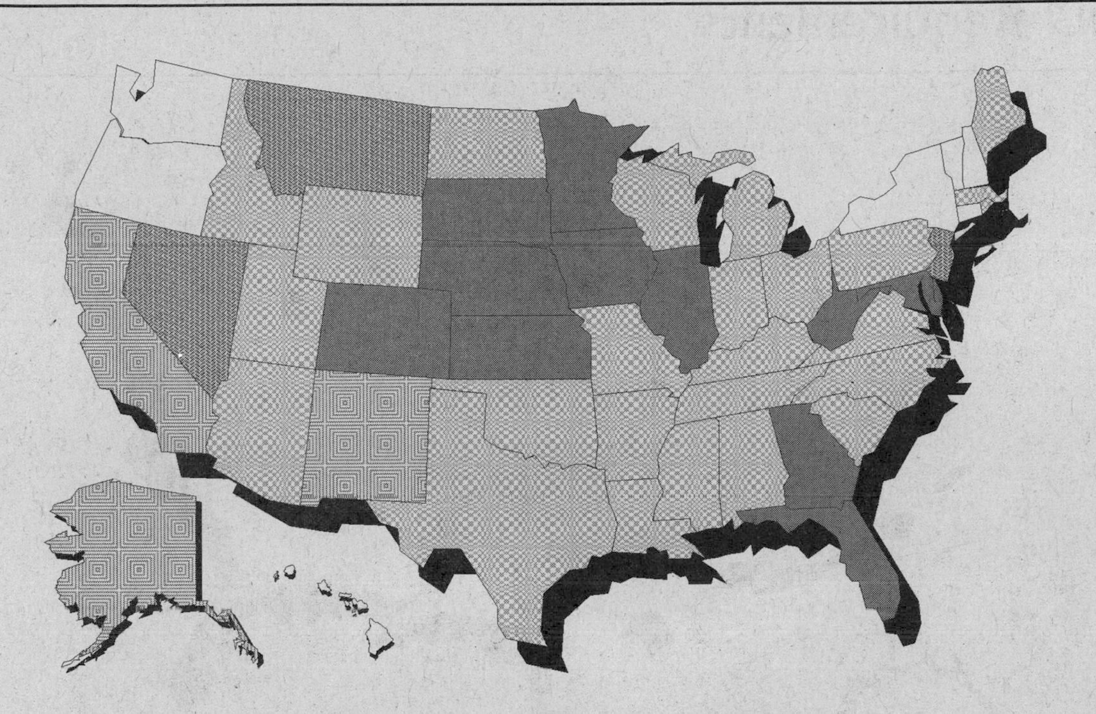

Thirty-seven state parental involvement laws are currently in effect:

Twenty-five states require parental consent for minors seeking abortion: AL, AR, AZ, ID, IN, KY, LA, ME, MA, MI, MS, MO, NC, ND, OH, OK, PA, RI, SC, TN, TX, UT, VA, WI, and WY.

Twelve states require parental notice for minors seeking abortion: CO, DE, FL, GA, IL, IA, KS, MD, MN, NE, SD, and WV.

Six state parental involvement laws are enjoined, in litigation, or not enforced:

Three states have parental consent laws that are enjoined, in litigation, or the state's Attorney General has issued an opinion against enforcement: AK, CA, and NM.

Three states have parental notice laws that are enjoined, in litigation, or not enforced: MT, NV, and NJ.

Parental Involvement Enhancements: ID Requirements

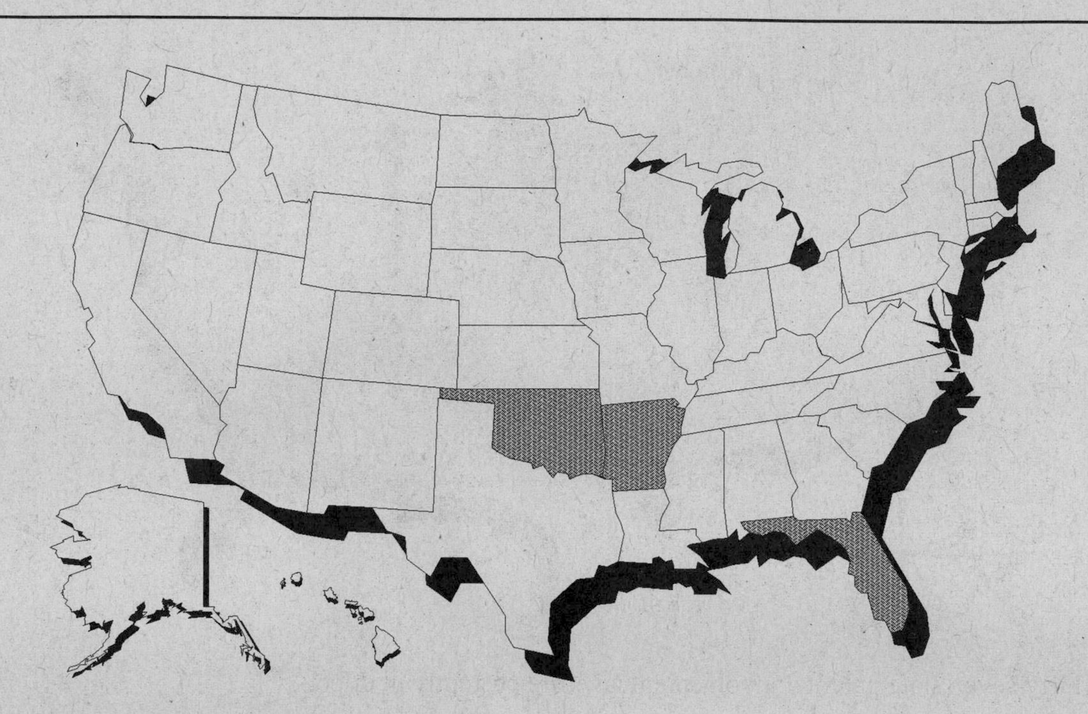

At least three states require a parent or guardian to provide identification: AR, FL, and OK.

Parental Involvement Enhancements: Notarization Requirements

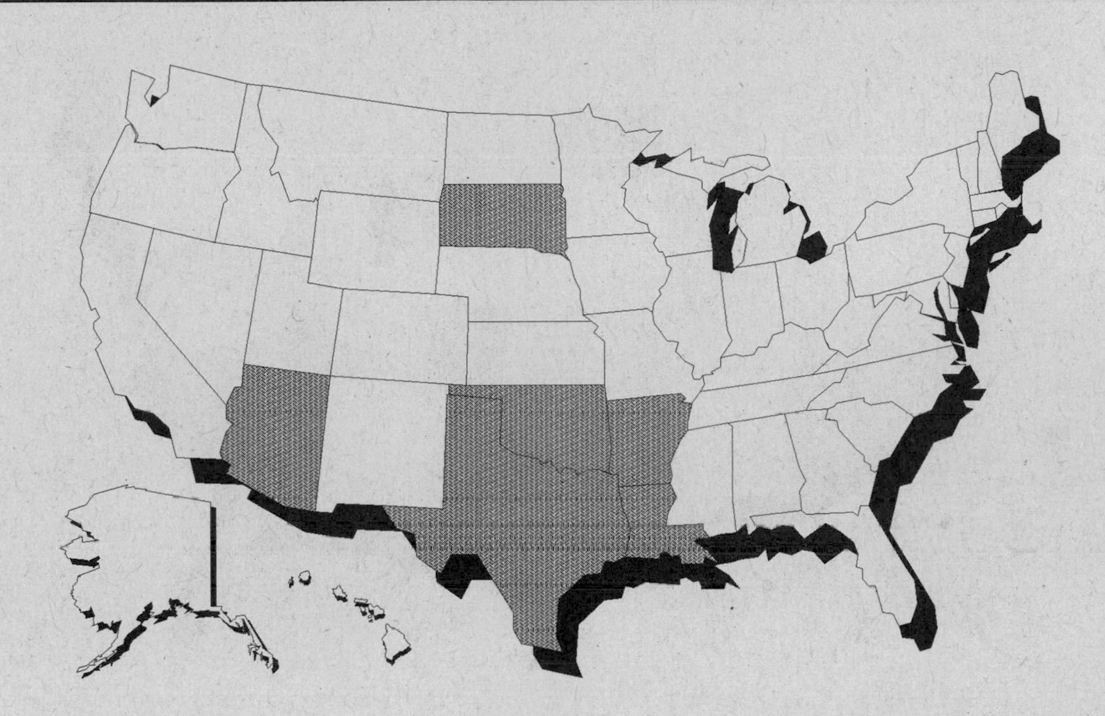

At least six states require a notarized signature by a parent or guardian: AZ, AR, LA, OK, SD, and TX.

Parental Involvement Enhancements: Judicial Bypass Standards

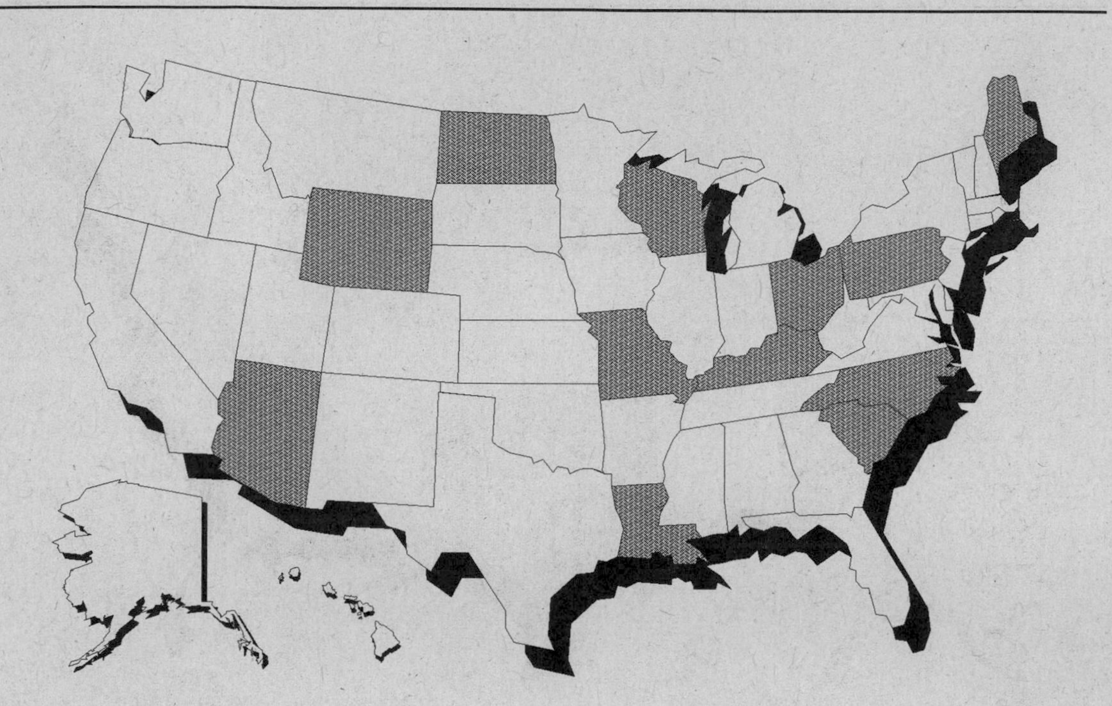

At least 12 states provide varying degrees of standards for judges to use when considering the "maturity" and/or "best interests of minors" in judicial bypass proceedings: AZ, KY, LA, ME, MO, NC, ND, OH, PA, SC, WI, and WY.

Regulating Abortion Facilities and Providers:
Combating the true back alley[1]

By Denise M. Burke
Vice President of Legal Affairs, Americans United for Life

Since the 1960s, abortion proponents have continued to argue that legalized abortion is beneficial to the health and well-being of American women. In support of this assertion, they have put forth a litany of purported advantages. The primary advantage they often cite is increased medical safety for women undergoing abortions.

When their campaign to legalize abortion began, proponents argued that if abortion was legal the procedure would be safer for women because it would become an accepted part of mainstream medical care, proper surgical procedures would be followed, and skilled and reputable gynecologists and surgeons would perform the procedure. Unskilled and incompetent butchers would no longer perform abortions. Thus, legalized abortion would eliminate the 5,000 to 10,000 deaths abortion advocates disingenuously claimed resulted from illegal or "back alley" abortions each year.[2]

Proponents also argued that legalizing abortion would ensure women receive proper care before, during, and after the procedure. Proper care would obviously include appropriate post-operative monitoring and follow-up care. Legalized abortion would ensure that no woman would bleed to death alone and in pain following an unsafe abortion.

These were the promises. But has it proven to be the reality? Has 37 years of legalized abortion eliminated these problems from our national consciousness? Plainly, it has not. Instead, abortion clinics across the nation have become the true back alleys of abortion mythology.

There is abundant evidence to support the contention that abortion clinics are the true back alleys abortion advocates warned us about. A quick review of just a few cases of substandard abortion care poignantly contrasts the reality of abortion in America today with what abortion advocates promised legalized abortion would eradicate.

CASE STUDY – South Carolina:
In 1994, several women testified before the General Assembly of the South Carolina legislature that when they walked into some of the state's abortion clinics they saw bloody, unwashed sheets, bloody cots in recovery rooms, and dirty bathrooms. Clinic workers testified the remains of unborn children were not disposed of properly, but rinsed down sinks.[3]

CASE STUDY – Texas:
Witnesses disclosed that abortion clinic personnel without medical licenses or formal medical training performed abortions.[4]

CASE STUDY – Arizona:
A young mother bled to death from a two-inch laceration in her uterus. As she lay in what medical assistants described as a pool of blood

that soaked the bedding and ran down the woman's legs, she was heard crying for help and asking what was wrong with her. Where was her doctor? He was eating lunch in the break room, refusing requests to check her condition, and later left her bleeding and unconscious to visit his tailor. The woman died after bleeding for two to three hours. Sadly, a hospital emergency room was less than five minutes down the street.[5]

CASE STUDY – Kansas:

Two inspections of the same Topeka, Kansas, abortion clinic revealed fetal remains stored in the same refrigerator as food; a dead rodent in the clinic hallway; overflowing, uncovered disposal bins containing medical waste; unlabeled, pre-drawn syringes with controlled substances in an unlocked refrigerator; improperly labeled and expired medicines; a carpeted floor in the surgical procedure room; and visible dirt and general disarray throughout the clinic. Dr. Krishna Rajanna, who operated the unsanitary clinic, also consistently violated the practice guidelines for conscious sedation.[6]

Tragically, these case studies are indicative of what some American women experience when they enter an abortion clinic. The question is what can be done about it. Each of the states involved in these case studies (South Carolina, Texas, Arizona, and Kansas) have since enacted comprehensive abortion clinic regulations requiring clinics to be licensed by the state, to be inspected by state health department officials, and to meet minimum health and safety standards.

Enacting comprehensive abortion clinic regulations is a critical and sensible solution to the problem of unsafe, back-alley abortions in America. These regulations are designed to safeguard against unsanitary conditions, inferior equipment, and the employment of unsuitable and untrained personnel. They are also intended to put an end to substandard medical practices that injure and kill untold numbers of women each year.

Moreover, to further ensure women's health and safety, states also should consider additional common sense laws including physician-only mandates, admitting privileges requirements, and comprehensive reporting requirements for abortions and abortion complications .

ISSUES

Abortion Clinic Regulations

Abortion providers do not foster or maintain a patient-physician relationship with women.

A significant percentage of all abortions are performed in clinics devoted solely to providing abortions and family planning services. Most women who seek abortions at these facilities do not have any relationship with the physician who performs the abortion, before or after the procedure. They do not return to the facility for post-surgical care. In most instances, the woman's only actual contact with the physician occurs simultaneously with the abortion procedure, with little opportunity to ask questions about the procedure, potential complications, and proper follow-up care.

Abortion is an invasive surgical procedure that can lead to numerous and serious medical complications.

Potential complications for first-trimester abortions include, among others, bleeding, hemorrhage, infection, uterine perforation, blood clots, cervical tears, incomplete abortion (retained tissue), failure to actually terminate the pregnancy, free fluid in the abdomen, acute abdomen, missed ectopic pregnancies, cardiac arrest, sepsis, respiratory arrest, reactions to anesthesia, fertility problems, emotional problems, and even death.[7]

The risks for second-trimester abortions are greater than for first-trimester abortions. The risk of hemorrhage, in particular, is greater, and the resultant complications may require a hysterectomy, other reparative surgery, or a blood transfusion.

As the author of a leading abortion textbook writes, "[T]here are few surgical procedures given so little attention and so underrated in its potential hazard as abortion."[8]

The courts have historically supported the need for abortion clinic regulations.

Since *Roe v. Wade*, the U.S. States Supreme Court has repeatedly recognized that a state has "a legitimate interest in seeing to it that abortion, like any other medical procedure, is performed under circumstances that ensure maximum safety for the patient."[9]

Federal courts have also repeatedly recognized that for the purposes of regulation, abortion is rationally distinct from other routine medical services because of the "particular gravitas of the moral, psychological, and familial aspects of the abortion decision."[10]

Comprehensive abortion clinic regulations passed in the years immediately following the 1992 U.S. Supreme Court decision in *Planned Parenthood v. Casey* were derived, in substantial part, from standards and protocols promulgated by abortion providers and abortion advocacy groups, specifically the Planned Parenthood Federation of America (Planned Parenthood) and the National Abortion Federation (NAF). The use of national abortion care standards and protocols has been a significant factor cited by federal courts in upholding these regulations against constitutional challenges by abortion providers.[11]

AUL has drafted the "Women's Health Protection Act" based on these national abortion care standards. Further, for states wishing to impose more exacting standards, AUL has drafted the "Abortion Patients' Enhanced Safety Act," which imposes standards similar to those followed in ambulatory surgical centers.

Physician-Only Laws and Admitting Privileges Requirements

The number of abortion providers nationwide is declining and pro-abortion groups are seeking ways to incorporate and increase the number of non-physician providers.

In recent years, pro-abortion organizations like the NAF and the Center for Reproductive Rights (CRR) have pushed to expand access to RU-486 ("the abortion pill") and Plan B ("emergency contraception"), while simultaneously bemoaning the declining number of abortion providers in the U.S. To deal with these competing issues, they have vowed to work "in collaboration with partner organizations to explore different strategies for expanding scope of practice [of physician assistants, nurses, midwives, and others] in states."[12] At this juncture, this concerted effort by pro-abortion groups and their allies is focused on access to abortifacients, but their tactics and goals are readily transferable to efforts to expand the scope of practice for surgical abortions.

Abortion Reporting

The current voluntary abortion reporting system administered by the CDC is seriously flawed, resulting in inaccurate, unreliable, and incomplete abortion data.

Although the majority of the states require the reporting of some abortion-related information to state agencies, the states are not required to submit these reports to the Centers for Disease Control and Prevention (CDC) or other federal or national reporting agency.[13] The individual states are responsible for setting up and enforcing abortion reporting policies and systems, and for deciding what information (if any at all) should be submitted to the CDC. Some estimates suggest state reports to the CDC lack information on as many as 45-50% of the abortions performed annually.[14]

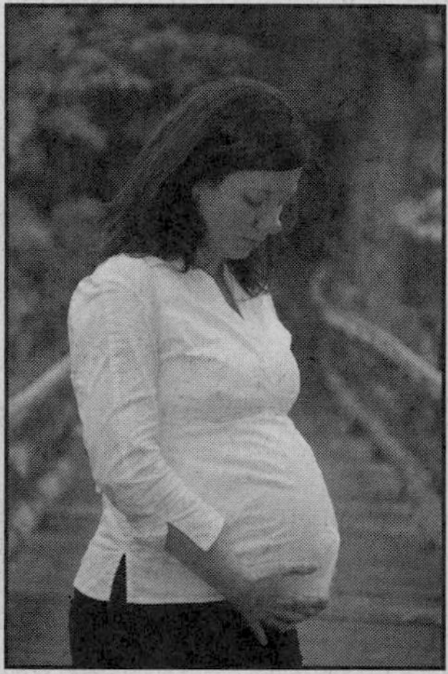

Accurate data on late-term abortions is virtually non-existent.

The states do not specifically require abortion providers to report late-term abortions. Although many states require reporting the gestational age of the unborn child at the time of the abortion, the majority of the states do not. Hence, there is no way of knowing how many late-term abortions are performed. Consequently, important information on the safety, efficacy, and complications of late-term abortions is lacking. Even the pro-abortion Alan Guttmacher Institute has admitted "specific data on the frequency of late-term abortions are limited, and data on the use of dilation and extraction [*i.e.*, partial-birth abortion] do not exist either at the state or national level."[15]

The majority of the states do not require reporting on long-term complications.

Abortion complications can be severe and lasting, and may even lead to death.[16] Unfortunately, the abortion reporting laws of the majority of the states, as well as the U.S. Standard Report of Induced Termination of Pregnancy form,[17] do not require abortion providers to report on long-term complications.

Additionally, many women who suffer complications are treated at hospitals, and not at the clinic where they underwent their abortions. Abortion providers are not required to record or report complications (including deaths) that occur and are treated outside their facilities.

However, one state, Mississippi, has made a noticeably positive step in improving abortion complication reporting. Mississippi's statute requires all physicians treating abortion patients—not just abortion providers—to file "a written report with the State Department of Health regarding each patient who comes under the physician's professional care and requires medical treatment or suffers death that the attending physician has a reasonable basis to believe is a primary, secondary, or tertiary result of an induced abortion."[18] Mississippi is currently the only state with this requirement.

RU-486's unique risks and complications necessitate reporting requirements tailored to

the use of abortifacients.
Since the FDA's September 2000 approval of RU-486, the number of nonsurgical abortions performed each year has increased.[19] Reliable information on the number and complications of non-surgical abortions (including RU-486) is unavailable partly because not all state abortion reporting laws require reporting on non-surgical abortions, and even those that do require reporting on non-surgical abortions do not require this information to be reported to the CDC.

In addition, there is an insufficient understanding of the risks and complications associated with nonsurgical abortions. Nonsurgical abortions carry unique risks because, unlike with surgical abortions, abortifacients can be prescribed by anyone with a "medical license," such as untrained psychiatrists, podiatrists, and dentists.[20] In addition, side effects are often confusingly similar to that of an ectopic pregnancy. Lastly, RU-486 is routinely and openly administered to women contrary to its FDA-approved regimen, resulting in severe complications, including death.[21]

Lack of uniform reporting hinders research on nationwide abortion trends.
As there is no uniform method for abortion reporting among the states, abortion data collected by the different states is, in many respects, incomparable.[22] For example, states vary in their definitions of abortion complications, as well as in their methods of determining gestational age. States also differ in how they submit information to the CDC—some states submit aggregated data prepared by a state statistical agency, whereas some states submit the reports without passing them through a state agency.[23] Some states submit information on abortions that occurred in the state, whereas other states submit information on abortions performed on residents of the state.[24] In addition, the reporting forms issued by the various state health departments have changed throughout the years. All of these inconsistencies make it hard to compare data from the different states, track trends, understand sociological motives that lead to abortion, or state conclusively anything that accurately reflects the country as a whole.[25]

To remedy these concerns, AUL has drafted the "Abortion Complication Reporting Act."

KEY TERMS

Abortion surveillance is the collection, analysis, and dissemination of information related to abortion procedures, abortion morbidity, and abortion mortality with the objective of preventing morbidity and mortality associated with induced abortion. Abortion surveillance is an established branch of epidemiological surveillance.[26]

Abortion complications are the adverse short- and long-term physical, emotional, and psychological effects of abortion on women.

The U.S. Standard Report of Induced Termination of Pregnancy form is the abortion reporting form issued by the CDC, and has been used as a model by the states. The form requests reporting on: (1) name and location of the abortion facility; (2) demographic and geographic information about the patient; (3) patient ID number; (4) obstetric history (*e.g.*, date of last menses, number of prior pregnancies and abortions); (5) type of abortion procedure (including RU-486); and (6) names of physician and person filling out the report. Some states generally follow this model report form, and some do not. The abortion reporting laws of the various states may call for more or less than what is required in the standard form.[27]

Voluntary abortion reporting is the submission of state abortion reports and/or aggregated abortion report information by state agencies to the CDC on a voluntary and discretionary, rather than contractual, basis.

MYTHS & FACTS

Myth: Abortion clinic regulations unfairly single out abortion providers for regulation and oversight.
Fact: Federal courts have repeatedly held abortion to be "rationally distinct from other routine medical services."[28] Therefore, a state may choose to regulate abortion while leaving other types of medical or surgical procedures unregulated. As the Fourth Circuit noted, "In adopting an array of regulations that treat the relatively simple medical procedures of abortion more seriously than other medical procedures, [the State] recognizes the importance of abortion practice while yet permitting it to continue, as protected by the Supreme Court's cases on the subject."[29]

Myth: Individual abortion providers are already licensed (as physicians) by the state medical board and their offices are already regulated under a variety of federal and state regulations. Thus, there is no need for additional and/or specifically-tailored abortion clinic regulations.
Fact: These arguments have been made and repeatedly and summarily rejected by federal courts.[30] Abortion clinic regulations are designed to specifically address and meet the needs of abortion patients. Physician licensing standards and other federal or state regulations (such as those applicable to onsite laboratory services, employee safety, etc.) are not designed to meet the specific medical needs of women undergoing abortions.

Myth: These regulations will create an undue burden on women seeking abortions by increasing the cost of abortions and/or by decreasing the number of providers.
Fact: Federal courts have also summarily and repeatedly rejected these arguments.[31] The abortion right is the right of the "woman herself—not her husband, her parent, her doctor or others—to make the decision to have an abortion."[32] It is not the right of the woman to pay a certain price for an abortion or the right of an abortion provider to remain in practice or to have a financially lucrative practice.

Further, in evaluating challenges to abortion clinic regulations, federal courts have repeatedly determined that the simple fact the regulations may inconvenience some abortion providers and/or may result in an expenditure of time and money to come into compliance with the regulations does not create a burden on the woman seeking an abortion (as opposed to the abortion provider) and, therefore, are not enough to invalidate such regulations.

Finally, even assuming the specific regulatory scheme would lead to an increase in the cost of abortions in the state and/or result in fewer providers, the U.S. Supreme Court has held "the fact that a law which serves a valid purpose, one not designed to strike at the [abortion] right itself, has the incidental effect of making it more difficult or more expensive to procure an abortion cannot be enough to invalidate it."[33] Clearly, protecting maternal health is a valid and compelling reason for regulating abortion clinics.

Myth: Abortion reporting laws are unconstitutional.
Fact: The U.S. Supreme Court has held that abortion reporting is constitutional and does not impose an undue burden on a woman's right to an abortion. For example, in *Planned Parenthood v. Casey*, the Court held "[t]he collection of information with respect to actual patients is a vital element of medical research, and so it cannot be said that the requirements serve no purpose other than to make abortions more difficult."[34]

Myth: Abortion reporting laws violate women's privacy.
Fact: Abortion reporting laws specifically protect women's privacy. Every state abortion reporting law contains provisions prohibiting the inclusion of patient names in abortion reporting forms. Many states even mandate that any information that can "reasonably lead" to the identification of a patient must not be included in an abortion report and/or publication.

Myth: There is no need for abortion reporting laws because the data and reports published by the Alan Guttmacher Institute (AGI) are reliable and accurate.
Fact: Abortion data published by AGI is unreliable for many reasons. First, the foremost purpose of the AGI's abortion reporting system is to promote the availability of abortion. AGI has stated "[t]he CDC, consistent with its federal function, focuses particular attention on the safety of the procedure, while AGI concerns itself with the availability of abortion services throughout the country."[35] AGI's emphasis on abortion access rather than on women's health and safety comes as no surprise, as the AGI has long been known as the unofficial research arm of Planned Parenthood.[36]

Second, AGI is a privately-funded organization and its ability to collect data and produce statistics is limited. Notably, for financial reasons, AGI has been forced to limit its collection of abortion data to every four years.[37]

Third, AGI collects information on a voluntary basis directly from abortion providers. Although AGI claims it collects abortion information from "all known abortion providers," they only collect information from those providers who voluntarily respond to phone call surveys or questionnaires that AGI sends through the mail. None of the abortion providers contacted are under any obligation to respond, and there is no way to assure that responses are truthful and accurate. Moreover, AGI has revealed it does not use an authentic, comprehensive list of abortion providers. Rather, AGI has admitted they compile a list of provider names by searching through the telephone yellow pages, the membership directory of NAF, and the Internet.[38] Thus, AGI cannot accurately claim they collect information from all known abortion providers.

Fourth, AGI's scope is limited to abortion providers who are known as or advertise themselves as abortion providers. Abortions performed by private practice physicians (outside of established abortion clinics) remain mostly unreported.[39]

Lastly, AGI does not ask abortion providers for

information on short- and long-term complications, medical care provided for complications, or follow-up examinations.[40]

Myth: The current abortion reporting system is on par with other vital statistics data collection systems.

Fact: The CDC and the medical community have long recognized that the current abortion system is substantially below par in comparison to all other systems of vital statistics data collection. In 1978, in an attempt to establish an abortion reporting system on par with other vital statistics collection systems, the National Center for Health Statistics (NCHS) sought to establish a new system that would collect information from the states on a contractual, rather than voluntary, basis. However, as a result of inadequate financial planning, NCHS failed to institute the planned system.[41] Interestingly, since 1978, the CDC and NCHS have never again attempted to establish an abortion reporting system that is on par with other vital statistics collecting systems.

Myth: Abortion reporting laws will endanger women's health.

Fact: The medical and public health communities have emphasized that improved methods of abortion reporting are essential for improving women's health care. Accurate statistics on abortion procedures and their outcomes and complications contribute to the body of medical knowledge that informs practicing abortion providers and physicians-in-training on (1) which abortion techniques are safest and most effective; (2) how to safely perform a specific abortion procedure; and (3) how to improve the procedure to make it safer and to avoid complications.[42]

Endnotes

[1] Portions of the information contained in this overview were excerpted from D. Burke, *Abortion Clinic Regulation: Combating the True Back-Alley*, The Cost of Choice 122-131 (2004).

[2] However, the numbers of deaths from illegal abortion were greatly exaggerated, as were the claims that abortions were inherently unsafe before *Roe v. Wade*. For example, in 1960, Planned Parenthood's Director Mary Calderone wrote:

> Abortion is no longer a dangerous procedure. This applies not just to therapeutic abortions as performed in hospitals but also so-called illegal abortions as done by physicians . . . abortion, whether therapeutic or illegal, is in the main no longer dangerous, because it is being done well by physicians.

Mary Calderone, *Illegal Abortion as a Public Health Problem*, 50 Am. J. Pub. Health 949 (July 1960).

Moreover, Dr. Bernard Nathanson, a founder of National Abortion and Reproductive Rights Actions League (NARAL), later conceded these statistics were intentionally misleading:

> How many deaths were we talking about when abortion was illegal? In NARAL, we generally emphasized the drama of the individual case, not the mass statistics, but when we spoke of the latter it was always "5,000 to 10,000 deaths a year." I confess that I knew the figures were totally false, and I suppose the others did too if they stopped to think of it . . . The overriding concern was to get the laws eliminated, and anything within reason which had to be done was permissible.

Bernard Nathanson, Aborting America 193 (1979).

[3] Dial, *Abortion: A Dirty Industry*, Citizen Magazine, July 2001

[4] Dial, *supra*.

[5] Phoenix Police Department Report, July 15, 1998; testimony of Dr. John I. Biskind, *State v. Biskind*, No.CR99-00198 (Ariz. Superior Ct.), Feb. 13, 2001.

[6] Consent Order, Board of Healing Arts of the State of Kansas, Docket No. 50-H, Feb. 14, 2005; Final Order, Board of Healing Arts of the State of Kansas, Docket No. 50-H-58, June 14, 2005.

[7] Information on abortion complications is drawn from depositions, responses to interrogatories, and other discovery in *Tucson Woman's Clinic v. Eden*, No. CIV 00-141-TUC-RCC (D. Ariz. Oct. 1, 2002).

[8] Warren M. Hern, Abortion Practice 101 (1990).

[9] *Roe v. Wade*, 410 U.S. 113, 150 (1973). *See also Planned Parenthood of Southeastern Penn. v. Casey*, 505 U.S. 833, 847 (1992).

[10] *Greenville Women's Clinic v. Bryant*, 222 F.3d 157, 173 (4th Cir. 2000), *cert. denied*, 531 U.S. 1191 (2001).

[11] For example, in upholding South Carolina's abortion clinic regulations, the Fourth Circuit Court of Appeals noted, with approval, that the regulations were "little more than a codification of national medical- and abortion-association recommendations designed to ensure the health and appropriate care of women seeking abortions." *Greenville Women's Clinic*, 222 F.3d 157.

[12] *See e.g.*, http://www.prochoice.org/cfc/legal_practice.html

(last visited August 24, 2009).

[13] *State Policies in Brief: Abortion Reporting Requirements*, The Alan Guttmacher Institute, October 2007. *See also* Rebekah Saul, *Abortion Reporting in the United States: An Examination of the Federal-State Partnership*, The Alan Guttmacher Institute, Family Planning Perspectives, Vol. 30, Number 5 (1998); Willard Cates, Jr., David A. Grimes, & Kenneth F. Schultz, *Abortion Surveillance at the CDC: Creating Public Health Light Out of Political Heat*, Am. J. Prev. Med., Vol. 19, Number 1S (2000); and Smith & Cates, *supra*, n. 1.

[14] *Issues in Brief: The Limitations of U.S. Statistics on Abortion*, The Alan Guttmacher Institute (1997).

[15] Rebekah Saul, *supra*, n. 2. *See also, Issues in Brief, supra*, n. 3 ("There are few authoritative data to support claims regarding how many late-term abortions are performed…").

[16] Abortion complications include, but are not limited to: death, uterine perforation, cervical perforation, infection, bleeding, hemorrhage, blood clots, failure to actually terminate the pregnancy, incomplete abortion (retained tissue), pelvic inflammatory disease, endometritis, missed ectopic pregnancy, cardiac arrest, respiratory arrest, renal failure, metabolic disorder, shock, embolism, coma, placenta previa, preterm delivery in subsequent pregnancies, free fluid in the abdomen, adverse reactions to anesthesia and other drugs, and mental and psychological complications such as depression, anxiety, sleeping disorders, psychiatric hospitalization, and emotional problems.

[17] The "U.S. Standard Report of Induced Termination of Pregnancy" was introduced in 1978 by the National Center for Health Statistics (NCHS). The form has been generally used by the states as a model for state reporting forms. *See* Rebekah Saul, *supra*, n. 2.

[18] CMSR 15-301-044.

[19] Rachael K. Jones, Mia R. Zolna, Stanley K. Henshaw & Lawrence B. Finer, *Abortion Incidence in the United States: Incidence and Access to Services, 2005*, Perspectives on Sexual and Reproductive Health, The Alan Guttmacher Institute (March 2008), at 6, 15.

[20] Even the Alan Guttmacher Institute has admitted that untrained personnel are given unfettered authority to perform medical abortions. *See supra*, n. 13 ("Early medication abortion requires less training and equipment than surgical abortion and can be more easily provided by family planning clinics and physicians' offices.…Mifepristone has made it easier for health care providers, including those that do not specialize in obstetrics and gynecology, to provide abortion services.").

[21] Mailee R. Smith, *The Deadly Convenience of RU-486 and Plan B*, Defending Life 2009: A State-by-State Legal Guide to Abortion, Bioethics, and the End of Life, published by Americans United for Life. *Available at* http://dl.aul.org/abortion/the-deadly-convenience-of-ru-486-and-plan-b (last visited August 24, 2009).

[22] *See e.g.*, Rebekah Saul, *supra*, n. 2 ("…accurate, complete and consistent data that is comparable across the years…simply do not now exist.").

[23] Lawrence B. Finer & Stanley K. Henshaw, *Estimates of U.S. Abortion Incidence, 2001-2003*, The Alan Guttmacher Institute (2006).

[24] *Id.*

[25] *See e.g., Issues in Brief, supra*, n. 3.

[26] Smith & Cates, *supra*, n. 1, at 194.

[27] For example, all states with abortion reporting laws prohibit the inclusion of the patient name, and sometimes also the patient ID number on the reporting form. All states that require reporting of the patient ID have strict requirements for maintaining the confidentiality of the patient's identity. The abortion reporting laws of Hawaii, Kentucky, New Mexico, New York, Oregon, Tennessee, Vermont and Virginia require only a general abortion report, with no specific requirements (*e.g.*, the total number of abortions performed in a given time period, or merely that "all abortions shall be reported to the State"). For abortions performed on minors, Arkansas, Georgia, Louisiana, Oklahoma, South Carolina, Utah and Wisconsin require reporting on whether or not the applicable parental notification and/or consent law was followed. Only three states—Alaska, West Virginia, and Montana—require reporting on whether or not informed consent was obtained prior to the abortion. Only three states—Arizona, Oregon, and Washington—require reporting on medical treatment provided for abortion complications. Only one state, Louisiana, requires reporting on the name and address of the facility or hospital where post-abortion complication treatment was given.

[28] *See, e.g. Greenville Women's Clinic*, 222 F.3d at 172-75; *Casey*, 505 U.S. at 852.

[29] *Greenville Women's Clinic*, 222 F.3d at 175.

[30] *See Tucson Woman's Clinic*, No. CIV 00-141-TUC-RCC; *Greenville Women's Clinic*, 222 F.3d 157; *Women's Med. Ctr. of Northwest Houston v. Bell*, 248 F.3d 411 (5th Cir. 2001).

[31] *See Greenville Women's Clinic*, 222 F.3d 157; *Bristol Reg'l Women's Ctr., P.C. v. Tenn. Dep't of Health*, No. 3:99-0465 (D. Tenn. Oct. 22, 2001); *Bell*, 248 F.3d 411.

[32] *Casey*, 505 U.S at 877.

[33] *Casey*, 505 U.S at 874.

[34] 505 U.S. 833 at 900-901 (1992).

[35] *Issues in Brief, supra*, n. 3.

[36] The connection between these two organizations is well-known—Alan Guttmacher himself was one of the original founders of Planned Parenthood.

[37] *Issues in Brief, supra*, n. 3 ("…the difficulties inherent in raising private funds, repeatedly, for a massive information-gathering effort limit AGI's ability to go into the field with greater regularity."). *See also State Policies in Brief, supra*, n. 2; Rebekah Saul, *supra*, n. 2.; Willard Cates, Jr. *et al.*, *supra*, n. 2; and Smith & Cates, *supra*, n. 1.

[38] *Supra*, n. 13, at 7, 15-16.

[39] *Id.*

[40] *Supra*, n. 13, at 7. The AGI questionnaire asks providers for information on the number of surgical and nonsurgical abortions performed, gestational age at the time of the abortion, and the distance traveled by women receiving nonsurgical abortions. Hospitals are not asked any questions about nonsurgical abortions.

[41] Rebekah Saul, *supra*, n. 2.

[42] In addition to physician training, abortion statistics are necessary in order to prepare hospitals and health facilities for the medical needs of women who have abortions. Hospitals and health facilities must be prepared to provide women with adequate medical care before and during an abortion, as well as any emergency care she may need after the abortion has been performed. Good abortion statistics will inform hospitals and health facilities as to what care a woman will need before, during, and after an abortion. Moreover, an improved abortion reporting system requiring increased accountability will improve women's health care because it will provide incentive for abortion providers to ensure adequate safety precautions are taken when performing an abortion, and better health care is provided to women after the abortion procedure.

Abortion Provider Requirements & Regulations Talking Points

Abortion Clinic Regulations

- Abortion clinic regulations consist of minimal health and safety standards necessary to ensure basic medical care for women before, during, and after an abortion. Typical abortion clinic regulations include provisions relating to:
  - Licensing and training requirements for abortion providers;
  - Requirement that all surgical instruments be sterilized;
  - Maintenance and confidentiality of patient medical records;
  - Availability of functioning emergency care equipment;
  - Having a sink for personnel to wash their hands prior to a procedure;
  - Prohibition on the use of expired medications;
  - Post-procedural patient care and observation; and
  - Written protocol for patient follow-up.

- Abortion clinic regulations are consistent with equal protection guarantees and do not single out abortion providers for unfair treatment. The federal courts have summarily rejected the argument that clinic regulations violate abortion providers' right to equal protection. Instead, the courts have held abortion to be "a unique act" that is "rationally distinct" from all other types of medical procedures. As such, a state may choose to regulate abortion while leaving other types of medical or surgical procedures unregulated.[1]

- Abortion clinic regulations do not impose an undue burden on a woman's "right to choose." Federal courts have summarily rejected the argument that abortion clinic regulations will create an undue burden on women seeking abortions by increasing the cost of abortions and/or by decreasing the number of providers.[2] The abortion right has been specifically defined by the U.S. Supreme Court as "the right of the women herself," not the right of doctors to practice without oversight or to charge a certain price for an abortion.[3] The U.S. Supreme Court has frequently held that "incidental cost increases" are not sufficient to strike down clinic regulations protecting women's health and safety.[4]

- Another option for ensuring the health and safety of women at abortion clinics is to define and regulate abortion clinics as ambulatory surgical centers. Missouri enacted such a law in 2007, but the law remains in litigation. However, a federal court has—thus far—refused to enter a permanent injunction against the law.[5]

Physician-Only Requirements

- Forty-three states and the District of Columbia limit the performance of surgical abortions to licensed physicians. Additionally, a small number of states also specifically preclude healthcare providers such as chiropractors and nurses from performing surgical and/or chemical abortions.

Admitting Privileges

- Eleven states have enforceable requirements mandating abortion providers have admitting privileges at a hospital within a specified distance of the abortion clinic.

- Moreover, some counties in Indiana have enacted a similar requirement.

Abortion Reporting/Abortion Complication Reporting

- Thirty-nine states require reporting (to varying degrees) on both surgical and nonsurgical abortions, while seven states require reporting only on surgical abortions.

- Only twenty-two of these states specifically require reporting on (at last some) abortion complications.

- The U.S. Supreme Court has repeatedly held that abortion reporting requirements are constitutional and do not impose an "undue burden" on a woman's right to choose abortion. For example, in *Planned Parenthood v. Casey*, the Court held "[t]he collection of information with respect to actual [abortion] patients is a vital element of medical research, and so it cannot be said that the requirements serve no purpose other than to make abortions more difficult."[6]

- The current abortion reporting system administered by the Centers for Disease Control and Prevention (CDC) is inherently limited and will always result in inaccurate data, in large part, because it is a voluntary surveillance system. Although the majority of the states have laws requiring abortion providers to submit confidential abortion reports to state agencies, the states are not required to submit these reports to the CDC.[7]

- There is little to no data being compiled to contribute to an understanding of long-term abortion complications. States with abortion complication reporting requirements typically only require reporting on short-term complications.[8] Moreover, most women who suffer abortion complications are treated at hospitals and not at the abortion clinics where they underwent their abortions. Abortion providers are not required to record or report complications (including death) treated outside their facilities.

- Accurate information on the number and complications of late-term abortions is virtually non-existent. The states do not specifically require abortion providers to report late-term abortions. Even the pro-abortion Alan Guttmacher Institute has admitted "specific data on the frequency of late-term abortions are limited, and data on the use of dilation and extraction [*i.e.*, partial-birth abortion] do not exist either at the state or national level."[9]

- There is no reliable information on the number and complications of nonsurgical abortions (including RU-486) because not all states require reporting on these abortions.[10] The number of nonsurgical abortions performed each year is increasing, but, in light of inadequate data collection, there is an insufficient understanding of the risks and complications associated with these abortions. Clearly, the risks are different. For example, RU-486 patients have reported significantly longer bleeding and higher levels of pain, nausea, vomiting, and diarrhea than women who have surgical abortions. RU-486 abortions have also been shown to be less effective than surgical abortions.[11] Moreover, unlike surgical abortions, RU-486 can be provided by anyone with a "medical license," such as untrained psychiatrists and dentists. Lastly, RU-486 is routinely and openly administered to women contrary to its FDA-approved regimen; this has resulted in severe complications, including death.[12]

Endnotes

[1] *See Planned Parenthood v. Casey*, 505 U.S. 833, 852 (1992); *Greenville Women's Clinic v. Bryant*, 222 F.3d 157, 172-175 (4th Cir. 2000), *cert denied*, 531 U.S. 1191 (2001); and *Women's Medical Center of Northwest Houston v. Bell*, 248 F.3d 411 (5th Cir. 2001).

[2] *Greenville Women's Clinic v. Bryant*, 222 F.3d 157, 172-175 (4th Cir. 2000), *cert denied*, 531 U.S. 1191 (2001); *Women's Medical Center of Northwest Houston v. Bell*, 248 F.3d 411 (5th Cir. 2001); *Bristol Reg'l Women's Ctr., P.C. v. Tenn. Dep't of Health,* No. 3:99-0465 (D. Tenn. Oct. 22, 2001).

[3] *Casey*, 505 U.S. at 833, 877 (1992) (joint opinion of O'Connor, Kennedy, and Souter, JJ.).

[4] *See e.g. Webster v. Reproductive Health Svcs.*, 492 U.S. 490, 530 (1989) and *Planned Parenthood v. Ashcroft*, 462 U.S. 476, 490 (1983).

[5] *Planned Parenthood v. Drummond,* Case Number 07-04164 (W.D. Mo. 2007).

[6] 505 U.S. 833 at 900-901 (1992).

[7] *State Policies in Brief: Abortion Reporting Requirements*, The Alan Guttmacher Institute, October 2007. *See also* Rebekah Saul, *Abortion Reporting in the United States: An Examination of the Federal-State Partnership*, The Alan Guttmacher Institute, Family Planning Perspectives, Vol. 30, Number 5 (1998); Jack C. Smith & Willard Cates, Jr., *The Public Need for Abortion Statistics*, Public Health Reports, Vol. 93, pp.194-197 at 12; and Willard Cates, Jr. *et al.*, *supra*, n.1. Some states do not have abortion reporting statutes. As a result, the CDC has been forced to use its own guesses on the number and results of abortions in those states for purposes of its published abortion data. For example, the District of Columbia, Maryland, New Hampshire, and New Jersey do not have abortion reporting laws, and the abortion reporting law in California is permanently enjoined.

[8] Willard Cates, Jr. *et al.*, *supra*, n.1; and Smith & Cates, *supra*, n. 4, at 12.

[9] Rebekah Saul, *supra*, n. 4. *See also, Issues in Brief: The Limitations of U.S. Statistics on Abortion*, The Alan Guttmacher Institute (1997) ("There are few authoritative data to support claims regarding how many late-term abortions are performed…"). Although many states require reporting the gestational age of the fetus at the time of the abortion, the majority of the states do not. Hence, there is no way of knowing how many late-term abortions are performed, and whether or not those late-term abortions included partial-birth abortions.

[10] In 1998, only 17 states required abortion providers to report nonsurgical abortions. As of October 2007, only 29 states require abortion providers to report nonsurgical abortions.

[11] Jeffrey T. Jensen *et al.*, *Outcomes of Suction Curettage and Mifepristone Abortion in the United States: A Prospective Comparison Study*, Contraception 59:153, 156 (1999). (one study revealed RU-486 abortions failed in 18.3 percent of participating patients, compared to the 4.7 percent failure rate of patients who underwent surgical abortions).
[12] Mailee R. Smith, *The Deadly Convenience of RU-486 and Plan B*, in Defending Life 2009: A State-by-State Legal Guide to Abortion, Bioethics, and the End of Life, published by Americans United for Life. *Available at* http://dl.aul.org/abortion/the-deadly-convenience-of-ru-486-and-plan-b (last viewed on August 24, 2009).

Abortion Clinic Regulations

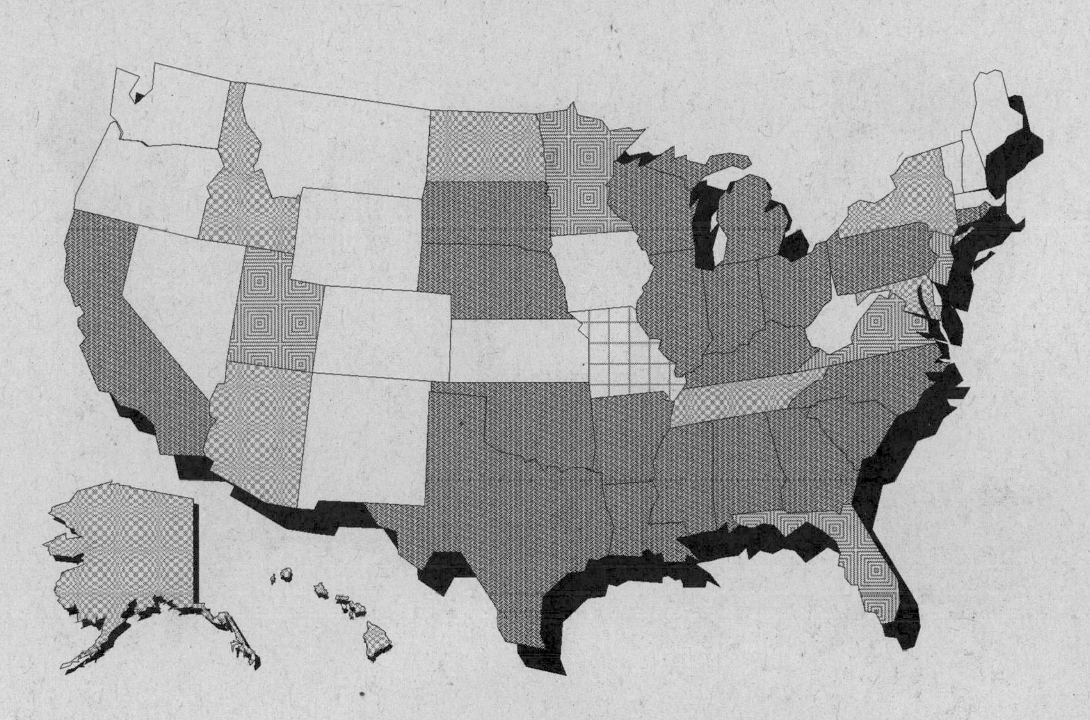

One state imposes stringent ambulatory surgical center standards on clinics performing any abortions: MO.

Twenty-one states maintain varying degrees of abortion clinic regulations that apply to all abortions: AL, AR, CA, CT, GA, IL, IN, KY, LA, MI, MS, NE, NC, OH, OK, PA, RI, SC, SD, TX, and WI.

Five states regulate facilities performing post-first trimester abortions only: FL, MN, NJ, UT, and VA.

Eight states have clinic regulations that are enjoined or otherwise not enforced: AK, AZ, HI, ID, MD, NY, ND, and TN.

Physician-Only Requirements

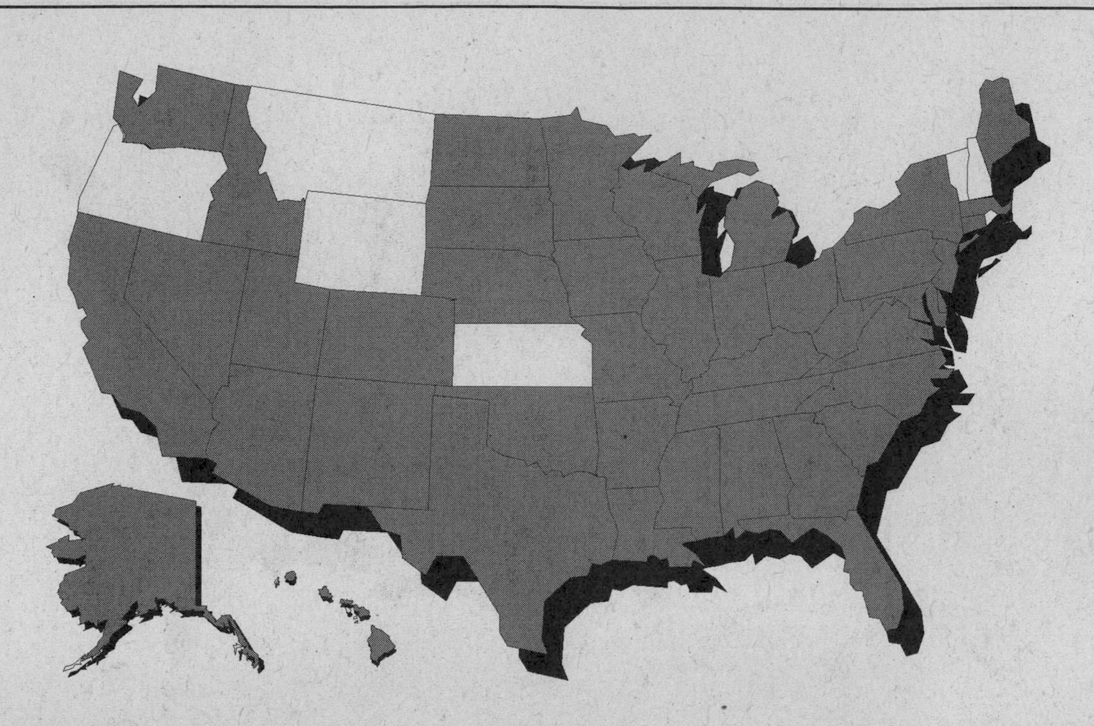

Forty-three states and the District of Columbia limit the performance of surgical abortions to licensed physicians: AL, AK, AZ, AR, CA, CO, CT, DE, DC, FL, GA, HI, ID, IL, IN, IA, KY, LA, ME, MD, MA, MI, MN, MS, MO, NE, NV, NJ, NM, NY, NC, ND, OH, OK, PA, SC, SD, TN, TX, UT, VA, WA, WI, and WY.

Admitting Privileges for Abortion Providers

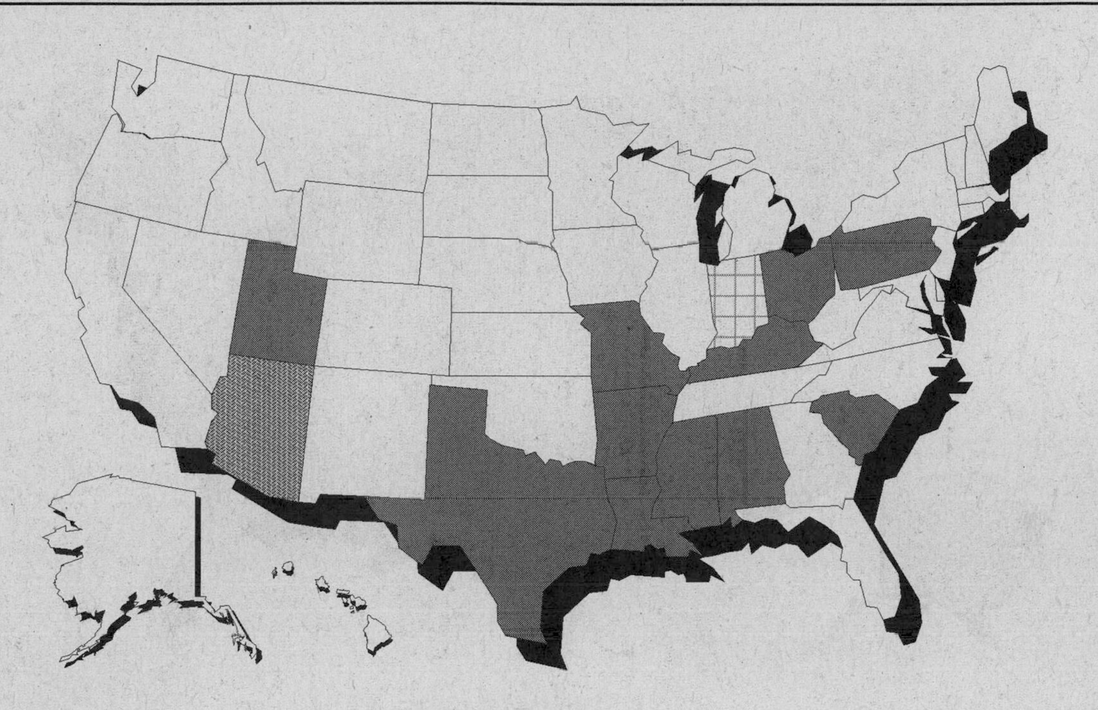

Eleven states require abortion providers to maintain admitting privileges: AL, AR, KY, LA, MS, MO, OH, PA, SC, TX, and UT.

Abortion providers in some counties in one state must maintain admitting privileges: IN.

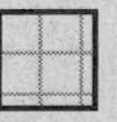

One state's admitting privileges' requirement is enjoined pending the outcome of litigation: AZ.

Abortion Reporting

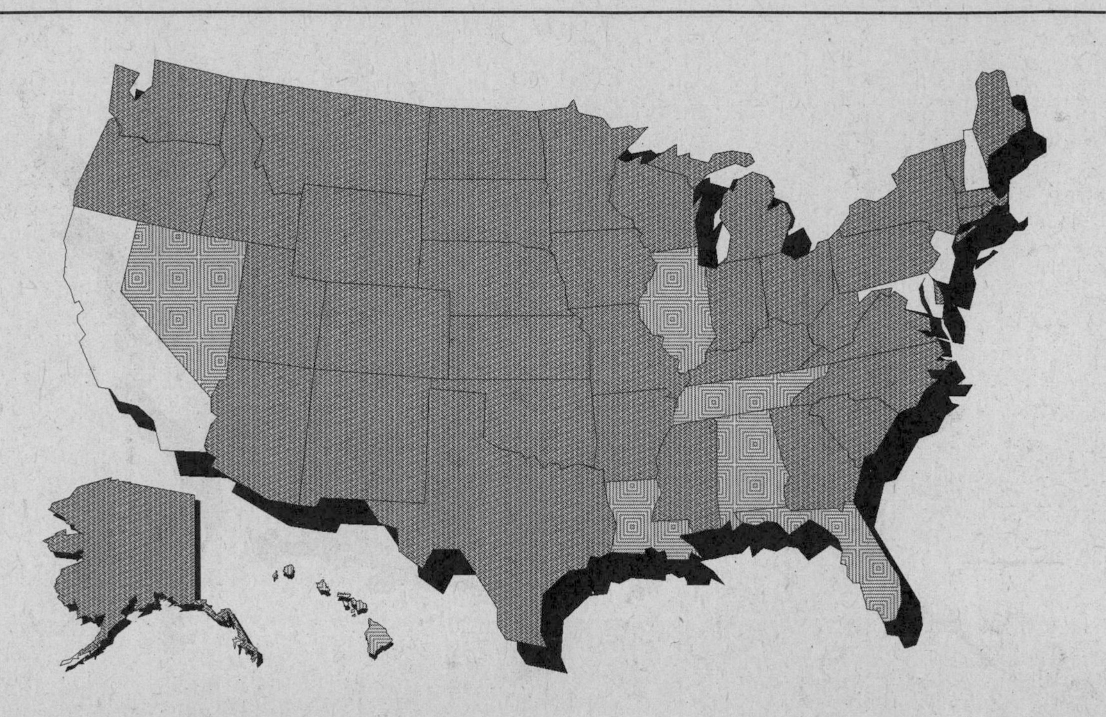

Thirty-nine states require reporting (to varying degrees) on both surgical and nonsurgical abortions: AK, AZ, AR, CO, CT, DE, GA, ID, IN, IA, KS, KY, ME, MA, MI, MN, MS, MO, MT, NE, NM, NY, NC, ND, OH, OK, OR, PA, RI, SC, SD, TX, UT, VT, VA, WA, WV, WI, and WY.

Seven states require reporting (to varying degrees) on surgical abortions only: AL, FL, HI, IL, LA, NV, and TN.

Abortion Complication Reporting

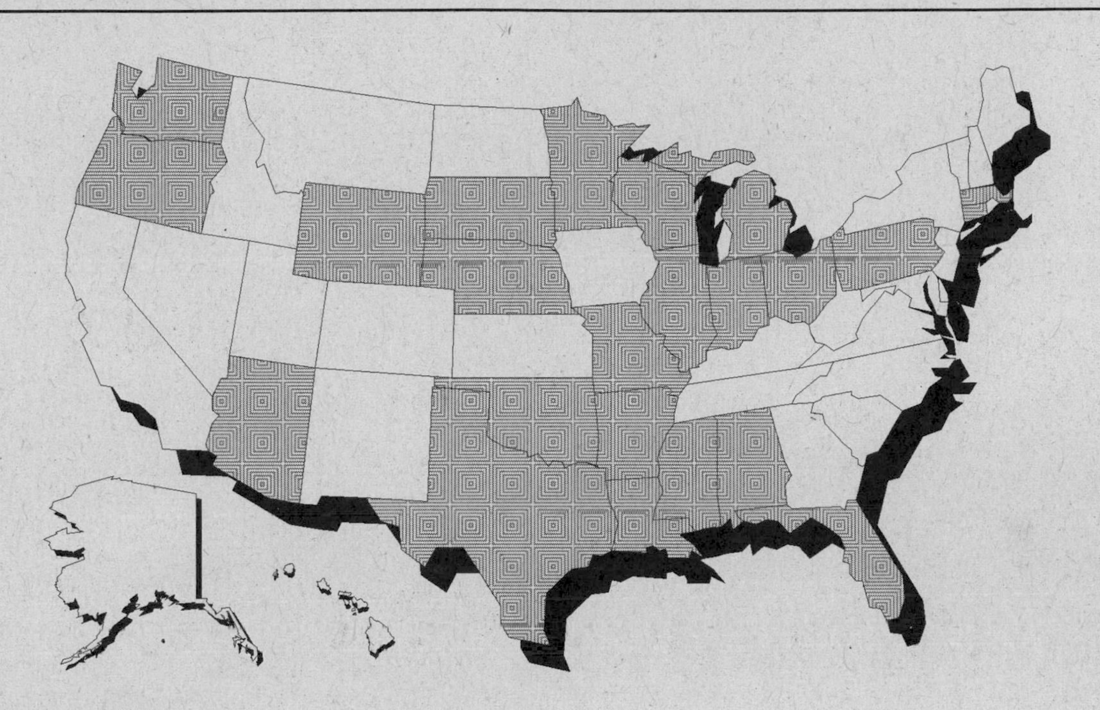

Twenty-three states require reporting (to varying degrees) on abortion complications: AL, AZ, AR, CT, FL, IL, IN, LA, MA, MI, MN, MS, MO, NE, OH, OK, OR, PA, SD, TX, WA, WI, and WY.

Planned Parenthood:
What can be done to stop their radical agenda for America?

By Denise M. Burke
Vice President of Legal Affairs, Americans United for Life

Planned Parenthood's legacy is a troubling one of ruined lives and deceptive, politically-motivated promises. For more than 90 years, it has relentlessly pursued an agenda of unapologetic abortion-on-demand, putting profits and ideology above women's health and safety. Again and again, Planned Parenthood has proven they are not the defenders of women's rights and health they hold themselves out to be.

What has Planned Parenthood wrought over nearly a century?

- They have performed a significant percentage of the nearly 50 million abortions this country and its families have suffered since 1973, when *Roe v. Wade* was decided.
- In their quest to further enrich their already-bulging coffers, they have made American taxpayers involuntarily complicit in their radical agenda. For example, in 2007 Congress and state governments appropriated more than $300 million to Planned Parenthood. Given Planned Parenthood's sizeable abortion market share, this undoubtedly means taxpayers are indirectly subsidizing abortions, abortion counseling, and abortion referrals (by freeing up money Planned Parenthood receives from other sources to be used for abortion rather than operational, program, and other expenses incurred by Planned Parenthood). Notably, with the Obama Administration now in power, Planned Parenthood and its supporters are now seeking to more than double the funding it receives from the federal government.
- They have prioritized their profit margin and political agenda over women's health and safety by (among other things):
    - Ignoring the ever-mounting evidence of the negative impact of abortion on women and misleading women about the physical risks and emotional impact of abortion.[1] In fact, on its website Planned Parenthood goes so far as to claim abortion offers health benefits.[2]
    - Opposing common sense, protective laws supported by the majority of Americans, including parental involvement, informed consent for abortion, and laws permitting only licensed physicians to perform abortions.
    - Purportedly failing to report sexual crimes committed against children.[3]
    - Dispensing the dangerous abortion drug RU-486 in direct violation of the FDA-approved protocol for the drug, endangering women's lives and health.[4]
- They advocate violating the constitu-

- tional rights of those who disagree with them. Specifically, they seek to compel healthcare professionals, Catholic hospitals, and other unwilling groups and individuals to participate in abortions regardless of their religious, moral, or ethical convictions against the practice.[5]
- And America is not large enough to contain their ambitious agenda. They are on a quest to make "abortion the law of the world," bullying countries around the world into complying with their demands and goals.[6]

An understanding of the history of Planned Parenthood, its unrelenting abortion advocacy, and its growing record of scandals is critical to developing effective and comprehensive strategies to counter its influence.

Planned Parenthood at a Glance

Planned Parenthood is the collective name of domestic and international organizations that comprise the International Planned Parenthood Federation (IPPF). The Planned Parenthood Federation of America (PPFA) is the U.S. affiliate and one of IPPF's larger members. PPFA maintains a network of state and regional affiliates across the 50 states.

PPFA operates approximately 880 clinics in the United States[7], has a total annual budget of nearly $1 billion[8], and provides abortion, family planning, sex education, and other services to 3 million people each year.[9] PPFA claims that one in four American women will visit one of their clinics in her lifetime.[10]

Critically, Planned Parenthood is also the most prominent provider of abortions in the U.S. In 2006, Planned Parenthood and its affiliates performed nearly 300,000[11] abortions, more than one-quarter of the abortions performed that year.

Federal and state government grants and contracts provide nearly one-third of Planned Parenthood's annual revenues. In fiscal year 2007, this amounted to $336.7 million from American taxpayers.[12] Planned Parenthood is also supported by private individuals, with (reportedly) over 900,000 active individual contributors.[13] Moreover, large donors such as the Rockefeller Foundation, the Carnegie Foundation, and the Bill & Melinda Gates Foundation contribute a substantial part of the organization's budget.[14]

Founding of Planned Parenthood

Margaret Sanger, a birth-control activist and eugenics supporter, founded Planned Parenthood in 1916. In October of that year, Sanger opened the first American birth control clinic in Brooklyn, New York. In 1923, she incorporated the American Birth Control League, which was influential in liberalizing birth control laws in the 1920s and 1930s. Later, in 1942 the League was reorganized as the Planned Parenthood Federation of America by Edris Rice-Wray Carson, Alice Carver Lee, Cornelia Vansant Lewis, Mary Scribner, and others.[15]

After its initial focus on contraceptives, Planned Parenthood later increasingly turned its attention to more expansive reproductive rights, especially abortion.

Planned Parenthood's Promotion of Abortion

Planned Parenthood supports unregulated and unrestricted abortion-on-demand and opposes common sense regulation of abortion, including:

- Informed consent and reflection periods;
- Parental involvement for minors;
- Requirements that only licensed physicians perform abortions;
- Limits on the use of taxpayer funding for abortions, abortion referrals, or abortion counseling;
- Bans on partial-birth abortion; and
- Laws protecting the freedom of conscience of healthcare providers and institutions that decline to participate in abortions.

More ominously, Planned Parenthood actively supports both federal and state "Freedom of Choice Acts" (FOCA), radical attempts to enshrine abortion-on-demand into American law, to sweep aside all existing laws regulating or restricting abortion—laws the majority of Americans support—and to prevent states and the federal government from enacting similar protective measures in the future.[16] Planned Parenthood readily admits the draconian nature of FOCA, arguing it will "invalidate existing and future laws that interfere with or discriminate against" an unfettered "right to abortion."[17]

One of Planned Parenthood's more notable FOCA advocacy efforts was in April 2007, just after the U.S. Supreme Court upheld the federal "Partial Birth Abortion Ban Act of 2003"[18], a decision embraced by a vast majority of Americans but denounced by Planned Parenthood and its allies. In late April of that year, Planned Parenthood, in a message to its supporters, stated, "Every American who values freedom and privacy should be troubled by the Supreme Court's reckless decision to uphold the federal abortion ban. And every American can fight back. Wednesday, April 25, 2007, the third anniversary of the history *[sic]* March for Women's Lives, is a national call-in day—a day for the pro-choice community to flood the phone lines of the U.S. House and Senate, urging our members of Congress to stand up for women's health and safety and to co-sponsor FOCA."[19]

Planned Parenthood and the U.S. Supreme Court

Over the past 35 years, Planned Parenthood and its state and regional affiliates have been very active in federal and state courts, seeking to invalidate state and federal regulations of and restrictions on abortion. Notably, Planned Parenthood has been prominently involved in key abortion-related cases that have, ultimately, reached the U.S. Supreme Court.

Some of Planned Parenthood's more notable attempts to invalidate common-sense abortion regulations and restrictions include:

- *Planned Parenthood of Central Missouri v. Danforth* (U.S. Supreme Court 1976): Planned Parenthood succeeded in striking down portions of a Missouri law that required parental consent for a minor's abortion, prohibited saline abortions, and required abortion providers to use professional skill and care to preserve the life of a viable unborn child marked for abortion.[20]

- *Planned Parenthood v. Casey* (U.S. Supreme Court 1992): Planned Parenthood unsuccessfully challenged a Pennsylvania law requiring informed consent for abortion, parental consent for a minor's abortion, and mandating statistical reporting requirements for abortions.[21]
- *Ayotte v. Planned Parenthood* (U.S. Supreme Court 2006): Planned Parenthood unsuccessfully sought to strike down New Hampshire's parental notification law.[22]
- *Gonzales v. Planned Parenthood* (U.S. Supreme Court 2007): Companion case to *Gonzales v. Carhart*, unsuccessfully seeking to strike down federal ban on partial-birth abortion.[23]

Growing Scandals Involving Planned Parenthood

Planned Parenthood is no stranger to scandal and controversy. Recent scandals have included failures to comply with state laws regarding the reporting of suspected child sexual abuse, the willful failure to comply with state parental involvement laws, arguably seeking to impede investigations by state authorities into allegations that state and local affiliates of Planned Parenthood violated state laws, and purported acceptance of donations earmarked for racially-discriminatory abortions.

Disturbingly, numerous allegations have surfaced over the past six years concerning Planned Parenthood's failure to report the sexual abuse of young girls. For example, in 2003 a Planned Parenthood affiliate in Arizona was found civilly liable after failing to report that the clinic had performed an abortion on a 13-year-old girl who had been impregnated by her 23-year-old foster brother. The young girl was returned to the home where she continued to be abused and was impregnated a second time.[24]

In a more recent case, a 14-year-old girl walked into a Planned Parenthood clinic in Cincinnati, accompanied by her soccer coach, John Haller. He was 21 years old and had initiated sexual activity with the girl when she was 13 years old. Now that she was pregnant, Haller wanted her to have an abortion. The soccer coach signed the parental notification forms then required by Ohio law. The teenager's parents later found out about her abortion and the sexual abuse perpetrated by her soccer coach. The soccer coach was prosecuted and served three years in prison. The parents are now suing Planned Parenthood for failing to report the sexual abuse and for failing to comply with Ohio's parental involvement law.

Similarly, in October 2005 Planned Parenthood of Minnesota/North Dakota/South Dakota was fined $50,000 for violating Minnesota's parental notification law.[25]

Further, over a three-year period from 2004 to 2006, a Kansas Planned Parenthood affiliate refused to comply with a subpoena from then-Kansas Attorney General Phill Kline, who was seeking access to clinic records related to late-term abortions that may have been performed in violation of Kansas law. Comprehensive Health, an abortion clinic operated by Planned Parenthood of Kansas and Mid-Missouri (along with the other targeted clinic), eventually petitioned the Kansas Supreme Court to block the subpoena. However, in February 2006 the Kansas Supreme Court refused the request, ruling that Attorney General Kline could seek access to the clinic records, but first had to present his evidence against the clinics to the district court with jurisdiction over the matter.[26]

Similarly, in 2005 Indiana Attorney General Steve Carter was investigating whether family planning clinics, including Planned Parenthood, were properly reporting cases of rape and molestation of children under the age of 14.[27] Planned Parenthood filed a lawsuit seeking to avoid producing its records and was ultimately successful.

Finally, Planned Parenthood affiliates in several states were recently subjected to a series of phone calls by students on the staff of a University of California at Los Angeles (UCLA) student-run, pro-life magazine, *The Advocate*. The calls included one in July 2007 to Planned Parenthood of Idaho offering a donation if it could be earmarked for abortions for African-American women. The organization's vice president of development and marketing did not reject the offer and was later suspended.[28]

What Can Be Done To Counter Planned Parenthood and its Influence?

There is much that can be done to counter the influence of Planned Parenthood and its radical abortion-on-demand agenda. A comprehensive plan would necessarily include:

- Increasing public educational efforts on Planned Parenthood, its history, and its agenda;
- Increasing research into the negative impact of abortion on women to counter Planned Parenthood's false assertions that abortion has "health benefits" for women or is safer than childbirth, and to reduce demand for abortions;
- Enacting more common sense, medically-appropriate regulations of abortion, including informed consent, ultrasound requirements, parental involvement, and abortion clinic regulations. These types of regulations have been proven to reduce the abortion rate;
- Enacting comprehensive legislation to ensure all healthcare providers, employees, and volunteers at Planned Parenthood clinics are required to report suspected child sexual abuse and sexual crimes against minors. AUL has developed the "Child Protection Act" to meet this goal.
- Funding and supporting pregnancy care centers that, unlike Planned Parenthood, offer women facing unplanned pregnancy with real choices and support;
- Enacting broad limits on the appropriation of state family planning funds to ensure such funds are not commingled with funding used to provide abortions. AUL's "Title X Consistency and Transparency Act" is designed to ensure that federal and state family planning funds are not directly or indirectly used to pay the costs associated with abortions; and
- Limiting (and, ultimately, eliminating) federal and state taxpayer funding of Planned Parenthood and its affiliates.

Clearly, the American public needs to learn more about the history, agenda, and practices of this dangerous and radical organization and voice their opposition to what Planned Parenthood represents. When they do, Planned Parenthood may not be around to celebrate its centennial.

Endnotes

[1] For a list of just some of the medical studies showing the negative impact of abortion on women, *see Medical Studies on the Impact of Abortion*, Defending Life 2009: Proven Strategies for a Pro-Life America, pp. 1041-47 (hereinafter, Defending Life 2009).

[2] *See* http://www.plannedparenthood.org/issues-action/abortion-issues-5946.htm (last visited August 26, 2009).

[3] *See e.g.,* Patrick Lavin, *Sexual Abuse Reporting Laws: Ending the Abortion Industry's Complicity n the Sexual Abuse of Minors,* Defending Life 2009, pp.183-85.

[4] *See* http://www.nrlc.org/news/2006/NRL04/TwoMoreDie.html (last visited August 26, 2009).

[5] *See e.g.,* http://www.plannedparenthood.org/files/PPFA/fact-refusal-clauses.pdf (last visited August 26, 2009).

[6] *See e.g.,* http://www.ippf.org/en/Resources/Guides-toolkits/Access+to+safe+abortion.htm (last visited August 26, 2009).

[7] *See* http://www.plannedparenthood.org/about-us/who-we-are-4648.htm (last visited August 26, 2009).

[8] *See e.g.,* http://www.plannedparenthood.org/files/PPFA/PPFA_990.pdf (last visited August 26, 2009).

[9] http://www.plannedparenthood.org/about-us/who-we-are/planned-parenthood-glance-5552.htm (last visited August 26, 2009).

[10] *Id.*

[11] *See* http://www.plannedparenthood.org/issues-action/birth-control/teen-pregnancy/reports/pp-services-17317.htm (last visited August 26, 2009).

[12] *See* http://en.wikipedia.org/wiki/Planned_Parenthood (last visited August 26, 2009)

[13] *See* http://www.plannedparenthood.org/files/AR_2007_vFinal.pdf (last visited August 26, 2009)

[14] *See e.g.,* http://en.wikipedia.org/wiki/Planned_Parenthood (last visited August 26, 2009).

[15] *Id.*

[16] For more information about FOCA, *see* Denise Burke, *The Freedom of Choice Act: Radical Attempt to Prematurely End Debate Over Abortion, infra,* and visit www.fightfoca.com (a project of Americans United for Life).

[17] http://www.plannedparenthood.org/issues-action/abortion/freedom-of-choice-act/articles/foca-14191.htm (last visited August 26, 2009).

[18] *Gonzales v. Carhart*, 127 S.Ct. 1610 (2007).

[19] *Id.*

[20] 428 U.S. 52 (1976).

[21] 505 U.S. 833 (1992)

[22] 126 S.Ct. 961 (2006). The New Hampshire law was ultimately repealed by the state legislature.

[23] U.S. Supreme Court Case No. 05-1382; *see also Gonzales v. Carhart*, 127 S.Ct. 1610 (2007).

[24] *Jane Doe v. Planned Parenthood of Central and Northern Ariz., et al.*, No. CV 2001-014876, Order of Partial Summary Judgment (Superior Ct., Ariz., Cty. of Maricopa, Nov. 26, 2002); *Glendale Teen Files Lawsuit Against Planned Parenthood*, ARIZ. REPUBLIC, Sept. 2, 2001, at B3, and *Arizona Trial Judge Concludes Planned Parenthood Negligently Failed To Report Abortion*, HEALTH L. WK., Jan. 10, 2003, at 7.

[25] Prather, *Judge Faults St. Paul Clinic in Abortion Lawsuit*, St. Paul Pioneer Press, p.A1 (October 13, 2005).

[26] *See* http://www.medicalnewstoday.com/articles/50913.php (last visited August 26, 2009).

[27] *See* http://www.medicalnewstoday.com/articles/21387.php (last visited August 26, 2009).

[28] S. Forester, *Response to caller "a serious mistake" says Planned Parenthood of Idaho*, Idaho Statesman, (Feb. 28, 2008).

State Funding Limitations:
A proven weapon in reducing abortions

By Denise M. Burke
Vice President of Legal Affairs, Americans United for Life

In recent years, Dr. Michael New of the University of Alabama has analyzed the impact of incremental state laws on the abortion rate in each state. In his paper entitled *Analyzing the Impact of State Level Pro-Life Legislation in the 1990s*, he showed that pro-life laws, particularly state limitations on the funding of abortions when coupled with other measures such as parental involvement laws, were driving down the national abortion rate. Specifically, his research disclosed a 17% decline in abortions during the 1990s due in large part to state laws, including limitations on state funding of abortions.

His work illustrates that pro-life laws already save tens of thousands of lives every year. It also spotlights unprecedented opportunities to save more lives in states without common sense prohibitions and limitations on the use of state funds for abortion and abortion-related counseling and advocacy. These commonsense limitations include:

- Limits on state Medicaid funding for abortion;
- Prohibitions or limits on state funding to organizations that perform, counsel on behalf of, or affiliate with organizations that perform or advocate on behalf of abortion, including eliminating or restricting funding of organizations like Planned Parenthood;
- Limits on the use of state facilities and employees for the performance of abortions; and
- Limits on insurance coverage for abortions for public employees.

ISSUES

State Medicaid Funding

Enacted in 1976, the Hyde Amendment[1] forbids the use of federal funds for abortions except in cases where continued pregnancy endangers the life of the woman or where the pregnancy resulted from rape or incest. This standard guides both federal and state funding for abortions under joint federal-state Medicaid programs for low-income women. At a minimum, states must provide coverage for abortions performed in accordance with the Hyde Amendment exceptions. However, a state may, using non-federal funds, pay for other abortions. Currently, 32 states follow the funding limitations provided for in the Hyde Amendment, while 17 states provide broader funding for abortion.

With the current leadership in Congress and the White House, the Hyde Amendment could be in jeopardy. Importantly, the discussions in Congress concerning the possible repeal of the Hyde Amendment create urgency for states to consider enacting their own limitations on the use of state funding for abortions, abortion referrals, and abortion counseling.

Prohibitions on Recipients of State Funding:

There are several tools states can use to limit and exercise control over who receives state family planning and other similar funding, eliminating indirect subsidies to and unintentional support of abortion.

A state can prohibit the use of state-appropriated funds for abortion counseling and/or referrals. Opponents of this type of limitation frequently refer to it as a "gag rule."

A state may also restrict organizations that receive state funds from associating with entities that perform and/or provide counseling or referrals for abortion. For example, it may prohibit the commingling of state funding with other sources of funding used to provide, refer for, or counsel on behalf of abortions. In the same vein, a state can also require the segregation of staff, facilities, and administrative support services between segments of a business providing family planning and other state-supported services and those providing abortions, abortion referrals, or abortion counseling.

To this end, AUL has developed the "Title X Consistency and Transparency Act."

A number of states, such as Colorado, Missouri, and Texas[2], have already placed significant limitations on recipients of state family planning and similar funding. In 2003, Planned Parenthood unsuccessfully challenged the limitations imposed in Texas. Earlier that year, the Texas legislature had diverted about $13 million away from clinics that provided abortions and abortion-related services. In response, Texas Health Commissioner Eduardo Sanchez sent out a letter to Planned Parenthood and other state clinics receiving state family planning funding ordering them to cease providing abortions or face a loss of state funding. Ultimately, the State of Texas prevailed in a four-year legal challenge to the limitations.

Currently, 18 states have implemented restrictions and limitations on recipients of state family planning and other funding.

Restrictions on the Use of State Facilities

Only a small number of states have restricted the use of public facilities for the performance of abortions. The types of facilities typically covered by such restrictions include public hospitals and hospitals and health clinics maintained through the state school, college, or university system.

Limitations on Insurance Coverage

Since state taxpayer funds are used to pay for insurance policies for state employees, 12 state legislatures have enacted restrictions on the amount and type of coverage provided for abortions. Two states strictly prohibit abortion coverage for public employees, while three states have an exception for circumstances where the life of the woman is endangered by a continued pregnancy. Seven states provide exceptions beyond the women's life to cases of rape, incest, or fetal abnormality.

Five states have passed laws restricting private health insurance plans from covering abortions. These state laws permit insurance coverage for abortions only in limited circumstances, such as where the woman's life is endangered or where the pregnancy is the result of rape or incest. Policyholders must pay an additional premium or purchase a separate policy rider for abortion coverage.

MYTHS & FACTS

Myth: State Medicaid funding restrictions discriminate against poor women and unfairly restrict them from exercising their constitutional right to abortion.
Fact: The Hyde Amendment, which guides both federal and state funding for abortions under joint federal-state Medicaid programs for low-income women, has been upheld by the U.S. Supreme Court. The Court specifically found that the restrictions on the use of federal funds to pay for abortions for low-income women were not unconstitutional.[3]

Moreover, abortion providers, such as Planned Parenthood, often purposely set the average cost for a first-trimester abortion below what the market would bear, in part, to facilitate the delivery of abortion services to lower income women. The average cost for a first-trimester abortion is approximately $300-$400, well below the average costs for most other office or clinic-based surgical procedures.

Myth: Restrictions on abortion counseling and referrals violate an organization or individual's First Amendment (free speech) rights.
Fact: Eighteen states currently restrict the use of state funds for abortion counseling or referral and none of these state laws have been declared unconstitutional for any reason. It is perfectly legitimate for states, through the allocation of state funds and other programs, to demonstrate and implement a preference for childbirth and adoption over abortion. •

Endnotes

[1] Hyde Amendment to the Medicaid Act, Title XIX of the Social Security Act (1976).

[2] *See e.g., Planned Parenthood of Mid-Missouri & Eastern Kansas, Inc. v. Dempsey*, 167 F.3d 458 (8th Circuit 1999) and *Planned Parenthood v. Sanchez*, 403 F.3d 324 (5th Circuit 2005).

3 *Harris v. McRae*, 448 U.S. 297 (1980).

State Funding Limitations Talking Points

- In his paper entitled *Analyzing the Impact of State Level Pro-Life Legislation in the 1990s*, Dr. Michael New of the University of Alabama showed that incremental pro-life laws—particularly state limitations on the funding of abortions when coupled with other measures such as parental involvement laws—were driving down the national abortion rate. Specifically, his research disclosed a 17% decline in abortions during the 1990s, due in large part to incremental state laws, including limitations on state funding of abortions.

- Common-sense limitations on state funding include:
  - Limits on state Medicaid funding for abortion;
  - Prohibitions or limits on state funding to organizations that perform, counsel on behalf of, or affiliate with organizations that perform or advocate on behalf of abortion, including eliminating or restricting funding of organizations like Planned Parenthood;
  - Limits on the use of state facilities and employees for the performance of abortions; and
  - Limits on insurance coverage for abortion for public employees.

- Enacted in 1976, the federal Hyde Amendment[1] forbids the use of federal funds for abortions except in cases where continued pregnancy endangers the life of the woman or where the pregnancy resulted from rape or incest. This standard guides both federal and state funding for abortions under joint federal-state Medicaid programs for low-income women. At minimum, states must provide coverage for abortions performed in accordance with the Hyde Amendment exceptions.

- Currently, 32 states follow the funding limitations provided for in the Hyde Amendment, while 17 states provide broader funding for abortion.[1]

- There are several tools states can use to limit and exercise control over who receives state family planning and other similar funding, eliminating indirect subsidies to and unintentional support of abortion.

  A state can prohibit the use of state-appropriated funds for abortion counseling and/or referrals. Opponents of this type of limitation frequently refer to it as a "gag rule."

  A state may also restrict organizations that receive state funds from associating with entities that perform and/or provide counseling or referrals for abortion. For

example, it may prohibit the commingling of state funding with other sources of funding used to provide, refer for, or counsel on behalf of abortions. In the same vein, a state can also require the segregation of staff, facilities, and administrative support services between segments of the business providing family planning and other state-supported services and those providing abortions, abortion referrals, or abortion counseling.

- State funding limitations for abortion do not discriminate against poor or low-income women. Rather, they protect women from the negative consequences of abortion and avoid making taxpayers indirectly complicit in abortion.

Endnotes

[1] Twenty-six states (and the District of Columbia) generally follow the federal funding standard: Alabama, Arkansas, Colorado, Delaware, Florida, Georgia, Idaho, Kansas, Kentucky, Louisiana, Maine, Michigan, Missouri, Nebraska, Nevada, New Hampshire, North Carolina, North Dakota, Ohio, Oklahoma, Pennsylvania, Rhode Island, South Carolina, Tennessee, Texas, and Wyoming.

Two states generally follow the federal funding standard but also provide funding for abortions when a woman's physical health is threatened by a continued pregnancy: Indiana and Wisconsin.

Three states generally follow the federal funding standard but also provide funding for abortions in cases involving fetal abnormalities: Iowa, Mississippi, and Virginia.

One state generally follows the federal funding standard but also provides funding when a woman's physical health is threatened by a continued pregnancy and in cases of fetal abnormalities: Utah.

One state provides state funding for abortions only in the case of life-endangerment, in apparent violation of the federal standard: South Dakota.

State Medicaid Funding

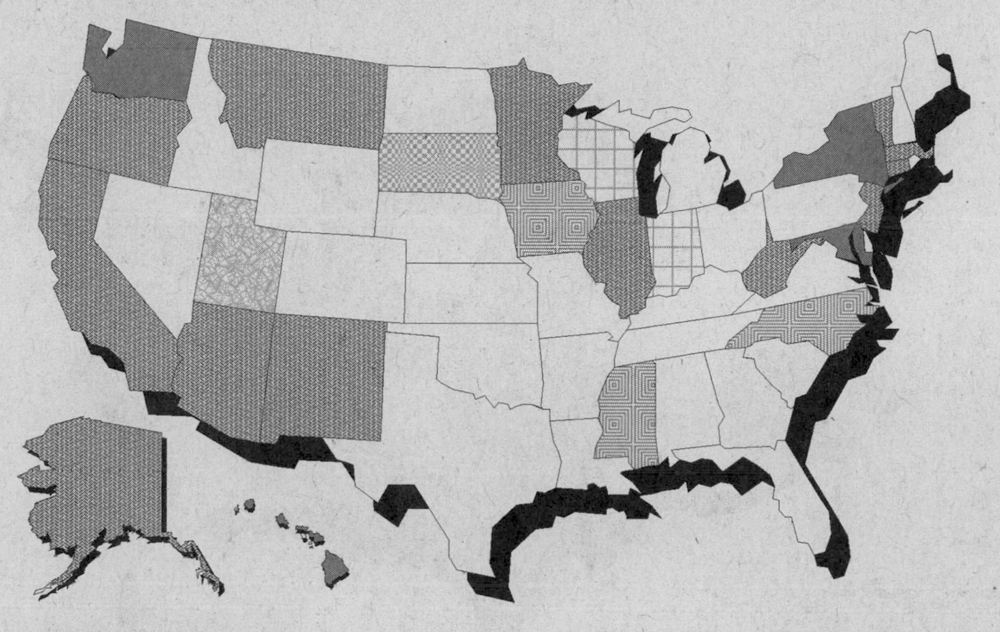

Twenty-six states (and the District of Columbia) generally follow the federal funding standard: AL, AR, CO, DC, DE, FL, GA, ID, KS, KY, LA, ME, MI, MO, NE, NV, NH, NC, ND, OH, OK, PA, RI, SC, TN, TX, and WY.

Two states generally follow the federal funding standard but also provide funding for abortions when a woman's physical health is threatened by a continued pregnancy: IN and WI.

Three states generally follow the federal funding standard but also provide funding for abortions in cases involving fetal abnormalities: IA, MS, and VA.

One state generally follows the federal funding standard but also provides funding when a woman's physical health is threatened by a continued pregnancy and in cases of fetal abnormalities: UT.

One state provides state funding for abortions only in the case of life-endangerment, in apparent violation of the federal standard: SD.

Thirteen states, pursuant to a court order, use state funds to provide all or most "medically necessary" abortions: AK, AZ, CA, CT, IL, MA, MN, MT, NJ, NM, OR, VT, and WV.

Four states have chosen to voluntarily use state funds to provide all or most "medically necessary" abortions: HI, MD, NY, and WA.

Prohibitions on Recipients of State Funding

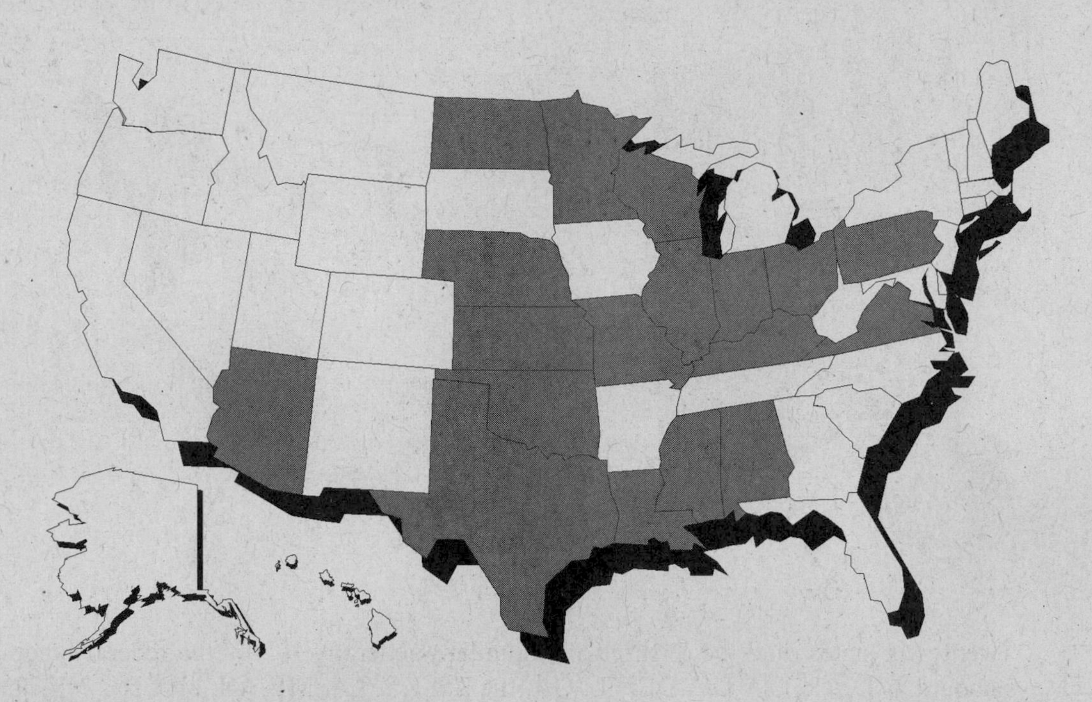

Eighteen states currently prohibit organizations that receive state funds from using those funds to provide abortion counseling or to make referrals for abortion, and/or prohibit organizations that receive state funds from associating with entities that provide counseling or referrals for abortion: AL, AZ, IL, IN, KS, KY, LA, MN, MS, MO, NE, ND, OH, OK, PA, TX, VA, and WI.

Restrictions on the Use of State Facilities

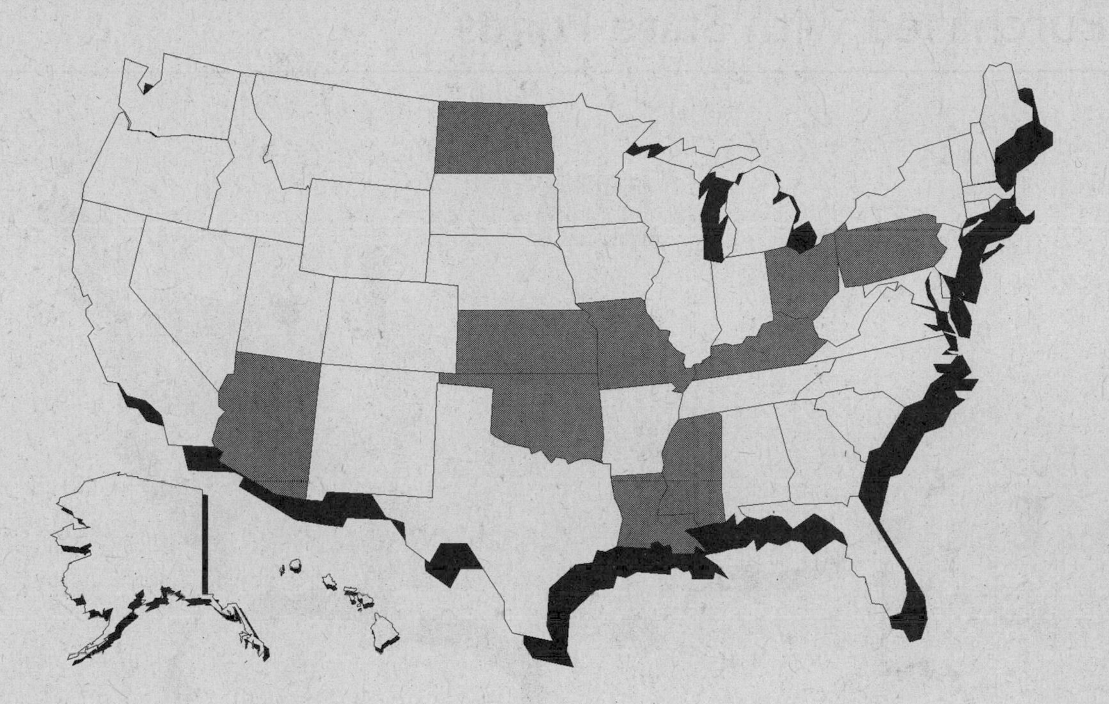

Ten states have enacted restrictions on the use of some or all state facilities, such as public hospitals, for the performance of abortions: AZ, KS, KY, LA, MS, MO, ND, OH, OK, and PA.

Limitations on Insurance Coverage Purchased with State Funds

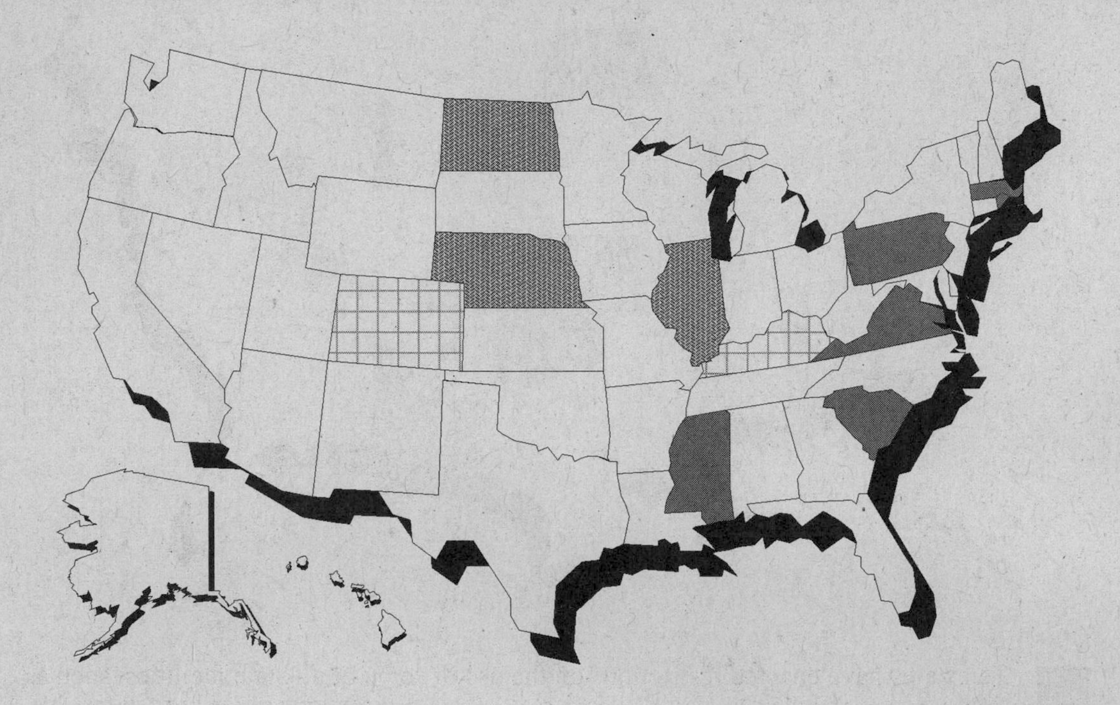

Two states completely ban insurance coverage for abortion for public employees: CO and KY.

Three states provide abortion coverage only when a woman's life is endangered: IL, NE, and ND.

Six states provide coverage when a woman's life or health is endangered or in cases of rape, incest, or fetal abnormality: MA, MS, PA, RI, SC, and VA.

Limitations on Private Insurance Coverage of Abortion

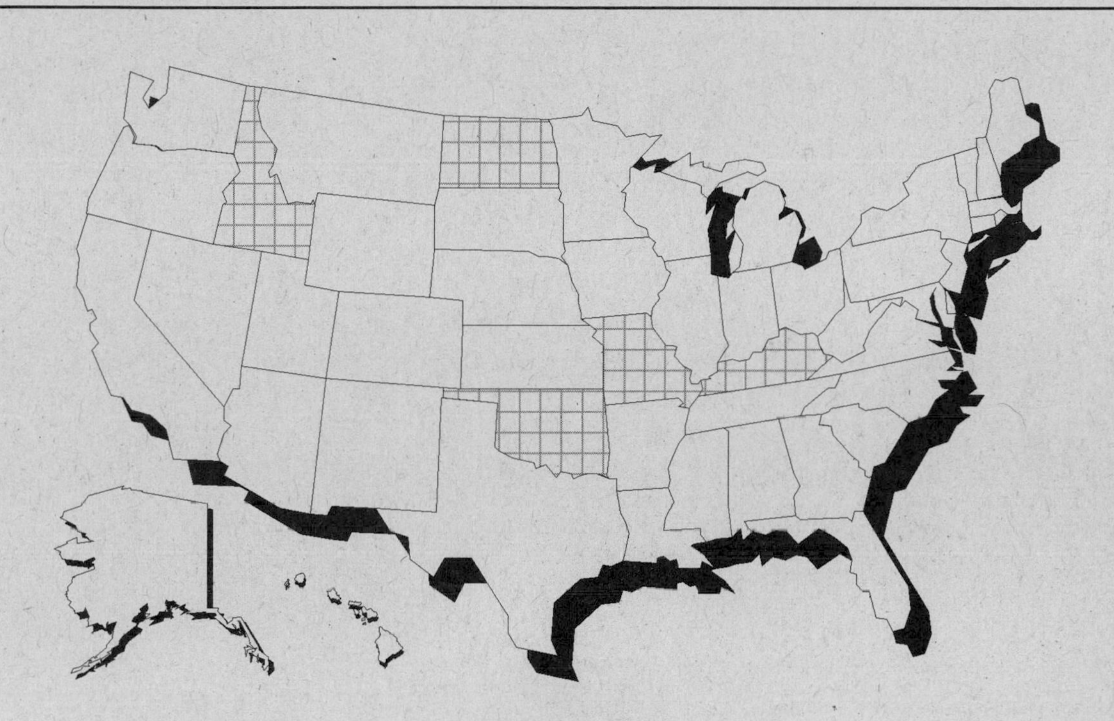

Five states places limits on the availability of private insurance coverage for abortion: ID, KY, MO, ND, and OK.

Deadly Convenience:
RU-486, Plan B, and the danger of "contraceptive equity"

By Mailee R. Smith
Staff Counsel, Americans United for Life

Chemical abortion is the new frontier for abortion advocates. More and more abortion clinics are turning from surgical abortions in the first trimester to focus exclusively on chemical abortions—more commonly referred to as the RU-486 regimen. Because some state laws do not define "abortion" in such a way as to include chemical abortions, the RU-486 regimen may fly under the radar, so to speak, and allow clinics to dispense it without regard to abortion regulations in the state.

Another recent development—a repackaging of the "safe, legal, and rare" mantra of the 1990s—is President Barack Obama's claim that he wants to reduce the number of abortions in the United States. This rings of the abortion advocates' claims that reduction of abortion is dependent upon prevention of pregnancy. Prevention of pregnancy, they claim, is in turn dependent upon access to "emergency contraception" and regular contraception. Further, access to contraception is not enough; pro-abortion advocates want employers to pay for it.

These arguments come at the detriment to women. RU-486 and "emergency contraception" are dangerous and potentially deadly, and contraceptive equity laws serve only to endanger a healthcare system already in crisis.

ISSUES

RU-486

The Population Council filed a new drug application with the FDA in 1996 for approval of RU-486 and granted Danco Laboratories the exclusive license to distribute RU-486 in the United States. A Chinese drug manufacturer—which has previously been cited by the FDA for tainted drugs—manufactures the pills. On September 28, 2000, the FDA approved RU-486 under Subpart H, its accelerated approval regulations specifically enacted to quickly approve drugs for HIV patients.

Taken alone, RU-486 fails in one-third of cases.[1] Thus, a prostaglandin must also be ingested.[2] A woman first takes three RU-486 tablets at a doctor's office or abortion clinic. This initial ingestion blocks progesterone from getting to the baby, and the baby starves to death. Under the regimen approved by the FDA, the woman is to return 36 to 48 hours later to take a second drug, misoprostol (a prostaglandin), which causes the woman to expel the baby. The woman returns for a third visit three weeks later for an exam to confirm that the baby has been completely expelled and to monitor bleeding. If the procedure fails, a woman must undergo a surgical abortion.

In order to protect women against the risks of RU-486, AUL has drafted the "Unlawful Distribution of Abortion-Inducing Drug (RU-486) Act."

Emergency Contraception

In 1999, the FDA approved the distribution of "emergency contraception" (EC), also known as Plan B, by prescription. EC is allegedly prescribed after a woman has had sex without contraception. Within 72 hours after intercourse, the woman takes the first dose; 12 hours later, she takes a second dose. When taken according to this regimen, EC is only 75 to 85 percent effective in preventing pregnancy or implantation.[3]

On August 24, 2006, the FDA approved over-the-counter sales of Plan B to women 18 years of age and over. But this was not enough for pro-abortion groups, who continued litigation and pushed for the availability of EC to minors. On March 23, 2009, a federal district court in New York ruled that Plan B must be made available to 17-year-old minors and directed the FDA to reconsider its policies regarding minors' access. The Obama Administration did not appeal and the FDA intends to comply with the ruling.

Contraceptive Equity

In recent years, abortion advocates have begun clamoring for contraceptive equity laws. In sum, such laws require that employers and insurers who offer prescription drug coverage to include coverage for contraception. These laws mandate employers and insurers with convictions against contraceptive use must violate their consciences or beliefs. While most contraceptive equity laws offer an exemption for organizations dedicated to inculcating religious values or beliefs (*e.g.* churches), many of these laws do not provide the same protection for religiously-affiliated organizations that serve the general public. For example, religiously-affiliated groups or para-church organizations—such as adoption agencies and charitable organizations —are not exempt and must provide prescription coverage for contraceptives.

In addition to this obvious infringement on the right of conscience, contraceptive equity laws also worsen a healthcare situation that is already in crisis. The American public is demanding better healthcare. But if religiously-affiliated organizations are forced to choose between following their beliefs and providing prescription coverage, it is likely many if not most will choose simply to stop providing prescription coverage to their employees. Contrary to abortion advocates' claims that contraceptive equity laws will improve women's health, this would leave a greater number of women—and men—without prescription coverage.

And as if these dangers were not enough, contraceptive equity laws open the door for laws requiring employers and insurers to provide coverage for abortion. The abortion lobby will likely use the same rationalization—that it is allegedly key to vital healthcare service—to justify mandated insurance coverage of abortion.

KEY TERMS

- An **abortifacient** is a drug that causes an abortion.

- **Emergency contraception (EC)** is allegedly used to prevent pregnancy after unprotected sexual intercourse. It is also referred to as the **morning-after pill** or **postcoital contraception**. The two particular products approved by the FDA are known as **Plan B** and **Preven**. While other forms of EC include massive doses of regular birth control pills or insertion of an intrauterine device, any references to EC in this overview deal specifically with the morning-after pill.

- **RU-486** is a chemical abortifacient which is also known as **mifepristone,** or by its brand name, **Mifeprex**. It is taken to end pregnancy, not to prevent it.

MYTHS & FACTS

Myth: Proper clinical trials demonstrate that RU-486 is "safe and effective."
Fact: One of the FDA's rules is that "uncontrolled studies or partially controlled studies are not acceptable as the sole basis for the approval claims of effectiveness." Yet neither the French trials nor the U.S. trial solely relied upon in approving RU-486 were blinded or controlled, and they did not yield "safe and effective" results. Almost 86 percent of patients in the first French trial and 93 percent in the second French trial experienced at least one adverse effect as a result of using RU-486.[4] Ninety-nine percent of patients in the U.S. trial experienced adverse effects—23 percent of which were severe.[5]

Furthermore, RU-486 has not been tested on females under the age of 18, yet it is given to females in this age group.

Myth: A chemical abortion is safer than surgical abortion and carries fewer and less severe side effects.
Fact: The common side effects of RU-486 are painful contractions, nausea, vomiting, diarrhea, pelvic pain and spasms, dizziness, and headaches.[6] Most women experience excessive bleeding, which can last for weeks. RU-486 patients report "significantly longer bleeding" and "significantly higher levels" of pain, nausea, vomiting, and diarrhea than women who have surgical abortions.[7] In one study, RU-486 failed in 18.3 percent of patients, while surgical abortions failed in only 4.7 percent of patients.[8] In addition, the potential long-term effects of chemical abortion, such as effects on fertility and future pregnancies, are not known.

Myth: RU-486 was properly approved through the FDA's channels, so it must be safe.
Fact: RU-486 was actually approved through the FDA's "Accelerated Approval Regulations." These regulations were designed for drugs "that have been studied for their safety and effectiveness in treating serious or life-threatening illnesses and that provide meaningful therapeutic benefit to patients over existing treatments."[9] Yet, as demonstrated above, RU-486 was not adequately tested for its safety and effectiveness and it does not provide meaningful therapeutic benefit over the surgical abortions already available. In addition, pregnancy is not a serious or life-threatening illness. RU-486 should not have been approved under this accelerated procedure.

Myth: Over-the-counter access to "emergency contraception" like Plan B will reduce the number of unplanned pregnancies and abortions.

Fact: Studies reveal that "emergency contraception" does not reduce pregnancy and abortion rates. In one study, abortions increased by nearly 6,000 in a one-year period, jumping 3.2 percent.[10] Once EC became available without prescription in the United Kingdom, use among teenage girls doubled from 1 in 12 to 1 in 5.[11] In fact, one study reported that 4 out of 12 women were influenced to have unprotected sex because of the easy access to EC.[12] With the increased rate of sexual activity and the substantial failure rate of EC, the over-the-counter availability of Plan B cannot be expected to reduce the number of pregnancies or abortions. Furthermore, in those areas with easy access to EC, the number of sexually transmitted diseases has skyrocketed.

Myth: Plan B is safe for females under the age of 18.
Fact: The maker of Plan B has not researched what happens when adolescents take Plan B. Moreover, the maximum safe dose for levornorgestrel, the active ingredient in Plan B, and the effects of overdose have not been determined by scientific study on any age group.

Myth: Given the FDA's approval, there is nothing that the states can do to limit or regulate Plan B.
Fact: While abortion advocates are focused on increasing access to Plan B (*e.g.* mandating immediate availability in hospital emergency rooms) and eliminating restrictions on minors' access, there are steps states can consider to responsibly limit access and to protect minors, including (1) limiting the number of packets of Plan B that can be obtained at one time and in one pharmacy; (2) requiring that purchases of Plan B be logged by drug store and pharmacy employees (similar to what currently occurs in many states with over-the-counter cold and allergy medicines); and (3) prohibiting registered sex offenders—especially those that prey on minors—from purchasing Plan B.

Myth: Women need contraceptive equity laws to combat their employers' gender discrimination because women spend as much as 68 percent more than men in out-of-pocket healthcare costs, due in large part to the cost of prescription contraceptives and the various costs of unintended pregnancies.
Fact: The abortion lobby has neither established that a significant connection exists between lack of coverage for contraceptives and unintended pregnancies, nor has it proven that the higher healthcare costs are not a result of factors other than differences in plan coverage, such as differing illness or medical service usage levels.

Myth: Contraceptive equity laws are cost-effective because they save employers the costs resulting from their employees' unintended pregnancies.
Fact: The abortion lobby relies on an assumption that employees not using contraceptives because of the costs will begin using contraceptives if their states enact contraceptive equity laws. No studies validate this assumption. Instead, rising healthcare costs have reduced the number of employers offering their employees any health benefits and increased the number of employees turning down their employers' offer of health coverage. Insurance mandates such as contraceptive equity laws will further compromise the ability of employers to offer affordable health plans to their employees.[13]

Endnotes

[1] Wendy Wright, *RU-486: Deadly Approval*, Family Voice 7, 10 (Jan./Feb. 2003).

[2] *See* Americans United for Life, *Citizen Petition to the U.S. Food and Drug Administration*, at 6 (1995).

[3] Bethanie Swendsen, *Does Plan-B Approval Really Put Science on the Line?*, available at http://www.cwfa.org/articles/7967/CWA/life/index.htm (last visited June 16, 2009).

[4] *See* AAPLOG et al., *Citizen Petition and Request for Administrative Stay*, at 26-27.

[5] *See id.* at nn.313 & 317 & accompanying text.

[6] Wendy Wright, *RU-486: Killer Pills*, available at http://www.cwfa.org/articles/1561/CWA/life/index.htm (last visited June 16, 2009).

[7] Jeffrey T. Jensen et al., *Outcomes of Suction Curettage and Mifepristone Abortion in the United States: A Prospective Comparison Study*, Contraception 59:153, 156 (1999).

[8] *Id.*

[9] 21 C.F.R. § 314.500.

[10] *UK Reports Nearly 6000 More Abortions in 2003 over 2002* (July 21, 2004), available at http://www.lifesite.net/ldn/2004/jul/04072110.html (last visited June 16, 2009).

[11] S. Doughty, *Morning-After Pill Lures Teens*, Herald Sun (Mar. 28, 2003).

[12] P. Bissell et al., *The Sale of Emergency Hormonal Contraception in Community Pharmacies in the UK: The Views of Users*, Int'l J. Pharm. Practice R47 (Supp. 2002).

[13] For more information on the topics discussed in this article, please visit AUL's website at http://www.AUL.org.

RU-486, Plan B, & Contraceptive Equity Talking Points

RU-486:

- The approved RU-486 regimen is dangerous and does not adequately protect women. It does not require an ultrasound, which is necessary to determine the gestational age of the pregnancy and whether the pregnancy is ectopic. RU-486 is particularly dangerous because its side effects are confusingly similar to the symptoms of an ectopic pregnancy.

- Moreover, anyone with a medical license—including untrained psychiatrists, podiatrists, and other non-related specialists—can prescribe RU-486.

- Doctors and clinics are not using RU-486 as approved by the FDA, which is "for the medical termination of intrauterine pregnancies through 49 days' pregnancy."[1] The approved regimen also requires at least three office visits. Yet RU-486 is openly administered to women with pregnancies beyond seven weeks, and the second office visit is often eliminated.[2] Failing to follow the approved regimen of an already dangerous drug puts women's health and lives even more at risk.

- "The FDA has acknowledged the deaths of 8 women associated with the drug, 9 life-threatening incidents, 232 hospitalizations, 116 blood transfusions, and 88 cases of infection. These and other cases have added up to a total of 950 adverse event reports as of March 31, 2006."[3]

Plan B/"Emergency Contraception":

- Because Plan B is only 75 to 89 percent effective, it is 11 to 25 percent ineffective.[4]

- Plan B is believed to act principally by blocking ovulation, but it also prevents the implantation of an already fertilized egg.[5] Thus, Plan B may act as an abortifacient.

- Over-the-counter access to Plan B is inherently unsafe. First, over-the-counter access makes Plan B available to a larger population of women than any trial has tested. Second, if the hormones in regular birth control pills render such drugs unsafe for non-prescription status, the higher amounts found in Plan B cannot be safe either. Third, a study has revealed that one-third of women who read the instructions for Plan B do not understand that it is not to be used as a regular form of birth control.[6] Over one-third did not understand that a second dose must be taken 12 hours after the first.[7]

- Plan B is used to exploit women. A study done in Thailand, where emergency contraception has been available without prescription for almost 20 years, had the following comments: "Although many feminists believe that the morning-after pill gives them more control over their own bodies, it would seem, judging from the few studies conducted so far, that it is actually being used by men to exploit women."[8] Indeed, studies revealed men were the most frequent buyers. Many women did not even know what they were taking; they were simply told by their partners that the pill was a health supplement. Easy access to an easily-administered drug encourages the continued exploitation of women by sexual predators.

Contraceptive Equity:

- Most contraceptive equity laws do not protect the rights of conscience of employers and insurers possessing religious or moral objections to contraception. Though many contraceptive equity laws offer an exemption for organizations dedicated to inculcating religious values or beliefs (*e.g.* churches), many of these laws do not provide the same protection for religiously-affiliated organizations that serve the general public.

- There is no evidence or study establishing that contraceptive equity laws save employers the costs resulting from their employees' unintended pregnancies. On the other hand, contraceptive equity laws increase the cost of healthcare. This rise in healthcare costs has reduced the number of employers offering their employees any health benefits and increased the number of employees turning down their employers' offer of health coverage. Insurance mandates such as contraceptive equity laws will further compromise the ability of employers to offer affordable health plans to their employees.

- As contraceptive equity laws without comprehensive rights of conscience protections are increasingly adopted in the states, it will become easier for abortion advocates to justify mandated insurance coverage of abortion using the same rationalizations used to support mandatory contraception coverage.

- Providing coverage for contraception is not analogous to providing coverage for Viagra. Most health plans pay for Viagra only when a man seeks it to address impotence rather than to enhance sexual performance. When a man utilizes Viagra in this context, he is using it to treat infertility, a medical disorder he possesses. On the other hand, a woman uses contraceptives solely to prevent a pregnancy, a completely natural condition.

- Women do not need contraceptive equity laws to combat their employers' gender discrimination. There is no evidence showing any connection between lack of coverage for contraceptives and unintended pregnancies, nor has it been proven that higher healthcare costs are not merely a result of factors such as differing illness or medical service usage levels, rather than a result of differences in plan coverage.

Endnotes

[1] Letter from FDA/CDER to Sandra P. Arnold, Population Council (Sept. 28, 2000).

[2] *See* AAPLOG et al., *Citizen Petition and Request for Administrative Stay*, at nn.313 & 317 & accompanying text. Instead, the patients administer misoprostol vaginally—not orally, as approved—at home. *Id.*

[3] Dave Andrusko, *Investigations Proving RU-486's Lethal Dangers*, available at http://www.nrlc.org/news/2006/NRL06/LethalDangers.html (last visited June 17, 2009).

[4] *See* Wendy Wright et al., *The Morning-After Pill* at 3 (2006), available at http://www.cwfa.org/articles/6085/CWA/life/index.htm (last visited June 17, 2009).

[5] Food & Drug Administration, *FDA's Decision Regarding Plan B: Questions and Answers* (2006), available at http://www.fda.gov/CDER/DRUG/infopage/planB/planBQandA.htm (last visited June 17, 2009).

[6] Wendy Wright et al., *supra.*

[7] *Id.*

[8] Karnjariya Sukrung, *Morning-After Blues*, Bangkok Post, June 10, 2002.

RU-486 Regulations

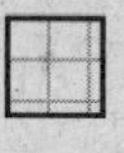
Two states require that RU-486 be administered in compliance with the approved FDA protocol and the drug label (but both laws are in litigation): OH and OK

Four states specifically impose minimal administrative regulations on the dispensation of RU-486: CA, GA, NC, and RI.

"Emergency Contraception" Collaborative Practice Agreements

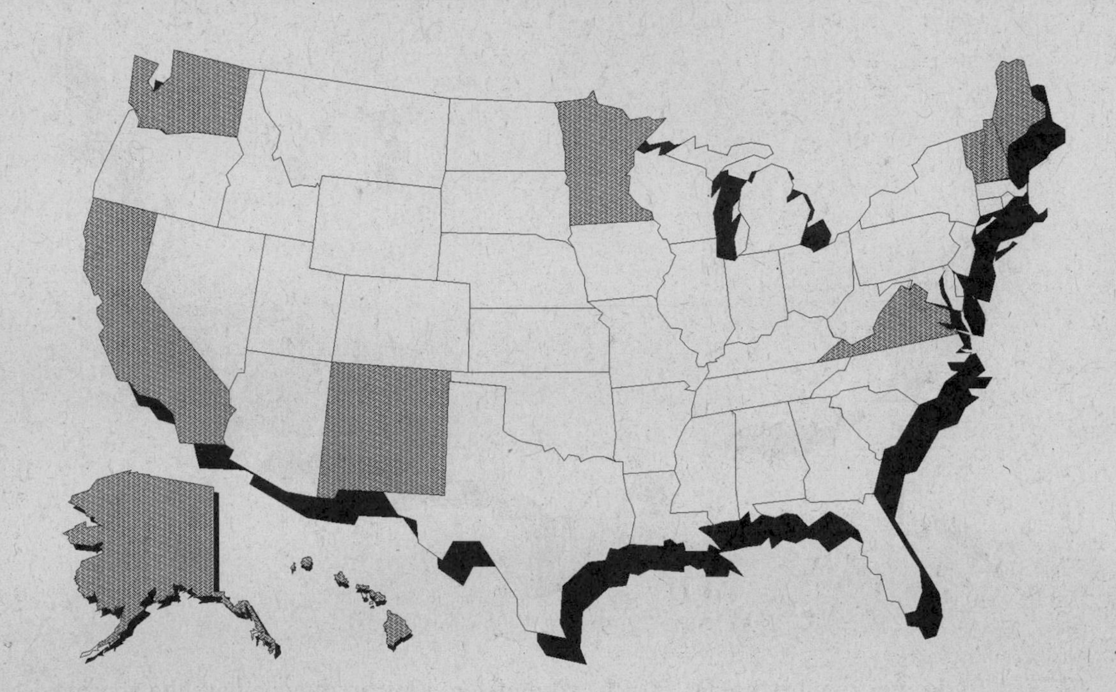

At least 10 states maintain laws that allow pharmacists or nurses to dispense "emergency contraception" to women (possibly including minors under the age of 17) without a prescription: AK, CA, HI, ME, MN, NH, NM, VT, VA, and WA.

"Emergency Contraception" Access

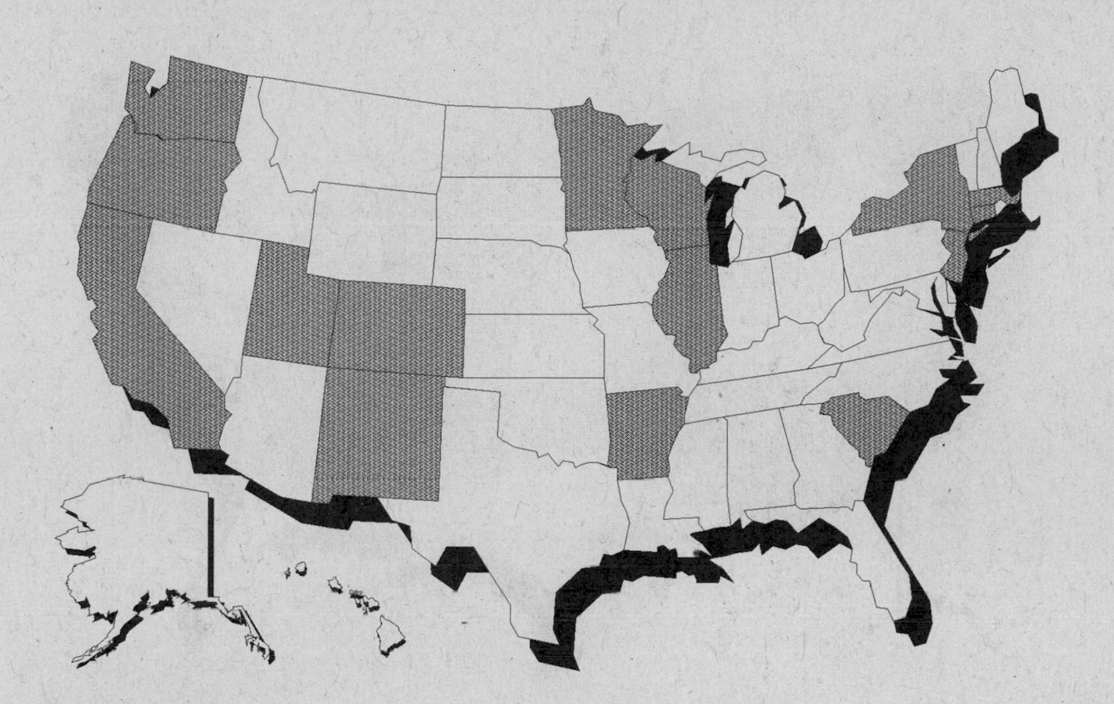

At least 15 states require healthcare facilities or providers to provide information about and/or access to "emergency contraception" to assault victims: AR, CA, CO, CT, IL, MA, MN, NJ, NM, NY, OR, SC, UT, WA, and WI.

Contraceptive Equity Laws

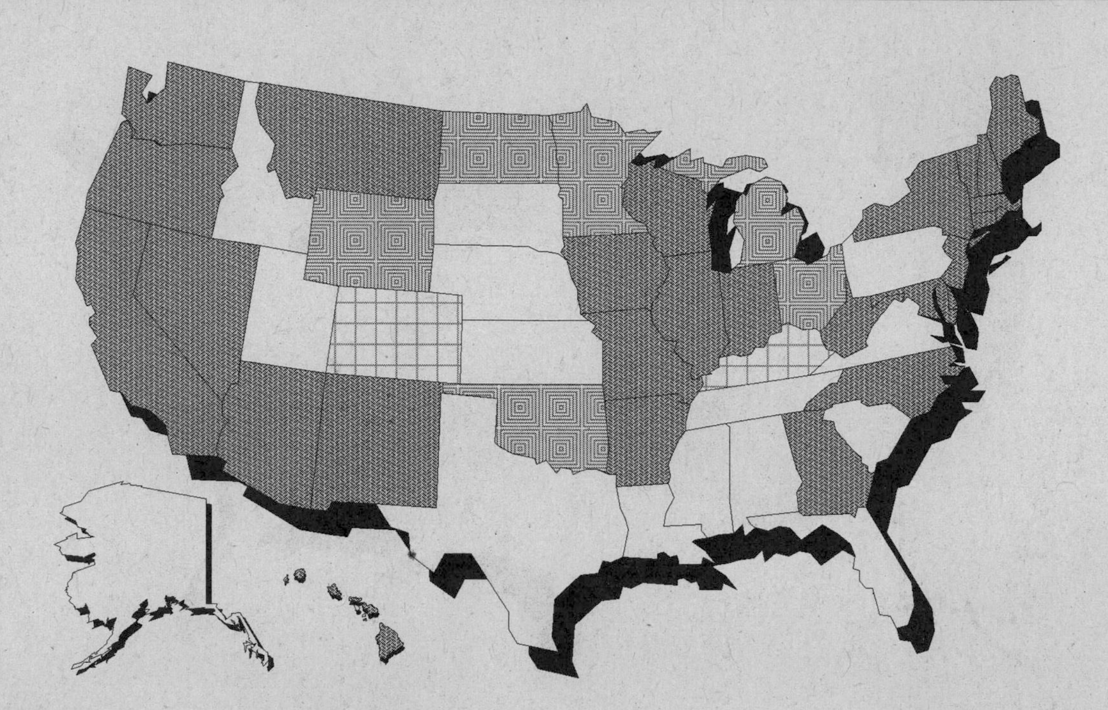

Twenty-seven states have enacted "contraceptive equity" laws: AZ, AR, CA, CT, DE, GA, HI, IL, IN, IA, ME, MD, MA, MO, MT (AG opinion), NV, NH, NJ, NM, NY, NC, OR, RI, VT, WA, WV, and WI.

Two states without "contraceptive equity" laws require insurers providing prescription drug coverage for individuals and small employers to offer contraceptive coverage: CO and KY.

Six states without "contraceptive equity" laws require health maintenance organizations (HMOs) to cover prescription contraceptives or family planning services: MI, MN, ND, OH, OK, and WY.

Other Contraceptive Equity Laws

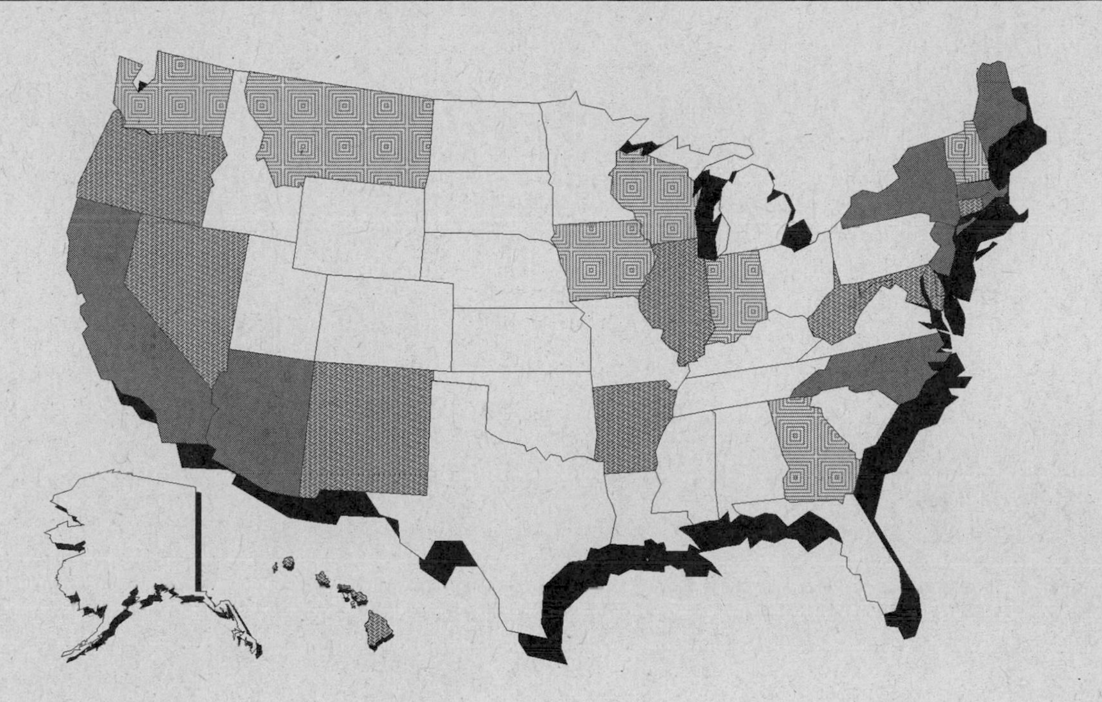

Ten states provide exemptions to certain employers and insurers who object (on moral or religious grounds) to providing contraceptives: AR, CT, DE, HI, IL, MD, NV, NM, OR, and WV.

Eight states provide a narrow exemption excluding the ability of most employers and insurers with moral or religious objections from exercising the exemption: AZ, CA, ME, MA, NJ, NY, NC, and RI.

Eight states do not specifically provide an exemption for employers and insurers with moral or religious objections to providing contraceptives: GA, IN, IA, MT, NH, VT, WA, and WI.

Pregnancy Care Centers:
On the frontline in the cause for life

By Denise M. Burke
Vice President of Legal Affairs, Americans United for Life

The life-affirming impact of pregnancy care centers (also known as crisis pregnancy centers and pregnancy resource centers) on the women and the communities they serve is considerable. Each year the reach and influence of pregnancy care centers (PCCs) grows as more centers open, as public opinion on abortion increasingly shifts to a pro-life ethic, and as the centers receive more favorable attention for their important work. Today, thousands of PCCs operate across the country, serving women with compassion and integrity and offering them positive alternatives for unplanned pregnancies.

Perhaps there is no better indicator of the positive impact that PCCs are having by supporting women emotionally and financially, by protecting women from the adverse health consequences of abortion, and by helping to reduce the number of abortions performed each year than the vitriol directed toward these centers by pro-abortion advocacy groups. These groups refer to them as "fake centers" and produce and market kits for activists to target and expose pregnancy care centers with negative publicity and protests. Even they, in their zeal to promote abortion-on-demand, cannot ignore the very real and increasingly powerful impact pregnancy care centers are having on women and on public opinion about abortion.

As the positive outreach of the nation's PCCs has expanded, so too have attempts by pro-life legislators around the country to support their important work through specialty vehicle license plate programs and direct taxpayer-funded subsidies.

ISSUES

Each year, more than 2,500 PCCs across the United States provide invaluable free services to hundreds of thousands of women facing unplanned pregnancies. Services offered by PCCs typically include:

- Free pregnancy tests;
- One-on-one, nonjudgmental options counseling;
- Temporary housing, food, clothing, furniture, and other material assistance;
- Childbirth and parenting classes;
- Ultrasounds, pre-natal vitamins, and other medical care;
- Education and employment counseling;
- 24-hour telephone hotlines; and/or
- Referrals for health care and to adoption agencies and other support services.

Funding Options for Pregnancy Care Centers

"Choose Life" License Plates:
Currently, 22 states have "Choose Life" specialty license plate programs where the pro-

ceeds benefit PCCs and other organizations providing abortion alternatives such as adoption.[1]

Notably, many of these programs specifically preclude agencies and organizations that provide, counsel in favor of, or refer for abortions from receiving any proceeds from the programs.

Since organizations that advocate on behalf of abortion are often excluded from receiving any proceeds from these programs, national abortion advocacy groups, along with the American Civil Liberties Union (ACLU), have lodged multiple constitutional challenges against many of these state license plate programs. The results have been mostly positive, with judges ruling against or dismissing such challenges.

To date, only one "Choose Life" specialty license plate program has been declared unconstitutional by a federal court. In the litigation surrounding South Carolina's initial license plate program, the U.S. Court of Appeals for the Fourth Circuit found the program violated the First Amendment, failing to provide a forum for opposing views. In 2004, the U.S. Supreme Court refused to review the ruling and the program was ended. However, in November 2008 South Carolina enacted a second, unchallenged specialty program providing revenue to pregnancy care centers.

In a recent development, pro-life advocates in several states—including Arizona, Illinois, Missouri, New Jersey, and New York—have challenged the states' failure to approve "Choose Life" license plates. In each case, proponents of the plates met requirements for the state's specialty license plate program and are alleging the state discriminated against the plates' pro-life message.

In January 2008, the Ninth Circuit ruled that Arizona's denial of the "Choose Life" plate was unconstitutional. In October 2008, the U.S. Supreme Court denied review and the plates are now available.

Recently, the U.S. Court of Appeals for the Eight Circuit ordered "Choose Life" plates issued in Missouri, ruling that the state statute providing for the issuance of specialty license plates was unconstitutional

Direct State Funding of Pregnancy Care Centers

A smaller number of states currently provide direct taxpayer funding to pregnancy care centers.[2] Typically, this funding comes through appropriation or budget measures and includes specific conditions on the types of organizations that can apply for and receive the funding. Careful attention has been paid to whether or not faith-based pregnancy care centers, such as CareNet, can participate in the funding without jeopardizing their status and faith-based mission.

Limitations on/Attempted Regulation of Pregnancy Care Centers

In recent years, a small number of states have targeted PCCs for hostile regulation or unnecessary oversight. For example, in 2007 in one of the most direct and insidious attacks on the mission of PCCs, Oregon, at the behest of Planned Parenthood Advocates of Oregon and NARAL Pro-Choice Oregon, considered a measure establishing and funding a study committee to "review the policies and procedures"

of state PCCs. The legislation then proposed Oregon fund a "study commission" that would seek to confirm its premise: PCCs are fake clinics that intentionally lie to and mislead women. Although the legislation was handily defeated by an educational campaign lead by national and local PCC supporters, it is, arguably, a new and provocative tactic being pursued by abortion advocates to close down PCCs and to short-circuit meaningful debate about abortion and its negative impact on women. In 2008, a similar attack was launched in Maryland.

Sadly, Oregon and Maryland have not been the only states to target PCCs with proposed legislation rooted in pro-abortion rhetoric and bias. Fortunately, these measures have received little attention from most legislators and the public, but one can only imagine the outrage that would have resulted had the legislation instead asserted that abortion clinics were provided false or misleading information to women.

MYTHS & FACTS

Myth: Pregnancy care centers provide medically inaccurate information to women.
Fact: PCCs distribute medically accurate information regarding fetal development, pregnancy, and the risks—physical and mental—of abortion. All information used and distributed by approved providers is medically accurate, recently published, and includes citations to legitimate authorities, such as the Centers for Disease Control and Prevention (CDC), medical journals, and other reputable sources. If there is medical debate regarding whether or not abortion carries particular risks (*e.g.*, the abortion-breast cancer link), information on this conflict is brought to the attention of the woman and is not hidden or withheld from her.

Myth: PCC personnel are poorly or inadequately trained.
Fact: PCC staff and volunteers are appropriately trained for the services they provide. Those PCCs that offer ultrasounds and/or other medical services hire medically-trained staff and comply with state and federal regulations regarding licensing and certification.[3]

Myth: PCCs engage in false advertising, misleading women into believing they provide abortions and abortion counseling.
Fact: Advertising by PCCs is honest and discloses to women the types of services provided by the centers. Most PCCs, including those affiliated with national organizations such as Birthright International and CareNet, have strict standards of integrity regarding truth in advertising and require the full disclosure of the types of services provided.[4]

Pregnancy care centers are most often listed under "Abortion Alternatives" in the Yellow Pages or other telephone directories. In many areas, it is the Yellow Pages publisher who determines how to categorize PCCs.[5] PCCs do not advertise under names such as "Abortion Services."

Myth: PCC personnel are judgmental and do not provide a woman with counseling on "all her reproductive care options."
Fact: PCCs provide women with compassionate and confidential counseling in a non-judgmental manner regardless of their pregnancy outcomes. Women who have used the services of a PCC reported a 98% positive effect, including 71% who had a very positive effect, according to a survey of 630 women conducted by the Wirthlin Group.[6] Of those women who were aware of PCCs, 87% believed they have a positive impact on the women they serve, including a majority of those who identified themselves as "pro-choice."[7]

Myth: Faith-based PCCs are not eligible for governmental funding.
Fact: PCCs receiving federal and state funds strictly adhere to the "Charitable Choice Act." Under this Act, an organization is not prohibited from receiving TANF (federal Temporary Aid to Needy Families) funds solely because it is a faith-based organization. Faith-based organizations are allowed to receive TANF funds if they conduct religious and spiritual activities separately, in time or location, from the TANF-funded activities.

Endnotes

[1] Alabama, Arizona, Arkansas, Connecticut, Florida, Georgia, Hawaii, Indiana, Kentucky, Louisiana, Maryland, Mississippi, Missouri, Montana, North Dakota, Ohio, Oklahoma, Pennsylvania, South Carolina, South Dakota, Tennessee, and Virginia.

[2] In 2009, at least eleven states were providing direct funding or approved such funding: California, Florida, Louisiana, Minnesota, Missouri, North Dakota, Ohio, Oklahoma, Pennsylvania, Texas, and Wisconsin. Conversely, Kansas Governor Mark Patterson disapproved $355,000 in funding for PCCs.

[3] Amy Contrada, *Saving More Babies with Ultrasound: Crisis Pregnancy Centers Have Success Using Pictures*, MASSACHUSETTS NEWS (2002), available at http://www.massnews.com/2002_editions/01_Jan/12302preg.htm (last visited August 20, 2009).

[4] *Id.* at 15; Kristin Hansen, *Pregnancy Centers Respond to Another Attempt By Abortion Proponents to Shut Down Competition*, CARENET (2006), available at http://www.carenet.production.digiknow.com/newsroom/press_release.php?id=46 (last visited August 20, 2009).

[5] Scott and Bainbridge, *The Making of a Controversy*, at 5.

[6] National Right to Life News, *Most Americans—Even "Pro-Choicers"—approve of CPCs*, (May 1998), available at http://www.accessmylibrary.com/coms2/summary_0286-405023_ITM (last visited August 20, 2009).

[7] *Id.* This positive attitude is shared by both those who support abortion [86%], those who are pro-life (87%) and those without a consistent stand on the issue of abortion (88%).

Pregnancy Care Centers Talking Points

- More than 2,500 pregnancy care centers (PCCs) across the United States provide invaluable free services to hundreds of thousands of women facing unplanned pregnancies. Services offered by PCCs typically include:
    - Free pregnancy tests;
    - One-on-one, nonjudgmental options counseling;
    - Temporary housing, food, clothing, furniture, and other material assistance;
    - Childbirth and parenting classes;
    - Ultrasounds, pre-natal vitamins, and other medical care;
    - Education and employment counseling;
    - 24-hour telephone hotlines; and/or
    - Referrals to healthcare, adoption agencies, and other support services.

- PCC staff and volunteers are appropriately trained for the services they provide. Those PCCs that offer ultrasounds and/or other medical services hire medically-trained staff and comply with state and federal regulations regarding licensing and certification.[1]

- Advertising by PCCs is honest and discloses to women the types of services provided by the centers. Most PCCs, including those affiliated with national organizations such as Birthright International and CareNet, have strict standards of integrity regarding truth in advertising and require the full disclosure of the types of services provided.[2] Pregnancy care centers are most often listed under "Abortion Alternatives" in the Yellow Pages or other telephone directories. In many areas, it is the Yellow Pages publisher who determines how to categorize PCCs.[3] PCCs do not advertise under names such as "Abortion Services."

- PCCs distribute medically accurate information regarding fetal development, pregnancy, and the risks—physical and mental—of abortion. All information used and distributed by approved providers is medically accurate, recently published, and includes citations to legitimate authorities, such as the Centers for Disease Control and Prevention (CDC), medical journals, and other reputable sources.

- If there is medical debate regarding whether or not abortion carries particular risks (*e.g.*, the abortion-breast cancer link), information on this conflict is brought to the attention of the client and is not hidden or withheld from her.

- PCCs receiving federal and state funds strictly adhere to the "Charitable Choice Act." Under this Act, an organization is not prohibited from receiving TANF (federal Temporary Aid to Needy Families) funds solely because it is a faith-based organization. Faith-

based organizations are allowed to receive TANF funds if they conduct religious and spiritual activities separately, in time or location, from the TANF-funded activities.

- PCCs provide women with compassionate and confidential counseling in a nonjudgmental manner regardless of their pregnancy outcomes. Women who have used the services of a PCC reported a 98% positive effect, including 71% who had a very positive effect, according to a survey of 630 women conducted by the Wirthlin Group.[4] Of those women who were aware of PCCs, 87% believed they have a positive impact on the women they serve, including a majority of those who identified themselves as "pro-choice."[5]

- As PCCs play a critical role in encouraging women to make positive life choices, it is imperative they be supported and protected from unwarranted attacks.
    - State legislatures should vigorously oppose legislation impeding the ability of PCCs to provide important support and resources for women who have exercised their right to choose alternatives to abortion.
    - States should show their support for PCCs by passing pro-PCC resolutions that commend PCCs for the positive, invaluable services PCCs provide to hundreds of thousands of women. In addition, legislators should support legislative initiatives to provide direct federal funding for PCCs (including religiously-affiliated centers) and funding to assist PCCs with the purchase of ultrasound equipment.

Endnotes

[1] Amy Contrada, *Saving More Babies with Ultrasound: Crisis Pregnancy Centers Have Success Using Pictures*, Massachusetts News (2002), available at http://www.massnews.com/2002_editions/01_Jan/12302preg.htm (last visited August 20, 2009).

[2] *Id.* at 15; Kristin Hansen, *Pregnancy Centers Respond to Another Attempt By Abortion Proponents to Shut Down Competition*, CareNet (2006), available at http://www.carenet.production.digiknow.com/newsroom/press_release.php?id=46 (last visited August 20, 2009).

[3] Scott and Bainbridge, *The Making of a Controversy*, at 5.

[4] National Right to Life News, *Most Americans—Even "Pro-Choicers"—approve of CPCs*, (May 1998), available at http://www.accessmylibrary.com/coms2/summary_0286-405023_ITM (last visited August 20, 2009).

[5] *Id.* This positive attitude is shared by both those who support abortion [86%], those who are pro-life (87%) and those without a consistent stand on the issue of abortion (88%).

Direct Funding of Pregnancy Care Centers

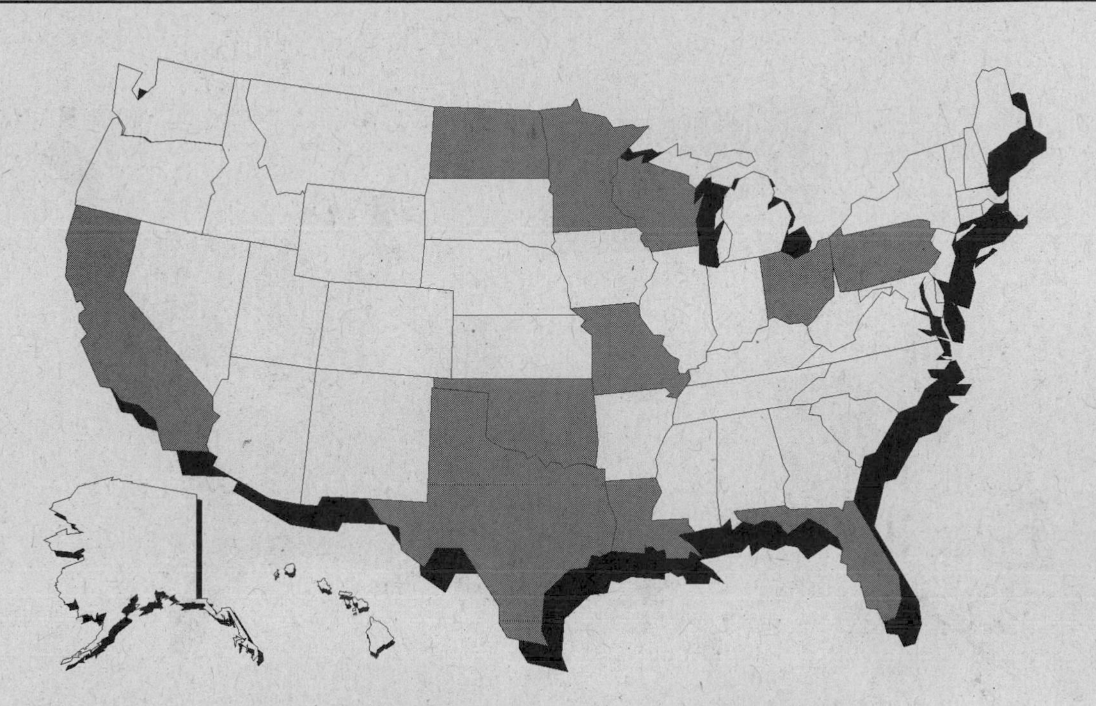

At least 11 states currently provide direct funding to pregnancy care centers or have recently approved such funding: CA, FL, LA, MN, MO, ND, OK, OH, PA,TX, and WI.

"Choose Life" License Plate Programs

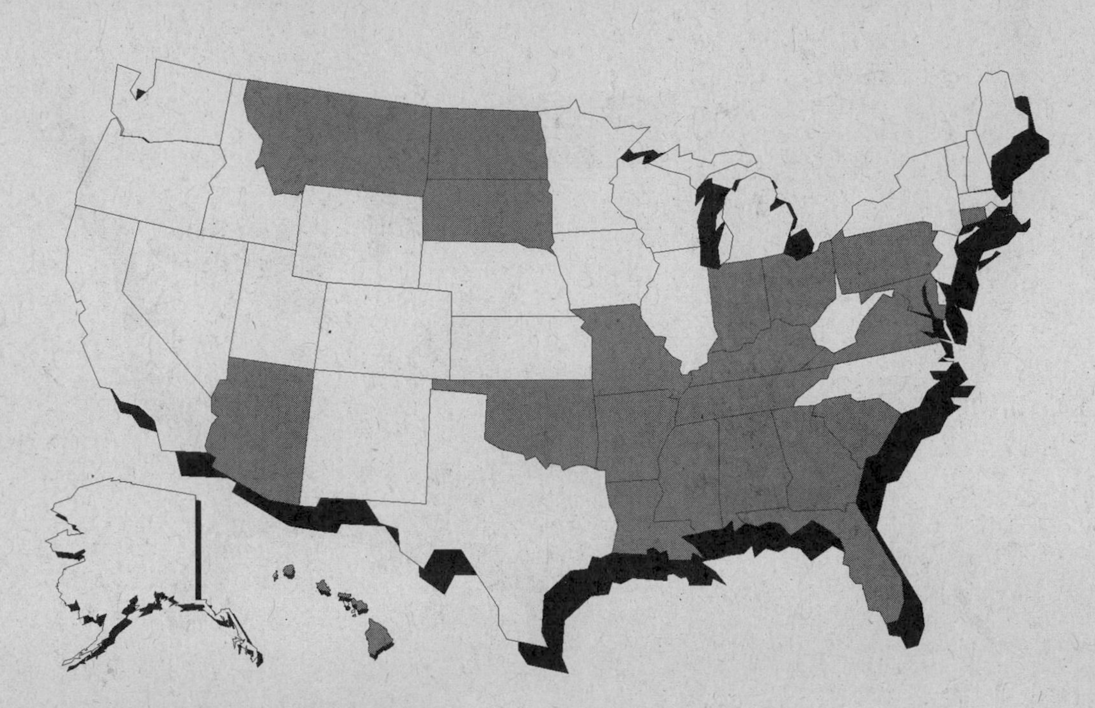

Twenty-two states have "Choose Life" specialty license plate programs where the proceeds benefit pregnancy care centers and/or other organizations providing abortion alternatives: AL, AZ, AR, CT, FL, GA, HI, IN, KY, LA, MD, MS, MO, MT, ND, OH, OK, PA, SC, SD, TN, and VA.

AUL Model Legislation

STATE CONSTITUTIONAL AMENDMENT

States seeking a meaningful and effective mechanism to protect human life should consider the following state constitutional amendment. A version of these sections was originally drafted by Paul Benjamin Linton[1], adopting language from the Arkansas and Rhode Island state constitutions.

Section 1. The policy of [*Insert name of State*] is to protect the life of every unborn child from conception to birth, to the extent permitted by the federal constitution.

Section 2. Nothing in this constitution shall be construed to grant or secure any right relating to abortion or the public funding thereof.

Section 3. No public funds shall be used to pay for any abortion, except to save the life of the mother [*or as may be required by federal law*].

Besides being simple, practical, and clear, there are several merits to this proposed language: it has been enacted in other states, it has been shown to be effective, and it can actually go into effect and do some good now and after *Roe v. Wade* is overturned.

Section 1 of the proposed amendment is based on §2 of Amendment 68 of the Arkansas Constitution. It is aspirational and would guide the interpretation of existing and future state laws by all branches of state government.

Section 2 is based on Article I, § 2, of the Rhode Island Constitution. It is intended to prevent any branch of state government, including the judiciary, from manufacturing a right to abortion under the state constitution. It would also effectively overturn any existing state judicial decisions creating such a right.

Section 3 is based on §1 of Amendment 68 of the Arkansas Constitution. It is intended to prevent state funding of abortion to the extent permitted by federal law.

Endnotes

[1] Paul Benjamin Linton, Esq. is an attorney in private practice in Illinois and a former General Counsel of Americans United for Life. He is also the author of *Abortion and State Constitutions: A State-by-State Analysis* (Carolina Academic Press 2008).

JOINT RESOLUTION OPPOSING THE FEDERAL "FREEDOM OF CHOICE ACT"

JOINT RESOLUTION No. ______
By Representatives/Senators ___________

WHEREAS, since 1989, some members of the United States Congress have repeatedly introduced and recommended for passage the federal "Freedom of Choice Act" which purports to classify abortion as a "fundamental right," equal in stature to the right to free speech and the right to vote – rights that, unlike abortion, are specifically enumerated in the Constitution of the United States;

[*OR, when introduced: WHEREAS, the 111th United States Congress has introduced the "Freedom of Choice Act", [H.R. ____ /S.____] which purports to classify abortion as a "fundamental right," equal in stature to the right to free speech and the right to vote – rights that, unlike abortion, are specifically enumerated in the Constitution of the United States;*]

WHEREAS, the federal "Freedom of Choice Act" is strongly supported by Barack Obama, President of the United States; members of the current Administration; and national and state abortion-advocacy groups;

WHEREAS, the federal "Freedom of Choice Act" would invalidate any "statute, ordinance, regulation, administrative order, decision, policy, practice, or other action" of any federal, state, or local government or governmental official (or any person acting under government authority) that would "deny or interfere with a woman's right to choose" abortion, or that would "discriminate against the exercise of the right . . . in the regulation or provision of benefits, facilities, services, or information";

WHEREAS, the federal "Freedom of Choice Act" would nullify any federal or state law "enacted, adopted, or implemented before, on, or after the date of [its] enactment" and would effectively prevent the State of [*Insert name of State*] from enacting similar protective measures in the future;

WHEREAS, the federal "Freedom of Choice Act" could be passed as a whole by Congress or, alternatively, implemented piecemeal through legislation, budgetary measures, Executive Orders, and other policy determinations;

WHEREAS, the 10th Amendment to the Constitution of the United States provides that "[t]he powers not delegated to the United States by the Constitution, nor prohibited by it to the States, are reserved to the States respectively, or to the people";

WHEREAS, the power to determine an individual state's abortion-related laws and policy including the delineation of appropriate medical requirements and standards for its provision has not been delegated in any manner to the federal government;

WHEREAS, beginning with *Roe v. Wade* in 1973, the Supreme Court of the United States has expressly and repeatedly recognized the right and authority of the states to regulate the provision of abortion;

WHEREAS, the Supreme Court of the United States has long recognized that an individual state, such as the State of [*Insert name of State*], "has a legitimate interest in seeing to it that abortion, like any other medical procedure, is performed under circumstances that insure maximum safety for the patient. This interest obviously extends ***at least*** to the performing physician and his staff, to the facilities involved, to the availability of after-care, and to adequate provision for any complication or emergency that might arise." *Roe v. Wade*, 410 U.S. 113, 150 (1973) (emphasis added);

WHEREAS, the State of [*Insert name of State*] and the other states thus retain the authority to regulate the provision of abortion and, in the interest of protecting both women and the unborn, have acted accordingly and appropriately;

WHEREAS, the federal "Freedom of Choice Act" would invalidate more than 550 federal and state abortion-related laws, laws supported by the majority of the American public;

WHEREAS, the federal "Freedom of Choice Act" would specifically invalidate the following common sense, protective laws properly enacted by the State of [*Insert name of State*]:
[*Drafter's Note: Insert bulleted list of state laws that would be invalidated by the federal "Freedom of Choice Act." AUL is available for assistance in compiling a complete list of affected state laws.*]

WHEREAS, the federal "Freedom of Choice Act" will not make abortion safe or rare, but will instead actively promote and subsidize abortion with State and Federal tax dollars and do nothing to ensure its safety; and

WHEREAS, the federal "Freedom of Choice Act" will protect and promote the abortion industry, sacrifice women and their health to a radical political ideology of unregulated abortion-on-demand, and silence the voices of everyday Americans who want to engage in a meaningful public discussion and debate over the availability, safety, and even desirability of abortion.

NOW, THEREFORE, BE IT RESOLVED BY THE LEGISLATURE OF THE STATE OF [*Insert name of State*]:

Section 1. That the [*Legislature*] strongly opposes [*if yet available, insert: H.R. ____ /S.____*], the federal "Freedom of Choice Act" and urges the United States Congress to summarily reject it.

Section 2. That the [*Legislature*] strongly opposes the federal "Freedom of Choice Act" because it seeks to circumvent the States' general legislative authority as guaranteed by the 10th Amendment to the U.S. Constitution.

Section 3. That the [*Legislature*] strongly opposes the federal "Freedom of Choice Act" because it seeks to undermine the right and responsibility of the States and the people to debate, vote on, and determine abortion-related laws and policy.

Section 4. That the [*Legislature*] strongly opposes the federal "Freedom of Choice Act" because the protection of women's health through state regulations on abortion is a compelling State interest that should not be nullified by Congress.

Section 5. That the [*Legislature*] strongly opposes the federal "Freedom of Choice Act" because its enactment would nullify [*Insert appropriate number*] laws in the State of [*Insert name of State*], laws that the [*Legislature*] and the people of [*Insert name of State*] strongly support.

Section 6. That the Secretary of State of [*Insert name of State*] transmit a copy of this resolution to the Governor; to the President of the United States; to the President of the Senate and the Speaker of the House of Representatives of the United States Congress; and to each individual member of [*Insert name of State*]'s Congressional delegation.

JOINT RESOLUTION PROPOSING A CONSTITUTIONAL AMENDMENT RETURNING DETERMINATIONS ON ABORTION LAW AND POLICY TO THE AMERICAN PEOPLE

JOINT RESOLUTION No. ____
By Representatives/Senators __________________

WHEREAS, no right to abortion is rooted in the traditions of the American people and no national right to abortion is conferred by the Constitution of the United States;

WHEREAS, the Supreme Court's decisions in *Roe v. Wade* and *Doe v. Bolton* have no basis in the text or history of the Constitution of the United States;

WHEREAS, the Supreme Court's abortion decisions have taken away the American people's right of self-government and have not respected the authority of the American people, through their elected representatives, to establish abortion law and policy;

WHEREAS, the authority of the people of each state to determine public policy and to protect human life and health is fundamental;

WHEREAS, the appropriate forum for the resolution of the abortion issue in a democracy is the legislature;

WHEREAS, state legislatures are ultimate guardians of the liberties and welfare of the people in quite as great a degree as the courts;

WHEREAS, the Supreme Court's abortion decisions have resulted in the most extreme abortion policy of any democracy in the world and have resulted in significant damage to the physical and psychological health of American women;

WHEREAS, the State of [*Insert name of State*] has a duty to protect innocent human life;

WHEREAS, human life founded on inherent and inalienable rights is entitled to the full protection of law and due process and the Supreme Court's abortion decisions have failed to protect the lives of unborn children;

WHEREAS, because of the Supreme Court's abortion decisions, it is impossible for the State of [*Insert name of State*] to protect the life, health, and welfare of women and unborn human life; to protect parental rights; to maintain accurate statistical data to aid in providing proper

maternal health regulations; and to properly regulate the practice of medicine; and

WHEREAS, the State of [*Insert name of State*] is prevented, by the Supreme Court, from providing adequate legal remedies to protect the life, health, and welfare of pregnant women and unborn human life.

NOW, THEREFORE, BE IT RESOLVED BY THE LEGISLATURE OF THE STATE OF [*Insert name of State*]:

Section 1. That, because the people in a republic have the only legitimate authority to determine abortion law and policy, the Legislature of this State, as duly-elected representatives of the people, calls upon the United States Congress to propose a constitutional amendment, pursuant to Article V of the Constitution of the United States, reaffirming that a right to abortion is not conferred by the Constitution of the United States.

Section 2. That the Secretary of State of [*Insert name of State*] transmit a copy of this resolution to the Governor, to the President of the United States, and to the President of the Senate and the Speaker of the House of Representatives of the United States Congress.

PARTIAL-BIRTH ABORTION BAN ACT

HOUSE/SENATE BILL No.______
By Representatives/Senators______________

Section 1. Title

This Act may be known and cited as the "Partial-Birth Abortion Ban Act."

Section 2. Legislative Findings and Purposes

(a) The [*Legislature*] of the State of [*Insert name of State*] finds that:

(1) Partial-birth abortion is a gruesome and inhumane procedure that is never medically necessary and, as such, should be prohibited.

(2) In 2003, the 108th United States Congress passed the "Partial-Birth Abortion Ban Act of 2003" (18 U.S.C. §1531) and President George W. Bush signed it into law.

(3) Later, on April 18, 2007, the Supreme Court of the United States upheld the "Partial-Birth Abortion Ban Act of 2003" ("the federal ban") in *Gonzales v. Carhart*, 127 S. Ct. 1610 (2007), specifically ruling that a ban on partial-birth abortion need not include a maternal "health" exception to be constitutional.

(4) This Act's language stems from and uses as its primary influence the language of the federal ban as upheld in *Gonzales v. Carhart*.

(5) This Act—a state ban on partial-birth abortion—is needed to supplement the federal ban. Importantly, the federal ban was narrowly tailored to reach only those partial-birth abortion procedures that implicate Congress' power to regulate interstate or foreign commerce. U.S. Const. art. 1, §8, cl. 3. Without this Act, partial-birth abortions performed, but not affecting these narrow categories of commerce, are not prohibited under the federal ban.

(6) Partial-birth abortion poses serious risks to women's long-term health and is not universally embraced by the mainstream medical community.

(7) There is a substantial evidentiary record upon which the [*Legislature*] of the State of [*Insert name of State*] has based its conclusion that a state ban on par-

tial-birth abortion is not constitutionally required to contain a maternal "health" exception.

(8) Moreover, the medical evidence clearly supports the informed judgment of the State of [*Insert name of State*] that a partial-birth abortion is never medically necessary to preserve a woman's health and instead poses serious health risks, lying outside the standard of medical care.

(9) Specifically, partial-birth abortion poses serious risks including, but not limited to: an increased risk of cervical incompetence, a result of cervical dilation that makes it difficult or impossible for a woman to successfully carry a subsequent pregnancy to term; an increased risk of uterine rupture, abruption, amniotic fluid embolus, and trauma to the uterus as a result of converting the child to a footling breech position—a procedure which, according to a leading obstetrics textbook, "there are very few, if any, indications for other than for delivery of a second twin"; and a risk of lacerations and secondary hemorrhaging as a result of the physician blindly forcing a sharp instrument into the base of the unborn child's skull while he or she is lodged in the birth canal—an act which could result in severe bleeding and subsequent shock.

(10) There is no credible medical evidence that partial-birth abortions are safer than other abortion procedures. No controlled studies of partial-birth abortion have been conducted nor have any comparative studies been conducted to demonstrate its safety and efficacy compared to other abortion methods. Furthermore, there have been no articles published in peer-reviewed journals that establish that partial-birth abortions are superior in any way to established abortion procedures.

(11) In light of this overwhelming evidence, the State of [*Insert name of State*] has a compelling interest in prohibiting partial-birth abortion. Both *Roe v. Wade*, 410 U.S. 113 (1973), and *Planned Parenthood v. Casey*, 505 U.S. 833 (1992), recognized a governmental interest in protecting the life of a child during the birth [*or delivery*] process. This interest is specifically implicated during a partial-birth abortion because labor is induced and the birth process is begun before an abortion is attempted or the child is actually aborted [*or killed*].

(12) In fact, partial-birth abortion kills a child who is mere inches away from birth and becoming a "person" under *Roe*. Thus, the State clearly has a heightened interest in protecting the life of the partially-born child.

(13) The public's perception of the appropriate role of a physician during a child's

birth [*or delivery*] is undermined by aborting a child in the manner that purposefully seeks to kill the child inches from birth [*or legal personhood*].

(14) Partial-birth abortion is disturbingly similar to the killing of a newborn infant and blurs the legal and moral lines between infanticide and abortion. This Act reinforces that line at birth—just as the Supreme Court established in *Roe v. Wade*—while also preserving the integrity of the medical profession and promoting respect for human life.

(15) The vast majority of infants killed during partial-birth abortions are alive up through the very end of the procedure. Medical science has established that an unborn infant can feel pain when subjected to painful stimuli like that inflicted during a partial-birth abortion procedure. Moreover, an unborn child's perception of pain is even more intense than that of newborn infants and older children subjected to the same stimuli.

(b) For these reasons, the [*Legislature*]'s purposes in promulgating this Act are to conclusively establish that partial-birth abortion is never medically indicated to preserve the health of the mother and poses significant health risks to her; to clearly define the line between abortion and infanticide by killing; and to safeguard the role of a physician during childbirth.

Section 3. Definitions

(a) "**Partial-birth abortion**" means an abortion in which the person performing the abortion:

(1) Deliberately and intentionally vaginally delivers a living fetus until, in the case of a head-first presentation, the entire fetal head is outside the body of the mother, or, in the case of breech presentation, any part of the fetal trunk past the navel is outside the body of the mother, for the purpose of performing an overt act that the person knows will kill the partially-delivered living fetus; and

(2) Performs the overt act, other than completion of delivery, that kills the partially-delivered living fetus.

(b) "**Physician**" means a doctor of medicine or osteopathy legally authorized to practice medicine and surgery by the State in which the doctor performs such activity, or any other individual legally authorized by the State to perform abortions; *provided, however,* that any individual who is not a physician or not otherwise legally authorized by the State to perform abortions, but who nevertheless directly performs a partial-birth abortion, shall be subject to the provisions of this Act.

Section 4. Prohibition.

A person shall not knowingly perform or attempt to perform a partial-birth abortion.

Section 5. Limitations.

No person shall perform or induce a partial-birth abortion on a viable fetus unless such person is a physician and has a documented referral from another physician not legally or financially affiliated with the physician performing or inducing the abortion and both physicians determine that the life of the mother is endangered by a physical disorder, physical illness, or physical injury, including a life-endangering physical condition caused by or arising from the pregnancy itself.

Section 6. Reporting

(a) If a physician determines in accordance with the provisions of Section 5 that a partial-birth abortion is necessary and performs a partial-birth abortion on the woman, the physician shall report such determination and the reasons for such determination in writing to the medical care facility in which the abortion is performed for inclusion in the report of the medical care facility to the [*Insert appropriate State department, department head, or regulatory body*]; or if the abortion is not performed in a medical care facility, the physician shall report the reasons for such determination in writing to the [*Insert appropriate State department, department head, or regulatory body*] as part of the written report made by the physician to [*Insert appropriate State department, department head, or regulatory body*]. The physician shall retain a copy of the written reports required under this Section for not less than five years.

(b) Failure to report under this Section does not subject physician to criminal or civil penalties under Sections 7 and 8.

(c) Subsection (b) does not preclude sanctions, disciplinary action, or any other appropriate action by the [*Insert appropriate citation or reference to State Medical Board or other appropriate agency*].

Section 7. Criminal Penalties

(a) Any person who intentionally or knowingly violates this Act is guilty of a [*Insert class of felony or misdemeanor*].

(b) Any physician who intentionally or knowingly performs a partial-birth abortion and thereby kills a human fetus shall be fined not less than ten thousand nor more than one-hundred thousand dollars under this Act, or be imprisoned [*at hard labor*] not less than one year nor more than ten years, or both.

Section 8. Civil Penalties

(a) The father, if married to the mother at the time she receives a partial-birth abortion procedure, and, if the mother has not attained the age of 18 years at the time of the abortion, the maternal grandparents of the fetus may in a civil action obtain appropriate relief, unless the pregnancy resulted from the plaintiff's criminal conduct or the plaintiff consented to the abortion.

(b) Such relief shall include—

(1) money damages for all injuries, psychological and physical, occasioned by the violation of this Act; and

(2) statutory damages equal to [*Insert number*] times the cost of the partial-birth abortion.

Section 9. Review by State Medical Board [*of Medical Licensure and Supervision*].

(a) A physician-defendant accused of an offense under this Act may seek a hearing before the State Medical Board [*or other appropriate State agency*] as to whether the physician's conduct was necessary to save the life of the mother whose life was endangered by a physical disorder, physical illness, or physical injury, including a life-endangering physical condition caused by or arising from the pregnancy itself.

(b) The findings on this issue are admissible on this issue at the civil and criminal trial(s) of the physician-defendant. Upon a motion of the physician-defendant, the court shall delay the beginning of the trial(s) for not more than 30 days to permit such a hearing to take place.

Section 10. Penalties for Ambulatory Healthcare Facilities.

(a) An ambulatory healthcare [*surgical*] facility licensed pursuant to [*Insert appropriate statutes or regulations*] in which the partial-birth abortion is performed in violation of this Act shall be subject to immediate revocation of its license by the [*Insert appropriate department or agency*].

(b) An ambulatory healthcare [*surgical*] facility licensed pursuant to [*Insert appropriate statutes or regulations*] in which the partial-birth abortion is performed in violation of this Act shall lose all state funding for [*Insert number*] years and will be required to reimburse the state for funds from the calendar [*fiscal*] year in which the partial-birth abortion was performed.

Section 11. Prosecutorial Exclusion.

A woman upon whom a partial-birth abortion is performed may not be prosecuted under this Act for a conspiracy to violate Section 4 of this bill.

Section 12. Construction.

(a) Nothing in this Act shall be construed as creating or recognizing a right to abortion.

(b) It is not the intention of this Act to make lawful an abortion that is currently unlawful.

Section 13. Severability

Any provision of this Act held to be invalid or unenforceable by its terms, or as applied to any person or circumstance, shall be construed so as give it the maximum effect permitted by law, unless such holding shall be one of utter invalidity or unenforceability, in which event such provision shall be deemed severable herefrom and shall not affect the remainder hereof or the application of such provision to other persons not similarly situated or to other, dissimilar circumstances.

Section 14. Right of Intervention

The [*Legislature*], by joint resolution, may appoint one or more of its members, who sponsored or cosponsored this Act in his or her official capacity, to intervene as a matter of right in any case in which the constitutionality of this law is challenged.

Section 15. Effective Date.

This Act shall take effect on [*Insert date*].

BAN ON ABORTIONS PERFORMED FOR REASONS OF SEX SELECTION, POTENTIAL GENETIC DEFORMITY, OR POTENTIAL DISABILITY

[***Drafter's Note:*** AUL is providing this model to spark and encourage discussion about the need for states to ban abortions performed for reasons of sex selection and potential genetic deformities or disabilities as identified during prenatal care or testing. This model was originally drafted as proposed federal legislation, but has been adapted for the States. **However, it should not be introduced or filed in any legislature, in whole or in part, without consulting AUL.]**

HOUSE/SENATE BILL No. _____
By Representatives/Senators _____

Section 1. Short Title.

This Act may be cited as the "Abortion Act of [*Insert appropriate year*]."

Section 2. Legislative Findings.

The [*Legislature*] finds and declares the following:

(a) In regard to sex-selective abortion:

(1) A sex-selective abortion is used to prevent the birth of a child of an undesired sex. The victims of sex-selective abortion are overwhelmingly female.

(2) The United States, along with other countries, has petitioned the United Nations General Assembly to declare sex-selective abortion a crime against women.

(3) Countries such as India, Great Britain, and China have taken steps to end sex-selective abortion. For example, China and India do not allow doctors to reveal the sex of an unborn child.

(4) Women are a vital part of our society and culture and possess the same fundamental human rights as men.

(5) The United States prohibits discrimination on the basis of sex in various areas, including: employment, education, athletics, and health insurance.

(6) It is undesirable to have a sex imbalance within a society, particularly when there is a shortage of women. Countries with high rates of male-preference have experienced ill effects due to an increasing number of young, unmarried men.

(7) A large population of young, unmarried men can be a cause of increased violence and militancy within a society.

(8) There is currently no evidence of a strong preference for males among American citizens. However, because of [*Legislature*]'s commitment to the equality of women and desire to never face a sex-imbalance problem, it considers sex-selective abortion to be a problem worthy of a prohibition.

(b) In regard to abortion and Down syndrome:

(1) Studies have revealed that unborn children that are diagnosed with Down syndrome or a potential for Down syndrome are disproportionately aborted.

(2) Studies have found that between 70% and 100% of unborn children diagnosed with Down syndrome are aborted.

(3) Recent years have seen an increase in the use of amniocentesis and other prenatal testing to diagnose potential health problems in unborn children.

(4) Amniocentesis and other prenatal testing often give correct results, but also give many false-positives.

(5) Roughly 1 in every 700 to 1,000 children is born with Down syndrome.

(6) Down syndrome is not considered a severe disability.

(7) In various circumstances, the United States prohibits discrimination against persons with Down syndrome.

(8) In many situations, such as education, the United States requires that concessions be made for the benefit of persons with Down syndrome.

(9) Persons with Down syndrome contribute to American culture and are a valuable part of our society.

(10) Many persons with Down syndrome are able to maintain employment, obtain

an education, and live with varying degrees of independence.

(11) As technology advances and as medical treatments and educational methods improve, persons with Down syndrome will increasingly be self-dependent and productive citizens.

(12) Persons with Down syndrome possess the same fundamental human rights as all other human beings.

(c) In regard to abortion and genetic abnormalities:

(1) Studies have revealed that unborn children who are diagnosed with a genetic abnormality or a potential for a genetic abnormality are often aborted.

(2) Studies have found that between 70% and 100% of unborn children diagnosed with genetic abnormalities are aborted.

(3) Recent years have seen an increase in the use of amniocentesis and other prenatal testing to diagnose potential health problems in unborn children.

(4) Amniocentesis and other prenatal testing often give correct results, but also give false-positives.

(5) There are approximately 4,000 known genetic abnormalities.

(6) The United States prohibits discrimination against persons with physical or mental deformities or handicaps in various circumstances, such as housing and employment.

(7) In many situations the United States requires that concessions be made for the benefit of persons with physical or mental handicaps.

(8) Persons with physical or mental deformities or handicaps contribute to American culture and are a valuable part of our society.

(9) Many persons with physical or mental deformities or handicaps are able to support themselves financially, obtain an education, and live independently.

(10) As technology advances and as medical treatments and educational methods improve, persons with physical or mental deformities or handicaps will increasingly be self-dependent and productive citizens.

(11) Persons with physical or mental deformities or handicaps possess the same fundamental human rights as all other human beings.

Section 3: Definitions.

As used in this Act only:

(a) "**Abortion**": The act of using or prescribing any instrument, medicine, drug, or any other substance, device, or means with the intent to terminate the clinically diagnosable pregnancy of a woman with knowledge that the termination by those means will with reasonable likelihood cause the death of the unborn child. Such use, prescription, or means is not an abortion if done with the intent to:

(1) Save the life or preserve the health of an unborn child;

(2) Remove a dead unborn child caused by spontaneous abortion; or

(3) Remove an ectopic pregnancy.

(b) "**Down syndrome**" refers to a chromosome disorder associated either with an extra chromosome 21 (in whole or in part) or an effective trisomy for chromosome 21. Down syndrome is sometimes referred to as trisomy 21 syndrome.

(c) "**Genetic abnormality**" means any defect, disease, or disorder that is inherited genetically. The term genetic abnormality includes, but is not limited to: any physical disability, any mental disability or retardation, any physical disfigurement, scoliosis, dwarfism, Down syndrome, albinism, Amelia, or any other type of physical or mental abnormality or disease.

(d) "**Incompetent**" means any person who has been adjudged a disabled person and has had a guardian appointed for her under the [*State Probate Act or other appropriate state law*].

(e) "**Minor**" means any person under the age of eighteen (18) who is not and has not been married and has not been legally emancipated.

(f) "**Physician**" means any person licensed to practice medicine in this State. The term includes medical doctors and doctors of osteopathy.

(g) "**Pregnant woman**" means any female, including those who have not reached the age of 18 [*or minors*], who is in the reproductive condition of having an unborn child in the woman's uterus.

(h) "**Sex-selective abortion**" means an abortion performed solely on account of the sex of the unborn child.

(i) "**Unborn child**" means the offspring of human beings from conception until birth.

Section 4. Prohibition on Sex-Selective Abortion.

(a) No person may intentionally perform or attempt to perform an abortion with the knowledge that the pregnant woman is seeking the abortion solely on account of the sex of the unborn child.

(b) Nothing in this Section shall be construed to proscribe the performance of an abortion because the unborn child has a genetic disorder that is linked to the unborn child's sex.

(c) If this Section is held invalid as applied to the period of pregnancy prior to viability, then it shall remain applicable to the period of pregnancy subsequent to viability.

Section 5. Prohibition on Abortion for Down Syndrome.

(a) No person may intentionally perform or attempt to perform an abortion with knowledge that the pregnant woman is seeking the abortion solely because the unborn child has been diagnosed with either:

(1) Down syndrome, or

(2) a potential for Down syndrome.

(b) If this Section is held invalid as applied to the period of pregnancy prior to viability, then it shall remain applicable to the period of pregnancy subsequent to viability.

Section 6. Prohibition on Abortion for a Genetic Abnormality.

(a) No person may intentionally perform or attempt to perform an abortion with knowledge that the pregnant woman is seeking the abortion solely because the unborn child has been diagnosed with either:

(1) a genetic abnormality, or

(2) a potential for a genetic abnormality.

(b) If this Section is held invalid as applied to the period of pregnancy prior to viability, then it shall remain applicable to the period of pregnancy subsequent to viability.

Section 7. Criminal Penalties

(a) Any physician or other person who intentionally or knowingly violates this Act is guilty of a [*Insert class of felony*].

(b) Any physician or other person who intentionally or knowingly performs or attempts to perform an abortion prohibited by this Act shall be fined not less than [*Insert appropriate amount or possible range of fine*], or be imprisoned [*at hard labor*] not less than [*Insert appropriate time period or range*], or both.

Section 8. Civil Penalties

(a) Any physician or person who intentionally or knowingly violates this Act shall be liable for damages, and shall, if applicable, have his or her medical license suspended or revoked. He/She may also be enjoined from such acts as proscribed in this Act.

(b) A pregnant woman upon whom an abortion has been performed in violation of this Act, the parent or legal guardian of the woman if she is an unemancipated minor as defined in [*Insert citation(s) or other reference(s) to appropriate State statute*], or the legal guardian [*or conservator*] of the woman if she has been adjudged incompetent under [*Insert citation(s) or other reference(s) to State statute(s) relating to petition and hearing; independent evaluation*] may commence a civil action for any knowing or reckless violation of the Act and may seek both actual and punitive damages. Such damages shall include, but are not limited to –

(1) money damages for all injuries, psychological and physical, occasioned by the violation(s) of this Act; and

(2) statutory damages equal to [*Insert number*] times the cost of the abortion performed in violation of this Act.

(c) Any physician who performs an abortion in violation of this Act shall be considered to have engaged in unprofessional conduct for which his or her [*certificate or*] license to provide healthcare services in the State of [*Insert name of State*] shall be suspended or revoked by the [*Insert name of State Medical Board or other appropriate entity*].

(d) A cause of action for injunctive relief against any physician or other person who had knowingly violated this Act may be maintained by the woman upon whom the abortion was performed or attempted to be performed in violation of this Act; any person who is the spouse, parent, guardian, conservator, or a current or former licensed healthcare provider of, the woman upon whom an abortion has been performed or attempted to be performed in violation of this Act; by the Office of the Attorney General of [*Insert name of State*]; or by a District [*County or*

City Attorney] with appropriate jurisdiction. The injunction shall prevent the physician or person from performing further abortions in violation of this Act.

(e) Any physician or other person who knowingly violates the terms of an injunction issued in accordance with this Act shall be subject to [*civil and/or criminal*] contempt and shall be fined not less than [*Insert appropriate amount or possible range of fine*], or be imprisoned [*at hard labor*] not less than [*Insert appropriate time period or range*], or both.

[***Drafter's Note***: *If only civil contempt is selected as the appropriate remedy for failure to comply with a validly-issued injunction, then any reference(s) to imprisonment or other criminal penalties should be removed from subparagraph 7(e).*]

Section 9. Exclusion of Liability for Woman Who Undergoes Abortion Prohibited Under this Act.

(a) Any woman upon whom an abortion in violation of this Act is performed or attempted may not be prosecuted under this Act for a conspiracy to violate this Act or otherwise held criminally or civilly liable for any violation(s).

(b) In any criminal proceeding or action brought under this Act, any woman upon whom an abortion in violation of this Act is performed or attempted is entitled to all rights, protections, and notifications afforded to crime victims under [*Insert citation(s) or other reference(s) to State law(s) or administrative policies associated with the State's Victim-Witness Protection or similar program*].

(c) In every civil proceeding or action brought under this Act, the anonymity of the any woman upon whom an abortion is performed or attempted shall be preserved from public disclosure unless she gives her consent to such disclosure. A court of competent jurisdiction, upon motion or *sua sponte*, shall issue orders to the parties, witnesses, and counsel, and shall direct the sealing of the record and exclusion of individuals from courtrooms or hearing rooms, to the extent necessary to safeguard her identity from public disclosure. In the absence of written consent of the woman upon whom an abortion has been performed or attempted, anyone who initiates a proceeding or action under Section 7 of this Act shall do so under a pseudonym.

Section 10. Construction.

(a) Nothing in this Act shall be construed as creating or recognizing a right to abortion.

(b) It is not the intention of this Act to make lawful an abortion that is currently unlawful.

Section 11. Severability.

Any provision of this Act held to be invalid or unenforceable by its terms, or as applied to any person or circumstance, shall be construed so as to give it the maximum effect permitted by law, unless such holding shall be one of utter invalidity or unenforceability, in which event such provision shall be deemed severable herefrom and shall not affect the remainder hereof or the application of such provision to other persons not similarly situated or to other, dissimilar circumstances.

Section 12. Right of Intervention

The [*Legislature*], by joint resolution, may appoint one or more of its members, who sponsored or cosponsored this Act in his or her official capacity, to intervene as a matter of right in any case in which the constitutionality of this law is challenged.

Section 13. Effective Date.

This Act takes effect on [*Insert date*].

WOMAN'S RIGHT TO KNOW ACT

HOUSE/SENATE BILL No. _____
By Representatives/Senators _____

Section 1. Title.

This Act may be known and cited as the "Woman's Right to Know Act." [*or alternatively as the "Woman's Health Information Act" or the "Informed Consent for Abortion Act"*].

Section 2. Legislative Findings and Purposes.

(a) The [*Legislature*] of the State of [*Insert name of State*] finds that:

(1) It is essential to the psychological and physical well-being of a woman considering an abortion that she receive complete and accurate information on abortion and its alternatives.

(2) The knowledgeable exercise of a woman's decision to have an abortion depends on the extent to which she receives sufficient information to make an informed choice between two alternatives: giving birth or having an abortion.

(3) [*Insert percentage*] of all abortions are performed in clinics devoted solely to providing abortions and family planning services. Most women who seek abortions at these facilities do not have any relationship with the physician who performs the abortion, before or after the procedure. They do not return to the facility for post-surgical care. In most instances, the woman's only actual contact with the physician occurs simultaneously with the abortion procedure, with little opportunity to receive counseling concerning her decision.

(4) The decision to abort "is an important, and often a stressful one, and it is desirable and imperative that it be made with full knowledge of its nature and consequences." *Planned Parenthood v. Danforth,* 428 U.S. 52, 67 (1976).

(5) "The medical, emotional, and psychological consequences of an abortion are serious and can be lasting. . . ." *H.L. v. Matheson,* 450 U.S. 398, 411 (1981).

(6) Abortion facilities or providers often offer only limited or impersonal counseling opportunities.

(7) Many abortion facilities or providers hire untrained and unprofessional "coun-

selors" to purportedly provide pre-abortion counseling, but whose primary goal is actually to "sell" or promote abortion services.

(b) Based on the findings in Subsection (a) of this Section, the purposes of this Act are to:

(1) Ensure that every woman considering an abortion receive complete information on abortion and its alternatives and that every woman submitting to an abortion do so only after giving her voluntary and fully-informed consent to the abortion procedure;

(2) Protect unborn children from a woman's uninformed decision to have an abortion;

(3) Reduce "the risk that a woman may elect an abortion, only to discover later, with devastating psychological consequences, that her decision was not fully informed." *Planned Parenthood v. Casey,* 505 U.S. 833, 882 (1992); and

(4) Adopt the construction of the term "medical emergency" accepted by the U.S. Supreme Court in *Planned Parenthood v. Casey*, 505 U.S. 833 (1992).

Section 3. Definitions.

For purposes of this Act only:

(a) "**Abortion**" means the act of using or prescribing any instrument, medicine, drug, or any other substance, device, or means with the intent to terminate the clinically diagnosable pregnancy of a woman with knowledge that the termination by those means will with reasonable likelihood cause the death of the unborn child. Such use, prescription, or means is not an abortion if done with the intent to:

(1) Save the life or preserve the health of an unborn child;

(2) Remove a dead unborn child caused by spontaneous abortion; or

(3) Remove an ectopic pregnancy.

(b) "**Complication**" means that condition which includes, but is not limited to, hemorrhage, infection, uterine perforation, cervical laceration, pelvic inflammatory disease, endometritis, and retained products of conception ("incomplete abortion"). The Department may further define "complication."

(c) "**Conception**" means the fusion of a human spermatozoon with a human ovum.

(d) "**Department**" means the Department of [*Insert appropriate title*] of the State of [*Insert name of State*].

(e) "**Facility**" or "**medical facility**" means any public or private hospital, clinic, center, medical school, medical training institution, healthcare facility, physician's office, infirmary, dispensary, ambulatory surgical treatment center, or other institution or location wherein medical care is provided to any person.

(f) "**First trimester**" means the first 12 weeks of gestation.

(g) "**Gestational age**" means the time that has elapsed since the first day of the woman's last menstrual period.

(h) "**Hospital**" means an institution licensed pursuant to the provisions of the law of this State.

(i) "**Medical emergency**" means that condition which, on the basis of the physician's good faith clinical judgment, so complicates the medical condition of a pregnant woman as to necessitate the immediate termination of her pregnancy to avert her death or for which a delay will create serious risk of substantial and irreversible impairment of a major bodily function.

(j) "**Physician**" means any person licensed to practice medicine in this State. The term includes medical doctors and doctors of osteopathy.

(k) "**Pregnant**" or "**pregnancy**" means that female reproductive condition of having an unborn child in the [*woman's*] uterus.

(l) "**Qualified person**" means an agent of the physician who is a psychologist, licensed social worker, licensed professional counselor, registered nurse, or physician.

(m) "**Unborn child**" means the offspring of human beings from conception until birth.

(n) "**Viability**" means the state of fetal development when, in the judgment of the physician based on the particular facts of the case before him or her and in light of the most advanced medical technology and information available to him or her, there is a reasonable likelihood of sustained survival of the unborn child outside the body of his or her mother, with or without artificial support.

Section 4. Informed Consent Requirement.

No abortion shall be performed or induced without the voluntary and informed consent of the woman upon whom the abortion is to be performed or induced. Except in the case of a medical

emergency, consent to an abortion is voluntary and informed if and only if:

(a) At least 24 hours before the abortion, the physician who is to perform the abortion or the referring physician has informed the woman, orally and in person, of the following:

(1) The name of the physician who will perform the abortion;

(2) Medically accurate information that a reasonable patient would consider material to the decision of whether or not to undergo the abortion, including (a) a description of the proposed abortion method; (b) the immediate and long-term medical risks associated with the proposed abortion method including, but not limited to, the risks of infection, hemorrhage, cervical or uterine perforation, danger to subsequent pregnancies, and increased risk of breast cancer; and (c) alternatives to the abortion;

(3) The probable gestational age of the unborn child at the time the abortion is to be performed;

(4) The probable anatomical and physiological characteristics of the unborn child at the time the abortion is to be performed;

(5) The medical risks associated with carrying her child to term; and

(6) Any need for anti-Rh immune globulin therapy if she is Rh negative, the likely consequences of refusing such therapy, and the cost of the therapy.

(b) At least 24 hours before the abortion, the physician who is to perform the abortion, the referring physician, or a qualified person has informed the woman, orally and in person, that:

(1) Medical assistance benefits may be available for prenatal care, childbirth, and neonatal care, and that more detailed information on the availability of such assistance is contained in the printed materials and informational video given to her and described in Section 5.

(2) The printed materials and informational video in Section 5 describe the unborn child and list agencies that offer alternatives to abortion.

(3) The father of the unborn child is liable to assist in the support of this child, even in instances where he has offered to pay for the abortion. In the case of rape or incest, this information may be omitted.

(4) She is free to withhold or withdraw her consent to the abortion at any time

without affecting her right to future care or treatment and without the loss of any state or federally-funded benefits to which she might otherwise be entitled.

(c) The information required in Sections 4(a) and 4(b) is provided to the woman individually and in a private room to protect her privacy, to maintain the confidentiality of her decision, and to ensure that the information focuses on her individual circumstances and that she has an adequate opportunity to ask questions.

(d) At least 24 hours before the abortion, the woman is given a copy of the printed materials and a viewing of, or a copy of, the informational video described in Section 5. If the woman is unable to read the materials, they shall be read to her. If the woman asks questions concerning any of the information or materials, answers shall be provided to her in a language she can understand.

(e) Prior to the abortion, the woman certifies in writing on a checklist form provided or approved by the Department that the information required to be provided under Subsections 5(a), 5(b), and 5(d) has been provided. All physicians who perform abortions shall report the total number of certifications received monthly to the Department. The Department shall make the number of certifications received available to the public on an annual basis.

(f) Except in the case of a medical emergency, the physician who is to perform the abortion shall receive and sign a copy of the written certification prescribed in Subsection 5(e) of this Section prior to performing the abortion. The physician shall retain a copy of the checklist certification form in the woman's medical record.

(g) In the event of a medical emergency requiring an immediate termination of pregnancy, the physician who performed the abortion shall clearly certify in writing the nature of the medical emergency and the circumstances which necessitated the waiving of the informed consent requirements of this Section. This certification shall be signed by the physician who performed the emergency abortion, and shall be permanently filed in both the records of the physician performing the abortion and the records of the facility where the abortion takes place.

(h) A physician shall not require or obtain payment for a service provided to a patient who has inquired about an abortion or scheduled an abortion until the expiration of the 24-hour reflection period required in Sections 4(a), 4(b), and 4(d).

Section 5. Publication of Materials.

The Department shall cause to be published printed materials and an informational video in English and [*Spanish and other appropriate language(s)*] within [*Insert appropriate number*] days after this Act becomes law. On an annual basis, the Department shall review and update, if necessary, the following easily comprehensible printed materials and informational video:

(a) Geographically indexed materials that inform the woman of public and private agencies and services available to assist a woman through pregnancy, upon childbirth, and while her child is dependent, including but not limited to adoption agencies.

The materials shall include a comprehensive list of the agencies, a description of the services they offer, and the telephone numbers and addresses of the agencies, and shall inform the woman about available medical assistance benefits for prenatal care, childbirth, and neonatal care.

The Department shall ensure that the materials described in this Section are comprehensive and do not directly or indirectly promote, exclude, or discourage the use of any agency or service described in this Section. The materials shall also contain a toll-free 24-hour-a-day telephone number which may be called to obtain information about the agencies in the locality of the caller and of the services they offer.

The materials shall state that it is unlawful for any individual to coerce a woman to undergo an abortion [*Insert reference to State's anti-coercion statute(s), if any*] and that if a minor is denied financial support by the minor's parents, guardian, or custodian due to the minor's refusal to have an abortion performed, the minor shall be deemed emancipated for the purposes of eligibility for public-assistance benefits, except that such benefits may not be used to obtain an abortion. The materials shall also state that any physician who performs an abortion upon a woman without her informed consent may be liable to her for damages in a civil action at law and that the law permits adoptive parents to pay costs of prenatal care, childbirth, and neonatal care. The materials shall also include the following statement:

"There are many public and private agencies willing and able to help you to carry your child to term, and to assist you and your child after your child is born, whether you choose to keep your child or to place her or him for adoption. The State of [*Insert name of State*] strongly urges you to contact one or more of these agencies before making a final decision about abortion. The law requires that your physician or his agent give you the opportunity to call agencies like these before you undergo an abortion."

(b) Materials that include information on the support obligations of the father of a child who is born alive, including but not limited to the father's legal duty to support his child, which may include child support payments and health insurance, and the fact that paternity may be established by the father's signature on a birth certificate or statement of paternity, or by court action. The printed material shall also state that more information concerning establishment of paternity and child support services and enforcement may be obtained by calling State or county public assistance agencies.

(c) Materials that inform the pregnant woman of the probable anatomical and physiological characteristics of the unborn child at two-week gestational increments from fertilization to full term, including color photographs of the developing unborn child at two-week gestational increments. The descriptions shall include information about brain and heart functions, the presence of external members and internal organs during the applicable stages of development, and any relevant information on the possibility of the unborn child's survival. If a photograph is not available, a picture must contain the dimensions of the unborn child and must be realistic. The materials shall be objective, nonjudgmental, and designed to convey only accurate scientific information about the unborn child at the various gestational ages.

(d) Materials which contain objective information describing the various surgical and drug-induced methods of abortion, as well as the immediate and long-term medical risks commonly associated with each abortion method including, but not limited to, the risks of infection, hemorrhage, cervical or uterine perforation or rupture, danger to subsequent pregnancies, increased risk of breast cancer, the possible adverse psychological effects associated with an abortion, and the medical risks associated with carrying a child to term.

(e) A checklist certification form to be used by the physician or a qualified person under Subsection 4(e) of this Act, which will list all the items of information which are to be given to the woman by a physician or the agent under this Act.

(f) The materials shall be printed in a typeface large enough to be clearly legible.

(g) The Department shall produce a standardized videotape that may be used statewide, presenting the information described in Subsections 5(a), 5(b), 5(c), and 5(d), in accordance with the requirements of those Subsections. In preparing the video, the Department may summarize and make reference to the printed comprehensive list of geographically indexed names and services described in Subsection 5(a). The videotape shall, in addition to the information described in Subsections 5(a), 5(b), 5(c), and 5(d), show an ultrasound of the heartbeat of an unborn child at four to five weeks gestational age, at six to eight weeks gestational age, and each month thereafter, until viability. That information shall be presented in an objective, unbiased manner designed to convey only accurate scientific information.

(h) The materials required under this section and the videotape described in Subsection 5(g) shall be available at no cost from the Department upon request and in appropriate number to any person, facility, or hospital.

Section 6. Medical Emergencies.

When a medical emergency compels the performance of an abortion, the physician shall inform the woman, before the abortion if possible, of the medical indications supporting the physician's judgment that an immediate abortion is necessary to avert her death or that a 24-hour delay will cause substantial and irreversible impairment of a major bodily function.

Section 7. Criminal Penalties.

Any person who intentionally, knowingly, or recklessly violates this Act is guilty of a [*Insert class felony or misdemeanor*].

Section 8. Civil Penalties.

(a) In addition to any and all remedies available under the common or statutory law of this State, failure to comply with the requirements of this Act shall:

(1) Provide a basis for a civil malpractice action for actual and punitive damages.

(2) Provide a basis for a professional disciplinary action under [*Medical Malpractice Act*].

(b) No civil liability may be assessed against the female upon whom the abortion is performed.

(c) When requested, the court shall allow a woman to proceed using solely her initials or a pseudonym and may close any proceedings in the case and enter other protective orders to preserve the privacy of the woman upon whom the abortion was performed.

(d) If judgment is rendered in favor of the plaintiff, the court shall also render judgment for a reasonable attorney's fee in favor of the plaintiff against the defendant.

(e) If judgment is rendered in favor of the defendant and the court finds that the plaintiff's suit was frivolous and brought in bad faith, the court shall also render judgment for reasonable attorney's fee in favor of the defendant against the plaintiff.

Section 9. Reporting.

(a) For the purpose of promoting maternal health and life by adding to the sum of medical and public health knowledge through the compilation of relevant data, and to promote the State's interest in protecting the unborn child, a report of each abortion performed shall be made to the Department on forms prescribed by it. The reports shall be completed by the hospital or other licensed facility in which the abortion occurred, signed by the physician who performed the abortion, and transmitted to the Department within 15 days after each reporting month. The report forms shall not identify the individual patient by name and shall include the following information:

(1) Identification of the physician who performed the abortion, the facility where the abortion was performed, and the referring physician, agency or service, if any. Notwithstanding any provision of law to the contrary, the Department shall ensure that the identification of any physician or other healthcare provider reporting under this Section shall not be released or otherwise made available to the general public.

(2) The county and state in which the woman resides.

(3) The woman's age.

(4) The number of prior pregnancies and prior abortions of the woman.

(5) The probable gestational age of the unborn child.

(6) The type of procedure performed or prescribed and the date of the abortion.

(7) Preexisting medical condition(s) of the woman which would complicate pregnancy, if any.

(8) Medical complication(s) which resulted from the abortion, if known.

***[Drafter's Note:** Please refer to AUL's "Abortion Complication Reporting Act" for more detail regarding reporting of abortion complications.]*

(9) The length and weight of the aborted child for any abortion performed pursuant to a medical emergency as defined in Section 6 of this Act.

(10) Basis for any medical judgment that a medical emergency existed which excused the physician from compliance with any provision of this Act.

(b) When an abortion is performed during the first trimester of pregnancy, the tissue that is removed shall be subjected to a gross or microscopic examination, as needed, by the physician or a qualified person designated by the physician to determine if a pregnancy existed and was terminated. If the examination indicates no fetal remains, that information shall immediately be made known to the physician and sent to the Department within 15 days of the analysis.

(c) When an abortion is performed after the first trimester of pregnancy, the physician must certify whether or not the child was viable, and the dead unborn child and all tissue removed at the time of the abortion shall be submitted for tissue analysis to a board-eligible or certified pathologist. If the report reveals evidence of viability or live birth, the pathologist shall report such findings to the Department within 15 days, and a copy of the report shall also be sent to

the physician performing the abortion. The Department shall prescribe a form on which pathologists may report any evidence of live birth, viability, or absence of pregnancy.

(d) Every facility in which an abortion is performed within this State during any quarter year shall file with the Department a report showing the total number of abortions performed within the hospital or other facility during that quarter year. This report shall also show the total abortions performed in each trimester of pregnancy. These reports shall be submitted on a form prescribed by the Department that will enable a facility to indicate whether or not it is receiving any State-appropriated funds. The reports shall be available for public inspection and copying only if the facility receives State-appropriated funds within the 12-calendar-month period immediately preceding the filing of the report. If the facility indicates on the form that it is not receiving State-appropriated funds, the Department shall regard that facility's report as confidential unless it receives other evidence that causes it to conclude that the facility receives State-appropriated funds.

(e) After 30 days public notice following the law's enactment, the Department shall require that all reports of maternal deaths occurring within the State arising from pregnancy, childbirth, or intentional abortion state the cause of death, the duration of the woman's pregnancy, when her death occurred, and whether or not the woman was under the care of a physician during her pregnancy prior to her death. The Department shall issue any necessary regulations to assure that information is reported, and conduct its own investigation, if necessary, to ascertain such data.

Known incidents of maternal mortality of nonresident women arising from induced abortion performed in this State shall be included in the report as incidents of maternal mortality arising from induced abortions.

Incidents of maternal mortality arising from continued pregnancy or childbirth and occurring after induced abortion has been attempted but not completed, including deaths occurring after induced abortion has been attempted but not completed as a result of ectopic pregnancy, shall be included as incidents of maternal mortality arising from induced abortion.

(f) Every physician who is called upon to provide medical care or treatment to a woman who is in need of medical care because of a complication or complications resulting, in the good faith judgment of the physician, from having undergone an abortion or attempted abortion, shall prepare a report. The report must be filed with the Department within 30 days of the date of the physician's first examination of the woman. The report shall be on forms prescribed by the Department. The forms shall contain the following information, as received, and such other information except the name of the patient, as the Department may from time to time require:

(1) Age of the patient.

(2) Number of pregnancies patient may have had prior to the abortion.

(3) Number and type of abortions patient may have had prior to this abortion.

(4) Name and address of the facility where the abortion was performed.

(5) Gestational age of the unborn child at the time of the abortion, if known.

(6) Type of abortion performed, if known.

(7) Nature of complication or complications.

(8) Medical treatment given.

(9) The nature and extent, if known, of any permanent condition caused by the complication.

(g) Reports filed pursuant to Subsections 9(a) or 9(f) shall not be deemed public records and shall remain confidential, except that disclosure may be made to law enforcement officials upon an order of a court after application showing good cause. The court may condition disclosure of the information upon any appropriate safeguards it may impose.

(h) The Department shall prepare a comprehensive annual statistical report for the Legislature based upon the data gathered from reports under Subsections 9(a) and 9(f). The statistical report shall not lead to the disclosure of the identity of any physician or person filing a report under Subsections 9(a) or 9(f), nor of any patient about whom a report is filed. The statistical report shall be available for public inspection and copying.

(i) Original copies of all reports filed under Subsections 9(a), 9(d), and 9(f) shall be available to the [*State Medical Board*] for use in the performance of its official duties.

(j) The following penalties shall attach to any failure to comply with the requirements of this Section:

(1) Any person required under this Section to file a report, keep any records, or supply any information, who willfully fails to file such report, keep such records, or supply such information at the time or times required by law or regulation, is guilty of "unprofessional conduct," and his or her license for the practice of medicine and surgery shall be subject to suspension or revocation in

accordance with procedures provided under the [*Medical Practice Act*].

(2) Any person who willfully delivers or discloses to the Department any report, record, or information known by him or her to be false is guilty of a [*Insert class of misdemeanor or felony*].

(3) Any person who willfully discloses any information obtained from reports filed pursuant to Subsection 9(a) or 9(f), other than that disclosure authorized under Subsection 9(g), or as otherwise authorized by law, is guilty of a [*Insert class of misdemeanor or felony*].

(4) Intentional, knowing, reckless, or negligent failure of the physician to submit an unborn child or tissue remains to a pathologist as required by Subsection 9(b), or intentional, knowing, or reckless failure of the pathologist to report any evidence of live birth or viability to the Department in the manner and within the time prescribed in Subsection 9(b) is a [*Insert class of misdemeanor or felony*].

(5) In addition to the above penalties, any person, organization, or facility who willfully violates any of the provisions of this Section requiring reporting shall upon conviction:

a. For the first time, have his, her, or its license suspended for a period of six months.

b. For a second time, have his, her, or its license suspended for a period of one year.

c. For the third time, have his, her, or its license revoked.

(k) The Department shall create the forms required by this Act within 60 days after the effective date of this Act and shall cause to be published, within 90 days after the effective date of this Act, the printed materials described in this Act.

No provision of this Act requiring the reporting of information on forms published by the Department, or requiring the distribution of printed materials published by the Department pursuant to this Act, shall be applicable until 10 days after the requisite forms are first created and printed materials are first published by the Department or until the effective date of this Act, whichever is later.

Section 10. Construction.

(a) Nothing in this Act shall be construed as creating or recognizing a right to abortion.

(b) It is not the intention of this law to make lawful an abortion that is currently unlawful.

Section 11. Right of Intervention.

The [*Legislature*], by joint resolution, may appoint one or more of its members, who sponsored or cosponsored this Act in his or her official capacity, to intervene as a matter of right in any case in which the constitutionality of this law is challenged.

Section 12. Severability.

Any provision of this Act held to be invalid or unenforceable by its terms, or as applied to any person or circumstance, shall be construed so as give it the maximum effect permitted by law, unless such holding shall be one of utter invalidity or unenforceability, in which event such provision shall be deemed severable herefrom and shall not affect the remainder hereof or the application of such provision to other persons not similarly situated or to other, dissimilar circumstances.

Section 13. Effective Date.

This Act takes effect on [*Insert date*].

THE WOMAN'S ULTRASOUND RIGHT TO KNOW ACT

HOUSE/SENATE BILL NO. _______
By Representatives/Senators ____________

Section 1. Title

This Act may be known and cited as the "Woman's Ultrasound Right to Know Act."

Section 2. Legislative Findings and Purposes.

(a) The [*Legislature*] of the State of [*Insert name of State*] finds that:

(1) It is essential to the psychological and physical well-being of a woman considering an abortion that she receive complete and accurate information on the reality and status of her pregnancy and of her unborn child.

(2) The decision to abort "is an important, and often a stressful one, and it is desirable and imperative that it be made with full knowledge of its nature and consequences." *Planned Parenthood v. Danforth,* 428 U.S. 52, 67 (1976).

(3) The knowledgeable exercise of a woman's decision to have an abortion depends on the extent to which the woman receives sufficient information to make an informed choice between two alternatives: giving birth or having an abortion.

(b) Based on the findings in Subsection (a) of this Section, the purposes of this Act are to:

(1) Ensure that every woman considering an abortion receive complete information on the reality and status of her pregnancy and of her unborn child and that every woman submitting to an abortion do so only after giving her voluntary and informed consent to the abortion procedure;

(2) Protect unborn children from a woman's uninformed decision to have an abortion;

(3) Reduce "the risk that a woman may elect an abortion, only to discover later, with devastating psychological consequences, that her decision was not fully informed." *Planned Parenthood v. Casey,* 505 U.S. 833, 882 (1992); and

(4) Adopt the construction of the term "medical emergency" accepted by the U.S. Supreme Court in *Planned Parenthood v. Casey,* 505 U.S. 833 (1992).

Section 3. Definitions

For purposes of this Act only:

(a) "**Abortion**" means the act of using or prescribing any instrument, medicine, drug, or any other substance, device, or means with the intent to terminate the clinically diagnosable pregnancy of a woman with knowledge that the termination by those means will with reasonable likelihood cause the death of the unborn child. Such use, prescription or means is not an abortion if done with the intent to:

(1) Save the life or preserve the health of an unborn child;

(2) Remove a dead unborn child caused by spontaneous abortion; or

(3) Remove an ectopic pregnancy.

(b) "**Auscultation**" means the act of listening for sounds made by internal organs of the fetus, specifically for a fetal heartbeat, utilizing an ultrasound transducer and fetal heart rate (FHR) monitor.

(c) "**Department**" means the Department of [*Insert appropriate title*] of the State of [*Insert name of State*].

(d) "**Facility**" or "**medical facility**" means any public or private hospital, clinic, center, medical school, medical training institution, healthcare facility, physician's office, infirmary, dispensary, ambulatory surgical treatment center, or other institution or location wherein medical care is provided to any person.

(e) "**Medical emergency**" means that condition which, on the basis of the physician's good faith clinical judgment, so complicates the medical condition of a pregnant woman as to necessitate the immediate termination of her pregnancy to avert her death or for which a delay will create serious risk of substantial and irreversible impairment of a major bodily function.

(f) "**Physician**" means any person licensed to practice medicine in this State. The term includes medical doctors and doctors of osteopathy.

(g) "**Pregnant**" or "**pregnancy**" means that female reproductive condition of having an unborn child in the [*woman's*] uterus.

(h) **"Qualified person"** means an agent of the physician who is a psychologist, licensed social worker, licensed professional counselor, registered nurse, or physician.

(i) **"Unborn child"** means the offspring of human beings from conception until birth.

(j) **"Ultrasound"** means the use of ultrasonic waves for diagnostic or therapeutic purposes, specifically to monitor a developing fetus.

Section 4. Informed Consent Ultrasound Requirement.

No abortion shall be performed or induced without the voluntary and informed consent of the woman upon whom the abortion is to be performed or induced. Except in the case of a medical emergency, consent to an abortion is voluntary and informed if and only if:

(a) At least 24 hours before the abortion, the physician who is to perform the abortion on the pregnant woman or the referring physician or qualified person assisting the physician has informed the woman, orally and in person, of the following:

> (1) That fetal ultrasound imaging and auscultation of fetal heart tone services are available that enable a pregnant woman to view the image and hear the heartbeat of her unborn child before the abortion is performed, and
>
> (2) That she has the right to view an active ultrasound of the unborn child and hear the heartbeat of the unborn child if the heartbeat is audible.

(b) At the woman's request, the physician or qualified person assisting the physician must, at least 24 hours prior to the performance of the abortion,

> (1) provide the real-time ultrasound image to the pregnant woman for her to view and auscultation of fetal heart tone for her to hear or, alternatively,
>
> (2) provide a list of healthcare providers, facilities, and clinics that offer to perform ultrasounds free of charge. The list shall be arranged geographically and shall include the name, address, hours of operation, and telephone number of each listed entity.

(c) The active ultrasound image must be of a quality consistent with standard medical practice in the community, shall contain the dimensions of the unborn child, and shall accurately portray the presence of external members and internal organs, if present or viewable, of the unborn child.

(d) The auscultation of fetal heart tone must be of a quality consistent with standard medical practice in the community.

(e) At least 24 hours prior to the performance of the abortion, a physician or qualified person assisting the physician shall obtain the woman's signature on a certification form stating the following:

(1) That the woman has been informed that fetal ultrasound imaging and auscultation of fetal heart tone services are available that enable a pregnant woman to view the image and to hear the heartbeat of her unborn child;

(2) That she has been informed that she has a right to view the active ultrasound image of the unborn child and to hear the heartbeat of the unborn child if the heartbeat is audible; and

(3) That the woman either (A) requested ultrasound imaging and auscultation of fetal heart tone services and received the requested services or was provided with the list of entities outlined in Subsection 4(b)(2); or (B) that the woman opted not to receive ultrasound imaging and auscultation of fetal heart tone services.

(f) Before the abortion is performed or induced, the physician who is to perform or induce the abortion shall receive a copy of the written certification prescribed by Section 4(e). The physician shall retain a copy of the signed certification form in the woman's medical record.

(g) The [*Department*] shall enforce the provisions of this Act at all facilities and medical facilities that provide abortion services.

Section 5. Medical Emergencies

When a medical emergency compels the performance of an abortion, the physician shall inform the woman, before the abortion if possible, of the medical indications supporting the physician's judgment that an immediate abortion is necessary to avert her death or that a 24-hour delay will cause substantial and irreversible impairment of a major bodily function.

Section 6. Civil Penalties.

(a) In addition to any and all remedies available under the common or statutory law of this State, failure to comply with the requirements of this Act shall:

(1) Provide a basis for a civil malpractice action for actual and punitive damages. Any intentional violation of this Act shall be admissible in a civil suit as *prima facie* evidence of a failure to obtain informed consent, which, except in the case of a medical emergency as defined by this Act, constitutes medical malpractice.

(2) Provide a basis for a professional disciplinary action under [*Medical Malpractice Act*].

(3) Provide a basis for recovery for the woman for the wrongful death of her unborn child under the [*Wrongful Death Act*], whether or not the unborn child was born alive or was viable at the time the abortion was performed.

(b) When requested, the court shall allow a woman to proceed using solely her initials or a pseudonym and may close any proceedings in the case and enter other protective orders to preserve the privacy of the woman upon whom the abortion was performed.

(c) If judgment is rendered in favor of the plaintiff, the court shall also render judgment for a reasonable attorney's fee in favor of the plaintiff against the defendant.

(e) If judgment is rendered in favor of the defendant and the court finds that the plaintiff's suit was frivolous and brought in bad faith, the court shall also render judgment for reasonable attorney's fee in favor of the defendant against the plaintiff.

Section 7. Criminal Penalties

Any person who purposefully, knowingly, or recklessly performs or attempts to perform or induce an abortion without complying with this Act is guilty of a [*Insert class felony or misdemeanor*].

Section 8. Construction.

(a) Nothing in this Act shall be construed as creating or recognizing a right to abortion.

(b) It is not the intention of this law to make lawful an abortion that is currently unlawful.

Section 9. Right of Intervention.

The [*Legislature*], by joint resolution, may appoint one or more of its members, who sponsored or cosponsored this Act in his or her official capacity, to intervene as a matter of right in any case in which the constitutionality of this law is challenged.

Section 10. Severability.

Any provision of this Act held to be invalid or unenforceable by its terms, or as applied to any person or circumstance, shall be construed so as give it the maximum effect permitted by law, unless such holding shall be one of utter invalidity or unenforceability, in which event such provision shall be deemed severable herefrom and shall not affect the remainder hereof or the application of such provision to other persons not similarly situated or to other, dissimilar circumstances.

Section 11. Effective Date.

This Act takes effect on [*Insert date*].

THE FETAL PAIN AWARENESS AND PREVENTION ACT

HOUSE/SENATE BILL No. ______
By Representatives/Senators ______________

Section 1. Title.

This Act may be known and cited as the "Fetal Pain Awareness and Prevention Act."

Section 2. Legislative Findings and Purposes.

(a) The [*Legislature*] of the State of [*Insert name of State*] finds that:

(1) It is essential to the psychological and physical well-being of a woman considering an abortion that she receive complete and accurate information on the reality and status of her pregnancy and of her unborn child.

(2) The decision to abort "is an important, and often a stressful one, and it is desirable and imperative that it be made with full knowledge of its nature and consequences." *Planned Parenthood v. Danforth,* 428 U.S. 52, 67 (1976).

(3) Adequate and legitimate informed consent includes information which "relat[es] to the consequences to the fetus." *Planned Parenthood v. Casey,* 505 U.S. 833, 882-883 (1992).

(4) A state may take measures to protect unborn children from suffering pain needlessly during performance of an abortion.

(b) Based on the findings in Subsection (a) of this Section, the purpose of this Act is to:

(1) Ensure that every woman considering an abortion receive complete information on the reality and status of her pregnancy and of her unborn child and that every woman submitting to an abortion do so only after receiving accurate information on the ability of her unborn child to feel pain;

(2) Protect unborn children from a woman's uninformed decision to have an abortion;

(3) Take measures to protect unborn children from suffering pain needlessly during performance of an abortion;

(4) Reduce "the risk that a woman may elect an abortion, only to discover later, with devastating psychological consequences, that her decision was not fully informed." *Planned Parenthood v. Casey,* 505 U.S. 833, 882 (1992); and

(5) Provide a woman considering an abortion the opportunity to choose anesthesia or analgesia for her unborn child, thereby alleviating or eliminating the pain that an unborn child may feel during an abortion.

Section 3. Definitions.

For purposes of this Act only:

(a) "**Abortion**" means the act of using or prescribing any instrument, medicine, drug, or any other substance, device, or means with the intent to terminate the clinically diagnosable pregnancy of a woman with knowledge that the termination by those means will with reasonable likelihood cause the death of the unborn child. Such use, prescription, or means is not an abortion if done with the intent to:

(1) Save the life or preserve the health of an unborn child;

(2) Remove a dead unborn child caused by spontaneous abortion; or

(3) Remove an ectopic pregnancy.

(b) "**Anesthesia**" or "**analgesic**" means a drug, administered for medical or surgical purposes, that induces a partial or total loss of sensation.

(c) "**Department**" means the Department of [*Insert appropriate title*] of the State of [*Insert name of State*].

(d) "**Facility**" or "**medical facility**" means any public or private hospital, clinic, center, medical school, medical training institution, healthcare facility, physician's office, infirmary, dispensary, ambulatory surgical treatment center, or other institution or location wherein medical care is provided to any person.

(e) "**Gestation**" means Estimated Gestational Age (EGA) as determined by the time that has elapsed since the first day of the woman's last menstrual period.

(f) "**Medical emergency**" means that condition which, on the basis of the physician's good faith clinical judgment, so complicates the medical condition of a pregnant woman as to necessitate the immediate termination of her pregnancy to avert her death or for which a delay will create serious risk of substantial and irreversible impairment of a major bodily function.

(g) "**Pain**" means a basic bodily sensation that is induced by a noxious stimulus or stimuli, is received by naked nerve endings, is often characterized by physical discomfort, and can be indicated by observable physiological and behavioral responses.

(h) "**Physician**" means any person licensed to practice medicine in this State. The term includes medical doctors and doctors of osteopathy.

(i) "**Qualified person**" means an agent of the physician who is a psychologist, licensed social worker, licensed professional counselor, registered nurse, or physician.

(j) "**Registered nurse**" means any person licensed to practice nursing in this State, and certified to perform anesthetic and/or analgesic services.

(k) "**Unborn child**" means a member of the species *homo sapiens* from fertilization until birth.

Section 4. Fetal Pain Informed Consent and Prevention Requirements.

(a) Except in the case of a medical emergency, at least 24 hours prior to an abortion being performed or induced on an unborn child who is 20 weeks gestation or more, the physician performing the abortion on the pregnant woman, the referring physician, or a qualified person assisting the physician shall, orally and in person, offer information on fetal pain to every patient. This information and counseling shall include, but shall not be limited to, the following:

(1) That, by 20 weeks, the unborn child possesses all anatomical links in its nervous system (including spinal cord, nerve tracts, thalamus, and cortex) that are necessary in order to feel pain.

(2) That an unborn child who is 20 weeks gestation or more is fully capable of experiencing pain.

(3) A description of the actual steps in the abortion procedure to be performed or induced, and at which steps in the abortion procedure the unborn child is capable of feeling pain.

(4) That maternal anesthesia typically offers little pain prevention for the unborn child.

(5) That an anesthetic or analgesic is available in order to minimize and/or alleviate pain to the fetus.

(b) At the woman's request, the physician or registered nurse assisting the physician must administer an anesthetic or analgesic to eliminate or alleviate pain to the fetus caused by the particular method of abortion to be performed or induced.

(c) The administration of anesthesia and/or analgesic must be performed in a manner consistent with standard medical practice in the community.

Section 5. Exceptions.

(a) The requirements of the entirety of Section 4 of this Act do not apply when the physician who is to perform the abortion or the referring physician deems, according to his best medical judgment, that

(1) A medical emergency exists, or

(2) The administration of an anesthetic or analgesic would to a medically significant degree decrease the possibility of sustained survival of the fetus apart from the body of the mother, with or without artificial support, or

(3) The administration of an anesthetic or analgesic would increase the risk to the woman's life or physical health.

(b) The requirements of Subsection 4(b) and 4(c) only of this Act do not apply when the woman, upon being informed of the possibility of pain to the fetus and the availability of anesthesia or analgesics to alleviate such pain, refuses her consent to the administration of such analgesic or anesthetic.

Section 6. Certification Required.

(a) At least 24 hours prior to the performance of the abortion, the physician or qualified person assisting the physician shall obtain the woman's signature on a certification form stating the following:

(1) That the woman has been given the information described in Section 4(a) of this Act;

(2) That the woman has been given the choice to have anesthesia or an analgesic administered to the unborn child, and

(3) That the woman either (A) requested administration of anesthesia or an analgesic, or (B) opted not to receive administration of anesthesia or an analgesic.

(b) Before the abortion is performed or induced, the physician who is to perform or induce the abortion shall receive a copy of the written certification prescribed by this Section. The physician shall retain a copy of the signed certification form in the woman's medical record.

Section 7. Medical Emergencies.

When a medical emergency compels the performance of an abortion, the physician shall inform the woman, before the abortion if possible, of the medical indications supporting the physician's judgment that an immediate abortion is necessary to avert her death or that a 24-hour delay will cause substantial and irreversible impairment of a major bodily function.

Section 8. Enforcement.

The [*Department*] shall enforce the provisions of this Act at all facilities and medical facilities that provide abortion services.

Section 9. Civil Penalties.

(a) In addition to any and all remedies available under the common or statutory law of this State, failure to comply with the requirements of this Act shall:

(1) Provide a basis for a civil malpractice action for actual and punitive damages.

(2) Provide a basis for a professional disciplinary action under [*Medical Malpractice Act*].

(b) No civil liability may be assessed against the female upon whom the abortion is performed.

(c) When requested, the court shall allow a woman to proceed using solely her initials or a pseudonym and may close any proceedings in the case and enter other protective orders to preserve the privacy of the woman upon whom the abortion was performed.

(d) If judgment is rendered in favor of the plaintiff, the court shall also render judgment for a reasonable attorney's fee in favor of the plaintiff against the defendant.

(e) If judgment is rendered in favor of the defendant and the court finds that the plaintiff's suit was frivolous and brought in bad faith, the court shall also render judgment for reasonable attorney's fee in favor of the defendant against the plaintiff.

Section 10. Criminal Penalties.

(a) Any person who knowingly or recklessly performs an abortion in violation of this Act shall be guilty of a [*Insert class of felony or misdemeanor*].

(b) No criminal penalty may be assessed against the female upon whom the abortion is performed.

Section 11. Construction.

(a) Nothing in this Act shall be construed as creating or recognizing a right to abortion.

(b) It is not the intention of this law to make lawful an abortion that is currently unlawful.

Section 12. Right of Intervention.

The [*Legislature*], by joint resolution, may appoint one or more of its members, who sponsored or cosponsored this Act in his or her official capacity, to intervene as a matter of right in any case in which the constitutionality of this law is challenged.

Section 13. Severability.

Any provision of this Act held to be invalid or unenforceable by its terms, or as applied to any person or circumstance, shall be construed so as give it the maximum effect permitted by law, unless such holding shall be one of utter invalidity or unenforceability, in which event such provision shall be deemed severable herefrom and shall not affect the remainder hereof or the application of such provision to other persons not similarly situated or to other, dissimilar circumstances.

Section 14. Effective Date.

This Act takes effect on [*Insert date*].

COERCIVE ABUSE AGAINST MOTHERS PREVENTION ACT

HOUSE/SENATE BILL No. ______
By Representatives/Senators __________________

Section 1. Title.

This Act shall be known as the "Coercive Abuse Against Mothers Prevention Act."

Section 2. Legislative Findings and Purposes.

(a) The [*Legislature*] of the [*Insert name of State*] finds that:

(1) Research indicates that violence against pregnant women is a serious problem across the nation. Many women report that they were coerced into abortion and have suffered grievous physical, emotional, psychological, and spiritual harm as a result.

(2) Reproductive healthcare facilities are often the only and last opportunities of hope for victims of coercive abuse and, as such, are in a unique position to help such victims.

(3) More cases of coerced or attempted coerced abortions are reported if women are informed of their rights and given information concerning treatment and protective options.

(4) More victims receive treatment for coercive abuse if women are informed of their rights and given information concerning treatment and protective options.

(5) Coercive abuse is a serious women's health issue because it violates their right to physical and emotional health, right of conscience, and their right to freely choose either pregnancy or abortion.

(b) The [*Legislature*] seeks to make it illegal to coerce or otherwise force a woman or minor into aborting her unborn child and intends to empower all mothers in the State of [*Insert name of State*] to exercise their freedom of conscience in choosing life for their pre-born children free of violent and abusive coercion.

Section 3. Definitions.

For the purposes of this Act only:

(a) "**Abortion**" means the act of using or prescribing any instrument, medicine, drug, or any other substance, device, or means with the intent to terminate the clinically diagnosable pregnancy of a woman with knowledge that the termination by those means will with reasonable likelihood cause the death of the unborn child. Such use, prescription, or means is not an abortion if done with the intent to:

(1) Save the life or preserve the health of an unborn child;

(2) Remove a dead unborn child caused by spontaneous abortion; or

(3) remove an ectopic pregnancy.

(b) "**Abuser**" means any person who coerces, forces, attempts to coerce, or attempts to force a woman into having an abortion.

(c) "**Coerce**" or "**force**" an abortion means that a person coerces an abortion if he or she knows of or suspects the pregnancy of a woman and engages or conspires with another to engage in any conduct described below that is intentionally and purposely aimed at causing or directing the woman to have an abortion and solely conditioned upon the pregnant female disregarding or refusing the person's demand that she seek an abortion:

(1) Committing, attempting to commit, or threatening to commit physical harm to the woman, unborn child, or another person;

(2) Committing, attempting to commit, or threatening to commit any act prohibited by any statute of this State [*or insert specific citation(s) or reference(s) to State's criminal and civil code*], (*including any common law tort not codified in a State statute*);

(3) Revoking, attempting to revoke, or threatening to revoke a scholarship awarded to the woman by a public or private institution of higher education;

(4) Discharging, attempting to discharge, or threatening to discharge the woman or another person; or changing, attempting to change, or threatening to change her or the other person's compensation, terms, conditions, or privileges of employment;

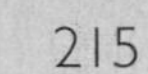

(5) Denying, attempting to deny, or threatening to deny any social assistance for which a pregnant woman or another person has applied, has been approved for, or has been receiving and for which she or the other person is otherwise eligible; or

(6) Denying, removing, or threatening to deny or remove financial support or housing from a dependent.

The terms "coerce" and "force" do not include or encompass constitutionally-protected speech, conduct, or expressions of conscience.

(d) "**Coercion**" means with purpose to restrict a pregnant woman's freedom of action to her detriment, any person engaging in conduct defined in Section 3(c) of this Act.

(e) "**Course of conduct**" means a pattern of conduct composed of a series of two or more separate acts evidencing a continuity of purpose.

(f) "**Dependent**" means [*Insert definition from and citation to appropriate federal or state law*].

(g) "**Mandatory reporter**" means any individual who provides healthcare services, including a physician, surgeon, physical therapist, psychiatrist, psychologist, medical resident, medical intern, hospital staff member, licensed nurse, nurse's aide, any emergency medical technician, paramedic, and any employee, staff member, or volunteer at a reproductive healthcare facility.

(h) "**Physician**" or "**attending physician**" means any person licensed to practice medicine in this State. The term includes medical doctors and doctors of osteopathy.

(i) "**Pregnant woman**" means any female, including those who have not reached the age of 18 [*or minors*], who is in the reproductive condition of having an unborn child in the mother's uterus.

(j) "**Reproductive healthcare facility**" or "**facility**" means any office, clinic, or facility that provides surgical or medical abortions, abortion counseling, abortion referrals, contraceptives, contraceptive counseling, sex education, or gynecological care and services.

(k) "**Solely**" means that the conduct described in Section 4 of this Act must be such that it would not have occurred but for the woman's pregnancy. This does not preclude the possibility that an actor may have multiple motives for engaging in the conduct described in Section 4 of this Act.

(l) **"Threat"** means at least one statement, or a course of conduct, by an individual that would cause a reasonable person to believe that the individual is likely to act in accordance with the statements or as implied by a course of conduct. A threat does not include constitutionally-protected speech or any generalized statement regarding a lawful pregnancy option, including, but not limited to, an emotional expression by a family or household member of the pregnant female.

(m) **"Unborn child"** or **"pre-born child"** means the offspring of human beings from conception until birth.

Section 4. Forced or Coerced Abortion Prohibited; Penalties.

(a) ***Prohibition***: It shall be illegal to coerce or force a pregnant woman to have an abortion.

(b) ***Penalties***:

(1) A pregnant woman injured by reason of an abuser's violation of this Act may bring a civil suit for recovery of damages for such injury, including wrongful death on behalf of an aborted child (*as provided for in* [*Insert citation to State's Wrongful Death Act*]), whether or not the perpetrator is criminally prosecuted or convicted and whether or not the pregnant woman has an abortion. In such a civil suit, the pregnant woman shall be entitled to recover, in addition to any other damages, her reasonable attorney's fees and costs if she is the prevailing party.

(2) Anyone who is guilty of engaging in conduct described in and proscribed by this Section is, in addition to any other crimes described in [*State's criminal code*], guilty of a [*Insert appropriate class felony or misdemeanor*].

(3) If a violation of this Section is committed by the father or putative father of the unborn child against a pregnant female who is less than 18 years of age, and the father or putative father is 18 years of age or older, the father or putative father is guilty of a [*Insert reference to a higher level of crime*].

(4) Any minor [*or woman*] who is threatened with such coercion may apply to a court of competent jurisdiction for relief. The court shall provide the minor with counsel, give the matter expedited consideration, and grant such relief as may be necessary to prevent such coercion.

(5) If a minor is denied financial support by the minor's parents, guardian, or cus-

todian because of the minor's refusal to have an abortion, the minor must be considered an emancipated minor for the purposes of eligibility for public assistance benefits. The public assistance benefits may not be used to obtain an abortion.

Section 5. Reproductive Healthcare Facility Requirements; Penalties.

(a) ***Sign Postage Requirement***:

(1) A reproductive healthcare facility shall conspicuously post signs visible to all who enter so as to be clearly readable, which state: "It is against the law for anyone, regardless of his or her relationship to you, to force you to have an abortion. You have the right to contact any local or state law enforcement or social service agency to receive protection from any actual or threatened physical, emotional, or psychological abuse. It is against the law to perform, induce, prescribe for, or provide you with the means for an abortion without your voluntary consent."

(2) Such signs must be posted in the waiting room(s), consultation room(s), and procedure room(s).

(3) The continued posting of such signs shall be a condition of licensure of any reproductive healthcare facility under [*Insert reference(s) to State licensure law or administrative requirements*]. The display of such a sign does not discharge the duty of a reproductive healthcare facility to have a physician orally inform the pregnant woman of information contained in Sections 5(b)(5) and 5(c) of this Act.

(b) ***Mandatory Reporting Requirements***:

(1) Requirement: A mandatory reporter must report every instance of alleged or suspected coerced abortion as defined in Sections 3(c) and 4(a) of this Act. The mandatory reporter may not use his or her discretion in deciding what cases should or should not be reported to the appropriate law enforcement or relevant state agency.

(2) Standard: The standard to be applied to a mandatory reporter in determining a reportable suspicion is reasonability in good faith.

(3) Procedure: If a mandatory reporter has cause to believe that a pregnant woman is or was a victim of conduct described in and proscribed by Sections 3 and 4

of this Act, the mandatory reporter shall make a report no later than the 48th hour after such coercion, force, attempted coercion, or attempted force has been brought to his or her attention or suspicion. A mandatory reporter may not delegate the responsibility to report such coercion, force, attempted coercion, or attempted force to any other person but must personally make the report. A mandatory reporter must make a report to [*Designate local or state law enforcement agency or other appropriate social services agency*].

(4) Content: The person making the report must identify the name and address of the woman, and, in a case of a minor, the name and address of the person who is responsible for the care or custody of the minor. The person making the report must also file any pertinent information he or she may have relating to the alleged or suspected coercion, force, attempted coercion, or attempted force.

(5) The attending physician shall orally inform the female that no one can force her to have an abortion.

(6) It shall be unlawful for any reproductive healthcare facility to willfully and knowingly continue to employ a mandatory reporter who has violated Section 4 or 5 of this Act.

(c) In a private room, the attending physician shall orally ask the pregnant woman if she is being coerced or forced to have an abortion. If it is reasonably suspected that the woman is being coerced or forced into having an abortion, the physician shall inform the woman that such coercion is illegal, that the woman may have civil remedies, that a request or demand by the father to have an abortion does not relieve his financial support responsibilities, and provide the patient with information about assistance, counseling, and protective services offered by social programs and local or state law enforcement.

(d) No person shall perform an abortion upon a woman who is known or suspected to be a victim of conduct described in and proscribed by Sections 3(c) and 4(a) of this Act within 24 hours of when this fact or suspicion arises and informing the woman of her rights as provided in Sections 5(b)(5) and 5(c) of this Act.

The mandatory 24-hour reflection period may be waived if, in the physician's best medical judgment, an abortion is necessary to prevent the death of the woman or to prevent substantial and irreversible injury to a major bodily function.

(e) ***Penalties***:

(1) A pregnant woman injured by reason of a facility's violation of this Act may

bring a civil suit for recovery of damages for such injury, including wrongful death on behalf of an aborted child (*as provided for in* [*Insert citation to state's Wrongful Death Act*]), whether or not the attending physician or the facility is criminally prosecuted or convicted and whether or not the pregnant woman has an abortion. In such a civil suit, the pregnant woman shall be entitled to recover, in addition to any other damages, her reasonable attorney's fees and costs if she is the prevailing party.

(2) Any mandatory reporter who has reason to believe a woman is or has been a victim of conduct described in and proscribed by Sections 3(c) and 4(a) of this Act and willfully and knowingly does not report such coercion, force, attempted coercion, or attempted force as required by this Act is guilty of a [*Insert appropriate class of felony or misdemeanor*].

(3) Any person who performs an abortion which is inconsistent with Section 5(d) of this Act is guilty of a [*Insert appropriate class of felony or misdemeanor*].

(4) Any person who performs, induces, or assists in performing or inducing an abortion on a woman, and is unaware that the woman is or has been a victim of conduct described in and proscribed by Sections 3(c) and 4(a) as a result of a willful, knowing, or purposeful failure to comply with the requirements of Section 5(c) of this Act is guilty of a [*Insert appropriate class of felony or misdemeanor*].

(5) Initial and continuing adherence to the requirements of Section 5 of this Act shall be a condition of licensure for any reproductive healthcare facility under [*Insert reference(s) to State licensure law or administrative requirements*].

(6) A woman receiving an abortion inconsistent with any provision of this Act cannot be prosecuted.

Section 6. Duties of Law Enforcement [*or Other Designated State Social Services or Public Agency*].

(a) Upon the request of the complainant (including a pregnant woman, a woman who was coerced or forced into having an abortion and later reports the coercion or force, or any woman whose rights under this Act were denied by any physician or facility), a law enforcement agency [*or designated social services agency*] investigating a violation of this Act shall notify the complainant not less than 24 hours before initially contacting the person(s) alleged to have violated Section 4 or 5 of this Act.

(b) This Act does not preclude or prohibit an alleged perpetrator from being charged with, convicted of, or punished for any other crime committed while also violating this Act.

(c) A court of competent jurisdiction may order that a term of imprisonment imposed for violating this Act be served consecutively to a term of imprisonment imposed for any other crime committed while also violating this Act.

Section 7. Construction.

(a) This Act does not create, recognize, endorse, or condone a right to an abortion.

(b) It is not the intention of this Act to make lawful an abortion that is currently unlawful.

Section 8. Severability.

Any provision of this Act held to be invalid or unenforceable by its terms, or as applied to any person or circumstance, shall be construed so as to give it the maximum effect permitted by law, unless such holding shall be one of utter invalidity or unenforceability, in which event such provision shall be deemed severable herefrom and shall not affect the remainder hereof or the application of such provision to other persons not similarly situated or to other, dissimilar circumstances.

Section 9. Right of Intervention.

The [*Legislature*], by a joint resolution, may appoint one or more of its members, who sponsored or cosponsored this Act in his or her official capacity, to intervene as a matter of right in any case in which the constitutionality of this Act is challenged.

Section 10. Enforcement Date.

This Act takes effect on *[Insert date]*.

PARENTAL CONSENT FOR ABORTION ACT

HOUSE/SENATE BILL No. ______
By Representatives/Senators ____________

Section 1. Short Title.

This Act may be cited as the "Parental Consent for Abortion Act."

Section 2. Legislative Findings and Purposes.

(a) The Legislature of the State of [*Insert name of State*] finds that:

(1) Immature minors often lack the ability to make fully informed choices that take into account both immediate and long-range consequences.

(2) The medical, emotional, and psychological consequences of abortion are sometimes serious and can be lasting, particularly when the patient is immature.

(3) The capacity to become pregnant and the capacity for mature judgment concerning the wisdom of an abortion are not necessarily related.

(4) Parents ordinarily possess information essential to a physician's exercise of his or her best medical judgment concerning the child.

(5) Parents who are aware that their minor daughter has had an abortion may better ensure that she receives adequate medical attention after her abortion.

(6) Parental consultation is usually desirable and in the best interests of the minor.

(b) The [*Legislature*]'s purposes in enacting this parental consent law is to further the important and compelling State interests of:

(1) Protecting minors against their own immaturity.

(2) Fostering family unity and preserving the family as a viable social unit.

(3) Protecting the constitutional rights of parents to rear children who are members of their household.

(4) Reducing teenage pregnancy and unnecessary abortion.

(5) In light of the foregoing statements of purpose, allowing for judicial bypasses of the parental consent requirement to be made only in exceptional or rare circumstances.

Section 3. Definitions.

For purposes of this Act only:

(a) "**Abortion**" means the act of using or prescribing any instrument, medicine, drug, or any other substance, device, or means with the intent to terminate the clinically diagnosable pregnancy of a woman with knowledge that the termination by those means will with reasonable likelihood cause the death of the unborn child. Such use, prescription, or means is not an abortion if done with the intent to:

(1) Save the life or preserve the health of an unborn child;

(2) Remove a dead unborn child caused by spontaneous abortion; or

(3) Remove an ectopic pregnancy.

(b) "**Coercion**" means restraining or dominating the choice of a minor female by force, threat of force, or deprivation of food and shelter.

(c) "**Consent**" means a notarized written statement signed by the mother, father, or legal guardian (or alternate person as described in Section 5) of the minor declaring that the affiant has been informed that the minor intends to seek an abortion and that the affiant consents to the abortion.

(d) "**Department**" means the Department of [*Insert appropriate title*] of the State of [*Insert name of State*].

(e) "**Emancipated minor**" means any person under eighteen (18) years of age who is or has been married or who has been legally emancipated.

(f) "**Incompetent**" means any person who has been adjudged a disabled person and has had a guardian appointed for her under the [*State Probate Act or other appropriate state law*].

(g) "**Medical emergency**" means a condition that, on the basis of the physician's good-faith clinical judgment, so complicates the medical condition of a pregnant woman as to necessitate the immediate abortion of her pregnancy to avert her death or for which a delay will create serious risk of substantial and irreversible impairment of a major bodily function.

(h) "**Neglect**" means the failure of a parent or legal guardian to supply a child with necessary food, clothing, shelter, or medical care when reasonably able to do so or the failure to protect a child from conditions or actions that imminently and seriously endanger the child's physical or mental health when reasonably able to do so.

(i) "**Physical abuse**" means any physical injury intentionally inflicted by a parent or legal guardian on a child.

(j) "**Physician**" or "**attending physician**" means any person licensed to practice medicine in this State. The term includes medical doctors and doctors of osteopathy.

(k) "**Sexual abuse**" means any sexual conduct or sexual penetration as defined in [*Insert citation(s) or other reference(s) to appropriate section(s) of the State criminal code or other appropriate law(s)*] and committed against a minor by an adult family member as defined in this Act or a family member as defined in [*Insert citation(s) or other reference(s) to appropriate section of the State criminal code or other appropriate law(s)*].

Section 4. Consent of One Parent Required.

Except in the case of a medical emergency, or except as provided in Sections 5, 6, or 9, if a pregnant woman is less than 18 years of age and not emancipated, or if she has been adjudged an incompetent person under [*Insert citation(s) or other reference(s) to State statute(s) relating to petition and hearing; independent evaluation*], no person shall perform an abortion upon her unless, in the case of a woman who is less than 18 years of age, he or she first obtains the notarized written consent of both the pregnant woman and one of her parents or a legal guardian; or, in the case of a woman who is an incompetent person, he or she first obtains the notarized written consent of her guardian. In deciding whether to grant such consent, a pregnant woman's parent or guardian shall consider only their child's or ward's best interests.

Section 5. Alternate Consent.

If the minor patient declares in a signed written statement that she is a victim of sexual abuse, neglect, or physical abuse by either of her parents or her legal guardian(s), then the attending physician shall obtain the notarized written consent required by this Act from a brother or sister of the minor who is over 21 years of age, or from a stepparent or grandparent specified by the minor. The physician who intends to perform the abortion must certify in the patient's medical record that he or she has received the written declaration of abuse or neglect. Any physician relying in good faith on a written statement under this Section shall not be civilly or criminally liable under any provisions of this Act for failure to obtain consent.

Section 6. Exceptions.

Consent shall not be required under Section 4 or 5 of this Act if:

(a) The attending physician certifies in the patient's medical record that a medical emergency exists and there is insufficient time to obtain the required consent; or

(b) Consent is waived under Section 9.

Section 7. Coercion Prohibited.

A parent, guardian, or any other person shall not coerce a minor to have an abortion performed. If a minor is denied financial support by the minor's parents, guardian, or custodian due to the minor's refusal to have an abortion performed, the minor shall be deemed emancipated for the purposes of eligibility for public-assistance benefits, except that such benefits may not be used to obtain an abortion.

Section 8. Reports.

A monthly report indicating the number of consents obtained under this law, the number of times in which exceptions were made to the consent requirement under this Act, the type of exception, the minor's age, and the number of prior pregnancies and prior abortions of the minor shall be filed with the [*Department of Public Health*] on forms prescribed by the Department. No patient names are to be used on the forms. A compilation of the data reported shall be made by the Department on an annual basis and shall be available to the public.

Section 9. Procedure for Judicial Waiver of Consent.

(a) The requirements and procedures under this Section are available to minors and incompetent persons whether or not they are residents of this state.

(b) The minor or incompetent person may petition any [*circuit*] court for a waiver of the consent requirement and may participate in proceedings on her own behalf. The petition shall include a statement that the complainant is pregnant and is unemancipated. The petition shall also include a statement that consent has not been waived and that the complainant wishes to abort without obtaining consent under this Act. The court shall appoint a guardian *ad litem* for her. Any guardian *ad litem* appointed under this Act shall act to maintain the confidentiality of the proceedings.

[***Drafter's Note:*** *Because of concern for confidentiality, unless a judicial decision or other state law requires it, it might be better to say: "The court may appoint a guardian ad litem for her."*]

The [*circuit*] court shall advise her that she has a right to court-appointed counsel and shall provide her with counsel upon her request.

(c) Court proceedings under this Section shall be confidential and shall ensure the anonymity of the minor or incompetent person. All court proceedings under this Section shall be sealed. The minor or incompetent person shall have the right to file her petition in the [*circuit*] court using a pseudonym or using solely her initials. All documents related to this petition shall be confidential and shall not be available to the public. These proceedings shall be given precedence over other pending matters to the extent necessary to ensure that the court reaches a decision promptly. The court shall rule, and issue written findings of fact and conclusions of law, within 48 hours of the time that the petition was filed, except that the 48-hour limitation may be extended at the request of the minor or incompetent person. If the court fails to rule within the 48-hour period and an extension was not requested, then the petition shall be deemed to have been granted, and the consent requirement shall be waived.

(d) If the court finds, by clear and convincing evidence, that the minor is both sufficiently mature and well-informed to decide whether to have an abortion, the court shall issue an order authorizing the minor to consent to the performance or inducement of an abortion without the consent of a parent or guardian and the court shall execute the required forms. If the court does not make the finding specified in this subparagraph or subparagraph (e) of this Section, it shall dismiss the petition.

(e) If the court finds, by clear and convincing evidence, that there is a pattern of physical, sexual, or emotional abuse of the complainant by one or both of her parents, her guardian, or her custodian, or that the notification of a parent or guardian is not in the best interest of the complainant, the court shall issue an order authorizing the minor to consent to the performance or inducement of an abortion without the consent of a parent or guardian. If the court does not make the finding specified in this subparagraph or subparagraph (d) of this Section, it shall dismiss the petition.

(f) A court that conducts proceedings under this Section shall issue written and specific factual findings and legal conclusions supporting its decision and shall order that a confidential record of the evidence and the judge's findings and conclusions be maintained. At the hearing, the court shall hear evidence relating to the emotional development, maturity, intellect, and understanding of the minor.

(g) An expedited confidential appeal shall be available, as the Supreme Court provides by rule, to any minor or incompetent person to whom the [*circuit*] court denies a waiver of consent. An order authorizing an abortion without consent shall not be subject to appeal.

(h) No filing fees shall be required of any pregnant minor who petitions a court for a waiver of parental consent under this Act at either the trial or the appellate level.

Section 10. Appeal Procedure.

The Supreme Court is respectfully requested to establish rules to ensure that proceedings under this Act are handled in an expeditious and confidential manner and to satisfy the requirements of federal courts.

[***Drafter's Note:*** *This Section should be drafted to comport with whatever procedure the State uses to establish appeals procedures. If the legislature has this authority, those procedures should be included in the legislation.*]

Section 11. Penalties.

(a) Any person who intentionally performs an abortion with knowledge that or with reckless disregard as to whether the person upon whom the abortion is to be performed is an unemancipated minor or an incompetent without obtaining the required consent is guilty of a [*Insert appropriate class of felony or misdemeanor*]. In this Section, "**intentionally**" is defined by Section [*Insert section number*] of the [*State criminal penal code*].

It is a defense to prosecution under this Act that the minor falsely represented her age or identity to the physician to be at least 18 years of age by displaying an apparently valid governmental record of identification such that a careful and prudent person under similar circumstances would have relied on the representation. The defense does not apply if the physician is shown to have had independent knowledge of the minor's actual age or identity or failed to use due diligence in determining the minor's age or identity. In this subparagraph, "**defense**" has the meaning and application assigned by Section [*Insert section number*] of the [*State criminal penal code*].

(b) Failure to obtain consent from person(s) from whom consent is required under this Act is *prima facie* evidence of failure to obtain consent and of interference with family relations in appropriate civil actions. Such *prima facie* evidence shall not apply to any issue other than failure to inform the parents or legal guardian and interference with family relations in appropriate civil actions. The civil action may be based on a claim that the act was a result of simple negligence, gross negligence, wantonness, willfulness, intention, or other legal standard of care. The law of this State shall not be construed to preclude the award of exemplary damages in any appropriate civil action relevant to violations of this Act. Nothing in this Act shall be construed to limit the common law rights of parents or legal guardians.

(c) Any person not authorized to provide consent under this Act who provides consent is guilty of a [*Insert appropriate class of felony or misdemeanor*].

(d) Any person who coerces a minor to have an abortion is guilty of a [*Insert appropriate class of felony or misdemeanor*].

Section 12. Construction.

(a) Nothing in this Act shall be construed as creating or recognizing a right to abortion.

(b) It is not the intention of this Act to make lawful an abortion that is currently unlawful

Section 13. Severability.

Any provision of this Act held to be invalid or unenforceable by its terms, or as applied to any person or circumstance, shall be construed so as give it the maximum effect permitted by law, unless such holding shall be one of utter invalidity or unenforceability, in which event such provision shall be deemed severable herefrom and shall not affect the remainder hereof or the application of such provision to other persons not similarly situated or to other, dissimilar circumstances.

Section 14. Right of Intervention.

The [*Legislature*], by joint resolution, may appoint one or more of its members who sponsored or co-sponsored this Act, as a matter of right and in his or her official capacity, to intervene to defend this law in any case in which its constitutionality is challenged.

Section 15. Effective Date.

This Act takes effect on [*Insert date*].

PARENTAL NOTIFICATION OF ABORTION ACT

HOUSE/SENATE BILL No. _____
By Representatives/Senators ________________

Section 1. Short Title.

This Act may be cited as the "Parental Notification of Abortion Act."

Section 2. Legislative Findings and Purposes.

(a) The [*Legislature*] of the State of [*Insert name of State*] finds that:

(1) Immature minors often lack the ability to make fully informed choices that take into account both immediate and long-range consequences.

(2) The medical, emotional, and psychological consequences of abortion are sometimes serious and can be lasting, particularly when the patient is immature.

(3) The capacity to become pregnant and the capacity for mature judgment concerning the wisdom of an abortion are not necessarily related.

(4) Parents ordinarily possess information essential to a physician's exercise of his or her best medical judgment concerning the child.

(5) Parents who are aware that their minor daughter has had an abortion may better ensure that she receives adequate medical attention after her abortion.

(6) Parental consultation is usually desirable and in the best interests of the minor.

(b) The [*Legislature*]'s purpose in enacting this parental notice law is to further the important and compelling State interests of:

(1) Protecting minors against their own immaturity.

(2) Fostering family unity and preserving the family as a viable social unit.

(3) Protecting the constitutional rights of parents to rear children who are members of their household.

(4) Reducing teenage pregnancy and unnecessary abortion.

(5) In light of the foregoing statements of purpose, allowing for judicial bypasses of parental notification to be made only in exceptional or rare circumstances.

Section 3. Definitions.

For purposes of this Act only:

(a) "**Abortion**" means the act of using or prescribing any instrument, medicine, drug, or any other substance, device, or means with the intent to terminate the clinically diagnosable pregnancy of a woman with knowledge that the termination by those means will with reasonable likelihood cause the death of the unborn child. Such use, prescription, or means is not an abortion if done with the intent to:

(1) Save the life or preserve the health of an unborn child;

(2) Remove a dead unborn child caused by spontaneous abortion; or

(3) Remove an ectopic pregnancy.

(b) "**Actual notice**" means the giving of notice directly, in person or by telephone.

(c) "**Constructive notice**" means notice by certified mail to the last known address of the parent or guardian with delivery deemed to have occurred 48 hours after the certified notice is mailed.

(d) "**Coercion**" means restraining or dominating the choice of a minor female by force, threat of force, or deprivation of food and shelter.

(e) "**Department**" means the Department of [*Insert appropriate title*] of the State of [*Insert name of State*].

(f) "**Emancipated minor**" means any person under eighteen (18) years of age who is or has been married or who has been legally emancipated.

(g) "**Incompetent**" means any person who has been adjudged a disabled person and has had a guardian appointed for her under the [*State Probate Act or other appropriate State law*].

(h) "**Medical emergency**" means a condition that, on the basis of the physician's good-faith clinical judgment, so complicates the medical condition of a pregnant woman as to necessitate the immediate abortion of her pregnancy to avert her death or for which a delay will create serious risk of substantial and irreversible impairment of a major bodily function.

(i) "**Neglect**" means the failure of a parent or legal guardian to supply a child with necessary food, clothing, shelter, or medical care when reasonably able to do so or the failure to protect a child from conditions or actions that imminently and seriously endanger the child's physical or mental health when reasonably able to do so.

(j) "**Physical abuse**" means any physical injury intentionally inflicted by a parent or legal guardian on a child.

(k) "**Physician,**" "**attending physician**," or "**referring physician**" means any person licensed to practice medicine in this State. The term includes medical doctors and doctors of osteopathy.

(l) "**Sexual abuse**" means any sexual conduct or sexual penetration as defined in [*Insert citation(s) or other reference(s) to appropriate section(s) of the State criminal code or other appropriate law(s)*] and committed against a minor by an adult family member as defined in this Act or a family member as defined in [*Insert citation(s) or other reference(s) to appropriate section of the State criminal code or other appropriate law(s)*].

Section 4. Notice of One Parent Required.

No person shall perform an abortion upon an unemancipated minor or upon an incompetent unless that person has given at least 48 hours actual notice to one parent or the legal guardian of the pregnant minor or incompetent of his or her intention to perform the abortion. The notice may be given by a referring physician. The person who performs the abortion must receive the written statement of the referring physician certifying that the referring physician has given notice to the parent or legal guardian of the unemancipated minor or incompetent who is to receive the abortion. If actual notice is not possible after a reasonable effort, the person or his or her agent must give 48 hours constructive notice.

Section 5. Alternate Notification.

If the minor patient declares in a signed written statement that she is a victim of sexual abuse, neglect, or physical abuse by either of her parents or her legal guardian, then the attending physician shall give the notice required by this Act to a brother or sister of the minor who is over 21 years of age, or to a stepparent or grandparent specified by the minor. The physician who intends to perform the abortion must certify in the patient's medical record that he or she has received the written declaration of abuse or neglect. Any physician relying in good faith on a written statement under this Section shall not be civilly or criminally liable under any provisions of this Act for failure to give notice.

Section 6. Exceptions.

Notice shall not be required under Section 4 or 5 of this Act if:

(a) The attending physician certifies in the patient's medical record that a medical emergency exists and there is insufficient time to provide the required notice; or

(b) Notice is waived in writing by the person who is entitled to notice; or

(c) Notice is waived under Section 9.

Section 7. Coercion Prohibited.

A parent, legal guardian, or any other person shall not coerce a minor to have an abortion performed. If a minor is denied financial support by the minor's parents, legal guardian, or custodian due to the minor's refusal to have an abortion performed, the minor shall be deemed emancipated for the purposes of eligibility for public-assistance benefits, except that such benefits may not be used to obtain an abortion.

Section 8. Reports.

A monthly report indicating the number of notices issued under this law, the number of times in which exceptions were made to the notice requirement under this Act, the type of exception, the minor's age, and the number of prior pregnancies and prior abortions of the minor shall be filed with the [*Department of Public Health*] on forms prescribed by the Department. No patient names are to be used on the forms. A compilation of the data reported shall be made by the Department on an annual basis and shall be available to the public.

Section 9. Procedure for Judicial Waiver of Notice.

(a) The requirements and procedures under this Section are available to minors and incompetent persons whether or not they are residents of this State.

(b) The minor or incompetent person may petition any [*circuit*] court for a waiver of the notice requirement and may participate in proceedings on her own behalf. The petition shall include a statement that the complainant is pregnant and is unemancipated. The petition shall also include a statement that notice has not been waived and that the complainant wishes to abort without giving notice under this Act. The court shall appoint a guardian *ad litem* for her. Any guardian *ad litem* appointed under this Act shall act to maintain the confidentiality of the proceedings.

[***Drafter's Note:*** *Because of concern for confidentiality, unless a judicial decision or other state*

law requires it, it might be better to say: "the court may appoint a guardian ad litem for her."]

The [*circuit*] court shall advise her that she has a right to court-appointed counsel and shall provide her with counsel upon her request.

(c) Court proceedings under this Section shall be confidential and shall ensure the anonymity of the minor or incompetent person. All court proceedings under this Section shall be sealed. The minor or incompetent person shall have the right to file her petition in the [*circuit*] court using a pseudonym or using solely her initials. All documents related to this petition shall be confidential and shall not be available to the public. These proceedings shall be given precedence over other pending matters to the extent necessary to ensure that the court reaches a decision promptly. The court shall rule, and issue written findings of fact and conclusions of law, within 48 hours of the time that the petition was filed, except that the 48-hour limitation may be extended at the request of the minor or incompetent person. If the court fails to rule within the 48-hour period and an extension was not requested, then the petition shall be deemed to have been granted, and the notice requirement shall be waived.

(d) If the court finds, by clear and convincing evidence, that the minor is both sufficiently mature and well-informed to decide whether to have an abortion, the court shall issue an order authorizing the minor to consent to the performance or inducement of an abortion without the notification of a parent or guardian and the court shall execute the required forms. If the court does not make the finding specified in this subparagraph or subparagraph (e) of this Section, it shall dismiss the petition.

(e) If the court finds, by clear and convincing evidence, that there is a pattern of physical, sexual, or emotional abuse of the complainant by one or both of her parents, her guardian, or her custodian, or that the notification of a parent or guardian is not in the best interest of the complainant, the court shall issue an order authorizing the minor to consent to the performance or inducement of an abortion without the notification of a parent or guardian. If the court does not make the finding specified in this subparagraph or subparagraph (d) of this Section, it shall dismiss the petition.

(f) A court that conducts proceedings under this Section shall issue written and specific factual findings and legal conclusions supporting its decision and shall order that a confidential record of the evidence and the judge's findings and conclusions be maintained. At the hearing, the court shall hear evidence relating to the emotional development, maturity, intellect, and understanding of the minor.

(g) An expedited confidential appeal shall be available, as the Supreme Court provides by rule, to any minor or incompetent person to whom the [*circuit*] court denies a waiver of notice. An order authorizing an abortion without notice shall not be subject to appeal.

(h) No filing fees shall be required of any pregnant minor who petitions a court for a waiver of parental notification under this Act at either the trial or the appellate level.

Section 10. Appeal Procedure.

The Supreme Court is respectfully requested to establish rules to ensure that proceedings under this Act are handled in an expeditious and confidential manner and to satisfy the requirements of federal courts.

[***Drafter's Note:*** *This Section should be drafted to comport with whatever procedure the State uses to establish appeals procedures. If the legislature has this authority, those procedures should be included in the legislation.*]

Section 11. Penalties.

(a) Any person who intentionally performs an abortion with knowledge that or with reckless disregard as to whether the person upon whom the abortion is to be performed is an unemancipated minor or an incompetent without providing the required notice is guilty of a [*Insert appropriate class of felony or misdemeanor*]. In this Section, "**intentionally**" is defined by Section [*Insert section number*] of the [*State criminal penal code*].

It is a defense to prosecution under this Act that the minor falsely represented her age or identity to the physician to be at least 18 years of age by displaying an apparently valid governmental record of identification such that a careful and prudent person under similar circumstances would have relied on the representation. The defense does not apply if the physician is shown to have had independent knowledge of the minor's actual age or identity or failed to use due diligence in determining the minor's age or identity. In this subparagraph, "**defense**" has the meaning and application assigned by Section [*Insert section number*] of the [*State criminal penal code*].

(b) Failure to provide person(s) with the notice required under this Act is *prima facie* evidence of failure to provide notice and of interference with family relations in appropriate civil actions. Such *prima facie* evidence shall not apply to any issue other than failure to inform the parents or legal guardian and interference with family relations in appropriate civil actions. The civil action may be based on a claim that the act was a result of simple negligence, gross negligence, wantonness, willfulness, intention, or other legal standard of care. The law of this State shall not be construed to preclude the award of exemplary damages in any appropriate civil action relevant to violations of this Act. Nothing in this Act shall be construed to limit the common law rights of parents or legal guardians.

(c) Any person not authorized to receive notice under this Act who signs a waiver of notice under subsection (b) of Section 6 is guilty of a [*Insert appropriate class of felony or misdemeanor*].

(d) Any person who coerces a minor to have an abortion is guilty of a [*Insert appropriate class of felony or misdemeanor*].

Section 12. Construction.

(a) Nothing in this Act shall be construed as creating or recognizing a right to abortion.

(b) It is not the intention of this Act to make lawful an abortion that is currently unlawful.

Section 13. Severability.

Any provision of this Act held to be invalid or unenforceable by its terms, or as applied to any person or circumstance, shall be construed so as give it the maximum effect permitted by law, unless such holding shall be one of utter invalidity or unenforceability, in which event such provision shall be deemed severable here from and shall not affect the remainder hereof or the application of such provision to other persons not similarly situated or to other, dissimilar circumstances.

Section 14. Right of Intervention.

The [*Legislature*], by joint resolution, may appoint one or more of its members who sponsored or co-sponsored this Act, as a matter of right and in his or her official capacity, to intervene to defend this law in any case in which its constitutionality is challenged.

Section 15. Effective Date.

This Act takes effect on [*Insert date*].

ABORTION PATIENTS' ENHANCED SAFETY ACT

[***Drafter's Note:*** *This model is based, in significant part, on a Missouri law still in litigation; therefore, lawmakers and policy groups should consult with AUL experts prior to introducing it in their state. The best candidates for this legislation have an established record of enacting protective legislation, such as comprehensive informed consent requirements, parental consent, ultrasound requirements, and comprehensive and specifically-targeted abortion clinic regulations. Moreover, several issues will need to be considered carefully before introducing this legislation, including whether or not the administration of abortifacients such as RU-486 will be covered or excluded.*]

HOUSE/SENATE BILL No. ______
By Representatives/Senators ____________

Section 1. Title.

This Act may be known and cited as the "Abortion Patients' Enhanced Safety Act."

Section 2. Legislative Findings and Purposes.

(a) The Legislature of the State of [*Insert name of State*] finds that:

(1) [*Insert percentage*] of all abortions are performed in clinics devoted solely to providing abortions and family planning services. Most women who seek abortions at these facilities do not have any relationship with the physician who performs the abortion either before or after the procedure. They do not return to the facility for post-surgical care. In most instances, the woman's only actual contact with the abortion provider occurs simultaneously with the abortion procedure, with little opportunity to ask questions about the procedure, potential complications, and proper follow-up care.

(2) For most abortions, the woman arrives at the clinic on the day of the procedure, has the procedure in a room within the clinic, and recovers under the care of clinic staff, all without a hospital admission.

(3) "The medical, emotional, and psychological consequences of an abortion are serious and can be lasting …." *H.L. v. Matheson*, 450 U.S. 398, 411 (1981).

(4) Abortion is an invasive, surgical procedure that can lead to numerous and serious medical complications. Potential complications for first trimester abortions

include, among others, bleeding, hemorrhage, infection, uterine perforation, blood clots, cervical tears, incomplete abortion (retained tissue), failure to actually terminate the pregnancy, free fluid in the abdomen, acute abdomen, missed ectopic pregnancies, cardiac arrest, sepsis, respiratory arrest, reactions to anesthesia, fertility problems, emotional problems, and even death.

(5) The risks for second trimester abortions are greater than for first trimester abortions. The risk of hemorrhage, in particular, is greater, and the resultant complications may require a hysterectomy, other reparative surgery, or a blood transfusion.

(6) The State of [*Insert name of State*] has a legitimate concern for the public's health and safety. *Williamson v. Lee Optical*, 348 U.S. 483, 486 (1985).

(7) The State of [*Insert name of State*] "has legitimate interests from the outset of pregnancy in protecting the health of women." *Planned Parenthood of Southeastern Pennsylvania v. Casey*, 505 U.S. 833, 847 (1992). More specifically, the State of [*Insert name of State*] "has a legitimate concern with the health of women who undergo abortions." *Akron v. Akron Ctr. for Reproductive Health, Inc.*, 462 U.S. 416, 428-29 (1983).

(8) Moreover, the State of [*Insert name of State*] has "a legitimate interest in seeing to it that abortion, like any other medical procedure, is performed under circumstances that ensure maximum safety for the patient." *Roe v. Wade*, 410 U.S. 113, 150 (1973).

(9) Since the Supreme Court's decision in *Roe v. Wade*, courts have repeatedly recognized that for the purposes of regulation, abortion services are rationally distinct from other routine medical services, because of the "particular gravitas of the moral, psychological, and familial aspects of the abortion decision." *Greenville Women's Clinic v. Bryant*, 222 F.3d 157, 173 (4th Cir. 2000), *cert. denied*, 531 U.S. 1191 (2001).

(10) In adopting an array of regulations that treat abortion more seriously than other medical procedures, the State of [*Insert name of State*] recognizes the importance of the abortion practice while permitting it to continue, as protected by the Supreme Court's cases on the subject. *Greenville Women's Clinic v. Bryant*, 222 F.3d 157, 175 (4th Cir. 2000), *cert. denied*, 531 U.S. 1191 (2001).

(11) An ambulatory surgical center (ASC) [*or other appropriate term as used in existing State statutes*] is a healthcare facility that specializes in providing sur-

gery services in an outpatient setting. ASCs generally provide a cost-effective and convenient environment that may be less stressful than what many hospitals offer. Particular ASCs may perform surgeries in a variety of specialties or dedicate their services to one specialty.

(12) Patients who elect to have surgery in an ASC arrive on the day of the procedure, have the surgery in an operating room, and recover under the care of the nursing staff, all without a hospital admission.

(b) Based on the findings in subsection (a) of this Act, it is the purpose of this Act:

(1) To define certain abortion clinics as "ambulatory surgical centers" [*or other appropriate term as used in existing State statutes*] under the laws of this State, and to subject them to licensing and regulation as such.

(2) To promote and enforce the highest standard for care and safety in facilities performing abortions in this State.

(3) To provide for the protection of public health through the establishment and enforcement of a high standard of care and safety in abortion clinics.

(4) To regulate the provision of abortion consistent with and to the extent permitted by the decisions of the Supreme Court of the United States.

Section 3. Definitions.

As used in this Act only:

(a) "**Abortion**" means the act of using or prescribing any instrument [*,medicine, drug, or any other substance, device, or means*] with the intent to terminate the clinically diagnosable pregnancy of a woman, with knowledge that the termination by those means will with reasonable likelihood cause the death of the unborn child. Such use [*,prescription, or means*] is not an abortion if done with the intent to:

(1) Save the life or preserve the health of the unborn child;

(2) Remove a dead unborn child caused by spontaneous abortion; or

(3) Remove an ectopic pregnancy.

(b) "**Abortion clinic**" means a facility, other than an accredited hospital, in which five or more first trimester abortions in any month or any second or third trimester abortions are performed.

(c) "**Department**" means the [*Insert name of State department or agency that licenses and regulates ambulatory surgical centers or similar State-regulated entities*] of the State of [*Insert name of State*].

Section 4. Statutory Definition of "Ambulatory Surgical Center" [*Or Other Appropriate Term*] Modified to Include Certain Facilities Performing Abortions.

(a) The term "**ambulatory surgical center**" [*or other appropriate term as used in existing State statutes, administrative rules, or other regulatory materials*] as used in [*Insert specific reference(s) to State statute(s), administrative rules, or other regulatory materials governing ambulatory surgical centers or similar State-regulated entities*] shall include abortion clinics which do not provide services or other accommodations for abortion patients to stay more than twenty-three hours within the clinic.

(b) All ambulatory surgical centers [*or other appropriate term as used in existing State statutes, administrative rules, or other regulatory materials*] operating in this State, including abortion clinics, must meet the licensing and regulatory standards prescribed in [*Insert specific reference(s) to State statute(s), administrative rules, or other regulatory materials providing licensing and regulatory standards for ambulatory surgical centers or similar State-regulated entities*].

Section 5. Criminal Penalties.

Whoever operates an abortion clinic as defined in this Act without a valid ambulatory surgical center [*or other appropriate term as used in existing State statute(s). administrative rules, or other regulatory materials*] license issued by the Department is guilty of a [*Insert appropriate felony or misdemeanor classification*].

Section 6. Civil Penalties and Fines.

(a) Any violation of this Act may be subject to a civil penalty or fine up to [*Insert appropriate amount*] imposed by the Department.

(b) Each day of violation constitutes a separate violation for purposes of assessing civil penalties or fines.

(c) Both the Office of the Attorney General and the Office of the District Attorney [*or other appropriate classification such as "County Attorney"*] for the county in which the violation occurred may institute a legal action to enforce collection of civil penalties or fines.

Section 7. Injunctive Remedies.

In addition to any other penalty provided by law, whenever, in the judgment of the Director of the [*Insert name of State department or agency that licenses and regulates ambulatory surgical centers or similar State-regulated entities*], any person has engaged, or is about to engage, in any acts or practices which constitute, or will constitute, a violation of this Act, the Director shall make application to any court of competent jurisdiction for an order enjoining such acts and practices, and upon a showing by the Director that such person has engaged, or is about to engage, in any such acts or practices, an injunction, restraining order, or such other order as may be appropriate shall be granted by such court without bond.

Section 8. Construction.

(a) Nothing in this Act shall be construed as creating or recognizing a right to abortion.

(b) It is not the intention of this Act to make lawful an abortion that is currently unlawful.

Section 9. Right of Intervention.

The [*Legislature*], by joint resolution, may appoint one or more of its members, who sponsored or cosponsored this Act in his or her official capacity, to intervene as a matter of right in any case in which the constitutionality of this Act or any portion thereof is challenged.

Section 10. Severability.

If any provision, word, phrase, or clause of this Act or the application thereof to any person or circumstance is held invalid, such invalidity shall not affect the provisions, words, phrases, clauses, or applications of this Act which can be given effect without the invalid provision, word, phrase, clause, or application and to this end, the provisions, words, phrases, and clauses of this Act are declared severable.

Section 11. Effective Date.

This Act takes effect on [*Insert date*].

WOMEN'S HEALTH PROTECTION ACT

HOUSE/SENATE BILL No. ______
By Representatives/Senators ___________

Section 1. Title.

This Act may be known and cited as the "Women's Health Protection Act."

Section 2. Legislative Findings and Purposes.

(a) The [*Legislature*] of the State of [*Insert name of State*] finds that:

(1) [*Insert percentage*] of all abortions are performed in clinics devoted solely to providing abortions and family planning services. Most women who seek abortions at these facilities do not have any relationship with the physician who performs the abortion either before or after the procedure. They do not return to the facility for post-surgical care. In most instances, the woman's only actual contact with the abortion provider occurs simultaneously with the abortion procedure, with little opportunity to ask questions about the procedure, potential complications, and proper follow-up care.

(2) "The medical, emotional, and psychological consequences of an abortion are serious and can be lasting …." *H.L. v. Matheson*, 450 U.S. 398, 411 (1981).

(3) "[T]he abortion decision … is more than a philosophic exercise. Abortion is a unique act. It is an act fraught with consequences for others: for the woman who must live with the implications of her decision; for the spouse, family, and society which must confront the knowledge that these procedures exist, procedures some deem nothing short of an act of violence against innocent human life; and, depending on one's beliefs, for the life or potential life that is aborted." *Planned Parenthood of Southeastern Pennsylvania v. Casey*, 505 U.S. 833, 852 (1992).

(4) Abortion is an invasive, surgical procedure that can lead to numerous and serious medical complications. Potential complications for first trimester abortions include, among others, bleeding, hemorrhage, infection, uterine perforation, blood clots, cervical tears, incomplete abortion (retained tissue), failure to actually terminate the pregnancy, free fluid in the abdomen, acute abdomen, missed ectopic pregnancies, cardiac arrest, sepsis, respiratory arrest, reactions to anes-

thesia, fertility problems, emotional problems, and even death.

(5) The risks for second trimester abortions are greater than for first trimester abortions. The risk of hemorrhage, in particular, is greater, and the resultant complications may require a hysterectomy, other reparative surgery, or a blood transfusion.

(6) The State of [*Insert name of State*] has a legitimate concern for the public's health and safety. *Williamson v. Lee Optical*, 348 U.S. 483, 486 (1985).

(7) The State of [*Insert name of State*] "has legitimate interests from the outset of pregnancy in protecting the health of women." *Planned Parenthood of Southeastern Pennsylvania v. Casey*, 505 U.S. 833, 847 (1992).

(8) More specifically, the State of [*Insert name of State*] "has a legitimate concern with the health of women who undergo abortions." *Akron v. Akron Ctr. for Reproductive Health, Inc.*, 462 U.S. 416, 428-29 (1983).

(9) The State of [*Insert name of State*] has "a legitimate interest in seeing to it that abortion, like any other medical procedure, is performed under circumstances that ensure maximum safety for the patient." *Roe v. Wade*, 410 U.S. 113, 150 (1973).

(10) Since the Supreme Court's decision in *Roe v. Wade*, courts have recognized that for the purposes of regulation, abortion services are rationally distinct from other routine medical services, because of the "particular gravitas of the moral, psychological, and familial aspects of the abortion decision." *Greenville Women's Clinic v. Bryant*, 222 F.3d 157, 173 (4th Cir. 2000), *cert. denied*, 531 U.S. 1191 (2001).

(11) In adopting an array of regulations that treat abortion more seriously than other medical procedures, the State of [*Insert name of State*] recognizes the importance of the abortion practice while yet permitting it to continue, as protected by the Supreme Court's cases on the subject. *Greenville Women's Clinic v. Bryant*, 222 F.3d 157, 175 (4th Cir. 2000), *cert. denied*, 531 U.S. 1191 (2001).

(b) Based on the findings in Subsection (a) of this Act, it is the purpose of this Act to:

(1) To regulate abortion consistent with and to the extent permitted by the decisions of the Supreme Court of the United States.

(2) To provide for the protection of public health through the development, establishment, and enforcement of standards of care in abortion clinics.

Section 3. Definitions.

As used in this Act only:

(a) "**Abortion**" means the act of using or prescribing any instrument, medicine, drug, or any other substance, device, or means with the intent to terminate the clinically diagnosable pregnancy of a woman with knowledge that the termination by those means will with reasonable likelihood cause the death of the unborn child. Such use, prescription, or means is not an abortion if done with the intent to:

(1) Save the life or preserve the health of the unborn child;

(2) Remove a dead unborn child caused by spontaneous abortion; or

(3) Remove an ectopic pregnancy.

(b) "**Abortion clinic**" means a facility, other than an accredited hospital, in which five or more first trimester abortions in any month or any second or third trimester abortions are performed.

(c) "**Born-alive**," with respect to a member of the species *homo sapiens*, means the complete expulsion or extraction from his or her mother of that member, at any stage of development, who after such expulsion or extraction breathes or has a beating heart, pulsation of the umbilical cord, or definite movement of voluntary muscles, regardless of whether the umbilical cord has been cut, and regardless of whether the expulsion or extraction occurs as a result of natural or induced labor, cesarean section, or induced abortion.

(d) "**Conception**" and "**fertilization**" each mean the fusion of the human spermatozoon with a human ovum.

(e) "**Department**" means the [*Insert name of state health department or other appropriate agency*].

(f) "**Director**" means the Director of the [*Insert name of state health department or other appropriate agency*].

(g) "**Gestation**" means the time that has elapsed since the first day of the woman's last menstrual period.

(h) "**Licensee**" means an individual, a partnership, an association, a limited liability company, or a corporation authorized by the [*Insert name of state health department or other appropriate agency*] to operate an abortion clinic.

(i) "**Physician**" means a person licensed to practice medicine in the State of [*Insert name of State*]. This term includes medical doctors and doctors of osteopathy.

Section 4. Licensure requirements.

(a) Beginning on [*Insert effective date*], all abortion clinics shall be licensed by the [*Insert name of State health department or other appropriate agency*]. Any existing abortion clinic as defined by this Act shall make application for license within 90 days.

(b) An application for a license shall be made to the Department on forms provided by it and shall contain such information as the Department reasonably requires, which may include affirmative evidence of ability to comply with such reasonable standards, rules, and regulations as are lawfully prescribed hereunder. Additional information required by the Department shall be supplied on supplemental forms as needed.

(c) Following receipt of an application for license, the Department shall issue a license if the applicant and the facility meet the requirements established by this Act and the minimum standards, rules, and regulations adopted in pursuance thereof, for a period of one year.

(d) A temporary or provisional license may be issued to an abortion clinic for a period of six months in cases where sufficient compliance with minimum standards, rules, and regulations require an extension of time, if a disapproval has not been received from any other state or local agency otherwise authorized to inspect such facilities. The failure to comply must not be detrimental to the health and safety of the public.

(e) A license shall apply only to the location and licensee stated on the application and such license, once issued, shall not be transferable from one place to another or from one licensee to another. If the location of the facility is changed, the license shall be automatically revoked. A new application form shall be completed prior to all license renewals.

(f) An application for a license or renewal to operate an abortion clinic shall be accompanied by a fee of [*Insert appropriate amount*], which is hereby levied as the license fee for operation of an abortion clinic for a period of one year. The fees herein levied and collected shall be paid into the general fund.

(g) Each license issued hereunder shall be for a period of one year from the date of issuance unless sooner revoked, shall be on a form prescribed by the Department, and may be renewed from year to year upon application and payment of the license fee as in the case of procurement of the original license.

(h) The Department may deny, suspend, revoke, or refuse to renew a license in any case in which it finds that there has been a substantial failure of the applicant or licensee to comply with the requirements of this Act or the minimum standards, administrative rules, and regulations adopted by the Department pursuant to this Act. In such case, the Department shall furnish the person, applicant, or licensee 30 days notice specifying reasons for the action.

(i) Any person, applicant, or licensee who feels aggrieved by the action of the Department in denying, suspending, revoking, or refusing to renew a license may appeal the Department's action in accordance with the delay, notice, and other procedures established [*Insert reference to agency/administrative appeal procedures within Department*].

(j) Any person, applicant, or licensee aggrieved by the action of the appellate board may, within 30 days after notification of such action, appeal suspensively to the [*Insert name of court*]. A record of all proceedings before the appellate board shall be made and kept on file with the board. The board shall transmit a certified copy of the record to the [*Name of court*]. The [*Name of court*] shall try the appeal *de novo*.

Section 5. Inspections and Investigations.

(a) The Department shall establish policies and procedures for conducting pre-licensure and re-licensure inspections of abortion clinics. Prior to issuing or reissuing a license, the Department shall conduct an onsite inspection to ensure compliance with the minimum standards, administrative rules, and regulations promulgated by the Department under the authority of this Act.

(b) The Department shall also establish policies and procedures for conducting inspections and investigations pursuant to complaints received by the Department and made against any abortion clinic. The Department shall receive, record, and dispose of complaints in accordance with the established policies and procedures.

Section 6. Minimum standards, administrative rules, and regulations for abortion clinics.

The Department shall establish minimum standards, administrative rules, and regulations for the licensing and operation of abortion clinics. Such minimum standards, administrative rules, and regulations become effective upon approval by the Director of [*Insert name of State health department or other appropriate agency*].

Section 7. Administrative rules for abortion clinics.

(a) The Director shall adopt rules for an abortion clinic's physical facilities. At a minimum these rules shall prescribe standards for:

(1) Adequate private space that is specifically designated for interviewing, counseling, and medical evaluations.

(2) Dressing rooms for staff and patients.

(3) Appropriate lavatory areas.

(4) Areas for pre-procedure hand washing.

(5) Private procedure rooms.

(6) Adequate lighting and ventilation for abortion procedures.

(7) Surgical or gynecologic examination tables and other fixed equipment.

(8) Post-procedure recovery rooms that are supervised, staffed, and equipped to meet the patients' needs.

(9) Emergency exits to accommodate a stretcher or gurney.

(10) Areas for cleaning and sterilizing instruments.

(11) Adequate areas for the secure storage of medical records and necessary equipment and supplies.

(12) The display in the abortion clinic, in a place that is conspicuous to all patients, of the clinic's current license issued by the Department.

(b) The Director shall adopt rules to prescribe abortion clinic supplies and equipment standards, including supplies and equipment that are required to be immediately available for use or in an emergency. At a minimum these rules shall:

(1) Prescribe required equipment and supplies, including medications, required for the conduct, in an appropriate fashion, of any abortion procedure that the medical staff of the clinic anticipates performing and for monitoring the progress of each patient throughout the procedure and recovery period.

(2) Require that the number or amount of equipment and supplies at the clinic is adequate at all times to assure sufficient quantities of clean and sterilized durable equipment and supplies to meet the needs of each patient.

(3) Prescribe required equipment, supplies, and medications that shall be available and ready for immediate use in an emergency and requirements for written protocols and procedures to be followed by staff in an emergency, such as the loss of electrical power.

(4) Prescribe required equipment and supplies for required laboratory tests and requirements for protocols to calibrate and maintain laboratory equipment at the abortion clinic or operated by clinic staff.

(5) Require ultrasound equipment in those facilities that provide abortions after 12 weeks' gestation.

(6) Require that all equipment is safe for the patient and the staff, meets applicable federal standards, and is checked annually to ensure safety and appropriate calibration.

(c) The Director shall adopt rules relating to abortion clinic personnel. At a minimum these rules shall require that:

(1) The abortion clinic designate a medical director of the abortion clinic who is licensed to practice medicine and surgery in the State of [*Insert name of State*].

(2) Physicians performing surgery are licensed to practice medicine and surgery in the State of [*Insert name of State*], demonstrate competence in the procedure involved and are acceptable to the medical director of the abortion clinic.

(3) A physician with admitting privileges at an accredited hospital in this state is available.

(4) If a physician is not present, a registered nurse, nurse practitioner, licensed practical nurse, or physician's assistant is present and remains at the clinic when abortions are performed to provide post-operative monitoring and care until each patient who had an abortion that day is discharged.

(5) Surgical assistants [*or other appropriate classification of healthcare provider*] receive training in counseling, patient advocacy, and the specific responsibilities of the services the surgical assistants [*or other appropriate classification of*

healthcare provider] provide.

(6) Volunteers receive training in the specific responsibilities of the services the volunteers provide, including counseling and patient advocacy as provided in the rules adopted by the Director for different types of volunteers based on their responsibilities.

(d) The Director shall adopt rules relating to the medical screening and evaluation of each abortion clinic patient. At a minimum these rules shall require:

(1) A medical history including the following:

a. Reported allergies to medications, antiseptic solutions, or latex.

b. Obstetric and gynecologic history.

c. Past surgeries.

(2) A physical examination including a bimanual examination estimating uterine size and palpation of the adnexa.

(3) The appropriate laboratory tests including:

a. For an abortion in which an ultrasound examination is not performed before the abortion procedure, urine or blood tests for pregnancy performed before the abortion procedure.

b. A test for anemia.

c. Rh typing, unless reliable written documentation of blood type is available.

d. Other tests as indicated from the physical examination.

(4) An ultrasound evaluation for all patients who elect to have an abortion after 12 weeks' gestation. The rules shall require that if a person who is not a physician performs an ultrasound examination, that person shall have documented evidence that the person completed a course in the operation of ultrasound equipment as prescribed in rule. The physician or other healthcare professional shall review, at the request of the patient, the ultrasound evaluation results with the patient before the abortion procedure is performed, including the probable gestational age of the fetus.

(5) That the physician is responsible for estimating the gestational age of the fetus based on the ultrasound examination and obstetric standards in keeping with established standards of care regarding the estimation of fetal age as defined in rule and shall write the estimate in the patient's medical history. The physician shall keep original prints of each ultrasound examination of a patient in the patient's medical history file.

(e) The Director shall adopt rules relating to the abortion procedure. At a minimum these rules shall require:

(1) That medical personnel is available to all patients throughout the abortion procedure.

(2) Standards for the safe conduct of abortion procedures that conform to obstetric standards in keeping with established standards of care regarding the estimation of fetal age as defined in rule.

(3) Appropriate use of local anesthesia, analgesia, and sedation if ordered by the physician.

(4) The use of appropriate precautions, such as the establishment of intravenous access at least for patients undergoing second or third trimester abortions.

(5) The use of appropriate monitoring of the vital signs and other defined signs and markers of the patient's status throughout the abortion procedure and during the recovery period until the patient's condition is deemed to be stable in the recovery room.

(f) The Director shall adopt rules that prescribe minimum recovery room standards. At a minimum these rules shall require that:

(1) Immediate post-procedure care consists of observation in a supervised recovery room for as long as the patient's condition warrants.

(2) The clinic arrange hospitalization if any complication beyond the management capability of the staff occurs or is suspected.

(3) A licensed healthcare professional who is trained in the management of the recovery area and is capable of providing basic cardiopulmonary resuscitation and related emergency procedures remains on the premises of the abortion clinic until all patients are discharged.

(4) A physician with admitting privileges at an accredited hospital in this state remains on the premises of the abortion clinic until all patients are stable and are ready to leave the recovery room and to facilitate the transfer of emergency cases if hospitalization of the patient or a child born alive is necessary. A physician shall sign the discharge order and be readily accessible and available until the last patient is discharged.

(5) A physician discusses RhO(d) immune globulin with each patient for whom it is indicated and assures it is offered to the patient in the immediate post-operative period or that it will be available to her within 72 hours after completion of the abortion procedure. If the patient refuses, a refusal form approved by the Department shall be signed by the patient and a witness and included in the medical record.

(6) Written instructions with regard to post-abortion coitus, signs of possible problems, and general aftercare are given to each patient. Each patient shall have specific instructions regarding access to medical care for complications, including a telephone number to call for medical emergencies.

(7) There is a specified minimum length of time that a patient remains in the recovery room by type of abortion procedure and duration of gestation.

(8) The physician assures that a licensed healthcare professional from the abortion clinic makes a good faith effort to contact the patient by telephone, with the patient's consent, within 24 hours after surgery to assess the patient's recovery.

(9) Equipment and services are located in the recovery room to provide appropriate emergency resuscitative and life support procedures pending the transfer of the patient or a child born alive to the hospital.

(g) The Director shall adopt rules that prescribe standards for follow-up care. At a minimum these rules shall require that:

(1) A post-abortion medical visit is offered and, if requested, scheduled for two to three weeks after the abortion, including a medical examination and a review of the results of all laboratory tests.

(2) A urine pregnancy test is obtained at the time of the follow-up visit to rule out continuing pregnancy. If a continuing pregnancy is suspected, the patient shall be evaluated and a physician who performs abortions shall be consulted.

(h) The Director shall adopt rules to prescribe minimum abortion clinic incident reporting.

At a minimum these rules shall require that:

(1) The abortion clinic records each incident resulting in a patient's or a child born-alive's serious injury occurring at an abortion clinic and shall report them in writing to the Department within 10 days after the incident. For the purposes of this paragraph, "**serious injury**" means an injury that occurs at an abortion clinic and that creates a serious risk of substantial impairment of a major body organ.

(2) If a patient's death occurs, other than a fetal death properly reported pursuant to law, the abortion clinic reports it to the Department not later than the next Department work day.

(3) Incident reports are filed with the Department and appropriate professional regulatory boards.

(i) The Department shall not release personally identifiable patient or physician information.

(j) The rules adopted by the Director pursuant to this Act do not limit the ability of a physician or other healthcare professional to advise a patient on any health issue.

(k) The provisions of this Act and the rules and regulations adopted pursuant hereto shall be in addition to any other laws, rules, and regulations which are applicable to facilities defined as "**abortion clinics**" under this Act.

Section 8. Criminal Penalties.

(a) Whoever operates an abortion clinic as defined in this Act without a valid license issued by the Department is [*Insert appropriate misdemeanor classification*].

(b) Any person who intentionally, knowingly, or recklessly violates this Act or any rules and regulations adopted under this Act is guilty of [*Insert appropriate misdemeanor classification*].

Section 9. Civil Penalties and Fines.

(a) Any violation of this Act or any rules and regulations adopted under this Act may be subject to a civil penalty or fine up to [*Insert appropriate amount*] imposed by the [*Insert name of State health department or other appropriate agency*].

(b) Each day of violation constitutes a separate violation for purposes of assessing civil penalties or fines.

(c) In deciding whether and to what extent to impose fines, the Department shall consider the following factors:

(1) Gravity of the violation including the probability that death or serious physical harm to a patient or individual will result or has resulted;

(2) Size of the population at risk as a consequence of the violation;

(3) Severity and scope of the actual or potential harm;

(4) Extent to which the provisions of the applicable statutes or regulations were violated;

(5) Any indications of good faith exercised by licensee;

(6) The duration, frequency, and relevance of any previous violations committed by the licensee; and

(7) Financial benefit to the licensee of committing or continuing the violation.

(d) Both the Office of the Attorney General and the Office of the District Attorney [*or other appropriate classification such as "County Attorney"*] for the county in which the violation occurred may institute a legal action to enforce collection of civil penalties or fines.

Section 10. Injunctive Remedies.

In addition to any other penalty provided by law, whenever in the judgment of the Director of the [*Insert name of State health department or other appropriate agency*], any person has engaged, or is about to engage, in any acts or practices which constitute, or will constitute, a violation of this Act, or any rule or regulation adopted under the provision of this Act, the Director shall make application to any court of competent jurisdiction for an order enjoining such acts and practices, and upon a showing by the Director that such person has engaged, or is about to engage, in any such acts or practices, an injunction, restraining order, or such other order as may be appropriate shall be granted by such court without bond.

Section 11. Construction.

(a) Nothing in this Act shall be construed as creating or recognizing a right to abortion.

(b) It is not the intention of this Act to make lawful an abortion that is currently unlawful.

Section 12. Right of Intervention.

The [*Legislature*], by joint resolution, may appoint one or more of its members, who sponsored or cosponsored this Act in his or her official capacity, to intervene as a matter of right in any case in which the constitutionality of this Act or any portion thereof is challenged.

Section 13. Severability.

Any provision of this Act held to be invalid or unenforceable by its terms, or as applied to any person or circumstance, shall be construed so as give it the maximum effect permitted by law, unless such holding shall be one of utter invalidity or unenforceability, in which event such provision shall be deemed severable herefrom and shall not affect the remainder hereof or the application of such provision to other persons not similarly situated or to other, dissimilar circumstances.

Section 14. Effective Date.

This Act takes effect on [*Insert date*].

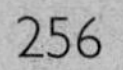

ABORTION COMPLICATION REPORTING ACT

HOUSE/SENATE BILL No. ______
By Representatives/Senators ____________

Section 1. Title.

This Act may be known and cited as the "Abortion Complication Reporting Act."

Section 2. Legislative Findings and Purposes.

(a) The [*Legislature*] of the State of [*Insert name of State*] finds:

(1) The State "has legitimate interests from the outset of pregnancy in protecting the health of women." *Planned Parenthood of Southeastern Pennsylvania v. Casey*, 505 U.S. 833, 847 (1992).

(2) Specifically, the State "has a legitimate concern with the health of women who undergo abortions." *Akron v. Akron Ctr. for Reproductive Health, Inc.* 462 U.S. 416, 428-29 (1983).

(3) Abortion is an invasive, surgical procedure that can cause severe physical and psychological short- and long-term complications for the woman, including but not limited to: uterine perforation, cervical perforation, infection, bleeding, hemorrhage, blood clots, failure to actually terminate the pregnancy, incomplete abortion (retained tissue), pelvic inflammatory disease, endometritis, missed ectopic pregnancy, cardiac arrest, respiratory arrest, renal failure, metabolic disorder, shock, embolism, coma, placenta previa in subsequent pregnancies, preterm delivery in subsequent pregnancies, free fluid in the abdomen, adverse reactions to anesthesia and other drugs, and psychological or emotional complications such as depression, anxiety, and sleeping disorders.

(4) To facilitate reliable scientific studies and research on the safety and efficacy of abortion, it is essential the medical and public health communities have access to accurate information on the abortion procedure and complications resulting from abortion.

(5) Abortion "record keeping and reporting provisions that are reasonably directed to the preservation of maternal health and that properly respect a patient's confidentiality and privacy are permissible." *Planned Parenthood v. Danforth*, 428

U.S. 80 at 52, 79-81 (1976).

(6) Abortion and complication reporting provisions do not impose an undue burden on a woman's right to choose whether or not to terminate a pregnancy. "The collection of information with respect to actual patients is a vital element of medical research, and so it cannot be said that the requirements serve no purpose other than to make abortions more difficult." *Planned Parenthood v. Casey*, 505 U.S. 833 at 900-901 (1992).

(7) To promote its interest in maternal health and life, the State of [*Insert name of State*] maintains an interest in:

a. Collecting information on all complications from all abortions performed in the state; and

b. Compiling statistical reports based on abortion complication information collected pursuant to this Act for future scientific studies and public health research.

(8) Since the Supreme Court's decision in *Roe v. Wade*, courts have recognized that for the purposes of regulation, abortion services are rationally distinct from other routine medical services, because of the "particular gravitas of the moral, psychological, and familial aspects of the abortion decision." *Greenville Women's Clinic v. Bryant*, 222 F.3d 157, 173 (4th Cir. 2000), *cert. denied*, 531 U.S. 1191 (2001).

(b) Based on the findings in subsection (a) of this Act, it is the purpose of this Act to promote maternal health and life, the health and safety of minors, the protection of parental rights, and the protection of born human life, by adding to the sum of medical and public health knowledge through the compilation of relevant data on all complications and maternal deaths resulting from abortion in the State of [*Insert name of State*].

Section 3. Definitions.

For the purposes of this Act only:

(a) "**Abortion**" means the act of using or prescribing any instrument, medicine, drug, or any other substance, device, or means with the intent to terminate the clinically diagnosable pregnancy of a woman with knowledge that the termination by those means will with reasonable likelihood cause the death of the unborn child. Such use, prescription, or means is not an abortion if done with the intent to:

(1) Save the life or preserve the health of the unborn child,

(2) Remove a dead unborn child caused by spontaneous abortion, or

(3) Remove an ectopic pregnancy.

(b) "**Complication**" means any adverse physical or psychological condition arising from the performance of an abortion, which includes but is not limited to: uterine perforation, cervical perforation, infection, bleeding, hemorrhage, blood clots, failure to actually terminate the pregnancy, incomplete abortion (retained tissue), pelvic inflammatory disease, endometritis, missed ectopic pregnancy, cardiac arrest, respiratory arrest, renal failure, metabolic disorder, shock, embolism, coma, placenta previa in subsequent pregnancies, preterm delivery in subsequent pregnancies, free fluid in the abdomen, adverse reactions to anesthesia and other drugs; any psychological or emotional complications such as depression, anxiety, and sleeping disorders; and any other "adverse event" as defined by the Food and Drug Administration (FDA) criteria given in the Medwatch Reporting System.

(c) "**Department**" means the Department of [*Insert title*] of the State of [*Insert name of State*].

(d) "**Facility**" means any public or private hospital, clinic, center, medical school, medical training institution, healthcare facility, physician's office, infirmary, dispensary, ambulatory surgical center, or other institution or location wherein medical care is provided to any person.

(e) "**Hospital**" means any institution licensed as a hospital pursuant to the law of this State.

(f) "**Physician**" means any person licensed to practice medicine in this State. The term includes medical doctors and doctors of osteopathy.

(g) "**Pregnant**" or "**pregnancy**" means that female reproductive condition of having an unborn child in the mother's [*woman's*] uterus.

Section 4. Abortion Complication Reporting.

(a) A facility shall file a written report with the Department regarding each patient who comes under the facility's care and reports any complication, requires medical treatment, or suffers death that the attending physician or facility staff has reason to believe is a primary, secondary, or tertiary result of an abortion.

(b) These reports shall be submitted within 30 days of the discharge or death of the patient treated for the complication.

(c) The Department shall summarize aggregate data from the reports required under this Act and submit the data to the Centers for Disease Control and Prevention (CDC) for the purpose of inclusion in the annual Vital Statistics Report. The aggregated data shall also be made independently available to the public by the Department in a downloadable format.

(d) The Department shall develop and distribute or make available online in a downloadable format a standardized form for the report required under Section 4(a) of this Act.

(e) The Department shall communicate this reporting requirement to all medical professional organizations, licensed physicians, hospitals, emergency rooms, abortion facilities, Department of Health clinics, and ambulatory surgical facilities operating in the state.

(f) The report required under this Section shall not contain:

(1) The name of the woman;

(2) Common identifiers, such as her social security number or motor vehicle operator's license number; or

(3) Other information or identifiers that would make it possible to identify in any manner or under any circumstances an individual who has obtained or seeks to obtain an abortion.

(g) Neither the Department, any other state department, agency, or office, nor any employees thereof shall compare data concerning abortions or abortion complications maintained in an electronic or other information system file with data in any another electronic or other information system that could result in identifying in any manner or under any circumstances an individual obtaining or seeking to obtain an abortion.

(h) Statistical information that may reveal the identity of a woman obtaining or seeking to obtain an abortion shall not be maintained by the Department or any other state department, agency, or office.

(i) The Department or an employee of the Department shall not disclose to a person or entity outside the Department the reports or the contents of the reports required under this Act in a manner or fashion as to permit the person or entity to whom the report is disclosed to identify in any way or under any circumstances the person who is the subject of the report.

(j) Disclosure of confidential identifying information in violation of this Act shall constitute a [*Insert appropriate felony or misdemeanor classification*] which, upon conviction, shall be punished by [*Insert penalty*].

Section 5. Reporting Requirements.

Each report of death or medical treatment for complications following abortion required under Section 4 of this Act shall contain at minimum the following information:

(a) The age and race of the patient;

(b) The characteristics of the patient, including residency status, county of residence, marital status, education, number of previous pregnancies, number of miscarriages, number of stillbirths, number of living children, and number of previous abortions;

(c) The date the abortion was performed, the reason for the abortion if known, and the method used if known;

(d) The type of facility where the abortion was performed;

(e) The specific complication(s) that led to the treatment, including, but not limited to, failure to actually terminate the pregnancy, missed ectopic pregnancy, uterine perforation, cervical perforation, incomplete abortion (retained tissue), bleeding, infection, hemorrhage, blood clots, cardiac arrest, respiratory arrest, pelvic inflammatory disease, damage to pelvic organs, endometritis, renal failure, metabolic disorder, shock, embolism, free fluid in the abdomen, acute abdomen, adverse reaction to anesthesia or other drugs, hemolytic reaction due to the administration of ABO-incompatible blood or blood products, hypoglycemia where onset occurs while patient is being cared for in the abortion facility, physical injury associated with therapy performed in the abortion facility, coma, death, and psychological or emotional complications including but not limited to depression, anxiety, and sleep disorders; and

(f) The amount billed to cover the treatment of the specific complication(s), including whether the treatment was billed to Medicaid, insurance, private pay, or other method. This should include charges for any physician, hospital, emergency room, prescription or other drugs, laboratory tests, and any other costs for the treatment rendered.

Section 6. Penalties.

The following penalties shall apply to violations of this Act:

(a) Any person required under this Act to file a report, keep any records, or supply any information, who willfully fails to file such report, keep such records, or supply such information at the time or times required by law or regulation, is guilty of unprofessional conduct, and his or her license for the practice of medicine [and surgery] shall be subject to suspension or revocation in accordance with procedures provided under the [*State Medical Practice Act or other*

appropriate statute].

(b) Any person who willfully delivers or discloses to the Department any report, record or information known by him or her to be false is guilty of a [*Insert appropriate misdemeanor or felony classification*].

(c) Any person who willfully discloses any information obtained from reports filed pursuant to this Act, other than the disclosure authorized by the Act or otherwise authorized by law, is guilty of a [*Insert appropriate misdemeanor or felony classification*].

(d) In addition to the above penalties, any person, organization, or facility who willfully violates any of the provisions of this Act requiring reporting shall upon conviction:

(1) For the first time, have its license suspended for a period of six months.

(2) For the second time, have its license suspended for a period of one year.

(3) For the third time, have its license revoked.

Section 7. Right of Intervention.

The [*Legislature*], by joint resolution, may appoint one or more of its members, who sponsored or cosponsored this Act in his or her official capacity, to intervene as a matter of right in any case in which the constitutionality of this law is challenged.

Section 8. Severability.

Any provision of this Act held to be invalid or unenforceable by its terms, or as applied to any person or circumstance, shall be construed so as give it the maximum effect permitted by law, unless such holding shall be one of utter invalidity or unenforceability, in which event such provision shall be deemed severable herefrom and shall not affect the remainder hereof or the application of such provision to other persons not similarly situated or to other, dissimilar circumstances.

Section 9. Effective Date.

This Act takes effect on [*Insert date*].

CHILD PROTECTION ACT

HOUSE/SENATE BILL No. _____
By Representatives/Senators ___________

Section 1. Short Title.

This Act may be cited as the "[*Insert name of State*] Child Protection Act."

Section 2. Legislative Findings and Purposes.

(a) The [*Legislature*] finds that:

(1) Children are increasingly being preyed upon, victimized, and coerced into illegal sexual relationships by adults.

(2) [*Insert name of State*] law requires caretakers, healthcare facilities, healthcare providers, teachers, and other specified individuals to report suspected incidents of sexual crimes against children. [*Insert references to appropriate State statute(s)*].

(3) However, many of these suspected criminal acts go unreported and perpetrators are not investigated or prosecuted.

(4) [*Insert name of State*] may better prevent future sexual crimes against children by investigating, prosecuting, incarcerating, and treating those who prey upon and victimize children.

(5) To prevent future and continuing sexual crimes against children, all crimes of this nature must be reported to state investigators and state agencies that are specifically-trained and equipped to professionally, thoroughly, and compassionately investigate cases of suspected crimes against children, relieving mandatory reporters of this responsibility.

(6) The physical, emotional, developmental, and psychological impact of sexual crimes on child victims can be severe and long-lasting.

(7) The societal costs of these crimes are also significant and affect the entire populace.

(8) The collection, maintenance, and preservation of evidence—including forensic tissue samples—furthers [*Insert name of State*]'s interest in protecting children from sexual crimes and provides the State with the tools necessary for successful investigations and prosecutions.

(9) Parents and guardians have both the right and responsibility to be involved in medical treatment decisions involving their child/children and no one has the right to knowingly or willfully impede or circumvent this right.

(10) There are documented cases of individuals other than a parent or guardian aiding, abetting, and assisting minor girls to procure abortions without their parents or guardians' knowledge, consent, or involvement. This includes transporting children across state lines to avoid parental involvement requirements in the child's home state.

(11) Such actions violate both the sanctity of the familial relationship and [*Insert name of State*]'s parental involvement law for abortion.

(b) The [*Legislature*]'s purposes in enacting the [*Child Protection Act*] are to further the important and compelling state interests of:

(1) Protecting children from sexually-predatory adults;

(2) Ensuring that adults who are involved in illegal sexual relationships or contact with children are reported, investigated, and, when warranted, prosecuted;

(3) Relieving medical professionals and other mandatory reporters of suspected sexual crimes against children from any responsibility to personally investigate the allegation or suspicion. Mandatory reporters must simply report allegations, suspicions, and pertinent facts. Trained law enforcement or social services personnel will then be responsible for any investigation and for the ultimate disposition of the allegation or case;

(4) Reducing the physical, emotional, developmental, and psychological impact of sexual crimes on child victims;

(5) Reducing the societal and economic burden on the populace that results from sexual crimes against children;

(6) Providing law enforcement officials with the tools and evidence necessary to investigate and prosecute child predators; and

(7) Protecting and respecting the right of parents and guardians to be involved in the medical decisions and treatment of their child/children and preventing anyone from knowingly or willfully subverting or circumventing those rights.

Section 3. Definitions.

For the purposes of this Act:

(a) "**Abuse**" means the involvement of a child in any sexual act with a parent or another adult; any sexual activity involving a child under the age of 12; the aiding or toleration of a parent or caretaker of the child's sexual involvement with any other adult; the child's involvement in pornographic displays; or any other involvement of a child in sexual activity constituting a crime under the laws of this State. [*Drafter's Note: Depending on the specific provisions and prohibitions of the State's criminal code, more definitive exclusion of sexual acts or conduct between two (consenting) children may be appropriate in light of recent federal court decisions. Please consult AUL for specific drafting assistance.*]

(b) "**Adult**" means one who has attained the age [*of 18 or the legal age of majority in this state*].

(c) "**Caretaker**" means any person legally obligated to provide or secure adequate care for the child, including a parent, guardian, tutor, legal custodian, foster home parent, or anyone else providing the child with a residence.

(d) "**Child**" or "**children**" means anyone under the age of 18 *or, if appropriate, state's age of consent for sexual activity*].

(e) "**Child pornography**" means visual depiction of a child engaged in actual or simulated sexual intercourse, deviate sexual intercourse, bestiality, masturbation, sadomasochistic abuse, or lewd exhibition of the genitals.

(f) "**Coercion**" means restraining or dominating the choice of a child by force, threat of force, or deprivation of food and shelter.

(g) "**Mandatory reporter**" means any of the following individuals performing their occupational duties:

(1) "**Health practitioner**" means any individual who provides healthcare services, including a physician, surgeon, physical therapist, psychiatrist, psychologist, medical resident, medical intern, hospital staff member, licensed nurse, nurse's

aid, any emergency medical technician, paramedic, and any employee, staff member, or volunteer at a reproductive healthcare facility.

(2) "**Member of the clergy**" means any priest, rabbi, duly-ordained deacon, or minister, except that he or she is not required to report a confidential communication that is protected as a function of the church, but must then encourage that person to come forward and report the allegations to the proper authorities.

(3) "**Teaching or child care provider**" means anyone who provides training and supervision of a child, including any public or private school teacher, teacher's aide, public or private school principal, public or private school staff member, social worker, probation officer, foster home parent, group home or other child care institutional staff member, personnel of residential home facilities, a licensed or unlicensed day care provider, or any individual who provides such services to a child.

(4) **Police officers or law enforcement officials**.

(5) "**Commercial film and photographic print processor**" is any person who develops exposed photographic film into negatives, slides, or prints, or who makes prints from negatives or slides for compensation.

(6) "**Physician**" means any person licensed to practice medicine in this State. The term includes medical doctors and doctors of osteopathy.

(7) "**Reproductive healthcare facility**" means any office, clinic, or any other facility that provides abortions, abortion counseling, abortion referrals, contraceptives, contraceptive counseling, sex education, or gynecological care and services.

(h) For the purposes of this Act only, "**abortion**" means the act of using or prescribing any instrument, medicine, drug, or any other substance, device, or means with the intent to terminate the clinically diagnosable pregnancy of a woman with knowledge that the termination by those means will with reasonable likelihood cause the death of the unborn child. Such use, prescription, or means is not an abortion if done with the intent to:

(1) Save the life or preserve the health of an unborn child;

(2) Remove a dead unborn child caused by spontaneous abortion; or

(3) Remove an ectopic pregnancy.

(i) **"Sexual abuse"** means any sexual conduct, sexual contact, or sexual penetration as defined in [*Insert appropriate reference(s) to State criminal code provision(s)*] and committed against a child by an adult or involving a child under the age of 12.

Section 4. Mandatory Reporter Requirements.

A mandatory reporter must report every instance of alleged or suspected abuse, sexual abuse, or sexual crimes against a child as defined by [*Insert appropriate reference(s) to State criminal code provision(s)*]. The mandatory reporter may not use his or her discretion in deciding what cases should or should not be reported to the appropriate law enforcement or designated state agencies.

Section 5. Mandatory Reporting Procedure.

If a mandatory reporter has cause to believe that a child has been abused, sexually abused, or has been the victim of a sexual crime as defined in [*Insert appropriate reference(s) to State criminal code provision(s)*], the mandatory reporter shall make a report no later than the 48th hour after such abuse, sexual abuse, or crime has been brought to his or her attention or he or she suspects such abuse, sexual abuse, or crime. A mandatory reporter may not delegate the responsibility to report such abuse, sexual abuse, or crime to any other person but must personally make the report. The mandatory reporter must make a report to [*Designate appropriate local or State law enforcement agency and/or other State agencies*].

Section 6. Contents of the Report.

The person making the report must identify the name and address of the child as well as the name and address of the person(s) who is responsible for the care or custody of the child. The person making the report must also file any pertinent information he or she may have relating to the alleged or suspected abuse, sexual abuse, or sexual crime.

Section 7. Failure to Report.

Any mandatory reporter who has reason to believe that a child's physical or mental health or welfare has been adversely affected because of abuse, sexual abuse, or a sexual crime and does not report such abuse, sexual abuse, or sexual crime as provided by this Act shall be subject to [*Insert reference to appropriate civil remedy, fine, or other penalty*].

Section 8. Maintenance of Forensic Samples from Abortions Performed in Cases Involving Suspected Sexual Crime Against a Child.

(a) Any physician who performs an abortion on a child who is less than 14 years of age at the time of the abortion procedure shall preserve, in accordance with rules and regulations adopted by the [*State Attorney General or other appropriate law enforcement agency charged with the collection and preservation of evidence*] pursuant to this Act, fetal tissue extracted during such abortion. The physician shall submit such tissue to the [*Insert name of proper State agency such as State Department of Public Safety, Bureau of Investigation, or to the State Crime Laboratory*].

(b) The [*State Attorney General or other appropriate law enforcement agency charged or familiar with the forensic collection and preservation of evidence*] shall adopt rules and regulations prescribing:

(1) The amount and type of fetal tissue to be preserved and submitted by a physician pursuant to this Section;

(2) Procedures for the proper preservation of such tissue for the purpose of DNA testing and examination;

(3) Procedures for documenting the chain of custody of such tissue for use as evidence;

(4) Procedures for proper disposal of fetal tissue preserved pursuant to this Section;

(5) A uniform reporting instrument mandated to be utilized by physicians when submitting fetal tissue under this Section which shall include the name and address of the physician submitting the fetal tissue and the name and complete address of residence of the parent or legal guardian of the child upon whom the abortion was performed; and

(6) Procedures for communication with law enforcement agencies regarding evidence and information obtained pursuant to this Section.

(c) Failure of a physician to comply with any provision of this Section or any rule or regulation adopted thereunder:

(1) Shall constitute unprofessional conduct for the purposes of [*Insert appropriate statutory reference*]; and

(2) Is a [*Insert appropriate criminal offense classification*] and a [*Insert appropriate higher classification of offense*] upon a second or subsequent conviction.

Section 9. Prohibition on Intentionally Causing, Aiding, Abetting, or Assisting Child to Obtain an Abortion Without Parental [*Consent or Notification*].

(a) No person shall intentionally cause, aid, or assist a child to obtain an abortion without the [*consent or notification required by (insert reference to State parental involvement for abortion law)*].

(b) A person who violates subsection (a) of this Section shall be civilly liable to the child and to the person or persons required to [*give the consent/receive notice under (insert reference to state parental involvement for abortion law)*]. A court may award damages to the person or persons adversely affected by a violation of subsection (a) of this Section, including compensation for emotional injury without the need for personal presence at the act or event, and the court may further award attorneys' fees, litigation costs, and punitive damages. Any adult who engages in or consents to another person engaging in a sex act with a child in violation of the provisions of [*Insert appropriate reference(s) to criminal penal code provision(s)*], which results in the child's pregnancy, shall not be awarded damages under this Section.

(c) It shall not be a defense to a claim brought under this Section that the abortion was performed or induced pursuant to consent to the abortion given in a manner that is otherwise lawful in the state or place where the abortion was performed or induced.

(d) An unemancipated child does not have capacity to consent to any action in violation of this Section.

(e) A court of competent jurisdiction may enjoin conduct that would be in violation of this Section upon petition by the Attorney General, a prosecuting or district attorney, or any person adversely affected or who reasonably may be adversely affected by such conduct, upon a showing that such conduct:

(1) Is reasonably anticipated to occur in the future; or

(2) Has occurred in the past, whether with the same child or others, and that it is not unreasonable to expect that such conduct will be repeated.

Section 10. Right of Intervention.

The [*Legislature*], by joint resolution, may appoint one or more of its members, who sponsored or cosponsored this Act in his or her official capacity, to intervene as a matter of right in any case in which the constitutionality of this law is challenged.

Section 11. Severability.

Any provision of this Act held to be invalid or unenforceable by its terms, or as applied to any person or circumstance, shall be construed so as to give it the maximum effect permitted by law, unless such holding shall be one of utter invalidity or unenforceability, in which event such provision shall be deemed severable herefrom and shall not affect the remainder hereof or the application of such provision to other persons not similarly situated or to other, dissimilar circumstances.

Section 12. Effective Date.

This Act takes effect on [*Insert date*].

ABORTION-INDUCING DRUGS SAFETY ACT

HOUSE/SENATE BILL No. ________
By Representatives/Senators ______________

Section 1. Title.

This Act may be known and cited as the "Abortion-Inducing Drugs Safety Act."

Section 2. Legislative Findings and Purposes.

(a) The [*Legislature*] of the State of [*Insert State*] finds that:

(1) The Food and Drug Administration (FDA) approved the drug mifepristone as an abortion-inducing drug with a specific gestation, dosage, and administration protocol.

(2) As tested and approved by the FDA, and as outlined in the drug label, an abortion by mifepristone consists of three oral doses of 200 mg of mifepristone, followed by a single oral dose of .4 mg misopristol, (more commonly known as the "RU-486 regime") through 49 days LMP (a gestational measurement using the first day of the woman's "last menstrual period" as a marker).

(3) As tested and approved by the FDA, and as outlined in the drug label, the aforementioned treatment requires three office visits by the patient, and the dosages may only be administered in a clinic, medical office, or hospital under supervision of a physician.

(4) Specifically, on Day One, three 200 mg tablets are taken in a single oral dose; on Day Three, the patient returns and, unless an abortion has occurred and is confirmed, the patient takes two 200 Ag (400 Ag) tablets of misoprostol orally. On Day 14, the patient is to return for a follow-up visit in order to confirm that a complete termination of pregnancy has occurred.

(5) Court testimony by Planned Parenthood and other physicians demonstrates that physicians routinely fail to follow the mifepristone protocol as tested and approved by the FDA, and as outlined in the drug label. *See* e.g., *Planned Parenthood Cincinnati Region v. Taft*, 459 F. Supp. 2d 626 (S.D. Oh. 2006).

(6) Specifically, Planned Parenthood and other physicians are administering a

single oral dose of 200 mg of mifepristone, followed by a single *vaginal* dose of .8 mg misopristol, through 63 days LMP, without medical supervision, and without follow-up care. *See* e.g., *Planned Parenthood Cincinnati Region*, 459 F. Supp. 2d at 630n.7.

(7) The use of mifepristone presents significant medical risks to women, including but not limited to *C. sordellii* bacterial infection, septic shock, toxic shock syndrome, adult respiratory distress syndrome from sepsis, *Escheria coli* sepsis, group B Streptococcus septicemia, disseminated intravascular coagulopathy (DIC) with heptic and renal failure, severe pelvic infection, and massive hemorrhage.

(8) "Off-label" use of mifepristone can be deadly. As of September 2007, at least eight American women had died from mifepristone abortions.

(9) Medical studies have indicated that 1 to 2 out of every 1,000 women who undergo drug-induced abortions will require emergency blood transfusion for massive hemorrhage. The FDA has reported that at least 116 women have required blood transfusions for massive bleeding after drug-induced abortions, with at least 54 losing more than half of their blood volume.

(10) The absence of proper follow-up care after drug-induced abortions has resulted in at least 17 women having undetected ectopic pregnancies, 11 of which resulted in ectopic rupture.

(11) These dangerous risks demand strict adherence to the FDA-approved protocol outlined above.

(b) Based on the findings in subsection (a) of this Section, it is the purpose of this Act to:

(1) Protect women from the dangerous and potentially deadly off-label use of abortion-inducing drugs, such as mifepristone.

(2) Ensure that physicians abide by the protocol tested and approved by the FDA for such abortion-inducing drugs, as outlined in the drug labels.

Section 3. Definitions.

(a) "**Abortion-inducing drug**" means a medicine, drug, or any other substance prescribed or dispensed with the intent of terminating the clinically diagnosable pregnancy of a woman, with knowledge that the termination will with reasonable likelihood cause the death of the unborn child.

(b) "**Abortion**" means the act of using or prescribing any instrument, medicine, drug, or any other substance, device, or means with the intent to terminate the clinically diagnosable pregnancy of a woman, with knowledge that the termination by those means will with reasonable likelihood cause the death of the unborn child. Such use, prescription, or means is not an abortion if done with the intent to:

(1) Save the life or preserve the health of an unborn child;

(2) Remove a dead unborn child caused by spontaneous abortion; or

(3) Remove an ectopic pregnancy.

(c) "**Department**" means the Department of [*Insert appropriate title*] of the State of [*Insert State*].

(d) "**Drug label**" means the pamphlet accompanying an abortion-inducing drug which outlines the protocol tested and authorized by the FDA and agreed upon by the drug company applying for FDA authorization of that drug. Also known as "final printing labeling instructions," it is the FDA document which delineates how a drug is to be used according to the FDA approval.

(e) "**LMP**" or "**gestational age**" means the time that has elapsed since the first day of the woman's last menstrual period.

(f) "**Mifepristone**" means the specific abortion-inducing drug regimen also known as RU-486.

(g) "**Physician**" means any person licensed to practice medicine in this State. The term includes medical doctors and doctors of osteopathy.

(h) "**Pregnant**" or "**pregnancy**" means that female reproductive condition of having an unborn child in the mother's [*woman's*] uterus.

(i) "**Unborn child**" means the offspring of human beings from conception until birth.

Section 4. Unlawful Distribution of Abortion-Inducing Drug

(a) It shall be unlawful to knowingly give, sell, dispense, administer, otherwise provide, or prescribe any abortion-inducing drug to a pregnant woman for the purpose of inducing an

abortion in that pregnant woman, or enabling another person to induce an abortion in a pregnant woman, unless the person who gives, sells, dispenses, administers, or otherwise provides or prescribes the abortion-inducing drug is a physician, and the provision or prescription of the abortion-inducing drug satisfies the protocol tested and authorized by the FDA and as outlined in the label for the abortion-inducing drug.

(b) Every pregnant woman to whom a physician gives, sells, dispenses, administers, otherwise provides, or prescribes any abortion-inducing drug shall be provided with a copy of the drug's label.

(c) The physician giving, selling, dispensing, administering, otherwise providing, or prescribing the abortion-inducing drug must have a signed contract with a physician who agrees to handle complications and be able to produce that signed contract on demand by the patient or by the Department. Every pregnant woman to whom a physician gives, sells, dispenses, administers, otherwise provides, or prescribes any abortion-inducing drug shall receive the name and phone number of the physician who will be handling emergencies, and the hospital at which any emergencies will be handled. The physician who contracts to handle emergencies must have active admitting privileges and gynecological/surgical privileges at the hospital designated to handle any emergencies associated with the use or ingestion of the abortion-inducing drug.

Section 5. Reporting.

If a physician provides an abortion-inducing drug to another for the purpose of inducing an abortion as authorized in Section 4 of this Act, and if the physician knows that the person who uses the abortion-inducing drug for the purpose of inducing an abortion experiences during or after the use an adverse event, the physician shall provide a written report of the serious event within 24 hours of the event to the FDA via the Medwatch Reporting System [*and to the State Medical Board*].

[*The State Medical Board shall compile and retain all reports it receives under this Section. All reports the board receives are public records open to inspection under [citation to or appropriate reference to applicable State code section(s) regarding public records]. In no case shall the State Medical Board release to any person or entity the name or any other personal identifying information regarding a person who uses an abortion-inducing drug for the purpose of inducing an abortion and who is the subject of a report the State Medical Board receives under this provision.*]

An "**adverse event**" shall be defined for purposes of this Act according to the FDA criteria given in the Medwatch Reporting System.

Section 6. Criminal Penalties.

A person who intentionally, knowingly, or recklessly violates any provision of this Act is guilty of a [*Insert appropriate class of felony or misdemeanor*]. In this Section, "**intentionally**" is defined by Section [*Insert section number*] of the [*State Criminal Penal Code*].

No criminal penalty may be assessed against the pregnant woman upon whom the drug-induced abortion is performed.

Section 7. Civil Penalties.

(a) In addition to whatever remedies are available under the common or statutory law of this State, failure to comply with the requirements of this Act shall:

> (1) Provide a basis for a civil malpractice action for actual and punitive damages.
>
> (2) Provide a basis for a professional disciplinary action under [*Medical Malpractice Act*].
>
> (3) Provide a basis for recovery for the woman's survivors for the wrongful death of the woman under the [*Wrongful Death Act*].

(b) No civil liability may be assessed against the pregnant woman upon whom the drug-induced abortion is performed.

(c) When requested, the court shall allow a woman to proceed using solely her initials or a pseudonym and may close any proceedings in the case and enter other protective orders to preserve the privacy of the woman upon whom the abortion was performed.

(d) If judgment is rendered in favor of the plaintiff, the court shall also render judgment for a reasonable attorney's fee in favor of the plaintiff against the defendant.

Section 8. Construction.

(a) Nothing in this Act shall be construed as creating or recognizing a right to abortion.

(b) It is not the intention of this Act to make lawful an abortion that is currently unlawful.

Section 9. Right of Intervention.

The [*Legislature*], by joint resolution, may appoint one or more of its members, who sponsored or cosponsored this Act in his or her official capacity, to intervene as a matter of right in any case in which the constitutionality of this law is challenged.

Section 10. Severability.

Any provision of this Act held to be invalid or unenforceable by its terms, or as applied to any person or circumstance, shall be construed so as give it the maximum effect permitted by law, unless such holding shall be one of utter invalidity or unenforceability, in which event such provision shall be deemed severable herefrom and shall not affect the remainder hereof or the application of such provision to other persons not similarly situated or to other, dissimilar circumstances.

Section 11. Effective Date.

This Act takes effect on [*Insert date*].

TITLE X CONSISTENCY AND TRANSPARENCY ACT

HOUSE/SENATE BILL No. ______
By Representatives/Senators ____________

[**Drafter's Note:** *This Act may be introduced independently or, alternatively, as part of a state Appropriations Act or budgetary rider.*]

Section 1. Title.

This Act may be known and cited as the "Title X Consistency and Transparency Act."

Section 2. Legislative Findings and Purposes.

(a) The [*Legislature*] of the State of [*Insert name*] finds that:

(1) The State of [*Insert name of State*] voluntarily participates in several federal programs that provide funds for family planning services. Among these programs are Title X of the "Public Health Service Act," which provides project grants to public and private agencies for family planning services, and Title XX of the "Social Security Act," which provides block grants to the states for social services, including family planning.

(2) The regulations for Title X specify that funds may not be used to finance abortions or abortion-related activity. Specifically, Title X provides that "none of the funds appropriated … shall be used in programs where abortion is a method of family planning." 42 U.S.C. §300a-6.

(3) Title XX funds may not be used for the provision of medical care. Moreover, any Title XX funds used to match Title X funds may not be used to finance abortions or abortion-related activity.

(4) In addition to federal family planning funds, the State of [*Insert name of State*] also provides state-originated funds under [*Insert reference to any direct State subsidies, grants, or other allocations for family planning services, education, etc.*] for family planning.

(5) The [*Insert name of State*] Department of Health [*or other appropriate State department or agency*] appropriates and distributes both federal and state funds for family planning services to [*"family planning contractors" or other appropriate term*].

(6) [*Insert reference(s) to applicable State law(s)*] prohibits the use of public funds for elective abortion: abortions performed in cases not involving rape, incest, or threats to the life of the mother [*or insert specific exemption language from applicable State law*].

(7) Left unrestricted or unregulated, federal and state funds for family planning services can, in some cases, effectively and indirectly subsidize contractors, individuals, organizations, or entities performing or inducing abortions, referring for abortions, or counseling in favor of abortions through shared administrative costs, overhead, employee salaries, rent, utilities, and various other expenses.

(8) When a State appropriates public funds to establish a program it is entitled to define the limits of that program. *Rust v. Sullivan*, 500 U.S. 173, 194 (1991).

(9) The decision not to fund abortion places no governmental obstacle in the path of a woman who chooses to terminate her pregnancy. *Rust v. Sullivan*, 500 U.S. 173, 201 (1991).

(10) It is permissible for a State to engage in unequal subsidization of abortion and other medical services to encourage alternative activity deemed in the public interest. *Rust v. Sullivan*, 500 U.S. 173, 201 (1991).

(11) Requiring abortion-related activity to be completely separate from other activities that receive state funding in no way denies any right to engage in abortion-related activities. *Rust v. Sullivan*, 500 U.S. 173, 198 (1991).

(b) It is the intent of the [*Legislature*] that no federal family planning funds appropriated or dispersed by this State shall be used to pay the direct or indirect costs (including, but not limited to, administrative costs or expenses, overhead, employee salaries, rent, and telephone and other utilities) of abortion procedures, abortion referrals, or abortion counseling provided by [*"family planning contractors" or other appropriate term*] and that these activities are not to be subsidized, either directly or indirectly, by those funds.

(c) It is also the intent of the [*Legislature*] that no state family planning funds appropriated or dispersed pursuant to [*Insert reference(s) to specific State statute(s) regarding family planning funds and/or State family planning policies or programs*], shall be appropriated to or distributed to individuals, organizations, entities, or affiliates of individuals, organizations, or entities that perform, induce, refer for, or counsel on behalf of elective abortions.

(d) The [*Legislature*]'s purpose in enacting this funding law is to ensure that family planning funds are used for family planning services and not to subsidize, directly or indirectly, elective abortions.

(e) The [*Legislature*], through this Act, is not seeking to enact any impermissible prohibition upon the ability of family planning contractors [*or other appropriate term*] or other individuals, organizations, or entities to continue providing abortion services using their own funds and with no direct or indirect federal or state family planning funds.

(f) Further, with respect to federal family planning funds, the Legislature is not seeking to prohibit all contracting with contractors, individuals, organizations, or entities that may provide abortion services using other independent sources of funds. For example under existing federal law, in order to receive family planning funds under Title X, a family planning contractor may form and maintain completely separate and distinct affiliates *(e.g.,* by dividing its operations into "family planning affiliates" and "abortion services affiliates"). *Planned Parenthood of Mid-Missouri & Eastern Kansas, Inc. v. Dempsey*, 167 F.3d 458 (8th Circuit 1999) and *Planned Parenthood v. Sanchez*, 403 F.3d 324 (5th Circuit 2005).

(g) Finally, this Act is not directed at primary conduct of physicians or individual health-care providers.

Section 3. Definitions.

As used in this Act only:

(a) "**Abortion**" means the act of using or prescribing any instrument, medicine, drug, or any other substance, device, or means with the intent to terminate the clinically diagnosable pregnancy of a woman with the knowledge that the termination by those means will with reasonable likelihood cause the death of the unborn child. Such use, prescription, or means is not an abortion if done with the intent to:

(1) Save the life or preserve the health of an unborn child;

(2) Remove a dead unborn child caused by spontaneous abortion; or

(3) Remove an ectopic pregnancy.

Further, an "**elective abortion**" means an abortion performed for reasons other than rape, incest, or threats to the life of the mother [*or insert specific exemption language from State law*].

(b) "**Affiliate**" means an organization that owns or controls, or is owned or controlled, in whole or in part, by the other; related by shareholdings or other means of control; or a subsidiary, parent, or sibling corporation.

(c) "**Associate**" means enter into any written or oral contract or agreement with another contractor, individual, organization, or entity that provides, induces, refers for, or counsels on behalf of abortions; exert any degree of ownership of or control over another contractor, individual, organization, or entity that provides, induces, refers for, or counsels on behalf of abortions; or own, direct, or control shares in another contractor, individual, organization, or entity that provides, induces, refers for, or counsels on behalf of abortions.

(d) "**Department**" means the [*Insert name of State*] Department of Health [*or insert name of responsible Department or agency*].

(e) "**Family planning contractor**" and "**contractor**" mean an individual, organization, or entity that enters into a contract or agreement with the [*Department of Health or other responsible department or agency*] to receive funds for and provide family planning services.

(f) "**Family planning services**" means a range of acceptable methods to prevent, delay, space, or otherwise time pregnancy, including natural family planning methods and infertility services. Family planning services do not include abortion, abortion referrals, or counseling in favor of abortion.

(g) "**Federal family planning funds**" means any federal money appropriated or dispersed by any state official, branch, department, or agency, in whole or in part, for family planning services, including (but not limited to) funds under Title X, Title XX, or other federal money accepted by the state, in whole or in part, for family planning services.

(h) "**State family planning funds**" means funds dispersed under [*Insert references to specific state statute(s) regarding State family planning funds or State family planning policies or programs*].

Section 4. Prohibitions on Use of Funds.

(a) No federal or state family planning funds shall be used by contractors of the Department to pay the direct or indirect costs (including, but not limited to, administrative costs and expenses, overhead, employee salaries, rent, telephone and other utilities) of performing, inducing, referring for, or counseling in favor of abortion procedures.

(b) No state family planning funds shall be granted, appropriated, or distributed to contractors or affiliates of contractors that perform, induce, refer for, or counsel in favor of elective abortions.

Section 5. Limited Waiver.

If the Department concludes that compliance with Subsection 4(b) would result in a significant reduction in family planning services in any public health region of the State, the Department may waive the requirements of Subsection 4(b) for the affected region to the extent necessary to avoid a significant reduction in family planning services to the region. This waiver shall expire on [*Insert appropriate year, date, or time period*], and no waiver shall extend beyond that date.

Section 6. Mandatory Certification of Compliance.

(a) A family planning contractor, individual, organization, or entity applying for federal family planning funds appropriated and distributed by the Department must certify in writing on forms provided by the Department that it will not, directly or indirectly, use the funds to perform, induce, refer for abortion, or counsel in favor of abortions. Recipients of federal family planning funds through the Department will annually submit a written certification of continued compliance. Funds shall not be granted to any family planning contractor, individual, organization, or entity until the required certification has been received.

(b) A family planning contractor, individual, organization, or entity applying for state family planning funds must certify in writing on forms provided by the Department that it will not perform, induce, refer for, or counsel in favor of elective abortions and will not associate with, contract with, or provide financial or other support to individuals, organizations, or entities performing, inducing, referring for, or counseling in favor of elective abortions. Recipients of state family planning funds through the Department will annually submit a written certification of continued compliance. Funds shall not be granted to any family planning contractor, individual, organization, or entity until required certification has been received.

(c) The Department shall include in its financial audit a review of the use of appropriated federal and state funds to ensure compliance with this Act.

Section 7. Failure to Comply/Recoupment of Funds.

(a) A family planning contractor that receives any family planning funds and is found not to be in compliance with the requirements of this Act will be enjoined from receiving any future family planning funds and will be liable to return to the State the full amount of family planning funds received.

(b) Both the Office of the Attorney General and the Office of the District Attorney [*or other appropriate designation such as "County Attorney"*] for the county in which the violation occurred may institute a legal action to enforce recoupment, collection, or reimbursement of

family planning funds.

Section 8. Penalties for Failure to Comply.

(a) In addition to any and all remedies available under the common or statutory law of this State, failure to comply with the requirements of this Act shall:

(1) Enjoin the family planning contractor, individual, organization, or entity from eligibility to receive any future family planning funds; and

(2) Require the family planning contractor, individual, organization, or entity to reimburse the State the full amount of family planning funds received through the Department.

(b) Any violation of this Act may subject the family planning contractor, individual, organization, or entity to a civil penalty or fine up to [*Insert appropriate amount*] imposed by the [*Insert name of Department of Health or other appropriate state department or agency*].

(c) Both the Office of the Attorney General and the Office of the District Attorney for the county in which the violation occurred may institute a legal action to enforce collection of civil penalties or fines.

Section 9. Construction.

(a) Nothing in this Act shall be construed as creating or recognizing a right to abortion.

(b) Nothing in this Act shall be construed as creating or recognizing a right to funds for family planning services.

Section 10. Right of Intervention.

The Legislature, by joint resolution, may appoint one or more of its members, who sponsored or cosponsored this Act in his or her official capacity, to intervene as a matter of right in any case in which the constitutionality of this law is challenged.

Section 11. Severability.

Any provision of the Act held to be invalid or unenforceable by its terms, or as applied to any person or circumstance, shall be construed so as to give it the maximum effect permitted by law, unless such holding shall be one of utter invalidity or unenforceability in which event such provision shall be deemed severable herefrom and shall not affect the remainder hereof or the application of such provision to other persons not similarly situated or to other, dissimilar circumstances.

Section 12. Effective Date.

This Act takes effect on [*Insert appropriate date*].

JOINT RESOLUTION HONORING PREGNANCY CARE CENTERS

JOINT RESOLUTION No. ______
By Representatives/Senators ___________

WHEREAS, the life-affirming impact of pregnancy care centers on the women, men, children, and communities they serve is considerable and growing;

WHEREAS, pregnancy care centers serve women in [*Insert name of State*] and across the United States with integrity and compassion;

WHEREAS, more than 2,500 pregnancy care centers across the United States provide comprehensive care to women and men facing unplanned pregnancies, including resources to meet their physical, psychological, emotional, and spiritual needs;

WHEREAS, pregnancy care centers offer women free, confidential, and compassionate services, including pregnancy tests, peer counseling, 24-hour telephone hotlines, childbirth and parenting classes, and referrals to community, healthcare, and other support services;

WHEREAS, many medical pregnancy care centers offer ultrasounds and other medical services;

WHEREAS, many pregnancy care centers provide information on adoption and adoption referrals to pregnant women;

WHEREAS, pregnancy care centers encourage women to make positive life choices by equipping them with complete and accurate information regarding their pregnancy options and the development of their unborn children;

WHEREAS, pregnancy care centers provide women with compassionate and confidential peer counseling in a nonjudgmental manner regardless of their pregnancy outcomes;

WHEREAS, pregnancy care centers provide important support and resources for women who choose childbirth over abortion;

WHEREAS, pregnancy care centers ensure that women are receiving prenatal information and services that lead to the birth of healthy infants;

WHEREAS, many pregnancy care centers provide grief assistance for women and men who regret the loss of their children from past choices they have made;

WHEREAS, many pregnancy care centers work to prevent unplanned pregnancies by teaching effective abstinence education in public schools;

WHEREAS, both federal and state governments are increasingly recognizing the valuable services of pregnancy care centers through the designation of public funds for such organizations;

WHEREAS, pregnancy care centers operate primarily through reliance on the voluntary donations and time of caring individuals who are committed to caring for the needs of women and promoting and protecting life. [; and]

[OPTIONAL (*consider adding only in states where PCCs have been publically accused by a legislator, abortion-advocacy group, or another party of false advertising or other deceptive practices)*: WHEREAS, pregnancy care centers provide full disclosure, in both their advertisements and direct contact with women, of the types of services they provide].

NOW, THEREFORE, BE IT RESOLVED BY THE LEGISLATURE OF THE STATE OF [*Insert name of State*]:

Section 1. That the [*Legislature*] strongly supports pregnancy care centers in their unique, positive contributions to the individual lives of women, men, and babies—both born and unborn.

Section 2. That the [*Legislature*] commends the compassionate work of tens of thousands of volunteers and paid staff at pregnancy care centers in [*Insert name of State*] and across the United States.

Section 3. That the [*Legislature*] strongly encourages the Congress of the United States and other federal and state government agencies to grant pregnancy care centers assistance for medical equipment and abstinence education in a manner that does not compromise the mission or religious integrity of these organizations.

Section 4. That the [*Legislature*] disapproves of the actions of any national, state, or local groups attempting to prevent pregnancy care centers from effectively serving women and men facing unplanned pregnancies.

Section 5. That the Secretary of State of [*Insert name of State*] transmit a copy of this resolution to each pregnancy care center in [*Insert name of State*], to the Governor, to the President of the United States, and to the President of the Senate, and the Speaker of the House of Representatives of the United States Congress.

Legal Recognition of UNBORN & NEWLY BORN

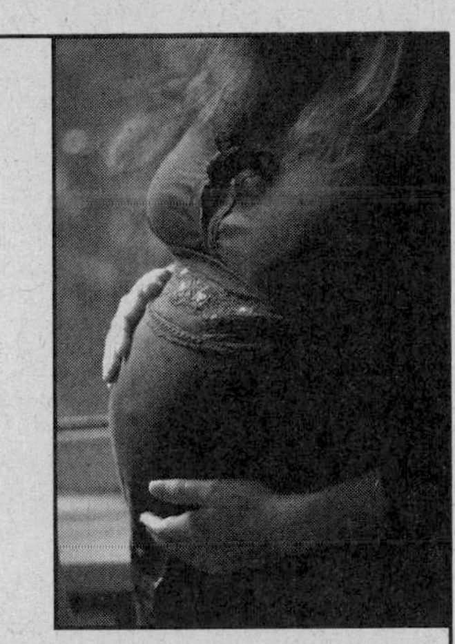

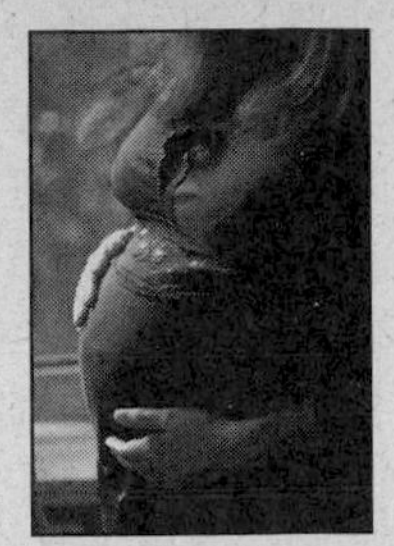

Legal Recognition of Unborn & Newly Born

Teresa Keeler was eight months pregnant when she was beaten unconscious by her jealous ex-husband, Robert Keeler, who told her during the attack that he was going to "stomp it out of her." Later, at the hospital, Keeler delivered her daughter, who was stillborn and suffered from a fractured skull. Prosecutors attempted to charge Robert Keeler for the beating of his ex-wife and for the murder of her unborn daughter. However, this was 1969 and California did not yet have an unborn victims of violence law (*i.e.* fetal homicide statute).

The California Supreme Court ultimately dismissed the murder charge against Robert Keeler, ruling that only someone who had been born-alive could be murdered, as the state criminal code then defined the offense. Intense public pressure resulted in a change to the state's homicide statute which now recognizes an unborn child as a potential victim. It was this amended law that was used, in 2004, to successfully prosecute Scott Peterson for the murders of his wife, Laci Peterson, and their unborn son, Conner. That case galvanized national attention on the need for these types of protective laws and led to the enactment of the federal "Unborn Victims of Violence Act."

As the pro-life movement focuses significant time and attention on protecting unborn children from abortion and laments existing constraints on its ability to provide full legal protection to the unborn in this context, it is often easy to forget there are many opportunities to protect and to provide legal recognition and protection for unborn and newly-born children (outside the context of abortion). Among these opportunities are enacting state unborn victims of violence protections; permitting assailants to be prosecuted for nonfatal assaults on the unborn; providing a civil cause of action in the death of an unborn child because of the negligence of a third party (such as a drunk driver); and requiring that infants who survive an abortion are given proper medical care and attention.

This Section outlines these opportunities to protect the unborn and newly born and provides resources for their enactment.

Primer on Legal Recognition of Unborn & Newly Born

By Denise M. Burke
Vice President of Legal Affairs, Americans United for Life

The unimaginable grief and suffering endured by Laci and Conner Peterson's family was, largely due to their own courageous advocacy, transformed into a blow for justice on behalf of unborn victims of criminal violence. In April 2004, President Bush signed the "Unborn Victims of Violence Act", more commonly known as "Laci and Conner's Law," and filled an important gap in federal law. Federal prosecutors may now charge an assailant in the death of an unborn child when the death occurs on federal property, such as a military installations, or when the death stems from the commission of a federal crime.

More importantly, Laci and Conner lived in a state (California) where prosecutors could press murder charges for the deaths of both this young mother and her unborn son. Thirty-six states carry such provisions in their criminal law, often referred to as "fetal homicide laws." As for the remaining 14 states, Laci Peterson's mother, Sharon Rocha, has said it best, that they are in effect telling grieving families that "innocent victims [like Conner] are not really victims—indeed that they never existed at all."

Unborn victims of violence laws are just one example of how states may establish the legal "personhood" of an unborn child, providing them with legal recognition and protection outside the context of abortion. There are several more available under both criminal and civil law.

Issues

Fetal Homicide

In recent years, several high-profile cases from across the nation have highlighted the need for laws protecting unborn victims from criminal violence. Currently, 36 states provide some degree of protection for unborn victims of homicide.

Under common law,[1] the killing of an unborn child was not considered a homicide unless the child was first born alive and then died as a result of a criminal prenatal act. This rule, called "the born-alive rule," is still followed in a majority of states that have not enacted special legislation to protect unborn children from criminal violence. Thus, if someone shoots a pregnant woman, killing her child, he or she is not subject to criminal prosecution for the murder of the child unless the child is first born alive and then dies as a result of the injuries which the child sustained before birth. The purpose of the laws protecting unborn victims of homicide, also known as "fetal homicide laws," is to overturn the common law born-alive rule and criminalize conduct causing the death of an unborn child. These laws are not directed at abortion which, under current constitutional doctrine, is protected.

AUL has drafted the "Crimes Against the Unborn Child Act," providing protection to the unborn (from conception) from fatal and nonfatal criminal assaults.

Nonfatal Assaults on the Unborn

On occasion, the assailant's attack does not result in the death of the unborn child, but instead injures the child *in utero* (perhaps also resulting in a premature delivery). In such instances, 21 states permit the prosecution of the assailant for assault.

One-Victim Laws

A minority of jurisdictions—11 states—have enacted one-victim laws that permit prosecutions and enhanced penalties in cases where a woman is assaulted and suffers a miscarriage, stillbirth, or "damage to [her] pregnancy." Notably, of these states, six do not have another law (such as a fetal homicide law) that recognizes the unborn child as a second victim of the attack.[2]

Use of Force to Protect the Unborn

All 50 states permit the use of force (including, when appropriate, deadly force) in specified circumstances: for self defense, in the defense of others, or when a person reasonably believes force is being used or imminently will be used against them or someone else. In 2002, a Michigan court examined the applicability of these affirmative defenses (to criminal liability) to the use of force to protect the unborn.

In 1999, Jaclyn Kurr suffered a miscarriage after being physically attacked by her boyfriend, Antonio Pena. Jaclyn was more than 16 weeks pregnant with quadruplets when Pena punched her stomach multiple times during an argument. Jaclyn stabbed Pena in defense of her unborn children. Pena subsequently died, and Jaclyn was charged with and found guilty of manslaughter. On appeal, the Michigan Court of Appeals held that Jaclyn, as a pregnant woman, was justified in using force—in this case, deadly force—to protect the lives of her unborn children.[3]

This ruling brought attention to an area of law that had long been neglected. Applying the affirmative defense of "defense of others" to protect the unborn is a victory for women and children, and opens a new chapter in the fight to protect the lives of the unborn

In April 2009, Oklahoma enacted AUL's "Pregnant Woman's Protection Act" that specifically provides that women may use force to protect their unborn children from criminal assaults.

Born-Alive Infant Protection

Jill Stanek, a nurse at Christ Hospital in Oak Lawn, Illinois, held a tiny, 21-week-old baby boy in her hands. He weighed about half a pound and was around ten inches long. "He was too weak to move very much, expending any energy he had trying to breathe," Jill recalled. The baby had survived an abortion and was going to be left alone in a filthy utility room because his parents did not want to hold him as he died, and the attending nurse was too busy to bother with him. Jill intervened. "I could not stand the thought of this suffering child dying alone in the soiled utility room, so I cradled and rocked him for the 45 minutes that he lived," she testified before the House of Representatives. "Toward the end, he was so quiet, I couldn't tell if he was alive unless I held him up to the light to see if I could see his heart beating through his chest wall."[4]

To her horror, Jill discovered that babies who were born alive as a result of failed abortions were routinely left alone to die on the cold metal countertop in the hospital's utility room.[5] Distraught and filled with disbelief, Jill spoke out against the practice and was subsequently fired.

Jill worked to have the hospital prosecuted for violating "Illinois Abortion Law of 1975," which required physicians to provide medical care for born-alive infants. However, then-Illinois Attorney General Jim Ryan found that there was "no basis for legal action."[6] Similarly, the Office for Civil Rights at the U.S. Department of Health and Human Services wrote a letter to Jill stating that federal "civil rights laws do not cover abortions or the rights of newborns."[7]

Undeterred, Jill took her story all the way to the U.S. House of Representatives in 2001, where she testified in support of the "Federal Born-Alive Infants Protection Act" (BAIPA).

The Federal Born-Alive Infants Protection Act (BAIPA) of 2002

The federal BAIPA clarifies that, for the purposes of "any Act of Congress, or any ruling, regulation, or interpretation of the various administrative bureaus and agencies of the United States," the legal terms "person," "human being," "child" and "individual" include infants who are born alive at any stage of development, including those born as a result of a failed abortion. Through this definition, the Act requires that infants who are born alive as a result of a failed abortion must be given immediate and complete medical care and attention.

On March 12, 2002, the federal BAIPA passed the House of Representatives by a resounding voice vote. Later, on June 19, 2002, it was approved by a 98-0 vote in the U.S. Senate. All Democrats were present for that vote, and all of them—including Senators Hillary Clinton, Ted Kennedy, Barbara Boxer and John Kerry—voted in favor of the bill. On the Senate floor, Sen. Boxer voiced her strong support for the bill, exclaiming, "Who would be more vulnerable than a newborn baby?" She continued, stating that "all of our people deserve protection, from the very tiniest infant to the most elderly among us."[8]

State Born-Alive Infant Protection Acts

Since its enactment, the federal BAIPA has been used as a model for similar state legislation. Currently, the majority of the states have some form of a BAIPA. At least 24 states have laws creating a specific affirmative duty of physicians to provide medical care and treatment to born-alive infants at any stage of development, and at least 3 states require such care and treatment after viability. One state protects born-alive infants at any stage of development from "deliberate acts" undertaken by a physician that result in the death of the infant, but does not create a specific affirmative duty to provide care and treatment.

Like their federal counterpart, state BAIPAs specifically declare they do not implicate or infringe on the right to abortion. For example, the Illinois BAIPA contains two "neutrality clauses"—one of which is identical to that in the federal BAIPA, and a second one which reinforces the point that *Roe v. Wade* and the right to abortion are not implicated or altered by the

BAIPA. This second clause specifically states: "Nothing in this Section shall be construed to affect existing federal or State law regarding abortions."[9]

State BAIPAs are necessary for a several reasons. First, as a federal law, the federal BAIPA only applies in limited circumstances. For example, the federal BAIPA would only extend to those hospitals and employees operated by the federal government, or which receive federal funding; it would not prohibit private or state-operated clinics and hospitals from denying care or medical attention to born-alive infants. Second, the states can enact state versions of the BAIPA that are more comprehensive and protective than the federal version. Lastly, state versions of federal laws function as reinforcement mechanisms for their federal counterpart. The federal government has limited resources for law enforcement and prosecution so state BAIPAs will help ensure the intent and requirements of BAIPAs are enforced, and violators are prosecuted.

To assist states in enacting a BAIPA, AUL has drafted the "Born-Alive Infant Protection Act."

Prevention and Treatment of Maternal Drug and Alcohol Abuse

In recent years, a number of states have passed laws providing protection for women and their children from the ravages of drug and alcohol abuse. The intent of most of these laws is not to criminalize the mother's use of drugs and/or alcohol, but to provide, encourage, and, in some cases, mandate reporting and treatment. Notably, 20 states fund special drug and alcohol treatment programs for pregnant women and newborns.

Civil Causes of Action for the Wrongful Death of an Unborn Child

By court decision or statute, 38 states allow a wrongful death (civil) cause of action for the death of an unborn child.[10] Of these, 29 states allow a wrongful death suit if the child is viable; 9 states allow suits for a pre-viable unborn child; and 12 states still require a live birth, barring a cause of action for the death of the unborn child unless the child is born alive and dies thereafter.

To assist states in providing for this civil cause of action, AUL has drafted the "Unborn Wrongful Death Act."

Refusal to Recognize Wrongful Life or Wrongful Birth Lawsuits

A number of states also refuse to recognize wrongful life or wrongful birth causes of action. Wrongful life is an "action…brought by or on behalf of the child…[who] alleges, because of the defendant's negligence, his parents either decided to conceive him ignorant of the risk of an impairment or birth defect, or were deprived of information during gestation that would have prompted them to terminate the pregnancy."[11] Simply put, in a wrongful life action, a child is arguing that (1) the pregnancy should have been terminated; (2) that "but for the defendant's negligence" the plaintiff would not have been born; and (3) the plaintiff's life would have been better not lived.

Meanwhile, wrongful birth is an "action brought by the parent of a child born with an impairment or birth defect." The basic argument made by the parent is that he/she would have aborted the child if he/she had known that the child would be disabled.[12] Since the birth defect is naturally occurring, "[t]he parent alleges that the negligence of those charged with prenatal testing or genetic counseling deprived them of the right to make a timely decision regarding whether to terminate a pregnancy because of the likelihood their child would be born physically or mentally impaired."[13]

Wrongful life and wrongful birth claims raise significant issues because the core argument attacks the sanctity of life of every human person—these claims assert that some lives are better off not lived, that the disabled are better off dead.[14] To term children with disabilities "defective" and advocate for their elimination prior to birth is to dangerously re-classify the disabled as less human, to grant these citizens fewer rights, and to attribute a lower value to their lives and contributions to humanity. "[15]

Currently, 29 states have either refused to recognize or limited a wrongful life action, while 3 states expressly permit this controversial cause of action.

Unfortunately, wrongful birth causes of action have found significantly greater acceptance by state courts, legislatures, and the public. Thirty-two states permit wrongful birth causes of action, while only eleven states expressly prohibit such causes of action.

MYTHS & FACTS

Myth: Laws extending legal recognition and protection to unborn children are unconstitutional because they give legal status to an unborn child and/or contradict the established tenets of *Roe v. Wade*.

Fact: Despite numerous challenges, no law protecting unborn children outside the context of abortion have been struck down as unconstitutional. Moreover, these laws do not directly implicate the right to choose an abortion. For example, unborn victims of violence laws, also known as fetal homicide laws, specifically exclude the performance of a legal abortion from potential criminal liability. They also do not apply to conduct to which the mother of the unborn child (or her legal guardian) consents, such as medical treatment or an abortion.

Myth: Crimes that result in the death of or injury to an unborn child are merely offenses against the pregnant woman, with death or harm to the unborn child being an incidental or accidental consequence.

Fact: The failed effort by Senator Dianne Feinstein (D-CA) to gut "Laci and Conner's Law" (by making assault on a pregnant woman an "enhanced offense" if her unborn child also dies) sought to perpetuate this view. Nothing, in fact, could be further from the truth. In many cases involving violence against pregnant women, the assailant attacks a pregnant woman with the intent of killing the unborn child by causing a miscarriage or stillbirth. In some, the woman refused to have an abortion and the child's father, rather than respecting her choice, reacts violently to end the pregnancy. In these situations, women have been savagely beaten, pushed down flights of stairs, and suffered blows, stab wounds, and gunshots targeted to the abdomen. Sometimes, this violence takes a less savage, but no less deadly turn. For example, in 2002 an Ohio physician whose pregnant girlfriend had refused to have an abortion spiked her drink with a prescription drug known to cause miscarriage.

Myth: Now that we have the federal "Unborn Victims of Violence Act," there is no need to pass similar state protections.
Fact: Murder and assaults, except in limited circumstances, are typically state crimes. The vast majority of the criminal prosecutions for homicide and assault take place in state courts, not in federal courts, so it is critical that each state protect the unborn from criminal violence. Conversely, "Laci and Conner's Law" only applies to federal crimes and federal jurisdictions, such as military installations.

Thus, the biggest impact of "Laci and Conner's Law" may be in its revisions to the Uniform Code of Military Justice (UCMJ). Military prosecutors can now pursue charges against military personnel stationed anywhere in the world if their actions cause the death of an unborn child; previously, they were limited to filing such charges only in those states with laws protecting unborn victims of violence. A case such as that of Airman Gregory L. Roberts, who in 1996 savagely beat his pregnant wife, rupturing her uterus and killing their unborn daughter, resulted in manslaughter charges only because Ohio, where he was stationed, had a fetal homicide law on its books. Had Roberts been stationed in Colorado or North Carolina—states with a significant military presence, but no laws protecting an unborn child from violence—he could not have been charged with his daughter's death and would have faced prosecution only for the assault on his wife.

Myth: There are no supposed adult abortion survivors.
Fact: There are many adult abortion survivors. For example, Gianna Jessen of California, born April 6, 1977, is a saline abortion survivor. Gianna's biological mother had a third-trimester saline abortion at the age of 17. After being burned alive for 18 hours in the womb from the saline solution, Gianna was born alive in a Los Angeles County abortion clinic. The procedure left her with cerebral palsy, which led doctors to assert that she would never be able to hold up her head, sit up, crawl, or walk. However, Gianna began to walk with the assistance of braces and a walker by the age of three and now runs marathons across the world.[16]

Myth: Pro-abortion advocates strongly oppose BAIPAs.
Fact: Not all pro-abortion advocates oppose BAIPAs. For example, the National Abortion Rights Action League (NARAL) publicly supported the federal BAIPA, stating in a July 20, 2000 press release that "NARAL does not oppose passage of the Born Alive Infants Protection Act" because the Act "is not targeted at *Roe v. Wade* or a woman's right to choose."[17]

Myth: The requirements of BAIPAs may put the mother's life at risk in some circumstances.
Fact: Physicians are not liable for denying a born-alive infant medical care and treatment if, in the physician's reasonable judgment, such denial was necessary to protect the life of the mother.

Endnotes

[1] As distinguished from laws created by the enactments of legislatures, the common law comprises the body of those principles and rules of action, relating the government and security of persons and property, that derive their authority solely from usages and customs of immemorial antiquity, or from the judgments and decrees of courts recognizing, affirming, and enforcing such usages and customs. The most common source of American common law is English common law.

[2] These states are Arkansas, Colorado, Indiana, Iowa, Kansas, Maine, Michigan, Mississippi, New Hampshire, New Mexico,

and Wyoming. Five states, Arkansas, Indiana, Kansas, Michigan, and Mississippi, have so-called one-victim laws on the books, but also define certain offenses against the unborn child as "homicide."

[3] *See State v. Kurr*, 654 N.W.2d 651, 657 (Mich. Ct. App. 2002).

[4] Testimony of Jill Stanek during the hearing before the Subcommittee on the Constitution on the Committee on the Judiciary, U.S. House of Representatives, 107th Congress, on H.R. 2175 (Born Alive Infant Protection Act), July 12, 2001, Serial No. 32, at 19.

[5] *Id.* One instance involved the failed abortion of a baby boy who was supposed to have spina bifida. What appeared on the ultrasound to be a mass on the baby's back was actually an incompletely formed twin. The healthy baby was born alive with an intact spine after the failed abortion procedure, and was left to die on the cold countertop of the utility room.

[6] *Id.* at 25, 42

[7] *Id.* at 25, 41.

[8] Congressional Record, S7062-S7064, June 28, 2001. In addition, Sen. Kennedy stated, "Madam President, I am going to urge the Senate to accept the amendment tomorrow. I think we had a good discussion about it. I hope that we will move ahead and accept it."

[9] 5 ILCS 70 § 1.36 (d).

[10] *See* Dena M. Marks, *Person v. Potential: Judicial Struggles to Decide Claims Arising from the Death of an Embryo or Fetus and Michigan's Struggle to Settle the Question*, 37 Akron L. Rev. 41 (2004). *See also* Amber Dina, *Wrongful Death and the Legal Status of the Previable Embryo*, 19 Regent U. L. Rev. 251 (2006/2007). (Nebraska and Texas have changed their law by statute since 2004).

[11] *See e.g., Willis v. Wu*, 607 S.E.2d 63, 66 (S.C. Dist. Ct. 1980).

[12] *Id.*

[13] *Id.*

[14] *Id.*

[15] Darpana M. Sheth, *Better Off Unborn? An Analysis of Wrongful Birth and Wrongful Life Claims Under the Americans with Disabilities Act*, 73 Tenn. L. Rev. 641, n.23 (2006) (arguing that wrongful birth and wrongful life claims violate the "Americans with Disabilities Act").

[16] Gianna Jessen's Biography, available at http://www.giannajessen.com/EPK/bio.html (last visited August 19, 2009), and *Gianna Jessen's Story*, available at http://bornalivetruth.org/giannastory.aspx (last visited August 19, 2009).

[17] *Timeline on the Federal Born-Alive Infants Protection Act*, National Right to Life Committee, *available at* http://www.nrlc.org/ObamaBAIPA/TimelineFederalBAIPA.html (last visited August 19, 2009).

Legal Recognition of Unborn & Newly Born Talking Points

Unborn Victims of Violence Protections (Fetal homicide and assault statutes)

- Unborn victims of violence laws do not directly impact or implicate the woman's right to choose abortion. These laws deal with criminal violence against a woman and her unborn child, not legal abortion. Indeed, these laws uniformly and specifically exclude legal abortion from potential criminal liability.

- These laws recognize that criminal violence against pregnant women inherently involves and endangers two victims—the woman and her unborn child. Importantly, in a significant number of assaults against pregnant women, the assailant's true target is the unborn child.

- While 36 states recognize the unborn child as a separate victim of criminal violence against a pregnant woman, a minority of states (six states) statutorily recognize only one victim of such assaults. In these states, an assault on a pregnant woman that results in a miscarriage or stillbirth is typically considered an enhanced offense for sentencing purposes.

- Despite repeated challenges, no state or federal law criminalizing violence against an unborn child has been declared unconstitutional by any court.

- Typically, unborn victims of violence laws do not apply to any act committed by the mother of an unborn child; to any medical procedure (including abortion) performed by a physician (or other licensed medical professional) at the request of the pregnant woman (or her legal guardian); or to the lawful dispensation or administration of lawfully prescribed medication.

- The authority of the states to prohibit self-abortion or other conduct by the pregnant woman herself which may be injurious to the life or health of her unborn child is unclear. It should be noted that prior to *Roe*, women were not prosecuted for self-abortion. In the absence of special legislation, courts generally have refused to hold a pregnant woman liable under child neglect or other criminal statutes for prenatal injuries, regardless of how inflicted. Thus, to avoid any possible constitutional problems, laws protecting unborn victims of violence are intended to reach nonconsensual conduct only and typically exclude conduct of the pregnant woman herself.

Pregnant Woman's Protection Act (Use of Force to Protect the Unborn)

- In *People v. Kurr*, the Michigan Court of Appeals recognized that women are justified in using (deadly) force when necessary to protect the lives of their unborn children from criminal violence.[1] Moreover, in April 2009, the Oklahoma legislature unanimously passed AUL's "Pregnant Woman's Protection Act," statutorily acknowledging a pregnant woman's right to use force, including deadly force, to protect her unborn child.

- The statutes of all 50 states allow the use of force (and deadly force) in certain circumstances for self-defense, in defense of others, and in defense of property. In *Kurr*, the court applied the "defense of others" theory to situations where a woman believes that the life of her unborn child is at risk.

- Permitting a woman to use force to protect her unborn child is not the only instance where legal status has been granted to the unborn. For example, the federal "Unborn Victims of Violence Act" as well as the laws of 36 states recognize an unborn child as a separate victim of criminal violence and treat the killing of an unborn child as a form of homicide.

- Michigan courts have held that a woman's use of (deadly) force to protect her unborn child is constitutional, does not affect the right to abortion, and does not criminalize abortion. The use of (deadly) force to protect the unborn is a narrow defense available solely to the pregnant woman. Even then, the defense is available only against the unlawful use of (deadly) force. Thus, allowing such a defense in no way implicates a woman's right to choose legal abortion and in no way affects the performance of legal abortions.

- The use of (deadly) force to protect the unborn does not apply to the defense of embryos that exist outside of a woman's body (*i.e.,* frozen embryos). Thus, case and statutory law on this issue will not interfere with any research or reproductive endeavors that involve frozen embryos.

Born-Alive Infant Protection (BAIPA)

- Federal and state BAIPAs in no way implicate, alter, or infringe upon the right to abortion, and in no way affect the holdings of *Roe v. Wade* or its progeny. All BAIPAs contain neutrality clauses clarifying this. For example, Section C of the federal BAIPA states: "Nothing in this [S]ection shall be construed to affirm, deny, expand, or contract any legal status or legal right applicable to any member of the species *homo sapiens* at any point prior to being born alive as defined by this Section."

- Even the National Abortion Rights Action League-Pro Choice America (NARAL) has acknowledged that BAIPAs do not violate the right to choose abortion. For example, NARAL stated in a July 20, 2000 press release that it did not "oppose passage of the [federal] Born Alive Infants Protection Act" because the Act "is not targeted at *Roe v. Wade* or a woman's right to choose."[2]

- Once a living human being is outside of the mother, it is no longer a "fetus" but a "person," an American citizen with civil rights to equal protection under the law.

- The denial of basic medical care to born-alive infants which causes their death—regardless of whether they were born as a result of natural or induced labor, cesarean section, or induced abortion—is infanticide.

- The right to abortion is the right of a pregnant woman to decide "whether or not to terminate a pregnancy."[3] However, when the child is no longer in the womb (as a result of the birth process or an attempted abortion), the woman is no longer pregnant and her right to choose an abortion does not translate to a right to a dead child. The right to abortion does not extend so far as to justify the denial of civil rights and other legal protection to born, living human persons.

- BAIPAs are unique from other laws because they create a specific affirmative duty for physicians to provide medical care and treatment to born-alive infants.

- BAIPAs do not endanger the lives of women. BAIPA's contain exceptions for the life or the health of the mother. Physicians are not liable for denying a born-alive infant medical care and treatment if, in the physician's reasonable judgment, such denial was necessary to protect the life of the mother.

- The majority of the states have some form of a BAIPA. At least 24 states have laws creating a specific affirmative duty of physicians to provide medical care and treatment to born-alive infants at any stage of development,[4] and at least 3 states require such care and treatment after the child is viable.[5]

Endnotes

[1] 654 N.W.2d 651, 657 (Mich. Ct. App. 2002).

[2] *Timeline on the Federal Born-Alive Infants Protection Act*, National Right to Life Committee, *available at* http://www.nrlc.org/ObamaBAIPA/TimelineFederalBAIPA.html (last visited August 19, 2009).

[3] *Roe v. Wade*, 410 U.S. 113 (1973).

[4] Alabama, Arizona, California, Delaware, Georgia, Illinois, Indiana, Kansas, Louisiana, Maine, Michigan, Mississippi, Missouri, Montana, Nebraska, New York, Oklahoma, Pennsylvania, Rhode Island, South Dakota, Tennessee, Texas, Washington, and Wisconsin.

[5] Florida, Iowa, Indiana, Montana, North Dakota, and Nevada.

Fetal Homicide

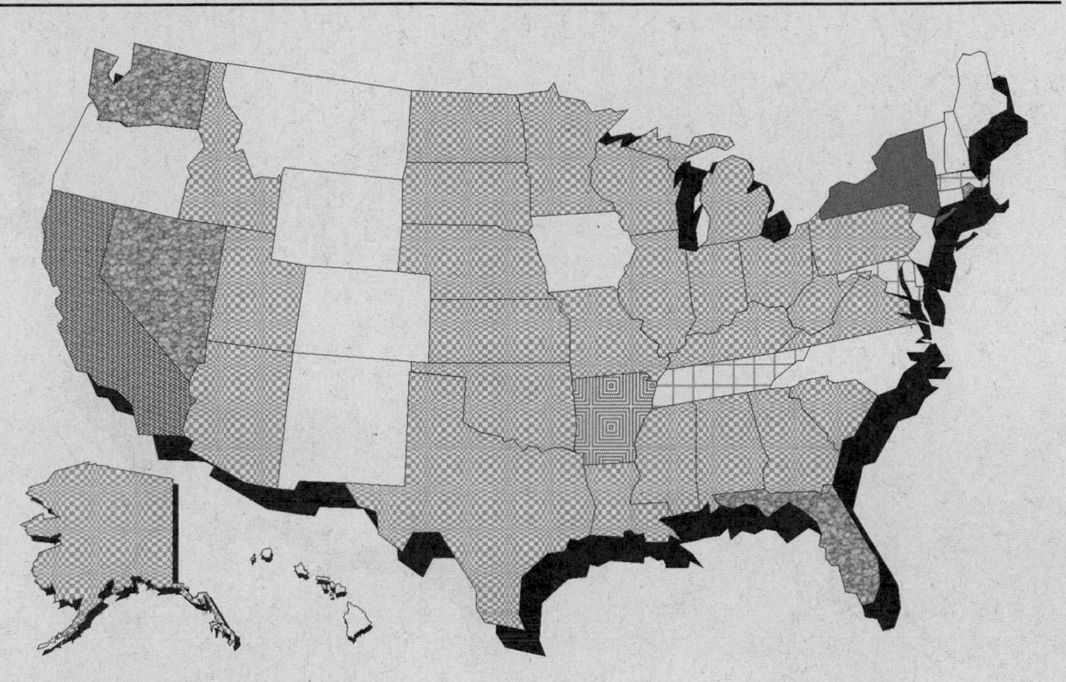

Thirty-six states treat the killing of an unborn child as a form of homicide:

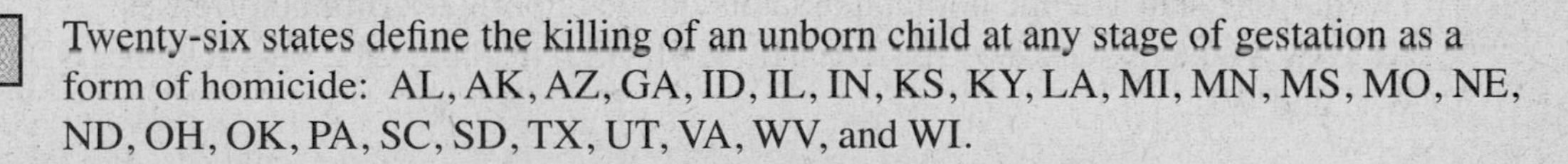

Twenty-six states define the killing of an unborn child at any stage of gestation as a form of homicide: AL, AK, AZ, GA, ID, IL, IN, KS, KY, LA, MI, MN, MS, MO, NE, ND, OH, OK, PA, SC, SD, TX, UT, VA, WV, and WI.

One state defines the killing of an unborn child after the embryonic stage (seven to eight weeks) as a form of homicide: CA.

One state defines the killing of an unborn child after 12 weeks of gestation as a form of homicide: AR.

Four states define the killing of an unborn child after "quickening" (discernible movement within the womb) as a form of homicide: FL, NV, RI, and WA.

Three states define the killing of an unborn child after viability as a form of homicide: MD, MA, and TN.

One state defines the killing of an unborn child after 24 weeks gestation as a form of gestation: NY.

Nonfatal Assaults on the Unborn

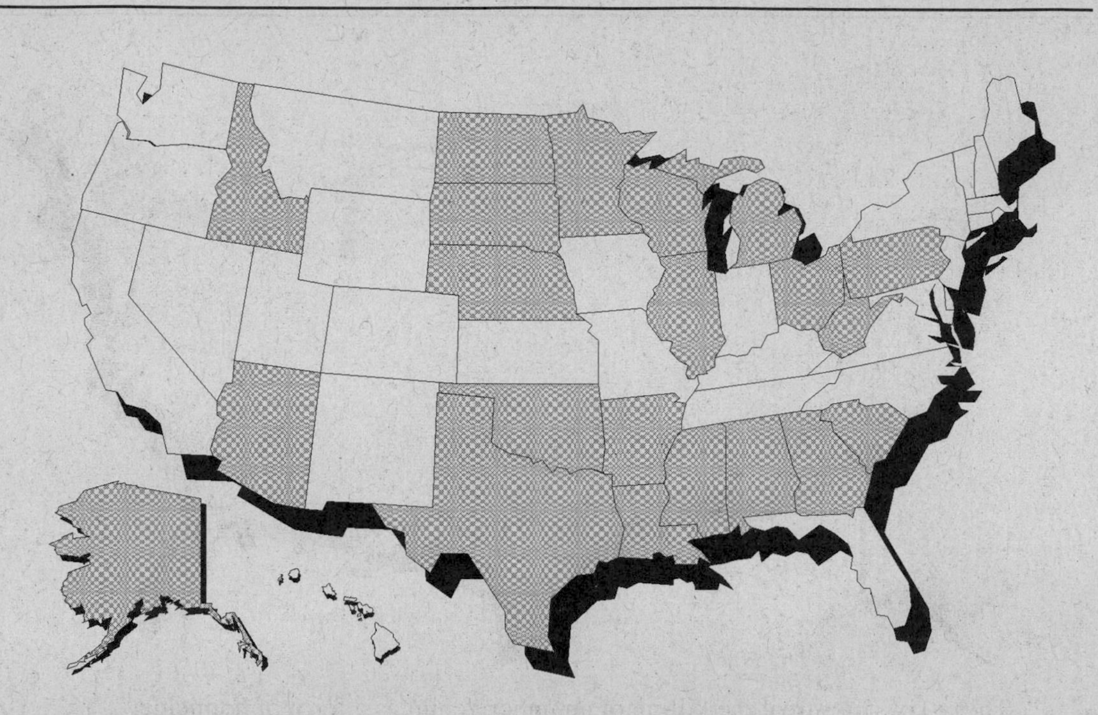

Twenty-one states define nonfatal assaults on the unborn as criminal offenses: AL, AK, AZ, AR, GA, ID, IL, LA, MI, MN, MS, NE, ND, OH, OK, PA, SC, SD, TX, WV, and WI.

One-Victim Laws

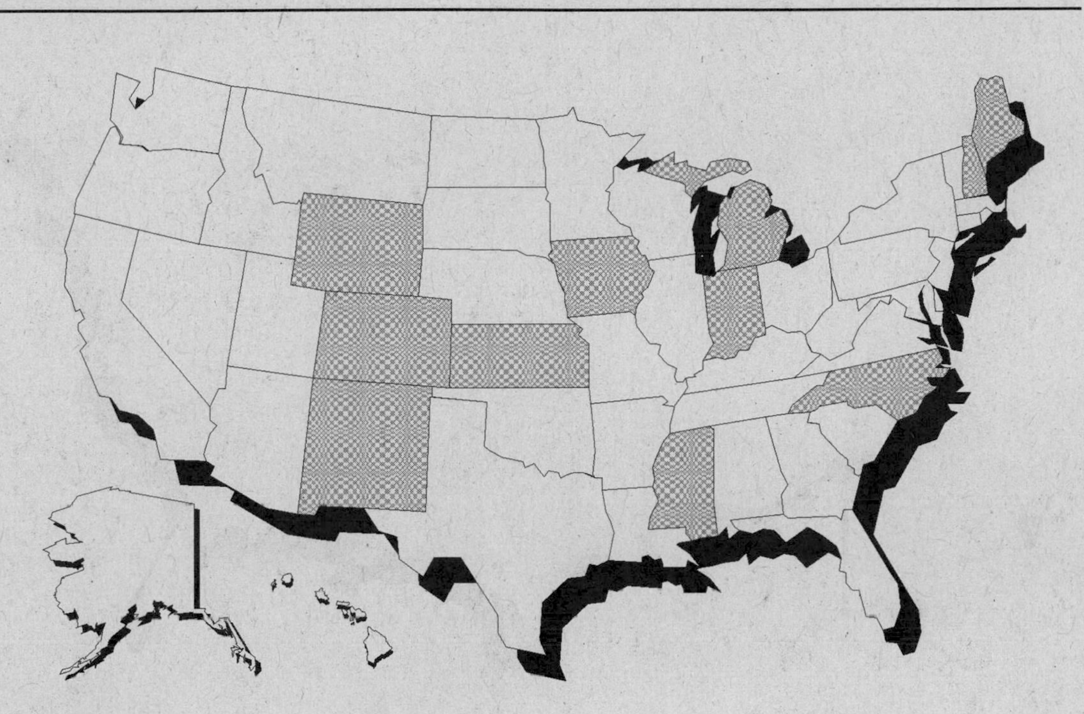

 Eleven states define criminal assaults on a pregnant woman that result in miscarriage, stillbirth, or "damage to a pregnancy" as an enhanced offense for sentencing purposes: CO, IN, IA, KS, ME, MI, MS, NH, NM, NC, and WY.

Use of Force to Protect the Unborn

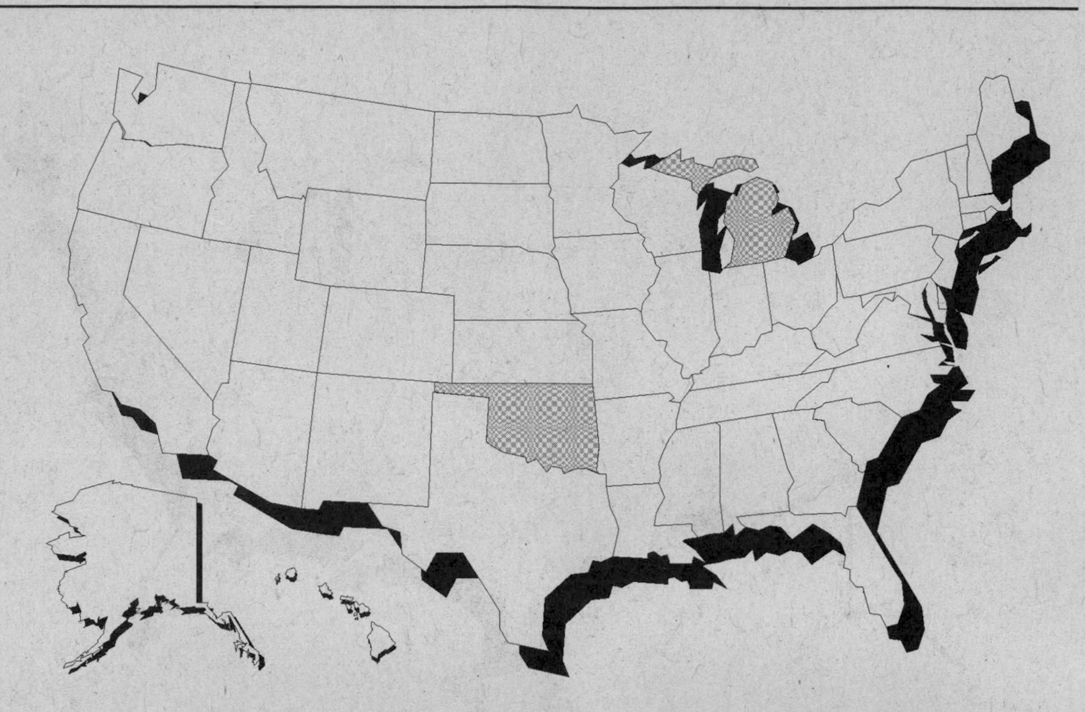

Two states specifically permit the application of the affirmative defense of "defense of others" to cases where a woman uses force (including deadly force) to protect her unborn child: MI and OK.

Born-Alive Infants Protection Act (BAIPA)

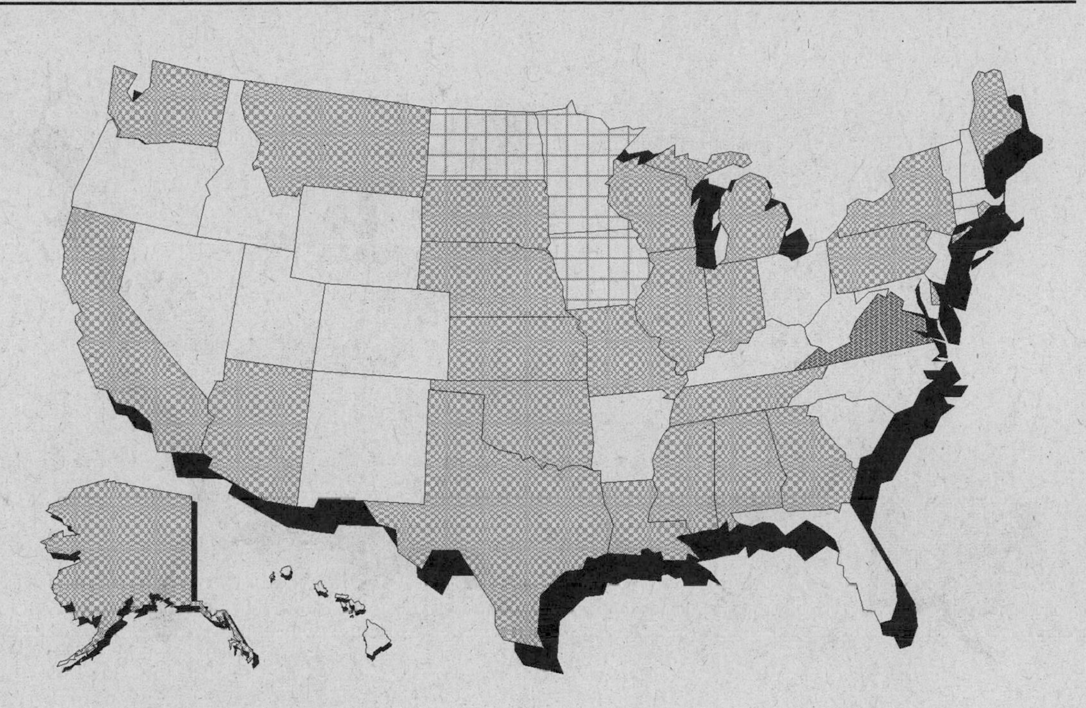

Twenty-four states have laws creating a specific affirmative duty for physicians to provide medical care and treatment to born-alive infants at any stage of development: AL, AZ, CA, DE, GA, IL, IN, KS, LA, ME, MI, MS, MO, MT, NE, NY, OK, PA, RI, SD, TN, TX, WA, and WI.

Three states have laws creating a specific affirmative duty for physicians to provide medical care and treatment to born-alive infants only after viability: IA, MN, and ND.

One state protects born-alive infants at any stage of development from "deliberate acts" undertaken by a physician that result in the death of the infant: VA.

Prenatal Use of Drugs and Alcohol by the Mother

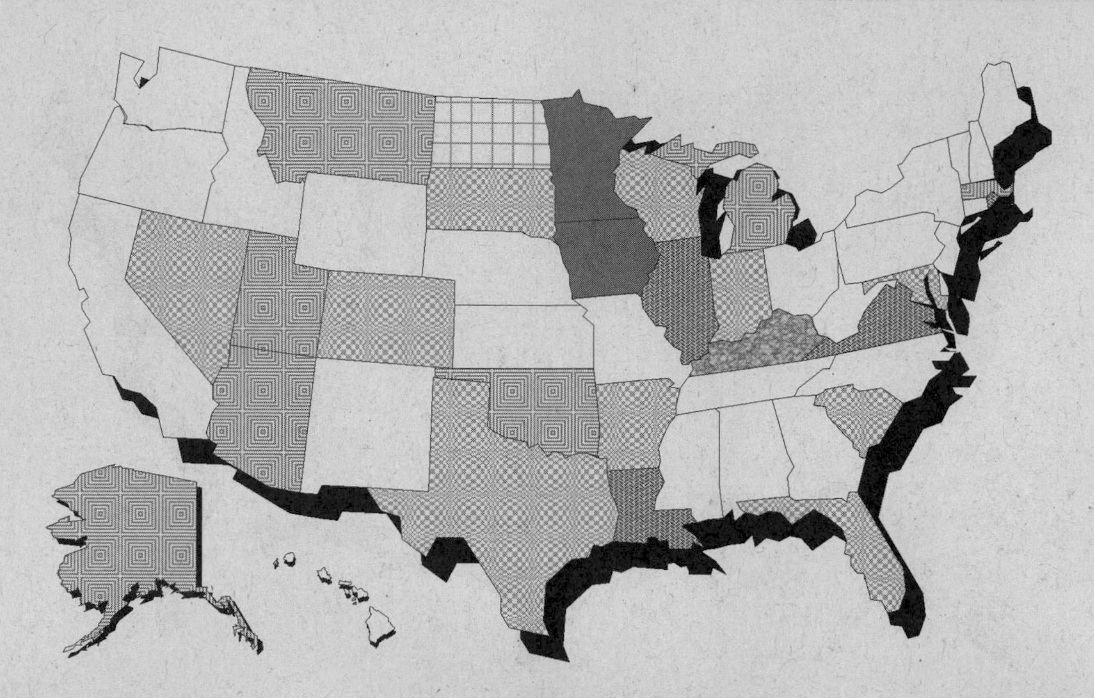

Two states define substance abuse during pregnancy as "child abuse," require healthcare professionals to report suspected prenatal drug use, and require testing of newborns when there is a suspicion of prenatal drug use: IA and MN.

Four states define substance abuse during pregnancy as "child abuse" and require healthcare professionals to report suspected prenatal drug use: IL, LA, RI, and VA.

One state requires healthcare professionals to report suspected prenatal drug use, and requires testing of newborns when there is a suspicion of prenatal drug use: ND.

Ten states also define substance abuse during pregnancy as "child abuse" and/or "neglect" under civil child-welfare statutes: AR, CO, FL, IN, MD, NV, SC, SD, TX, and WI.

Seven states only require healthcare professionals to report suspected prenatal drug use: AK, AZ, MA, MI, MT, OK, and UT.

One state only requires healthcare professionals to test newborns for prenatal drug exposure when there is suspicion of prenatal drug abuse: KY.

Drug Treatment Programs for Pregnant Women

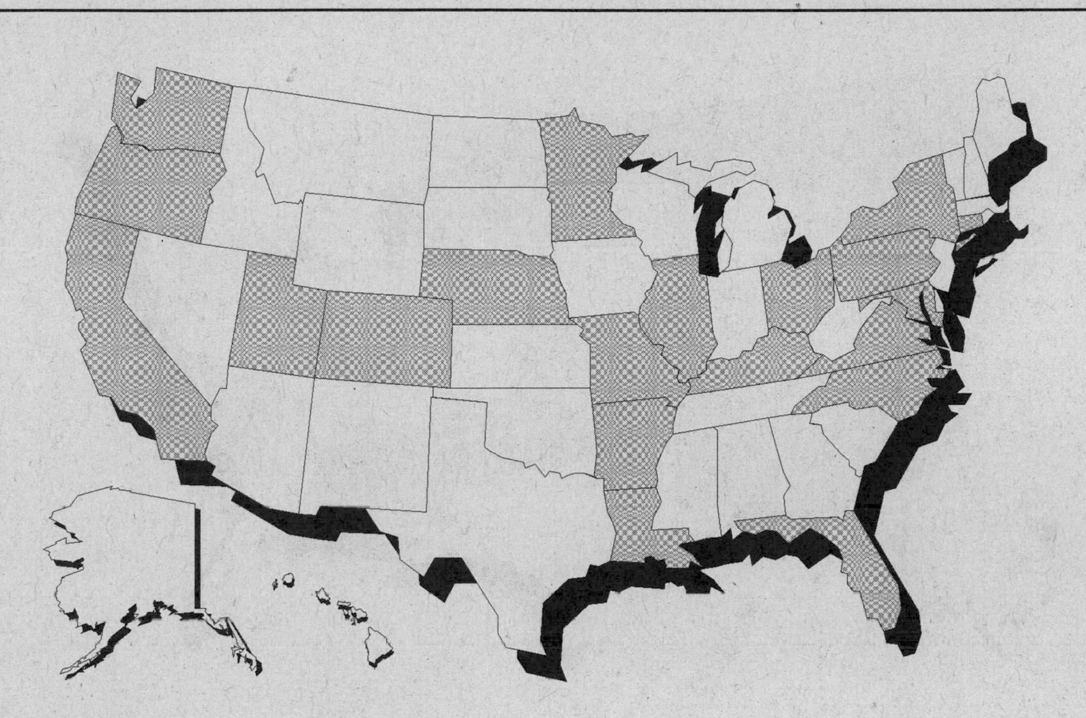

Twenty states fund drug treatment programs for pregnant women and newborns: AR, CA, CO, CT, FL, IL, KY, LA, MD, MN, MO, NE, NY, NC, OH, OR, PA, UT (requiring priority admission to exist for pregnant women), VA, and WA.

Wrongful Death (Civil Action)

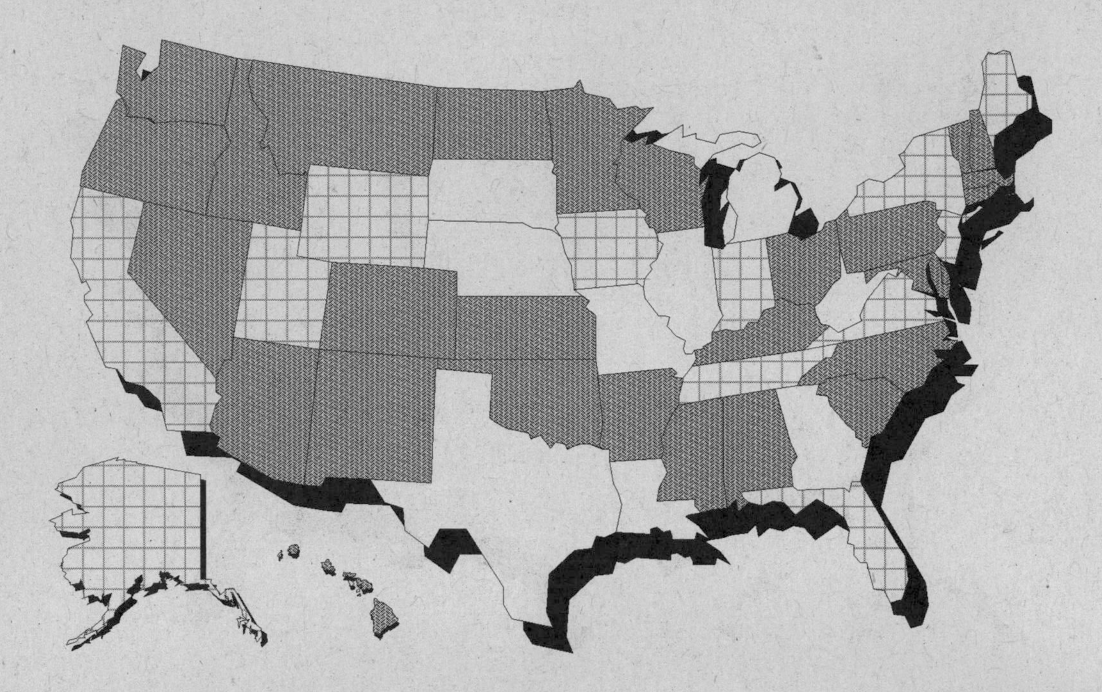

Twenty-nine states permit a wrongful death action if the unborn child was viable at the time of his/her death: AL, AZ, AR, CO, CT, DE, HI, ID, KS, KY, MD, MA, MN, MS, MT, NV, NH, NM, NC, ND, OH, OK, OR, PA, RI, SC, VT, WA, and WI.

Nine states allow suits for a pre-viable unborn child: GA (limited to quickening), IL, LA, MI, MO, NE, SD, TX, and WV.

Twelve states still require live birth (and bar a cause of action for the death of the unborn child unless the child is born alive and dies thereafter): AK, CA, FL, IN, IA, ME, NJ, NY, TN, UT, VA, and WY.

Wrongful Life Causes of Action

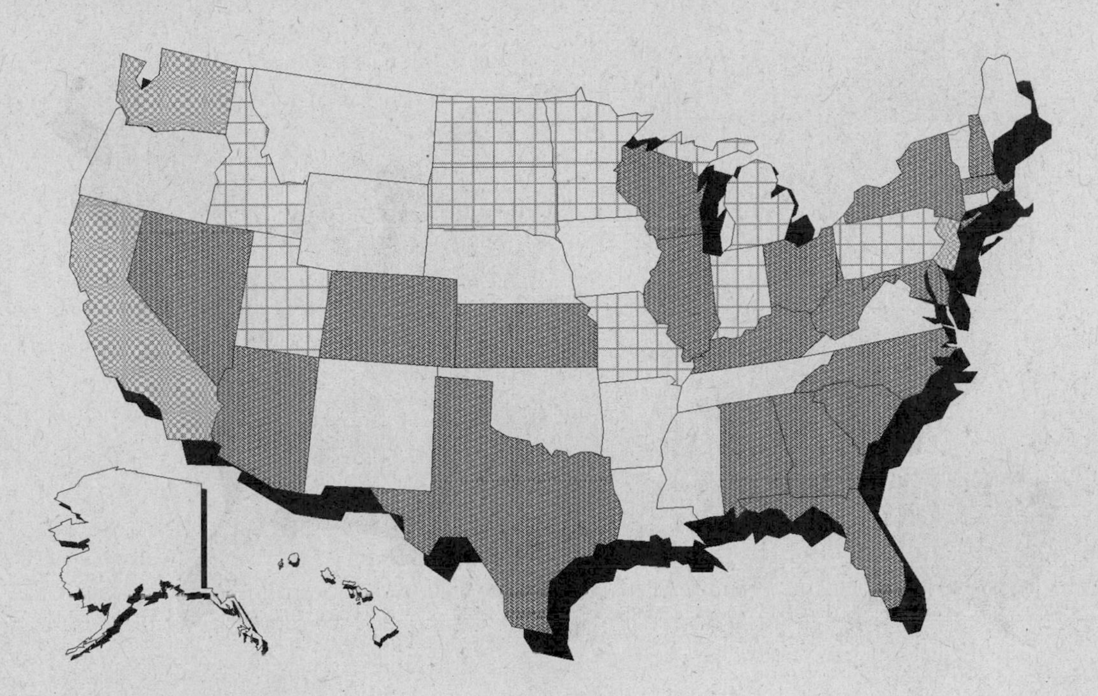

Twenty states have rejected wrongful life actions through judicial opinion: AL, AZ, CO, DE, FL, GA, IL, KS, KY, MD, MA, NV, NH, NY, NC, OH, SC, TX, WV, and WI.

Nine states have passed statutes barring or limiting wrongful life actions: ID, IN, MI, MN, MO, ND, PA, SD, and UT.

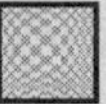

Three states expressly permit wrongful life causes of action: CA, NJ, and WA.

Wrongful Birth Causes of Action

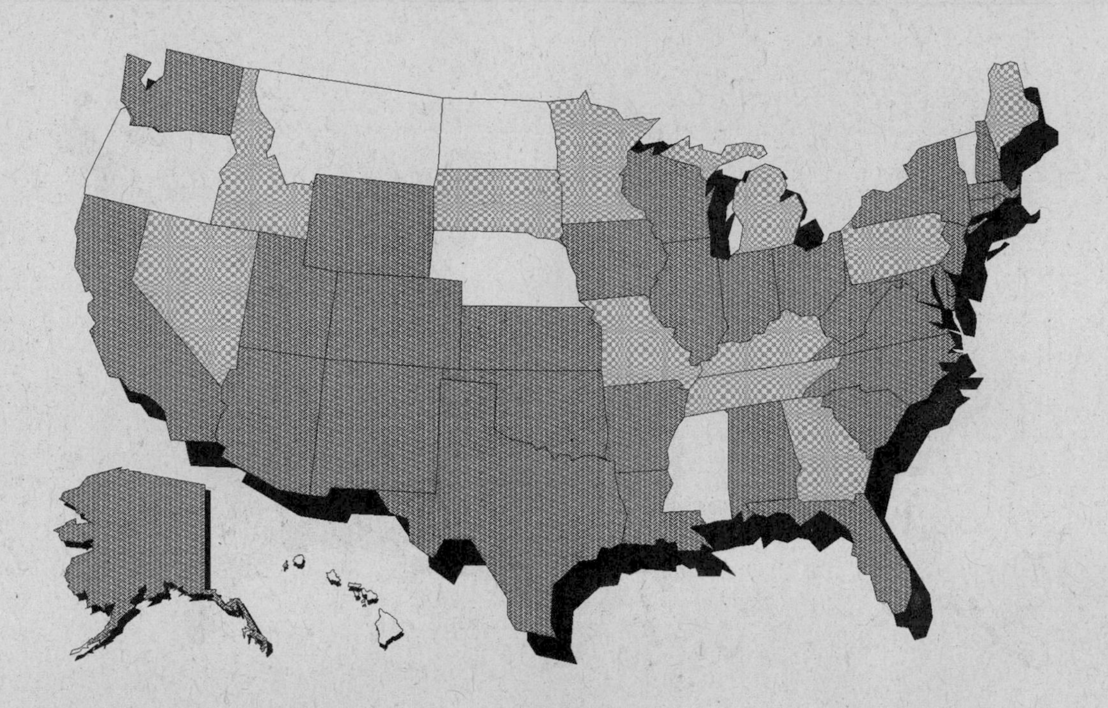

Eleven states have expressly prohibited wrongful birth causes of action: GA, ID, KY, ME, MI, MN, MO, NV, PA, SD, and TN.

Thirty-two states permit wrongful birth causes of action: AL, AK, AZ, AR, CA, CO, CT, DE, FL, IL, IN, IA, KS, LA, MD, MA, NH, NJ, NM, NY, NC, OH, OK, RI, SC, TX, UT, VA, WA, WV, WI, and WY.

2009 State Legislative Sessions in Review:
Legal recognition & protection of unborn & newly born

By Denise M. Burke
Vice President of Legal Affairs, Americans United for Life

State laws protecting unborn victims of violence received significant public and media attention over the past few years. For example, in January 2008, Marine Lance Corporal Maria Lauterbach and her unborn child were murdered near Camp Lejeune, North Carolina. Lauterbach was nearing her due date at the time of her murder. Fellow Marine Cesar Armando Laurean has been charged in the Lauterbach's murder, but will not face charges for killing Lauterbach's child since North Carolina is one of only 14 states that does not have a law protecting unborn victims of violence (*i.e.*, fetal homicide laws).

Conversely, in April 2008, Maryland prosecutors secured the state's first conviction under its new fetal homicide law when 25-year-old David Miller was convicted of two counts of first-degree murder for killing Elizabeth Walters and their unborn daughter. A witness to the murders testified that Miller, who was married to another woman, climbed into the back seat of the car she was sitting in with Walters and told the pregnant woman she was "not going to ruin [his] life," then pulled out a gun and shot Walters in the head. Friends of the popular Baltimore waitress said she had enthusiastically made the choice to keep and raise her daughter and was eagerly preparing for the birth.

Finally, laws protecting infants who survive attempted abortions, most commonly referred to as "born-alive infant protection laws," became a centerpiece of the 2008 Presidential campaign.

In 2009, 28 states considered more than 80 measures providing legal protection to and recognition of the unborn and newly born, roughly comparable to activity levels from 2008.

Protection of Unborn Victims of Violence

At least 15 states—including Hawaii, Illinois, Indiana, Montana, Nebraska, New York, Oregon, Rhode Island, Tennessee, West Virginia, and Wyoming—introduced measures to protect unborn victims of violence.

Indiana enacted a measure criminalizing the killing of an unborn child at any stage of gestation and increasing the penalties for performing an illegal abortion. It also enacted a measure providing an option for enhanced sentencing for any person who kills an unborn child while committing murder or felony-murder.

One-Victim/Enhanced Penalty Laws

At least six states—including Hawaii, North Carolina, Oklahoma, Rhode Island, West Virginia, and Wyoming—considered measures criminalizing assaults on pregnant women and providing for enhanced penalties for such actions. However, these measures do not recognize the unborn child as a second victim.

Protection for Pregnant Women

Oklahoma enacted AUL's "Pregnant Woman's Protection Act," which provides an affirmative defense to women who use force to protect their unborn children from a criminal assault.

Substance Abuse by Pregnant Women

Continuing a significant legislative trend over the past few years, at least 19 states—including Alabama, Arkansas, California, Hawaii, Illinois, Kentucky, Maine, Minnesota, Missouri, New Mexico, Rhode Island, Tennessee, and Texas—introduced measures designed to curb substance abuse by pregnant women and/or provide for needed treatment.

Arkansas enacted a measure defining "neglect" to include the presence of an illegal substance in a newborn's blood and permitting the use of such test result as evidence of neglect in subsequent proceedings.

Texas enacted a measure creating a task force charged, in part, with advising on potential criminal liability for women who expose their unborn children to controlled substances.

Born-Alive Infant Protection

A small number of states, including South Carolina, considered measures to protect infants born alive following a botched abortion and to ensure they receive appropriate medical care.

Stillborn/Fetal Death Certificates

At least nine states—including Alaska, Illinois, Maine, New Mexico, New York, Pennsylvania, Tennessee, and West Virginia—introduced measures to provide for a death certificate when an infant is stillborn.

Alaska enacted a measure that permits, upon a parent's request, the issuance of a death certificate and requires medical providers to inform parents of this option.

Indiana enacted a measure requiring the state Department of Health to develop an electronic death registration system that will include information on stillbirths.

Maine enacted a measure permitting the issuance of a death certificate upon a parent's request, while Pennsylvania enacted a measure providing for "fetal death registrations."

Infant Abandonment

At least 11 states—including Alaska, Arizona, California, Illinois, New York, North Dakota, Tennessee, and Washington—introduced legislation allowing for the legal abandonment of infants under circumstances that ensure their health and safety.

Tennessee enacted a measure to include police and fire stations and "emergency medical services facilities" as permissible locations to legally relinquish an infant.

Washington enacted a measure to include medical clinics (during their established hours of operations) as permissible locations to legally relinquish an infant.

Wrongful-Death (Civil) Causes of Action

At least three states—Alabama, Illinois, and New York—considered measures to provide for a wrongful-death (civil) cause of action in the death of an unborn child. The measures were equally divided between providing protection from conception and only after viability.

Wrongful Birth and Wrongful Life Causes of Action

New Jersey considered a measure to prohibit both wrongful birth and wrongful life causes of action.

AUL Model Legislation

CRIMES AGAINST THE UNBORN CHILD ACT

HOUSE/SENATE BILL No. ______
By Representatives/Senators ________________________

Section 1. Title.

This Act may be known and cited as the "Crimes Against the Unborn Child Act" [*or, alternatively, the "Unborn Victims of Violence Act"*].

Section 2. Legislative Findings and Purposes.[1]

(a) A significant loophole exists in [*Insert name of State*]'s criminal law, denying protection to pregnant women and certain children. Currently, an offender may not be held criminally responsible for the harm caused to a child unless that child has first been born alive. Thus, an unborn child is completely denied protection under this State's existing criminal laws.

(b) [*Insert name of State*] lags behind most states in this area of crime victims' protection. Thirty-six states now provide varying degrees of protection and justice for pregnant women and their unborn children who are victims of violence. Importantly, 26 states provide protection for unborn children at any stage of gestation.

(c) Recent statistics demonstrate that domestic abuse and violence against women increases during pregnancy. It is estimated that one in five women will be abused during pregnancy. Moreover, a study in the *Journal of the American Medical Association* found that in the State of Maryland, a pregnant woman is more likely to be a victim of a homicide than to die of any other cause.

(d) Compounding this tragedy is the loophole in [*Insert name of State*]'s current law, which denies effective protection and remedy to women, their children, and their extended families, telling them, in effect, that their loved ones never existed at all. When a woman makes a conscious choice to keep her baby and has that choice violently taken away from her by a brutal perpetrator, justice—through comprehensive, effective, and timely legal protections—must be available to them.

(e) The federal "Unborn Victims of Violence Act," enacted in April 2004, is limited, applying only to unborn children injured or killed during the course of specified federal crimes of violence. It does not reach many crimes of violence committed against pregnant women and their unborn children—crimes which are most commonly prosecutable only under state criminal laws.

(f) Thus, it is the intent of the [*Legislature*] that the affirmative right of a pregnant woman to carry her child to term be protected, and that perpetrators of crimes against pregnant women and their unborn children be held accountable for their crimes.

Section 3. Amendment of State Criminal Code.

For purposes of the offenses of **homicide**, **assault**, and **battery** [*Designate the specific crimes and sections of the state criminal code to be amended*], the term "**person**" [*or other appropriate term(s) as used in the state's criminal code*] includes an unborn child at every stage of gestation from conception until live birth.

Section 3. Definitions.

For the purposes of this Act only:

(a) "**Conception**" means the fusion of a human spermatozoon with a human ovum.

(b) "**Gestation**" means the time during which a woman carries an unborn child in her womb, from conception to birth.

(c) "**Unborn child**" means the offspring of human beings from conception until birth.

Section 4. Exclusions.

Nothing in this Act shall apply to an act committed by the mother of an unborn child; to a medical procedure performed by a physician or other licensed medical professional at the request of a mother of an unborn child or the mother's legal guardian; or to the lawful dispensation or administration of lawfully prescribed medication.

Section 5. Right of Intervention.

The [*Legislature*], by joint resolution, may appoint one or more of its members, who sponsored or cosponsored this Act in his or her official capacity, to intervene as a matter of right in any case in which the constitutionality of this law is challenged.

Section 6. Severability.

If any provision, word, phrase, or clause of this Act or the application thereof to any person or circumstance is held invalid, such invalidity shall not affect the provisions, words, phrases, clauses, or applications of this Act which can be given effect without the invalid provision, word, phrase, clause, or application and to this end, the provisions, words, phrases, and clauses of this Act are declared severable.

Section 7. Effective Date.

This Act takes effect on [*Insert date*].

Endnotes

[1] Much of the text of the Legislative Findings and Purposes section is modeled after language contained in legislation recently introduced in New York. *See e.g.* NY AB 4897 (2009).

PREGNANT WOMAN'S PROTECTION ACT

HOUSE/SENATE BILL No. ______
By Representatives/Senators ____________

[*Drafter's Note: This model provides general guidance and should be specifically tailored to the requirements of each state's criminal code. Please contact AUL for drafting assistance.*]

Section 1. Title.

This Act may be known and cited as the "Pregnant Woman's Protection Act."

Section 2. Legislative Findings and Purposes.

(a) The [*Legislature*] of the State of [*Insert name of State*] finds that:

(1) Violence and abuse are often higher during pregnancy than during any other time in a woman's life;

(2) Women are more likely to suffer increased abuse as a result of unintended pregnancies;

(3) Younger women are at a higher risk for pregnancy-associated homicide;

(4) A pregnant or recently-pregnant woman is more likely to be a victim of homicide than to die of any other cause;

(5) Homicide and other violent crimes are the leading cause of death for women of reproductive age;

(6) Husbands, ex-husbands, or boyfriends are often the perpetrators of pregnancy-associated homicide or violence;

(7) Moreover, when husbands, ex-husbands, or boyfriends are involved, the violence is often directed at the unborn child or intended to end or jeopardize the pregnancy; and

(8) Violence against a pregnant woman puts the life and bodily integrity of both the pregnant woman and the unborn child at risk.

(b) By adopting this Act, the [*Legislature*] intends to:

(1) Ensure that the affirmative right of a pregnant woman to carry her child to term is protected;

(2) Ensure that affirmative defenses to criminal liability provided for under [*Insert name of State*]'s criminal code at Section(s) [*Insert citations to appropriate criminal code section(s)*] explicitly provide for a pregnant woman's right to use force, including deadly force, to protect her unborn child; and

(3) Supplement, but not supersede, the applicability of any other affirmative defenses to criminal liability provided for under [*Insert name of State*]'s criminal code.

Section 3. Definitions.

As used in this Act only:

(a) "**Another**" means a person other than the pregnant woman.

(b) "**Deadly force**" means [*Insert specific language from and citation to appropriate State criminal code section(s)*] (*or "force which, under the circumstances in which it is used, is readily capable of causing death or serious physical harm"*).

(c) "**Force**" means [*Insert specific language from and citation to appropriate State criminal code section(s)*] (*or "violence, compulsion, or constraint exerted upon or against another"*).

(d) "**Embryo**" means an individual organism of species *homo sapiens* from the single cell stage to eight weeks development.

(e) "**Pregnant**" means the female reproductive condition of having an unborn child in the woman's body.

(f) "**Unborn child**" means the offspring of human beings from conception until birth.

(g) "**Unlawful force**" means [*Insert specific language from and citation to appropriate State criminal code section(s)*] (*or "force which is employed without the consent of the pregnant woman and which constitutes an offense under the criminal laws of this State or an actionable tort"*).

Section 4. Affirmative Defense to Criminal Liability.

A pregnant woman is justified in using force or deadly force against another to protect her unborn child if:

(a) Under the circumstances as the pregnant woman reasonably believes them to be, she would be justified under Section(s) [*Insert citation(s) to State criminal code section(s) on self-defense and use of deadly force*] in using force or deadly force to protect herself against the unlawful force or unlawful deadly force she reasonably believes to be threatening her unborn child; and

(b) She reasonably believes that her intervention and use of force or deadly force are immediately necessary to protect her unborn child.

Section 5. Exclusions.

The affirmative defense to criminal liability provided for under this Act does not apply to:

(a) Acts committed by anyone other than the pregnant woman (*which may otherwise be provided for under alternate sections of this State's criminal code)*;

(b) Acts where the pregnant woman would be obligated under Section(s) [*Insert State criminal code section(s) requiring retreat before acting in self-defense, if any*] to retreat, to surrender the possession of a thing, or to comply with a demand before using force in self-defense. However, the pregnant woman is not obligated to retreat before using force or deadly force to protect her unborn child, unless she knows that she can thereby secure the complete safety of her unborn child; or

(c) The defense of human embryos existing outside of a woman's body (*such as, but not limited to, frozen human embryos stored at fertility clinics or elsewhere*).

Section 6. Severability.

Any provision of this Act held to be invalid or unenforceable by its terms, or as applied to any person or circumstance, shall be construed so as to give it maximum effect permitted by law, unless such holding shall be one of utter invalidity or unenforceability, in which event such provision shall be deemed severable herefrom and shall not affect the remainder hereof or the application of such provision to other persons not similarly situated or to other, dissimilar circumstances.

Section 7. Effective Date.

This Act takes effect on *[Insert date]*.

BORN-ALIVE INFANT PROTECTION ACT

HOUSE/SENATE BILL NO. __________
Sponsored by Representatives/Senators ________________

Section 1. Title.

This Act may be known and cited as the "Born Alive Infant Protection Act".

Section 2. Legislative Findings and Purpose.

(a) The [*Legislature*] of the State of [*Insert name of State*] finds that:

(1) The State of [*Insert name of State*] has a paramount interest in protecting all human life.

(2) If an [attempted] abortion results in the live birth of an infant, the infant is a legal person for all purposes under the laws of this State.

(3) A woman's right to terminate a pregnancy ends when the pregnancy is terminated. The right to an abortion has never been legally or morally equated to the "right to a dead child."

(4) It is not an infringement on a woman's right to terminate her pregnancy for this State to assert its interest in protecting an infant whose live birth occurred as the result of an [attempted] abortion.

(5) Without proper legal protection, newly-born infants who survive [attempted] abortions have been denied proper life-saving or life-sustaining medical treatment and left to die.

(b) Accordingly, it is the purpose of this Act to ensure the protection and promotion of the health and well-being of all infants born alive in this State. Therefore, this Act mandates that healthcare providers give medically-appropriate and reasonable life-saving or life-sustaining medical care and treatment to all born-alive infants.

Section 3. Definitions.

For the purposes of this Act only:

(a) "**Abortion**" means the act of using or prescribing any instrument, medicine, drug, or any other substance, device, or means with the intent to terminate the clinically-diagnosable pregnancy of a woman with knowledge that the termination by those means will with reasonable likelihood cause the death of the unborn child. Such use, prescription, or means is not an abortion if done with the intent to:

(1) save the life or preserve the health of an unborn child;

(2) remove a dead unborn child caused by spontaneous abortion; or

(3) remove an ectopic pregnancy.

(b) "**Born alive**" or "**live birth**" means the complete expulsion or extraction of an infant from his or her mother, regardless of the state of gestational development, that, after expulsion or extraction, whether or not the umbilical cord has been cut or the placenta is attached, and regardless of whether the expulsion or extraction occurs as a result of natural or induced labor, cesarean section, or induced abortion, shows any evidence of life, including, but not limited to, one or more of the following:

(1) breathing;

(2) a heartbeat;

(3) umbilical cord pulsation; or

(4) definite movement of voluntary muscles.

(c) "**Consent**" means knowledge of and explicit or implicit agreement to or instruction to perform a violation of this Act.

(d) "**Facility**" or "**medical facility**" means any public or private hospital, clinic, center, medical school, medical training institution, healthcare facility, physician's office, infirmary, dispensary, ambulatory surgical treatment center, or other institution or location wherein medical care is provided to any person.

(e) "**Infant**" means a child of the species *homo sapiens* that has been completely expulsed or extracted from its mother, regardless of the stage of gestational development, until the age of thirty (30) days post birth.

(e) "**Premature**" or "**preterm**" means occurring prior to the thirty-seventh (37th) week of gestation.

Section 4. Requirements and Responsibilities.

(a) A person shall not deny or deprive an infant of nourishment with the intent to cause or allow the death of the infant for any reason including:

(1) the infant was born with a handicap;

(2) the infant is not wanted by the parent(s) or guardian(s); or

(3) the infant is born alive by natural or artificial means.

(b) A person shall not deprive an infant of medically-appropriate and reasonable medical care and treatment or surgical care.

(c) The requirements of this Section shall not be construed to prevent an infant's parent(s) or guardian(s) from refusing to give consent to medical treatment or surgical care which is not medically necessary or reasonable, including care or treatment which either:

(1) is not necessary to save the life of the infant;

(2) has a potential risk to the infant's life or health that outweighs the potential benefit to the infant of the treatment or care; or

(3) is treatment that will do no more than temporarily prolong the act of dying when death is imminent.

(d) The physician performing an abortion must take all medically-appropriate and reasonable steps to preserve the life and health of a born-alive infant. If an abortion performed in a hospital results in a live birth, the physician attending the abortion shall provide immediate medical care to the infant, inform the mother of the live birth, and request transfer of the infant to a resident or on-duty or emergency care physician who shall provide medically-appropriate and reasonable medical care and treatment to the infant. If an abortion performed in a facility other than a hospital results in a live birth, a physician attending the abortion shall provide immediate medical care to the infant and call 9-1-1 for an emergency transfer of the infant to a hospital that shall provide medically-appropriate and reasonable care and treatment to the infant.

(e) If the physician described in paragraph (d) of this Section is unable to perform the duties in that paragraph because he is assisting the woman on whom the abortion was performed, then an attending physician's assistant, nurse, or other licensed healthcare provider must assume the duties outlined in that paragraph.

(f) Any born-alive infant, including one born in the course of an abortion procedure, shall be treated as a legal person under the laws of this State, with the same rights to medically-appropriate care and treatment, and birth and death (if death occurs) certificates shall be issued accordingly.

(g) If, before the abortion, the mother, [and if married, her husband,] has [or have] stated in writing that she does [or they do] not wish to keep the infant in the event that the abortion results in a live birth, and this writing is not retracted before the [attempted] abortion, the infant, if born alive, shall immediately upon birth become a ward of [*Insert name of appropriate State child welfare department or agency*].

(h) No person may use any premature born-alive infant for any type of scientific research or other kind of experimentation except as necessary to protect or preserve the life and health of the premature born alive infant.

[*Optional:* ***Section 5. Infanticide.*** *[Optional if the State's criminal code does not include the crime of infanticide or if the State does not wish to add another definition to the existing crime of infanticide.*

*(a) "**Infanticide**" means any deliberate act that:*

(1) is intended to kill an infant who has been born alive; and

(2) that does kill such infant.

(b) Any physician, nurse, or other licensed healthcare provider who deliberately fails to provide medically-appropriate and reasonable care and treatment to a born-alive infant and, as a result of that failure, the infant dies, shall be guilty of the crime of infanticide.]

Section [6]. Exceptions.

The mother will not be liable, criminally or civilly, for actions of a physician, nurse, or other licensed healthcare provider, in violation of this Act to which she did not give her consent.

Section [7]. Criminal Penalties.

(a) Any physician, nurse, or other licensed healthcare provider who knowingly and intentionally or negligently fails to provide medically-appropriate and reasonable care and treatment to a born-alive infant in the course of an [attempted] abortion shall be guilty of a [*Insert appropriate classification*] felony and upon conviction shall be fined an amount not exceeding [*Insert appropriate amount*], or imprisoned not less than [*Insert appropriate term*] years and not exceeding [*Insert appropriate term*] years, or both.

[*Optional:* (b) *Any person found guilty of the crime of infanticide shall be fined an amount not exceeding [Insert appropriate amount], or imprisoned not less than [Insert appropriate term] years and not exceeding [Insert appropriate term] years, or both [or will be punished according to the sentencing guidelines found in the Criminal Code of [Insert name of State]]*].

[(c)] Any violation of Section 4, paragraph (h) of this Act [concerning the research use of a born- alive infant] is a [*Insert appropriate classification*] felony and upon conviction shall be fined an amount not exceeding [*Insert appropriate amount*], or imprisoned not less than [*Insert appropriate term*] years and not exceeding [*Insert appropriate term*] years, or both.

Section [8]. Civil and Administrative Action.

In addition to whatever remedies are available under the common or statutory law of this State, failure to comply with the requirements of this Act shall:

(a) Provide a basis for a civil action for compensatory and punitive damages. Any conviction under this Act shall be admissible in a civil suit as *prima facie* evidence of a failure to provide medically-appropriate and reasonable care and treatment to a born-alive infant. Any civil action may be based on a claim that the death of or injury to the born-alive infant was a result of simple negligence, gross negligence, wantonness, willfulness, intentional conduct, or another violation of the legal standard of care.

(b) Provide a basis for professional disciplinary action under [*Insert appropriate reference(s) to State statute(s) and/or administrative rules concerning State Medical Board's oversight and review authority*] for the suspension or revocation of any license for physicians, licensed and registered nurses, or other licensed or regulated persons. Any conviction of any person for any failure to comply with the requirements of this Act shall result in the automatic suspension of his or her license for a period of at least one year [*or other appropriate penalty*] and shall be reinstated after that time only under such conditions as the [*Insert reference(s) to appropriate regulatory or licensing body*] shall require to ensure compliance with this Act.

(c) Provide a basis for recovery for the parent(s) of the infant or the parent(s) or guardian(s) of the mother if the mother is a minor, for the wrongful death of the infant under [*Insert reference(s) to State's wrongful death statute(s)*], whether or not the infant was viable at the time the [attempted] abortion was performed.

Section [9]. Construction.

(a) Nothing in this Act shall be construed to affirm, deny, expand, or contract any legal status or legal right applicable to any member of the species *homo sapiens* at any point prior to being born alive, as defined in this Act.

(b) Nothing in this Act shall be construed to affect existing Federal or State law regarding abortion.

(c) Nothing in this Act shall be construed as creating or recognizing a right to abortion.

(d) Nothing in this Act shall be construed to alter generally accepted medical standards.

Section [10]. Severability.

Further, any provision of this Act held to be invalid or unenforceable by its terms, or as applied to any person or circumstance, shall be construed so as to give it the maximum effect permitted by law, unless such holding shall be one of utter invalidity or unenforceability, in which event such provision shall be deemed severable here from and shall not affect the remainder hereof or the application of such provision to other persons not similarly situated or to other, dissimilar circumstances.

Section [11]. Right of Intervention.

The [*Legislature*], by joint resolution, may appoint one or more of its members, who sponsored or cosponsored this Act in his or her official capacity, to intervene as a matter of right in any case in which the constitutionality of this law is challenged.

Section [12]. Effective Date.

This Act takes effect on [*Insert date*].

UNBORN WRONGFUL DEATH ACT

HOUSE/SENATE BILL NO. ____
Sponsored by Representatives/Senators ______

Section 1. Title.

This Act may be known and cited as the "Unborn Wrongful Death Act."

Section 2. Legislative Findings and Purposes

(a) The [*Legislature*] of the State of [*Insert name of State*] finds that:

(1) This State has statutorily recognized a wrongful death civil cause of action [*Insert appropriate code section(s)*] since [*Insert date*].

(2) The wrongful death cause of action is intended to correct a flaw in the common law: At common law, no cause of action survived a victim's death. Thus, a tortfeasor (wrongdoer) could escape liability merely because he inflicted injuries so severe they resulted in the death of his victim.

(3) The wrongful death cause of action provides for damages to be paid by the wrongdoer to his victim's survivors, thus deterring tortuous and harmful behavior and providing for restitution to the victim's estate.

(4) This State has an interest in protecting every human being, including unborn children, from tortious and harmful acts.

(5) Parents of unborn children have protectable interests in the life, health, and well-being of their children.

(6) Tortious behavior which results in the death of an unborn child carries the same social and emotional cost as that which results in the death of a born and living human being, including bereavement, a loss to society, and the lawlessness and disregard for life which characterizes all negligent, harmful, and wrongful behavior.

(b) For these reasons, the [*Legislature*] finds the exclusion of unborn children from coverage under the State's wrongful death cause of action is at cross purposes with the justifications for the statute(s), and a cause of action for the wrongful death of an unborn child

should be permitted under the laws of this State.

Section 3. Definitions.

For the purposes of this Act only:

(a) "**Abortion**" means the act of using or prescribing any instrument, medicine, drug, or any other substance, device, or means with the intent to terminate the clinically diagnosable pregnancy of a woman with knowledge that the termination by those means will with reasonable likelihood cause the death of the unborn child. Such use, prescription, or means is not an abortion if done with the intent to:

(1) Save the life or preserve the health of the unborn child,

(2) Remove a dead unborn child caused by spontaneous abortion, or

(3) Remove an ectopic pregnancy.

(b) "**Born alive**" means the substantial expulsion or extraction of an infant from its mother, regardless of the duration of the pregnancy, that after expulsion or extraction, whether or not the umbilical cord has been cut or the placenta is attached, and regardless of whether the expulsion or extraction occurs as a result of natural or induced labor, cesarean section, or induced abortion, shows any evidence of life, including, but not limited to, one or more of the following:

(1) Breathing.

(2) A heartbeat.

(3) Umbilical cord pulsation.

(4) Definite movement of voluntary muscles.

(c) "**Conception**" means the fusion of a human spermatozoon with a human ovum.

(d) "**Physician**" means a doctor legally authorized to practice medicine or surgery in this State, or any other individual legally authorized by this State to perform abortions; *provided, however,* that any individual who is not a physician and not otherwise legally authorized by this State to perform abortions, but who nevertheless performs an abortion, shall be subject to the provisions of this Act.

(e) **"Unborn child"** means the offspring of human beings from conception until birth.

Section 4. Cause of Action.

The state or location of gestation or development of an unborn child when an injury is caused, when an injury takes effect, or at death, shall not foreclose maintenance of a cause of action under the law of this State arising from the death of the unborn child caused by wrongful act, neglect, carelessness, lack of skill, or default.

Section 5. Exceptions.

(a) There shall be no cause of action against a physician or a medical institution for the wrongful death of an unborn child caused by an abortion where the abortion was permitted by law and the requisite consent was lawfully given; *provided, however*, that a cause of action is not prohibited where an abortion is performed in violation of state law or where the child is born-alive and subsequently dies.

(b) There shall be no cause of action against a physician or a medical institution for the wrongful death of an unborn child *in utero* based on the alleged misconduct of the physician or medical institution where the defendant did not know and, under the applicable standard of good medical care, had no medical reason to know of the pregnancy of the mother or the existence of the unborn child.

Section 6. Construction.

(a) This Act does not create, recognize, endorse, or condone a right to an abortion.

(b) It is not the intention of this Act to make lawful an abortion that is currently unlawful.

Section 7. Severability.

Any provision of this Act held to be invalid or unenforceable by its terms, or as applied to any person or circumstance, shall be construed so as give it the maximum effect permitted by law, unless such holding shall be one of utter invalidity or unenforceability, in which event such provision shall be deemed severable herefrom and shall not affect the remainder hereof or the application of such provision to other persons not similarly situated or to other, dissimilar circumstances.

Section 8. Right of Intervention.

The [*Legislature*], by joint resolution, may appoint one or more of its members, who sponsored or cosponsored this Act in his or her official capacity, to intervene as a matter of right to defend this law in any case in which its constitutionality is challenged.

Section 9. Effective Date.

This Act takes effect on [*Insert date*].

BIOETHICS & BIOTECHNOLOGY

Bioethics & Biotechnology

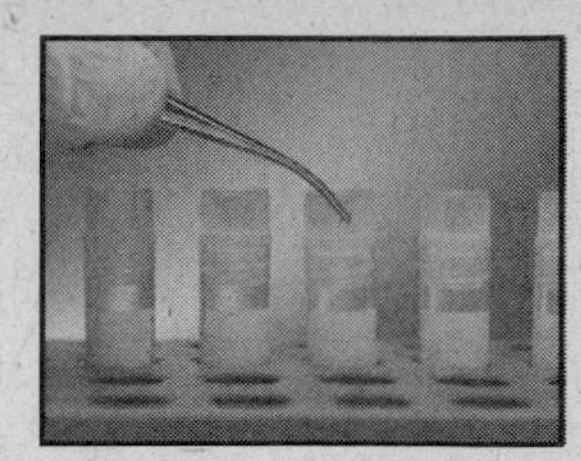

With each passing year, we face new and increasingly complex challenges to the sanctity of human life. Medical research and new biotechnologies are advancing far faster than our society's ethical and legal constraints ensuring their moral use. When Aldous Huxley wrote *Brave New World* in 1932, human cloning was just science fiction. Today, human cloning is a reality.

We have seen extraordinary advances in medical research over the past 10 years. The once languishing area of stem cell research has surged to life. Every day, new treatments developed from adult stem cells are being used to treat real people suffering from once incurable diseases and serious injuries. Others, while not cured, have made such progress that their illnesses or injuries no longer dominate their everyday lives, and they once again engage in life in a way they never thought possible.

Scientists have been able to help patients suffering from over 70 different diseases and injuries—including brain cancer, leukemia, lymphoma, Crone's disease, Lupus, heart damage, Parkinson's, Sickle cell anemia, and end-stage bladder disease—using adult stem cells. Conversely, morally-problematic embryonic stem-cell research has not helped a single human patient.

Despite the promising advances in adult stem-cell research, many scientists and politicians continue to seek unfettered freedom (and our tax dollars) for immoral uses of biotechnology in the hope of miracle cures. If we do not act with greater urgency, the abuse of nascent human life will become more entrenched and far more difficult to regulate. Powerful ethical and legal limits are needed to preserve and protect the sanctity of all human life.

In this section, we have focused on providing accurate and up-to-date information on advances in biotechnology, including human cloning, destructive embryo research (DER), and ethical alternatives to DER—such as adult stem cells, human skin cells, and cord blood.

Moreover, capitalizing on the national debate over the "Octo-Mom" and

the ethical limits of assisted reproduction, we hope to spark thoughtful, responsible discussion and debate on the regulation of assisted reproductive technologies (ART), including *in vitro* fertilization (IVF). For example, we argue in favor of informed consent for IVF and limitations on the number of embryos that may be implanted during an IVF treatment cycle. We also urge that embryo adoption be given as an option to parents of IVF-created embryos, and that such an adoption be recognized under state law. It is critical we provide meaningful oversight and regulation of IVF and other reproductive technologies, as the so-called leftover embryos in IVF clinics around the nation are at the heart of ongoing debates over DER and human cloning.

"The Brave New World" of Bioethics

A survey of federal and state laws

By Mailee R. Smith
Staff Counsel, Americans United for Life

Continuing advances in biomedical science and technology are raising challenging and profound ethical issues—for individuals and families, for scientists and healthcare professionals, and for the broader society. Many important human values are implicated, among them health and the relief of suffering, respect for life and the human person, human freedom, and human dignity. The flourishing field of modern bioethics arose to explore these issues, and various bodies, including the U.S. Congress, state legislatures, local research review boards, academic bioethics institutes, and several national commissions, continue to wrestle with them.

The term "bioethics" commonly refers to the moral questions and implications raised by biological discoveries and biomedical advances, and particularly those questions raised by experimentation on living human beings. As such, the field covers a variety of scientific and medical areas, including destructive embryo research, cloning, assisted reproduction, and genetic testing—areas lacking significant protective regulation under either federal or state law.

ISSUES

Destructive Embryo Research (DER)

Obtaining embryonic stem cells requires the destruction of a living human embryo. It is done by taking a days-old embryo that has grown to the several hundred-cell stage, breaking it apart, and taking the cells from the embryo's inner mass.[1] These unspecialized cells are then grown and used for research.

More than ten years after the first isolation of embryonic stem cells, there is not a single disease that these cells have been used to cure, regardless of whether the cells obtained from embryos are created through sperm and egg or through cloning. Scientists have been conducting research on mouse embryonic stem cells for over 25 years and are still unable to cure mice.[2] Research on humans that necessitates destroying human embryos would be repugnant even if it led to cures. However, such research on humans is even more unseemly given the fact that this research has rarely (and never consistently) worked in animals.

There are successful, ethical alternatives to using human embryos as a source of stem cells for research and therapeutic purposes. One important source is umbilical cord blood—a very rich source of stem cells. Another is adult stem cells from various organs. Researchers have long known, for example, that bone marrow can form into blood cells. We now know that bone-marrow cells can form into fat, cartilage, and bone tissue. A third promising source is neural stem cells. These stem cells have been successfully isolated and cultured from living human neural tissue and even from adult cadavers. Moreover, research breakthroughs since 2007 are opening the door for the reprogramming of adult stem cells into the embryonic stem cell state—without the use or destruction of human embryos.

Adult stem cells have helped patients with over 70 different diseases, with more being continually added. The future of human cures is not in destroying some humans to treat others. It is in ethical treatments that treat all human life with dignity and respect. But proponents of embryonic stem-cell research have purposely created a false impression that embryonic stem cells have a proven therapeutic use, when they have in reality never helped a single human patient.

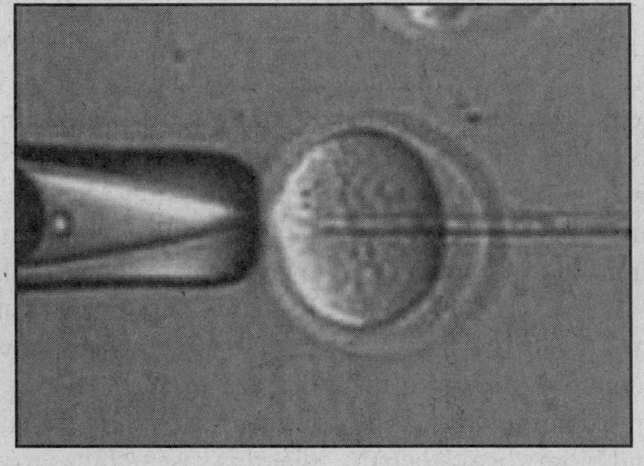

In addition to the facts that 1) it is necessary to destroy nascent human life to obtain embryonic stem cells for research, and 2) embryonic stem-cell research has never helped a human patient, such research is also immoral because the only way to obtain the human eggs necessary to create embryos is to exploit women. A woman normally only produces one or two eggs per reproductive cycle. To obtain enough eggs for research, a woman must take drugs that will cause her to super-ovulate, releasing 10-15 eggs at a time, and undergo an invasive surgical procedure in order to retrieve them. Thus, it is simply not possible to obtain enough eggs from willing women to adequately pursue this research or treat possible diseases that may come from any breakthroughs using embryonic stem cells.[3]

The U.S. Supreme Court has never ruled on the legal status of a human embryo outside of the mother's womb. In August 2001, President George W. Bush announced that federal funding would be allowed only for research on then-existing embryonic stem-cell lines. But in March 2009, President Barack Obama signed an Executive Order reversing that policy.

It is, therefore, up to the states to institute protective measures. Currently, seven states either expressly or impliedly ban DER on embryos created through *in vitro* fertilization (IVF) or cloned human embryos, and 19 states ban fetal experimentation. In addition to these direct bans on research, at least six states restrict funding or the use of state facilities for DER, and 16 states have passed legislation encouraging the use of adult stem cells or umbilical cord blood and/or the donation of umbilical cord blood.

AUL has drafted several models to help states curb ineffective, unethical research and promote ethical research that is already making a difference. These models include the "Destructive Embryo Research Act" banning destructive embryo research; a "Prohibition on Public Funding of Human Cloning and Destructive Embryo Research Act"; and an "Egg Provider Protection Act," focused on preventing the exploitation of women.

Human Cloning

One of the inherent problems in using embryonic stem cells in therapies is the problem of transplantation. If a transplanted cell's DNA is even somewhat different from the DNA of the person being treated, the body usually sees those cells as invaders and kills them off—much like what happens when whole-organ transplants are rejected because of the recipient's immune system response. Without the use of drugs to suppress the patient's immune system, transplanted tissue generally survives only a few hours or days.

To overcome this inherent problem, scientists began pursuing human cloning as a method for obtaining genetically-compatible cells for transplantation. Human cloning is the process through which an human egg is taken from a woman, the nucleus is removed, and then it is replaced with a nucleus from a patient's body cell. Using electrical shock or "chemical bath," the egg is tricked into believing it has been fertilized, and it begins to divide, becoming a human embryo.

A general misconception exists that there are two types of human cloning: therapeutic cloning (or "cloning-for-biomedical-research") and reproductive cloning (or "cloning-to-produce-children"). However, these designations are simply two different rationales or justifications offered for the same procedure, known medically as "somatic cell nuclear transfer," or human cloning.

Both rationales are morally wrong because both scientifically begin with the creation of a cloned human being at the embryonic stage of life. The differing justifications that one clone is destined to be destroyed for its stem cells and the other for implantation in a womb do not—and cannot—change the basic scientific fact that the cloned human embryos created for therapeutic or reproductive purposes are simultaneously human beings. For this reason and others, comprehensive bans on human cloning should be enacted in the 50 states and by the U.S. Congress.

Currently, no federal law bans human cloning for any purpose, and the U.S. Supreme Court has not yet spoken on the subject. However, seven states ban human cloning for any purpose, while eight states ban cloning-to-produce-children. Five states have no laws banning human cloning, but do possess statutes which may be interpreted as prohibiting harmful experimentation on IVF-created or cloned human embryos. Conversely, at least seven states fund cloning or embryonic stem-cell research.

AUL has drafted a "Human Cloning Prohibition Act" to assist states seeking to ban human cloning for all purposes. And as previously mentioned, AUL has also drafted a model bill prohibiting the public funding of such unethical research.

Assisted Reproductive Technologies (ART)

In vitro fertilization (IVF) is the fertilization of a human egg by a human sperm outside a woman's body, in a laboratory. The term "assisted reproductive technology" (ART) encompasses both IVF as well as other newer forms of ART. Despite the increasingly wide-spread use of these reproductive technologies, there is a lack of common-sense regulation of these procedures at both the federal and state levels.

This lack of regulation has resulted in the storage of more than 400,000 cryopreserved (frozen) human embryos in laboratories across the United States.

In 2004, the President's Council on Bioethics issued a report, *Reproduction & Responsibility*, outlining the lack of regulation of ART. As the Council's report points out, "[t]here is only one federal statute that aims at the regulation of assisted reproduction: the 'Fertility Clinic Success Rate and Certification Act of 1992' (sometimes called the 'Wyden Act')," and it only serves two purposes: 1) providing consumers with information about the effectiveness of ART services, and 2) providing states with a model certification process for embryo laboratories.[4] Additionally, the "Clinic Laboratory Improvement Amendments of 1988" govern quality assurance and control in clinical laboratories including those involved in ART, and the Centers for Disease Control and Prevention (CDC) has announced a new national ART Surveillance System. These regulations pale in comparison to those in place in Great Britain, Germany, Sweden, Switzerland, and many other European nations, where, for example, the number of embryos transferred per reproductive cycle is limited by law.

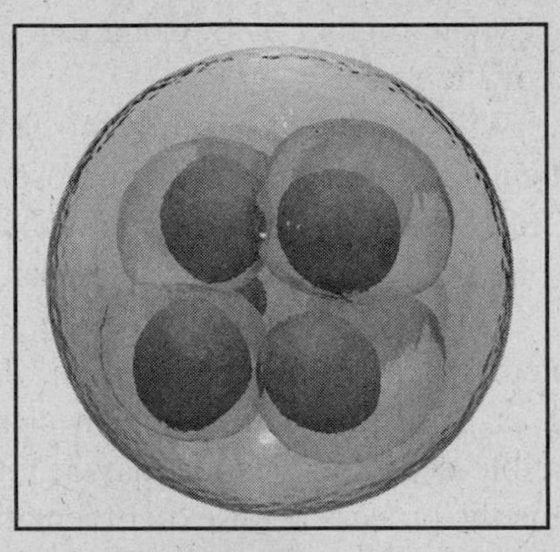

The Council's March 2004 report further confirmed that ART is little regulated by the states. In fact, as the report noted, "[t]he vast majority of state statutes directly concerned with assisted reproduction … are concerned mostly with the question of access to such services."[5] For example, at least 14 states address insurance coverage of ART.

Meanwhile, a small number of states have various provisions providing that only physicians may perform ART, placing limits on assisted insemination procedures, defining the legal status of the child created by ART, defining the legal status of the parent or donor, regulating the use of public funds or facilities for ART, mandating informed consent for ART, or governing the treatment of human embryos.

Responsible state and federal regulation is necessary for several reasons:

- Assisted reproductive technologies, primarily IVF, are the gateway to all future genetic engineering. The current lack of regulation promotes the creation and destruction of excess embryos and, if not adequately responded to, promotes conditions conducive for human cloning and other immoral experimentation on human life in its earliest forms.

- The health of women undergoing IVF, who are often injected with hormones that may cause cancer and other diseases, may be compromised, and subsequently-born children may suffer genetic damage from the procedures.

- There are increasing numbers of multiple births (with associated health and safety concerns), as well as the use of so-called selective reductions (*i.e.*, abortions) of unborn children.

AUL has drafted model legislation, entitled the "Assisted Reproductive Technologies Disclosure and Risk Reduction Act," aimed at ensuring truly informed consent by couples undergoing ART processes as well as regulating the number of embryos that can be transferred in a single reproductive cycle.

Embryo Adoption

The lack of ART regulation has left hundreds of thousands of embryos frozen in time. But through embryo adoption, couples can adopt so-called leftover embryos from other couples who have already undergone IVF. This process represents an emerging alternative to the traditional options left to IVF parents: indefinite cryopreservation, donation to anonymous persons, or donation for research.

Not only does embryo adoption allow parents to choose an alternative other than destruction for research, but it also offers a more attractive option than donation. When the embryos are donated to other couples, as opposed to adopted by them, the process is anonymous and the placement is usually determined by the fertility clinic's physician. Receiving couples usually undergo only basic medical screening and psychological counseling.

When embryos are adopted, on the other hand, the process is typically much more open. The adopting family will likely have access to the child's history, a potential match for future organ donation, and the possibility of a relationship with the placing family. Programs such as the Snowflake Embryo Adoption Program require adopting couples to undergo extensive screening, such as fingerprinting, background checks, home studies, infant CPR, and parenting classes. Placing families and adoptive families prepare informational portfolios about themselves—dossiers including everything from photographs to information regarding religious backgrounds. Like birth mothers, genetic parents use this information to choose adoptive parents to bear and raise their embryos.

Currently, however, embryos are usually stranded in a sort of legal no man's-land. Many courts are reluctant to classify embryos as property, but they also do not characterize them as human beings. Laws regarding embryo donation and adoption are, at best, unsettled. There are no federal laws which specifically address these issues, but three states have provided general guidance for embryo donation and allow for embryo adoption.

AUL has crafted a model bill, entitled the "Embryo Adoption Act," for states interested in explicitly permitting embryo adoption and bringing it under the auspices of their existing adoption laws.

Genetic Testing and Discrimination

Genetic testing is currently available for 1,500 diseases, and tests for hundreds of others are currently being developed.[6] But, as with other areas of biotechnological success, ethical issues have arisen with the advancement of genetic testing. For example, can health insurance companies use the results of genetic testing in granting or denying coverage? Or can employers screen the genetic information of potential employees before making hiring or promotion decisions?

Denying health insurance coverage on the basis of genetic disease is not new. In the 1970s, some insurance companies denied coverage or charged higher premiums to African Americans who carried the Sickle cell anemia gene. More recently, young children were denied health insurance because they carried a recessive genetic disease. In another example, the health insurance coverage of a young boy with Fragile X Syndrome (an inherited form of mental retardation) was dropped; the company claimed the syndrome was a pre-existing condition. On the employment front, workers for Burlington Northern Sante Fe Railroad were tested for genetic predisposition to carpal tunnel syndrome.

In 2008, Congress took an initial step toward protecting patients against such discrimination by passing the "Genetic Information Nondiscrimination Act" (GINA). GINA prohibits employers and health insurers from discriminating against persons on the basis of their genetic information.

But this is only an initial step. GINA only protects against discrimination by employers and health insurers—it does not prohibit discrimination by life, disability, or long-term care insurers. Further, no current federal law or U.S. Supreme Court precedent addresses the issue of prenatal testing and the proper use of the results of genetic testing performed on the unborn. Therefore, it is up to the states to ensure that their citizens are not discriminated against by health, life, disability, and long-term care insurers.

Some states already address prenatal testing in one way or another—either by affirming life or, sadly, by encouraging abortion. While most states and the District of Columbia encourage life by prohibiting discrimination by insurance companies, there are a number of states that encourage the "prevention" (*i.e.*, abortion) of birth defects through the use of amniocentesis and prenatal testing. At least 14 states encourage such genetic testing or allow discrimination by insurance companies.

KEY TERMS

- **Adult stem cells**—semi-specialized cells that create the end-stage cells that do the work of the body. Present throughout life, they continually work to replace dying end-stage cells. There are no ethical difficulties associated with using these cells as there are with embryonic stem cells. Sometimes referred to as "multipotent stem cells," more than 70 different diseases have been treated with these cells.

- **Cloning**—the creation, by whatever technique, of an entity genetically identical to another entity already in existence. Through cloning, the new entity has only one genetic parent, not two as in normal reproduction.

- **Cloning-for-biomedical-research**—the creation of a new human being at the embryonic stage of life genetically identical to a single parent, with the intention of harvesting the clone's stem cells for experimentation, thereby resulting in the destruction of the cloned human being.

- **Cloning-to-produce-children**—the creation of a new human being at the embryonic stage of life genetically identical to a single parent, with the intention that the cloned human being will be implanted in a womb and born.

- **Cord blood stem cell**—an adult stem cell found in the umbilical cord blood of newborn infants. Umbilical cords, which are routinely discarded, were discovered to have an unusually high concentration of adult stem cells which are very easy to obtain and are capable of treating a host of diseases. In 2006, Congress passed legislation that will create a national umbilical cord blood bank similar to the national bone marrow system for the public.

- **Embryo**—an entity that, through whatever means (normal reproduction, cloning, or other method), has a full complement of DNA and, with the proper environment and nutrition and unless otherwise interrupted, will develop along the natural course of progression for that species into further stages of development until natural death.

- **Embryonic stem cell**—an early-stage stem cell obtained by destroying embryos of the same species. Embryonic stem cells can become virtually any type of cell in the body, but only if properly directed in their development. This naturally happens in the organized human embryo, but is something that scientists have yet to learn how to control. The primary ethical issues associated with using these cells are that they currently require the destruction of a living human embryo and that use of such cells in medical research constitutes unethical experimentation when there has not been adequate research using animals. Sometimes referred to as "pluripotent stem cells," there is not a single disease that scientists can treat with these cells.

- **Genetic discrimination**—discrimination which "occurs if people are treated unfairly because of differences in their DNA that increase their chances of getting a certain disease. For example, a health insurer might refuse to give coverage to a woman who has a DNA difference that raises her odds of getting breast cancer. Employers also could use DNA information to decide whether to hire or fire workers."[7]

- **Genetic testing**—testing "developed to find DNA differences that affect our health."[8] In other words, these are tests which "look for alterations in a person's genes or changes in the level of key proteins coded for by specific genes."[9] It is believed that healthcare providers will be able to utilize "information about each person's DNA to develop more individualized ways of detecting, treating and preventing disease."[10]

- **Somatic cell nuclear transfer (SCNT)**—a type of cloning. A process in which the nucleus (and therefore the original DNA) is removed from an egg and discarded, the nucleus of a somatic (or body) cell containing the genetic material of another entity is transplanted into the egg, and an electric shock or chemical solution is used to trick the egg into believing it has been fertilized. The egg, containing another entity's DNA, begins dividing as any other early embryo.

- **Zygote**—a one-cell embryo. From this one cell will arise every cell in the body. Sometimes referred to as a fertilized egg or "totipotent cell."

MYTHS & FACTS

Myth: Embryonic stem-cell researchers are close to finding cures for a host of terrible diseases, like cancer, diabetes, and neurological disorders such as Parkinson's.
Fact: Embryonic stem cells are unable to cure anyone of anything. Instead, use of the cells in humans does little good and can do great harm. Adult stem-cell research is helping cure or treat more than 70 diseases, with more work being prepared for or currently in clinical trials.

Myth: Embryonic stem-cell research, including the destruction of embryos for their parts, is morally and ethically acceptable.
Fact: Even if breakthroughs using embryonic stem cells do occur, it is still unethical to destroy human embryos for their "parts." Regardless of the perceived or real benefit of destroying human embryos, there is no ethical justification for destroying nascent human life regardless of its origins. It is never right to intentionally kill innocent human life to save another's life, especially in such a systematic manner.

Myth: Cloned human embryos are not really human.
Fact: This would mean that Dolly, the first mammal clone, was not a sheep, despite the fact she was created using a sheep egg and sheep DNA and after birth looked and acted like a sheep. If cloned human embryos are not human, then what are they? The only logical answer is that a cloned human embryo is fully human.

Myth: We do not owe a right to life to cloned embryos. They are an unnatural aberration.
Fact: Regardless of the ethical issues surrounding the creation of human clones or why a clone was created, if created it should not be forbidden to live. We do not require the destruction of human life when created through other unethical means (*e.g.*, rape). Laws against creating cloned embryos should not require the clone's destruction.

Myth: A ban on destructive human embryo research or human cloning will stifle scientific research or economic development in my state.
Fact: Few companies even do this research, in part because there are no foreseeable cures that will recoup the dollars needed for investment. And, if embryonic stem-cell research ends up not producing cures, companies may not survive long enough to produce any benefit.

Myth: Embryos left over from *in vitro* fertilization (IVF) procedures are just going to die anyway. We should get some benefit from them.
Fact: It is not necessarily the case that embryos left over from IVF procedures will be destroyed. Some parents change their mind and decide to implant the embryos to give

them a chance at survival. Increasingly, infertile couples are adopting embryos that would otherwise be destroyed or languish in cryopreservation. Even if these embryos would be destroyed, it does not give us the right to use them for research material.

Myth: You cannot compare a clump of cells smaller than the tip of pencil to an existing human being who is suffering and may die without this research.
Fact: It is not your size or location that gives you value and dignity; rather, it is your status as a member of the human race. Every human being, whether as small as the tip of a pencil or as large as a sumo wrestler, deserves the protections accorded to all other human beings. If we decide that some members of the human race should not receive those protections, then we are all at risk if the rich, powerful, or a simple majority decides some of us are no longer worthy of life.

Myth: Adult stem cells are not as capable as embryonic stem cells.
Fact: While it is generally agreed that embryonic stem cells are more flexible in becoming different tissue types than adult stem cells, the idea that adult cells are not as capable as embryonic cells for use in treatments is pure speculation. Currently, adult cells are much more capable of treating human beings than embryonic cells, which have yet to cure a single disease.

Myth: Promoting embryo adoption will limit the availability of embryos for research and will therefore prevent us from discovering important cures for debilitating diseases.
Fact: The vast majority of embryos in storage (over 80 percent) are reserved for the genetic parents' possible future use. Encouraging embryo adoption will simply lessen the number of embryos that remain indefinitely suspended in frozen storage, and further allow loving families to bear and raise children.

Myth: Now that the federal government has passed GINA, patients are fully protected.
Fact: GINA does not cover everyone. For example, GINA does not cover members of the military. In addition, GINA only pertains to employers and health insurers. It does not prohibit discrimination by life, disability, or long-term care insurers. Furthermore, GINA is only a minimum standard of protection that must be met in all states. States are free to pass laws providing more protection and more restrictions on the use of genetic information by insurers and others.

Myth: Americans who possess certain genetic traits are already protected under the "Americans with Disabilities Act" (ADA).
Fact: While it is true that the ADA prohibits employers from discriminating against disabled persons who are capable of performing their duties with reasonable accommodation, and the Equal Employment Opportunities Commission (EEOC) has stated that healthy persons with genetic predispositions to a disease fall within the scope of the ADA, this carries no weight with insurance companies, who are not held accountable to the EEOC in their decisions of who and who not to insure. Thus, GINA and state laws are necessary to protect individuals from such discrimination on the part of insurance companies.

Myth: My state adequately protects me against genetic discrimination.
Fact: While at least 40 states and the District

of Columbia prohibit discrimination in health insurance policies based upon the results of genetic testing, the degree of protection differs. For example, some states specifically prohibit health insurers from requiring testing, while others allow health insurers to consider the results of tests only if the patients voluntarily submit favorable results. On the other hand, some states actually encourage genetic testing or allow discrimination in certain types of health insurance policies. Thus, states are encouraged to enact further restrictions limiting the use of genetic information by all insurance companies.

Endnotes

[1] Michael J. Schlambott et. al., *Derivation of pluripotent stem cells from cultured human primordial germ cells*, Proc. Nat'l Acad. Sci. USA 95:23, 13726-731 (1998).

[2] See M. J. Evans & M. H. Kaufman, *Establishment in culture of pluripotential cells from mouse embryos*, Nature 292, 154–56 (1981).

[3] *See* David Prentice, *Under the Microscope: A Scientific Look at Cloning,* Family Policy 15:3. *See also* Wesley J. Smith, *Lessons From the Cloning Debate: The Need for a Secular Approach*, in Human Dignity in the Biotech Century 194-96 (Charles W. Colson & Nigel M. de S. Cameron, eds. 2004) (explaining that it is not physiologically possible to obtain enough eggs to treat disease through stem cell research and human cloning).

[4] President's Council on Bioethics, *Reproduction & Responsibility* (March 2004).

[5] *Id.* at 51.

[6] Genetic & Public Policy Center of Johns Hopkins University, *Genetic Privacy & Discrimination* (updated March 2009), available at http://www.dnapolicy.org/policy.privacy.php (last visited July 17, 2009).

[7] National Human Genome Research Institute, *Genetic Discrimination Fact Sheet: Genetic Information Nondiscrimination Law of 2008* (updated January 9, 2009), available at http://www.genome.gov/10002328 (last visited July 17, 2009).

[8] *Id.*

[9] National Human Genome Research Institute, *Frequently Asked Questions About Genetic Testing* (February 5, 2009), available at http://www.genome.gov/19516567 (last visited July 17, 2009).

[10] National Human Genome Research Institute, *Genetic Discrimination Fact Sheet: Genetic Information Nondiscrimination Law of 2008, supra.*

Laws Related to Human Cloning

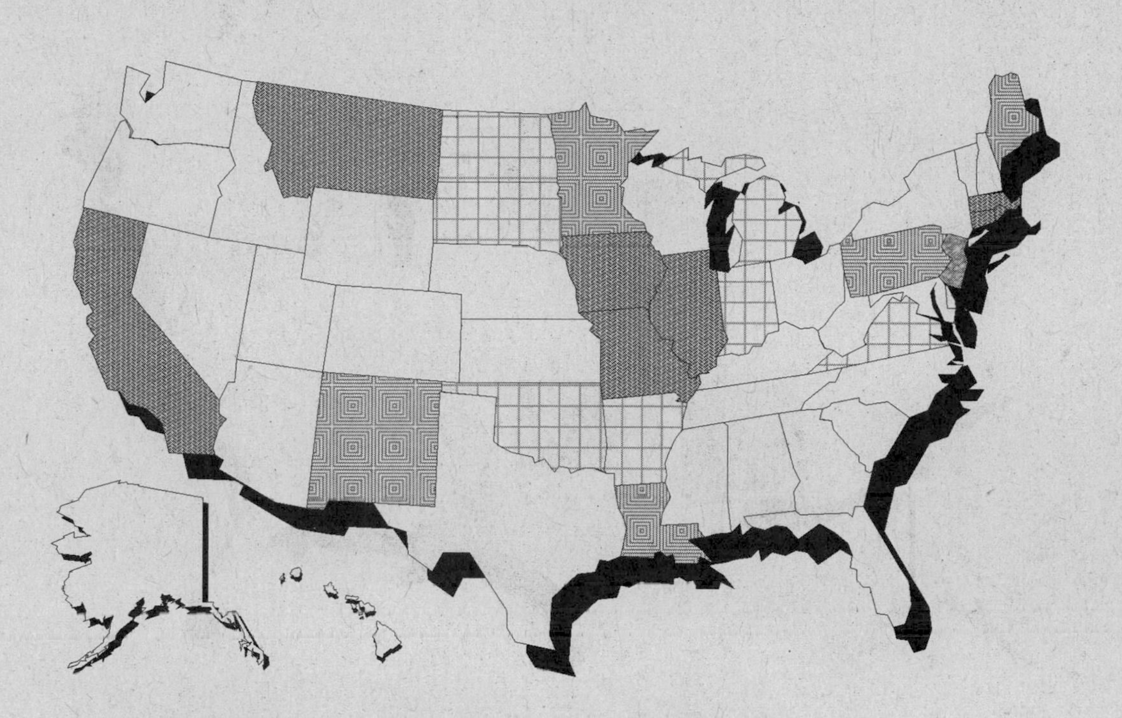

Seven states ban cloning for any purpose, including both cloning-to-produce-children and cloning-for-biomedical-research: AR, IN, MI, ND, OK, SD, and VA.

Eight states allow human cloning for destructive embryo research (cloning-for-biomedical-research) but prohibit attempting to bring a cloned child to term (cloning-to-produce-children): CA, CT, IL, IA, MA, MO, MT, and RI.

Five states have no specific law on human cloning, but have other statutes that either expressly or implicitly ban destructive human embryo research on IVF-created embryos and possibly on cloned human embryos: LA, ME, MN, NM, and PA.

One state permits destructive experimentation on both cloned human embryos and cloned human fetuses up to live birth: NJ.

Laws Related to Destructive Embryo Research

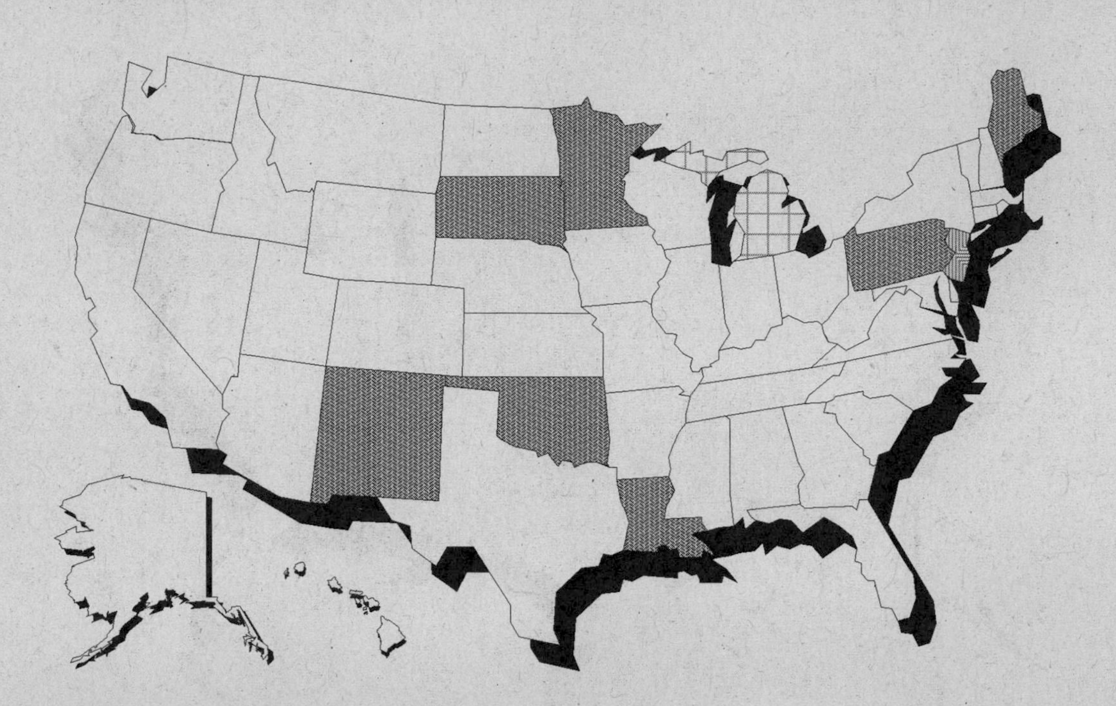

Seven states either expressly or implicitly ban destructive human embryo research on IVF-created embryos and/or cloned human embryos: LA, ME, MN, NM, OK, PA, and SD.

One state expressly permits destructive experimentation on IVF-created embryos: MI

One state permits destructive experimentation on both cloned human embryos and cloned human fetuses up to live birth: NJ

Funding of Cloning & Destructive Human Embryo Research

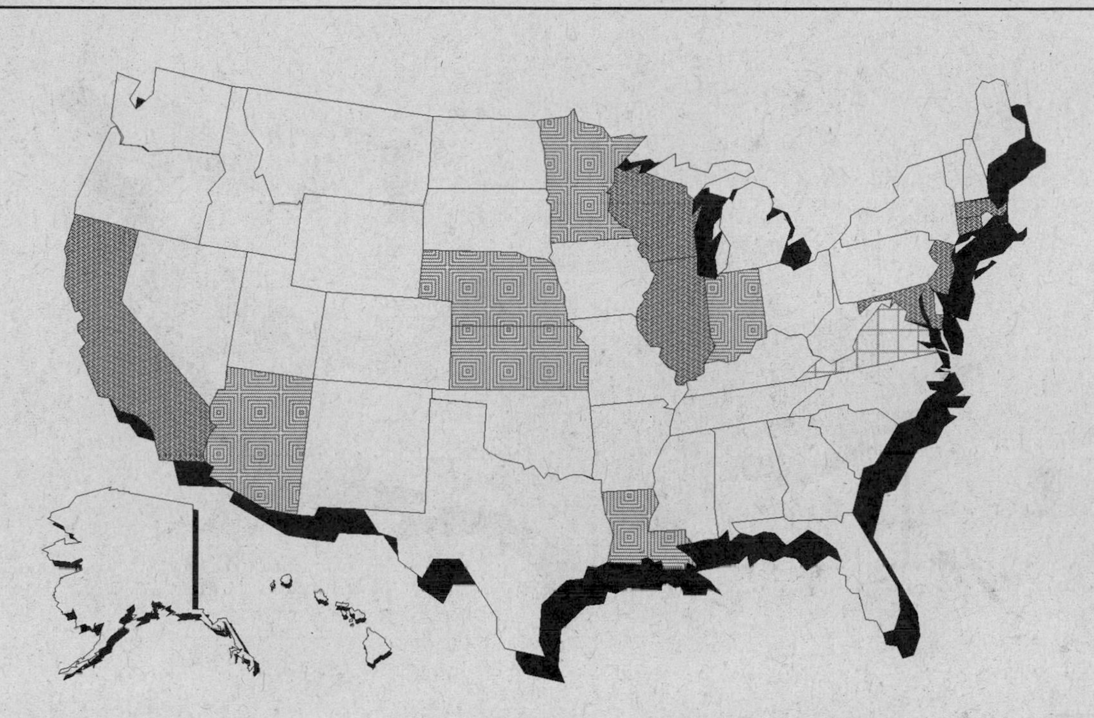

Seven states use state tax dollars to fund destructive human embryo research: CA, CT, IL, MD, MA, NJ, and WI.

Six states restrict funding or use of state facilities for human cloning and/or destructive human embryo research: AZ, IN, KS, LA, MN, and NE.

One state restricts funding for human cloning and/or destructive embryo research and prohibits loans for entities conducting destructive human embryo research, but also allows tax incentives for destructive human embryo research by providing that research equipment is not taxed: VA

Ethical Research Alternatives

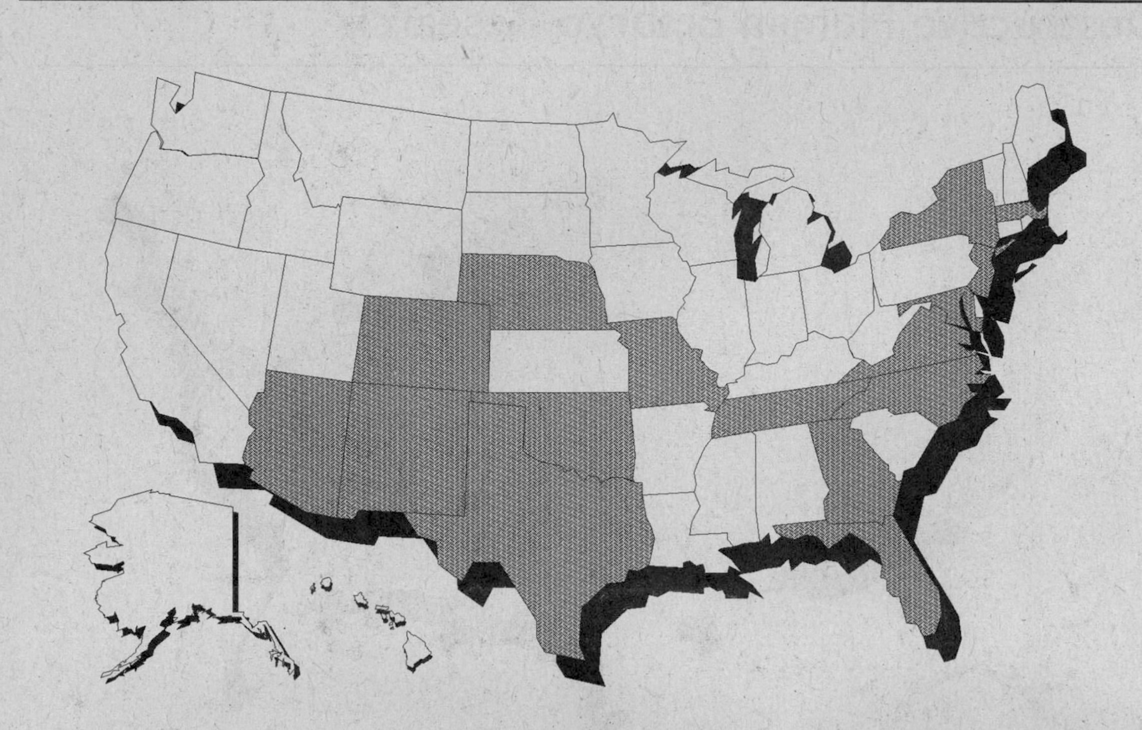

At least 16 states promote or encourage the use of umbilical cord cells and/or other forms of adult stem cells for research: AZ, CO, FL, GA, MD, MA, MO, NE, NJ, NM, NY, NC, OK, TN, TX, and VA.

Other Restrictions on Cloning & Destructive Human Embryo Research

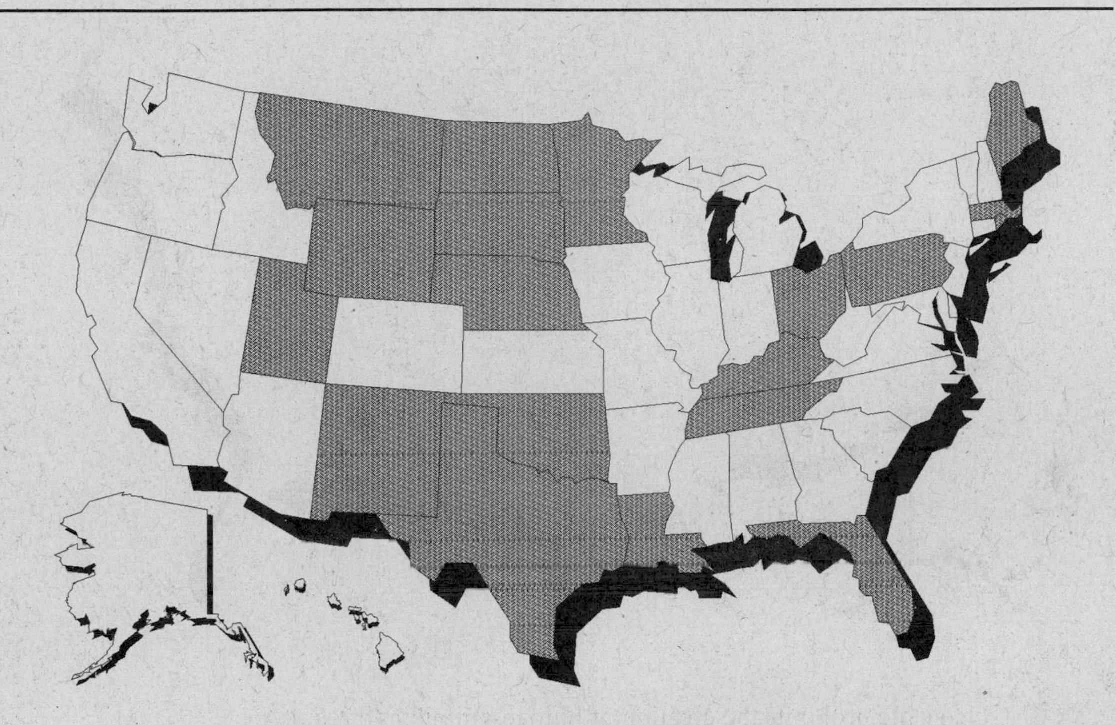

Nineteen states continue to ban so-called fetal experimentation (however, four federal courts have invalidated other states' fetal experimentation laws): FL, KY, LA, ME, MA, MN, MT, NE, NM, ND, OH, OK, PA, RI, SD, TN, TX, UT, and WY.

Laws Related to Chimeras

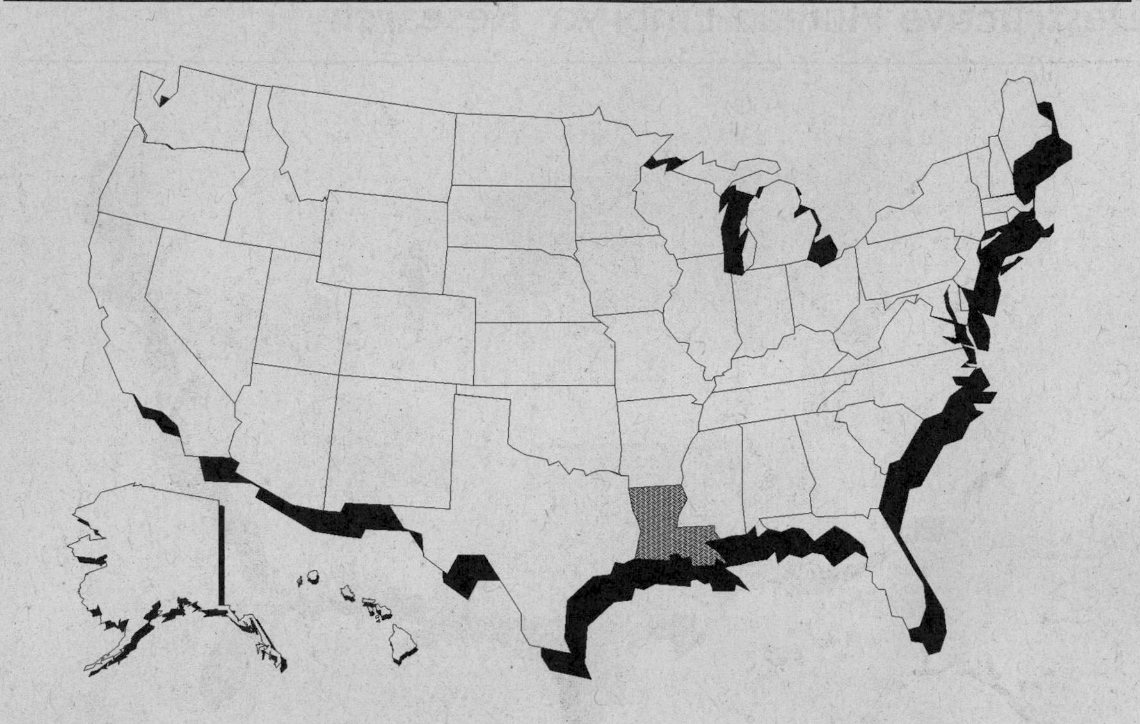

One state prohibits the creation of human-animal hybrids: LA.

State Regulation of ART/IVF

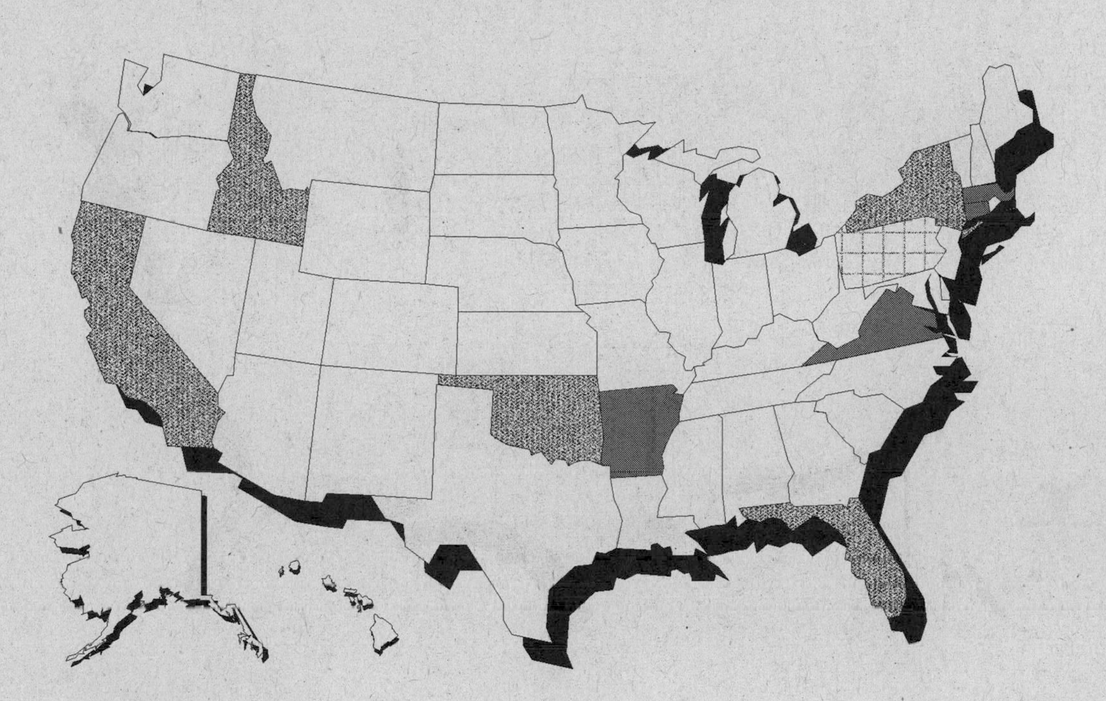

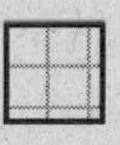

Only one state comprehensively regulates ART/IVF and facilities performing such procedures: PA

At least five states regulate the donation and/or transfer of human sperm, human eggs, or pre-embryos: CA, FL, ID, NY, and OK

Four states require some form of informed consent or impose specific contractual requirements for ART/IVF: AR, CT, MA, and VA

Other State Regulations of ART/IVF

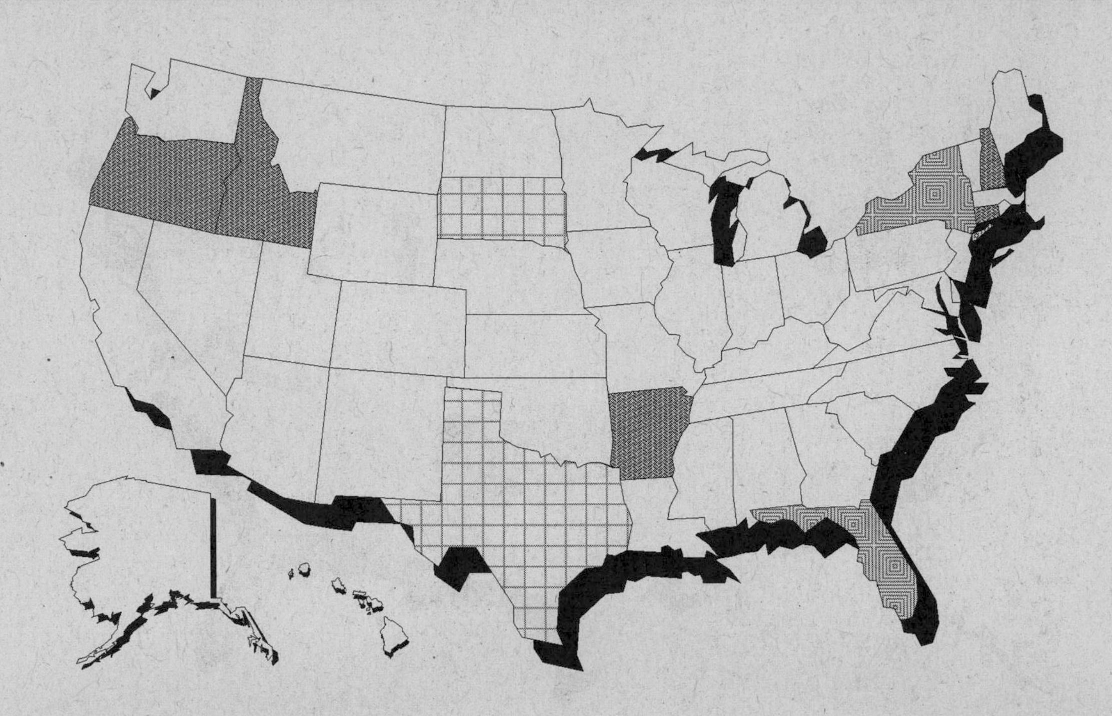

At least five states regulate the types of healthcare providers that can perform ART/IVF: AR, CT, ID, NH, and OR

Two states regulate gestational surrogacy: FL and NY

At least two other states provide minimal regulation of ART/IVF: SD and TX

Laws Regarding Life & Parenthood in ART/IVF

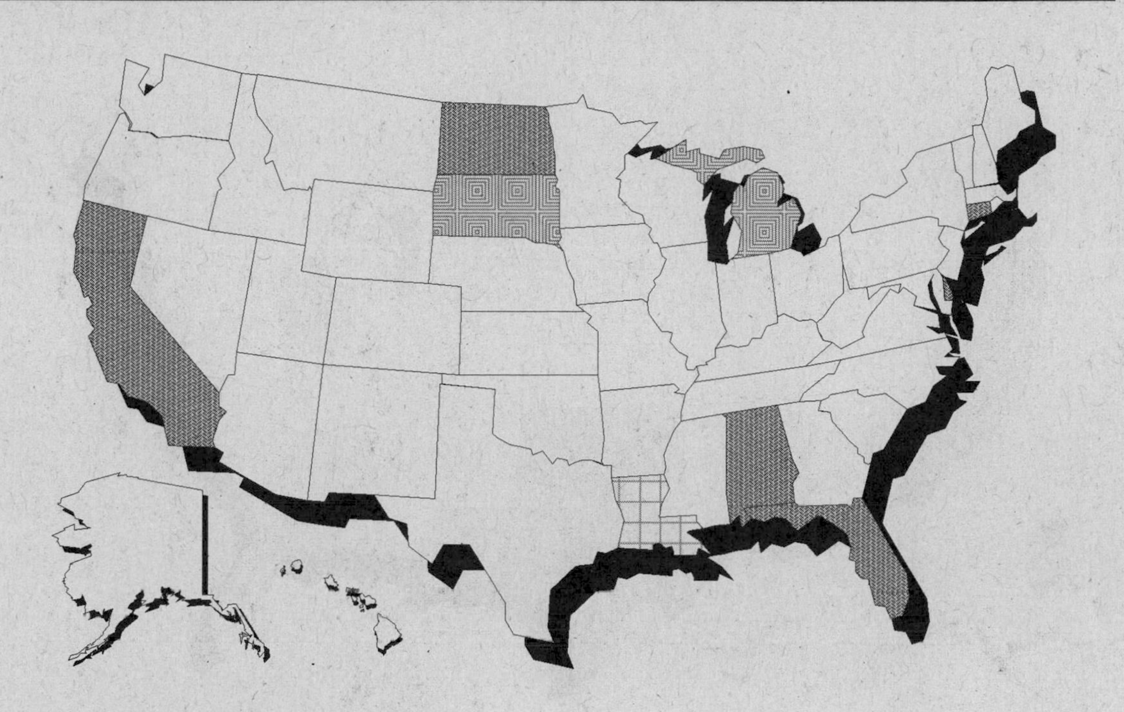

Only one state by law defines an embryo conceived through ART/IVF as a "juridical (or legal) person": LA

Two states regulate the use and treatment of gametes, neonates, embryos, or fetuses: MI and SD

At least six states terminate parental rights/responsibilities of donors or otherwise govern the legal status of children conceived through the use of ART/IVF: AL, CA, CT, DE, FL, and ND

Laws Related to Embryo Donation & Adoption

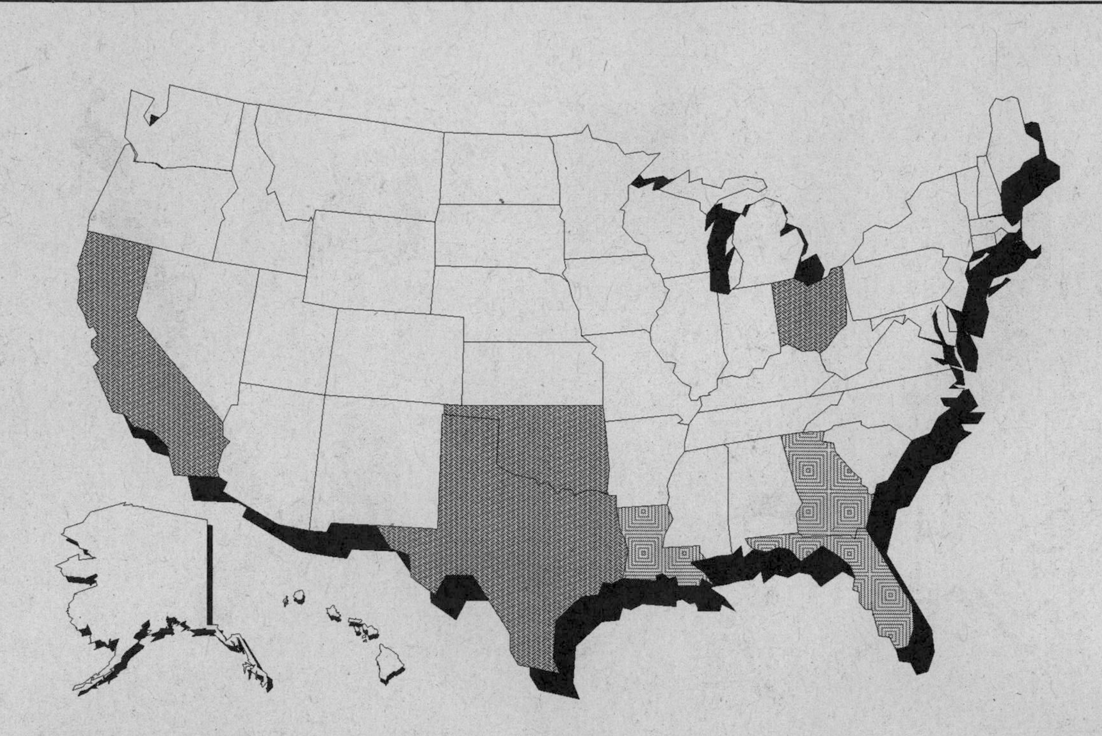

Four states have laws in effect providing some general guidance for embryo donation: CA, OH, OK, and TX.

Three states have laws in effect providing some general guidance for embryo donation and allow for embryo adoption: FL, GA, and LA.

2009 State Legislative Sessions in Review:
Bioethics & biotechnology

By Mailee R. Smith
Staff Counsel, Americans United for Life

One of the basic foundations of American society is that human beings have inherent dignity and, therefore, are always to be treated as ends and never merely as means to an end. Consequently, even the noble goal of healing people must not be achieved by the immoral means of destroying other human beings, including those at the embryonic stage of life. Of all human beings, embryos are the most defenseless against abuse. The intentional destruction of some human beings for the alleged good of other human beings is always morally wrong. Therefore, destroying human embryos to harvest their stem cells should be legally proscribed, as should all forms of human cloning.

Unfortunately, the ongoing legislative debates in state houses around the nation over measures to proscribe or support stem cell research and human cloning are filled with hyperbole and misinformation. The following is just a sampling of important information all too often missing or withheld from crucial public discussions over the desirability and morality of research and experimentation on human beings at the earliest stages of life:

- The American people and their elected representatives should be cautious of the seductive claims of medical utopia made by biotech research firms who have a strong financial interest in using human beings as commodities. Biotech companies advocating for the legalization and government funding of embryonic stem-cell research usually neglect to inform the public that embryonic research is far superceded in successful current applications by those derived from ethical research, principally that involving adult stem cells.

- Bans on medical research that destroys human life at its earliest stages or that creates human life for further research or experimentation (*i.e.*, human cloning) would have the indirect benefit of allowing research money and effort to be directed to the already productive field of adult stem-cell transplantation and somatic cell gene therapies. These procedures are free of the ethical dilemmas associated with destructive human embryo research.

- Importantly, adult stem cells have a proven record of effective clinical remedies, which cannot be said for embryonic stem cells. To date, scientists have been able to help patients suffering from over 70 different diseases and injuries—including brain cancer, leukemia, lymphoma, Crone's disease, Lupus, heart damage, Parkinson's,

Sickle cell anemia, and end-stage bladder disease—using adult stem cells. No clinical use of human embryonic stem cells has yet been published in the scientific literature.

- A general misconception exists that there are two types of human cloning—"cloning-to-produce-children" and "cloning-for-biomedical-research." In truth, these designations are simply two different rationales or justifications offered for the same procedure, known medically as "somatic cell nuclear transfer," or human cloning. Both rationales are morally wrong because scientifically both begin with the creation of a cloned human being at the embryonic stage of life. The differing justifications that one clone is destined for implantation in a womb and the other is destined to be destroyed for its stem cells do not—and cannot—change the basic scientific fact that the cloned human embryos created for both reproductive or therapeutic purposes are simultaneously human beings.

In 2009, legislators in 31 states considered more than 95 measures related to biotechnologies. This level of activity represents an almost 20 percent increase from 2008. Over the last several years, however, we have seen a significant downward trend in legislation concerning these critical and emerging areas. Thus, even with the increase in bioethics-related legislation in 2009, this level of activity does not compare favorably to the 500 bills introduced in 2005.

Human Cloning

At least 11 states—including Alabama, Georgia, Michigan, Minnesota, Montana, New Mexico, New York, Oklahoma, Oregon, Texas, and West Virginia—considered measures related to human cloning.

Montana enacted a measure that bans cloning for reproductive purposes (cloning-to-produce-children), but it does not ban cloning for all purposes.

Oklahoma enacted a measure that prohibits human cloning for all purposes (both cloning-to-produce-children and cloning-for-biomedical-research).

Destructive Embryo Research

At least 12 states—including Alabama, California, Georgia, Illinois, Maryland, Michigan, Minnesota, Mississippi, New Mexico, New York, Oklahoma, and Oregon—considered measures banning or promoting destructive embryo research. In addition, West Virginia considered a measure prohibiting the use of "unborn children" in research experiments.

Oklahoma enacted a measure which prohibits nontherapeutic research that destroys human embryos or subjects embryos to risk of injury or death.

Ethical Forms of Research

At least seven states—Illinois, Maine, Michigan, Minnesota, North Carolina, Ohio, and Texas—considered measures promoting ethical forms of stem cell research, including the use of adult stem cells and umbilical cord blood.

North Carolina enacted legislation requiring the Department of Health and Human Services to make publications available to the public regarding umbilical cord stem cells and umbilical cord blood banking. The new law also requires that the Department encourage healthcare professionals to provide the publications to their pregnant patients.

State Funding of Biotechnology

Funding measures ran the gamut in 2009, from prohibiting taxpayer funding of destructive embryo research and/or cloning, to funding ethical forms of research, to funding destructive embryo research. In all, eight states considered funding measures related to biotechnologies.

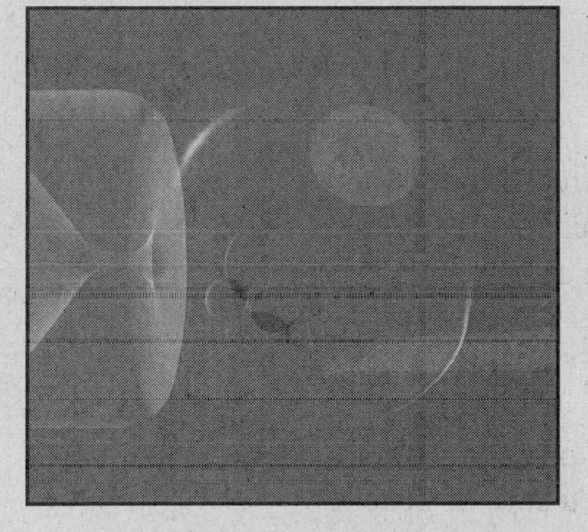

Four states—Minnesota, Missouri, New York, and Texas—considered measures prohibiting or limiting the use of public funding for human cloning or destructive embryo research. Minnesota enacted a measure prohibiting the funding of human cloning.

Three states—Maine, Nebraska, and Oklahoma—considered measures funding ethical forms of research. Nebraska enacted a measure that funds programs enacted in 2008 that support ethical research, and Oklahoma directed funding toward ethical research.

Only one state, Oregon, considered legislation funding destructive embryo research.

Chimeras

Only three states—Georgia, Louisiana, and Michigan—considered measures prohibiting the creation of human-animal hybrids, with Louisiana enacting its bill.

Assisted Reproductive Technology

At least 19 states considered measures related to assisted reproductive technologies (ART), including *in vitro* fertilization (IVF). As usual, most of these bills involved access to—not regulation of—the ART industry.

At least 11 states—including Arkansas, Georgia, Illinois, Kentucky, Maryland, Massachusetts, Michigan, Mississippi, Missouri, Oregon, and Rhode Island—considered measures broadening insurance coverage for assisted reproductive technologies.

At least eight states—including California, Georgia, Hawaii, Michigan, Minnesota, Missouri, New York, and Oklahoma—considered measures regulating (to varying degrees) the ART industry. Missouri's bill would have limited the number of embryos a physician could implant in a woman per reproductive cycle.

A handful of states—including Georgia, Iowa, New York, North Dakota, and Oklahoma—considered measures related to parentage. North Dakota enacted a law involving ART and inheritance rights.

Nebraska considered a measure calling for an

interim study to examine *in vitro* fertilization.

Embryo Adoption

While only one state considered a measure related to embryo adoption in 2008, five states—Georgia, Massachusetts, Mississippi, Oklahoma, and Tennessee—considered such measures in 2009.

Georgia enacted a law changing the definition of "child" to include a human embryo and providing specific procedures for embryo adoption.

Human Egg Donation

At least three states—California, Florida, and Minnesota—considered legislation regulating the donation of or solicitation of human eggs.

Genetic Discrimination

Colorado enacted a measure providing for liability and limitations on disclosure of genetic information and preventing genetic information from being used to deny access to healthcare insurance or Medicare supplemental insurance coverage.

AUL Model Legislation

HUMAN CLONING PROHIBITION ACT

HOUSE/SENATE BILL No. ______
By Representatives/Senators ____________

Section 1. Title.

This Act may be known and cited as the "Human Cloning Prohibition Act."

Section 2. Legislative Findings.

(a) The [*Legislature*] of the state of [*Insert name of State*] finds that:

(1) At least one company has announced that it has successfully cloned a human being at an early embryonic stage of life, and others have announced that they will attempt to clone a human being using the technique known as somatic cell nuclear transfer.

(2) Efforts to create human beings through cloning mark a new and decisive step toward turning human reproduction into a manufacturing process in which human beings are made in laboratories to preordained specifications and, potentially, in multiple copies.

(3) Creating cloned live-born human children, or "cloning-to-produce-children," begins by creating cloned human beings at the embryonic stage of life, a process which some also propose as a way of creating human embryos for destructive research as sources of stem cells and tissues for possible treatment of other humans, or "cloning-for-biomedical-research;"

(4) Many scientists agree that attempts at "cloning-to-produce-children" pose a massive risk of producing children who are stillborn, unhealthy, or severely disabled, and that attempts at "cloning-for-biomedical-research" always result in the destruction of human beings at the embryonic stage of life when their stem cells are harvested.

(5) The prospect of creating new human life, solely to be exploited ("cloning-to-produce-children") or destroyed ("cloning-for-biomedical-research") in these ways, has been condemned on moral grounds by many as displaying a profound disrespect for life.

(6) The distinction between so-called therapeutic cloning and reproductive cloning is a false distinction scientifically because both begin with the reproduction of a human being at the embryonic stage of life, one destined for implantation in a womb and one destined for destructive farming of its stem cells. Regardless of its ultimate destiny, all human embryos are simultaneously human beings.

(7) It will be nearly impossible to ban only attempts at "cloning-to-produce-children" if "cloning-for-biomedical-research" is allowed because cloning would take place within the privacy of a doctor-patient relationship; the implantation of embryos to begin a pregnancy is a simple procedure; and any government effort to prevent the implantation of an existing cloned embryo or to prevent birth once implantation has occurred would raise substantial moral, legal, and practical issues.

(b) Based on the above findings, it is the purpose of this Act to prohibit the use of cloning technology to initiate the development of new human beings at the embryonic stage of life for any purpose.

Section 3. Definitions.

For purposes of this Act:

(a) "**Human cloning**" means human asexual reproduction, accomplished by (1) introducing the genetic material from one or more human somatic or embryonic cells into a fertilized or unfertilized oocyte whose nuclear material has been removed or inactivated before or after introduction, so as to produce an organism at any stage of development with a human or predominantly human genetic constitution; (2) artificially subdividing a human embryo at any time from the two-cell stage onward, such that more than one human organism results; or (3) introducing pluripotent cells from any source into a human embryo, nonhuman embryo, or artificially-manufactured human embryo or trophoblast, under conditions where the introduced cells generate all or most of the body tissues of the developing organism.

(b) "**Somatic cell**" means a cell having a complete set of chromosomes obtained from a living or deceased human body at any stage of development.

(c) "**Embryo**" means an organism of the species *homo sapiens* from the single cell stage to eight weeks development.

(d) "**Fetus**" means an organism of the species *homo sapiens* from eight weeks development until complete expulsion or extraction from a woman's body, or removal from an artificial womb or other similar environment designed to nurture the development of such organism.

(e) "**Pluripotent cells**" means stem cells possessing the ability to give rise to most or all of the various cell types that make up the body. One demonstration of pluripotency is the ability, even after prolonged culture, to form derivatives of all three embryonic germ layers from the progeny of a single cell.

Section 4. Prohibitions.

It shall be unlawful for any person or entity, public or private, to intentionally or knowingly:

(a) perform or attempt to perform human cloning;

(b) participate in an attempt to perform human cloning;

(c) transfer or receive the product of human cloning for any purpose; or

(d) transfer or receive, in whole or in part, any oocyte, embryo, fetus, or human somatic cell for the purpose of human cloning.

Section 5. Exceptions.

Nothing in this Act shall restrict areas of scientific research not specifically prohibited by this Act, including *in vitro* fertilization; the administration of fertility-enhancing drugs; or research in the use of nuclear transfer or other cloning techniques to produce molecules, DNA, tissues, organs, plants, animals other than humans or cells other than human embryos.

Section 6. Penalties.

(a) Criminal Penalties:

(1) Any person or entity that violates Sections 4(a) or 4(b) of this Act shall be guilty of a [*Insert degree of felony*].

(2) Any person or entity that violates Sections 4(c) or 4(d) of this Act shall be guilty of a [*Insert degree of misdemeanor*].

(b) Civil Penalty. Any person or entity that violates any provision of this Act and derives a pecuniary gain from such violation shall be fined [*Insert appropriate amount*] or twice the amount of gross gain, or any amount intermediate between the foregoing, at the discretion of the court.

(c) Unprofessional Conduct. Any violation of this Act shall constitute unprofessional conduct pursuant to [*Insert appropriate statutes for 1) medical doctors and surgeons and 2) osteopathic doctors*] and shall result in permanent revocation of the violator's license to practice medicine.

(d) Trade, Occupation, or Profession. Any violation of this Act may be the basis for denying an application for, denying an application for the renewal of, or revoking any license, permit, certificate, or any other form of permission required to practice or engage in a trade, occupation, or profession.

Section 7. Severability.

Any provision of this Act held to be invalid or unenforceable by its terms, or as applied to any person or circumstance, shall be construed so as give it the maximum effect permitted by law, unless such holding shall be one of utter invalidity or unenforceability, in which event such provision shall be deemed severable herefrom and shall not affect the remainder hereof or the application of such provision to other persons not similarly situated or to other, dissimilar circumstances.

Section 8. Right of Intervention

The [*Legislature*], by joint resolution, may appoint one or more of its members who sponsored or co-sponsored this Act, as a matter of right and in his or her official capacity, to intervene to defend this law in any case in which its constitutionality is challenged.

Section 9. Effective Date

This Act takes effect on [*Insert date*].

DESTRUCTIVE HUMAN EMBRYO RESEARCH ACT

HOUSE/SENATE BILL No. ____
Sponsored by Representatives/Senators __________

Section 1. Title.

This Act may be known and cited as the "Destructive Human Embryo Research Act."

Section 2. Legislative Findings and Purpose.

(a) The [*Legislature*] of the State of [*Insert name of State*] finds that:

(1) Human embryos are human beings at the earliest stage of development;

(2) Some human embryos are being created and then destroyed to obtain stem cells for research;

(3) Destructive human embryo research to obtain embryonic stem cells raises grave moral, ethical, scientific, and medical issues that must be addressed;

(4) The moral justification of medical or scientific research cannot be based upon the dehumanizing and utilitarian premise that the end justifies any means; and

(5) Medical research and treatment does not require the destruction of human life, because it can be ethically pursued in other ways, including the use of adult stem cells.

(b) Accordingly, it is the purpose of this Act to prohibit destructive human embryo research.

Section 3. Definitions.

For purposes of this Act:

(a) "**Human embryo**" means a genetically complete living organism of the species *homo sapiens*, from the single cell stage to eight weeks development, that is not located in a woman's body.

(b) "**Gamete**" means a human sperm or unfertilized human ovum.

(c) "**Destructive research**" means medical procedures, scientific or laboratory research, or other kinds of investigation that kill or injure the subject of such research. It does not include:

(1) *in vitro* fertilization and accompanying embryo transfer to a woman's body, or

(2) any diagnostic procedure that may benefit the human embryo subject to such tests.

Section 4. Prohibitions.

It shall be unlawful for any person to:

(a) intentionally or knowingly conduct destructive research on a human embryo;

(b) buy, sell, receive, or otherwise transfer a human embryo with the knowledge that such embryo will be subjected to destructive research; or

(c) buy, sell, receive, or otherwise transfer gametes with the knowledge that a human embryo will be produced from such gametes to be used in destructive research.

Section 5. Sanctions.

(a) Whoever violates Section 4(a) shall be guilty of a [*Insert degree of felony or misdemeanor*] for each violation.

(b) Whoever violates Section 4(b) shall be guilty of a [*Insert degree of felony or misdemeanor*] for each violation.

(c) Whoever violates Section 4(c) shall be guilty of a [*Insert degree of felony or misdemeanor*] for each violation.

Section 6. Severability.

Any provision of this Act held to be invalid or unenforceable by its terms, or as applied to any person or circumstance, shall be construed so as give it the maximum effect permitted by law, unless such holding shall be one of utter invalidity or unenforceability, in which event such provision shall be deemed severable herefrom and shall not affect the remainder hereof or the application of such provision to other persons not similarly situated or to other, dissimilar circumstances.

Section 7. Right of Intervention.

The [*Legislature*], by joint resolution, may appoint one or more of its members who sponsored or co-sponsored this Act, as a matter of right and in his or her official capacity, to intervene to defend this law in any case in which its constitutionality is challenged.

Section 8. Effective Date.

This Act takes effect on [*Insert date*].

PROHIBITION ON PUBLIC FUNDING OF HUMAN CLONING AND DESTRUCTIVE EMBRYO RESEARCH ACT

HOUSE/SENATE Bill No.____
By Representatives/Senators______________

Section 1. Short Title.

This Act may be cited as the "Prohibition on Public Funding of Human Cloning and Destructive Embryo Research Act."

Section 2. Legislative Findings and Purpose.

(a) The [*Legislature*] of the State of [*Insert name of State*] finds that:

(1) The prospect of creating new human life solely to be exploited or destroyed has been condemned on moral grounds by many as displaying a profound disrespect for human life.

(2) Destructive human embryo research reduces the status of human beings from ends in themselves to a mere means to another's possible benefit.

(3) The moral justification of medical or scientific research cannot be based upon the dehumanizing and utilitarian premise that the potential ends justify any means.

(4) Ethical research—research not involving human cloning and destructive embryo research—has proven more promising than destructive research. For example, so-called therapeutic cloning has, thus far, made no valuable therapeutic advancements, while research with ethically-obtained adult stem cells has already produced significant and valuable contributions and improved patient health. Adult stem-cell contributions have included heart tissue regeneration; corneal reconstruction; treatment for autoimmune diseases such as diabetes, lupus, Crohn's disease, and multiple sclerosis; and treatment for leukemia and other related bone and blood cancers.

(5) Moreover, recent and promising advances in reprogramming human cells to behave as if in an embryonic state render controversial cloned human embryos unnecessary for use in embryonic stem-cell research.

(6) Cloning embryos and destructive embryo research require human egg cells, which are highly expensive to obtain.

(7) Harvesting human egg cells also poses significant health risks to women. Such risks include ovarian hyperstimulation syndrome, damage to internal organs or blood vessels, infertility, depression, and death.

(8) Harvesting human egg cells for research, whether women are compensated or not, could result in the commoditization of women.

(9) Public opinion is divided over the deep, conflicting moral and ethical concerns on matters related to payment to women for access to their human egg cells. Providing public funds to be exchanged in these transactions would be a misuse of revenue collected from concerned [*citizens or Americans*].

(10) Public opinion is similarly divided over the deep, conflicting moral and ethical concerns surrounding the creation and destruction of human embryos. Providing public funds to such research would be a misuse of revenue collected by this State.

(b) The [*Legislature's*] purpose in enacting this ban on taxpayer funding is to further the important and compelling state interests of:

(1) Respecting life and fostering a culture of life;

(2) Limiting public expenditures;

(3) Directing public expenditures away from funding research that has not yielded any significant scientific contributions;

(4) Directing public expenditures toward funding research that has already yielded significant contributions for patients;

(5) Relieving the consciences of taxpayers concerned about the possible exploitation of women that may result from the collection of and payment for human egg cells; and

(6) Relieving the consciences of those resident taxpayers who object to human cloning and destructive embryo research.

Section 3. Definitions.

For the purposes of this Act:

(a) "**Human cloning**" means human asexual reproduction, accomplished by (1) introducing the genetic material from one or more human somatic or embryonic cells into a fertilized or unfertilized oocyte whose nuclear material has been removed or inactivated before or after introduction, so as to produce an organism at any stage of development with a human or predominantly human genetic constitution; (2) artificially subdividing a human embryo at any time from the two-cell stage onward, such that more than one human organism results; or (3) introducing pluripotent cells from any source into a human embryo, nonhuman embryo, or artificially-manufactured human embryo or trophoblast, under conditions where the introduced cells generate all or most of the body tissues of the developing organism.

(b) "**Somatic cell**" means a cell having a complete or nearly complete set of chromosomes obtained from a living or deceased human body at any stage of development.

(c) "**Human embryo**" means an organism with a human or predominately human genetic constitution, from a single cell up to eight weeks of development, that is derived by fertilization, parthenogenesis, cloning (also known as 'somatic cell nuclear transfer'), or any other means from one or more human gametes or human diploid cells.

(d) "**Embryonic stem cell**" means a stem cell obtained from an embryo of the same species.

(e) "**Destructive research**" means medical procedures, scientific or laboratory research, or other kinds of investigation that kill or injure the subject of such research. It does not include:

(1) *In vitro* fertilization and accompanying embryo transfer to a woman's body;

(2) Research in the use of nuclear transfer or other cloning techniques to produce molecules; deoxyribonucleic acid; cells other than human embryos, tissues, organs, plants, or animals other than humans; or

(3) Any diagnostic procedure that benefits the human embryo subject to such tests, while not imposing risks greater than those considered acceptable for other human research subjects.

(f) "**Pluripotent cells**" means stem cells possessing the ability to give rise to most or all of the various cell types that make up the body. One demonstration of pluripotency is the ability, even after prolonged culture, to form derivatives of all three embryonic germ layers from the

progeny of a single cell.

(g) "**Public funds**" means, but is not limited to:

(1) Any monies received or controlled by the State or any official, department, division, agency, or educational or political subdivision thereof, including but not limited to monies derived from federal, state, or local taxes, gifts, or grants from any source; settlements of any claims or causes of action, public or private; bond proceeds or investment income; federal grants or payments; or intergovernmental transfers; and

(2) Any monies received or controlled by an official, department, division, or agency of state government or any educational or political subdivision thereof, or to any person or entity pursuant to appropriation by the [*Legislature*] or governing body of any political subdivision of this State.

Section 4. Human Cloning and Destructive Embryonic Stem-Cell Research Against Public Policy.

The [*Legislature*] declares that public funding of human cloning and destructive embryo research is against public policy.

Section 5. Prohibition.

(a) No public funds shall be used to finance human cloning or destructive embryo research. The State, a state educational institution, or a political subdivision of the State may not use public funds, facilities, or employees to knowingly destroy human embryos for the purpose of research or knowingly participate in human cloning or attempted human cloning.

(b) No public funds shall be used to buy, receive, or otherwise transfer a human embryo with the knowledge that such embryo will be subjected to destructive research; and

(c) No public funds shall be used to buy, receive, or otherwise transfer gametes with the knowledge that a human embryo will be produced from such gametes to be used in destructive research.

This Section will go into effect notwithstanding any other law in the State.

Section 6. Exceptions.

Nothing in this Act shall restrict the funding of areas of scientific research not specifically prohibited by this Act, including:

(a) *In vitro* fertilization and accompanying embryo transfer to a woman's body;

(b) The administration of fertility enhancing drugs;

(c) Research in the use of nuclear transfer or other cloning techniques to produce molecules; deoxyribonucleic acid; tissues, organs, plants, or animals other than humans, or cells other than human embryos; and

(d) Any diagnostic procedure that benefits the human embryo subject to such tests, while not imposing risks greater than those considered acceptable for other human research subjects

Section 7. Penalties.

(a) Criminal Penalty. Any person or entity that knowingly fails or refuses to comply with this Act is guilty of a [*Insert class felony or misdemeanor*].

(b) Civil Penalty. Any person or entity that knowingly fails or refuses to comply with this Act shall be fined [*Insert amount*].

(c) Trade, Occupation, or Profession. Any violation of this Act may be the basis for denying an application for, denying an application for the renewal of, or revoking any license, permit, certificate, or any other form of permission required to practice or engage in a trade, occupation, or profession.

Section 8. Severability.

Any provision of this Act held to be invalid or unenforceable by its terms, or as applied to any person or circumstance, shall be construed so as give it the maximum effect permitted by law, unless such holding shall be one of utter invalidity or unenforceability, in which event such provision shall be deemed severable herefrom and shall not affect the remainder hereof or the application of such provision to other persons not similarly situated or to other, dissimilar circumstances.

Section 9. Right of Intervention.

The [*Legislature*], by joint resolution, may appoint one or more of its members, who sponsored or cosponsored this Act in his or her official capacity, to intervene as a matter of right to defend this law in any case in which its constitutionality is challenged.

Section 10. Standing.

The provisions of this Act shall inure to the benefit of all residents of this State. Any taxpayer of this State or any political subdivision of this State shall have standing to bring suit against the State or any official, department, division, agency, or political subdivision of this State, and any recipient of public funds who or which is in violation of this Act in any court with jurisdiction to enforce the provisions of this Act.

Section 11. Effective Date.

This Act takes effect on [*Insert date*].

ASSISTED REPRODUCTIVE TECHNOLOGIES (ART) DISCLOSURE AND RISK REDUCTION ACT

HOUSE/SENATE BILL No. ______
By Representatives/Senators ____________

Section 1. Title.

This Act may be known and cited as the "Assisted Reproductive Technology (ART) Disclosure and Risk Reduction Act."

Section 2. Legislative Findings and Purposes.

(a) The [*Legislature*] of the State of [*Insert name of Sstate*] finds that:

(1) Infertility is of grave concern to many couples and individuals who want to be parents.

(2) Assisted reproductive technology (ART) is a growing, $4 billion annual industry that serves an increasing number of patients.

(3) ART procedures are expensive. Each cycle can cost $10,000 to 15,000 or more.

(4) Full information about the costs and risks of ART is necessary for patients to evaluate ART, including the risks associated with multiple gestation.

(5) Only one federal statute, the "Fertility Clinic Success Rate and Certification Act of 1992" (42 USCA §263a-1 *et seq*), directly regulates ART procedures by requiring the reporting of clinic success rates.

(6) ART is subject to little state regulation. For example, Connecticut and Virginia require the disclosure and reporting of ART success rates. New Hampshire and Pennsylvania impose some regulations on ART clinics, while several states require insurance coverage for ART.

(7) A number of countries regulate certain aspects of ART. Brazil, Denmark, Germany, Hungary, Saudi Arabia, Singapore, Sweden, and Switzerland limit the number of embryos (from two to four) that can be transferred per treatment

cycle. For example, Germany, Sweden, Denmark, and Switzerland limit transfers to three embryos, at most, per cycle. The United Kingdom limits the number transferred to two.

(8) Voluntary self-regulation of ART programs is not completely effective. Not all ART programs or facilities are members of professional organizations, like the Society for Assisted Reproductive Technology (SART) or the American Society for Reproductive Medicine (ASRM). Moreover, the professional organizations do not independently confirm that their members follow their voluntary guidelines.

(9) In most cases, ART involves the creation of multiple embryos, some of which are not subsequently used in an implantation (transfer) procedure.

(10) This State has an interest in ensuring protection for mothers who undergo ART and for the future health of children conceived through ART.

(11) Informed consent is one of the core principles of ethical medical practice and every patient has a right to information pertinent to an invasive medical procedure. Further, ART is unique because it produces a third party, the prospective child, who must also be considered and protected.

(12) Thorough recordkeeping and reporting is necessary for public education about the rates of success and the costs, risks, and benefits of ART and to ensure proper accountability.

(13) One problem associated with ART is high-order multiple pregnancies (three or more embryos implanting) and their associated health risks to mother and children, for which the economic burdens for parents and society are significant.

(14) Fetal reduction in the event of a high-order multiple pregnancy involves significant risks to the mother and to prospective children subsequently born.

(b) Based on the findings in Subsection (a) of this Section, the purpose of this Act is to:

(1) Protect the safety and well-being of women using ART and the children conceived through ART;

(2) Establish standards for obtaining informed consent from couples and individuals seeking ART;

(3) Require adequate reporting for facilities providing ART services;

(4) Reduce the risk of high-order multiple gestations and the risk of pre-maturity and other complications to mothers and children by limiting the number of embryos transferred in any reproductive cycle;

(5) Reduce the risks of fetal reduction to mothers and children; and

(6) Institute annual reporting requirements to the [*Insert name of State health department or other appropriate agency*].

Section 3. Definitions.

For purposes of this Act only:

(a) "**Assisted reproductive technology (ART)**" means all treatments and procedures which include the handling of human eggs and sperm, including *in vitro* fertilization, gamete intrafallopian transfer (GIFT), zygote intrafallopian transfer (ZIFT), and such other specific technologies as the [*Department of Health*] may include in this definition.

(b) "**ART program**" or "**program**" means all treatments or procedures which include the handling of both human eggs and sperm.

(c) "**Department**" means the [*Insert name of State health department or other appropriate agency*].

(d) "**Embryo**" means the developing human organism however generated, beginning with the diploid cell resulting from the fusion of the male and female pronuclei, or from somatic cell nuclear transfer, or by other means, until approximately the end of the second month of development.

(e) "**Gamete**" means human egg (oocyte) and sperm.

(f) "**Fetal reduction**" means the induced termination of one or more embryos or fetuses.

Section 4. Informed Consent.

(a) All ART programs providing assisted reproductive technologies must, at least 24 hours prior to obtaining a signed contract for services, provide patients with the following information in writing, and obtain a signed disclosure form before services commence:

(1) Description of the procedure(s)

(2) Outcomes and success:

a. The likelihood that the patient will become pregnant, based on experience at that particular program with patients of comparable age and medical conditions;

b. Statistics on the facility's success rate, including the total number of live births, the number of live births as a percentage of completed retrieval cycles, the rates for clinical pregnancy and delivery per completed retrieval cycle bracketed by age groups consisting of women under 30 years of age, women aged 30 through 34 years, women aged 35 through 39 years, and women aged 40 years and older;

c. The likelihood of the patient having a live-born child based on a forthright assessment of her particular age, circumstances, and embryo transfer options;

d. The program's most recent outcome statistics, as reported to the Centers for Disease Control and Prevention (CDC);

e. The existence of, and availability of data from, the "Fertility Clinic Success Rate and Certification Act" regarding pregnancy and live-birth success rates of ART programs, and a copy of the annual report by the ART program to the CDC pursuant to said Act; and

f. Statistics reported by the program to federal and state agencies are to be provided to the patient, along with reported statistics from all other clinics in the state and national ART statistics as reported to the CDC, along with an explanation of the relevance of the statistics.

(3) Costs:

a. The anticipated price (to the patient) of all procedures, including any charges for procedures and medications not covered in the standard fee; and

b. Average cost to patients of a successful assisted pregnancy.

(4) Major known risks:

a. All major known risks and side effects to mothers and children conceived, including psychological risks, associated with all ART drugs and procedures considered;

b. The risks associated with any drugs or fertility-enhancing medications proposed;

c. The risks associated with egg retrieval and embryo or oocyte transfer; and

d. The risks associated with multiple gestation to mother and child(ren).

(5) Multiple gestation and fetal reduction:

a. The likelihood that fetal reduction might be recommended as a response to multiple gestation; and

b. A clear explanation of the nature of fetal reduction and the associated risks for mother and any surviving child.

c. Decisions about embryo conception and transfer, including the patient's right to determine the number of embryos or oocytes to conceive and transfer.

(6) Donor gametes: If relevant, the testing protocol used to ensure that gamete donors are free from known infection, including human immunodeficiency viruses, and free from carriers of known genetic and chromosomal diseases.

(7) Non-transferred embryos:

a. The availability of embryo adoption for non-transferred embryos and information on agencies in the State that process embryo adoption;

b. The risks of cryopreservation for embryos, including information concerning the current feasibility of freezing eggs rather than embryos, and any influence that may have on the likelihood of a live-birth;

c. The current law governing disputes concerning excess embryos; and

d. Information concerning disposition of non-transferred embryos that may be chosen by the patient, and the rights of patients regarding that disposition, and the need to state their wishes and intentions regarding disposition.

(8) Changes that may affect the contract:

g. The effect on treatment, embryos, and the validity of informed consent of clinic closings, divorce, separation, failure to pay storage fees for excess embryos, failure to pay treatment fees, inability to agree on fate of embryos; death of patient or others, withdrawal of consent for transfer after fertilization but before cryopreservation, incapacity, unavailability of agreed upon disposition of embryos, or loss of contact with the clinic; and

h. The patient's right to revoke consent at any time and that charges will be limited to only the services provided, with exceptions possibly made for some shared-risk programs, if relevant.

(b) This information must be discussed with the patient, and the ART program must provide written documentation that all relevant information required by this Section has been given to the patient.

(c) Patients shall be informed of the option of additional counseling throughout future procedures, even if counseling was refused in the past.

(d) Each time a new cycle is undertaken, informed consent must be obtained and information provided to the patient with the latest statistics and findings concerning the patient's status.

(e) The [*Commissioner of Health or other appropriate office/individual*] is authorized to promulgate additional regulations providing more specific guidance for ensuring fully informed consent to ART.

Section 5. Data Collection & Reporting Requirements.

(a) All ART programs shall confidentially collect and maintain the following information, pertaining to the particular ART program, and confidentially report, on such forms as the Department prescribes, the following information to [*Insert name of state health department or other appropriate agency*], no later than February 1 following any year such procedures were performed:

(1) Success rates

a. Rates of success, defined as the total number of live births achieved, the percentage of live births per completed cycle of egg retrieval, and the numbers of both clinical pregnancy and actual delivery as ratios against the number of retrieval cycles completed. These statistics must be broken down into the age group of patients: <30, 30-34, 35-37, 38-40, 41-42, and >43;

b. Rate of live births per transfer; and

c. Number of live births per ovarian stimulation, broken down into age groups.

(2) Storage

a. Information regarding the safekeeping of embryos including:

i. storage location (if stored);

ii. location to which relocated (if transferred to another facility);

iii. purpose for which relocated (if transferred to another facility); and

iv. time and date of disposal of each patient's embryos, if destroyed.

(3) Technologies: Percentage usage of types of ART, including IVF, GIFT, ZIFT, combination, or other.

(4) Multiples:

a. Percentage of pregnancies resulting in multi-fetal pregnancies, broken down by number of fetuses; and

b. Percentage of live births having multiple infants.

(5) Fetal reduction:

a. Number of fetal reductions performed, individually reported, identifying the number of embryos transferred before the reduction;

b. Percentage of transferred embryos that implant;

c. Percentage of premature births per singleton and multiple births; and

d. The use of pre-implantation genetic diagnosis (PGD), if used in the ART program, including data on it safety and efficacy.

(6) Prematurity and other abnormalities:

a. Percentage of birth defects per singleton and multiple births; and

b. Percentage of fetal reductions that resulted in a miscarriage.

(b) The program's medical director shall verify in writing the accuracy of the foregoing data.

(c) The [*Commissioner of Health or other appropriate office or individual*] is authorized to promulgate additional regulations requiring additional or more specific data collection and reporting, as needed. [*The Commissioner shall make the data available in such form as the Commissioner prescribes.*]

Section 6. Limits on transfer of embryos in any reproductive cycle.

(a) It shall be unlawful for any ART clinic or its employees to transfer more than [*two*] embryos per reproductive cycle.

(b) In subsequent assisted reproductive cycles, transfer shall first be attempted with cryopreserved embryos from previous cycles, if they exist. Only after transfer is attempted with cryopreserved embryos may new embryos be conceived through ART. [*In the alternative, Section 6(b) could require presenting patients with the option of emphasizing the use of existing, cryopreserved embryos in future cycles.*]

Section 7. Embryo Donation and Adoption

No ART program may limit or inhibit the option or availability by patients of embryo donation or adoption through psychological evaluations, increased costs or payments, or other conditions.

Section 8. Penalties.

(a) Civil Penalty. Any person or entity that violates any provision of this Act and derives a pecuniary gain from such violation shall be fined [*Insert appropriate amount*] or twice the amount of gross gain, or any amount intermediate between the foregoing, at the discretion of the court [*as is just*].

(b) Unprofessional Conduct. Any violation of this Act shall constitute unprofessional conduct pursuant to [*Insert appropriate state statutes/regulations for 1) medical doctors/surgeons and 2) osteopathic doctors*] and shall result in sanctions increasing in severity from censure to temporary suspension of license to permanent revocation of license.

(c). Trade, Occupation, or Profession. Any violation of this Act may be the basis for denying an application for, denying an application for the renewal of, or revoking any license, permit, certificate, or any other form of permission required to practice or engage in a trade, occupation, or profession.

(d) Facility Licensing. Any violation of this Act by an individual in the employ and under the auspices of a licensed healthcare facility to which the management of said facility consents, knows, or should know may be the basis for denying an application for, denying an application for the renewal of, temporarily suspending, or permanently revoking any operational license, permit, certificate, or any other form of permission required to operate a healthcare facility.

Section 9. Severability.

Any provision of this Act held to be invalid or unenforceable by its terms, or as applied to any person or circumstance, shall be construed so as give it the maximum effect permitted by law, unless such holding shall be one of utter invalidity or unenforceability, in which event such provision shall be deemed severable herefrom and shall not affect the remainder hereof or the application of such provision to other persons not similarly situated or to other, dissimilar circumstances.

Section 9. Right of Intervention

The [*Legislature*], by joint resolution, may appoint one or more of its members who sponsored or co-sponsored this Act, as a matter of right and in his or her official capacity, to intervene to defend this law in any case in which its constitutionality is challenged.

Section 11. Effective Date.

This Act takes effect on [*Insert date*].

EGG PROVIDER PROTECTION ACT

HOUSE/SENATE Bill No. _____
By Representatives/Senators _____________

Section 1. Title.

This Act may be known as the "Egg Provider Protection Act."

Section 2. Legislative Findings and Purposes.

(a) The [*Legislature*] of the State of [*Insert name of State*] finds that:

(1) Human eggs used for research and fertility treatments are obtained from female human providers.

(2) Egg providers tend to be young, single women without children.

(3) Egg providers are usually compensated financially for their eggs or for the time, pain, and inconvenience of the extraction procedure.

(4) Egg harvesting requires preliminary hormone treatment.

(5) This hormone therapy is accompanied by serious health risks, including an increased risk of uterine, ovarian, and breast cancers and complications with future pregnancies.

(6) Many egg providers are not fully informed of the health risks associated with egg harvesting.

(7) Many egg providers suffer emotionally and psychologically for extended periods after their eggs are harvested.

(8) Many egg providers will choose to have children sometime after having their eggs harvested.

(b) Based on the findings in subsection (a) of this Section, it is the purpose of this Act to:

(1) Safeguard the health and welfare of egg providers;

(2) Require fully informed consent that ensures egg providers understand the physical, psychological, and reproductive risks that accompany egg harvesting;

(3) Prevent egg harvesting institutions from exploiting women and commodifying women's bodies; and

(4) Establish an egg provider registry in order to contribute to a more accurate and complete understanding of the effects of egg harvesting on the providers.

Section 3. Definitions.

For purposes of this Act only:

(a) "**Compensation**" means any consideration or payment given to a woman in exchange for the harvesting and use of her eggs. It does not include reimbursement for time and trouble.

(b) "**Department**" means [*Insert reference to appropriate State department or agency responsible for implementing and administering this Act*].

(c) "**Destructive human embryo research**" means medical procedures, scientific or laboratory research, or other kinds of investigation that kill or injure the human embryo. It does not include:

(1) *in vitro* fertilization and accompanying embryo transfer to a woman's body, or

(2) any diagnostic procedure that is intended to benefit the human embryo subject to such tests.

(d) "**Egg**" means the unfertilized gamete, or oocyte, of a human female.

(e) "**Egg harvesting**" means the extraction of an egg or eggs from the reproductive organs of a provider for purposes other than the impregnation of the provider with those same eggs.

(f) "**Egg provider**" or "**provider**" means any woman who provides or agrees to provide her eggs for purposes other than her own impregnation with those same eggs.

(g) "**Human cloning**" means human asexual reproduction, accomplished by (1) introducing the genetic material from one or more human somatic or embryonic cells into a fertilized or unfertilized oocyte whose nuclear material has been removed or inactivated before or after introduction, so as to produce an organism at any stage of development with a human or predominantly human genetic constitution; (2) artificially subdividing a human embryo at any time from the two-cell stage onward, such that more than one human organism results; or (3) introducing pluripotent cells from any source into a human embryo, nonhuman embryo, or artificially-manufactured human embryo or trophoblast, under conditions where the introduced cells generate all or most of the body tissues of the developing organism.

(h) "**Licensed physician**" means any person licensed to practice medicine in this State. The term includes medical doctors and doctors of osteopathy.

(i) "**Medication**" means a hormone, birth control pill, GnRH agonist, GnRH antagonist, gonadotropin, estrogen suppressor, antibiotic, pain medication, or any other drug.

(j) "**Public funds**" means, but is not limited to:

(1) Any monies received or controlled by the State or any official, department, division, agency, or educational or political subdivision thereof, including but not limited to monies derived from federal, state, or local taxes, gifts, or grants from any source; settlements of any claims or causes of action, public or private; bond proceeds or investment income; federal grants or payments; or intergovernmental transfers; and

(2) Any monies received or controlled by an official, department, division, or agency of state government or any educational or political subdivision thereof, or to any person or entity pursuant to appropriation by the general assembly or governing body of any political subdivision of this State.

(k) "**Solicitation**" means any advertisement whether written, printed, or spoken, in newspaper or magazine, on radio, television, or internet, or otherwise published.

Section 4. Professional and Clinical Requirements for Egg Harvesting.

(a) No person shall harvest eggs unless he or she is a licensed physician.

(b) No person shall harvest eggs except in a hospital, clinic, or other medical facility that meets the normal licensing standards for such facilities in the State, as detailed in [*Insert appropriate State code provision(s) and/ or administrative regulation(s)*].

(c) No person or entity shall provide compensation, financial or otherwise, for eggs or the egg harvesting procedure.

(d) Any reimbursement for time and trouble to the provider shall not exceed an amount typically paid to research subjects for their time and trouble in unrelated medical tests at the

institution offering the compensation, or if no other live-subject medical tests are conducted at that institution, at other medical institutions in the State.

Section 5. Eligibility of Egg Providers.

No physician shall harvest the eggs of an egg provider unless that person:

(a) is over the age of twenty;

(b) has never had her eggs harvested by that physician or another person legally or financially affiliated with that physician; and

(c) has never had her eggs harvested for reproductive purposes in this State.

Section 6. Solicitation of Egg Providers.

(a) No solicitation of egg providers shall offer compensation, financial or otherwise, for eggs or the egg harvesting procedure.

(b) Any solicitation of egg providers shall include a summary of any drug or hormone treatments involved, the total number of office or other visits that a provider must make, and the intended use of the eggs to be harvested.

Section 7. Informed Consent.

(a) Before conducting any medical procedures on or prescribing any hormones or other drugs for an egg provider, a physician shall provide the prospective provider with the following information, described in basic terminology and written in a language understood by the prospective provider, and shall obtain the provider's signed consent on a form that the [*Insert name of State health department or other appropriate agency*] shall prescribe.

(1) Procedure

a. Description of all hormones and other drugs to be taken by an egg provider, including the dosage, frequency of administration, intended biochemical function of, and likely physiological response to each medication;

b. The number of times the egg provider will be expected to visit the physician, the purpose for each visit, and the duration of each visit, including recovery time;

c. Description of the procedure to be performed on the egg provider, including all blood tests, ultrasounds, injections, and egg extractions. The description shall include the purpose, duration, and estimated recovery time of each procedure; and

d. Description of all restrictions the egg provider will be asked to undertake and their duration, including abstinence from alcohol, cigarettes, illegal drugs, prescription drugs, and unprotected sexual intercourse, and restrictions on driving following medication and medical procedures.

(2) Nature of Egg Harvesting

a. The approximate number of eggs to be harvested; and

b. That eggs have the potential to develop into live human persons sharing their parents' DNA, when fertilized by sperm.

(3) Intended Use of Eggs

a. Description of the intended use of the eggs;

b. Whether the eggs may be fertilized by sperm and, if so, how many days the resulting embryos will be permitted to develop;

c. Whether the eggs may be turned into blastocysts through human cloning or some means other than fertilization by sperm and, if so, how many days the resulting entities will be permitted to develop;

d. Whether the eggs may be used for destructive human embryo research;

e. Whether the eggs may be implanted in other persons for reproductive or other purposes;

f. How many separate recipients may be impregnated with the provider's eggs;

g. What information the egg provider will be entitled to learn about any children produced with her eggs, and what contact she will be allowed to have with such children; and

h. Whether the eggs may be multiplied to produce more eggs. If so, sections (a) through (g) of this Subsection also apply to the resulting eggs.

(4) Side Effects

a. Description of any pain that may be experienced as a result of hormones, other drugs, the egg harvesting procedure, or any related procedure, including the likely degree and duration of such pain;

b. Description of any other possible physical side effects, including allergic reaction, ovarian hyperstimulation syndrome, ovary rupture, bleeding, infection, blood clots, kidney failure, fluid build-up in the lungs, damage to bowel or bladder, and scarring of the fallopian tubes, that may be experienced as a result of hormones, other drugs, the egg harvesting procedure, or any related procedure, including the likely degree and duration of such physical side effects;

c. Description of any emotional or psychological side effects, including depression, stress-related symptoms, and mood swings, that may be experienced as a result of hormones, other drugs, the egg harvesting procedure, or any related procedure, including the likely degree and duration of such emotional or psychological side effects;

d. Information on studies demonstrating an increased likelihood of the egg provider developing uterine, breast, or ovarian cancer, or any other type of cancer, after providing eggs, including the percentage of the general female population that develop each type of cancer, and the percentage of egg providers that develop each type of cancer; and

e. The adverse effects the hormones, other drugs, the egg harvesting procedure, and other related procedures have on future attempts of the egg provider to become pregnant, including scarred fallopian tubes and infection.

f. Acknowledgement that, to date, the process and risks related to egg harvesting are highly unstudied and unknown compared to other medical procedures and treatments, and thus the egg provider cannot be completely informed of all potential risks or effects.

(b) No person other than the egg provider shall consent on behalf of the provider.

Section 8. Data Collection and Reporting and Maintenance of State Registry.

(a) The [*Legislature*] of the State of [*Insert name of State*] further finds that there is a substantial lack of knowledge in regard to the effects and risks of the egg harvesting process.

In order to develop the breadth of knowledge necessary to adequately inform women of the risks involved and better understand the demographic targeted by researchers for egg harvesting purposes, the Department shall develop and maintain a state registry containing the following information about each woman who provides eggs to any person or institution within the State:

(1) The age of the egg provider;

(2) The current yearly income of the egg provider;

(3) The city and state of residence of the egg provider;

(4) The number of pregnancies of the egg provider;

(5) The number of live births of the egg provider;

(6) The number of times the egg provider has previously provided or attempted to provide eggs;

(7) The number of eggs harvested for each time the egg provider has previously provided eggs;

(8) All hormones and other drugs prescribed or administered to the egg provider, including dosage and frequency of administration, relating directly or indirectly to the egg harvesting procedure;

(9) The manner in which the egg provider was instructed to administer the hormones and drugs prescribed;

(10) Whether the egg provider was told that the medical community has not yet adequately studied the effects of the egg harvesting procedure and therefore the egg provider cannot be completely informed of all potential risks or effects;

(11) Whether the egg provider had a particular physician or other contact person within the institution harvesting the eggs and, if so, the name and position of that physician or other person;

(12) The total number of eggs harvested;

(13) The particular disposition [*or use*] of the eggs harvested;

(14) Whether and to what extent the egg provider received any follow-up care;

(15) Any side effects or adverse events in the health of the egg provider which happened during the administration of hormones or other drugs, during the harvesting procedure, or up to one year following the ingestion of hormones or drugs and/or the harvesting procedure, whichever is later;

(16) Any medical treatment or procedure provided to the egg provider as a result of the hormones or other drugs or egg harvesting procedure;

(17) The total amount of money paid to the egg provider for time, transportation, discomfort, or other services related to the egg harvesting procedure; and

(18) An itemized list of the amounts of money paid to the egg provider, the source of each amount, and the consideration for each amount.

For purposes of this Act, an "adverse event" shall be defined according to the Food and Drug Administration (FDA) criteria given in the Medwatch Reporting System.

(b) Any person or institution that harvests human eggs shall collect and maintain the information required in part (a) of this Section, and shall report it to the Department on such forms as the Department shall prescribe within 15 days after the last day of each calendar month.

(c) The Department shall summarize aggregate data from the reports required under this Section and submit the data to the Centers for Disease Control and Prevention (CDC) for the purpose of inclusion in the annual Vital Statistics Report. The aggregated data shall also be made independently available to the public by the Department in a downloadable format.

(d) In addition to the information enumerated in part (a) of this Section, any person or institution that harvests human eggs shall report to the Department the name of the egg provider for which the information was collected and reported. That name shall not be included in the Department's aggregate report. The Department shall assign a unique identification number for each egg provider for the purposes of the aggregate report.

(e) The Department shall maintain a separate registry containing the names of the egg providers with their unique identification numbers. This registry will be accessible only by petition to the Department and for good cause, including but not limited to statistical compilation and research on the effects and risks of the egg harvesting procedure.

Section 9. Prohibition on Use of Taxpayer Funds for Human Egg Harvesting.

(a) Notwithstanding any other law, no public funds shall be used to facilitate the harvesting of human eggs, pay for the procedure of egg harvesting, or compensate those who perform or undergo the procedure.

(b) For purposes of this section, "**egg harvesting**" includes the extraction of human oocytes from a woman's reproductive organs for the purpose of reproduction.

Section 10. Penalties.

(a) Criminal Penalty. Any person or entity that violates any section of this Act shall be guilty of a [*Insert appropriate degree of felony or misdemeanor*].

(b) Civil Penalty. Any person or entity that violates any provision of this Act shall be fined [*Insert appropriate amount*] or twice the amount of gross pecuniary gain derived from such a violation, or any amount intermediate between the forgoing, at the discretion of the court.

(c) Unprofessional Conduct. Any violation of this Act shall constitute unprofessional conduct pursuant to [*Insert appropriate statutes for 1) medical doctors and surgeons and 2) osteopathic doctors*] and shall result in permanent revocation of the violator's license to practice medicine.

(d) Trade, Occupation, or Profession. Any violation of this Act may be the basis for denying an application for, denying an application for the renewal of, or revoking any license, permit, certificate, or any other form of permission required to practice or engage in a trade, occupation, or profession.

Section 11. Severability.

Any provision of this Act held to be invalid or unenforceable by its terms, or as applied to any person or circumstance, shall be construed so as give it the maximum effect permitted by law, unless such holding shall be one of utter invalidity or unenforceability, in which event such provision shall be deemed severable herefrom and shall not affect the remainder hereof or the application of such provision to other persons not similarly situated or to other, dissimilar circumstances.

Section 12. Right of Intervention.

The [*Legislature*], by joint resolution, may appoint one or more of its members who sponsored or co-sponsored this Act, as a matter of right and in his or her official capacity, to intervene to defend this law in any case in which its constitutionality is challenged or questioned.

Section 13. Effective Date.

This Act takes effect on [*Insert date*].

EMBRYO ADOPTION ACT

HOUSE/SENATE BILL No. ______
By Representatives/Senators ______________

Section 1. Short Title.

This Act may be cited as the "Embryo [*Snowflakes*] Adoption Act."

Section 2. Legislative Purpose and Findings.

(a) The [*Legislature*] of the State of [*Insert name of State*] finds that:

(1) There are upwards of 400,000 cryopreserved (frozen) human embryos in laboratories and facilities in the United States, and that number grows annually;

(2) There is scant guidance from federal or state law for the disposition of frozen embryos given that few states have legislation governing the disposition of frozen embryos;

(3) The lack of clear guidance in federal or state law has resulted in numerous bitterly-contested lawsuits stemming from disputes over the status of and rights to frozen embryos, including cases decided by the Supreme Courts of Massachusetts, New Jersey, New York, Tennessee, and Washington;

(4) Embryo transfer is a haphazard process, with little consistency between *in vitro* fertilization (IVF) clinics and a general lack of dispositional agreements. The process provides insufficient protection for the best interests of the child and insufficient certainty for the rights and responsibilities of genetic and potential adoptive parents;

(5) The number of embryo transfers completed each year is unknown, and nearly all occur without the oversight of established adoption laws and procedures;

(6) It is doubtful that embryo adoption will lead to the production of more stored embryos because of the medical burden and financial expense of conceiving them;

(7) Despite growing use of the term "embryo adoption," the term, in the absence of legal changes, may create a "false sense of security" for donors who believe

that they have legally terminated their parental rights and responsibilities when they transfer an embryo to adoptive parents;

(8) Bringing embryo transfer within the auspices of existing state laws and adoption procedures will create greater protection for the child, greater certainty for the termination of rights of the genetic parents, and greater certainty for the parental rights of the adopting parents; and

(9) Whereas assisted reproductive technologies (ART) create the possibility that a child might have no parents or more than two parents (with sperm donors, egg donors, gestational surrogates, and commissioning couples), applying adoption procedures to embryo donation will help to ensure that a child does not have more than two legally-recognized parents at one time.

(b) The [*Legislature's*] purpose in enacting this Act is to:

(1) Clarify the rights of genetic and adoptive parents;

(2) Apply established procedures in adoption law to embryo adoption;

(3) Clarify the legal status of children placed for adoption as embryos; and

(4) Promote the best interests of the child.

Section 3. Definitions.

For purposes of this Act:

(a) "**Human embryo**" or "**embryo**" means an individual organism [*fertilized ovum*] of the human species, from the single cell stage to eight weeks development.

(b) "**Embryo transfer**" means the relinquishment of rights and responsibilities by the genetic parent(s) of a human embryo and the acceptance of said rights and responsibilities by adopting parent(s).

Section 4. Amends Definitions Section of State Adoption Law.

For purposes of this Act and the [*Insert definition section(s) of this State's adoption law(s)*], "**child**" [*or "***minor***"*] shall include a human embryo.

Section 5. Exclusivity.

The transfer of human embryos from genetic to adoptive parents shall be conducted pursuant to the adoption laws of this state.

Section 6. Time of Relinquishment of Rights.

Relinquishment of rights by genetic parents to a human embryo shall take place before implantation.

Section 7. Surrender of Rights.

Written surrender of rights shall be obtained from the genetic mother and father, unless the embryo was derived from donor gametes.

Section 8. Status of Prior Agreements for Disposition of Embryos.

A written surrender of rights to an embryo pursuant to Section 7 shall cancel any prior written agreement governing disposition of the embryo.

Section 9. Severability.

Any provision of this Act held to be invalid or unenforceable by its terms, or as applied to any person or circumstance, shall be construed so as give it the maximum effect permitted by law, unless such holding shall be one of utter invalidity or unenforceability, in which event such provision shall be deemed severable herefrom and shall not affect the remainder hereof or the application of such provision to other persons not similarly situated or to other, dissimilar circumstances.

Section 10. Right of Intervention.

The [*Legislature*], by joint resolution, may appoint one or more of its members who sponsored or co-sponsored this Act, as a matter of right and in his or her official capacity, to intervene to defend this law in any case in which its constitutionality is challenged or questioned.

Section 11. Effective Date.

This Act takes effect on [*Insert date*].

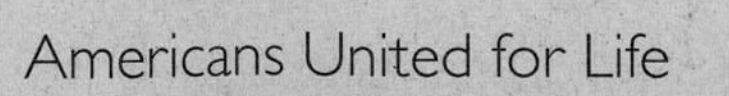

END OF LIFE

End of Life

In May 2008, Oregon resident Barbara Wagner received a chilling rejection letter from her healthcare insurance company. Wagner's state health plan denied coverage for medication that would treat her cancer and extend her life, but instead offered to pay for the cost-effective option of ending her life by lethal prescription.

Wagner's lung cancer, which had been in remission for two years, had returned. Her doctor had prescribed medication to treat the cancer. The medication cost $4,000 per month. A 64-year-old retired bus driver, Wagner could not personally afford the prescriptions. Relying on her Oregon Health Plan, she requested coverage for the cancer medications, only to receive a cold, flat denial. Her health insurance would not cover the $4,000-a-month cancer drugs, but would pay $50 for an assisted suicide.

Wagner and her family were devastated. "It was horrible," she said, tears flooding her eyes. "I got a letter in the mail that basically said if you want to take the pills, we will help you get that from the doctor and we will stand there and watch you die. But we won't give you the medication to live."

Physician-assisted suicide was legalized by Oregon in 1994 when it enacted its "Death with Dignity Act." On November 4, 2008, neighboring Washington became the second state to legalize the grisly practice of physician-assisted suicide when voters approved Initiative 1000. The Initiative took effect in March 2009 and a 66-year-old woman recently diagnosed with terminal pancreatic cancer was the first to legally commit suicide in May 2009.

Even more troubling, in December 2008, the First District Court of Montana became the first court in America to declare a constitutional "right to die" for competent, terminally ill patients. The judge claimed this "right to die" is encompassed in Montana's constitutional rights to individual privacy and human dignity—and this "right" includes assistance from physicians and exemptions from liability for the physicians under Montana homicide statutes. This one Montana judge effectively imposed physician-assisted suicide on the citizens of Montana with no safeguards or appropriate legislative limitations in place. She simply charged the legislature with the task of implementing this newfound "right to die."

What is happening in Washington and, particularly, in Montana is a wake up call to the nation and to those who want to protect the dying, the elderly, the sick, and the disabled. Compassion and Choices, the Death with Dignity National Center, and other euthanasia advocacy groups' deceptive mantra claim unbearable suffering for the terminally ill and patient choice as justifications to further their mission—to export the practice of physician-assisted suicide to all 50 states.

Prior to November 2008, the Death with Dignity National Center called its targeted plan "Oregon plus One." According to this plan, if just one other state besides Oregon were to legalize physician-assisted suicide, it would essentially trigger a domino effect and the rest of the nation would soon follow. Washington and now Montana have possibly set the domino effect in motion. It is critical to stop and possibly reverse a toppling toward assisted suicide, euthanasia, and the further devaluing of human life—a continuum on which the "right to die" has proven to become the duty to die.

Preserving Human Dignity at the End of Life:
A survey of federal and state laws

By Jessica J. Sage
Staff Counsel, Americans United for Life

Legal euthanasia in America seems to many to be an impossibility, but euthanasia advocates are diligently at work, incrementally advancing their agenda—accomplishing both big and small victories in public opinion, in legislatures, and in judicially-active courts. Euthanasia advocates cleverly cloak hastening the deaths of America's most vulnerable citizens as "Compassion and Choice." The marketing terms of "compassion" and "choice" deceptively portray self-destruction as morally correct and empowering. Unfortunately, they have gained "right to die" proponents significant momentum as Oregon, Washington, and Montana currently sanction physician-assisted suicide (PAS).

This primer is designed to educate and encourage lawmakers and citizens to continue the fight against the culture of death promulgated by supporters of euthanasia. As experienced in the Netherlands, once a nation permits voluntary euthanasia and assisted suicide, the principle of "universality" or "equal treatment" forces one to accept ending the lives of those without explicit request. Touting "Death with Dignity" and "choice" for the terminally-ill in insufferable pain is merely an incremental step in the continuum toward hastening death for the elderly, disabled, depressed, and others deemed to have a low quality of life at any age or stage of life.

Brief History of Euthanasia Advocacy in America

The euthanasia movement in America began by promoting living wills as a means to begin a euthanasia discussion and advance public acceptance of it. Two groups, the Euthanasia Society of America and Euthanasia Education Council, introduced living wills in 1967 and claimed they were necessary to give patients the right to refuse unwanted medical procedures in the event they later became incapacitated. Later, these groups introduced "mercy-killing" bills—to allow doctors to give disabled or dying patients lethal overdoses—in various state legislatures without success. In light of these failures, the living will started the discussion of withholding medical treatments and gave euthanasia advocates a more incremental and palatable step in the "right to die" campaign.

The Hemlock Society, founded in 1980 by Derek Humphry, sponsored "physician-aid-in-dying" initiatives in Washington in 1991 and California in 1992. Both measures permitted lethal injections and assisted suicide for terminally-ill patients, but both failed. Proponents correctly attributed the defeats to the public's reluctance to allow doctors to kill patients. After a time of re-strategizing, the group rebranded itself first as Compassion in Dying and more recently as Compassion & Choices—the organization that initiated and successfully directed the assisted suicide campaigns in Oregon and Washington for PAS.

Current Federal and State Laws

Federal and state laws generally address two end-of-life issues: 1) the refusal of medical treatment (to include the withdrawal of nutrition and hydration from terminally-ill patients or patients in persistent vegetative states), and 2) assisted suicide and euthanasia. While the United States Supreme Court did not rule on a related case until 1990, states have legislated in these areas since the beginning of the Nation. In fact, Anglo-American common law has addressed hastening death at the end of life for at least 700 years by punishing or prohibiting suicide, assisted suicide, and murder.[1]

State laws regarding the withdrawal of food and hydration were initially grounded in the common law of tort, battery, and informed consent.[2] From this common law sprung the right to refuse medical treatment, and the refusal and withdrawal of food and hydration was viewed as an exercise of this right. On the other hand, most states expressly prohibited assisted suicide and euthanasia. In fact, several of the American colonies would, as punishment, confiscate the property of individuals that committed suicide.[3] While the colonies eventually abolished such penalties, the courts continued to condemn suicide as "a grave public wrong."[4]

Since 1990, the Supreme Court has affirmed the states' interests in preserving life until its natural end. In *Cruzan v. Missouri Department of Health*, the Court for the first time was presented with a "right to die" issue.[5] The question before the Court was whether the Constitution forbids states from requiring "clear and convincing evidence" of a patient's wishes before the withdrawal of food and hydration. The Court held that it does not. Rather, the Court ruled that states may legitimately seek to safeguard patients through the imposition of heightened evidentiary requirements.[6] Thus, while patients may have a right to refuse food and hydration or have food and hydration withdrawn,[7] states may, in the interest of protecting the lives of patients, apply a clear and convincing standard when a guardian seeks to discontinue such life-sustaining treatments.[8]

In 1997, the Supreme Court took its next look at end-of-life issues in *Washington v. Glucksberg*[9] and *Vacco v. Quill*.[10] Through these cases, the Court declared there is no federal constitutional right to assisted suicide under the Due Process or Equal Protection Clauses of the Fourteenth Amendment, but implied that states have the power to decide whether to permit or prohibit PAS.

After examining the Nation's long history of forbidding suicide and assisted suicide, the Supreme Court in *Glucksberg* reaffirmed a state's "unqualified interest" in the preservation of human life.[11] Along with preserving life, the state's interests in preventing suicide include: protecting the ethics and integrity of the medical profession; protecting vulnerable groups of people from coercion, prejudice, stereotypes, and "societal indifference"; and preventing the slide toward euthanasia. The Court itself acknowledged that PAS would be "extremely difficult to police and contain" and that "[bans] on assisting suicide prevent such erosion." The Court concluded that these various interests are "unquestionably important and legitimate."[12]

In *Vacco*, the Supreme Court affirmed the distinction between assisting suicide and the withdrawal of life-sustaining treatment, stating it is a "distinction widely recognized and endorsed in the medical profession and in our legal traditions" and that it is important, logical, and rational.[13] The Supreme Court focused on the difference between causing death and allowing someone to die of his or her underlying disease. Finally, the Court termed the following as "valid and important public interests": prohibiting intentional killing and preserving life; preventing suicide; maintaining physicians' role as their patients' healers; protecting vulnerable people from indifference, prejudice, and psychological and financial pressure to end their lives; and avoiding a possible slide toward euthanasia.[14]

That same year, Congress passed the "Assisted Suicide Funding Restriction Act," which prohibits the use of federal funds for items and services "the purpose of which is to cause (or assist in causing) the suicide, euthanasia, or mercy killing of an individual."[15] While the Act was amended in 2000, it remains a barrier to the federal funding of PAS and euthanasia.

Most states prohibit assisted suicide. Thirty-five states expressly prohibit assisted suicide by statute, and another six states imply its prohibition through use of the common law or by interpreting their homicide statutes to apply to assistance in suicide. However, five states and the District of Columbia have neither express nor implied prohibitions against assisted suicide. Two states—Oregon and Washington—expressly authorize the practice. Moreover, in December 2008, a Montana trial court overturned the state's ban on PAS.[16] However, the case is pending before the Montana Supreme Court. Another state—California—now requires physicians to counsel their patients on how to end their lives, and also requires that physicians provide prescriptions for sedatives for patients wishing to starve or dehydrate themselves to death.

Unfortunately, euthanasia advocates have had some success in embedding their distorted view of end-of-life issues in the minds of the American people. The "right to die" is now a phrase of common household knowledge. While the issue of PAS appeared dormant in the years immediately following *Glucksberg* and *Vacco*, suicide proponents are again seeking to validate and legalize PAS in many states. Despite the explicit and implicit assisted suicide prohibitions in most states, nine states considered legislation to legalize PAS in 2009. Efforts must be made to prevent the spread of accepting and legalizing suicide as appropriate "medical treatment" and a legitimate "choice" before it infects more states across the nation.

ISSUES

The Oregon Experience

On November 8, 1994, Oregon became the first state in the Nation to authorize PAS of competent, terminally-ill patients.[17] Barbara Coombs

Lee, President of Compassion & Choices, authored and lobbied for Oregon's PAS initiative, known as the "Death with Dignity Act" (Act). While a federal district court initially enjoined enforcement of the voter initiative, the Ninth Circuit reversed. Five months following the Supreme Court decisions in *Glucksburg* and *Vacco*, the Act took effect in 1997.

In 2001, then-Attorney General John Ashcroft issued a directive stating that PAS is not a "legitimate medical purpose" and that substances regulated under the federal "Controlled Substances Act" could not legally be used for PAS. Supporters of PAS and euthanasia filed suit, and, in 2004, the Ninth Circuit ruled that the directive was illegal and unenforceable. On January 17, 2006, the Supreme Court affirmed the Ninth Circuit's ruling, holding that Congress did not intend for the Attorney General to have such authority. However, the Court's previous decisions denying a federal constitutional right to assisted suicide remained firm, but so did the implication that states have the right to determine whether to permit or prohibit PAS.[18]

Compassion & Choices is promoting Oregon's Act in numerous states as the model to legalize PAS and claims Oregon as a success story of how assisted suicide is to work, but the reality in Oregon exemplifies the inadequacy and circumvention of safeguards within the law and the inherent lack of transparency in PAS reporting.

Undiagnosed Depression and Inadequate Waiting Periods

To request PAS in Oregon, a person must be: a capable adult and resident of Oregon, and diagnosed with a terminal illness predicted to produce death within six months.[19] There is no requirement for the physician to determine the reason why a patient is requesting PAS and to address the real issue at hand—not insufferable pain, but depression and fear of the unknown.

Supporters of PAS offer horrific stories of extreme rarity, claiming terminally-ill patients need PAS to relieve their "unbearable pain and suffering." Often, the terminally-ill do express a fear of "unbearable pain and suffering," but it is a fear of possibility, not necessarily the realization of pain and suffering. Whereas in actuality, the most frequently cited concerns of terminally-ill patients in Oregon's annual reports are not pain and suffering, but the loss of personal autonomy and bodily function and the decreased ability to participate in activities that make life enjoyable.[20] The terminally-ill also fear becoming a burden to family members and friends and, ironically, physicians and family members reinforce this fear when they introduce the option of PAS as possible medical treatment. The better response is to reaffirm the value of the patient's life and compassionately support them through a natural end of their life.

Under Oregon's Act, physicians are only required to refer a patient for counseling or a psychological evaluation if they suspect a "psychiatric or psychological disorder or depression [is] causing impaired judgment." In the PAS reporting, the number of patients referred for counseling has consistently declined from ten patients in the second year to zero patients in the tenth year of reporting. In Oregon, physicians tend to utilize the psychiatric evaluation as a protective measure for themselves more than for the patient. Seemingly, as physicians contemplated less potential liability in assisting suicides, they made less psychiatric referrals. It is also unknown if the counseling referral is performed with any level of professional standards or if it is simply a meaningless exercise. When only six percent of Oregon psychiatrists surveyed said they were confident they could satisfactorily determine whether a patient was competent to commit suicide absent a long-term relationship with a patient, the consult simply becomes a rubber stamp.

The Oregon Act does not protect patients at their most vulnerable. Anyone receiving a prognosis for a terminal illness is in shock and understandably takes a period of time to come to terms with the news. They may react from an assumption that the diagnosis is correct, but what if it is not? Oregon's Act only requires the physician to make a "reasonable medical judgment" of six months to live. A physician's subjective determination of life expectancy is certainly not sufficient to make a life and death decision, and elect to commit suicide—particularly when physicians are often times wrong in their predictions.[21] Furthermore, the Act only requires a 48-hour waiting period from a written request for a lethal medication and the prescription and a 15-day waiting period for an oral request. The fact that there is no requirement that it be the same physician that receives the request and then fills the prescription further diminishes any protections these waiting periods supposedly offer. In other words, a request for PAS can be made to one physician who then refuses, but 2 or 15 days later a completely different doctor—most often times one located through the assisted suicide advocacy organization—can provide the prescription. Clearly, these waiting periods provide no protection when some doctors are willing to specialize in suicide and take advantage of those in a depressed and fearful state.

Encourages Physician Shopping and Germinates "Suicide Specialists"

Assisted-suicide advocates portray PAS as a personal choice to be made between the patient and a long-time, trusted physician—a very misleading picture. Helen, an Oregon woman diagnosed with metastatic breast cancer living in hospice, decided to request assisted suicide. Her own physician refused the request for undocumented reasons. A second physician found Helen to be depressed and refused her request. Helen's husband then called the predecessor to Compassion & Choices, Compassion in Dying, and received a referral to a physician willing to assist Helen's suicide. The prescribing physician knew Helen for about two weeks and consulted neither of the other doctors before he provided the prescribed protocol resulting in her death. [22]

Helen's story demonstrates how common it is for a patient seeking PAS to visit multiple doctors to find one that is willing to prescribe the lethal drug with little knowledge of the patient's physical, emotional, and psychological state—and with little interest in counseling on life-enhancing alternatives. In the first three years of Oregon's PAS experience, reports indicated that in 59 percent of the cases patients had to ask two or more physicians before receiving a prescription for lethal drugs.[23] More troubling, as demonstrated by Helen's case, a patient often locates a doctor specializing in suicide through an assisted suicide organization such as Compassion & Choices—far from a trusted, long-time family physician.[24]

Permits Involuntary Killing—No Witness at Death and Undefined Self-Administration

The Oregon Department of Human Services (ODHS) advertises the Act as allowing "terminally-ill Oregonians to end their lives through the voluntary self-administration of lethal medications, expressly prescribed by a physician for that purpose."[25] While the Act requires patient competence and witnesses at the time of the request for PAS, there are no such requirements at the time of administration of the drug. Once the lethal drug is prescribed there are no protective measures to know if the suicide is carried out voluntarily and actually self-administered. The Act itself contains no formal definition of self-administration. Rather, it refers to the patient's administration as a form of "ingest" or "ingesting" in the context of protecting insurance policies from nullification;[26] and the ODHS reporting requirements direct the attending physician to fill out its interview form within ten days of "a patient's ingestion of lethal medication."[27]

Moreover, self-administration does not require that only the patient administer the lethal prescription. Once the prescription is filled, the Act provides no protection from a third party administering the lethal medication—with or without the patient's express knowledge or consent. In addition, certain issues arise when the lethal drug does not actually cause death, leaving the physician or family members in a compromised situation of carrying out the suicide wishes through other final measures such as suffocation.

An interested or coercive third party may not allow the patient the purported "right to rescind" since no one will know how the death actually occurred once the prescription is written. The death will not provoke investigation because the acting physician may sign the death certificate and will classify the death as "natural." Oregon's Act significantly fails to recognize the real and dangerous conflict of interests inherent in both the suicide-enabling physician and inheriting family members at the actual time of death—offering little to no protection for the terminally-ill.

Lack of Transparency in Reporting Requirements

Oregon's Act permits little to no transparency and renders patient choice and protections illusory. It allows for unprecedented liability protection for doctors assisting suicides and promotes secrecy from the public. The Oregon Public Human Division (OPHD) is tasked with collecting and reporting information to ensure compliance with the law, in order to protect the welfare of those seeking assisted suicide. But in practice, it prioritizes immunities for physicians. The Act shields doctors from "civil or criminal liability or professional disciplinary action" if the physician acts in "good faith compliance" with the law.[28] This very subjective standard includes no consideration of reasonableness or professional community standards as seen in other areas of the law, which is especially troubling when the outcome for lack of compliance is the death of a vulnerable individual.

OPHD has failed to enact reporting requirements effective to its charge or an enforcement mechanism to ensure physicians comply with its oversight. As a result, the reporting requirements have become just a formality and provide less and less insight as to the ramifications of PAS, particularly when secrecy seems to be the objective. OPHD has epitomized patient-physician confidentiality in relation to PAS; and the Act specifically states that the information collected by OPHD "shall not be a public record and may not be made available for inspection by the public."[29] Not only is the collected information protected, the accuracy of what is collected is in question due to reliance upon the doctors self-reporting (and only those prescribing lethal drugs), the unknown number of PAS deaths not reported, the lack of witness requirements at time of death, and the undefined nature of self-administration within the law.

The shortcomings of Oregon's Act are not inconsequential, but are the subsequent and real consequences of accepting death as a choice in medical treatment and empowering physicians to take the life of their patients—voluntarily at first, but inevitably involuntary.

Acceptance of Physician-Assisted Suicide: The Inevitable Slide Toward Euthanasia

PAS Contradicts Suicide Prevention and Invites Abuse of Elderly and Disabled

Allowing assisted suicide runs completely contrary to the prevention of suicide, elder abuse, and discrimination against the disabled. First, in every other context America seeks to prevent suicide because it is understood to be self-destructive and harmful to the individual and society. It is the fourth leading cause of death among those aged 18 to 65 and eleventh overall in the United States. Over 60 percent of those who commit suicide suffer from severe depression even though it is among the most treatable of psychiatric illnesses. The first step in treatment is recognizing the depression. Between 80 and 90 percent of people with depression respond positively to treatment.[30] These responses to treatment for depression are profoundly similar for those seeking PAS; once treated, they want to continue living.

Second, PAS is a recipe for domestic and elder abuse. The National Center on Elder Abuse estimates one to two million Americans age 65 or older are injured, exploited, or otherwise abused physically, emotionally, psychologically, or financially each year by a caregiver or trusted individual they depend on for care or protection.[31] The physicians and family members to whom a terminally-ill patient looks to for support and protection are the same ones counseling that suicide may be the best option.

Third, PAS discriminates against and degrades the lives of people with disabilities. It denies people with disabilities the benefit of suicide prevention and the enforcement of homicide laws.[32] PAS encourages physicians and third parties to make a "quality of life" determination for those they deem to be suffering or living a life that they themselves would not want to live. The reasons cited by those requesting PAS are struggles people with disabilities cope with every day. Once assisted suicide is accepted as an answer to suffering, loss of autonomy, dependence on others, or the decreased ability to participate in enjoyment activities of life, there is nothing to prevent those life-value judgments from pervading American culture and imposing those same quality-of-life judgments on the disabled in-

voluntarily, and at any stage of life.

Switzerland and the Netherlands—Indisputable Evidence

Switzerland legalized assisted suicide in 1918 and has the most liberal law in the world. It is the only jurisdiction that permits nonresidents to travel to Switzerland to kill themselves. Dignitas, a Swiss suicide clinic, and its founder, Ludwig Minelli, demonstrate the persistent agenda of advocates for death to challenge and circumvent any safeguards in assisted suicide laws—the objective of making suicide available to all including the healthy but depressed. Dignitas is currently under investigation for assisting a healthy, but depressed man to commit suicide.[33] It has also publicized its intention to help a healthy wife commit suicide beside her terminally-ill husband.[34] Switzerland provides the United States with a vivid lesson that initially limiting assisted suicide to the terminally ill is the necessary first step—the incremental step toward society accepting killing as an alternative to human suffering

Even more striking, the Netherlands' clear track record establishes that assisted suicide is simply the next step toward euthanasia and infanticide. PAS has been available in the Netherlands since 1993.[35] Euthanasia is also legal for patients who explicitly request to be killed, as well as for those "with no free will," such as children, the severely mentally retarded, and those in persistent coma. The Netherlands was the first nation to legalize euthanasia—followed by Belgium—and now proponents of "mercy killings" are advocating for a "right to euthanasia" for people without explicit request. The practice of euthanasia, with and without request, is now prominent in both the Netherlands and Belgium, and many stories like the following have surfaced:

- One woman, unable to cope any longer with the illness of her husband, gave him an ultimatum: euthanasia or admission to a home for the chronically ill. Fearful of being left alone and at the mercy of strangers, the husband chose euthanasia. Despite the fact that the doctor was aware of the coercion, he euthanized the man anyway.[36]
- After stabilizing a cancer patient who did not desire euthanasia, a physician returned from the weekend to find that another physician had ended the patient's life without her consent. That physician admitted he did so because "she was not dying quickly enough and he needed space for another patient."[37]
- One physician ended the life of a nun without her consent because she was in excruciating pain and the doctor believed her faith would prohibit her from asking for death.[38]
- A hospital decided to administer lethal doses of sedatives to disabled and terminally-ill newborns. The hospital guideline permitted euthanasia on infants when the child's medical team and independent doctors agree the pain is untreatable, there is no hope for improvement, and the parents think it best. Since the passage of the Netherland's euthanasia bill in 1997, the Justice Ministry has documented 22 cases of newborn euthanasia. But judicial authorities have dismissed all 22 cases and no prosecutions occurred even though infanticide is illegal. [39]

While these stories seem nightmarish and unlikely to happen in the United States, the acceptance of PAS and the marketing of euthanasia in Oregon, Washington, Montana, and across the United States are already forcing our terminally-ill patients into similarly coercive situations.[40] The slippery slope argument is very pertinent and those nations who have gone before reveal the illusion of "autonomy" and "choice" within the assisted suicide movement. Death quickly becomes, not only an option, but the best option for the elderly, terminally ill, disabled, and those that some deem not worthy of life from birth.

To combat this slide toward euthanasia, AUL has developed the "Assisted Suicide Ban Act."

Pain Management and Palliative Care

Lack of physician knowledge and skill in the assessment and management of pain is one of the most consistently cited barriers to effective pain relief.[41] Consider Robert Wagner, an 81-year-old nursing home resident. He cried out in pain and tears welled in his eyes. Though the ophthalmologist had only bumped Robert's leg, the cancer in Robert's femur had gone undetected, largely because his doctors and the nursing home staff failed to notice that Robert was in pain.[42] Unfortunately, Robert Wagner's misunderstood grimace is not an isolated event. Today, where good pain management is most needed—in the nursing homes, hospitals, and hospice centers serving millions of Americans, many of whom die in those places—good pain management is notably lacking.

Terminally-ill patients repeatedly rank pain management and symptom control as an issue in their courses of treatment.[43] Yet, a 2004 study published in the *Journal of the American Medical Association* points out that nearly 25 percent of families report their loved ones did not receive good care at the end of life, especially in managing pain.[44] It is these bad experiences that make terminally-ill patients and their families consider the possibility of PAS. Moreover, patients are largely ill-informed when it comes to the breadth of possibilities in end-of-life care.[45]

Addressing this problem, some believe the Supreme Court decisions denying a constitutional right to PAS also created a right to good palliative care.[46] A movement toward better policies and more discourse in the medical community regarding methods for excellent end-of-life care embodies this notion. On the state level, the organizations exerting the most influence on pain law and policy are the state medical boards and the hospital accreditation agencies. While significant measures are underway to shape policy for better pain management, significant barriers still prevent many vulnerable Americans from receiving adequate relief, especially in end-of-life care. Among the most cited barriers is the simple truth that doctors remain uneducated about palliative care and specifically about the most current techniques in proper pain management.[47] Medical schools and nursing schools are not teaching palliative techniques to students, nor do textbooks and lectures address the use of pain medications.[48] As a result, healthcare providers enter their professions ill-equipped to manage chronic pain.[49]

Moreover, mistreating and undertreating pain symptoms are not trivial mistakes when healthcare costs are considered. Yet the greatest costs

of the perpetuated ignorance may be patients' lives. Sixty-nine percent of chronic pain sufferers would request PAS if they believed their pain could not be managed,[50] and many who request PAS would "withdraw that request if their depression and pain were treated."[51] Evidence supports that when suicide is an acceptable option, less energy is devoted to truly compassionate medical care including palliative services.[52] Creating a system of policies focused on palliative care is therefore antithetical to a system that accepts assisted suicide as a "treatment alternative."[53]

While the medical profession is making positive steps to improve its own practices in pain management, legislation can assist these efforts by encouraging more education, protecting doctors from litigation for prescribing certain medications for pain management, and fostering more communication between doctors and patients about palliative options for treatments. Such measures in the states will accelerate the popular trend toward confronting end-of-life issues with emphasis on compassion and dignity in life through pain management.

To encourage pain management education, AUL has developed the "Pain Medicine Education Act."

Nutrition and Hydration

In 2005, the case of Terry Schindler Schiavo brought the issue of artificial nutrition and hydration to the national spotlight. Terri suffered a cardio-respiratory arrest resulting in severe neurological injuries in 1990 at the age of 26. She lived from then until March 2005 with the delivery of her food and water through a tube, but required no other life-support measures to sustain her. She had not received any rehabilitative measures since 1992 and her family was restricted from caring for her in any way. She was not terminally ill and did not face a certain death in the near future. After a petition from her husband and guardian, a court declared her to be in a persistent vegetative state and ordered her food and water to be withheld. She died 13 days after the execution of the order from dehydration. She was 41.[54]

In 1990, the Supreme Court held that a state could choose to defer a third-party's decision to refuse medical treatment if there was no clear and convincing evidence of the patient's instruction to do so—the Constitution did not require the state to substitute the wishes of close family members in the absence of express patient wishes.[55] Even though food and water is a basic bodily necessity for sustainment, most medical professionals, and subsequently state legislatures, now consider food and water to be a form of medical treatment that may be refused by a patient's express instructions. In Terri's case, the court determined that she was in a persistent vegetative state and had made reliable oral statements that she would want her feeding tube removed under such circumstances.[56]

The issue is whether nutrition and hydration should be considered a medical treatment that can be refused, and if so, under what circumstances. There is disagreement even among like-minded individuals. Some consider the removal of food and water an act of euthanasia by starvation and dehydration; while others see it as a medical treatment permissibly withheld when a certain life condition is deemed no longer worth sustaining.

Those in favor of life are searching for ways to protect vulnerable individuals within this context and the broader context of "futile care theory" that is rapidly penetrating hospital care protocols. Futile care theory holds that a doctor may unilaterally withhold medical treatment because the doctor believes the quality of life of the patient is not worthwhile or is simply not cost effective, despite the wishes of the patient or patient's family. This theory contradicts the "choice" and "patient autonomy" arguments, but is akin to euthanasia as it rejects the ethic that all humans are equal and worthy of protection and adopts one where doctors decide which lives are worth saving and sustaining.[57]

Although some advance directive initiatives like living wills exacerbate these issues—particularly with the withdrawal of medical treatments including food and water—other options can provide some significant protections. In the absence of any form of advance directive, some states are creating rebuttable presumptions in favor of continuing food and water and restricting the powers of healthcare proxies or surrogates from removing artificial nutrition and hydration.

Advance Directives

"I'm not dead yet" has become a necessary statement by the disabled and those facing potentially life-threatening conditions. Charlotte Allen shares her experience with undergoing surgery for an early stage of breast cancer. She felt harassed by the hospital staff to fill out a living will instructing healthcare providers under what conditions she would want to be resuscitated, and whether she would want a ventilator or feeding tube if it became necessary.[58] Rather than assume a doctor will do everything in his power to save and sustain your life, the living will asks a patient to express what care a doctor may permissibly withhold. The persistent efforts of the healthcare community, lawyers, and policymakers to require a living will may be done with good intentions, but, in reality, it creates and projects an attitude that some lives are not worth saving—even if done so under the guise of patient choice and autonomy.

Advance directives are intentioned for a person to control—to a certain degree—future healthcare decisions in the event he or she later becomes unable to do so. The first type of advance directive implemented was the living will, which is a legal document indicating what treatments may be withheld if a patient faces a specified condition and is unable to make the decision. It was introduced and promoted by many euthanasia advocates attempting to initiate discussion on euthanasia and the notion that some lives are simply not worth saving.

A second type of advance directive is a durable power of attorney for healthcare decisions. This legal document empowers an appointed agent to act on the behalf of the principal in making healthcare decisions should the principal be unable to make those decisions. Assuming one selects a person who shares the patient's values on life and life-saving measures and is formidable enough to be an effective advocate, the agent is better able to address future healthcare decision than any written document of instructions.

Advance directives serve an important purpose in planning for the future. Without a healthcare proxy, patients will find that many healthcare providers and institutions will make important decisions for them or a court may appoint a guardian completely unfamiliar with the patient or their wishes. The International Task Force on Euthanasia and Assisted Suicide recommends a Protective Medical Decision Document, which names a durable power of attorney and specifically prohibits euthanasia and assisted suicide.[59]

Many states continue to promote advance directives and guidance for "do not resuscitate orders" —some to the benefit of patients and others to the detriment. Yet, a study published by the Archives of Internal Medicine found that 65 percent of physicians would not necessarily follow a living will if, for example, its instructions conflicted with the doctor's own ideas of the patient's prognosis or expected quality of life.[60] Many states encourage advance directives and some are creating registries to promote the adherence to them by the medical community. As the culture of death becomes more and more pervasive, it is critical to take protective measures against the underlying presumption of withholding certain medical treatments, inclusive of nutrition and hydration, and the propagation of futile care theory.

KEY TERMS

- **Advance directive** is a legal document expressing an individual's healthcare decision preferences in the circumstance where he or she becomes incapacitated or unable to make those decisions. A **living will** is a declaration, signed and witnessed (or notarized), instructing physicians and healthcare providers as to what treatments to withhold or withdraw if the person is in a terminal condition and unable to make the decision to refuse certain medical treatment. A **durable power of attorney for healthcare** is a document, signed and witnessed (or notarized), designating an agent to make healthcare decisions for the principal if the principal is temporarily or permanently unable to do so. A **combination advance directive** provides an agent specific instructions to follow in healthcare decisions if the person is unable to so.

- **Assisted suicide** is the act of suicide with the help of another party. **Physician-assisted suicide (PAS)** specifically involves the help of a physician in performing the act of suicide. Such assistance usually entails the prescribing or dispensing of controlled substances in lethal quantities that hasten death.

- **Euthanasia** involves the killing of one person by or with the physical assistance of another. **Voluntary euthanasia** is the ending of one life by another at the patient's request. **Nonvoluntary euthanasia** describes "a physician's ending the life of a patient *incapable* of giving or refusing consent."[61] **Involuntary euthanasia** describes the termination of a competent patient's life *without* his or her consent.[62]

- **Futile care theory** proposes that physicians may unilaterally disregard requests for life-sustaining treatment made by a patient or a family member if the quality of the patient's life is deemed not worth living. Advocates—including bioethicists, members of the medical academies, and social engineers—have drafted and proposed mandatory treatment guidelines on how to deny requested life-sustaining care—which have been adopted and put into practice by some hospitals.[63]

- **Pain** is an unpleasant sensory and emotional experience associated with actual or potential tissue damage or described in terms of such damage.[64] **Acute pain** is a temporary result of identifiable injury or disease.[65] **Chronic pain** is a state in which pain persists beyond the usual course of an acute disease or healing of an injury, or that may or may not be associated with an acute or chronic pathologic process that causes continuous or intermittent pain over months or years.[66] Chronic pain may be malignant—*i.e.*, caused by cancer—or nonmalignant.[67]

- **Palliative care** is "an approach [to medicine] that emphasizes pain relief, symptom control, and spiritual and emotional care for the dying and their families,"[68] rather than curing the underlying disease. It generally entails the use of analgesic medications, such as codeine and morphine.[69] However, other pain relief techniques, such as physical therapy and neurosurgery, are also used.[70]

- **Hospice** is "support and care for persons in the last phase of an incurable disease so that they may live as fully and comfortably as possible."[71] "Medicare regulations require that hospice patients must have a prognosis of less than six months if the disease runs its normal course."[72] In the U.S., approximately 3,300 hospices serve about 950,000 people each year.[73]

- **Opioids** are "strong pain medications derived from opium, or synthesized to behave like opium derivatives. Examples of opioids include morphine, codeine, oxycodone, methadone, and fentanyl."[74]

- **Palliative sedation** entails administrating sedatives to terminally-ill, conscious patients whose pain cannot be otherwise relieved to alleviate suffering, but with the effect of inducing unconsciousness. The phrase "palliative sedation" is preferred over "terminal sedation" in order to make clear the intent of administering the drug is not to induce unconsciousness.[75]

- **Double effect** is a traditional doctrine justifying palliative sedation. The doctrine holds three requirements: 1) the action itself (*e.g.,* sedation) is not morally wrong, 2) the secondary effect (*e.g.,* respiratory depression or death) is not merely a means to accomplish the intended benefit (*e.g.*, pain relief), and 3) proportionality exists between the intended effects and the unintended secondary effects (*e.g.,* established by the condition of the patient and consent of the patient or proxy.)[76]

- **Persistent vegetative state** is a clinical diagnosis of a condition in which an individual has lost cognitive neurological function and awareness of his or her surroundings with certain characteristics of maintaining sleep-wake cycles, responding to stimulation in only a reflexive way, and showing no evidence of meaningful response to the environment.[77]

MYTHS & FACTS

Physician-Assisted Suicide and Euthanasia

Myth: Allowing assisted suicide will not encourage the slide toward euthanasia. Safeguards and procedures can be put into place to ensure that PAS is only available for competent, terminally-ill patients.

Fact: In addition to the tragic example of the Netherlands is the fact that PAS is already available to terminally-ill patients in Oregon that are not enduring "unbearable pain and suffering." For example, if PAS is accepted for the terminally-ill without intractable pain, then those Americans with severe chronic pain who, unlike the terminally-ill, must live with such severe pain for many years to come, would also have a legitimate claim to PAS.[78] Thus, there is no reason not to expect PAS to be available to severe chronic pain sufferers, then non-severe chronic pain sufferers, and then to those suffering from psychological pain or distress, as in the Netherlands.[79] After examining the issues surrounding PAS and voluntary euthanasia, the British House of Lords concluded that it would not be possible to secure limits on its use.[80] It also does not appear that barricading one group of patients from PAS while allowing another group of patients to use PAS would pass constitutional muster.[81]

Myth: PAS allows terminally-ill patients a choice and preserves autonomy and dignity.

Fact: PAS "will ultimately weaken the autonomy of patients at the end of life."[82] Not only is human dignity found in more than a healthy body and autonomous lifestyle, but "the dignity of human life itself precludes policies that would allow it to be disposed of so easily."[83] Additionally, many PAS patients are coerced into suicide because of familial pressures and a desire not to be a burden on their families.[84] They often feel a need to justify their decisions to stay alive.[85] This is not the essence of choice, autonomy, or human dignity.

Myth: To say that "the so-called right to die all too easily becomes a duty to die"[86] is mere rhetoric.

Fact: The non-partisan New York State Task Force on Life and the Law issued that statement after examining end-of-life issues for almost 10 years. The 25-member task force, comprised of prominent physicians, nurses, lawyers, academics, and representatives of numerous religious communities, held differing views on PAS and euthanasia. However, the group unanimously concluded that the dangers of PAS vastly exceed any possible benefits.[87]

Moreover, the duty to die is already being played out in Oregon, where the state is actively promoting assisted suicide over medical care. In just one month in 2008, at least two different terminally-ill patients were denied medical treatment under the state health insurance plan, and instead were told that the state would pay for the patients' suicides.[88] The message was clear: We won't treat you, but we will help you die. The duty to die cannot be much clearer.

Pain Management and Palliative Care

Myth: The availability of PAS will not inhibit the availability of palliative care.

Fact: Palliative care actually "languishes as a consequence" of the easy availability of PAS and euthanasia.[89] Physicians are likely to grant requests for PAS before all avenues of palliative care have been explored.[90] In addition, physicians are not pushed to better educate themselves on palliative care, and researchers spend less time looking for better palliative medications and techniques.[91]

Myth: PAS is preferable because palliative medications result in unbearable side effects and may hasten death anyway.

Fact: Fears about side effects and the hastening of death are unfounded.[92] In fact, those patients with severe pain actually become tolerant of palliative medicines, minimizing side effects.[93] There is also no evidence that pain medications hasten death if such medications are used correctly.[94] In addition, doses can be increased to alleviate intensified pain as diseases progress.[95]

Myth: Opioids may cause addiction, even in patients experiencing severe pain.

Fact: "[I]t is a fact that when narcotics are prescribed for the legitimate purpose of treating pain, they essentially never cause addiction. In studies of addiction with a total population of over 24,000 patients, only seven could be documented as having become totally addicted as a result of receiving opioids for pain relief."[96]

Myth: Opioids pose a great risk for respiratory depression leading to hastened death, even when monitored carefully.

Fact: Where the pain is well-assessed and dosages are carefully monitored, the chances of causing an overdose in a suffering patient are extremely unlikely.[97] "[E]mpirical studies have failed to show an association between increases in doses of sedatives during the last hours of life and decreases in survival. Therefore, when dosed appropriately to relieve specific symptoms, such palliative medications do not appear to hasten death."[98] In fact, morphine use may prolong life by enabling a suffering patient to breathe more easily and effectively.[99]

Myth: Even a patient in severe pain can reach a maximum tolerable dose for morphine.

Fact: "Because of drug tolerance and individual responses to therapy, ceilings on dosage are not appropriate."[100]

Myth: Because pain is a subjective experience, no broad policies can improve management of individual cases.

Fact: While pain is different for each individual, there are objective ways to evaluate a patient's suffering. By establishing a system of pain management, such as that the JCAHO standards require, better services are provided. Objective evaluations of pain include: "the consistency of the patient's complaints and history during the evaluation; the course of the illness as documented in the medical records; the extent of objective findings, if any, due to injury or illness; findings of physical capabilities that contradict the patient's reports of limitations; and the presence of symptom magnification and somatization."[101]

Myth: Pain is an unfortunate and untreatable consequence of certain illnesses.

Fact: More than 90 percent of cancer pain can be controlled with proper treatment[102] and approximately 95 percent of all chronic pain in the terminally ill can be likewise controlled,[103] commonly through use of opioids.

Myth: If a physician prescribes or administers high doses of medication to relieve pain or other discomfort in a terminally ill patient, resulting in death, he or she will be criminally prosecuted.
Fact: If the death was not intended, such treatments are not murder or assisted suicide.[104]

Myth: In the small percentage of cases where a patient cannot be kept conscious while administering pain relief, there are no legal options and assisted suicide is necessary.
Fact: Palliative sedation is legal, even in states not authorizing assisted suicide, to relieve intractable symptoms.[105]

Nutrition and Hydration and Advance Directives

Myth: When food and hydration is withdrawn, the patient dies from an underlying disease or condition.
Fact: When food and hydration are withdrawn, the person dies of starvation and dehydration. It is not that they are in the process of dying, but a deliberate decision is made to remove food and water in order to no longer sustain the life—one deemed not worth living.

Myth: A persistent vegetative state (PVS) is a certain diagnosis and the person has no chance of recovery.
Fact: It is a clinical diagnosis based on subjective assessments from an attending physician. Louis Viljoen was diagnosed as PVS in 1996 following an accident and there were many times when his mother wondered whether her only child would be better off dead. But by 2005, he regained consciousness, demonstrated his good sense of humor and remembered everything from before his accident.[106] In many instances, patients will wake instantaneously without any warning within the first month of being in a persistent vegetative state. Generally, the first year holds the best odds for patients emerging from PVS: Children have 60 percent chance of recovery while adults have a 50 percent chance.[107]

Myth: The refusal of medical treatment is always at the decision of the patient or the patient's family.
Fact: Futile care theory is becoming more prevalent among hospital policies and procedures which promotes unilateral decisions by attending physicians to withdraw or withhold medical treatment if a life is considered unworthy of preserving against the wishes of the patient and the patient's family.

Endnotes

1 *Washington v. Glucksberg*, 521 U.S. 702, 711 (1997).
2 *Cruzan v. Director, Mo. Dept. of Health*, 497 U.S. 261, 269 (1990).
3 *See Glucksberg*, 521 U.S. at 712.
4 *Id.* at 141.
5 *Cruzan*, 497 U.S. at 277.
6 *Id.* at 280-81.
7 The Court stated that the "logical corollary of doctrine of informed consent is that the patient generally possesses the right not to consent, that is, to refuse treatment." *Id.* at 270.
8 *Id.* at 284.
9 521 U.S. 702.
10 521 U.S. 793 (1997).
11 *Glucksberg*, 521 U.S. at 728 (citing *Cruzan*, 497 U.S. at 282).
12 *Id.* at 702, 729-35.
13 *Vacco*, 521 U.S. at 800-01. *See also id.* at 808 (stating that "the two acts are different" and referring to the distinction as a "longstanding and rational distinction").
14 *Id.* at 801, 807-809.
15 Pub. L. No. 105-12, 111 Stat. 23-28, at § 2(b).
16 *Baxter v. State*, No. ADV-2007-787 (2008).
17 The initiative was voted on by Oregon citizens and was only

narrowly approved.

[18] *See Gonzales v. Oregon*, 546 U.S. 243 (2006); *Washington v. Glucksberg*, 521 U.S. 702 (1997); *Vacco v. Quill*, 521 U.S. 793 (1997).

[19] Oregon Death with Dignity Act, OR. REV. STAT. §§ 127.800, .805 (1997).

[20] In fact, in March 2008 Oregon disingenuously reported that more patients in 2007 were concerned with inadequate pain control than in previous years. However, if one looks at the summaries for the preceding years, in 2007 there was actually a 15 percent drop from 2006 in patients expressing a concern about pain control. *See, e.g.*, Oregon Department of Human Services, *Summary of Oregon's Death with Dignity Act—2007* (2008), available at http://www.oregon.gov/DHS/ph/pas/docs/year10.pdf (last visited June 11, 2009); Oregon Department of Human Services, *Summary of Oregon's Death with Dignity Act—2006* (2007), available at http://www.oregon.gov/DHS/ph/pas/docs/year9.pdf (last visited June 11, 2009); Oregon Department of Human Services, *Eighth Annual Report on Oregon's Death with Dignity Act* 14 (2006), available at http://www.oregon.gov/DHS/ph/pas/docs/year8.pdf (last visited Jun 11, 2009); Oregon Department Human Services, *Seventh Annual Report on Oregon's Death with Dignity Act* 15 (2005), available at http://egov.oregon.gov/DHS/ph/pas/docs/year7.pdf (last visited June 11, 2009); Oregon Department of Human Services, *Sixth Annual Report on Oregon's Death with Dignity Act* 14 (2004), available at http://egov.oregon.gov/DHS/ph/pas/docs/year6.pdf (last June 11, 2009).

[21] Nina Shapiro, *Terminal Uncertainty: Washington's new "Death With Dignity" law allows doctors to help people commit suicide—once they've determined that the patient has only six months to live. But what if they are wrong?* SEATTLE WEEKLY, Jan 14, 2009, *available at* www.seattleweekly.com/content/printVersion/553991 (last visited June 9, 2009).

[22] Herbert Hendin & Kathleen Foley, *Physician-Assisted Suicide in Oregon: A Medical Perspective*, 106 MICH. L. REV. 1616 (2008).

[23] DHS, Oregon's Death with Dignity Act: Three years of legalized physician-assisted suicide, Feb. 22, 2001, Table 3, available at http://egov.oregon.gov/DHS/ph/pas/docs/year3.pdf (last visited June 9, 2009).

[24] The Oregon branch of Compassion & Choices acknowledged its involvement in 79 percent of reported assisted-suicide deaths. Compassion in Dying of Oregon, Summary of Hastened Deaths, Data attached to Compassion in Dying of Oregon's IRS Form 990 for 2003.

[25] About Us, Oregon Department of Human Services *available at* http://www.oregon.gov/DHS/ph/pas/about_us.shtml (last visited June 13, 2009).

[26] OR. REV. STAT. § 127.875.

[27] Reporting Requirements of the Oregon Death with Dignity Act, Oregon Department of Human Services *available at* http://www.oregon.gov/DHS/ph/pas/oars.shtml (last visited June 13, 2009).

[28] OR. REV. STAT. § 127.885.

[29] OR. REV. STAT. § 127.865.

[30] National Statistics, American Foundation for Suicide Prevention (2006), *available at* http://www.afsp.org/index.cfm?fuseaction=home.viewpage&page_id=050FEA9F-B064-4092-B1135C3A70DE1FDA (last visited June 10, 2009).

[31] National Center on Elder Abuse, A Response to the Abuse of Vulnerable Adults (Washington, DC 2000).

[32] Nearly all end-of-life issues—access to competent health care, adequate pain relief, in-home personal care, peer counseling, family support—have been issues of disability rights for decades. Brief of *Amici Curiae* Disability, et al. at 3-4, *Baxter v. Montana*, (No. 09-0051).

[33] Steven Ertelt, *Dignitas Assisted Suicide Clinic in Switzerland Probed, Killed Man With Depression*, LifeNews.com, May 25, 2009, *available at* http://www.lifenews.com/bio2858.html (last visited May 27, 2009).

[34] David Brown, *Dignitas founder plans assisted suicide of healthy woman*, TIMESONLINE, Apr, 3, 2009 *available at* http://www.timesonline.co.uk/tol/news/world/europe/article6021947.ece (last visited June 15, 2009).

[35] New York State Task Force on Life and the Law, When Death is Sought: Assisted Suicide and Euthanasia in the Medical Context 2 (1994) [hereinafter Task Force].

[36] HERMAN HENDIN, SEDUCED BY DEATH: DOCTORS, PATIENTS, AND ASSISTED SUICIDE 142 (1998).

[37] *Id.* at 19.

[38] *Id.* at 141.

[39] Alexandra Colen, *Dutch Government Sanctions Infanticide*, THE BRUSSELS JOURNAL, Sept 25, 2005 *available at* http://www.brusselsjournal.com/node/297 (last visited June 16, 2009).

[40] In his book SEDUCED BY DEATH, Herbert Hendin relates the story of Louise, who suffered from an unnamed degenerative neurological disorder. *Id.* at 50-56. Death appeared imminent, and Louise requested that her doctor assist in her suicide. When Louise had second thoughts, her mother, a friend, her doctor, a reporter, and a member of Compassion in Dying (now Compassion & Choices) all acted to *convince* her that suicide was the right decision. *Id.*

[41] Ben A. Rich, *The Politics of Pain: Rhetoric or Reform?*, 8 DEPAUL J. HEALTH CARE L. 519, 523 (2005).

[42] Last Acts Program of the Robert Wood Johnson Foundation, *Means to a Better End: A Report on Dying in America Today* 33 (2002), available at http://www.rwjf.org/files/publications/other/meansbetterend.pdf (last visited October 24, 2008).

[43] Jane E. Brody, *Facing Up to the Inevitable: In Search of a Good Death*, NEW YORK TIMES, Dec. 30, 2003, at F5.

[44] Joan M. Teno et al., *Family Perspectives on End-of-Life Care at the Last Place of Care*, 291 JAMA 88 (2004).

[45] Maria J. Silveira et al., *Patients' Knowledge of Options at the End of Life: Ignorance in the Face of Death*, 284 JAMA 2483 (2000) ("A national poll conducted by the American Medical Association in 1997 found that 40% of respondents did not know it is legal to give pain medicine that could have the additional effect of hastening death (double effect), and 35% were not familiar with the terms *hospice* or *palliative care*.") (emphasis in original).

[46] Mark E. Chopko, *Responsible Public Policy at the End of Life*,

75 Det. Mercy L. Rev. 557, 574-75 (1998).

[47] S. Rep. No. 106-299 (2000) ("The problem is not that modern medicine is incapable of controlling pain, but that too many clinicians are inadequately trained in the most up-to-date techniques. In a survey of 1,177 physicians who had treated a total of more than 70,000 patients with cancer in the previous six months, 76 percent cited lack of knowledge as a barrier to their ability to control pain."); Andrea Petersen, *Negotiating the Terms of Your Death: Medical Advances Give Patients More Control Over How and When they Die*, Wall Street Journal, May 10, 2005, at D1 ("[A] number of more advanced pain treatments have been developed in recent years. And perhaps more significantly, palliative-care centers are finding success treating the dying with medications not necessarily meant for terminal illnesses.").

[48] *See e.g.*, S. Rep. No. 106-299, *supra* ("Perhaps 'the biggest obstacle' to adequate pain treatment of pain . . . is 'ignorance': Few medical schools or residency programs require training in pain management, and many rank-and-file physicals [sic] are unaware of modern advances in palliative care.");.

[49] *See e.g.*, Rabow, *supra*, at 771 ("In general, students and physicians feel ill prepared to provide end-of-life care.") *See also* Kwekkeboom et al., *supra*, at 91 ("In a recent survey of 352 practicing nurses, 66% rated their knowledge of end-of-life care as fair or poor. . . .62% of oncology nurses rated their basic nursing school education on end-of-life care as inadequate.

[50] Joseph P. Pestaner, *End-of-Life Care: Forensic Medicine v. Palliative Medicine*, 31 J.L. Med. & Ethics 365, 369 (2003).

[51] Herbert Hendin, Seduced by Death 24-25 (1997), *cited in Washington v. Glucksberg*, 521 U.S. 702, 730 (1997).

[52] *See e.g.*, Brief for Amicus National Hospice Organization at 18, *Vacco v. Quill*, 521 U.S. 793 (1997), and *Washington v. Glucksberg*, 521 U.S. 702 (1997) ("[T]he acceptance of assisted suicide as a way to deal with terminal illness would undercut further efforts to increase the public's awareness of hospice as a life-affirming option."); Chopko, *supra*, at 581-82 ("[I]mprovements [in pain relief techniques] could be dramatically undercut if assisted suicide were to become accepted practice . . . ."). *See also* Herbert Hendin, Med. Dir., Am. Found. Suicide Prevention, *Remarks for the President's Council on Bioethics* (Mar. 3, 2005), available at http://bioethicsprint.bioethics.gov/transcripts/march05/march03full.html (last visited Oct. 24, 2008) ("Euthanasia, intended for the exceptional case, became an accepted way of dealing with serious or terminal illness in The Netherlands. Palliative care became one of the casualties. Hospice care lagged behind that of other countries. Dutch deficiencies in palliative care have been attributed by Dutch palliative care experts to the easier alternative of euthanasia.").

[53] *See e.g.*, L. C. Kaldjian et al., *Internists' Attitudes Towards Terminal Sedation in End of Life Care*, 30 J. Med. Ethics 499, 499 (2004) ("Most internists who support aggressive palliation appear likely to draw an ethical line between terminal sedation and assisted suicide.").

[54] Terri's Story, Terri Schindler Schiavo Founation, *available at* http://www.terrisfight.org/pages.php?page_id=3 (last visited June 11, 2009).

[55] *Cruzan,* 497 U.S. at 286-87.

[56] Greer, George W., Circuit Judge (2000-02-11). "In re: the guardianship of Theresa Marie Schiavo, Incapacitated," File No. 90-2908GD-003". Florida Sixth Judicial Circuit. http://abstractappeal.com/schiavo/trialctorder02-00.pdf. pp. 9-10 (last visited Jun 11, 2009)

[57] *See* Wesley Smith, Forced Exit Euthanasia, Assisted Suicide, and the New Duty to Die 176-191 (Encounter Books 1997).

[58] Charlotte Allen, *BACK OFF! I'M NOT DEAD YET. I Don't Want a Living Will. Why Should I?* The Washington Post, Oct 14, 2007 B01 *available at* http://www.washingtonpost.com/wp-dyn/content/article/2007/10/12/AR2007101201882.html (last visited Jun 11, 2009).

[59] *Advance Directives*, International Task Force on Euthanasia and Assisted Suicide *available at* http://www.internationaltaskforce.org/advdir.htm (last visited Jun 11, 2009).

[60] Robin Marantz Henig, *Will We Ever Arrive at the Good Death?*, New York Times Magazine, Aug. 7, 2005 at 26.

[61] Hendin, *supra*, at 91 (emphasis added).

[62] *Id.* at 92.

[63] Smith, *supra* note 57, at 177, 185.

[64] Federation of State Medical Licensing Boards, *supra*, at 7.

[65] Wishik, *supra*, at 36.

[66] Federation of State Medical Licensing Boards, *supra*, at 7.

[67] Wishik, *supra*, at 36.

[68] Henig, *supra*, at 26.

[69] Task Force, *supra*, at 37.

[70] For a more in-depth explanation of palliative care, *see* Americans United for Life, Brief of *Amicus Curiae* in Support of Petitioners at 7-9, *Gonzales v. Oregon* (Sup. Ct. No. 04-623), available at http://www.aul.org/xm_client/client_documents/briefs/GonzalesvOregon04-623.pdf (last visited Oct. 24, 2008).

[71] *Center to Advance Palliative Care Manual: How to Establish a Palliative Care Program* (C. F. Von Gunten et al., eds. 2001), available at http://64.85.16.230/educate/content/elements/nhpcodefinition.html (last visited Oct. 24, 2008).

[72] Henig, *supra*, at 26.

[73] *Id.*

[74] Last Acts Program of the Robert Wood Johnson Foundation, *Means to a Better End: A Report on Dying in America Today* 33 (2002), available at http://www.rwjf.org/files/publications/other/meansbetterend.pdf (last visited Oct. 24, 2008).

[75] Bernard Lo & Gordon Rubenfeld, *Palliative Sedation in Dying Patients: "We Turn to It When Everything Else Hasn't Worked"*, 294 JAMA 1810, 1812 (2005).

[76] *Id.*

[77] Keith Andrews, *Misdiagnosis of the vegetative state: retrospective study in a rehabilitation unit*, BMJ 313: 13-16 (6 Jul 1996) *available at* http://www.bmj.com/cgi/content/full/313/7048/13 (last visited Jun 11, 2009).

[78] New York State Task Force on Life and the Law, When Death is Sought: Assisted Suicide and Euthanasia in the Medical Context 5 (Supp. 1997) [hereinafter Task Force Supp.]. Added to the plight of the non-terminally-ill chronic pain sufferers is the fact that the pain of the terminally-ill is actually *better* managed than that of chronic pain sufferers. Task Force, *supra*, at 23. An argument can be made that such sufferers actu-

ally have a stronger liberty interest in PAS than terminally-ill patients. Yale Kamisar, *The "Right to Die": On Drawing (and Erasing) Lines*, 35 Duq. L. Rev. 481, 510 (1996).

[79] *See, e.g.*, the story of "Netty Boomsma" in Hendin, *supra*, at 76-83. Few advocates of PAS argue that the right to PAS should be limited to the terminally-ill. Task Force, *supra*, at 74 n.113. One proposed model for PAS was limited to those with "incurable, debilitating disease who voluntarily request to end their lives." Hendin, *supra*, at 206. This would include patients with diabetes and arthritis. *Id.*

[80] *Report from the Select Committee on Medical Ethics*, House of Lords Session 1993-94, § 238. On May 12, 2006, the House of Lords again rejected proposed laws to allow PAS.

[81] Eric Chevlen, *The Limits of Prognostication*, 35 Duq. L. Rev. 337, 348 (1996). "If autonomy is the guiding principle and the determination of pain and suffering is so subjective, then any competent person… has the right to choose euthanasia." Hendin, *supra*, at 122. The New York State Task Force concluded that "it will be difficult, if not impossible, to contain the option to such a limited group…. [N]o principled basis will exist to deny [other patients] this right." Task Force Supp., *supra*, at 5. The Task Force explains that if the right to refuse medical treatment is not limited to the terminally-ill, then PAS will not be limitable, either. *Id.* at 12-13.

[82] Task Force Supp., *supra*, at 18; *see also* Task Force, *supra*, at 134 (stating that while the "autonomy" of some patients may be extended, the autonomy of many others would be compromised with the legalization of PAS).

[83] Task Force, *supra*, at 138.

[84] *See, e.g.*, Hendin, *supra*, at 50-56, 61, 128-32, 142.

[85] Task Force, *supra*, at 95. *See also id.* at 99 (stating that "the so-called 'right to die' all too easily becomes a duty to die").

[86] Task Force, *supra*, at 99.

[87] *Id.* at ix, 120.

[88] Steven Ertelt, *Oregon Tells Patients State Will Pay for Assisted Suicide, Not Health Care* (July 30, 2008), available at http://www.lifenews.com/bio2527.html (last visited October 24, 2008) [hereinafter Ertelt I]; Steven Ertelt, *Oregon State Health Care Plan Will Pay for Assisted Suicide, Not Treatment* (June 23, 2008), available at http://www.lifenews.com/nb139.html (last visited October 24, 2008). Randy Stroup, a patient with prostate cancer, was uninsured and needed expensive chemotherapy. *See* Ertelt I, *supra*. He applied to the Oregon health insurance plan for help, but was told that the state would not cover treatment, but would pay for an assisted suicide. *Id.*

[89] Hendin, *supra*, at 244.

[90] Task Force Supp., *supra*, at 4.

[91] The availability of euthanasia appears to have contributed to the failure of palliative care in the Netherlands. Hendin, *supra*, at 15.

[92] *See, e.g.*, *id.* at 44; Kamisar, *supra*, at 497.

[93] Task Force, *supra*, at 162; American Medical Association, *Report 4 of the Council on Scientific Affairs: Aspects of Pain Management in Adults* (1995), available at http://www.ama-assn.org/ama/pub/category/13672.html (last visited October 24, 2008).

[94] Task Force Supp., *supra*, at 17.

[95] Task Force, *supra*, at 162. Even the two percent of patients requiring sedation can die peacefully, without suffering. American Geriatrics Society, *supra*, at III.D.; Hendin, *supra*, at 14.

[96] Rosemary Ryan, *Medical Practice: Palliative Care and Terminal Illness*, 26 Nat'l Catholic Bioethics Quarterly 313, 316 (2001).

[97] *Id.* at 318. *See also* Brody, *supra*, at F5 (According to Elizabeth Ford Pitorak, director of the Hospice Institute of Hospice of the Western Reserve of Cleveland, no evidence supports that such drugs hasten death); Sarah E. M. Buzzee, Comment, *The Pain Relief Promotion Act: Congress's Misguided Intervention into End-of-Life*, 70 U. Cin. L. Rev. 217, 242 (2001).Lo & Rubenfeld, *supra*, at 1815; *see also* L. C. Kaldjian et al., *Internists' Attitudes Towards Terminal Sedation in End of Life Care*, 30 J. Med. Ethics 499 (2004) ("Although physiological concerns exist about the possibility that opioids and benzodiazepines may hasten death by suppressing respirations, there is a paucity of empirical data to support these concerns. . . .Even more provocative are suggestions that sedation toward the end of life may actually prolong life rather than hasten death, due to dampening of increased metabolic demands caused by pain and distress in patients who are fragile.").

[98] Lo & Rubenfeld, *supra*, at 1815; *see also* L. C. Kaldjian et al., *Internists' Attitudes Towards Terminal Sedation in End of Life Care*, 30 J. Med. Ethics 499 (2004) ("Although physiological concerns exist about the possibility that opioids and benzodiazepines may hasten death by suppressing respirations, there is a paucity of empirical data to support these concerns. . . .Even more provocative are suggestions that sedation toward the end of life may actually prolong life rather than hasten death, due to dampening of increased metabolic demands caused by pain and distress in patients who are fragile.").

[99] Ryan, *supra*, at 318.

[100] Lo & Rubenfeld, *supra*, at 1815. *See also* Ryan, *supra*, at 317.

[101] Wishik, *supra*, at 24.

[102] Furrow, *supra*, at 29.

[103] Wishik, *supra*, at 23.

[104] Meisel, *supra*, at 2499. *See also* Ryan, *supra*, at 317.

[105] Meisel, *supra*, at 2499.

[106] Julia Stuart, *Back from the Dead: A cure for comas*, Compassionate Healthcare Network, March 27, 2009 *available at* http://www.chninternational.com/pvs_recovery.htm (last visited June 16, 2009).

[107] *Persistent Vegetative State*, Brain and Spinal Cord.Org *available at* http://www.brainandspinalcord.org/recovery-traumatic-brain-injury/Vegetative-state-tbi.html (last visited June 16, 2009).

End of Life Talking Points

- Every court of final jurisdiction in the nation to consider the constitutionality of physician-assisted suicide (PAS) has held that the state's interest in preserving the lives of its people justifies its prohibition. Forty-one states have either an explicit or implied prohibition. The Supreme Court has acknowledged the legitimate government interests in: 1) preserving life; (2) preventing suicide; (3) avoiding the involvement of third parties and use of arbitrary, unfair, or undue influence; (4) protecting family members and loved ones; (5) protecting the integrity of the medical profession; and (6) avoiding future movement toward euthanasia and other abuses. *Washington v. Glucksburg*, 521 U.S. 702, 792-793 (1997).

- The "Oregon Death with Dignity Act" exemplifies how safeguards for legalized PAS are inadequate and being circumvented to allow suicide of the depressed and involuntary killing. It is impossible to hold physicians accountable when permitted to assist suicide. The lack of transparency in physician self-reporting measures and the failure of the Oregon Department of Human Services reporting requirements leave the elderly and disabled in danger.

- The Netherlands conclusively demonstrates that authorizing assisted suicide inevitably leads to involuntary euthanasia. Virtually every safeguard set up by the country has failed to protect patients. Regulation is impossible because 60 percent of cases are not reported.[1] One study revealed that .08 percent of all deaths in the Netherlands were a result of euthanasia performed without a contemporaneous request from the patient; in the United States, that would equal 16,000 deaths a year from involuntary euthanasia.[2] In other studies, one-fourth of physicians stated that they had "terminated the lives of patients without an explicit request."[3] In another study, no request for death was made in over 80 percent of the cases.[4]

- PAS is admittedly the first step in accepting death as an alternative to suffering—including depression and mental suffering. The Swiss experience reveals the abuses of legal assisted suicide and the difficulty in prosecuting violations of the law as advocates challenge the limits and safeguards. Dignitas, a Swiss assisted suicide facility, is under investigation for assisting a healthy, depressed man to commit suicide,[5] as well as, publicizing its intention to help a healthy wife commit suicide with her terminally-ill husband.[6]

- PAS is antithetical to the purpose and nature of the medical profession. The American Medical Association, the American Psychiatric Association, the American College of Physicians, and the American Academy of Geriatrics and the American Pain Society,

among other health care associations, have all issued position statements against PAS.

- PAS encourages a cost/benefit analysis and subjective determination of a patient's quality of life, especially with the current economic difficulties, efforts to cut health care costs, and the ongoing debate over nationalizing healthcare. Health insurance coverage in Oregon includes the "cost effective" medical treatment of ingesting a lethal prescription under "death with dignity."

- The vast majority of terminally-ill patients do not desire suicide—the overwhelming majority fight for life until the end.[7] PAS requests most often come from patients who are actually suffering from treatable mental disorders, typically depression. Often, patients withdraw their PAS request when physicians appropriately treat depression or address the pain and other concerns causing the depression.[8] An option of suicide provides little incentive for physicians to seek alternative remedies for alleviating pain and addressing the underlying causes of depression.

- Unbearable pain is often given as the reason to permit assisted suicide, but studies show it is not the reason patients request PAS. A study of HIV patients revealed, "The strongest predictors of interest in physician-assisted suicide were high scores on measures of psychological distress (depression, hopelessness, suicidal ideation, and overall psychological distress) and experience with terminal illness in a family member or friend."[9] The study concluded, "Patients' interest in physician-assisted suicide appeared to be more a function of psychological distress and social factors than physical factors."[10]

- Legalized PAS hides abuse of the elderly and disabled. It provides complete liability protection for doctors and promotes secrecy, particularly when PAS doctors are self-reporting, death certificates are required to report a "natural" death, and there are no witness requirements at time of death. As observed in Oregon, PAS—accompanied by any number of safeguards—permits absolutely no transparency and makes patient choice and protections simply illusions.

- PAS discriminates against and degrades the lives of people with disabilities. It denies people with disabilities the benefit of suicide prevention and enforcement of homicide laws.[11] Furthermore, PAS completely undermines suicide prevention efforts.

- Assisted suicide is unnecessary for the treatment of pain. Pain associated with terminal-illness patients can be relieved. Ninety-five to ninety-eight percent of pain can be addressed through palliative care.[12] The pain of the remaining patients can be relieved through sedation.[13] While PAS proponents market the hard cases—those cases where pain is claimed to be unbearable—proper palliative care makes the hard cases practically non-existent.

- A patient's pain and suffering is inherently subjective and cannot be used as a gauge for who should be eligible for PAS.[14] "Suffering is a distinctly human, not a medical, condition."[15] As such, public policies that hinge on the notion of pain and suffering are uncontainable.[16] In addition, any evaluation of pain and suffering would be left to a doctor's assessment which, ironically, depletes a patient's autonomy rather than preserves it.

- In contrast to using controlled substances for assisting suicide, using them to control pain is a "legitimate medical purpose" under the federal "Controlled Substances Act" and similar state statutes. The provision of pain medication and sedation is legally, medically, and ethically acceptable if it is intended to alleviate pain and is provided in accordance with accepted medical standards.

- The proper response to pain and suffering is training for healthcare professionals in the wider use of effective palliative techniques and education to patients to address unwarranted fears—not the elimination of the sufferer. [17]

Endnotes

[1] Herbert Hendin, Seduced by Death: Doctors, Patients, and Assisted Suicide 20, 136 (1998).

[2] New York State Task Force on Life and the Law, When Death is Sought: Assisted Suicide and Euthanasia in the Medical Context 134 (1994) [hereinafter Task Force]; Hendin, *supra*, at 91.

[3] Hendin, *supra*, at 139. In 48 percent of those cases there was no request of any kind. *Id.*

[4] *Id.* at 140.

[5] Steven Ertelt, *Dignitas Assisted Suicide Clinic in Switzerland Probed, Killed Man With Depression*, LifeNews.com, May 25, 2009, *available at* http://www.lifenews.com/bio2858.html (last visited May 27, 2009).

[6] David Brown, *Dignitas founder plans assisted suicide of healthy woman*, TIMESONLINE, Apr, 3, 2009 *available at* http://www.timesonline.co.uk/tol/news/world/europe/article6021947.ece (last visited June 15, 2009).

[7] Task Force, *supra*, at 9, 13, 72; Hendin, *supra*, at 34. Terminally-ill patients account for only two to four percent of all suicides. Hendin, *supra*, at 34 .

[8] Task Force, *supra*, at x, 13, 26, 108, 126. Treatment for depression resulted in 90 percent of patients ceasing their desire for suicide. In one study, every terminally-ill patient who expressed a wish to die was suffering from major depression. Hendin, *supra*, at 240.

[9] William Breitbart, MD, Barry D. Rosenfeld, PhD & Steven D. Passik, PhD, *Interest in Physician-Assisted Suicide Among Ambulatory HIV-Infected Patients*, Am J Psychiatry 1996; 153:238-242.

[10] *Id.*

[11] Nearly all end-of-life issues—access to competent health care, adequate pain relief, in-home personal care, peer counseling, family support—have been issues of disability rights for decades. Brief of *Amici Curiae* Disability, et al. at 3-4, *Baxter v. Montana*, (No. 09-0051).

[12] Timothy E. Quill & Christine K. Cassel, Professional Organizations' Position Statements on Physician-Assisted Suicide: A Case for Studied Neutrality, Annals of Internal Med. 138:3:208 (2003); Robert A. Burt, Constitutionalizing Physician-Assisted Suicide: Will Lightning Strike Thrice?, 35 Duq. L. Rev. 159, 166 (1996); see also Americans United for Life, Brief of Amicus Curiae in Support of Petitioners at 6-7, Gonzales v. Oregon (Sup. Ct. No. 04-623), available at http://www.aul.org/xm_client/client_documents/briefs/GonzalesvOregon04-623.pdf (last visited October 29, 2009).

[13] American Geriatrics Society, Brief as *Amicus Curiae* Urging Reversal of the Judgments Below at Part I.B, *Vacco v. Quill*, 521 U.S. 793 (1997); Wesley J. Smith, Forced Exit: The Slippery Slope from Assisted Suicide to Legalized Murder 207 (1997).

[14] *Id.* at 132.

[15] *Id.* at 22.

[16] Hendin, *supra*, at 192. "Suffering" may arise from a number of non-medical causes, such as social isolation, fear, and frustration of a goal, which are obviously unacceptable reasons to allow PAS. Task Force, *supra*, at 21, 135.

[17] Common barriers to palliative care are the *widespread* lack of training of physicians in palliative care and fears about the side effects of palliative care medications. Americans United for Life, *supra*, at 10-15. Thus, education of both physicians and patients is

a proper response to the pain and suffering of the terminally-ill.

Laws Regarding Assisted Suicide

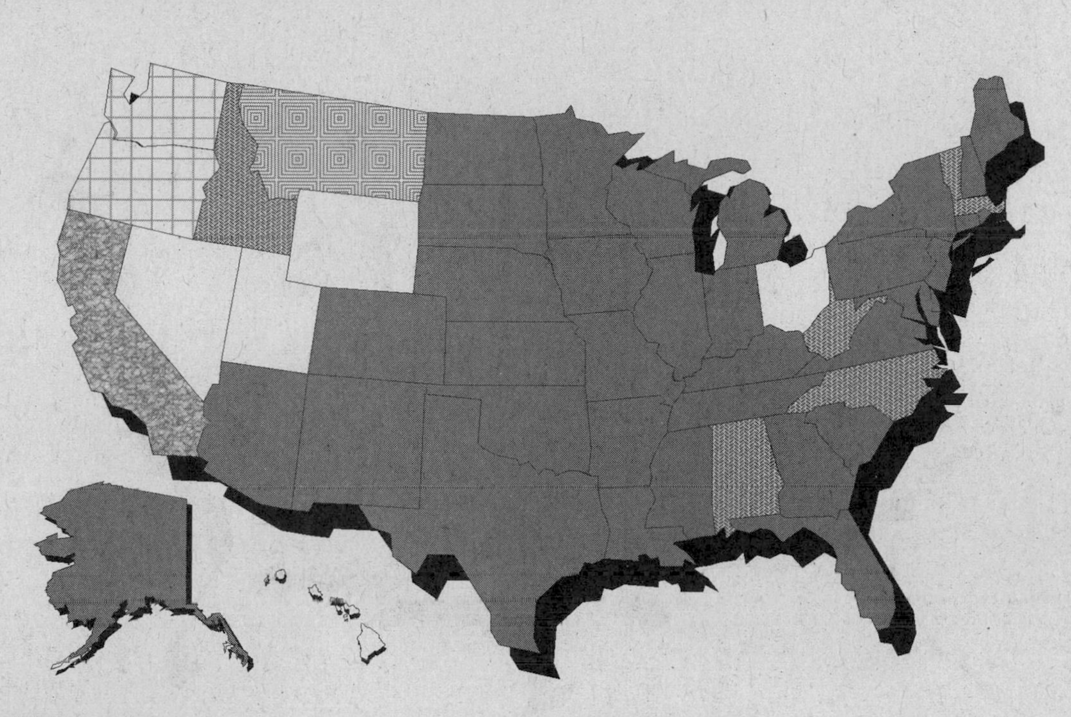

Thirty-five states expressly criminalize assisted suicide: AK, AZ, AR, CO, CT, DE, FL, GA, IL, IN, IA, KS, KY, LA, ME, MD, MI, MN, MS, MO, NE, NH, NJ, NM, NY, ND, OK, PA, RI, SC, SD, TN, TX, VA, and WI.

Six states prohibit assisted suicide under common law of crimes or judicial interpretation of homicide statutes: AL, ID, MA, NC, VT, and WV.

Two states approved assisted suicide by statute: OR and WA

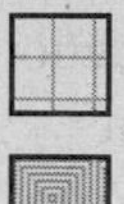

One state has pending constitutionally-declared "right to die" with physician-assisted suicide: MT

One state expressly criminalizes assisted suicide, but also requires physicians to counsel patients on how to commit suicide, going so far as to require physicians to provide prescriptions for those patients wishing to starve or dehydrate to death: CA

Pain Medicine Education

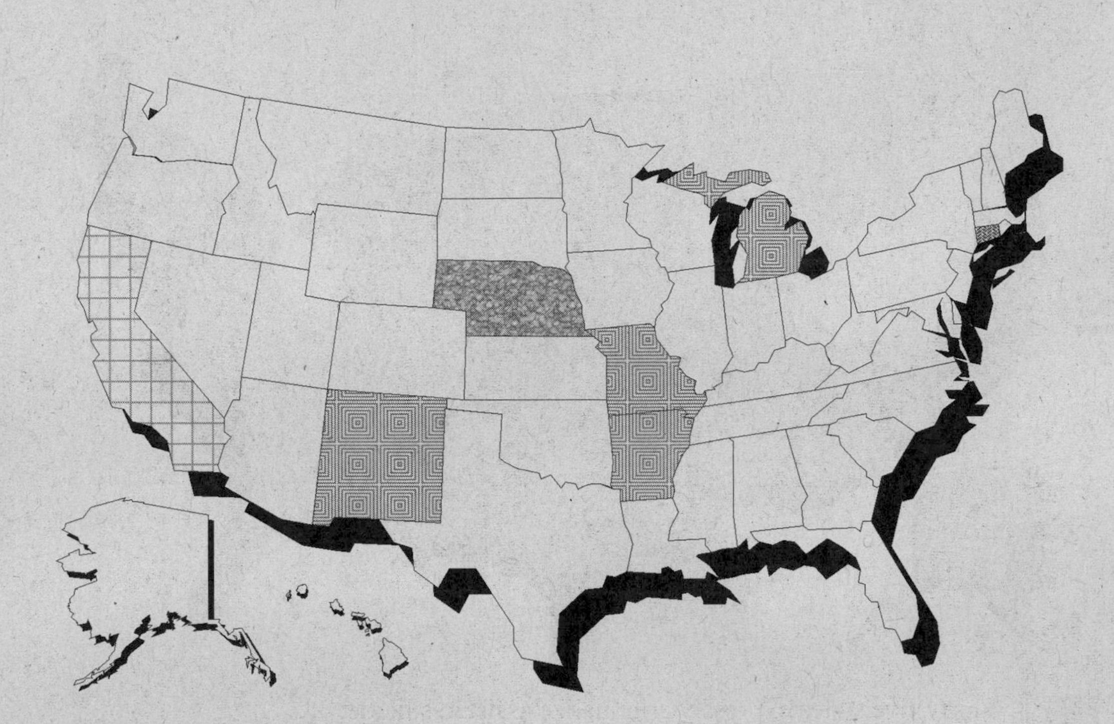

Only one state has amended its medical school curriculum requirements to add instruction on pain management and end-of-life issues: CA

One state requires annual training in pain recognition and management for nursing home staff: CT

Four states formed advisory councils on Pain Management to make recommendations on medical school curricula, continuing education, and other guidelines for pain management: AR, MI, MO, and NM

One state passed legislation encouraging licensing boards or individual physicians to pursue improving pain management education and treatment: NE

2009 State Legislative Sessions in Review: *End of Life*

By Jessica J. Sage
Staff Counsel, Americans United for Life

In most years, legislative and other state measures related to the end of life are few in number and do not receive much attention, except when, as in late 2008, Washington state voters approved physician-assisted suicide (PAS) and a Montana district court declared the state's constitutional rights to individual privacy and human dignity include the right for a patient to use the assistance of her physician to obtain lethal medication and commit suicide.

Just as in 2005 when the Terri Schindler-Schiavo case commanded the public's attention when a court ordered her feeding and hydration tube removed, the recent death of Linda Fleming, the first woman to commit suicide under the new PAS law in Washington, drew similar attention and much sorrow from pro-life advocates. Unfortunately, victories in Washington and Montana have energized the pro-euthanasia movement and emboldened it to introduce PAS legislation and other end-of-life related legislation across the country.

In 2009, approximately 140 measures related to end-of-life issues were considered in 44 states—a significant increase in activity from levels seen in 2008. This dramatic turn-of-events demands a meaningful public debate about PAS and euthanasia, the affirmative act of removing food and hydration from vulnerable patients, the scope and effectiveness of advance directives for health care and similar legal documents, and palliative care and pain management options.

Assisted Suicide and Euthanasia

Nearly a quarter of states dealt with PAS initiatives in the last two legislative years. In 2009, making use of titles such as *Death with Dignity*, *Compassionate Choices, Right to Die,* and *Patient Control* or *Choice*, at least eight states including Connecticut, Hawaii, Massachusetts, Montana, New Hampshire, New Mexico, and Vermont considered measures to legalize (or, in the case of Montana, regulate) PAS.

Importantly, euthanasia and PAS advocates have an aggressive agenda to see PAS legalized in all 50 states. Defeat does not deter them; rather, it causes them to re-strategize about how to gain acceptance for PAS and then re-attack. During the 2009 state legislative sessions, they did so by pursuing measures that advance their ideology, including lobbying state medical boards to pass resolutions or provide position statements of neutrality or affirmation for PAS, as well as promoting advance directives for individuals to explicitly refuse life-saving medical treatments and sustenance needs if they become incapacitated. In this vein, Maryland enacted a measure adding a nursing home industry representative to its State Advisory Council on Quality Care at End of Life.

Conversely, Wyoming considered a measure to criminalize assisted suicide.

Advance Directives, Living Wills, Healthcare Powers of Attorney, and Related Documents

The vast majority of end-of-life measures considered in 2009 dealt, in varying ways, with advance directives, "do not resuscitate" (DNR) orders, life-sustaining treatments, and the proper appointment of guardians and healthcare agents. In 2009, 12 states enacted new or revised current laws dealing with advance directives.

Arizona enacted two measures to amend existing statutes: First, to prohibit a fiduciary or trustee whose license has been revoked from serving as an agent under a healthcare power of attorney unless the person is related to the principal; and second, to require the court to give appointed guardian's authority to withhold or withdraw life-sustaining treatment, including artificial food and fluids. The second measure further created a rebuttable presumption in favor of food and fluids if no advance directive exists, and provided clarification for the process and standard of review to rebut that presumption.

Arkansas enacted two measures revising statutes to limit the power of the State Department of Human Services as custodian from withholding life-sustaining treatment without express court approval; and to clarify DNR procedures for nursing facility employees.

Louisiana passed resolutions for two studies. The first study requests the State Department of Health and Hospitals to study the use of living wills among Medicaid recipients, while the second creates a study committee to look at physician orders for life-sustaining care.

Maine enacted two measures, with the first developing two education programs about end-of-life directives for the public and the legal community and the second creating "Uniform Power of Attorney Act" relating to durable healthcare powers of attorney.

Minnesota amended applicable statutes to permit the release of medical records to healthcare agents.

Montana revised its guardianship law to prohibit a guardian from giving a DNR order if it conflicts with an incapacitated person's wishes.

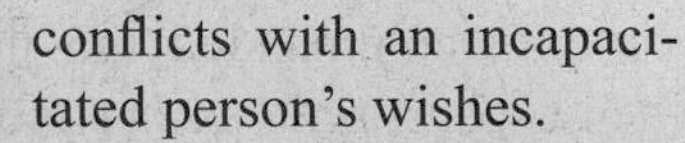

Both North Dakota and Oklahoma enacted measures creating registries for advance directives for healthcare.

Oregon amended its laws for advance directives, giving the healthcare representative the authority to approve short-term hospitalization for dementia patients.

Texas amended its Health and Safety Code to allow for electronic signatures on advance directives and to permit notarization of DNR orders (as an alternative to two witnesses).

Utah amended its "Advance Health Care Directive Act" to expand the list of healthcare professionals authorized to determine a patient's decision-making capacity and effectuate a patient's healthcare directive.

Finally, Virginia enacted measures creating a "Uniform Power of Attorney Act," clarifying the process for determining whether a patient lacks decision-making capacity, and specifying how a patient's DNR orders may be effectively revoked.

Preventing Starvation and Dehydration

At least eight states—including Arizona, Arkansas, Mississippi, Montana, New York, Ohio, Oregon, and Texas—considered measures related to life-sustaining treatments, including artificial food and hydration.

Arizona created a rebuttable presumption in favor of the continued provision of artificial food and fluids in the absence of an advance directive.

Arkansas amended its "Adult Maltreatment Custody Act" to limit the State Department of Human Services when functioning as a patient's legal custodian from making any decision to withhold life-sustaining treatment without express court approval.

Montana revised its guardianship law to prohibit a guardian from withholding or withdrawing life-sustaining treatment if it conflicts with incapacitated person's wishes.

Pain Management

At least 10 states—including California, Connecticut, Florida, Hawaii, Kansas, Massachusetts, Mississippi, Texas, Vermont, and West Virginia—considered measures related to proper pain management. Some measures encouraged training in and awareness of pain management, provided protection for physicians employing accepted pain management techniques, or enacted a patients' bill of rights, while others sought to regulate pain management clinics and the controlled substances used to treat pain.

California established September 2009 as "Pain Awareness Month" to inform healthcare providers of the need for effective pain management.

Connecticut enacted a measure requiring direct-care nursing home staff to complete annual training in pain recognition and the administration of pain management techniques.

Florida enacted the "Prescription Drug Monitoring Program" to monitor use of controlled substances in an electronic database system.

Texas enacted a measure to create licensing and regulation for pain management clinics.

West Virginia made minor changes to its "Management of Pain Act," specifically amending its definitions of "pain" and "pain-relieving controlled substances."

Palliative Care

At least four states—including Colorado, Illinois, New York, and Vermont—considered legislation to encourage training in and funding of palliative care. Illinois specifically considered pediatric palliative care; while New York sought to require healthcare practitioners to provide palliative care information and to counsel patients diagnosed with a terminal illness or condition on their options.

Colorado passed a resolution for a Hospice Palliative Care Interim study.

Vermont enacted a "Patient's Bill of Rights for Palliative Care and Pain Management" to ensure healthcare providers inform patients of all their treatment options.

AUL Model Legislation

ASSISTED SUICIDE BAN ACT

HOUSE/SENATE BILL No. ______
By Representatives/Senators ____________

Section 1. Title.

This Act may be known and cited as the "Assisted Suicide Ban Act."

Section 2. Legislative Findings and Purposes.

(a) The [*Legislature*] of the State of [*Insert name of State*] finds that:

(1) "In almost every State—indeed, in almost every western democracy—it is a crime to assist a suicide. The States' assisted-suicide bans are not innovations. Rather they are longstanding expressions of the States' commitment to the protection and preservation of all human life." *Washington v. Glucksberg*, 521 U.S. 702, 710 (1997).

(2) "Indeed, opposition to and condemnation of suicide—and, therefore, of assisting suicide—are consistent and enduring themes of our philosophical, legal and cultural heritages." This universal tradition has long rejected a right to assisted suicide and the State of [*Insert name of State*] "continues to explicitly reject it today, even for terminally ill, mentally competent adults." *Washington v. Glucksberg*, 521 U.S. 702, 711 and 723 (1997).

(3) The State of [*Insert name of State*] "has an unqualified interest in the preservation of human life…[and] in preventing suicide." *Washington v. Glucksberg*, 521 U.S. 702, 729-30 (1997).

(4) The State of [*Insert name of State*] "has an interest in protecting vulnerable groups—including the poor, the elderly, and disabled persons—from abuse, neglect, [*coercion*] and mistakes." A ban on assisted suicide reflects and reinforces our well-supported policy "that the lives of the terminally ill, disabled, and elderly people must be no less valued than the lives for the young and healthy, and that a seriously disabled [terminally-ill or elderly] person's suicidal impulses should be interpreted and treated the same way as anyone else's." *Washington v. Glucksberg*, 521 U.S. 702, 731-32 (1997).

(5) The State of [*Insert name of State*] has an interest in protecting the integrity

and ethics of the medical profession and affirms its responsibility to its patients as healers and those principles articulated in the Hippocratic Oath to:

a. Keep the sick from harm and injustice.
b. Refrain from giving anybody a deadly drug if asked for it, nor make a suggestion to this effect.

(6) More specifically, the State of [*Insert name of State*] recognizes the close link between physician-assisted suicide and euthanasia where a right to die easily becomes a "duty to die." A prohibition of assisted suicide is the only reasonable means to protect from foreseeable abuses. *Washington v. Glucksberg*, 521 U.S. 702, 734-35 (1997); *Vacco v. Quill*, 521 U.S. 793, 808-09 (1997).

(7) The State of [*Insert name of State*] recognizes the distinction between a patient refusing life-sustaining medical treatment (not to include the withdrawal of artificial nutrition and hydration), where he dies from the underlying fatal disease or pathology; and a patient ingesting or administering a lethal medication prescribed by a physician, where the medication is the cause of death. *Vacco v. Quill*, 521 U.S. 793, 801 (1997).

(8) The State of [*Insert name of State*] recognizes the importance of palliative care and pain management and emphasizes the distinction in the "legal principles of causation and intent" between pain management intended to alleviate pain and assisted suicide intended to cause death. *Vacco v. Quill*, 521 U.S. 793, 801-03 (1997).

(b) Based on the findings in Subsection (a) of this Act, it is the purpose of this Act to:

(1) Provide protection for our most vulnerable citizens by explicitly prohibiting assisted suicide within the State of [*Insert name of State*]'s criminal code.

(2) Reinforce and reflect the intended purpose of our medical professions to preserve life and act as healers.

Section 3. Definitions.

As used in this Act only:

(a) "**Deliberately**" means to consider carefully, done on purpose; or intentional.

(b) **“Healthcare provider”** means any individual who may be asked to participate in any way in a healthcare service, including, but not limited to, the following: a physician, physician’s assistant, nurse, nurses’ aide, medical assistant, hospital employee, clinic employee, nursing home employee, pharmacist, pharmacy employee, researcher, medical or nursing school faculty, student or employee, counselor, social worker, or any professional, paraprofessional, or any other person who furnishes, or assists in the furnishing of, healthcare services.

(c) **“Person”** means any natural person; and when appropriate, an “organization” to include:

(1) A public or private corporation, company, association, firm, partnership, or joint-stock company;
(2) Government or a governmental instrumentality; or
(3) A foundation, institution, society, union, club, or church.

(d) **“Physician”** means a person licensed to practice medicine in the State of [*Insert name of State*]. This term includes medical doctors and doctors of osteopathy.

(e) **“Suicide”** means the act or instance of taking one’s own life voluntarily and intentionally.

Section 4. Criminal Penalties.

(a) Any person who deliberately advises, assists, or encourages another to commit suicide, is guilty of [*Insert appropriate degree of felony*].

(b) Any physician or healthcare provider that:

(1) Prescribes any drug, compound, or substance to a patient with the intended purpose to assist in ending the patient’s life; or

(2) Assists or performs any medical procedure for the intended purpose to assist in ending the patient’s life

is guilty of [*Insert appropriate degree of felony*].

Section 5. Civil Penalties and Fines.

(a) Any person, physician, or healthcare provider who intentionally or knowingly violates this Act shall be liable for damages.

(b) If any person assists a suicide, any surviving family member, other beneficiary,

executor, or administrator of the decedent's estate may bring an appropriate action under [*Insert reference(s) to state's wrongful death statute(s)*].

(c) Any physician or other healthcare provider who assists a suicide in violation of this Act shall be considered to have engaged in unprofessional conduct for which his or her [*certificate or*] license to provide healthcare services in the State of [*Insert name of State*] shall be suspended or revoked by the State of [*Insert name of State Medical Board or other appropriate entity*].

Section 6. Construction.

Nothing in this Act shall be construed to prohibit a physician or healthcare provider from:

(1) Participating in the execution of a person sentenced by a court to death by lethal injection;

(2) Following a patient's clear, expressed, and documented wishes to withhold or withdraw life-sustaining treatment [*not necessarily inclusive of withdrawing artificial nutrition and hydration*].

(3) Prescribing and administering palliative care or pain medication treatment options intended to relieve pain while the patient's illness or condition follows its natural course.

Section 7. Right of Intervention.

The [*Legislature*], by joint resolution, may appoint one or more of its members, who sponsored or cosponsored this Act in his or her official capacity, to intervene as a matter of right in any case in which the constitutionality of this Act or any portion thereof is challenged.

Section 8. Severability.

If any provision, word, phrase, or clause of this Act or the application thereof to any person or circumstance is held invalid, such invalidity shall not affect the provisions, words, phrases, clauses, or applications of this Act which can be given effect without the invalid provision, word, phrase, clause, or application and to this end, the provisions, words, phrases, and clauses of this Act are declared severable.

Section 9. Effective Date.

This Act takes effect on [*Insert date*].

PAIN MEDICINE EDUCATION ACT

HOUSE/SENATE BILL No. _________
By Representatives/Senators ______________

Section 1. Title.

This Act may be known and cited as the "Pain Medicine Education Act."

Section 2. Legislative Findings and Purposes.

(a) The Legislature of the State of [*Insert name of State*] finds that:

(1) One goal of medicine is to relieve suffering.

(2) Inadequate pain relief is a serious public health problem in the United States, especially for those with chronic pain, the terminally ill, or those who are otherwise in the last stages of life. Approximately 80 [*or other number based on studies or other evidence*] percent of chronic-pain patients in this State do not receive adequate treatment for their pain symptoms.

(3) Clinical experience demonstrates that adequate pain management leads to enhanced functioning and increased quality of life, while uncontrolled pain contributes to disability and despair.

(4) Every person dies, suffers, and experiences pain at some point in his or her life. Diagnosis and treatment of pain is integral to the practice of medicine and appropriate management for each patient is the responsibility of the treating physician.

(5) Inappropriate pain treatment may result from healthcare providers' lack of knowledge about pain management.

(6) All healthcare providers should become knowledgeable about assessing patients' pain and effective methods of pain treatment, as well as statutory requirements for prescribing controlled substances.

(7) Many healthcare providers are ill-informed about current and effective management techniques for patients' pain symptoms because this topic is not adequately addressed in the normal course of healthcare provider schools' curricula.

(8) With proper management techniques, chronic pain may be reduced in the overwhelming majority of suffering patients.

(9) Controlled substances, including opioid analgesics, may be essential in the courses of treatment for all types of pain and are, therefore, necessary to the public health.

(10) Healthcare professionals' education has not provided appropriate training in the use of opioid medications for chronic pain.

(11) Patient pain should be assessed and treated promptly, and the quantity and frequency of doses should be adjusted to the intensity, duration of the pain, and treatment outcomes.

(12) Tolerance and physical dependence are normal consequences of sustained use of opioid analgesics and are not the same as addiction.

(13) The [*Legislature*] recognizes that some types of pain cannot be completely relieved.

(b) The [*Legislature's*] purpose in promulgating this Act is to further the important and compelling societal interests of:

(1) Expanding the opportunities for medical students, residents, and other healthcare providers to gain experience in treating severe pain symptoms in suffering patients.

(2) Ensuring the best possible medical care for all patients suffering from intractable and chronic pain.

(3) Improving the quality of life for all chronic pain sufferers, especially those in the last stages of life, by ensuring that patients undergo a peaceful, natural, and, as much as possible, pain-free end-of-life experience.

(4) Reducing patient requests for physician-assisted suicide (PAS) by addressing patient issues that may lead to depression and despair, the root causes and most-cited motivations for PAS.

(5) Broadening patient autonomy by presenting the greatest number of possible options for treatment through consultation with adequately knowledgeable physicians.

Section 3. Definitions.

As used in this Act only:

(a) "**Addiction**" means a primary, chronic, neurobiological disease, with genetic, psychosocial, and environmental factors influencing its development and manifestations. It is characterized by behaviors that include the following: impaired control over drug use, craving, compulsive use, and continued use despite harm. Physical dependence and tolerance are normal physiological consequences of extended opioid therapy for pain and are not the same as addiction.

(b) "**Classroom instruction**" means education conducted with a licensed instructor present, either by lecture or discussion, as an integrated part of a healthcare provider school course curriculum.

(c) "**Clinical instruction**" means education conducted through interaction with patients suffering from severe chronic or acute pain in hospital-based sites, nonhospital-based ambulatory care settings, and palliative care sites and hospices, and under the supervision of a licensed healthcare provider. This can include standardized patient experiences.

(d) "**Double Effect**" is a doctrine justifying palliative sedation and requiring three standards for ethical medical treatment: (1) the treatment itself is not morally wrong; (2) the intended benefit to the patient is not achieved by the secondary and unintended effects of the treatment; and (3) proportionality exists between the intended effects and the unintended secondary effects.

(e) "**Healthcare provider**" includes the following professionals:

(1) "**Nurses**" means licensees of the [*Insert name of the State Board of Nursing*], including advanced practice nurses.

(2) "**Pharmacists**" means licensees of the [*Insert the name of the State Board of Pharmacy*].

(3) "**Physicians**" means licensees of the [*Insert name of the State Board(s) licensing M.D.s and D.O.s*].

(4) "**Physician's assistants**" means licensees or registrants of the [*Insert the name of the State Board regulating physician assistants, which may include the Board of Medicine*].

(5) "**Nurse-practitioners**" means licensees of the [*Insert name of State Board(s) licensing nurse-practitioners*].

(f) "**Intractable pain**" means a state of pain, even if temporary, in which reasonable efforts to remove or remedy the cause of the pain have failed or have proven inadequate.

(g) "**Opioid**" means a strong pain medication derived from opium, or synthesized to behave like opium derivatives. Examples of opioids include but are not limited to morphine, codeine, oxycodone, methadone, and fentanyl.

(h) "**Pain**" is an unpleasant sensory and emotional experience associated with actual or potential tissue damage or described in terms of such damage.

(1) "**Acute pain**" is the normal, predicted physiological response to a noxious chemical, thermal, or mechanical stimulus and typically is associated with invasive procedures, trauma, and disease. It is generally time-limited.

(2) "**Chronic pain**" is a state in which pain persists beyond the usual course of an acute disease or healing of an injury, or that may or may not be associated with an acute or chronic pathologic process that causes continuous or intermittent pain over months or years.

(i) "**Palliative care**" means

(1) the active, total care of patients whose disease or medical condition is not responsive to curative treatment or whose prognosis is limited due to progressive, far-advanced disease; and

(2) the evaluation, diagnosis, treatment, and management of primary and secondary pain, whether acute, chronic, persistent, intractable, or associated with the end of life, the purpose of which is to diagnose and alleviate pain and other distressing signs and symptoms and to enhance the quality of life.

(j) "**Palliative sedation**" means the administration of sedatives to terminally ill, conscious patients whose pain cannot be otherwise relieved to alleviate suffering, but with the effect of inducing unconsciousness. The intent of administering the drug is to relieve pain, not to produce unconsciousness.

(k) "**Physical dependence**" means a state of adaptation that is manifested by drug class-specific signs and symptoms that can be produced by abrupt cessation, rapid dose reduction, decreasing blood level of the drug, and/or administration of an antagonist. Physical dependence by itself does not equate with addiction.

(l) "**Tolerance**" means a physiologic state resulting from regular use of a drug in which an increased dosage is needed to produce a specific effect, or a reduced effect is observed with a constant dose over time. Tolerance may or may nor be evident during opioid treatment and does not equate with addiction.

Section 4. Requirements for Healthcare Provider Education.

(a) **Objectives.** The instruction required by this Act is designed to meet the following objectives:

(1) That students will become more comfortable addressing the needs of patients experiencing chronic or severe pain.

(2) That students will be trained in the most current methods regarding the use of controlled substances, especially opioid analgesics.

(3) That students will realize the importance of developing a pain treatment plan for each patient in chronic or severe pain and learn methods and techniques necessary for developing such a plan.

(4) That students will learn objective methods for evaluating pain symptoms in patients.

(5) That students will understand the differences between addiction to opioid analgesics and tolerance and dependence on opioid analgesics.

(6) That students will understand the principle of double effect, especially with regard to palliative sedation.

(7) That students will understand the extreme unlikelihood of opioid administration hastening death when properly monitored.

(8) That students will understand relevant laws applicable to prescription of controlled substances.

(9) That students will become aware of differences in diverse cultural approaches to pain management and end-of-life care and become comfortable working with patients who may express preferences different than those of the student's own intuitions.

(b) **Curriculum.** The curriculum in each school educating healthcare providers and receiving public funds shall include at least eight (8) hours of classroom instruction and at least four (4) hours of clinical instruction on pain management. The curriculum shall be designed to accomplish all objectives listed in Sections 4(a)(1)-(9) of this Act. In developing a curriculum for pain management education, it is recommended that faculty educators are trained in or consult the "*Education for Physicians on End-of-Life Care (EPEC) Curriculum*" created by the Institute for Ethics at the American Medical Association.

(c) **Procedures for evaluating and monitoring pain.** Students shall be instructed in the following seven-step method for pain treatment:

(1) Evaluation of the patient. A medical history and physical examination must be obtained, evaluated, and documented in the medical record. The medical record should document the nature and intensity of the pain, current and past treatments for pain, underlying and co-existing diseases or conditions, the effect of pain on physical and psychological function, and history of substance abuse. The medical record should also document the presence of one or more recognized medical indications for the use of a controlled substance.

(2) Treatment plan. A written treatment plan should state objectives that will be used to determine treatment access, such as pain relief and improved physical and psychosocial function, and should indicate if any further diagnostic evalua tions or other treatments are planned. After treatment begins, the physician should adjust drug therapy to the individual medical needs of each patient. Other treatment modalities or a rehabilitation program may be necessary de pending on the etiology of the pain and the extent to which the pain is associ ated with physical and psychosocial impairment.

(3) Informed consent and agreement for treatment. The physician should discuss the risks and benefits of the use of controlled substances with the patient, persons designated by the patient, or the patient's surrogate or guardian if the patient is without medical decision-making capacity. The patient should receive prescriptions from one physician and one pharmacy whenever possible. If the patient is at high risk for medication abuse or has a history of substance abuse, the physician should consider the use of a written agreement between physician and patient outlining patient responsibilities, including:

a. Urine/serum medication levels screening when requested;

b. Number and frequency of all prescription refills; and

c. Reasons for which drug therapy may be discontinued (*e.g.*, violation of agreement).

(4) Periodic Review. The physician should periodically review the course of pain treatment and any new information about the etiology of the pain or the patient's state of health. Continuation or modification of controlled substances for pain management therapy depends on the physician's evaluation of progress toward treatment objectives. Satisfactory response to treatment may be indicated by the patient's decreased pain, increased level of function, or improved quality of life. Objective evidence of improved or diminished function should be moni tored and information from family members or other caregivers should be considered in determining the patient's response to treatment. If the patient's progress is unsatisfactory, the physician should assess the appropriateness of the continued use of the current treatment plan and consider the use of other therapeutic modalities.

(5) Consultation. The physician should be willing to refer the patient as necessary for additional evaluation and treatment in order to achieve treatment objectives. Special attention should be given to those patients with pain who are at risk for medication misuse, abuse, or diversion. The management of pain in patients with a history of substance abuse or with a comorbid psychiatric disorder may require extra care, monitoring, documentation, and consultation with or referral to an expert in the management of such patients.

(6) Medical records. The physician should keep accurate medical records to include:

a. The medical history and physical examination;

b. Diagnosis, therapeutic, and laboratory results;

c. Evaluations and consultations;

d. Treatment objectives;

e. Discussion of risks and benefits;

f. Informed consent;

g. Treatments;

h. Medications (including date, type, dosage, and quantity prescribed);

i. Instructions and agreements; and

j. Periodic reviews.

Records should remain current and be maintained in an accessible manner and readily available for review.

(7) Compliance with controlled substance laws and regulations. To prescribe, dispense, or administer controlled substances, the physician must be licensed in the State and comply with applicable federal and State regulations. Physicians are referred to the *Physician's Manual* of the U.S. Drug Enforcement Administration [*and any relevant documents issued by the State Medical Board*] for specific rules governing controlled substances as well as applicable State regulations.

(d) **Hours Requirements.** The following requirements apply to the core curriculum of any healthcare provider education program and are in addition to any course content required in elective courses or courses required for discrete areas of medicine. A board issuing a license or certification to any healthcare provider under [*Insert relevant citation(s)*] shall require that each applicant for initial licensure complete at least:

(1) Eight (8) hours of classroom instruction, and

(2) Four (4) hours of clinical instruction. This Section shall not apply to those seeking licensure from the [*Insert the name of the State Board of Pharmacy*].

(e) **Application.** The licensure requirements of this document shall apply to any student beginning healthcare provider education anytime after [*Insert date*].

Section 5. Pain Management Regulations Encouraged. [*for State Medical Boards who have not already done so*]

The [*Legislature*] strongly encourages [*Insert name of State Medical Licensing Board*] to adopt pain management regulations based on the *Pain Management Model Policy of the Federation of State Medical Licensing Boards* and the provisions of this Act.

Section 6. Severability.

Any provision of this Act held to be invalid or unenforceable by its terms, or as applied to any person or circumstance, shall be construed so as give it the maximum effect permitted by law, unless such holding shall be one of utter invalidity or unenforceability, in which event such provision shall be deemed severable herefrom and shall not affect the remainder hereof or the application of such provision to other persons not similarly situated or to other, dissimilar circumstances.

Section 7. Right of Intervention.

The [*Legislature*], by joint resolution, may appoint one or more of its members, who sponsored or cosponsored this Act in his or her official capacity, to intervene as a matter of right in any case in which the constitutionality of this Act or any portion thereof is challenged.

Section 8. Effective Date.

This Act takes effect [*Insert date*].

Healthcare RIGHTS OF CONSCIENCE

Healthcare
Rights of Conscience

Legal protection for healthcare rights of conscience affirms the need to provide quality care to patients, but also acknowledges that certain demands of patients, usually for procedures that are life-destructive and not life-saving, must not be blindly accommodated to the detriment of the rights of healthcare providers. Individuals and institutions do not lose their right to exercise their moral and religious beliefs and consciences once they decide to enter the healthcare profession.

Those who oppose laws protecting rights of conscience, primarily pro-abortion advocates, increasingly couch their arguments with references to women's right to healthcare access (including access to contraception) and seek to compel providers to act in violation of their consciences. However, the use of the term "access" is a red herring, as there is no real problem, when a conscientious objection is made, with a patient going to another (willing) healthcare provider for service.

However, protecting rights of conscience is necessary to avoid added stress on an already overtaxed healthcare system. Experts project that current shortages of physicians, nurses, and other healthcare professionals will worsen, failing to meet future requirements. Legal action and other pressure to compel healthcare providers to participate in procedures to which they conscientiously object threaten to make an already dangerous situation disastrous. By forcing healthcare professionals to choose between conscience and career, we will lose doctors, nurses, and other healthcare professionals who are already in short supply, especially in rural parts of the country. We will also effectively bar competent young men and women, desperately needed, from entering these vital professions. Without a doubt, the health of the nation demands protecting individual rights of conscience.

Many states have adopted conscience laws that give private hospitals, physicians, and nurses the right to conscientiously object only to participating in abortion. However, what is urgently needed are laws that recognize an affirmative civil right for all healthcare providers, including individuals (who may work for a private or public healthcare facility); institutions (whether those institutions are public or private); and payers (such as insurance companies) to refuse to participate in any healthcare service to which they conscientiously object.

This Section provides information on the increasing threat to healthcare rights of conscience by groups and individuals who believe that healthcare providers who oppose abortion, contraception, and immoral uses of biotechnology should "get out of the profession." A key component of this coercive agenda is legislation compelling individual pharmacists and pharmacies to stock and dispense "emergency contraception" regardless of conscience or other objections. This Section also seeks to provide the necessary resources to enact urgently-needed and comprehensive protection for all healthcare providers.

Healthcare Rights of Conscience:
A survey of federal and state laws

By Denise M. Burke
Vice President of Legal Affairs, Americans United for Life

"Much of the debate focused on strategy, with participants wondering whether it was better to work toward improving and narrowing conscience clauses or to fight to eliminate them altogether. ... Although reproductive rights activists should still work to improve conscientious objections, their ultimate goal should be getting rid of them."
-Then-ACLU Executive Director Ira Glasser, 2002 Executive Summary, "Conscientious Objections and Reproductive Rights"[1]

The threat to healthcare rights of conscience is real and growing. Currently, federal law and the laws of 47 states provide protection to healthcare providers and institutions who object to participating in abortions. However, the stated goal of many pro-abortion activists and groups is to abolish these protections and to force healthcare providers to participate in abortions without regard for their deeply-held religious, moral, or ethical beliefs. Much of the pro-abortion strategy in recent years has been focused on distorting, weakening, and ultimately eliminating federal laws and regulations that protect rights of conscience.

Overview of Federal Conscience Protections

Federal law currently provides limited statutory protection for healthcare rights of conscience. Congress first addressed the issue of conscience protections just weeks after the U.S. Supreme Court handed down *Roe v. Wade*. In 1973, Congress passed the first of the Church Amendments (named for its sponsor, Senator Frank Church). The Amendment provides that the receipt of funding through three federal programs cannot be used as a basis to compel a hospital or individual to participate in an abortion or sterilization procedure to which the hospital or individual has a moral or religious objection.

Taken together, the original and subsequent Church Amendments protect healthcare providers from discrimination by recipients of the U.S. Department of Health and Human Services (HHS) funds on the basis of their refusal, because of religious belief or moral conviction, to perform or participate in any lawful health service or research activity.

In 1995, when the Accreditation Council for Graduate Medical Education proposed mandating abortion training in all obstetrics and gynecology residency programs, Congress responded by enacting a measure[2] providing that any state or local government that receives federal financial assistance may not discriminate against healthcare entities that refuse to train, perform, refer for, or make arrangements for abortions.

Later, in 1996, Section 245 of the Public Health Service Act was enacted to prohibit the federal government and state or local governments that

receive federal financial assistance from discriminating against individual and institutional healthcare providers, including participants in medical training programs, who refused to, among other things, receive training in abortions; require or provide such training; perform abortions; or provide referrals for, or make arrangements for, such training or abortions.[3]

The most recent federal conscience protection, the Hyde-Weldon Amendment, was first enacted in 2005 and provides that no federal, state, or local government agency or program that receives funds in the Labor/Health and Human Services (HHS) appropriations bill may discriminate against a healthcare provider because the provider refuses to provide, pay for, provide coverage of, or refer for abortion. The Amendment is subject to annual renewal and has survived multiple legal challenges brought primarily by pro-abortion groups.

Recent Actions by HHS

On August 26, 2008, HHS published and solicited public comment on a proposed regulation[4] that would implement and strengthen the enforcement of existing federal conscience protections. Specifically, the regulation would require that recipients of HHS funding provide written certification of their compliance with federal conscience protections.

The regulation was specifically developed in response to increasing threats from and attacks by pro-abortion groups and others on the rights of conscience of healthcare providers who decline to provide, participate in, or refer for abortions. Specifically, in early 2008, the American College of Obstetricians and Gynecologists (ACOG) issued an ethics opinion that, when taken in conjunction with the American Board of Obstetrics and Gynecology's (ABOG) standards for physician certification, has the potential to force physicians to either violate their consciences by referring patients for abortions or risk losing their board certification.

"[The] proposed regulation is about the legal right of a healthcare professional to practice according to [his or her] conscience," then-HHS Secretary Mike Leavitt said. "Doctors and other healthcare providers should not be forced to choose between good professional standing and violating their conscience. Freedom of expression and action should not be surrendered upon the issuance of a healthcare degree."[5]

In his press release, Secretary Leavitt also noted that the proposed regulation would:

- Clarify that nondiscrimination protections apply to institutional healthcare providers as well as to individual employees working for recipients of certain funds from HHS;
- Require recipients of certain HHS funds to certify their compliance with laws protecting provider conscience rights;
- Designate the HHS Office for Civil Rights as the entity to receive complaints of discrimination addressed by the existing statutes and the proposed regulation; and
- Charge HHS officials to work with any state or local government or entity that may be in violation of existing statutes and the proposed regulation to encourage voluntary steps to bring that government or entity into compliance with the law.[6]

If compliance is not achieved, HHS officials will consider all legal options, including termination of funding and the return of funds paid out in violation of the nondiscrimination provisions.[7]

In a predictable and overwrought response, pro-abortion groups launched a massive misinformation campaign, alleging that HHS was trying to impede women's access to healthcare in general and to contraceptives in particular. However, in reality, it is the abortion advocates' campaign against conscience protections that is endangering access to healthcare for all Americans by threatening to drive providers from the profession.[8] After reviewing public comments, HHS adopted the regulation in December 2008.

Unfortunately, the abortion advocates campaign appears to have worked. On February 27, 2009, the Obama Administration announced its intent to rescind these rules.

Protections for Military Healthcare Providers

Notably, federal law also provides protections for military healthcare providers. Pursuant to Department of Defense (DOD) and individual service directives, military healthcare providers may refuse to participate, directly or indirectly, in medical procedures that they find morally or religiously objectionable. As with other rights of religious accommodation, this right will be balanced against military necessity and the potential adverse affect on unit readiness, individual readiness, unit cohesion, morale, discipline, safety, or health. Any refusals to provide medical care based on religious objections should be disclosed in advance to the provider's chain of command and to patients as the need arises.

DOD Directive (DODD) 6000.14, Patient Bill of Rights and Responsibilities in the Military Health System, dated 30 July 1998, provides, in pertinent part, that:

> (1) A provider who disagrees with a patient's wishes [as to a treatment], as a matter of conscience, should arrange for transfer of care to another qualified provider willing to proceed according to the patient's wishes within the limits of the law and medical ethics.
>
> (2) Military treatment facilities and Tricare [health insurance system for military dependents and retirees and their dependents] network providers and facilities shall disclose to patients... matters of conscience ... that could influence medical advice or treatment decisions.

While individual healthcare providers may refuse to participate in certain medical procedures, these procedures will still generally be provided by the military treatment facility (MTF) or an affiliated civilian facility or provider. Elective abortion is the only exception to this rule. Abortions are not performed in MTFs unless the mother's life is endangered by a continued pregnancy or the pregnancy results from rape or incest.

Military treatment facilities, both in the continental United States and at overseas locations, provide a range of contraceptive options to military members and their dependents, including sterilization. In April 2002, DOD issued a directive requiring "emergency contraception" be carried at all MTFs and military pharmacies. However, this mandate was rescinded in May 2002 and individual hospitals, clinics, and/or pharmacies must now decide for themselves whether or not to carry the controversial drug.

Sadly, healthcare professionals serving in the military are not immune from the radical agenda of pro-abortion advocates. One of the top objectives for abortion activists is to require that MTFs (both in the U.S. and overseas) provide elective abortions (paid for at taxpayer expense as is all military medical care). To achieve this objective, they would also need to circumvent DOD protections for healthcare rights of conscience as a majority of military physicians would likely refuse to provide or participate in the abortions.

Overview of State Conscience Protections

The battle over healthcare rights of conscience is being waged primarily in the 50 states. Currently, 47 states provide some degree of protection for certain healthcare providers to decline to provide or participate in abortions. However, only two states—Louisiana and Mississippi—provide comprehensive protections for all healthcare providers and for all healthcare procedures and services. Further, only three states—Alabama, New Hampshire, and Vermont—provide no protection for healthcare rights of conscience.

However, an increasing number of states are considering measures to compel conscience and force providers—primarily pharmacists—to provide services in violation of their consciences. These measures are originating from the Governor's mansion, the state legislature, and state medical governing and licensing agencies. For example, in 2005 then Illinois Governor Rod Blagojevich signed an Executive Order requiring pharmacists and pharmacies to fill prescriptions for contraceptives, including "emergency contraception," "without delay." In Washington in 2007, the State Board of Pharmacy issued a rule requiring pharmacies to fill, regardless of conscience or other objections, prescriptions for any drug including contraceptives or, if the particular drug is not in stock, facilitate the patient's access to that drug.

Endnotes

[1] *See* http://www.usccb.org/prolife/issues/abortion/THREAT.PDF (last visited August 19, 2009). Glasser was reporting on a 2002 national meeting involving the ACLU Reproductive Freedom Project, the Pro-Choice Resource Center, and the George Gund Foundation.

[2] 42 U.S.C. §238n (2008).

[3] *See* http://www.hhs.gov/news/press/2008pres/08/20080821a.html (last visited August 19, 2009).

[4] *See Federal Register*, Vol. 73, No. 155, 50274-85.

[5] *See* http://www.hhs.gov/news/press/2008pres/08/20080821a.html (last visited August 19, 2009).

[6] *Id.*

[7] *Id.*

[8] *See "Primer on Protecting Healthcare Rights of Conscience," infra.*

Healthcare Rights of Conscience Talking Points

In the ongoing debate over healthcare rights of conscience, misinformation and hyperbole abound (especially from those seeking to coerce conscience). However, a full and fair debate of the issue requires an understanding that:

- Health care is not a commodity, it is service. Those in the field are not clerks or automatons, but serious professionals trained to provide specialized care. As professionals, they engage in decision-making that is informed by their intellects and their consciences.

- Conscience is subjective but not relative, and is defined by the individual through his/her religious faith, morality, or ethics. Conscience is applied to all actions and decisions and cannot be ignored or compartmentalized.

- Freedom of conscience is an American ideal. That is, conscience is the freedom from coercion (by the government or other individuals) to act against one's will.

- Conscience is a check and balance in a healthcare provider's decision-making process. In the rapidly developing medical field, ethical challenges abound. We want our medical professionals to exercise ethical behavior (*i.e.*, behavior in accord with their conscience).

- Right of conscience protections affirm the need to provide quality care to patients and do not interfere with existing medical malpractice standards. They merely acknowledge that certain demands of patients, usually for procedures that are life-destructive and not life-saving, must not be blindly accommodated to the detriment of the rights of healthcare providers.

- Individuals and institutions do not lose their right to exercise their moral and religious beliefs and conscience once they decide to become healthcare providers.

- Nothing in the laws protecting healthcare rights of conscience prevents others from providing the healthcare service to which a conscientious objection has been made.

- Importantly, conscientious objections are most often raised concerning elective services, such as abortion, contraception, sterilization, physician-assisted suicide, and withdrawal of nutrition and hydration, rather than necessary or lifesaving services. Therefore, the lack of participation in these practices by a healthcare provider or institution will not endanger the lives or health of patients.

- However, protecting the rights of conscience of healthcare providers and institutions is necessary to avoid added stress on an already overtaxed healthcare system. Experts project that current shortages of physicians, nurses, and other healthcare professionals will worsen, failing to meet future requirements.

- Moreover, legal action and other pressure to compel healthcare providers to participate in procedures to which they conscientiously object threaten to make the already dangerous situation disastrous. By forcing healthcare professionals to choose between conscience and career, we will lose doctors, nurses, and other healthcare professionals who are already in short supply, especially in rural parts of the country. We will also effectively bar competent young men and women, desperately needed, from entering these vital professions.

- The strategy being used by abortion advocates and others to compel conscience is both clever and chilling. If they can create legal precedent to compel violation of conscience for one procedure (*e.g.*, dispensing contraceptives) or group of healthcare providers (*e.g.*, pharmacists), they will have established the legal precedent necessary to compel doctors to participate in surgical abortion and to compel all healthcare providers to participate in other objectionable procedures and services.

- Efforts to expand legal coercion are well underway and they include mandatory referral of patients. For example, on August 30, 2005, Michael Mennuti, the President of American College of Obstetrics and Gynecology (ACOG), wrote to the U.S. Congress, stating the official position of ACOG: "Doctors who morally object to abortion should be required to refer patients to other physicians who will provide the appropriate care." Recent actions by ACOG and the American Board of Obstetrics and Gynecology (ABOG) to make board certification or recertification dependent on compliance with ACOG's position on referrals for abortion furthers this coercive effort.

- Such efforts by ACOG and ABOG are only the first steps. After forcing complicity, the next step will be the coercion of active participation in abortion and other objectionable services and procedures by morally-objecting providers.

- Opponents of rights of conscience argue that only individuals can or should have (limited) rights of conscience. This is short-sighted and purposely misunderstands the notion that the mission of an organization or institution (such as a public or private hospital or a healthcare insurer) is informed by the individuals controlling that organization or institution.

Rights of Conscience Overview

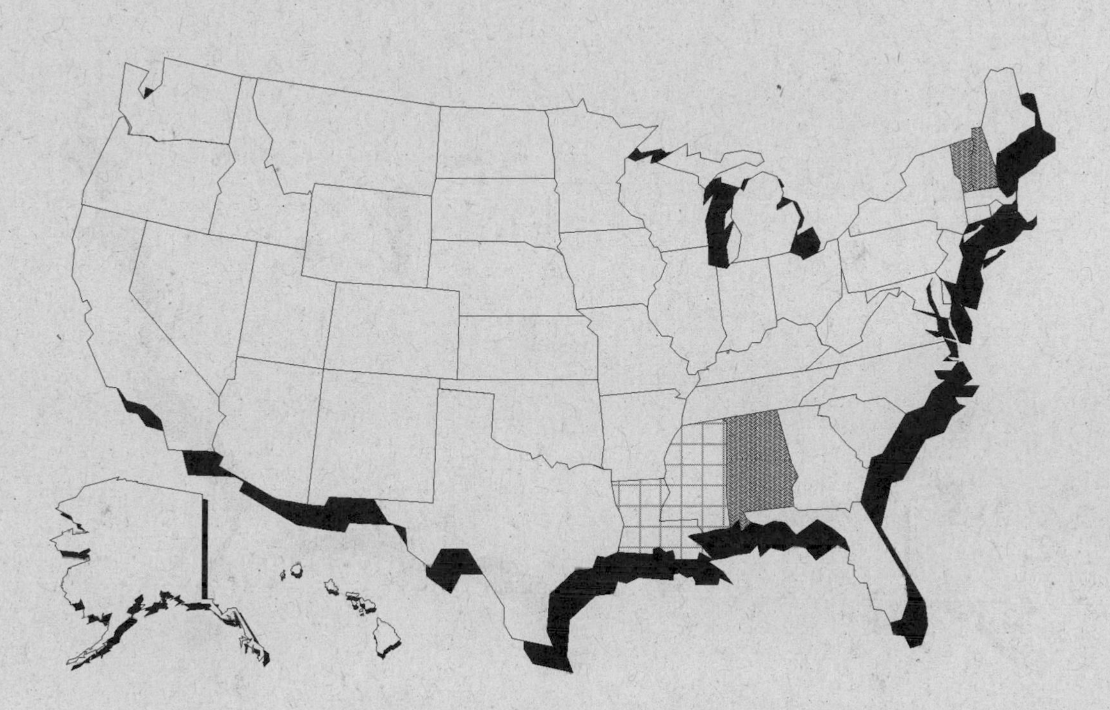

Two states protect the civil rights of all healthcare providers, whether individuals, institutions, payers (public or private) who conscientiously object to participating in any healthcare procedure or service: LA and MS

Forty-five states protect the civil rights of only certain healthcare professionals and/or institutions from participating in specific procedures (usually abortion only): AK, AZ, AR, CA, CO, CT, DE, FL, GA, HI, ID, IL, IN, IA, KS, KY, ME, MD, MA, MI, MN, MO, MT, NE, NV, NJ, NM, NY, NC, ND, OH, OK, OR, PA, RI, SC, SD, TN, TX, UT, VA, WA, WI, WV, and WY.

Three states provide no protection for the civil rights of healthcare providers, institutions, or payers: AL, NH, and VT.

Protection for Pharmacists

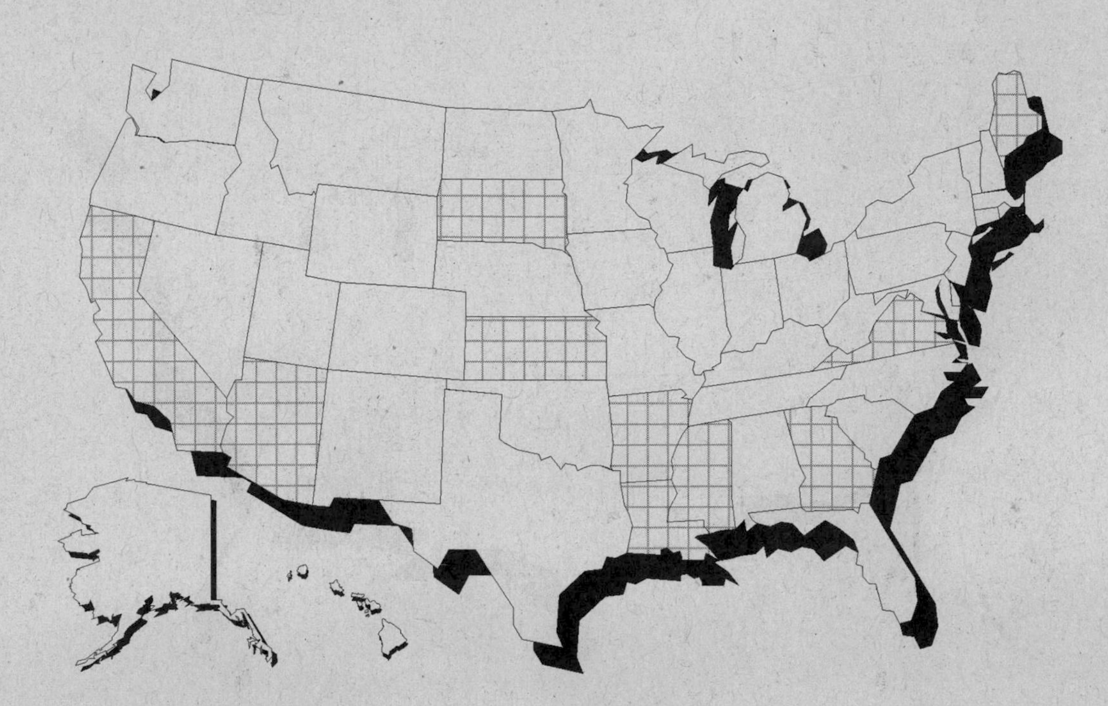

Ten states provide some specific protection for civil rights of pharmacists and pharmacies: AZ, AR, CA, GA, KS, LA, ME, MS, NC, and SD.

A Primer on Protecting Healthcare Rights of Conscience

By Denise M. Burke
Vice President of Legal Affairs, Americans United for Life

Over the last few decades, abortion advocates and their allies have launched a concerted campaign to force hospitals, healthcare institutions, health insurers, and individual healthcare providers to provide, refer, or pay for abortions. Their determined efforts to eviscerate the concept of conscience and the freedom to follow one's religious, moral, or ethical beliefs from the medical profession have resulted in the following:

- Catholic Charities in New York and California being forced by their state supreme courts to face the unenviable choice of offering healthcare coverage for contraceptives (even though the use of artificial contraception violates long-standing Catholic teachings) or, alternatively, to eliminate its prescription drug benefits for its employees (in contravention of Catholic Church teachings concerning the provision of just wages and benefits).
- An ambulance driver in Illinois being fired for refusing to take a woman to an abortion clinic.
- In 2004, New Mexico refusing to approve a community-owned hospital lease because of the hospital's refusal to perform elective abortions.
- A private hospital in Texas being sued for disregarding parental objections and providing life-sustaining care to an infant born after 23 weeks of gestation.
- The Washington Board of Pharmacy dictating that pharmacists must, regardless of conscience or other objections, fill all prescriptions including those for contraceptives and "emergency contraceptives."

Sadly, this represents only a small sampling of the mounting attacks on the rights of healthcare professionals to provide medical care without violating their religious, moral, or ethical beliefs.

In recent years, abortion advocates and their allies have prominently targeted pro-life pharmacists. Their goal is to require pharmacists to dispense contraceptives (including "emergency contraceptives"), forcing them to choose between their livelihood and their deeply-held religious, moral, or ethical beliefs. Although the U.S. Constitution protects the free exercise of religion, allowing one to follow what his or her conscience morally dictates, the abortion lobby is turning the debate into a referendum on alleged refusals to provide women access to controversial reproductive procedures.

These groups recognize that if they can establish legal precedent to coerce someone to violate their conscience regarding contraceptives, they can then easily extend that legal precedent to coerce healthcare providers to administer RU-486 (the so-called abortion pill), to coerce medical students to participate in abortion training, and to force doctors to participate in surgical abortion.

Often thought of as a contemporary problem, the issue of rights of conscience was referenced and considered by our Founding Fathers. For example, Thomas Jefferson wrote, "No provision in our Constitution ought to be dearer to man than that which protects the rights of conscience against the enterprises of the civil authority." Moreover, traditional western thought has understood individual conscience to be a guide for action and indispensable to appropriate action.

KEY TERMS

- **Right of conscience protection**: Shields physicians and other healthcare providers from liability, adverse administrative, and/or other negative consequences for refusing to participate in any healthcare procedure or service that would violate their moral conscience, ethical standards, or religious beliefs.

- **Conscience:** Moral standards that an individual has accepted and that regulate his/her actions and behavior.

  Archbishop John Myers (currently the Archbishop of Newark), in a pastoral letter, has stated, "By definition, conscience is the intellectual act of judgment of what is right and wrong to do or not to do. It is the last best judgment of what one ought to choose. Thus, conscience must be formed through education and prayer, and be informed by [religious faith]." Simply, conscience is at the heart of all decision-making.

- **Healthcare providers**: A broad term used to describe individuals working in the healthcare field. This includes doctors, nurses, medical students, pharmacists, medical assistants, pharmacist assistants, medical researchers, and others. All workers engage their conscience in their work; in a particular way, healthcare workers engage their conscience in caring for patients. To provide the fullest possible protection for individual freedom, this term should also be construed to include institutions such as public and private hospitals and health insurance companies and other payers.

- **Healthcare procedures**: Any procedure or service performed in a healthcare setting. All healthcare procedures—such as surgery, outpatient treatment, clinical care, and medical research—are acts during which healthcare providers engage their consciences.

MYTHS & FACTS

Myth: It is unconstitutional for healthcare providers to refuse to provide abortion because women have a legal right to obtain an abortion.
Fact: First, there is no right of access to abortion. In fact, the abortion "right" first announced in *Roe v. Wade*, 410 U.S. 113 (1973),

and reaffirmed in *Planned Parenthood v. Casey*, 404 U.S. 833 (1992), is the right of a woman to choose whether to terminate a pregnancy without interference from the government. Those cases cannot be read to give any patient, let alone the government, the authority to violate the fundamental freedom of conscience by forcing a healthcare provider to perform an abortion or any other controversial procedure.

Laws that protect the civil rights of healthcare providers do not forbid women from obtaining abortions. They merely protect healthcare providers from acting contrary to their consciences by providing them a right to refrain from participating in an abortion.

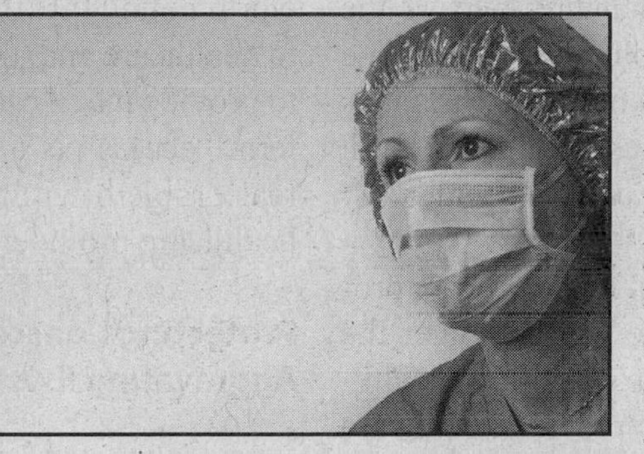

In fact, the U.S. Supreme Court has expressly recognized that (federal or state) governments are not required to facilitate abortions by funding them. In *Harris v. McRae*, 448 U.S. 297 (1980), the Court upheld a federal ban on the use of federal Medicaid funds to pay for elective abortions. In its reasoning, the Court noted that the abortion right created in *Roe* did not establish an entitlement to abortion. Rather, the Court said, *Roe* merely created limits on state action. Similarly, in *Webster v. Reproductive Health Services*, 492 U.S. 490 (1989), the Court upheld a state statute that prohibited state-run medical centers from providing elective abortions. Therefore, legislation protecting the rights of healthcare providers to refrain from participating in or facilitating abortion does not place an impermissible burden on a woman's right to abortion, because women do not have a right to force an individual or institution, including the government, to provide it.

Myth: Additional right of conscience protection is unnecessary because my state already has a conscience law.

Fact: Only two states—Louisiana and Mississippi—protect the rights of conscience of all healthcare providers, institutions, and payers (*e.g.*, health insurance companies) who refuse to provide any healthcare service based on a religious, moral, or ethical objection. Although 45 other states and the federal government have adopted conscience laws, these laws are inadequate because they usually protect the right to object only to participating in abortion and do not offer any affirmative protections. Moreover, many of the current laws do not protect all healthcare providers. For example, pharmacists are often excluded from coverage in these statutes and, therefore, are lacking affirmative protection of their right to decline to provide abortifacients or drugs that may used in an assisted suicide.

Myth: Conscience protection is a movement of the "religious right" and is designed to promote one religious viewpoint.

Fact: Conscience is at the heart of the American experience. Most Americans recognize the religious freedom found in the First Amendment of the United States Constitution. It reads: "Congress shall make no law respecting an establishment of religion, or prohibiting the free exercise thereof; or abridging the freedom of speech, or of the press; or the right of the people peaceably to assemble, and to petition the government for a redress of grievances."

What Americans may not realize is that an early draft of the Amendment written by James Madison included the following: "The Civil Rights of none shall be abridged on account of religious belief or worship, nor shall any national religion be established, nor shall the full and equal rights of conscience be in any manner, nor on any pretext infringed."

Obviously, conscience protections did not spring up recently—say, during the Vietnam War era—but are a long-standing part of the nation's baric. It is also a pluralistic right, one embraced by Christians and non-Christians alike. It is not based on respecting one faith but respecting the integrity of all individuals.

Myth: The legal protection for healthcare providers' rights of conscience will endanger the lives of patients because it will allow healthcare providers to decline to provide healthcare services and thereby deny access to patients.
Fact: Rights of conscience protections affirm the need to provide quality care to patients and do not interfere with existing medical malpractice standards. They merely acknowledge that certain demands of patients, usually for procedures that are life-destructive and not life-saving, must not be blindly accommodated to the detriment of the rights of healthcare providers

Individuals and institutions do not lose their right to exercise their moral and religious beliefs and conscience once they decide to become healthcare providers. Nothing in the laws protecting healthcare rights of conscience prevents others from providing the healthcare service to which a conscientious objection has been made. Conscientious objections are most often raised concerning elective services, such as abortion, contraception, sterilization, physician-assisted suicide, and withdrawal of nutrition and hydration, rather than necessary or lifesaving services. Therefore, the lack of participation in these practices by a healthcare provider or institution will not endanger the lives of patients.

Further, abortion proponents are increasingly couching their arguments with the language of women's "rights to healthcare access". It is worth noting that there is no fundamental right to healthcare and, therefore, no overriding duty to provide it against your conscience. Also, the term "access" is a red herring, as there is no real problem with a patient going to another healthcare provider for service.

Protecting Conscience Avoids Aggravating Existing Healthcare Crisis

Protecting the freedom of conscience of healthcare providers and institutions is necessary to avoid added stress on an already overtaxed healthcare system. Experts project that current shortages of physicians, nurses, and other healthcare professionals will worsen, failing to meet future requirements.

Legal action and other pressure to compel healthcare providers to participate in procedures to which they conscientiously object threaten to make the already dangerous situation disastrous. By forcing healthcare professionals to choose between conscience and career, we will lose doctors, nurses, and other healthcare providers who are already in short supply, especially in rural parts of the country.

We will also effectively bar competent young men and women, desperately needed, from entering these vital professions.

Many women have already experienced firsthand the current provider shortage, having a hard time finding obstetricians to deliver their babies. In 2006, 14 percent of ACOG members reported they had stopped delivering babies.[1] Further, the American Association of Medical Colleges (AAMC) projects an anticipated physician shortfall of 70,000 or more by 2025.[2]

As troubling as these predictions are, the nursing shortage is even worse. Some studies predict the shortage of registered nurses in the U.S. will reach 500,000 by 2025.[3] Health Resources and Services Administration (HRSA) officials have projected the nation's nursing shortage will grow to more than one million nurses by 2020, and analysts show that all 50 states will experience a shortage of nurses to varying degrees by the year 2015—just a few years from now.[4]

According to a July 2007 report released by the American Hospital Association, U.S. hospitals need approximately 116,000 RNs to fill current vacant positions nationwide.[5] Moreover, over half of the surveyed nurses reported that they intended to retire between 2011 and 2020.[6] The Council on Physician and Nurse Supply[7] has determined that 30,000 additional nurses must graduate annually to meet the nation's emerging healthcare needs, an expansion of 30% of the current number of annual nurse graduates.

Insufficient staffing raises stress levels, impacts job satisfaction, and is driving many to leave nursing.[8] Many recent studies also point to the connection between adequate staffing and safe patient care.[9] Increases in registered nurse staffing was associated with reductions in hospital-related mortality and "failure to rescue," as well as reduced length of stays; conversely, in settings with inadequate staffing, patient safety was compromised.[10] Most hospital RNs (93%) report major problems with having enough time to maintain patient safety, detect complications early, and collaborate with other healthcare team members.[11]

More nurses at the bedside could save thousands of patient lives each year.[12] Patients who have common surgeries in hospitals with high patient-to-nurse ratios have an up to 31% increased chance of dying.[13] Every additional patient in an average hospital nurse's workload increased the risk of death in surgical patients by 7%.[14] Having too few nurses may actually cost more money given the high costs of replacing burnt-out nurses and caring for patients with poor outcomes.

To slow—and not exacerbate—these shortages, there is a need for comprehensive conscience protections and proper enforcement of existing federal and state laws.[15] Model legislation providing such comprehensive protection is contained in AUL's "Healthcare Freedom of Conscience Act," which has already been enacted in Mississippi and provides protection for all healthcare providers and all procedures.

Protecting rights of conscience does not ban any procedure or prescription and does not mandate any particular belief or morality. Freedom of conscience simply provides American men and women the guarantees that this country was built upon: the right to be free from coercion. Protecting conscience helps ensure providers enter and remain in the healthcare professions, helping to meet the rising demand for quality healthcare. Failing to do so will compromise basic healthcare for the entire nation.

Endnotes

[1] Voice of America, *US Faces Obstetrician Shortage*, August 2006, available at: http://www.voanews.com/english/archive/2006-08/2006-08-07-voa51.cfm (last visited August 19, 2009).

[2] Myrle Croasdale, *Medical Schools on Target to Reach Enrollment Goals*, June 23/30, 2008, available at: http://amednews.com (last visited August 19, 2009).

[3] Report released by Dr. Peter Buerhaus in March 2003. *The Future of the Nursing Workforce in the United States: Data, Trends and Implications*. The report estimated demand for RNs growing 2% to 3% per year.

[4] *See* HRSA report, *What is Behind HRSA's Projected Supply, Demand, and Shortage of Registered Nurses?* Additionally, according to the latest projections from the U.S. Bureau of Labor Statistics published in the November 2007 *Monthly Labor Review*, more than one million new and replacement nurses will be needed by 2016. Government analysts project that more than 587,000 new nursing positions will be created through 2016 (a 23.5% increase), making nursing the nation's top profession in terms of projected job growth. Available at: www.bls.gov/opub/mlr/2007/11/art5full.pdf (last visited August 19, 2009).

[5] *See The 2007 State of America's Hospitals – Taking the Pulse* available at http://www.aha.org/aha/content/2007/PowerPoint/StateofHospitalsChartPack2007.ppt (last visited August 19, 2009).

[6] Bernard Hodes Group July 2006 study, *Nursing Management Aging Workforce Survey*, available at http://www.hodes.com/industries/healthcare/resources/research/agingworkforce.asp (last visited August 19, 2009).

[7] March 2008 statement released by an independent healthcare group study based at the University of Pennsylvania, The Council on Physician and Nurse Supply.

[8] In the March-April 2005 issue of *Nursing Economic$*, Dr. Peter Buerhaus and colleagues found that more than 75% of RNs believe the nursing shortage presents a major problem for the quality of their work life, the quality of patient care, and the amount of time nurses can spend with patients. Almost all surveyed nurses see future shortages as a catalyst for increasing stress on nurses (98%), lowering patient care quality (93%), and causing nurses to leave the profession (93%). According to a study in the October 2002 *Journal of the American Medical Association*, nurses reported greater job dissatisfaction and emotional exhaustion when they were responsible for more patients than they can safely care for. Researcher Dr. Linda Aiken concluded that "failure to retain nurses contributes to avoidable patient deaths."

[9] In March 2007, a comprehensive report initiated by the Agency for Healthcare Research and Quality was released on *Nursing Staffing and Quality of Patient Care*. Through meta-analysis, the authors found the shortage of registered nurses, in combination with an increased workload, poses a potential threat to the quality of care.

[10] Published in the March 2006 issue of *Nursing Economic$*, a comprehensive analysis of several national surveys on the nursing workforce found a majority of nurses reporting the RN shortage is negatively impacting patient care and undermining the quality of care goals set by the Institute of Medicine and the National Quality Forum.

[11] In an article published in the September/October 2005 issue of *Nursing Economic$*, Dr. Peter Buerhaus and associates found the majority of RNs (79%) and Chief Nursing Officers (68%) believe the nursing shortage is affecting the overall quality of patient care in hospitals and other settings, including long-term care facilities, ambulatory care settings, and student health centers.

[12] According to a study published in the October 23/30, 2002 issue of the *Journal of the American Medical Association*. Conducted by nurse researchers at the University of Pennsylvania and funded by the National Institute for Nursing Research.

[13] *Id.*

[14] *Id.*

[15] Forty-seven states provide some protections for healthcare freedom of conscience. Only Alabama, New Hampshire, and Vermont are without protective laws.

The Tip of the Spear:
Defending pharmacists' rights of conscience

By Elizabeth Rose
2006 AUL Summer Fellow

In recent years, pharmacists have faced an increasingly strident and public attack on their rights of conscience.[1] Not surprisingly, this attack directly relates to the ongoing battle over abortion. Following *Roe v. Wade*,[2] the issue of healthcare rights of conscience focused on the freedom of physicians, nurses, and other healthcare providers to abstain from participating in surgical abortions. Although this freedom is generally accepted by society, in the past decade pro-abortion groups have expanded their attacks on conscience, especially with regard to pharmacists' role in dispensing Plan B (also known as "emergency contraception"),[3] the abortifacient RU-486, and oral contraceptives. The growing trend is to demand access to these drugs for patients at the expense of the freedom of conscience of healthcare providers.[4] Heated political battles are taking place in state legislatures across the country as politicians attempt to pass laws either to protect pharmacists' right to abstain from participating in morally objectionable practices, or to force them to act in violation of their consciences or risk losing their jobs.

Freedom of conscience is a long-respected tradition in our nation, particularly for medical professionals. In fact, our nation's founding fathers recognized that rights of conscience and the free exercise of religion were essential to the foundation of a democratic nation. As James Madison stated:

> The Religion then of every man must be left to the conviction and conscience of every man; and it is the right of every man to exercise it as these may dictate . . . . It is the duty of every man to render to the Creator such homage, and such only, as he believes to be acceptable to him.[5]

Unfortunately, most commentators have slipped into the habit of using the language of tolerance and accommodation rather than framing this debate for what it truly is—a struggle to validate and protect the rights of conscience of individuals. In the words of the American Pharmacists Association: "We don't have a profession of robots. We have a profession of humans. We have to acknowledge that pharmacists have individual beliefs."[6] Nonetheless, instead of having their individual beliefs acknowledged and respected, pharmacists are increasingly faced with societal demands to go along with dispensing chemicals and devices that they know will be used to destroy human life.

Abortion proponents recognize the paramount importance of the issue of conscience generally and pharmacists' rights of conscience specifically. NARAL Pro-Choice America (NARAL) and its allies are engaged in a campaign to enact legislation that would force pharmacists to fill prescriptions for birth control and abortifacients regardless of an individual pharmacist's conscientious objection. NARAL has characterized these conscientious objectors as "renegade pharmacists . . . refusing to fill safe, legal prescriptions for birth control" and insists "pharmacies have a duty to dispense and have an ethical obligation not to endanger their patients [sic] health by withholding basic healthcare."[7] Clearly, these misrepresentations must be confronted, and an accurate understanding of this national crisis of conscience must be brought to the forefront.

As the pressure mounts on pharmacists to conform to societal demands, certain individuals face the distressing decision of whether to abandon their careers or their convictions. Pharmacists often risk dismissal or other disciplinary action for standing up for their beliefs. Luke Vander Bleek, a pharmacist and pharmacy owner, faced exactly this situation. In 1997, Vander Bleek, with his wife Joan, became the owner of a small town pharmacy in Morrison, Illinois. Over the next seven years, Vander Bleek opened or acquired three other pharmacies in small Illinois communities, providing pharmaceutical services that would otherwise not be available in these underserved markets. Vander Bleek established himself as a well-known, well-respected businessman who never dispensed Plan B because of his conscience and religious faith.

In April 2005, then-Illinois Governor Rod Blagojevich jeopardized Vander Bleek's ability to continue offering his services in these small towns. Blagojevich, through executive fiat and without legislative approval, issued an emergency Executive Order that required community pharmacies licensed in Illinois to procure and dispense all forms of contraceptives "without delay."[8] The Emergency Order—made permanent on August 16, 2005—directly contradicted an existing law, the "Illinois Health Care Right of Conscience Act,"[9] which provided broad conscience protection for healthcare workers in all healthcare settings. Vander Bleek recognized that he could not, in good conscience, follow the Governor's order and would be forced to leave his life-long profession as a pharmacist rather than "stock and dispense products that [he] believe[d] to be harmful to human life." Risking his livelihood and his reputation, Vander Bleek made the laudable decision to take a stand against the Governor's coercive order and, on June 8, 2005, filed a lawsuit challenging the Governor's order.[10]

Luke Vander Bleek is just one of thousands of individuals who have been forced to make similar decisions between following their consciences or maintaining their careers and protecting their families' livelihood. Many pharmacists view their profession as one of healing and oppose the use of medication to end human life. In Vander Bleek's own words: "I have spent my entire profession in pharmacy committed to easing suffering, curing, and diagnosing disease, and improving the quality of human life . . . . I will not practice in an environment, [in] which we are legally obliged to be involved in the destruction of human life."[11]

Especially when society cannot reach a consensus about the morality of a procedure, the law must protect pharmacists whose deep moral convictions dictate they cannot participate in behavior that is harmful to human life. For the conscientious objector, his or her moral, ethical, and religious convictions are not instruments for solving problems but form part of his or her identity and very self. Personal ethics cannot be bifurcated from professional ethics. Any law that forces pharmacists to act contrary to their convictions and to suppress their consciences imposes one set of value judgments over another.

Opponents of freedom of conscience contend that a pharmacist's right to conscientious objection must be subordinated to the needs of patients; however, conscientious objection does not prevent patients from obtaining contraceptives from other sources. Just as the exercise of freedom of speech does not force others to agree with the speaker, the exercise of freedom of conscience does not force others to agree with an objector. Objectors act primarily to preserve their own moral integrity, not to block access to services or to punish or control patients.[12] Their main concern is to avoid being implicated in what they understand to be an immoral act and, under the vast majority of circumstances, a patient who is denied a prescription from one pharmacist or pharmacy can conveniently obtain it elsewhere. It is inappropriate to reduce human persons to the status of tools or things under any circumstance, but it is particularly reprehensible in the healthcare setting where healthcare professionals are so valuable because of their knowledge and judgment. To demand the sacrifice of individual religious and personal rights of conscience in favor of patient convenience not only demeans an individual pharmacist but also the medical profession as a whole.

In order to protect the priceless rights of conscience of pharmacists, state legislatures must become more proactive in passing meaningful legislation. Although 47 states allow physicians and other healthcare providers to refuse to perform or participate in abortions,[13] this same protection is not widely granted to pharmacists and pharmacy owners. Although ten states currently have a law that protects pharmacists' rights of conscience to some degree,[14] opponents of rights of conscience continue to agitate for laws that would force a pharmacist to dispense prescriptions despite his or her conscientious objection.

For example, in 2008 approximately 70 measures related to healthcare rights of conscience were considered in state legislatures. Alarmingly, measures seeking to compel conscience and to force providers to act in opposition to their personal beliefs outpaced protective measures.

This alarming increase in efforts to compel conscience must be addressed and many states already have the tools to do so. Notabley, AUL has developed the "Pharmacists' Freedom of Conscience Act," which comprehensively protects the conscience rights of individual pharmacists, pharmacies, and entities such as insurance companies that pay for prescription drugs.

Further, for example, some states offer protection for the healthcare rights of conscience of public employees. These provisions explic-

itly provide that state or other public employees cannot be required to participate in family planning or birth control services.[15] In these states, lawmakers only need to extend the protection given to public employees to pharmacists who do not have the backing of state government. To adequately protect pharmacists and pharmacy owners, it is essential that every state enact comprehensive rights of conscience legislation.

As this national debate over the role and rights of pharmacists becomes more salient among state legislatures, it is of paramount importance that state legislators and public policy groups are apprised of the need to enact comprehensive legislation that respects pharmacists' rights of conscience and protects them from coercive action that contradicts their sincerely-held moral and religious beliefs.

Endnotes

[1] For an example of a pharmacists' conscience objection resulting in the loss of employment, *see* Jo Mannies, "'Pill' Dispute Here Costs Pharmacist Her Job," *St. Louis Post-Dispatch*, Jan. 27, 2006, A1.

[2] 410 U.S. 113 (1973).

[3] Although Plan B is also commonly referred to as the "morning-after pill," such a description is misleading because the drug actually functions as an abortifacient.

[4] "Access" is the frame promoted by pro-abortion groups. *See e.g.* "Illinois Rules on Access," Planned Parenthood of America, available at: http://www.plannedparenthood.org/pp2/portal/files/portal/media/pressreleases/pr-050816-pharmacist.xml (last visited August 19, 2009).

[5] James Madison, "Memorial and Remonstrance Against Religious Assessments," ¶ 15, reprinted in *Everson v. Bd. of Ed.*, 330 U.S. 1, 65-66 (Rutledge, J., dissenting).

[6] Susan C. Winckler, American Pharmacists Association, Vice President for Policy Communications

[7] Statements available at http://www.prochoiceamerica.org/assets/files/Birth-Control-Pharmacy-Access.pdf (last visited August 19, 2009).

[8] 68 Ill. Admin. Code § 1330.91 (2005)

[9] 745 Ill. Comp. Stat. Ann. 70/1 *et seq.* (2005)

[10] On December 18, 2008, the Illinois Supreme Court reversed a lower court's dismissal of this case and return the case to the trial court. The trial court has since entered an injunction prohibiting the State from enforcing the rule while litigation continues.

[11] Statements made before the United States House of Representatives' Small Business Committee on July 25, 2005, available at: http://wwwc.house.gov/smbiz/hearings/databaseDrivenHearingsSystem/displayTestimony.asp?hearingIdDateFormat=050725&testimonyId=377 (last visited August 19, 2009).

[12] For an exploration of some of the pharmacists' motivation, *see* Doug Moore, "Illinois Druggists Pledge to Defy Rule," *St. Louis Post-Dispatch,* Aug. 21, 2005, B1.

[13] Alabama, New Hampshire, and Vermont offer no protection for healthcare rights of conscience.

[14] Arizona, Arkansas, California, Georgia, Kansas, Louisiana, Maine, Mississippi, North Carolina, and South Dakota in some way protect pharmacists' conscientious objections.

[15] Colorado, Georgia, Oregon, West Virginia, Wisconsin, and Wyoming explicitly offer protection to a public employee who wishes to abstain from distributing contraception and/or family planning services. Colorado extends this protection only to city and county employees, while Oregon limits it to those who are employees of the Oregon Department of Human Services.

2009 State Legislative Sessions in Review:
Rights of Conscience

By Denise M. Burke
Vice President of Legal Affairs, Americans United for Life

"The conflict between social pressure and the demands of conscience can lead to the dilemma either of abandoning the medical profession or of compromising one's convictions... There is a middle path... It is the path of conscientious objection, which ought to be respected by all, especially legislators."
- Pope John Paul II, Rome (18 July 2001)

A right to conscientiously object must be a comprehensive civil right for any healthcare provider to refuse to participate in any healthcare procedure or service based on religious or moral convictions. All individuals, including healthcare providers, have a fundamental right to exercise their religious beliefs and conscience. Unfortunately, too frequently there is inadequate protection of the civil rights of healthcare providers who conscientiously object to participating in certain controversial healthcare procedures and services.

Current statutes that address this issue are largely inadequate because, for the most part, all they provide is a right for physicians, nurses, and private hospitals to refuse to participate in abortions. They often fail to address dispensing contraceptives and abortifacients, decisions regarding assisted suicide and euthanasia, and involvement in biotechnologies and certain research including human cloning and destructive forms of stem cell research. Moreover, these statutes often narrowly construe the word "participate" to exclude such activities as referral to and payment for the controversial service and preparation of the patient prior to that service.

As public opinion has shifted toward a more pro-life ethic, abortion advocates and, to a lesser extent, advocates of destructive and immoral research on human life at its earliest stages have grown increasingly strident in their attempts to force pro-life healthcare providers and hospitals to either compromise their convictions or leave the medical professions. For example, in the name of ensuring "reproductive freedom," abortion advocates are actively campaigning to coerce conscience. They are lobbying for legislation, pressuring medical schools and medical students, and seeking to force insurance companies to support their agenda.

Approximately 35 measures related to healthcare rights of conscience were considered in 20 states in 2009—a decrease of more than 50% from 2008 activity levels. However, for the first time in several years, protective measures outpaced measures seeking to violate or compel conscience by more than a 2 to 1 margin.

Comprehensive Protection for Rights of Conscience

At least ten states—Alabama, Hawaii, Louisiana, Montana, New York, Rhode Island, Tennessee, Texas, Washington, and West Virginia—considered measures providing comprehensive legal protection to healthcare providers.

Louisiana enacted a measure protecting both individual providers and healthcare institutions and permitting them to decline to participate in any healthcare service that violates their conscience.

The Michigan Senate passed a resolution condemning the professed intention of the Obama Administration, specifically the U.S. Department of Health and Human Services (HHS), to rescind the conscience rules approved in December 2008 by the Bush Administration. These rules seek to provide effective enforcement mechanisms for existing federal laws protecting conscience.

Notably, Texas introduced a constitutional amendment providing broad protection for conscience.

Abortion-Specific Protections

At least ten states, including New York and West Virginia, introduced measures protecting the right of individual healthcare providers and/or healthcare facilities to refuse to provide or participate in abortions.

Arizona enacted a measure expanding its existing protection for conscience. The measure permits individual providers, hospitals, and hospital employees to decline to facilitate an abortion.

Pharmacist-Specific Protection

At least 12 states—including Idaho, Missouri, Montana, North Carolina, and West Virginia—considered measures to specifically protect pharmacists and pharmacies from being compelled to dispense or otherwise provide drugs and devices, specifically abortifacient drugs and contraceptives, which violate their consciences.

Louisiana's new comprehensive conscience law specifically permits anyone to decline to provide abortifacients.

Protection for Health Insurers and Payers

At least five states introduced legislation intended to specifically protect insurance companies and other healthcare payers from being forced to violate their conscience by offering objectionable coverage.

Compulsion Measures

At least 12 states—including California, Florida, Indiana, New York, Missouri, Oklahoma, Rhode Island, Virginia, and Wisconsin—considered measures seeking to compel individual pharmacists and pharmacies to violate their consciences by dispensing contraceptives and abortifacients.

As part of the state budget, Wisconsin enacted a requirement that a pharmacy, when presented with a valid prescription, must dispense contraceptives—including "emergency contraception" (or Plan B) —within "the same timeframe" as they would dispense other drugs.

In Illinois, where litigation continues over a 2005 rule requiring pharmacists to fill prescriptions (including those for controversial "emergency contraception") "without delay," the legislature considered an amendment to the

"Pharmacy Practice Act" prohibiting the State from expending any funds to enforce any rule that requires a person or pharmacy to dispense "emergency contraception."

AUL Model Legislation

HEALTHCARE FREEDOM OF CONSCIENCE ACT

HOUSE/SENATE BILL NO. ________
By Representatives/Senators ________

Section 1. Title.

This Act may be known and cited as the "Healthcare Freedom of Conscience Act."

Section 2. Legislative Findings and Purposes.

(a) It is the public policy of [*Insert name of State*] to respect and protect the fundamental right of conscience of all individuals who provide healthcare services.

(b) Without comprehensive protection, healthcare rights of conscience may be violated in various ways, such as harassment, demotion, salary reduction, transfer, termination, loss of staffing privileges, denial of aid or benefits, and refusal to license or refusal to certify.

(c) It is the purpose of this Act to protect as a basic civil right the right of all healthcare providers, institutions, and payers to decline to counsel, advise, pay for, provide, perform, assist, or participate in providing or performing healthcare services that violate their consciences. Such healthcare services may include, but are not limited to, abortion, artificial birth control, artificial insemination, assisted reproduction, human cloning, euthanasia, destructive embryo research, fetal experimentation, physician-assisted suicide, and sterilization.

(d) Accordingly, it is the purpose of this Act to prohibit all forms of discrimination, disqualification, coercion, disability, or liability upon such healthcare providers, institutions, and payers that decline to perform any healthcare service that violates their consciences.

Section 3. Definitions.

(a) "**Healthcare service**" means any phase of patient medical care, treatment, or procedure, including, but not limited to, the following: patient referral, counseling, therapy, testing, diagnosis or prognosis, research, instruction, prescribing, dispensing or administering any device, drug, or medication, surgery, or any other care or treatment rendered by healthcare providers or healthcare institutions.

(b) "**Healthcare provider**" means any individual who may be asked to participate in any way in a healthcare service, including, but not limited to, the following: a physician, physician's assistant, nurse, nurses' aide, medical assistant, hospital employee, clinic employee, nursing home employee, pharmacist, pharmacy employee, researcher, medical or nursing school faculty, student or employee, counselor, social worker, or any professional, paraprofessional, or any other person who furnishes, or assists in the furnishing of, healthcare services.

(c) "**Healthcare institution**" means any public or private organization, corporation, partnership, sole proprietorship, association, agency, network, joint venture, or other entity that is involved in providing healthcare services, including but not limited to: hospitals, clinics, medical centers, ambulatory surgical centers, private physician's offices, pharmacies, nursing homes, university medical schools and nursing schools, medical training facilities, or other institutions or locations wherein healthcare services are provided to any person.

(d) "**Healthcare payer**" means any entity or employer that contracts for, pays for, or arranges for the payment of, in whole or in part, any healthcare service or product, including, but not limited to: health maintenance organizations, health plans, insurance companies, or management services organizations.

(e) "**Employer**" means any individual or entity that pays for or provides health benefits or health insurance coverage as a benefit to its employees, whether through a third party, a health maintenance organization, a program of self insurance, or some other means.

(f) "**Participate**" in a healthcare service means to counsel, advise, provide, perform, assist in, refer for, admit for purposes of providing, or participate in providing any healthcare service or any form of such service.

(g) "**Pay**" or "**payment**" means pay, contract for, or otherwise arrange for the payment of in whole or in part.

(h) "**Conscience**" means the religious, moral, or ethical principles held by a healthcare provider, the healthcare institution, or healthcare payer. For purposes of this Act, a healthcare institution or healthcare payer's conscience shall be determined by reference to its existing or proposed religious, moral, or ethical guidelines, mission statement, constitution, bylaws, articles of incorporation, regulations, or other relevant documents.

Section 4. Freedom of Conscience of Healthcare Providers.

(a) ***Freedom of Conscience***. A healthcare provider has the right not to participate, and no healthcare provider shall be required to participate in a healthcare service that violates his or her conscience.

(b) ***Immunity from Liability***. No healthcare provider shall be civilly, criminally, or administratively liable for declining to participate in a healthcare service that violates his or her conscience.

(c) ***Discrimination***. It shall be unlawful for any person, healthcare provider, healthcare institution, public or private institution, public official, or any board which certifies competency in medical specialties to discriminate against any healthcare provider in any manner based on his or her declining to participate in a healthcare service that violates his or her conscience. For purposes of this Act, discrimination includes, but is not limited to, the following: termination, transfer, refusal of staff privileges, refusal of board certification, adverse administrative action, demotion, loss of career specialty, reassignment to a different shift, reduction of wages or benefits, refusal to award any grant, contract, or other program, refusal to provide residency training opportunities, or any other penalty, disciplinary, or retaliatory action.

Section 5. Freedom of Conscience of Healthcare Institutions.

(a) ***Freedom of Conscience***. A healthcare institution has the right not to participate, and no healthcare institution shall be required to participate in a healthcare service that violates its conscience.

(b) ***Immunity from Liability***. A healthcare institution that declines to provide or participate in a healthcare service that violates its conscience shall not be civilly, criminally, or administratively liable if the institution provides a consent form to be signed by a patient before admission to the institution stating that it reserves the right to decline to provide or participate in healthcare services that violate its conscience.

(c) ***Discrimination***. It shall be unlawful for any person, public or private institution, or public official to discriminate against any healthcare institution, or any person, association, corporation, or other entity attempting to establish a new healthcare institution or operating an existing healthcare institution, in any manner, including but not limited to the following: any denial, deprivation, or disqualification with respect to licensure; any aid assistance, benefit, or privilege, including staff privileges; or any authorization, including authorization to create, expand, improve, acquire, or affiliate or merge with any healthcare institution, because such healthcare institution, or person, association, or corporation planning, proposing, or operating a healthcare institution declines to participate in a healthcare service which violates the healthcare institution's conscience.

(d) ***Denial of Aid or Benefit***. It shall be unlawful for any public official, agency, institution, or entity to deny any form of aid, assistance, grants, or benefits, or in any other manner to coerce, disqualify, or discriminate against any person, association, corporation, or other entity attempting to establish a new healthcare institution or operating an existing healthcare institution because the existing or proposed healthcare institution declines to participate in a healthcare service contrary to the healthcare institution's conscience.

Section 6. Freedom of Conscience of Healthcare Payers.

(a) ***Freedom of Conscience***. A healthcare payer has the right to decline to pay, and no healthcare payer shall be required to pay for or arrange for the payment of any healthcare service or product that violates its conscience.

(b) ***Immunity from Liability***. No healthcare payer and no person, association, corporation, or other entity that owns, operates, supervises, or manages a healthcare payer shall be civilly or criminally liable by reason of the healthcare payer's declining to pay for or arrange for the payment of any healthcare service that violates its conscience.

(c) ***Discrimination***. It shall be unlawful for any person, public or private institution, or public official to discriminate against any healthcare payer, or any person, association, corporation, or other entity (i) attempting to establish a new healthcare payer or (ii) operating an existing healthcare payer, in any manner, including but not limited to the following: any denial, deprivation, or disqualification with respect to licensure, aid, assistance, benefit, privilege, or authorization, including but not limited to any authorization to create, expand, improve, acquire, or affiliate or merge with any healthcare payer, because a healthcare payer, or a person, association, corporation, or other entity planning, proposing, or operating a healthcare payer declines to pay for or arrange for the payment of any healthcare service that violates its conscience.

(d) ***Denial of Aid or Benefits***. It shall be unlawful for any public official, agency, institution, or entity to deny any form of aid, assistance, grants, or benefits, or in any other manner to coerce, disqualify, or discriminate against any healthcare payer, or any person, association, corporation, or other entity attempting to establish a new healthcare payer or operating an existing healthcare payer because the existing or proposed healthcare payer declines to pay for or arrange for the payment of any healthcare service that is contrary to its conscience.

Section 7. Civil Remedies.

(a) ***Civil Action***. A civil action for damages or injunctive relief, or both, may be brought for the violation of any provision of this Act. It shall not be a defense to any claim arising out of the violation of this Act that such violation was necessary to prevent additional burden or expense on any other healthcare provider, healthcare institution, individual, or patient.

(b) ***Damage Remedies***. Any individual, association, corporation, entity, or healthcare institution injured by any public or private individual, association, agency, entity, or corporation by reason of any conduct prohibited by this Act may commence a civil action. Upon finding a violation of this Act, the aggrieved party shall be entitled to recover threefold the actual damages, including pain and suffering, sustained by such individual, association, corporation, entity, or healthcare institution, the costs of the action, and reasonable attorney's fees; but in no case shall recovery be less than $5,000 for each violation in addition to costs of the action and reasonable attorney's fees. These damage remedies shall be cumulative, and not exclusive of other remedies afforded under any other state or federal law.

(c) ***Injunctive Remedies***. The court in such civil action may award injunctive relief, including, but not limited to, ordering reinstatement of a healthcare provider to his or her prior job position.

Section 8. Severability.

Further, any provision of this Act held to be invalid or unenforceable by its terms, or as applied to any person or circumstance, shall be construed so as give it the maximum effect permitted by law, unless such holding shall be one of utter invalidity or unenforceability, in which event such provision shall be deemed severable herefrom and shall not affect the remainder hereof or the application of such provision to other persons not similarly situated or to other, dissimilar circumstances.

Section 9. Effective Date.

This Act takes effect on [*Insert date*].

PHARMACIST FREEDOM OF CONSCIENCE ACT

HOUSE/SENATE BILL NO. ________
By Representatives/Senators _________

Section 1. Title.

This Act may be known and cited as the "Pharmacist Freedom of Conscience Act."

Section 2. Legislative Findings and Purposes.

(a) It is the public policy of [*Insert name of State*] to respect and protect the fundamental rights of conscience of all individuals, organizations, and entities who prescribe, provide, administer, dispense, pay for, refer for, or participate or assist in providing or administering pharmaceuticals.

(b) Without comprehensive protection, the rights of conscience of pharmaceutical providers, institutions, and payers may be violated in various ways, such as hiring discrimination, harassment, demotion, salary reduction, transfer, termination, loss of staffing privileges, denial of aid or benefits, and refusal to license or refusal to certify.

(c) It is the purpose of this Act to protect as a basic civil right the right of all pharmaceutical providers, institutions, and payers to decline to prescribe, provide, administer, dispense, pay for, counsel on behalf of the administration or provision of any pharmaceutical product, medication, drug, device, or service; refer for the administration or provision of any pharmaceutical product, medication, drug, device, or service; or participate or assist in providing or administering any pharmaceutical product, medication, drug, device, or service that violate their consciences. Such pharmaceuticals may include, but are not limited to, abortifacients and medications used for artificial contraception, sterilization, artificial insemination, assisted reproduction, "mercy killing," physician-assisted suicide, and euthanasia.

(d) Accordingly, it is the purpose of this Act to prohibit all forms of discrimination, disqualification, coercion, disability, or liability upon such pharmaceutical providers, institutions, and payers that decline to provide pharmaceutical products, medications, drugs, devices, or services that violate their consciences.

Section 3. Definitions.

(a) "**Pharmaceutical**" means any product, medication, drug, or device that must be prescribed by a physician or obtained at a pharmaceutical institution.

(b) "**Pharmaceutical provider**" means any individual who may be asked to participate in any way in a pharmaceutical service, including, but not limited to, the following: a pharmacist, pharmacy owner, agent, employee, extern, technician, researcher, or any other person responsible to dispense or administer pharmaceuticals. This includes physicians, physician's assistants, nurses, nurses' aides, medical assistants, hospital employees, clinic employees, nursing home employees, counselors, social workers, medical and pharmacy school faculty or students, and professionals, paraprofessionals, or any other person who furnishes, or assists in the dispensing or administering of pharmaceuticals.

(c) "**Pharmaceutical service**" means any phase of patient pharmaceutical care, treatment, or procedure, including, but not limited to, the following: prescribing, providing, dispensing, or administering a pharmaceutical; patient referral, counseling, therapy, testing, or any other care or treatment rendered by pharmaceutical providers or pharmaceutical institutions related to prescribing, providing, administering, or dispensing of any product, medication, drug, or device.

(d) "**Pharmaceutical institution**" means any public or private organization, corporation, partnership, sole proprietorship, association, agency, network, joint venture, or other entity that is involved in providing pharmaceutical services, including but not limited to: pharmacies, hospitals, clinics, medical centers, ambulatory surgical centers, private physicians' offices, nursing homes, university medical or pharmacy schools, nursing schools, medical or pharmaceutical training facilities, or other institutions or locations wherein pharmaceutical services are provided to any person.

(e) "**Pharmaceutical payer**" means any entity or employer that contracts for, pays for, or arranges for the payment of, in whole or in part, any pharmaceutical product, medication, drug, device, or service.

(f) "**Healthcare payer**" means any entity or employer that contracts for, pays for, or arranges for the payment of, in whole or in part, any healthcare service or product, including, but not limited to health maintenance organizations, health plans, insurance companies, or management services organizations.

(g) "**Employer**" means any individual or entity that pays for or provides pharmaceutical coverage as a benefit to its employees, whether through a third party, a health maintenance organization, a program of self insurance, or some other means.

(h) "**Participate**" in pharmaceutical services means to prescribe, provide, dispense, administer, counsel on behalf of, refer for, or participate or assist in providing any pharmaceutical product, medication, drug, device, or service.

(i) "**Pay**" or "**payment**" means to pay, contract for, or otherwise arrange for the payment of in whole or in part.

(j) "**Conscience**" means the religious, moral or ethical principles held by a pharmaceutical provider, the pharmaceutical institution, or pharmaceutical payer. For purposes of this Act, a pharmaceutical institution or pharmaceutical payer's conscience shall be determined by reference to its existing or proposed.religious, moral or ethical guidelines, mission statement, constitution, bylaws, articles of incorporation, regulations, or other relevant documents.

Section 4. Freedom of Conscience of Pharmaceutical Providers.

(a) ***Freedom of Conscience***. A pharmaceutical provider has the right not to participate, and no pharmaceutical provider shall be required to provide or refer for any pharmaceutical services including but not limited to: prescribing, providing, administering, dispensing, paying for, counseling on behalf of the administration or provision of any pharmaceutical product, medication, drug, device, or service; referring for the administration or provision of any pharmaceutical product, medication, drug, device, or service; or participating or assisting in providing or administering any pharmaceutical product, medication, drug, device, or service that violate his or her conscience.

(b) ***Immunity from Liability***. No pharmaceutical provider shall be civilly, criminally, or administratively liable for declining to participate in a pharmaceutical service including, but not limited to: prescribing, providing, administering, dispensing, paying for, counseling on behalf of the administration or provision of any pharmaceutical product, medication, drug, device, or service; referring for the administration or provision of any pharmaceutical product, medication, drug, device, or service; or participating or assisting in providing or administering any pharmaceutical product, medication, drug, device, or service that violates his or her conscience.

(c) ***Discrimination***. It shall be unlawful for any person, pharmaceutical provider, pharmaceutical institution, public or private institution, public official, or any board which certifies competency in pharmacy to discriminate against any pharmaceutical provider in any manner based on his or her declining to participate in a pharmaceutical service including but not limited to: prescribing, providing, administering, dispensing, paying for, counseling on behalf of the administration or provision of any pharmaceutical product, medication, drug, device, or service; referring for the administration or provision of any pharmaceutical product, medication, drug, device, or service; or participating or assisting in providing or administering any pharmaceutical product, medication, drug, device, or service that violates his or her conscience. For purpose of this Act, discrimination includes, but is not limited to the following: termination, transfer, refusal of staff privileges, refusal of board certification, adverse administrative action, demotion, loss of career specialty, reassignment to a different

shift, discrimination in hiring, reduction of wages or benefits, refusal to award any grant, contract, or other program, refusal to provide training opportunities, or any other penalty, disciplinary, or retaliatory action.

Section 5. Freedom of Conscience of Pharmaceutical Institutions.

(a) ***Freedom of Conscience***. A pharmaceutical institution has the right not to participate, and no pharmaceutical institution shall be required to participate in any pharmaceutical service including but not limited to: prescribing, providing, administering, dispensing, paying for, counseling on behalf of the administration or provision of any pharmaceutical product, medication, drug, device, or service; referring for the administration or provision of any pharmaceutical product, medication, drug, device, or service; or participating or assisting in providing or administering any pharmaceutical product, medication, drug, device, or service that violates its conscience.

(b) ***Immunity from Liability***. A pharmaceutical institution that declines to provide or participate in a pharmaceutical service that violates its conscience shall not be civilly, criminally, or administratively liable if the institution provides notification posted in a clearly visible location where pharmaceuticals are provided, dispensed, or administered.

(c) ***Discrimination***. It shall be unlawful for any person, public or private entity or institution, or public official to discriminate against any pharmaceutical institution, or any person, association, corporation, or other entity attempting to establish a new pharmaceutical institution or operating an existing pharmaceutical institution, in any manner, including but not limited to the following: any denial, deprivation, or disqualification with respect to licensure; any aid assistance, benefit, or privilege including staff privileges; or any authorization including authorization to create, expand, improve, acquire, or affiliate or merge with any pharmaceutical institution, because such pharmaceutical institution, individual, association, or corporation planning, proposing, or operating a pharmaceutical institution, declines to participate in a pharmaceutical service which violates the pharmaceutical institution's conscience.

(d) ***Denial of Aid or Benefit***. It shall be unlawful for any public official, agency, institution, or entity to deny any form of aid, assistance, grants, or benefits, or in any other manner to coerce, disqualify, or discriminate against any person, association, corporation, or other entity attempting to establish a new pharmaceutical institution or operating an existing pharmaceutical institution because the existing or proposed pharmaceutical institution declines to participate in a pharmaceutical service contrary to the pharmaceutical institution's conscience.

Section 6. Freedom of Conscience of Healthcare and Pharmaceutical Payers.

(a) ***Freedom of Conscience***. A healthcare or pharmaceutical payer has the right to decline to pay, and no healthcare or pharmaceutical payer shall be required to pay for or arrange for the payment of any pharmaceutical product or service that violates its conscience.

(b) ***Immunity from Liability***. No healthcare or pharmaceutical payer and no person, association, corporation, or other entity that owns, operates, supervises, or manages a healthcare or pharmaceutical payer shall be civilly or criminally liable by reason of the healthcare or pharmaceutical payer's declining to pay for or arrange for the payment of any pharmaceutical product or service that violates its conscience.

(c) ***Discrimination***. It shall be unlawful for any person, public or private institution, or public official to discriminate against any healthcare or pharmaceutical payer, or any person, association, corporation, or other entity (i) attempting to establish a new healthcare or pharmaceutical payment plan, or (ii) operating an existing healthcare or pharmaceutical payment plan, in any manner, including but not limited to the following: any denial, deprivation, or disqualification with respect to licensure, aid, assistance, benefit, privilege, or authorization, including but not limited to any authorization to create, expand, improve, acquire, affiliate, or merge with any healthcare or pharmaceutical payment plan, because a prescription payer, or a person, association, corporation or other entity planning, proposing, or operating a healthcare or pharmaceutical payment plan declines to pay for or arrange for the payment of any pharmaceutical product or service that violates its conscience.

(d) ***Denial of Aid or Benefits***. It shall be unlawful for any public official, agency, institution, or entity to deny any form of aid, assistance, grants or benefits, or in any other manner to coerce, disqualify, or discriminate against any healthcare or pharmaceutical payer, or any person, association, corporation, or other entity attempting to establish a new healthcare or pharmaceutical payment plan or operating an existing healthcare or pharmaceutical payment plan because the existing or proposed healthcare or pharmaceutical payment plan declines to pay for, or arrange for the payment of any pharmaceutical product or service that is contrary to its conscience.

Section 7. Civil Remedies.

(a) ***Civil Action***. A civil action for damages or injunctive relief, or both, may be brought for the violation of any provision of this Act. It shall not be a defense to any claim arising out of the violation of this Act that such violation was necessary to prevent additional burden or expense on any other pharmaceutical provider, pharmaceutical institution, pharmaceutical payer, individual, or patient.

(b) ***Damage Remedies***. Any individual, association, corporation, entity, or pharmaceutical institution injured by any public or private individual, association, agency, entity, or corporation by reason of any conduct prohibited by this Act may commence a civil action. Upon finding a violation of this Act, the aggrieved party shall be entitled to recover threefold the actual damages, including pain and suffering, sustained by such individual, association, corporation, entity, or pharmaceutical institution, the costs of the action, and reasonable attorney's fees; but in no case shall recovery be less than $5,000 for each violation in addition to costs of the action and reasonable attorney's fees. These damage remedies shall be cumulative, and not exclusive of other remedies afforded under any other state or federal law.

(c) **Injunctive Remedies**. The court in such civil action may award injunctive relief, including, but not limited to, ordering reinstatement of a pharmaceutical provider to his or her prior job position.

Section 8. Severability.

Further, any provision of this Act held to be invalid or unenforceable by its terms, or as applied to any person or circumstance, shall be construed so as give it the maximum effect permitted by law, unless such holding shall be one of utter invalidity or unenforceability, in which event such provision shall be deemed severable herefrom and shall not affect the remainder hereof or the application of such provision to other persons not similarly situated or to other, dissimilar circumstances.

Section 9. Effective Date.

This Act takes effect on [*Insert date*].

STATE OF THE STATES

STATE OF THE STATES

Each year, we are making progress state by state and law by law toward a more pro-life America. In 2009 alone, there were more than 60 life-affirming measures enacted in the 50 states. This is especially notable given the economic and political turmoil we, as a nation, have endured over the past year. It is incredibly gratifying to see economic and other pressing issues have not deterred state lawmakers and everyday Americans from seeking to advance and restore a culture of life.

Recognizing the significance of state laws in protecting women and the unborn from the negative impact of abortion; in establishing legal recognition of and protection for unborn children in contexts other than abortion; in prohibiting the illicit use of emerging biotechnologies; in affirming the constitutional rights of healthcare providers; and in protecting those at the end of life, AUL has compiled an individual report card on the life-affirming laws in each of the 50 states and the District of Columbia.

These report cards summarize and highlight existing state laws on abortion, legal protection and recognition of the unborn, bioethics and biotechnologies, healthcare rights of conscience, and the end of life, as well as note critical gaps in legal protection. They also specifically discuss advances that have been made in each state over the past year.

In *Defending Life 2009*, we included a recommendation checklist for each state, allowing citizens, lawmakers, and others to readily assess each state's progress and develop a plan to further protect life in their state. In each checklist, we have made well-considered and specific recommendations as to what is needed, what are the best next steps toward a culture of life, and what is realistic and feasible for each state to accomplish.

We hope these report cards stir both thought and action intended to bring us closer to the day when every person—from conception until natural death—is welcomed in life and protected in law!

TEN BEST & WORST STATES FOR LIFE

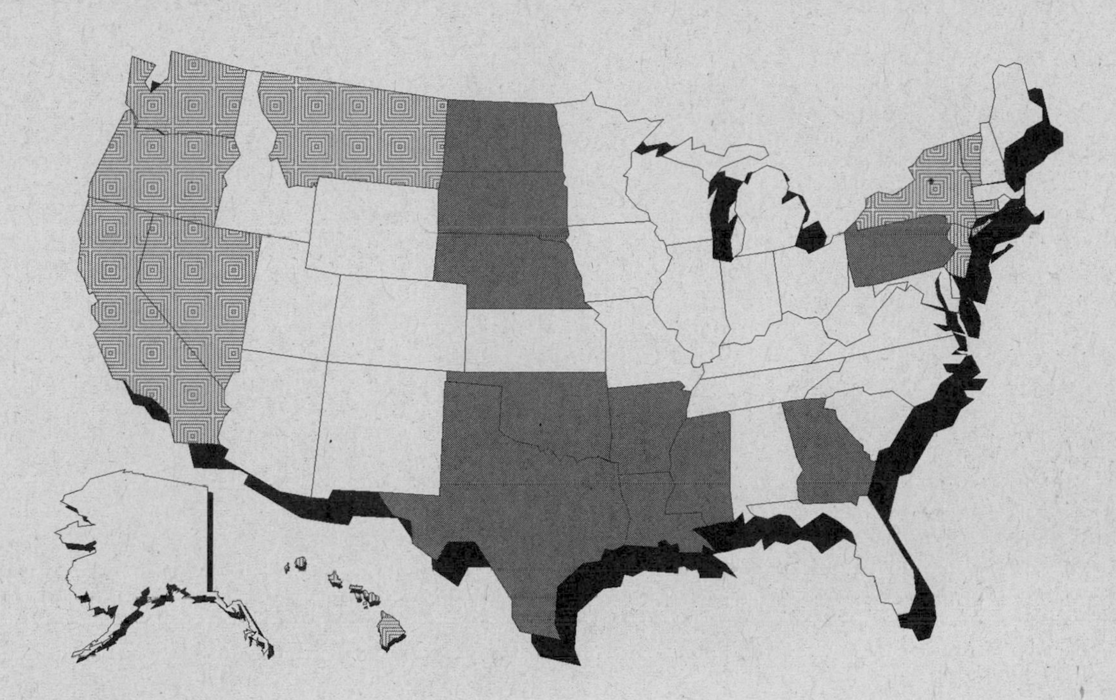

BEST STATES

1. Louisiana
2. Oklahoma
3. Pennsylvania
4. Texas
5. Arkansas
6. South Dakota
7. North Dakota
8. Georgia
9. Nebraska
10. Mississippi

WORST STATES

1. Washington
2. California
3. Hawaii
4. New Jersey
5. Vermont
6. Montana
7. Connecticut
8. Nevada
9. Oregon
10. New York

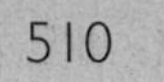

DEFENDING LIFE 2010 State Rankings

1. Louisiana
2. Oklahoma
3. Pennsylvania
4. Texas
5. Arkansas
6. South Dakota
7. North Dakota
8. Georgia
9. Nebraska
10. Mississippi
11. Missouri
12. Kentucky
13. Indiana
14. Kansas
15. Michigan
16. Virginia
17. Ohio
18. South Carolina
19. Alabama
20. Minnesota
21. Wisconsin
22. Arizona
23. Idaho
24. Colorado
25. Utah
26. Florida
27. North Carolina
28. Rhode Island
29. Maine
30. Tennessee
31. Delaware
32. Wyoming
33. West Virginia
34. Iowa
35. New Hampshire
36. Illinois
37. New Mexico
38. Massachusetts
39. Alaska
40. Maryland
41. New York
42. Oregon
43. Nevada
44. Connecticut
45. Montana
46. Vermont
47. New Jersey
48. Hawaii
49. California
50. Washington

Note:
Rankings are based on state laws that were enforceable or in effect on September 1, 2009.

ALABAMA

RANKING: 19

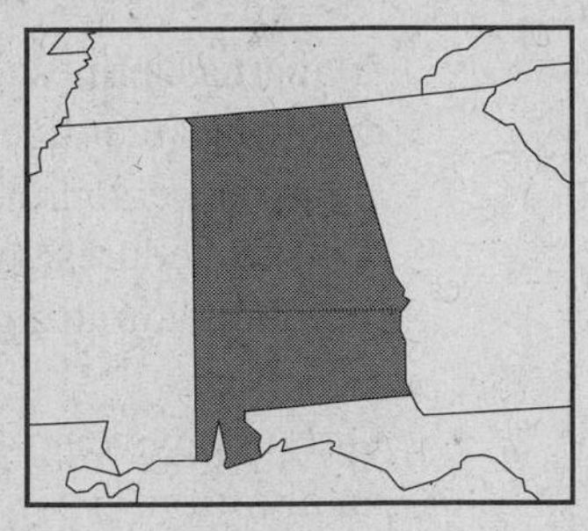

Alabama maintains some laws protecting women and the unborn, such as informed consent and parental consent requirements. However, it lags behind other states in laws related to bioethics and end-of-life issues. And unlike the majority of states, Alabama does not protect the freedom of conscience of any healthcare providers, failing even to protect physicians who do not wish to perform or participate abortions.

ABORTION:

- Alabama requires that a woman be given a 24-hour reflection period before a physician may perform an abortion and requires she be informed of the risks of and alternatives to abortion, the probable gestational age of her unborn child, and the probable anatomical and physiological characteristics of the child at the time of the abortion.

- Alabama also requires an abortion provider to perform an ultrasound prior to an abortion and provide the woman with an opportunity to review the ultrasound, along with a state-sponsored videotape and written material detailing sources of public and private support, adoption agencies, fetal development, abortion methods, and the father's legal responsibilities.

- The state requires abortion providers to state in their printed materials that it is illegal for someone to coerce a woman into having an abortion.

- One parent must consent before a physician may perform an abortion on a minor under the age of 18. A minor may obtain a judicial bypass of this requirement by demonstrating she is "mature and well informed enough to make her own decision or that abortion is in her best interests."

- Alabama prohibits public funds from being used for abortions unless the procedure is necessary to preserve the life of the woman or the pregnancy is the result of rape or incest.

- The state prohibits organizations that receive state funds from using those funds to provide abortion counseling or to make referrals for abortion. The Alabama Office of Women's Health may not advocate, promote, or otherwise advance abortion or abortifacients.

- Alabama defines "abortion and reproductive health centers" as hospitals and requires that they meet licensing requirements and minimum health and safety standards in such areas as personnel qualifications, records maintenance, admission requirements, abortion procedures, post-operative care, and infection control. Abortion providers must maintain admitting privileges.

- Only a physician licensed by the state to practice medicine or osteopathy may perform an abortion.

- Alabama offers "Choose Life" license plates, the proceeds of which benefit pregnancy care centers and/or other organizations providing abortion alternatives.

- The state maintains an enforceable abortion reporting law, but does not require the reporting of information to the Centers for Disease Control and Prevention (CDC). The measure requires abortion providers to report short-term complications.

LEGAL RECOGNITION OF UNBORN AND NEWLY BORN:

- Alabama defines a "person" under the homicide and assault laws to include the unborn child *in utero* at any stage of development.

- Alabama also defines a nonfatal assault on an unborn child as a criminal offense.

- The state allows wrongful death (civil) actions when a viable unborn child is killed through negligent or criminal act of another.

- Alabama has created a specific affirmative duty of physicians to provide medical care and treatment to born-alive infants at any stage of development.

- Alabama has enacted a "Baby Moses" law under which a mother or legal guardian who is unable to care for a newborn infant may anonymously and safely leave the infant in the care of a responsible person at a hospital, police station, fire station, or other prescribed location.

BIOETHICS LAWS:

- Alabama maintains no laws regarding human cloning or destructive embryo research.

- The state provides some guidance regarding parentage of children created through assisted reproductive technologies.

END OF LIFE LAWS:

- Alabama does not have a specific statute criminalizing assisted suicide. However, under the state's common law, assisted suicide remains a crime.

HEALTHCARE RIGHTS OF CONSCIENCE LAWS:

Participation in Abortion:

- Alabama currently provides no protection for the rights of conscience of healthcare providers.

Participation in Research Harmful to Human Life:

- Alabama currently provides no protection for the rights of healthcare providers who conscientiously object to participation in human cloning, destructive embryo research, or other forms of immoral medical research.

WHAT HAPPENED IN 2009:

- Alabama considered measures banning abortion and amending the state constitution to define "human being." The state also considered measures clarifying its definition of "medical emergency," amending an existing law requiring an ultrasound before abortion, and opposing the federal "Freedom of Choice Act." Conversely, Alabama considered a bill which would have exempted contraception from abortion-related regulations.

- The state also considered a measure defining "child" to include an unborn child for purposes of the state's wrongful death laws, as well as a measure creating a rebuttable presumption of guilt for exposing a child *in utero* to a controlled substance if both the mother and the child test positive for the same controlled substance.

- On the bioethics front, Alabama considered measures banning destructive embryo research and human cloning for all purposes.

- Alabama introduced a bill providing comprehensive right of conscience protection for healthcare providers, institutions, and payers.

RECOMMENDATIONS FOR ALABAMA		
	Short-term Priorities	**Additional Goals**
	ABORTION	
Informed Consent		Enhancements such as information on fetal pain or coercion
Parental Involvement		Enhancements such as notarized consent or identification requirements
State Rights & Policies		
Abortion Funding	Further prohibitions on use of public and family planning funds	
Abortion Provider Requirements		
Abortion Bans	Enforceable ban on partial-birth abortion or "delayed enforcement" law	
Regulation of Abortifacients		Regulation of RU-486 and other abortifacients
PCCs Support		State funding for PCCs
Abortion Reporting		Reporting on non-surgical abortions
	LEGAL RECOGNITION AND PROTECTION FOR UNBORN & NEWLY BORN	
Fetal Homicide		
Assault on Unborn		
Prohibitions on Wrongful Birth & Wrongful Life Lawsuits		Statutory prohibition on wrongful birth lawsuits

Permit Wrongful Death Lawsuits		
Born-Alive Infant Protection		
Abandoned Infant Protection		
BIOETHICS		
Human Cloning		Ban on all human cloning
DER		Ban on DER
State Funding of DER	Ban on state funding of DER & funding of ethical alternatives	
ART & IVF		Any medically-appropriate regulation of ART
END OF LIFE		
Assisted Suicide	Statutory ban on assisted suicide	
Pain Management Education		
RIGHTS OF CONSCIENCE		
Protection for Individual Providers	Comprehensive ROC protection	
Protection for Institutions	Comprehensive ROC protection	
Protection for Payers	Comprehensive ROC protection	

ALASKA

RANKING: 39

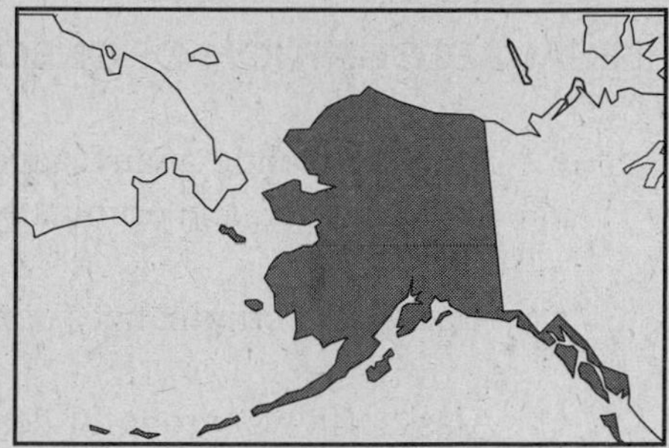

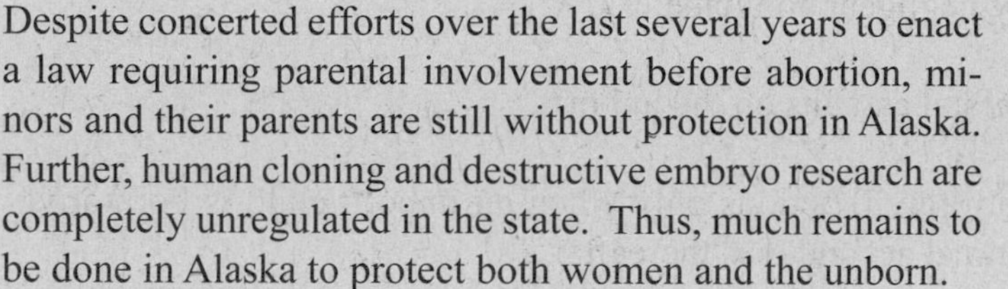

Despite concerted efforts over the last several years to enact a law requiring parental involvement before abortion, minors and their parents are still without protection in Alaska. Further, human cloning and destructive embryo research are completely unregulated in the state. Thus, much remains to be done in Alaska to protect both women and the unborn.

ABORTION:

- Alaska maintains an abortion information website and requires women seeking abortion certify in writing that a physician provided them with information on the following: fetal development, various abortion procedures, possible risks and complications associated with abortion and childbirth, eligibility requirements for medical assistance benefits, child support orders, and contraceptive options.

- The state includes information about the abortion-breast cancer link in the educational materials a woman must receive prior to abortion.

- The Alaska Supreme Court has determined the Alaska Constitution provides for a broader right to abortion than does the federal Constitution. As a result, the Alaska Attorney General has issued opinions that laws which require that only licensed physicians perform abortions and which seek to impose minimal health and safety regulations on abortion clinics are unconstitutional and unenforceable.

- Alaska taxpayers are required to fund "medically necessary" abortions. This requirement essentially equates to funding abortion-on-demand in light of the U.S. Supreme Court's broad definition of "health" in the context of abortion.

- Alaska limits the performance of abortions to licensed physicians.

- Prior to the FDA's August 2006 action allowing Plan B to be distributed over the counter, Alaska had enacted a law allowing pharmacists to dispense "emergency contraception" directly to women without a prescription. Under that law, a pharmacist must first be approved by a physician or advance practice nurse and by the Alaska Pharmacy Board.

- Alaska maintains an enforceable abortion reporting law, but the measure does not require the reporting of information to the Centers for Disease Control and Prevention (CDC). The measure applies to both surgical and nonsurgical abortions.

LEGAL RECOGNITION OF UNBORN AND NEWLY BORN:

- An unborn child at any stage of development is considered a separate victim of murder, manslaughter, and criminally negligent homicide.

- Alaska also criminalizes nonfatal assaults on the unborn.

- Alaska allows wrongful death (civil) actions only when an unborn child is born alive following a negligent or criminal act and dies thereafter.

- Alaska maintains a "Baby Moses" law, which provides immunity for a parent who leaves an unharmed infant no more than 21 days old with a police officer, medical provider, hospital employee, emergency services personnel, or any person the parent believes will act in the infant's best interest.

- Alaska requires healthcare professionals to report suspected prenatal drug exposure when there is suggestion of drug abuse or use during pregnancy.

- Alaska provides for stillbirth certificates. The person required to file a fetal death registration shall advise the mother and the father, if present, that he/she may request the preparation of a certificate of birth resulting in stillbirth.

BIOETHICS LAWS:

- Alaska maintains no laws regarding human cloning, destructive embryo research, or assisted reproductive technologies.

END OF LIFE LAWS:

- Alaska law specifically prohibits assisted suicide. Under the law, assisting a suicide constitutes manslaughter.

HEALTHCARE RIGHTS OF CONSCIENCE LAWS:

Participation in Abortion:

- Alaska law provides that no person or hospital may be required to participate in an abortion.

- However, subsequent court decisions have narrowed the protection for hospitals. Currently, nonsectarian hospitals built or operated with public funds may not refuse to offer or provide abortions.

Participation in Research Harmful to Human Life:

- Alaska currently provides no protection for the rights of conscience of healthcare providers who conscientiously object to participation in human cloning, destructive embryo research, or other immoral forms of medical research.

WHAT HAPPENED IN 2009:

- Alaska enacted a measure providing for stillbirth certificates. The measure provides that the person required to file a fetal death registration shall advise the mother and the father, if present, that he/she may request the preparation of a certificate of birth resulting in stillbirth.

- The state began the process to put a parental involvement measure on the 2010 ballot.

- The state considered legislation banning partial-birth abortion and requiring parental consent before a minor's abortion. It also considered a measure requiring that women be counseled on the pain an unborn child may feel during an abortion.

- Alaska considered legislation amending an existing law allowing for the legal abandonment of infants under circumstances that ensure their health and safety.

- Alaska did not consider any measure related to bioethics or healthcare rights of conscience.

RECOMMENDATIONS FOR ALASKA		
	Short-term Priorities	**Additional Goals**
	ABORTION	
Informed Consent	Reflection period	
Parental Involvement	Parental consent or notice	
State Rights & Policies	Constitutional amendment declaring no state right to abortion	
Abortion Funding	Limits on state funding of abortion	
Abortion Provider Requirements		Abortion clinic regulations
Abortion Bans		
Regulation of Abortifacients		Regulation of RU-486
PCCs Support		State funding for PCC's
Abortion Reporting		
	LEGAL RECOGNITION AND PROTECTION FOR UNBORN & NEWLY BORN	
Fetal Homicide		
Assault on Unborn		
Prohibitions on Wrongful Birth & Wrongful Life Lawsuits		
Permit Wrongful Death Lawsuits	Law permitting action for death of unborn child	

Born-Alive Infant Protection	Law requiring care for child who survives an abortion	
Abandoned Infant Protection		
BIOETHICS		
Human Cloning		Ban on all human cloning
DER		Ban on DER
State Funding of DER	Ban on state funding of DER & funding of ethical alternatives	
ART & IVF		Any medically-appropriate regulation of ART
END OF LIFE		
Assisted Suicide		
Pain Management Education		
RIGHTS OF CONSCIENCE		
Protection for Individual Providers	Comprehensive ROC protection	
Protection for Institutions	Comprehensive ROC protection	
Protection for Payers	Comprehensive ROC protection	

ARIZONA

RANKING: 22

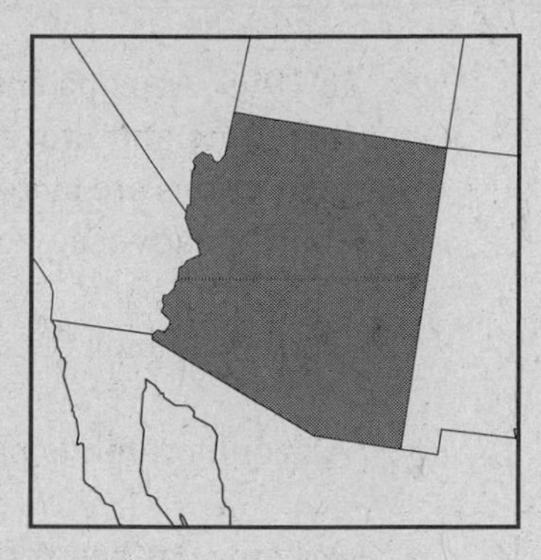

With the appointment of Janet Napolitano as Secretary of Homeland Security, the Arizona legislature was finally able to capitalize on an opportunity to enact life-affirming legislation without fear of unwarranted veto. The legislature took full advantage of this opportunity, enacting numerous pro-life bills—including informed consent requirements and a ban on partial-birth abortion—both of which had been vetoed on multiple occasions by former-Governor Napolitano.

ABORTION:

- Twenty-four hours prior to an abortion, a woman must receive information about the nature of the procedure, the immediate and long-term risks of abortion, the risks of childbirth, alternatives to the procedure, and the probable gestational age and anatomical and physiological characteristics of the unborn child. Women must also receive information about medical assistance benefits, the father's liability for child support, and that public and private agencies are available to assist the woman. This new law is currently under legal challenge.

- Women must also be informed that it is illegal for a person to intimidate or coerce a woman into having an abortion.

- One parent must consent before a physician may perform an abortion on a minor under the age of 18. That consent must be in writing and notarized. A minor may obtain judicial bypass of this requirement by demonstrating she is mature and capable of giving informed consent or that an abortion (without parental consent) is in her best interests. Arizona's law also includes evidentiary standards for judicial bypass hearings and prohibits a parent from refusing financial support as a means to coerce a minor into having an abortion.

- The Arizona Supreme Court has concluded state taxpayers must cover the costs of "medically necessary" abortions, implicitly recognizing a broader state constitutional right to abortion than provided by the U.S. Constitution.

- Arizona prohibits organizations that receive state funds from using those funds to provide abortion counseling or making referrals for abortion.

- A woman may not obtain an abortion at any university facility under the jurisdiction of the Arizona Board of Regents unless the procedure is necessary to save her life.

- In 1999, Arizona enacted comprehensive abortion clinic regulations in direct response to the tragic and preventable death of Lou Anne Herron at a Phoenix abortion clinic. The regulations are largely based on treatment protocols developed by abortion providers and abortion advocacy groups.

- Only physicians licensed in the state may perform surgical abortions.

- Arizona prohibits partial-birth abortion.

- Arizona has been directed to implement a "Choose Life" license plates program, with the proceeds benefitting organizations providing abortion alternatives.

- The state maintains an enforceable abortion reporting law, but does not require the reporting of information to the Centers for Disease Control and Prevention (CDC). The measure applies to both surgical and nonsurgical abortions and requires abortion providers to report short-term complications.

- Health insurance companies that provide prescription coverage must also provide coverage for contraceptives. The provision includes an exemption so narrow that it excludes the ability of most employers and insurers with moral or religious objections from exercising the exemption.

LEGAL PROTECTION OF UNBORN AND NEWLY BORN:

- Arizona law defines the killing of an unborn child at any stage of development as manslaughter.

- The state defines nonfatal assaults on the unborn as criminal offenses.

- The state allows wrongful death (civil) actions when a viable unborn child is killed through a negligent or criminal act.

- The state has created a specific affirmative duty of physicians to provide medical care and treatment to born-alive infants at any stage of development.

- Arizona maintains a "Dangerous Crimes Against Children Act," which allows for the prosecution of a woman for prenatal drug abuse that causes harm or injury to her unborn child. The woman could be specifically charged with child abuse and/or drug transfer to a minor under 12 years of age. The state further requires healthcare professionals to report suspected prenatal drug exposure.

BIOETHICS LAWS:

- Arizona requires health professionals to notify patients in the second trimester of pregnancy of options related to stem cells contained in the umbilical cord blood after the delivery, and options for donation or storage in a family donor banking program.

- Arizona prohibits taxpayer funding of human cloning and denies special tax credits to entities engaged in destructive embryo research. The state also maintains a stem cell research study committee.

- Arizona maintains no laws regarding assisted reproductive technologies.

END OF LIFE LAWS:

- Arizona has enacted a statute that expressly prohibits assisted suicide. Under this law, assisted suicide is considered manslaughter.

HEALTHCARE RIGHTS OF CONSCIENCE LAWS:

Participation in Abortion:

- Arizona law protects healthcare providers who conscientiously object to participation in abortions. Under this law, healthcare providers must object in writing and objections must be based on moral or religious beliefs.

- A pharmacy, hospital, or healthcare professional is not required to participate in or provide an abortion, abortion medication, "emergency contraception," or any medicine or device intended to inhibit or prevent implantation of a fertilized egg.

Participation in Research Harmful to Human Life:

- Arizona currently provides no protection for the rights of healthcare providers who conscientiously object to participation in human cloning, destructive embryo research, or other forms of immoral medical research.

WHAT HAPPENED IN 2009:

- Arizona enacted a number of pro-life measures this session, including a ban on partial-birth abortion; informed consent requirements; a measure limiting the performance of surgical abortions to physicians; a measure requiring written, notarized parental consent

before a minor obtains an abortion; and a measure prohibiting a person from coercing a woman into having an abortion.

- Arizona also enacted legislation providing that a pharmacy, hospital, or healthcare professional is not required to participate in or provide an abortion, abortion medication, "emergency contraception," or any medicine or device intended to inhibit or prevent implantation of a fertilized egg.

- The state enacted two measures to amend existing end-of-life statutes: First, to prohibit a fiduciary or trustee whose license has been revoked from serving as an agent under a healthcare power of attorney unless the person is related to the principal; and, second, to require the court to give appointed guardians authority to withhold or withdraw life sustaining treatment, including artificial food and hydration. The second measure further created a rebuttable presumption in favor of the provision of food and hydration if no advance directive exists, and provided clarification for the process and standard of review to rebut that presumption.

- Arizona considered legislation exempting contraception from abortion-related laws.

- The state did not consider any legislation related to bioethics or healthcare rights of conscience.

RECOMMENDATIONS FOR ARIZONA		
	Short-term Priorities	**Additional Goals**
	ABORTION	
Informed Consent	Enforceable ultrasound requirement	
Parental Involvement		
State Rights & Policies		
Abortion Funding	Constitutional amendment prohibiting taxpayer funding of elective abortions	
Abortion Provider Requirements		
Abortion Bans		
Regulation of Abortifacients		Regulation of RU-486
PCCs Support	Direct funding for PCC's	
Abortion Reporting		
	LEGAL RECOGNITION AND PROTECTION FOR UNBORN & NEWLY BORN	
Fetal Homicide		
Assault on Unborn		
Prohibitions on Wrongful Birth & Wrongful Life Lawsuits		Statutory prohibition on wrongful birth lawsuits
Permit Wrongful Death Lawsuits		

Born-Alive Infant Protection		
Abandoned Infant Protection		
BIOETHICS		
Human Cloning		Ban on all human cloning
DER		Ban on DER
State Funding of DER		
ART & IVF	Any medically-appropriate regulation of ART	
END OF LIFE		
Assisted Suicide	Combat attempts to legalize assisted suicide	
Pain Management Education		
RIGHTS OF CONSCIENCE		
Protection for Individual Providers	Comprehensive ROC protection (outside context of abortion)	
Protection for Institutions	Comprehensive ROC protection (outside context of abortion)	
Protection for Payers	Comprehensive ROC protection	

ARKANSAS

RANKING: 5

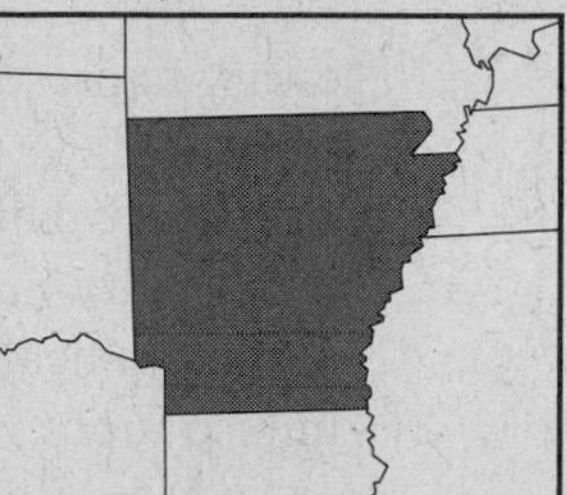
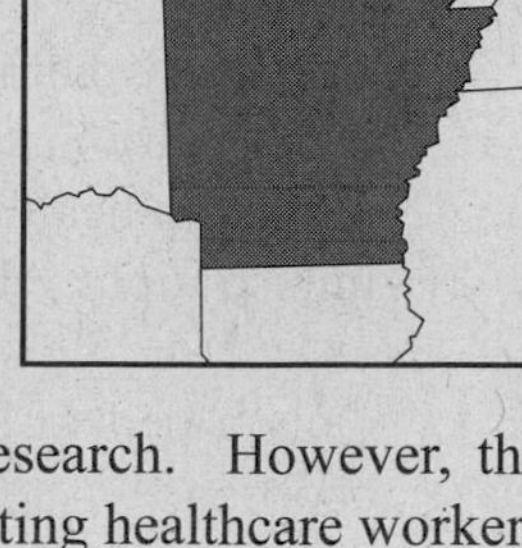

Arkansas has made great strides in protecting women from the harms of abortion, requiring not only basic informed consent but also requiring the provision of information on fetal pain and ultrasound availability. Arkansas is also one of only a small number of states that has banned both human cloning-to-produce-children and cloning-for-biomedical-research. However, the state maintains no laws regulating destructive embryo research or protecting healthcare workers who conscientiously object to participating in destructive research.

ABORTION:

- Arkansas requires that 24 hours prior to an abortion a physician provide a woman with information about the risks of abortion, the risks of continued pregnancy, and the probable gestational age of her unborn child. Further, state-prepared materials must be made available to her. These materials include pictures or drawings of the probable anatomical and physiological characteristics of the unborn child at two week gestational increments and a list of private and public agencies providing counseling and alternatives to abortion.

- The state requires that women considering abortion receive information about fetal pain.

- Arkansas requires that abortion providers offer a woman the opportunity to see the ultrasound image if an ultrasound is used in the preparation for the abortion.

- A woman must also receive a statement that her consent should be given voluntarily and not as a result of coercion, and abortion clinics must post signs with this statement.

- A physician may not perform an abortion on an unemancipated minor under the age of 18 without notarized written consent or in-person consent from a parent or legal guardian, unless the minor states by affidavit that she is the victim of physical or sexual abuse and that a parent is the perpetrator.

- Arkansas's policy, as explained in Amendment 68, § 2 to the state constitution, is to "protect the life of every unborn child from conception until birth, to the extent permitted by the Federal Constitution."

- Arkansas does not use taxpayer funds to pay for an abortion unless the procedure is nec-

essary to preserve the woman's life or the pregnancy resulted from rape or incest.

- Arkansas's comprehensive abortion clinic regulations apply to "any facility in which the primary function is the willful termination of pregnancy." The regulations prescribe minimum health and safety standards for the building or facility, staffing, and clinic administration. Abortion providers must maintain admitting privileges.

- Only a person licensed to practice medicine in the state of Arkansas may perform an abortion.

- Arkansas possesses an enforceable abortion prohibition should the U.S. Constitution be amended or certain U.S. Supreme Court decisions be reversed or modified.

- Arkansas prohibits partial-birth abortion.

- Hospitals must provide sexual assault victims with information about "emergency contraception." However, an individual provider may assert objections based on religious or moral beliefs.

- Arkansas has implemented a "Choose Life" license plate program, directing the proceeds to organizations providing abortion alternatives.

- The state has an enforceable abortion reporting law, but does not require the reporting of information to the Centers for Disease Control and Prevention (CDC). The measure applies to both surgical and nonsurgical abortions and requires abortion providers to report short-term complications.

- Arkansas requires insurance companies and employers providing prescription coverage also provide coverage for contraception. Coverage of "emergency contraception" is specifically excluded. The state provides an exemption to employers or insurers with a conscientious objection to contraceptives.

LEGAL RECOGNITION OF UNBORN AND NEWLY BORN:

- Under Arkansas law, the killing of an unborn child after 12 weeks of gestation is defined as a form of homicide.

- The state also criminalizes nonfatal assaults on the unborn.

- Arkansas allows parents and other relatives to bring wrongful death (civil) lawsuits when a viable unborn child is killed through the negligence or criminal act of another.

- Under the "Child Maltreatment Act," "neglect" includes prenatal drug use that causes the child to be born with an illegal substance in his or her system or a drug-related health problem. Moreover, such test results may be used as evidence of neglect in subsequent legal proceedings.

- In 2007, Arkansas allocated $5 million over two years to expand substance abuse treatment services for pregnant women and women with children.

- Arkansas allows a woman who loses a child after 20 weeks gestation to seek a "certificate of birth resulting in stillbirth," which is filed with the state registrar.

BIOETHICS LAWS:

- Arkansas bans both cloning-to-produce-children and cloning-for-biomedical-research. Fines levied for violating the ban are designated for the general revenue.

- Arkansas maintains no laws regarding destructive embryo research.

- Arkansas mandates artificial insemination procedures be done by a physician. In addition, the state requires insurance coverage of *in vitro* fertilization.

END OF LIFE LAWS:

- Assisted suicide is a felony in Arkansas.

HEALTHCARE RIGHTS OF CONSCIENCE LAWS:

Participation in Abortion:

- Arkansas law protects healthcare providers who conscientiously object to participating in abortions.

- Under the law, healthcare providers cannot be subject to civil liability or other recriminatory action for their refusal to participate in abortions.

- In addition, no hospital is required to permit an abortion within its facility.

- Arkansas provides some protection for the civil rights of pharmacists and pharmacies.

Participation in Research Harmful to Human Life:

- Arkansas currently provides no protection for the rights of healthcare providers who conscientiously object to participation in human cloning, destructive embryo research, or other forms of immoral medical research.

WHAT HAPPENED IN 2009:

- Arkansas enacted a measure prohibiting partial-birth abortion.

- The state also enacted a measure defining "neglect" to include the presence of an illegal substance in a newborn's blood and permitting the use of such test results as evidence of neglect in subsequent legal proceedings.

- Arkansas enacted two measures revising statutes to limit the power of the State Department of Human Services as custodian from withholding life-sustaining treatment without express court approval, and to clarify do-not-resuscitate procedures for nursing facility employees.

- The state considered a measure requiring healthcare facilities to provide information about and access to "emergency contraception," without exceptions.

- Arkansas considered a measure mandating health insurance coverage for *in vitro* fertilization.

- The state did not consider any legislation related to healthcare rights of conscience.

RECOMMENDATIONS FOR ARKANSAS		
	Short-term Priorities	**Additional Goals**
ABORTION		
Informed Consent	Penalties for failure to comply with informed consent law	
Parental Involvement		
State Rights & Policies		
Abortion Funding	Prohibition on use of state funds for abortion counseling or referrals	Prohibition on use of state facilities for abortion
Abortion Provider Requirements		
Abortion Bans		Ban on sex-selective abortions
Regulation of Abortifacients		
PCCs Support		State funding for PCCs
Abortion Reporting		
LEGAL RECOGNITION AND PROTECTION FOR UNBORN & NEWLY BORN		
Fetal Homicide		
Assault on Unborn		
Prohibitions on Wrongful Birth & Wrongful Life Lawsuits		Statutory prohibition on wrongful llife lawsuits
Permit Wrongful Death Lawsuits		

Born-Alive Infant Protection	Statutory protection for infants who survive abortion	
Abandoned Infant Protection		
BIOETHICS		
Human Cloning		
DER		Ban on DER
State Funding of DER	Ban on state funding of DER	
ART & IVF		Any medically-appropriate regulation of ART
END OF LIFE		
Assisted Suicide		
Pain Management Education		
RIGHTS OF CONSCIENCE		
Protection for Individual Providers	Comprehensive ROC protection	
Protection for Institutions	Comprehensive ROC protection	
Protection for Payers	Comprehensive ROC protection	

CALIFORNIA
RANKING: 49

The health and welfare of minors and unborn children continues to be at risk in California. Despite numerous attempts over the last several years, it has no parental involvement law. And while the state prohibits cloning-to-produce-children, it still allows cloning for research purposes and it directly funds destructive embryo research. Even adults are not necessarily safe in California, with the state maintaining a law requiring physicians provide material assistance to patients wishing to starve and/or dehydrate themselves to death.

ABORTION:

- California requires, prior to an abortion, a woman be informed of the nature of the abortion procedure, possible risks and complications, abortion alternatives, post-procedure medical services, and family planning information.

- A law requiring a physician have the consent of one parent or a court order prior to performing an abortion on a minor (under the age of 18) has been declared unconstitutional by the California Supreme Court.

- The California Supreme Court has found the state constitution provides a broader right to abortion than does the U.S. Constitution.

- The state also maintains a "Freedom of Choice Act." The Act mandates the right to abortion in California even if *Roe v. Wade* is eventually overturned, specifically providing "[e]very woman has the fundamental right to choose to bear a child or to choose and to obtain an abortion" and "[t]he state may not deny or interfere with a woman's right to choose or obtain an abortion prior to the viability of the fetus, or when the abortion is necessary to protect the life or health of the woman."

- The California Supreme Court has mandated that taxpayers pay for "medically necessary" abortions for women eligible for state medical assistance.

- California requires abortion clinics meet rudimentary standards for patient care, equipment, and staffing.

- Only licensed physicians and surgeons may perform surgical abortions.

- Emergency rooms are required to provide sexual assault victims with information about and access to "emergency contraception."

- The state allows pharmacists to dispense "emergency contraception" directly and without a prescription.

- California provides direct funding to pregnancy care centers.

- Health insurance plans that provide prescription coverage must also provide coverage for contraception. The provision includes an exemption so narrow it excludes the ability of most employers and insurers with moral or religious objections from exercising it.

- California "protects freedom of access" to abortion clinics and has established procedures for investigating "anti-reproductive-rights crimes."

LEGAL RECOGNITION OF UNBORN AND NEWLY BORN:

- Since 1970, California law has defined the killing of an unborn child after the embryonic stage (seven to eight weeks) as a form of homicide.

- The state allows wrongful death (civil) actions only when an unborn child is born alive following a negligent or criminal act and dies thereafter.

- The state has created a specific affirmative duty of physicians to provide medical care and treatment to born-alive infants at any stage of development.

- California maintains a "Baby Moses" law, under which a mother or legal guardian who is unable to care for a newborn infant may anonymously and safely leave the infant in the care of a responsible person at a hospital, police station, fire station, or other prescribed location.

- California funds drug treatment programs for pregnant women and newborns.

BIOETHICS LAWS:

- California bans cloning-to-produce-children, but explicitly allows and funds cloning-for-biomedical-research. Thus, it is a clone-and-kill state.

- California widely funds embryonic stem cell research and human cloning. Proposition 71, a ballot initiative passed in 2004, has created a constitutional right to engage in human cloning research. It also created a public body to issue $3 billion in bonds to fund embryonic stem cell research and the construction of human cloning facilities.

- California has enacted legislation relating to the prohibition of "therapeutic insemination" or use of sperm in assisted reproductive technologies (ART) if the sperm donor is found reactive for HIV or HTLV-1. It also regulates insurance coverage for ART.

- California provides that each individual undergoing fertility treatment must be informed of all possible options for unused embryos. It also details possible dispositions for embryos belonging to individuals or couples who die, separate, divorce, or fail to pay storage fees. Criminal law prohibits the use of embryos outside the parameters of that consent.

END OF LIFE LAWS:

- California expressly prohibits assisted suicide by statute. In 1996, the Ninth Circuit Court of Appeals upheld the felony charge that accompanies this prohibition.

- However, in 2008 the state enacted a measure that, while not explicitly legalizing assisted suicide, requires physicians to counsel their patients on how to end their lives. If patients elect to starve and/or dehydrate themselves to death, the physician must, if requested, provide material assistance by prescribing sedatives.

- California has amended its medical school curriculum requirements to include instruction on pain management and end-of-life issues.

HEALTHCARE RIGHTS OF CONSCIENCE LAWS:

Participation in Abortion:

- California currently provides legal protection for individual healthcare workers and private healthcare institutions that conscientiously object to participating in abortions. Protection also extends to medical and nursing students. However, this protection does not apply in medical emergencies.

- The state provides some protection for the civil rights of pharmacists and pharmacies.

Participation in Research Harmful to Human Life:

- California currently provides no protection for the rights of healthcare providers who conscientiously object to participation in human cloning, destructive embryo research,

or other forms of unethical medical research.

WHAT HAPPENED IN 2009:

- California enacted legislation recognizing September 2009 as "Pain Awareness Month" to inform healthcare providers of the need for effective pain management.

- California considered a measure related to informed consent, as well as a measure expanding the time in which an infant can be legally relinquished. California also considered a measure relating to substance abuse by pregnant women.

- Conversely, the state considered a measure requiring sexual assault victims receive information about and access to "emergency contraception," as well as a measure related to private insurance coverage of abortion.

- The state considered a measure promoting destructive embryo research. It also considered legislation regulating assisted reproductive technologies.

- California was one of the only states this session to address human egg harvesting, considering a bill that would have required any advertisement seeking oocyte donation (associated with the delivery of fertility treatment) to contain a notice relating to the potential health risks associated with human egg donation.

- California considered a draconian measure requiring pharmacists to dispense "emergency contraception" without regard to any ethical, moral, or religious objections.

RECOMMENDATIONS FOR CALIFORNIA

	Short-term Priorities	Additional Goals
ABORTION		
Informed Consent		
Parental Involvement	Parental consent or notice	
State Rights & Policies	Repeal of state FOCA	
Abortion Funding	Prohibitions on state funding for abortion	
Abortion Provider Requirements		Comprehensive abortion clinic regulations
Abortion Bans		
Regulation of Abortifacients	Regulation of RU-486	
PCCs Support		
Abortion Reporting		Mandatory reporting law for both surgical and nonsurgical abortions
LEGAL RECOGNITION AND PROTECTION FOR UNBORN & NEWLY BORN		
Fetal Homicide	Amend existing law to protect unborn child from conception	
Assault on Unborn		
Prohibitions on Wrongful Birth & Wrongful Life Lawsuits		Prohibitions on wrongful life and wrongful birth lawsuits
Permit Wrongful Death Lawsuits		

Born-Alive Infant Protection		
Abandoned Infant Protection		
BIOETHICS		
Human Cloning		Ban on human cloning
DER		Ban on DER
State Funding of DER	Constitutional amendment prohibiting state funding of DER and human cloning	
ART & IVF		Any medically-appropriate regulation of ART
END OF LIFE		
Assisted Suicide	Combat efforts to legalize assisted suicide	
Pain Management Education		
RIGHTS OF CONSCIENCE		
Protection for Individual Providers	Comprehensive ROC protection (especially pharmacists)	
Protection for Institutions	Comprehensive ROC protection	
Protection for Payers	Comprehensive ROC protection	

COLORADO

RANKING: 24

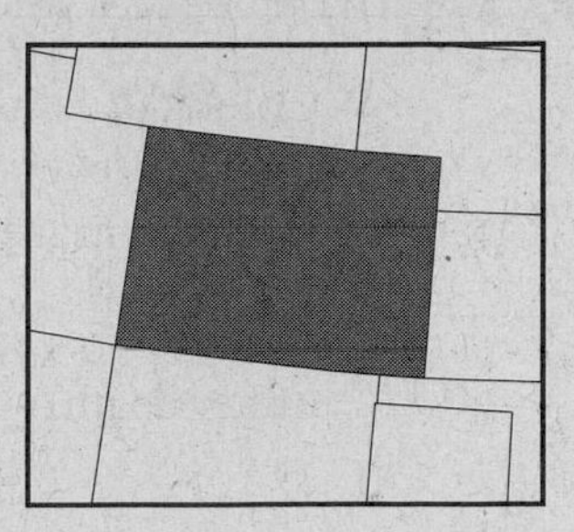

In 2009, Colorado was the only state to take a cue from the U.S. Congress and act to protect its citizens from genetic discrimination. Specifically, the state enacted legislation preventing genetic information from being used to deny access to healthcare insurance or Medicare supplement insurance coverage.

ABORTION:

- A physician may not perform an abortion on a minor under the age of 18 until at least 48 hours after written notice has been given to her parents, unless the parents waive the notice requirement or the minor declares she is a victim of abuse by a party entitled to notice and the abuse has been reported by the physician.
- The Colorado Constitution prohibits public funds from being used to pay for an abortion except when the abortion is necessary to preserve the woman's life. However, a federal court has declared this provision, along with two related statutes, in conflict with federal law. Currently the state prohibits public funds from being used for abortions unless the procedure is necessary to preserve the life of the woman or the pregnancy is the result of rape or incest.
- State family planning funds are prohibited from going to organizations that provide abortion services.
- The Colorado Attorney General has issued an opinion stating that group health insurance provided for state employees must exclude coverage for abortion.
- Only licensed physicians using accepted medical procedures may perform abortions.
- Hospitals must provide sexual assault victims with information about "emergency contraception," and pharmacies must post a notice when non-prescription "emergency contraception" is out of stock. However, hospitals are not required to provide the contraceptives, and individual providers may assert objections based upon religious or moral beliefs.
- Colorado has an enforceable abortion reporting law, but does not require the reporting of information to the Centers for Disease Control and Prevention (CDC). The measure applies to both surgical and nonsurgical abortions.
- Colorado requires insurers providing prescription drug coverage for individual and small employers to offer contraceptive coverage.

- Colorado defines "contraception" as "a medically accepted drug, device, or procedure used to prevent pregnancy," effectively preventing state abortion regulations from applying to contraception.
- Colorado requires death certificates indicate whether a woman was pregnant at the time of her death.

LEGAL RECOGNITION OF UNBORN AND NEWLY BORN:

- Actions by a third party designed to "intentionally, knowingly, recklessly, or with extreme indifference terminate or attempt to terminate a woman's pregnancy" are a felony in Colorado. However, the law does not recognize the unborn child as the second (and separate) victim of such a crime.
- Colorado allows parents and other relatives to bring wrongful death (civil) lawsuits when a viable unborn child is killed through the negligence or criminal act of another.
- In its definition of "child abuse or neglect," Colorado includes instances where an infant tests positive at birth for a controlled substance. The state also funds drug treatment programs for pregnant women and newborns.
- Women must be informed of the availability of stillbirth certificates and be given the option to request one following a miscarriage or stillbirth.

BIOETHICS LAWS:

- Colorado maintains no laws regarding destructive embryo research, human cloning, or assisted reproductive technologies.
- However, under the "Adult Stem Cells Cure Fund," the state has set standards for the collection of umbilical cord blood for those hospitals participating in donation programs. Voluntary financial contributions to the Fund may be designated on state income tax forms and an account for the proceeds has been created in the state treasury.
- Colorado has enacted legislation preventing genetic information from being used to deny access to healthcare insurance or Medicare supplement insurance coverage.

END OF LIFE LAWS:

- Colorado law expressly criminalizes assisted suicide. Assisting a suicide is considered manslaughter.

- Colorado protects medical caregivers from liability for manslaughter when prescribing or administering prescriptions for palliative care to terminally-ill patients. However, the statute does not permit assisted suicide.

HEALTHCARE RIGHTS OF CONSCIENCE LAWS:

Participation in Abortion:

- A hospital staff member or person associated with or employed by a hospital who objects in writing and on religious or moral grounds may not be required to participate in medical procedures that result in abortion.
- A hospital is not required to admit a woman for the purpose of performing an abortion.
- Private institutions and physicians and their agents may refuse to provide contraceptives and information about contraceptives based upon religious or conscientious objections. In addition, county and city employees may refuse on religious grounds to provide family planning and birth control services.

Participation in Research Harmful to Human Life:

- Colorado currently provides no protection for the rights of healthcare providers who conscientiously object to participation in human cloning, destructive embryo research, or other forms of immoral medical research.

WHAT HAPPENED IN 2009:

- Colorado reenacted a longstanding restriction prohibiting those who perform abortions from receiving state family planning funding.
- Colorado modified its definition of "contraception," listing it as "a medically acceptable drug, device, or procedure used to prevent pregnancy." The law was passed to ensure that state abortion regulations are not applied to the provision of contraception.
- Colorado also enacted legislation preventing genetic information from being used to deny access to healthcare insurance or Medicare supplement insurance coverage.
- The state enacted an end-of-life measure providing for a hospice palliative care interim study.
- The state did not consider any measures related to healthcare rights of conscience.

RECOMMENDATIONS FOR COLORADO		
	Short-term Priorities	**Additional Goals**
	ABORTION	
Informed Consent	Informed consent law with reflection period	
Parental Involvement		Amend parental notice law to require parental consent
State Rights & Policies		
Abortion Funding		
Abortion Provider Requirements	Comprehensive abortion clinic regulations	
Abortion Bans		Enforceable ban on partial-birth abortion
Regulation of Abortifacients		
PCCs Support		Funding for PCCs
Abortion Reporting		Reporting law for complications
	LEGAL RECOGNITION AND PROTECTION FOR UNBORN & NEWLY BORN	
Fetal Homicide	Law protecting unborn child from conception	
Assault on Unborn		
Prohibitions on Wrongful Birth & Wrongful Life Lawsuits		
Permit Wrongful Death Lawsuits		

Born-Alive Infant Protection	Law requiring care for infants who survive abortions	
Abandoned Infant Protection		
BIOETHICS		
Human Cloning		Ban on human cloning
DER		Ban on DER
State Funding of DER	Ban on state funding of DER	
ART & IVF		Any medically-appropriate regulation of ART
END OF LIFE		
Assisted Suicide		
Pain Management Education		
RIGHTS OF CONSCIENCE		
Protection for Individual Providers	Comprehensive ROC protection	
Protection for Institutions	Comprehensive ROC protection	
Protection for Payers	Comprehensive ROC protection	

CONNECTICUT

RANKING: 44

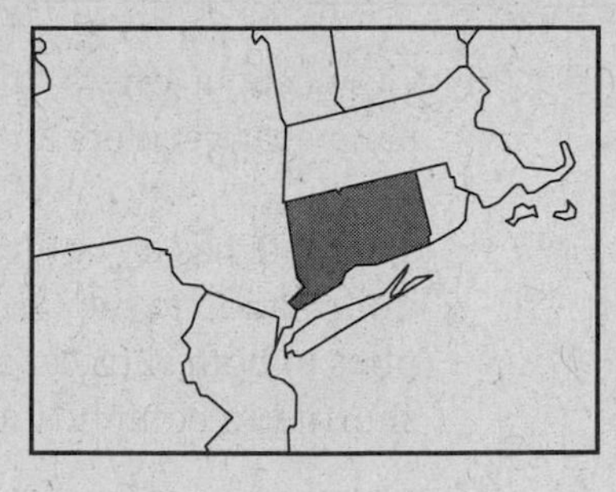

Connecticut law allows cloning-for-biomedical-research, but not cloning-to-produce-children, making it a clone-and-kill state. Researchers can clone human life, but they cannot allow it to survive. The state also permits destructive embryo research.

ABORTION:

- Connecticut law requires all women considering abortion receive counseling on the type of abortion procedure to be used and the discomfort and risks involved in that procedure.
- In addition to counseling on the type of abortion procedure and the inherent risks, minors must also receive information on the alternatives to abortion and public and private agencies that can provide assistance to them. Further, a qualified counselor must discuss the possibility of the minor involving a parent or other adult in her decision.
- The Connecticut Supreme Court has determined the state constitution protects the right to an abortion as a fundamental right and to a greater extent than the U.S. Constitution.
- The state maintains a "Freedom of Choice Act." The Act mandates the right to abortion even if *Roe v. Wade* is eventually overturned, specifically providing "[t]he decision to terminate a pregnancy prior to the viability of the fetus shall be solely that of the pregnant woman in consultation with her physician."
- Connecticut taxpayers are required to fund "medically necessary" abortions, theoretically mandating funding for most abortions given the U.S. Supreme Court's broad definition of "health" in the context of abortion.
- Connecticut mandates that abortion clinics meet rudimentary health and safety standards. The regulations prescribe minimum standards for the building or facility, patient medical testing, and the maintenance of patient records.
- Connecticut limits the performance of abortions to licensed physicians
- Hospitals must inform sexual assault victims about "emergency contraception" and provide the drug upon request (unless there is a positive pregnancy test). A hospital may contract with an independent medical professional to provide services related to "emergency contraception."

- Connecticut offers "Choose Life" license plates, the proceeds of which benefit pregnancy care centers and/or other organizations providing abortion alternatives.

- The state has an enforceable abortion reporting law, but does not require the reporting of information to the Centers for Disease Control and Prevention (CDC). The measure applies to both surgical and nonsurgical abortions and requires abortion providers to report short-term complications.

- Health insurance plans that provide prescription coverage must also provide coverage for contraception. Certain exemptions apply to religious employers or organizations.

LEGAL RECOGNITION OF UNBORN AND NEWLY BORN:

- Connecticut defines as a crime an assault on a pregnant woman resulting in "the termination of pregnancy that does not result in live birth." The law recognizes an affirmative defense if the defendant did not know that the victim was pregnant at the time of the assault.

- Connecticut allows parents and other relatives to bring wrongful death (civil) lawsuits when a viable unborn child is killed through the negligence or criminal act of another.

- The state funds drug treatment programs for pregnant women and newborns.

BIOETHICS LAWS:

- Connecticut prohibits cloning-to-produce-children. However, it permits destructive embryo research and cloning-for-biomedical-research, advancing and funding these destructive and immoral practices.

- Connecticut regulates assisted reproductive technologies to a degree. Only persons certified to practice medicine in the state of Connecticut may perform artificial insemination. The state requires the provision of information on how parents can relinquish or dispose of their ART-created embryos. In addition, the state regulates parentage of children created through ART, stating that an identified or anonymous sperm or egg donor has no right or interest in any child born as a result of artificial insemination.

- Connecticut requires health insurers to include coverage of infertility, including *in vitro* fertilization.

END OF LIFE LAWS:

- Connecticut has enacted a statutory prohibition on assisted suicide. Assisting a suicide constitutes manslaughter.

HEALTHCARE RIGHTS OF CONSCIENCE LAWS:

Participation in Abortion:

- Under Connecticut law, no person is required to participate in any phase of an abortion against his or her judgment or religious, moral, or philosophical beliefs.

Participation in Research Harmful to Human Life:

- Connecticut currently provides no protection for the rights of healthcare providers who conscientiously object to participation in human cloning, destructive embryo research, or other forms of immoral medical research.

WHAT HAPPENED IN 2009:

- Connecticut enacted legislation requiring direct care nursing home staff to have annual training in pain recognition and the administration of pain management techniques. Conversely, the state considered legislation allowing physician-assisted suicide.

- The state also considered measures bolstering informed consent and parental involvement.

- Connecticut did not consider any measure related to bioethics or healthcare rights of conscience.

- In January, Connecticut led a contingent of states filing a lawsuit against federal regulations issued under President George W. Bush guaranteeing healthcare freedom of conscience. The case, *Connecticut v. United States of America*, is currently stayed before the federal court for the District of Connecticut.

- In October, a state constitutional challenge to Connecticut's laws prohibiting assisted suiced was filed.

RECOMMENDATIONS FOR CONNECTICUT

	Short-term Priorities	Additional Goals
	ABORTION	
Informed Consent	Comprehensive informed consent with reflection period	
Parental Involvement	Mandatory parental notice or consent	
State Rights & Policies	Repeal of state FOCA	
Abortion Funding	Constitutional amendment banning state funding of abortions	
Abortion Provider Requirements		Comprehensive abortion clinic regulations
Abortion Bans		
Regulation of Abortifacients		
PCCs Support		Direct funding for PCCs
Abortion Reporting		
	LEGAL RECOGNITION AND PROTECTION FOR UNBORN & NEWLY BORN	
Fetal Homicide	Law protecting unborn child from conception	
Assault on Unborn		
Prohibitions on Wrongful Birth & Wrongful Life Lawsuits		
Permit Wrongful Death Lawsuits		

Born-Alive Infant Protection	Law requiring care for infants who survive abortions	
Abandoned Infant Protection		
BIOETHICS		
Human Cloning	Repeal of laws permitting any form of human cloning	
DER	Repeal of laws permitting DER	
State Funding of DER	Ban on state funding of DER	
ART & IVF		Any medically-appropriate regulation of ART
END OF LIFE		
Assisted Suicide		
Pain Management Education		
RIGHTS OF CONSCIENCE		
Protection for Individual Providers	Comprehensive ROC protection	
Protection for Institutions	Comprehensive ROC protection	
Protection for Payers	Comprehensive ROC protection	

DELAWARE

RANKING: 31

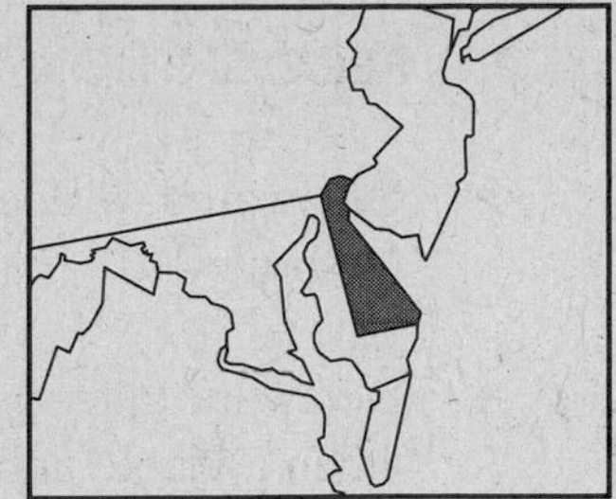

Yet again in 2009, Delaware considered few measures affecting human life. Importantly, it has yet to enact legislation protecting unborn victims of violence. Moreover, it also does not regulate destructive embryo research or human cloning, nor does it protect a health professional's right to conscientiously object to participation in such research.

ABORTION:

- Delaware's informed consent law requires that a woman be informed of the probable stage of her unborn child's development, the abortion procedure to be used and the inherent risks of the procedure, alternative abortion procedures, the probable effects of an abortion on future childbearing, and the alternatives to abortion. The portion of the law requiring a 24-hour reflection period has been ruled unconstitutional.

- Delaware prohibits coerced abortions, defining coercion as "restraining or dominating the choice of a minor female by force, threat of force, or deprivation of food and shelter." The state emancipates a minor for social assistance purposes if her parents or guardians deny financial support by reason of her refusal to undergo an abortion.

- Despite a law that prohibits a physician from performing an abortion on an unemancipated minor under the age of 16 until 24 hours after notice has been given to one parent, the Delaware Attorney General has issued a *Statement of Policy* providing that state officials will not prosecute abortion providers who fail to comply with this requirement.

- Taxpayer funds are not used to pay for abortions unless the life of the woman is endangered or the pregnancy is a result of rape or incest reported to the police.

- Only physicians licensed by the state of Delaware may perform abortions.

- Delaware has an enforceable abortion reporting law, but does not require the reporting of information to the Centers for Disease Control and Prevention (CDC). The measure applies to both surgical and nonsurgical abortions.

- If health insurance plans provide coverage for prescription drugs, coverage must also be provided for contraception. An exemption exists for religious employers.

LEGAL RECOGNITION OF UNBORN AND NEWLY BORN:

- Delaware law does not provide for the prosecution of third parties who kill or injure an unborn child.

- Delaware allows parents and other relatives to bring wrongful death (civil) lawsuits when a viable unborn child is killed through the negligence or criminal act of another.

- The state has created a specific affirmative duty of physicians to provide medical care and treatment to born-alive infants at any stage of development.

BIOETHICS LAWS:

- Delaware maintains no laws related to human cloning or destructive embryo research.

- Delaware declares, in regard to assisted reproductive technology (ART), a donor is not the parent of the resulting child. It also provides that consent for continued ART is withdrawn upon dissolution of a marriage.

END OF LIFE LAWS:

- Assisted suicide is a felony in Delaware.

HEALTHCARE RIGHTS OF CONSCIENCE LAWS:

Participation in Abortion:

- Delaware law provides that no person can be required to participate in any medical procedures that result in an abortion.

- Hospitals are not required to permit abortions within their facility.

Participation in Research Harmful to Human Life:

- Delaware currently provides no protection for the rights of healthcare providers who conscientiously object to participation in human cloning, destructive embryo research, or other forms of immoral medical research.

WHAT HAPPENED IN 2009:

- Delaware considered a measure requiring parental notification before a minor's abortion. It also considered a measure providing a "bubble zone" around "health care facilities," criminalizing entry into that area by sidewalk counselors or demonstrators.

- Delaware did not consider any actions related to bioethics or healthcare rights of conscience.

RECOMMENDATIONS FOR DELAWARE		
	Short-term Priorities	**Additional Goals**
	ABORTION	
Informed Consent	Comprehensive informed consent with reflection period	
Parental Involvement	Lift policy against enforcing parental notice law	Amend parental notice law to require parental consent
State Rights & Policies		
Abortion Funding	Ban on use of state funds for abortion counseling or referrals	Ban on use of state facilities for abortions
Abortion Provider Requirements		Comprehensive abortion clinic regulations
Abortion Bans		
Regulation of Abortifacients	Regulation of RU-486 and other abortifacients	
PCCs Support		Direct funding for PCCs
Abortion Reporting		
	LEGAL RECOGNITION AND PROTECTION FOR UNBORN & NEWLY BORN	
Fetal Homicide	Law protecting unborn child from conception	Law protecting unborn from nonfatal assaults
Assault on Unborn		
Prohibitions on Wrongful Birth & Wrongful Life Lawsuits		
Permit Wrongful Death Lawsuits		

Born-Alive Infant Protection		
Abandoned Infant Protection		
BIOETHICS		
Human Cloning		Ban on human cloning
DER		Ban on DER
State Funding of DER	Ban on state funding of DER	
ART & IVF		Any medically-appropriate regulation of ART
END OF LIFE		
Assisted Suicide		
Pain Management Education		
RIGHTS OF CONSCIENCE		
Protection for Individual Providers	Comprehensive ROC protection	
Protection for Institutions	Comprehensive ROC protection	
Protection for Payers	Comprehensive ROC protection	

DISTRICT OF COLUMBIA

Unlike the majority of states, the District of Columbia has no law or legal decision prohibiting assisted suicide. Other human life issues also remain untouched, such as basic protections for women and unborn children from the harms of abortion and regulation of human cloning and destructive embryo research.

ABORTION:

- Taxpayer funds may not be used for abortions unless the abortion is necessary to preserve the woman's life or the pregnancy was the result of rape or incest. However, in 2009, the U.S. House of Representatives voted to lift a 20-year-old ban on the use of locally-generated tax dollars for abortions in the District of Columbia.

- In the District of Columbia, abortions may only be performed under the direction of a licensed medical practitioner.

- No abortion may be performed after viability unless it is necessary to preserve the woman's life or health.

LEGAL RECOGNITION OF UNBORN AND NEWLY BORN:

- The laws of the District of Columbia do not provide for the prosecution of third parties who kill or injure an unborn child outside the context of abortion.

- The District of Columbia allows parents and other relatives to bring wrongful death (civil) lawsuits when a viable unborn child is killed through the negligence or criminal act of another.

BIOETHICS LAWS:

- The District of Columbia maintains no laws related to human cloning, destructive embryo research, or assisted reproductive technologies.

END OF LIFE LAWS:

- The legal status of assisted suicide in the District of Columbia remains undetermined. It has not enacted a special statute prohibiting assisted suicide, and it does not recognize common law crimes. There is also no judicial decision stating whether assisted suicide is a form of homicide under D.C.'s general homicide laws.

HEALTHCARE RIGHTS OF CONSCIENCE LAWS:

Participation in Abortion:

- Individuals may notify their supervisors in writing of any procedures conflicting with their religious or ethical beliefs. However, conscientious objection may not be exercised if a patient's safety is in jeopardy.

Participation in Research Harmful to Human Life:

- The District of Columbia currently provides no protection for the rights of healthcare providers who conscientiously object to participation in human cloning, destructive embryo research, or other forms of immoral medical research.

WHAT HAPPENED IN 2009:

- The U.S. House of Representatives voted to lift a 20-year-old ban on the use of locally generated tax dollars for abortions in the District of Columbia.

- The District of Columbia itself did not consider any measures related to abortion, protection of the unborn, bioethics, end-of-life issues, or healthcare rights of conscience.

FLORIDA

RANKING: 26

In the last several years, Florida has made strides—both legislatively and in the courts—to protect women and minors from the harms of abortion. The state also promotes nondestructive forms of stem cell research. However, Florida still does not specifically ban human cloning or destructive embryo research, and it does not protect healthcare providers who conscientiously object to such immoral research. Unfortunately, in 2009 Florida considered no measures regulating such practices.

ABORTION:

- Prior to an abortion, Florida requires women receive oral, in-person counseling regarding the nature and medical risks of abortion and pregnancy and the gestational age of the unborn child. Women must receive printed materials discussing pregnancy services and alternatives, providing a fetal description, and discussing medical benefits.

- Florida requires notice be given to one parent 48 hours prior to an abortion on a minor aged 17 years old and under. Notice may be provided in person, by telephone, or by mail. A judicial bypass mechanism is provided for minors aged 16 years and older. A judicial waiver may be given upon a showing of child abuse or sexual abuse and the court must report such abuse to law enforcement. There is an exception for medical emergencies, but notice must still be given to a parent within 24 hours of the abortion.

- The Florida Supreme Court has found the state constitution provides a broader right to abortion than does the U.S. Constitution. Under the auspices of this decision, Florida courts have struck down prior versions of the state's informed consent and parental involvement laws.

- Florida prohibits public funds from being used for abortions unless the procedure is necessary to preserve the life of the woman or the pregnancy is the result of rape or incest.

- Florida mandates health and safety standards for facilities performing abortions after the first trimester.

- Only physicians licensed by the state in medicine or osteopathy or those physicians practicing medicine or osteopathy and employed by the United States may perform abortions.

- Florida provides direct funding to pregnancy care centers, including faith-based centers.

- Florida also offers "Choose Life" license plates, the proceeds of which benefit pregnancy care centers and/or other organizations providing abortion alternatives.

- Florida has an enforceable abortion reporting law, but does not require the reporting of information to the Centers for Disease Control and Prevention (CDC). The measure requires abortion providers to report short-term complications only for second trimester abortions.

LEGAL RECOGNITION OF UNBORN AND NEWLY BORN:

- Under Florida criminal law, the killing of an unborn child after "quickening" (discernible movement in the womb) is defined as manslaughter. A person causing the death of an "unborn quick child" may be charged with the same level of offense applicable if the conduct had caused the death of the pregnant woman. A person may be charged with two offenses if both the pregnant woman and the unborn quick child are killed.

- The state allows wrongful death (civil) actions only when an unborn child is born alive following a negligent or criminal act and dies thereafter.

- Florida has enacted a "Baby Moses" law under which a mother or legal guardian who is unable to care for a newborn infant may anonymously and safely leave the infant in the care of a responsible person at a hospital, police station, fire station, or other prescribed location.

- The state defines substance abuse during pregnancy as child abuse under civil child-welfare statutes. The state also funds drug treatment programs for pregnant women and newborns.

BIOETHICS LAWS:

- Florida does not specifically ban human cloning or destructive embryo research, but it does ban fetal experimentation.

- Florida law encourages the use of adult stem cells, placental cells, and umbilical cord blood in research.

- Florida has enacted laws concerning the status of children conceived through *in vitro* fertilization; establishing an expedited affirmation of parental status for gestational surrogacy; governing the donation of eggs, sperm, and pre-embryos; and requiring health insurance coverage of *in vitro* fertilization. Embryo adoption is included in a listing of fertility techniques.

END OF LIFE LAWS:

- In Florida, assisted suicide is considered manslaughter.

HEALTHCARE RIGHTS OF CONSCIENCE LAWS:

Participation in Abortion:

- Under Florida law, a hospital staff member, person associated with or employed by a hospital, or physician's employee, who objects on religious or moral grounds, is not required to participate in any medical procedure that results in an abortion.

- Certain individuals, such as physicians, may refuse to furnish any contraceptive or family planning service, supplies, or information based on religious reasons.

- Hospitals are not required to perform abortions.

Participation in Research Harmful to Human Life:

- Florida does not expressly protect the rights of conscience of all healthcare providers who conscientiously object to participation in procedures other than abortion, such as destructive embryo research and human cloning.

WHAT HAPPENED IN 2009:

- Florida enacted the "Prescription Drug Monitoring Program" to monitor use of controlled substances, including those used for pain management and palliative care, in an electronic database system.

- Florida considered measures strengthening its parental notice law as well as measures promoting ultrasound use before abortion.

- Conversely, the state considered utilizing state funds to expand access to contraception, including "emergency contraception," and to promote its use.

- The state considered legislation prohibiting any person other than an attorney from receiving compensation for making a referral to an egg, sperm, or pre-embryo donor or gestational surrogate. The measure also prohibited any person other than an attorney from advertising for, or seeking, an egg, sperm, or pre-embryo donor or gestational surrogate.

- Florida considered legislation requiring pharmacists to fill all prescriptions for contraceptives "without delay."

RECOMMENDATIONS FOR FLORIDA		
	Short-term Priorities	**Additional Goals**
	ABORTION	
Informed Consent	Comprehensive informed consent with reflection period and appropriate penalties for noncompliance	
Parental Involvement		
State Rights & Policies	Amendment declaring no state right to abortion	
Abortion Funding	Ban on use of state funds for abortion counseling or referrals	Ban on use of state facilities for abortions
Abortion Provider Requirements		Comprehensive abortion clinic regulations beginning in first trimester
Abortion Bans		
Regulation of Abortifacients		Regulation of RU-486 and other abortifacients
PCCs Support		
Abortion Reporting		
	LEGAL RECOGNITION AND PROTECTION FOR UNBORN & NEWLY BORN	
Fetal Homicide	Amend law to protect unborn child from conception	
Assault on Unborn		
Prohibitions on Wrongful Birth & Wrongful Life Lawsuits		

Permit Wrongful Death Lawsuits		
Born-Alive Infant Protection	Law requiring care for infant who survives an abortion	
Abandoned Infant Protection		
BIOETHICS		
Human Cloning		Ban on human cloning
DER		Ban on DER
State Funding of DER	Ban on state funding of DER	
ART & IVF		Any medically-appropriate regulation of ART
END OF LIFE		
Assisted Suicide		
Pain Management Education		
RIGHTS OF CONSCIENCE		
Protection for Individual Providers	Comprehensive ROC protection	
Protection for Institutions	Comprehensive ROC protection	
Protection for Payers	Comprehensive ROC protection	

GEORGIA

RANKING: 8

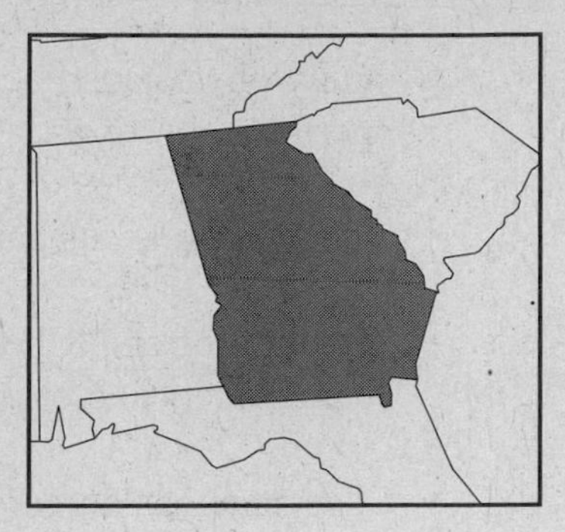

While Georgia provides some protection for the health and safety of women seeking abortions, it has yet to address several other important life issues. For example, Georgia does not ban destructive embryo research or human cloning, and it does not regulate assisted reproductive technologies, both common gateways to immoral and unethical medical research. In 2009, however, the state enacted legislation providing for embryo adoption, giving parents of cryopreserved embryos an established option other than destruction or donation for research.

ABORTION:

- Georgia requires that, 24 hours prior to an abortion, a woman receive information on the medical risks of abortion and pregnancy and the gestational age of the unborn child. A woman must also receive information on medical assistance benefits, child support, and the right to review state-prepared material on a state-sponsored website.

- In addition, a woman must be orally informed that information on fetal pain is available on the state-sponsored website.

- A woman must also be offered the opportunity to view any ultrasound performed as part of the preparation for the procedure. State-developed materials include resource information of organizations that provide ultrasounds.

- A physician may not perform an abortion on an unemancipated minor under the age of 18 until at least 24 hours after notice has been given to one parent. The notice may be given in person or over the telephone. A minor may obtain an abortion without parental notice if the parent has waived notice or the minor secures a court order stating that she is "mature and well-informed" enough to make her own decision or that parental notice is not in her best interest.

- Georgia law prohibits taxpayer funds from being used to pay for abortions unless the abortion is necessary to preserve the woman's life or the pregnancy is the result of rape or incest.

- Georgia imposes cursory administrative requirements on abortion clinics operating in the state. Further, second- and third-trimester abortions must be performed in hospitals or ambulatory surgical centers.

- Only physicians licensed to practice medicine and surgery in the state of Georgia may perform abortions.

- Georgia prohibits partial-birth abortions after viability.

- Georgia offers "Choose Life" license plates, the proceeds of which benefit pregnancy care centers and/or other organizations providing abortion alternatives.

- The state has an enforceable abortion reporting law, but does not require the reporting of information to the Centers for Disease Control and Prevention (CDC). The measure applies to both surgical and nonsurgical abortions.

- Health insurance plans that provide prescription coverage must also provide coverage for contraception. There is no exception for religious employers.

LEGAL RECOGNITION OF UNBORN AND NEWLY BORN:

- Under Georgia criminal law, the killing of an unborn child at any stage of gestation is defined as a form of homicide.

- Georgia also maintains the crime of feticide by vehicle, making the unborn child at any stage of development a victim under the state's homicide by vehicle law.

- Georgia defines nonfatal assaults on an unborn child as criminal offenses.

- Georgia allows parents and other relatives to bring wrongful death (civil) lawsuits when an unborn child is killed (after "quickening") through the negligence or criminal act of another.

- The state has created a specific affirmative duty of physicians to provide medical care and treatment to born-alive infants at any stage of development.

BIOETHICS LAWS:

- Georgia maintains no laws regulating human cloning, destructive embryo research, or assisted reproductive technologies.

- Georgia maintains the "Newborn Umbilical Cord Blood Bank" for postnatal tissue and fluid, thus encouraging the research of these promising cells.

- Georgia law provides for embryo adoption.

END OF LIFE LAWS:

- Under Georgia law, assisted suicide is a felony.

HEALTHCARE RIGHTS OF CONSCIENCE LAWS:

Participation in Abortion:

- A person who objects in writing to participating in abortions and whose objections are based on moral or religious grounds may not be required to participate in any medical procedure that results in an abortion.

- A hospital, medical facility, or physician is not required to admit a woman for the purpose of performing an abortion.

- The state provides some protection for the civil rights of pharmacists and pharmacies.

Participation in Research Harmful to Human Life:

- Georgia currently provides no protection for the rights of healthcare providers who conscientiously object to participation in human cloning, destructive embryo research, or other forms of immoral medical research.

WHAT HAPPENED IN 2009:

- Georgia enacted legislation providing for embryo adoption. Both houses adopted a resolution opposing the the federal "Freedom of Choice Act."

- Georgia considered measures banning abortion and defining an unborn child as a "person." Conversely, the state considered measures promoting "emergency contraception."

- On the bioethics front, the state considered legislation banning human cloning for all purposes and regulating assisted reproductive technologies. The state also considered a measure requiring health insurance coverage for the diagnosis and treatment of infertility.

- Georgia did not consider any measures related to healthcare rights of conscience.

RECOMMENDATIONS FOR GEORGIA

	Short-term Priorities	Additional Goals
ABORTION		
Informed Consent	Coerced abortion prevention	
Parental Involvement		Amend parental notice law to require consent
State Rights & Policies		
Abortion Funding	Ban on use of state funds for abortion counseling or referrals	Ban on use of state facilities for abortions
Abortion Provider Requirements	Comprehensive abortion clinic regulations beginning in first trimester	
Abortion Bans		Sex-selective abortion ban or "delayed enforcement" law
Regulation of Abortifacients		Regulation of RU-486 and other abortifacients
PCCs Support	Direct funding for PCCs	
Abortion Reporting		Mandatory reporting of abortion complications
LEGAL RECOGNITION AND PROTECTION FOR UNBORN & NEWLY BORN		
Fetal Homicide		
Assault on Unborn		
Prohibitions on Wrongful Birth & Wrongful Life Lawsuits		
Permit Wrongful Death Lawsuits		

Born-Alive Infant Protection		
Abandoned Infant Protection		
BIOETHICS		
Human Cloning		Ban on human cloning
DER		Ban on DER
State Funding of DER	Ban on state funding of DER	
ART & IVF		Any medically-appropriate regulation of ART
END OF LIFE		
Assisted Suicide		
Pain Management Education		
RIGHTS OF CONSCIENCE		
Protection for Individual Providers	Comprehensive ROC protection	
Protection for Institutions	Comprehensive ROC protection	
Protection for Payers	Comprehensive ROC protection	

HAWAII
RANKING: 48

Hawaii lacks the most basic protections for women, unborn children, and the terminally-ill. The state fails to provide for informed consent for abortion, to require parental involvement in a minor's abortion decision, or to ensure that abortion clinics maintain minimum health and safety standards. It also fails to ban destructive embryo research, human cloning, and assisted suicide.

ABORTION:

- Hawaii has no informed consent or parental involvement law.
- The state maintains a "Freedom of Choice Act." The Act mandates the right to abortion even if *Roe v. Wade* is eventually overturned, specifically providing that "[t]he State shall not deny or interfere with a female's right to choose or obtain an abortion of a nonviable fetus or an abortion that is necessary to protect the life or health of the female."
- Hawaiian taxpayers are required to pay for "medically necessary" abortions for women receiving state medical assistance.
- Hawaii maintains no enforceable abortion clinic regulations, but only licensed physicians, surgeons, or licensed osteopathic physicians or surgeons may perform abortions.
- Hawaii allows a pharmacist to provide "emergency contraception" to women without a prescription, provided the pharmacist has a collaborative therapy agreement with a licensed physician.
- Hawaii offers "Choose Life" license plates, the proceeds of which benefit pregnancy care centers and/or other organizations providing abortion alternatives.
- The state has an enforceable abortion reporting law, but does not require the reporting of information to the Centers for Disease Control and Prevention (CDC).
- Health insurance plans that provide prescription coverage must also provide coverage for contraception. An exemption exists for religious employers.

LEGAL RECOGNITION OF UNBORN AND NEWLY BORN:

- Hawaii does not protect unborn children from being killed or assaulted by third parties.

- The state allows wrongful death (civil) actions when a viable unborn child is killed through a negligent or criminal act.

- Hawaii does not require that appropriate medical care be given to infants who survive an attempted abortion.

- Hawaii has a "Baby Moses" law, which allows a person to leave an unharmed infant no more than 72 hours old at a hospital, fire station, or police station and be immune from prosecution for child abandonment. The professional receiving the child must inquire into the child's medical history and provide information on social services to the person relinquishing the infant.

BIOETHICS LAWS:

- Hawaii does not ban human cloning or destructive embryo research, nor does it maintain any meaningful regulation of assisted reproductive technologies.

- The state does, however, regulate insurance coverage of assisted reproductive technologies.

END OF LIFE LAWS:

- The legal status of assisted suicide in Hawaii remains undetermined. The state has not enacted a special statute prohibiting assisted suicide, and it does not recognize common law crimes. There is also no judicial decision stating whether assisted suicide is a form of homicide under Hawaii's general homicide laws.

HEALTHCARE
RIGHTS OF CONSCIENCE LAWS:

Participation in Abortion:

- Under Hawaiian law, no person or hospital is required to participate in abortions.

Participation in Research Harmful to Human Life:

- Hawaii currently provides no protection for the rights of healthcare providers who conscientiously object to participation in human cloning, destructive embryo research, or other forms of immoral medical research.

WHAT HAPPENED IN 2009:

- Hawaii considered measures prohibiting partial-birth abortion and requiring parental notice before abortion.
- The state considered several bills protecting unborn victims of violence, as well as a bill requiring the reporting of possible non-medical drug or alcohol abuse by a pregnant woman to the State Department of Human Services.
- Conversely, the state considered several bills urging hospital emergency rooms to provide information about and access to "emergency contraception."
- Hawaii considered measures regulating assisted reproductive technologies.
- The state considered legislation directing the state medical board to require physician clinical practitioners to complete two hours of continuing medical education on palliative care every four years. However, Hawaii also considered a number of measures allowing physician-assisted suicide.
- The state also considered healthcare rights of conscience legislation providing comprehensive protection for healthcare providers, institutions, and payers.

RECOMMENDATIONS FOR HAWAII		
	Short-term Priorities	**Additional Goals**
ABORTION		
Informed Consent	Comprehensive informed consent with reflection period	
Parental Involvement	Parental notice or consent	
State Rights & Policies	Repeal of state FOCA	
Abortion Funding	Prohibitions on state funding of abortion	
Abortion Provider Requirements		Comprehensive abortion clinic regulations beginning in first trimester
Abortion Bans		
Regulation of Abortifacients		
PCCs Support		Direct funding for PCCs
Abortion Reporting		
LEGAL RECOGNITION AND PROTECTION FOR UNBORN & NEWLY BORN		
Fetal Homicide	Comprehensive protections for unborn victims of violence	
Assault on Unborn		
Prohibitions on Wrongful Birth & Wrongful Life Lawsuits		
Permit Wrongful Death Lawsuits		

Born-Alive Infant Protection	Law requiring care for infant who survives an abortion	
Abandoned Infant Protection		
BIOETHICS		
Human Cloning		Ban on human cloning
DER		Ban on DER
State Funding of DER	Ban on state funding of DER	
ART & IVF		Any medically-appropriate regulation of ART
END OF LIFE		
Assisted Suicide	Statutory prohibition on assisted suicide & combat efforts to legalize the practice	
Pain Management Education		
RIGHTS OF CONSCIENCE		
Protection for Individual Providers	Comprehensive ROC protection	
Protection for Institutions	Comprehensive ROC protection	
Protection for Payers	Comprehensive ROC protection	

IDAHO

RANKING: 23

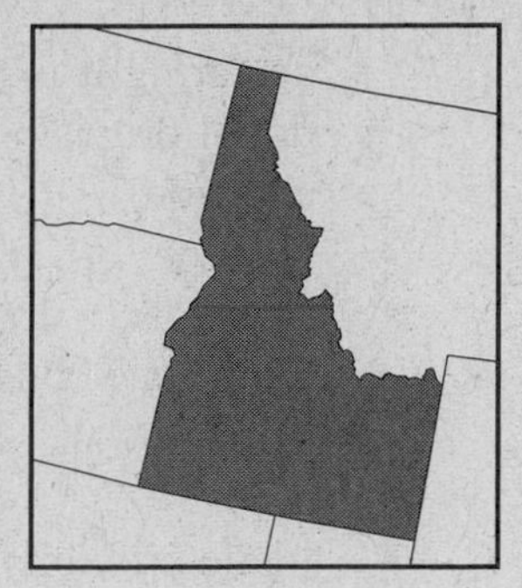

Over the last several years, Idaho has made great strides in ensuring that women receive adequate and medically-appropriate information before choosing abortion, including offering the woman the opportunity to view an ultrasound image and prohibiting coercion. However, Idaho does not regulate biotechnologies, nor does it protect researchers who conscientiously object to participating in human cloning or destructive embryo research.

ABORTION:

- Under Idaho law, a physician may not perform an abortion until 24 hours after he or she provides a woman with an "accurate and substantially complete" explanation of the abortion procedure to be used; the inherent risks and possible complications of the procedure, including possible effects on future childbearing; and alternatives to abortion and the risks of those alternatives. State-prepared material on fetal development, the availability of assistance from both public and private agencies, and a description of commonly-used abortion procedures and their specific risks must also be made available to the woman.

- In addition, abortion providers must offer a woman seeking an abortion the opportunity to view any ultrasound that is conducted in preparation for the procedure. Additionally, women have the right to ask for an ultrasound, even if the provider does not routinely conduct them.

- Idaho also prohibits anyone from coercing a woman into having an abortion, including in its definition of "coercion" the inflicting or threatening or conspiring to inflict physical harm. Violation of the statute becomes a felony if a pregnant woman suffers physical harm. The state allows a victim of coercive abuse to bring a civil suit against the abuser.

- Idaho requires written consent from one parent before an abortion is performed on a minor. Consent may be waived if there is a medical emergency, if the pregnancy is the result of rape or incest, or if a judicial order is obtained. Abortion providers must report information on abortions performed on minors, and courts must report information on waivers of the state's parental consent requirement.

- Idaho has adopted a legislative declaration providing that the state recognizes "the fundamental importance" of Idaho's interest in preserving the lives of unborn children and declaring it is the "public policy of this state that all state statutes, rules and constitutional provisions shall be interpreted to prefer, by all legal means, live childbirth over abortion."

- However, a 1996 decision by the Idaho Supreme Court has been interpreted as creating a state constitutional right to abortion that is broader than that provided by the U.S. Constitution.

- Idaho prohibits public funds from being used for abortions unless the procedure is necessary to preserve the life of the woman or the pregnancy is the result of rape or incest.

- Idaho prohibits private insurance companies from covering abortion, except in cases of life endangerment.

- Only physicians licensed by the state to practice medicine and surgery or osteopathic medicine and surgery may perform abortions.

- Idaho has an enforceable abortion reporting law, but does not require the reporting of information to the Centers for Disease Control and Prevention (CDC). The measure pertains to both surgical and nonsurgical abortions.

LEGAL RECOGNITION OF UNBORN AND NEWLY BORN:

- Idaho defines the killing of an unborn child at any stage of gestation as homicide.

- Idaho defines a nonfatal assault on an unborn child as a criminal offense.

- Idaho allows wrongful death (civil) actions when a viable unborn child is killed through negligent or criminal act.

BIOETHICS LAWS:

- Idaho has not enacted laws regarding human cloning or destructive embryo research.

- Idaho mandates that only physicians perform artificial insemination and regulates semen donation.

END OF LIFE LAWS:

- In Idaho, assisted suicide is a common law crime.

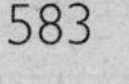

HEALTHCARE RIGHTS OF CONSCIENCE LAWS:

Participation in Abortion:

- A physician is not required to perform or assist in abortions.

- Nurses, medical technicians, hospital employees, and physician employees who object on religious, moral, or personal grounds are not required to participate in abortions. The objection must be in writing.

- A hospital, upon an objection of its governing board, is not required to admit a woman or permit the use of its facilities for the purposes of performing an abortion.

Participation in Research Harmful to Human Life:

- Idaho currently provides no protection for the rights of healthcare providers who conscientiously object to participation in human cloning, destructive embryo research, or other forms of immoral medical research.

WHAT HAPPENED IN 2009:

- Idaho did not consider any measures related to abortion, protection of the unborn, or bioethics.

- Idaho considered a measure providing that no person shall be required to provide for any pharmaceutical care or drug that violates his or her conscience.

RECOMMENDATIONS FOR IDAHO		
	Short-term Priorities	**Additional Goals**
ABORTION		
Informed Consent		Counseling on fetal pain
Parental Involvement		Enhancements like notarized consent or identification requirements
State Rights & Policies	Constitutional amendment declaring no state right to abortion	
Abortion Funding	Prohibition on use of state funds for abortion counseling or referrals	
Abortion Provider Requirements	Comprehensive abortion clinic regulations beginning in first trimester	
Abortion Bans		"Delayed enforcement" law
Regulation of Abortifacients		
PCCs Support		Direct funding for PCCs and/or "Choose Life" license plates
Abortion Reporting		
LEGAL RECOGNITION AND PROTECTION FOR UNBORN & NEWLY BORN		
Fetal Homicide		
Assault on Unborn		
Prohibitions on Wrongful Birth & Wrongful Life Lawsuits		

Permit Wrongful Death Lawsuits		
Born-Alive Infant Protection	Law requiring care for infant who survives an abortion	
Abandoned Infant Protection		
BIOETHICS		
Human Cloning		Ban on human cloning
DER		Ban on DER
State Funding of DER	Ban on state funding of DER	
ART & IVF		Any medically-appropriate regulation of ART
END OF LIFE		
Assisted Suicide		
Pain Management Education		
RIGHTS OF CONSCIENCE		
Protection for Individual Providers	Comprehensive ROC protection	
Protection for Institutions	Comprehensive ROC protection	
Protection for Payers	Comprehensive ROC protection	

ILLINOIS

RANKING: 36

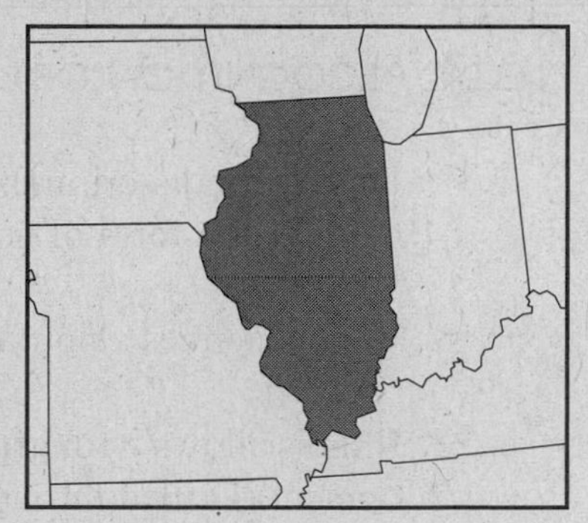

In 2009, the Seventh Circuit Court of Appeals rejected a challenge to Illinois' parental notice statute, ending federal litigation that has spanned a decade. However, Illinois still fails to provide meaningful protection for women and the unborn from the harms inherent in abortion..

ABORTION:

- Illinois' law prohibiting a physician from performing an abortion on a minor under the age of 18 without providing 48 hours notice to one parent is poised to go into effect, after more than a decade of litigation.

- Illinois taxpayers are required to fund "medically necessary" abortions, essentially funding abortion-on-demand given the federal courts' broad definition of "health" in the context of abortion.

- Illinois prohibits organizations that receive state funds from using those funds to provide abortion counseling or to make referrals for abortion.

- In the state health plan, Illinois provides abortion coverage only when a woman's life is endangered.

- Illinois' abortion clinic regulations are not uniformly applied to all of the state's abortion clinics.

- Only physicians licensed by the state of Illinois may perform abortions. A chiropractor's 1978 challenge to Illinois' requirement was rejected.

- Illinois requires emergency rooms provide information on "emergency contraception" to sexual assault victims.

- Illinois has an enforceable abortion reporting law, but does not require the reporting of information to the Centers for Disease Control and Prevention (CDC). The measure requires abortion providers to report short-term complications.

- Health insurance plans that provide prescription coverage must also provide coverage for contraception. An exemption is provided for religious employers.

LEGAL RECOGNITION OF UNBORN AND NEWLY BORN:

- Under Illinois criminal law, the killing of an unborn child at any stage of gestation is defined as a form of homicide.

- Illinois defines a nonfatal assault on an unborn child as a crime.

- Illinois allows wrongful death (civil) actions when an unborn child at any stage of development is killed through a negligent or criminal act.

- The state has created a specific affirmative duty of physicians to provide medical care and treatment to born-alive infants at any stage of development.

- Illinois maintains an "Abandoned Newborn Infant Protection Act," or "Baby Moses" law, which includes a prohibition preventing persons accepting an infant under the Act from publicly discussing the circumstances surrounding the infant's legal surrender.

- The state defines substance abuse during pregnancy as "child abuse" under civil child-welfare statutes. Illinois requires healthcare professionals to report suspected prenatal drug exposure and funds drug treatment programs for pregnant women and newborns.

BIOETHICS LAWS:

- Under the "Stem Cell Research and Human Cloning Prohibition Act," Illinois permits and funds destructive embryo research. While the Act prohibits cloning-to-produce-children, it specifically allows for "therapeutic cloning"—thus making it a clone-and-kill law.

- The Act also provides $15 million in grants for such destructive research.

- The state regulates insurance coverage for assisted reproductive technologies.

END OF LIFE LAWS:

- In Illinois, assisted suicide is a felony.

HEALTHCARE RIGHTS OF CONSCIENCE LAWS:

Participation in Abortion:

- By statute, Illinois protects the civil rights of all healthcare providers, whether individuals, institutions, or payers (public or private), who conscientiously object to participating in any healthcare services, including abortion. The law includes protection for medical and nursing students, counselors, and social workers.

- However, a 2005 Executive Order (implemented by former Governor Rod Blagojevich) directly threatens the broad applicability and the comprehensive protection provided by this statute. The Order demands that pharmacies dispense contraceptives—including "emergency contraception"—"without delay." In other words, a pharmacist must provide "emergency contraception" or transfer the prescription, even if such an action is a violation of his or her conscience. In essence, pharmacy owners who dispense contraceptives are mandated to provide "emergency contraception" on demand.

Participation in Research Harmful to Human Life:

- By statute, Illinois protects the civil rights of all healthcare providers who conscientiously object to participating in procedures such as human cloning and destructive embryo research.

WHAT HAPPENED IN 2009:

- Illinois enacted a measure that expands the age that an infant can be legally relinquished from 72 hours to 30 days.

- Illinois considered a state "Freedom of Choice Act," but also considered a measure opposing a federal "Freedom of Choice Act." Additional measures considered by the legislature included bills aimed at providing a woman the opportunity to view an ultrasound of her unborn child before having an abortion.

- The state considered measures mandating insurance coverage of contraception, but it also considered a bill prohibiting the use of certain state funds for the enforcement of any rule that forces pharmacists or pharmacies to provide "emergency contraception."

- Illinois considered a measure stating that the state is committed to supporting non-destructive stem cell research. It also considered a measure related to the health insurance coverage of infertility.

- The state considered a measure directing the State Department of Healthcare and Family Services to develop a pediatric palliative care pilot program under which a qualifying child may receive community-based pediatric palliative care from a trained interdisciplinary team while continuing to pursue aggressive curative treatments for a potentially life-limiting medical condition under the benefits available under the Medicaid program.

- Illinois did not consider any measures related to healthcare rights of conscience.

- In November of 2008, the Seventh Circuit Court of Appeals reversed a lower court ruling in *Choose Life Illinois v. White*, which had held that the state acted unconstitutionally in rejecting a "Choose Life" license plate. Later, the U.S. Supreme Court refused to review the case.

- On the other hand, the Seventh Circuit rejected a challenge to Illinois' parental notice act. However, in October 2009, a state law challenge to the law was filed.

- In *Morr-Fitz v. Quinn*, an Illinois circuit court enjoined the enforcement of a 2005 Executive Order requiring pharmacists and pharmacies to dispense "emergency contraception," regardless of moral or conscientious objection.

RECOMMENDATIONS FOR ILLINOIS		
	Short-term Priorities	**Additional Goals**
	ABORTION	
Informed Consent	Comprehensive informed consent with reflection period	
Parental Involvement		
State Rights & Policies		
Abortion Funding	Limits on state funding of abortion	
Abortion Provider Requirements	Comprehensive abortion clinic regulations beginning in first trimester	
Abortion Bans		
Regulation of Abortifacients		Regulation of RU-486
PCCs Support		Direct funding for PCCs
Abortion Reporting		Reporting requirements for complications
LEGAL RECOGNITION AND PROTECTION FOR UNBORN & NEWLY BORN		
Fetal Homicide		
Assault on Unborn		
Prohibitions on Wrongful Birth & Wrongful Life Lawsuits		
Permit Wrongful Death Lawsuits		

Born-Alive Infant Protection		
Abandoned Infant Protection		
BIOETHICS		
Human Cloning		Ban on human cloning
DER		Ban on DER
State Funding of DER	Ban on state funding of DER and human cloning	
ART & IVF		Any medically-appropriate regulation of ART
END OF LIFE		
Assisted Suicide		
Pain Management Education		
RIGHTS OF CONSCIENCE		
Protection for Individual Providers	Repeal of 2005 Executive Order	
Protection for Institutions	Repeal of 2005 Executive Order	
Protection for Payers		

INDIANA

RANKING: 13

In 2009, Indiana continued efforts to protect the unborn by enacting an unborn victims of violence law that protects unborn children from conception. Meanwhile, Indiana does not explicitly ban destructive embryo research, but it has banned all forms of human cloning and restricts the funding and practice of destructive embryo research.

ABORTION:

- Indiana law requires a woman receive, at least 18 hours before an abortion, information about the type of abortion procedure to be used; the risks of and alternatives to that particular procedure; the probable gestational age of the unborn child; the risks associated with carrying the pregnancy to term; and the name of the physician who will perform the abortion. Further, the woman must be told about state medical assistance benefits; the father's liability for child support; and abortion alternatives.

- Physicians must notify a pregnant woman of the availability of fetal ultrasound and fetal heart tone auscultation services at least 18 hours before a scheduled abortion and advise her that she may view the images or listen to the heart tone.

- A physician may not perform an abortion on a minor under the age of 18 without the written consent of one parent or a court order.

- Indiana funds abortions when it is necessary to preserve the woman's life or physical health or the pregnancy is the result of rape or incest.

- Indiana prohibits organizations that receive state funds from using those funds to provide abortion counseling or to make referrals for abortion.

- All facilities performing surgical abortions must be licensed by the state health department and meet comprehensive health and safety standards. Abortion providers in some Indiana counties must maintain admitting privileges.

- Indiana also requires that post-first-trimester abortions be performed in a hospital or ambulatory outpatient surgical center.

- Only physicians licensed to practice medicine in Indiana may perform abortions.

- Indiana prohibits partial-birth abortion.

- Indiana offers "Choose Life" license plates, the proceeds of which benefit pregnancy care centers and/or other organizations providing abortion alternatives.

- The state has an enforceable abortion reporting law, but does not require the reporting of information to the Centers for Disease Control and Prevention (CDC). The measure applies to both surgical and nonsurgical abortions and requires abortion providers to report short-term complications.

- Indiana has a "contraceptive equity" law, requiring health insurance coverage for contraception. No exemption is provided for employers or insurers with a moral or religious objection to contraception.

LEGAL RECOGNITION OF THE UNBORN AND NEWLY BORN:

- Under Indiana criminal law, the killing of an unborn child after viability is defined as a form of homicide.

- A person who, while committing murder or felony murder, causes the death of a child *in utero* may be sentenced to an additional fixed term of imprisonment that is equal to the advisory sentence for murder. This provision applies at any stage of gestation.

- Indiana defines criminal assaults on a pregnant woman that result in miscarriage, stillbirth, or "damage to pregnancy" as an enhanced offense for sentencing purposes.

- The state allows wrongful death (civil) actions only when an unborn child is born alive following a negligent or criminal act and dies thereafter.

- The state has created a specific affirmative duty of physicians to provide medical care and treatment to born-alive infants at any stage of development.

- The state defines substance abuse during pregnancy as "child abuse" under civil child-welfare statutes.

- The State Department of Health has been directed to develop a system of registry for stillbirth information.

BIOETHICS LAWS:

- Indiana bans human cloning for any purpose.

- Indiana restricts funding for destructive embryo research and only allows research to the extent permitted under federal law.

- However, Indiana does not regulate assisted reproductive technologies.

END OF LIFE LAWS:

- Indiana expressly prohibits assisted suicide by statute. Assisting a suicide constitutes a felony.

HEALTHCARE RIGHTS OF CONSCIENCE LAWS:

Participation in Abortion:

- A physician, hospital, facility employee, or staff member who objects on religious, moral, or ethical grounds is not required to participate in abortions.

- A private or religiously-affiliated hospital is not required to permit the use of its facilities for the performance of an abortion.

Participation in Research Harmful to Human Life:

- Indiana currently provides no protection for the rights of healthcare providers who conscientiously object to participation in human cloning, destructive embryo research, or other forms of immoral medical research.

WHAT HAPPENED IN 2009:

- Indiana enacted a law providing that a person who, while committing murder or felony murder, causes the death of a child *in utero* may be sentenced to an additional fixed term of imprisonment that is equal to the advisory sentence for murder. The measure also increased the penalties for providing an illegal abortion.

- The state also enacted a measure requiring the State Department of Health to develop a system of registry for stillbirth information.

- Indiana considered measures amending the state's informed consent requirement to require that a woman receive information about fetal pain before abortion, as well as undergo an ultrasound. The state also considered a measure requiring abortion providers have admitting privileges at a local hospital. Other measures considered involved wrongful death actions for unborn children and remedies for maternal substance abuse.

- Conversely, the state considered a measure forcing pharmacists and pharmacies to provide contraception in a "timely manner."

- The state did not consider any measures related to bioethics or end-of-life issues.

- Indiana considered draconian legislation requiring that prescriptions for contraceptives be filled "without delay."

RECOMMENDATIONS FOR INDIANA		
	Short-term Priorities	**Additional Goals**
	ABORTION	
Informed Consent	Enhancements such as counseling on fetal pain and coerced abortion prevention	
Parental Involvement		Enhancements such as notarized consent or identification requirements
State Rights & Policies		
Abortion Funding	State funding limits consistent with Hyde Amendment	Prohibition on the use of public facilities for abortions
Abortion Provider Requirements		
Abortion Bans		Sex-selective abortion ban or “delayed enforcement” law
Regulation of Abortifacients		Regulation of RU-486
PCCs Support		Direct funding for PCCs
Abortion Reporting		
	LEGAL RECOGNITION AND PROTECTION FOR UNBORN & NEWLY BORN	
Fetal Homicide		
Assault on Unborn		
Prohibitions on Wrongful Birth & Wrongful Life Lawsuits		
Permit Wrongful Death Lawsuits		

Born-Alive Infant Protection		
Abandoned Infant Protection		
BIOETHICS		
Human Cloning		
DER		
State Funding of DER	Funding of ethical alternatives to DER	
ART & IVF		Any medically-appropriate regulation of ART
END OF LIFE		
Assisted Suicide		
Pain Management Education		
RIGHTS OF CONSCIENCE		
Protection for Individual Providers	Comprehensive ROC protection	
Protection for Institutions	Comprehensive ROC protection	
Protection for Payers	Comprehensive ROC protection	

IOWA

RANKING: 34

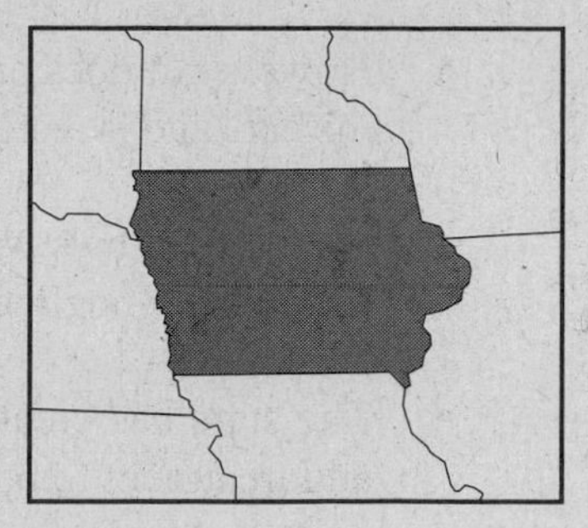

Since 2007, Iowa has explicitly permitted human cloning-for-biomedical-research and destructive embryo research. Further, Iowa still has not taken adequate steps to ensure the health and safety of women seeking or undergoing abortions or to protect unborn victims of violence. While it considered a number of life-affirming measures in 2009, none of those measures were enacted.

ABORTION:

- In 2002, Iowa issued an "Information, Not Criminalization" directive. The directive purportedly makes information on family planning, abortion, adoption, and other reproductive health information available to women at their request. However, the information is not mandated, and there are no penalties for failure to supply the information or to provide access to the information.

- A physician may not perform an abortion on an unmarried or never-married minor under the age of 18 until at least 48 hours after written notice has been provided to a parent or grandparent or a court order is issued.

- Iowa taxpayers are required to pay for abortions for women eligible for state medical assistance if the continued pregnancy endangers the woman's life; the unborn child is physically deformed, mentally deficient, or afflicted with a congenital condition; or the pregnancy is the result of reported rape or incest.

- Only physicians licensed to practice medicine and surgery in the state of Iowa or osteopathic physicians and surgeons may perform abortion.

- Iowa has an enforceable abortion reporting law, but does not require the reporting of information to the Centers for Disease Control and Prevention (CDC). The measure applies to both surgical and nonsurgical abortions.

- Health insurance plans that provide prescription coverage must also provide coverage for contraception. No exemption is provided for religious employers.

LEGAL RECOGNITION OF UNBORN AND NEWLY BORN:

- Iowa does not protect unborn children from criminal violence.

- However, it does provide that an attack on a pregnant woman that results in a stillbirth or miscarriage is a criminal assault.

- The state allows wrongful death (civil) actions only when an unborn child is born alive following a negligent or criminal act and dies thereafter.

- The state has created a specific affirmative duty of physicians to provide medical care and treatment to born-alive infants only after viability.

- The state defines substance abuse during pregnancy as "child abuse" under civil child-welfare statutes. Iowa requires healthcare professionals to report suspected prenatal drug exposure and healthcare professionals must test newborns for drug exposure when there is suspicion of prenatal drug use or abuse.

BIOETHICS LAWS:

- Under the "Stem Cell Research and Cures Initiative," Iowa allows and protects destructive embryo research and allows cloning-for-biomedical-research, while prohibiting cloning-to-produce-children—thus, making it a clone-and-kill state.

- Iowa does not regulate assisted reproductive technologies.

END OF LIFE LAWS:

- Iowa expressly prohibits assisted suicide. Under the law, assisting a suicide constitutes a felony.

HEALTHCARE RIGHTS OF CONSCIENCE LAWS:

Participation in Abortion:

- An individual who objects on religious or moral grounds is not required to participate in an abortion unless that abortion constitutes "emergency medical treatment" of a serious physical condition necessary to save the woman's life.

- A private or religiously-affiliated hospital is not required to perform or permit abortions that are not necessary to save the woman's life.

Participation in Research Harmful to Human Life:

- Iowa currently provides no protection for the rights of healthcare providers who conscientiously object to participation in human cloning, destructive embryo research, or other forms of immoral medical research.

WHAT HAPPENED IN 2009:

- Iowa continued its policy of paying for abortions within the Medicaid program in cases of fetal abnormality, rape, incest, and life endangerment.

- The state considered a number of life affirming bills, including measures requiring the reporting of information by abortion providers; mandating that a woman be offered the opportunity to view an ultrasound before abortion; requiring notarization or identification of a parent before a minor can obtain an abortion; and prohibiting state funds from being appropriated to facilities that perform abortions. The state also considered measures defining "life" as beginning at conception.

- Iowa considered a measure related to the status of posthumously-conceived children.

- Iowa did not consider any measures related to end-of-life issues or healthcare rights of conscience.

RECOMMENDATIONS FOR IOWA		
	Short-term Priorities	**Additional Goals**
	ABORTION	
Informed Consent	Comprehensive informed consent with reflection period	
Parental Involvement		Amend parental notice law to require parental consent
State Rights & Policies		
Abortion Funding		
Abortion Provider Requirements	Comprehensive abortion clinic regulations beginning in first trimester	
Abortion Bans		
Regulation of Abortifacients		Regulation of RU-486
PCCs Support		Direct funding for PCCs
Abortion Reporting		Reporting of complications
	LEGAL RECOGNITION AND PROTECTION FOR UNBORN & NEWLY BORN	
Fetal Homicide	Law recognizing unborn child at any stage of development as potential homicide victim	
Assault on Unborn		Law permitting prosecution for nonfatal assaults on the unborn
Prohibitions on Wrongful Birth & Wrongful Life Lawsuits		
Permit Wrongful Death Lawsuits		Law permitting wrongful death lawsuits in death of unborn

Born-Alive Infant Protection		
Abandoned Infant Protection		
BIOETHICS		
Human Cloning	Ban human cloning	
DER	Ban DER	
State Funding of DER	Ban on state funding of DER	
ART & IVF		Any medically-appropriate regulation of ART
END OF LIFE		
Assisted Suicide		
Pain Management Education		
RIGHTS OF CONSCIENCE		
Protection for Individual Providers	Comprehensive ROC protection	
Protection for Institutions	Comprehensive ROC protection	
Protection for Payers	Comprehensive ROC protection	

KANSAS

RANKING: 14

In 2009, former Kansas Governor Kathleen Sebelius and current Governor Mark Parkinson continued their assault on women and the unborn. Sebelius vetoed legislation strengthening Kansas' late-term abortion law and prohibiting partial-birth abortion. Meanwhile, Parkinson vetoed a measure eliminating state funding for Planned Parenthood, and then subsequently eliminated all state funding of abortion alternatives, endangering the health and welfare of women who do not want to end their pregnancies.

ABORTION:

- Under Kansas law, a physician may not perform an abortion until at least 24 hours after a woman has received complete and accurate information on the proposed abortion method; the risks of the proposed abortion method; the probable gestational age of the unborn child; the probable anatomical and physiological development of the unborn child; the medical risks of carrying a pregnancy to term; and the name of the physician who will perform the abortion. The woman must also be provided written information on medical assistance benefits, agencies offering alternatives to abortion, the father's legal liability, and the development of the unborn child.

- Women must also be given contact information for perinatal hospices and a list of organizations that provide free ultrasound examinations. Abortion providers must inform women the state-mandated written materials are also available online.

- Abortion providers must offer the opportunity to see an ultrasound image if an ultrasound is used in preparation for the abortion.

- The state includes information about the abortion-breast cancer link in the educational materials a woman must receive prior to abortion.

- The state requires abortion providers to state in their printed materials that it is illegal for someone to coerce a woman into having an abortion. Clinics must also post signs stating it is illegal to force a woman to have an abortion.

- A physician may not perform an abortion on an unemancipated minor under the age of 18 until notice has been given to one parent or a court order has been issued.

- Any physician who performs an abortion on a minor under the age of 14 must retain fetal

tissue extracted during the procedure and send it to the Kansas Bureau of Investigation. The tissue is to be submitted "for the purpose of DNA testing and examination" and will be used to investigate incidents of child rape and sexual abuse.

- Kansas prohibits public funds from being used for abortions unless the procedure is necessary to preserve the life of the woman or the pregnancy is the result of rape or incest.

- Contracts with the Kansas Department of Health and Environment's pregnancy maintenance program may not be awarded to groups that promote, refer for, or educate in favor of abortion.

- In addition, abortions may not be performed in any facility, hospital, or clinic owned, leased, or operated by the University of Kansas Hospital Authority unless necessary to preserve a woman's life or prevent "a serious risk of substantial and irreversible impairment of a major bodily function."

- Kansas prohibits partial-birth abortion after viability.

- Kansas permits abortions after viability only when an abortion provider has the documented referral from another physician not legally or financially affiliated with the abortion provider and both physicians determine: (1) The abortion is necessary to preserve the life of the pregnant woman; or (2) a continuation of the pregnancy will cause a substantial and irreversible impairment of a major bodily function of the pregnant woman.

- Kansas has an enforceable abortion reporting law, but does not require the reporting of information to the Centers for Disease Control and Prevention (CDC). The measure applies to both surgical and nonsurgical abortions.

LEGAL RECOGNITION OF UNBORN AND NEWLY BORN:

- Under Kansas law, an "unborn child" (from fertilization to birth) is a possible victim of murder, manslaughter, vehicular manslaughter, and battery.

- Kansas defines criminal assaults on a pregnant woman that result in miscarriage, stillbirth, or "damage to pregnancy" as an enhanced offense for sentencing purposes.

- The state allows wrongful death (civil) actions when a viable unborn child is killed through a negligent or criminal act.

- Kansas law requires that an attending physician take "all reasonable steps necessary to maintain the life and health" of a child who survives an attempted abortion at any stage of development.

BIOETHICS LAWS:

- Kansas maintains no laws regarding human cloning or assisted reproductive technologies.

- However, the state has enacted a measure promoting morally-responsible growth of the biotechnology industry. The state has specifically indicated the terms "bioscience," "biotechnology," and "life sciences" shall not be construed to include 1) induced human abortions or the use of cells or tissues derived therefrom, and 2) any research the federal funding of which would be contrary to federal laws.

END OF LIFE LAWS:

- In Kansas, assisting a suicide is a felony.

- Kansas maintains a "Pain Patient's Bill of Rights," which, among other provisions, allows physicians to prescribe a dosage of opiates deemed medically necessary to relieve pain. The law does not expand the scope of medical practice to allow physician-assisted suicide or euthanasia.

HEALTHCARE RIGHTS OF CONSCIENCE LAWS:

Participation in Abortion:

- No person may be required to participate in medical procedures that result in abortion.

- No hospital may be required to perform abortions in its facilities.

- The state provides some protection for the civil rights of pharmacists and pharmacies.

Participation in Research Harmful to Human Life:

- Kansas currently provides no protection for the rights of healthcare providers who conscientiously object to participation in human cloning, destructive embryo research, or other forms of immoral medical research.

WHAT HAPPENED IN 2009:

- Prior to her appointment as U.S. Secretary of Health and Human Services, then-Governor Kathleen Sebelius once again vetoed life-affirming measures. In addition to vetoing a bill that would have strengthened Kansas' law prohibiting late-term abortions, Sebelius vetoed a measure prohibiting partial-birth abortion.

- However, Sebelius signed a measure requiring an abortion provider to offer the woman the opportunity to see an ultrasound image if ultrasound is used in preparation for the abortion. Under the new law, abortion clinics must also post signs stating that it is illegal to force a woman to have an abortion. In addition, state informed consent materials must now include contact information for perinatal hospices and a list of organizations that provide free ultrasound examinations. Finally, abortion providers must inform women that the state-mandated written materials are also available online.

- Sebelius' successor, Governor Mark Parkinson, vetoed language in the budget bill that would have allowed funding for Planned Parenthood to lapse. And while the state legislature allocated $355,000 to abortion alternatives, Parkinson subsequently eliminated all state funding for abortion alternatives.

- The state considered a measure aimed at providing better pain relief and treatment to patients.

- Kansas did not consider any measures related to bioethics or healthcare rights of conscience.

RECOMMENDATIONS FOR KANSAS		
	Short-term Priorities	**Additional Goals**
	ABORTION	
Informed Consent	Fetal pain counseling	
Parental Involvement		Amend parental notice law to require parental consent
State Rights & Policies	Resolution opposing federal FOCA	
Abortion Funding		
Abortion Provider Requirements	Comprehensive abortion clinic regulations beginning in first trimester	
Abortion Bans		
Regulation of Abortifacients		Regulation of RU-486
PCCs Support		Funding for PCCs and/or "Choose Life" license plates
Abortion Reporting		
LEGAL RECOGNITION AND PROTECTION FOR UNBORN & NEWLY BORN		
Fetal Homicide		
Assault on Unborn		
Prohibitions on Wrongful Birth & Wrongful Life Lawsuits		
Permit Wrongful Death Lawsuits		

Born-Alive Infant Protection		
Abandoned Infant Protection		
BIOETHICS		
Human Cloning		Ban on human cloning
DER		Ban on DER
State Funding of DER	Ban on state funding of DER	
ART & IVF		Any medically-appropriate regulation of ART
END OF LIFE		
Assisted Suicide		
Pain Management Education		
RIGHTS OF CONSCIENCE		
Protection for Individual Providers	Comprehensive ROC protection	
Protection for Institutions	Comprehensive ROC protection	
Protection for Payers	Comprehensive ROC protection	

KENTUCKY
RANKING: 12

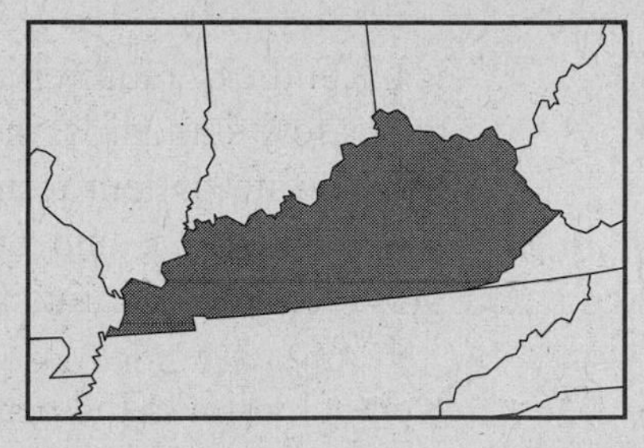

Kentucky has made great strides in protecting women and the unborn through its informed consent law, parental involvement law, abortion clinic regulations, and inclusion of unborn children under the protection of its homicide laws. The state also provides rights of conscience protection to certain healthcare providers. On the other hand, life-affirming regulations are still needed in the areas of human cloning and destructive embryo research.

ABORTION:

- Under Kentucky law, a physician may not perform an abortion until at least 24 hours after a woman has received information about the probable gestational age of her unborn child; the nature and risks of the proposed abortion procedure; and alternatives to abortion and the medical risks of carrying the pregnancy to term. She must also be told that state-prepared materials are available for her review, medical assistance may be available, and the father is liable for child support even if he offered to pay for the abortion.

- A physician may not perform an abortion on an unemancipated minor under the age of 18 until one parent consents or a court order is issued.

- Kentucky's legislature has declared its opposition to abortion, stating if the U.S. Constitution is amended or certain judicial decisions are reversed or modified, the recognition and protection of the lives of all human beings "regardless of their degree of biological development shall be fully restored."

- Kentucky prohibits public funds from being used for abortions unless the procedure is necessary to preserve the life of the woman or the pregnancy is the result of rape or incest.

- Kentucky prohibits organizations that receive state funds from using those funds to provide abortion counseling or to make referrals for abortion.

- All health insurance contracts, plans, and policies must exclude coverage for abortion unless the procedure is necessary to preserve the woman's life.

- Kentucky restricts the use of some or all state facilities for the performance of abortion.

- Kentucky has enacted comprehensive health and safety requirements for abortion clin-

ics. Kentucky requires abortion clinics meet licensing requirements and minimum health and safety standards, including maintaining written policies and procedures, conducting appropriate patient testing, ensuring proper staffing, maintaining necessary equipment and medication, and providing appropriate post-operative care. Further, all abortion providers must maintain admitting privileges.

- Kentucky limits the performance of abortions to licensed physicians.

- The state offers "Choose Life" license plates, the proceeds of which benefit pregnancy care centers and/or other organizations providing abortion alternatives.

- Kentucky has an enforceable abortion reporting law, but does not require the reporting of information to the Centers for Disease Control and Prevention (CDC). The measure applies to both surgical and nonsurgical abortions.

- Hospitals with emergency room services may not counsel victims of reported sexual offenses on abortion.

- Kentucky requires insurers providing prescription drug coverage for individual and small employers to offer contraceptive coverage.

LEGAL RECOGNITION OF UNBORN AND NEWLY BORN:

- The definition of "person" for purposes of Kentucky homicide laws includes "an unborn child from the moment of conception."

- Kentucky allows parents and other relatives to bring wrongful death (civil) lawsuits when a viable unborn child is killed through the negligence of another.

- Kentucky has enacted a "Baby Moses" law, under which a mother or legal guardian who is unable to care for a newborn infant may anonymously and safely leave the infant in the care of a responsible person at a hospital, police station, fire station, or other prescribed location.

- In 2008, Kentucky enacted legislation allocating $2 million over two years for substance abuse prevention and treatment programs for pregnant women. Healthcare professionals must test newborns for prenatal drug exposure when there is suspicion of prenatal drug use or abuse.

BIOETHICS LAWS:

- Kentucky maintains no laws regarding human cloning or destructive embryo research, but it does ban fetal experimentation.

- The state prohibits the use of public funds for assisted reproductive technologies.

END OF LIFE LAWS:

- In Kentucky, assisting a suicide is a felony.

HEALTHCARE RIGHTS OF CONSCIENCE LAWS:

Participation in Abortion:

- A physician, nurse, hospital staff member, or hospital employee who objects in writing and on religious, moral, or professional grounds is not required to participate in an abortion. Kentucky law also protects medical and nursing students.

- Private healthcare facilities and hospitals are not required to permit the performance of abortions if such performance violates the stated policy of that facility.

Participation in Research Harmful to Human Life:

- Kentucky currently provides no protection for the rights of healthcare providers who conscientiously object to participation in human cloning, destructive embryo research, or other forms of immoral medical research.

WHAT HAPPENED IN 2009:

- Kentucky considered measures strengthening its informed consent law, requiring an abortion provider to perform an ultrasound prior to abortion, and modifying the state's currently unenforceable partial-birth abortion ban to mirror federal law. The state also considered a bill expressing the legislature's support for pregnancy care centers and urging the U.S. Congress to grant pregnancy care centers assistance to purchase medical equipment and provide abstinence education without compromising the mission or integrity of those organizations.

- Conversely, Kentucky considered a bill requiring insurance coverage of contraception.

- The state also considered a measure related to health insurance coverage for the diagno-

sis and treatment of infertility.

- Kentucky did not consider any measures related to healthcare rights of conscience.

RECOMMENDATIONS FOR KENTUCKY		
	Short-term Priorities	**Additional Goals**
ABORTION		
Informed Consent	Ultrasound requirement	Enhancements like counseling on fetal pain or coercion
Parental Involvement		Enhancements like notarized consent or identification requirements
State Rights & Policies		
Abortion Funding		
Abortion Provider Requirements		
Abortion Bans		Sex-selective abortion ban or "delayed enforcement" law
Regulation of Abortifacients		Regulation of RU-486
PCCs Support	Direct funding for PCCs	
Abortion Reporting		Reporting of complications
LEGAL RECOGNITION AND PROTECTION FOR UNBORN & NEWLY BORN		
Fetal Homicide		
Assault on Unborn		
Prohibitions on Wrongful Birth & Wrongful Life Lawsuits		
Permit Wrongful Death Lawsuits		

Born-Alive Infant Protection	Law requiring care for infant who survives an abortion	
Abandoned Infant Protection		
BIOETHICS		
Human Cloning		Ban on human cloning
DER		Ban on DER
State Funding of DER	Ban on state funding of DER	
ART & IVF		Any medically-appropriate regulation of ART
END OF LIFE		
Assisted Suicide		
Pain Management Education		
RIGHTS OF CONSCIENCE		
Protection for Individual Providers	Comprehensive ROC protection	
Protection for Institutions	Comprehensive ROC protection	
Protection for Payers	Comprehensive ROC protection	

LOUISIANA

RANKING: 1

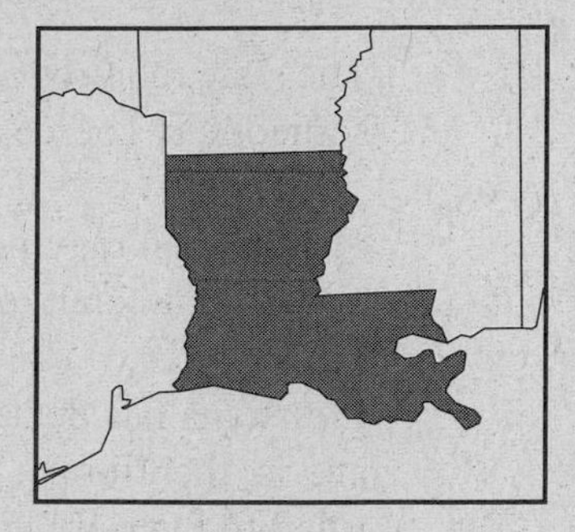

Louisiana maintains some of the most comprehensive and protective regulations regarding the health and safety of women seeking abortions and the protection of the unborn. In addition, while the state does not ban human cloning, it bans fetal experimentation, restricts the destruction of human embryos for research, and prohibits the public funding of human cloning.

ABORTION:

- A physician may not perform an abortion until at least 24 hours after a woman has been provided information about the proposed abortion procedure; the alternatives to abortion; the probable gestational age of the unborn child; the risks associated with abortion; and the risks associated with carrying the child to term. She must also be told about available medical assistance benefits; the father's legal responsibilities; and that her consent for an abortion may be withdrawn or withheld without any loss of government benefits.

- Louisiana also provides a booklet describing the development of the unborn child; describing abortion methods and their risks; providing a list of public and private agencies, including adoption agencies, that are available to provide assistance; providing information about state medical assistance benefits; and describing a physician's liability for failing to obtain her informed consent prior to an abortion.

- In addition, a woman considering abortion must receive information about fetal pain and also be given the option to undergo and review an ultrasound prior to an abortion. The woman must be told about the availability of anesthesia or analgesics to prevent pain to the unborn child. The mandatory informed consent materials state that, by 20 weeks gestation, an unborn child can experience and respond to pain and that anesthesia is routinely administered to unborn children for prenatal surgery at 20 weeks gestation or later.

- Louisiana requires an ultrasound at 20 weeks gestation and beyond to determine viability, and it requires the abortion provider offer the woman the opportunity to view the image.

- A woman seeking an abortion following rape or incest and using state funds to pay for the abortion must be offered the same informed consent information (without the 24-hour reflection period) as is required for other abortions in the state.

The state requires abortion providers to state in their printed materials that it is illegal for someone to coerce a woman into having an abortion.

- A physician may not perform an abortion on an unemancipated minor under the age of 18 without notarized, written consent from one parent or a court order.

- Louisiana has declared "the unborn child is a human being from the time of conception and is, therefore, a legal person for purposes of the unborn child's right to life and is entitled to the right to life from conception under the laws and Constitution of this state."

- Louisiana taxpayers are not required to fund abortions except when the abortion is necessary to preserve the woman's health or the pregnancy is the result of rape or incest.

- Louisiana prohibits organizations that receive public funds from using those funds to provide abortion counseling or to make referrals for abortion. The state has also enacted restrictions on the use of some or all state facilities for the performance of abortion.

- Louisiana requires the licensing of abortion clinics and imposes minimum health and safety standards in a variety of areas, including clinic administration, professional qualifications, patient testing, physical plant, and post-operative care. Abortion providers must maintain admitting privileges.

- Only physicians licensed to practice medicine in Louisiana may perform abortions.

- Louisiana has enacted a measure banning all abortions once *Roe v. Wade* is overturned. While the ban includes an exception for life endangerment, there is no exception for rape or incest.

- Louisiana bans partial-birth abortion throughout pregnancy, providing the banned procedure may be used only when necessary to save the life of the woman. The measure creates a civil cause of action for violations of the ban. It also contains more stringent criminal penalties than a similar federal law, imposing a sentence of hard labor or imprisonment for one to ten years and/or a fine of $10,000 to $100,000.

- Louisiana directly funds programs providing support for groups and organizations promoting abortion alternatives.

- Louisiana also offers "Choose Life" license plates, the proceeds of which benefit pregnancy care centers and/or other organizations providing abortion alternatives.

- The state has an enforceable abortion reporting law, but does not require the reporting of information to the Centers for Disease Control and Prevention (CDC). The measure requires abortion providers to report short-term complications and the name and address of the hospital of facility where treatment was provided for the complications.

LEGAL RECOGNITION OF UNBORN AND NEWLY BORN:

- Under Louisiana criminal law, the killing of an unborn child at any stage of gestation is defined as a form of homicide. In addition, an "unborn child" is a victim of feticide if killed during the perpetration of certain crimes, including robbery and cruelty to juveniles.

- Louisiana defines a nonfatal assault on an unborn child as a criminal offenses.

- The state allows wrongful death (civil) actions when an unborn child at any stage of gestation is killed through a negligent or criminal act.

- The state has created a specific affirmative duty of physicians to provide medical care and treatment to born-alive infants at any stage of development.

- Under the "Children's Code," "neglect" includes instances when a newborn is identified by a healthcare provider as having been affected by prenatal drug use or exhibiting symptoms of withdrawal. In 2007, Louisiana expanded the definition of "prenatal neglect" to include 1) "exposure to chronic or severe use of alcohol;" 2) the use of any controlled dangerous substance "in a manner not lawfully prescribed" that results in symptoms of withdrawal to the newborn; 3) the presence of a controlled substance or related metabolite in the newborn; or 4) observable and harmful effects in the newborn's appearance or functioning. The measure requires reporting by physicians to the appropriate state agency. The state also funds drug treatment programs for pregnant women and newborns.

BIOETHICS LAWS:

- Louisiana restricts the destruction of embryos that have been created through *in vitro* fertilization.

- Louisiana bans fetal experimentation and includes "embryo" as a stage of life protected by statute. While Louisiana has no specific statute banning human cloning, this statute may be interpreted to prohibit conducting harmful experimentation on cloned human embryos.The state also prohibits the public funding of cloning for any purpose.

- Louisiana bans the creation of chimeras, human-animal hybrids.

- By law, IVF-created embryos are defined as juridical (legal) persons.
- Louisiana law allows for embryo adoption if the biological parents renounce parental rights.

END OF LIFE LAWS:

- In Louisiana, assisted suicide is a felony.

HEALTHCARE RIGHTS OF CONSCIENCE LAWS:

Participation in Abortion:

- A physician, nurse, medical or nursing student, social service agency employee, or other person, hospital, medical facility, or corporation may not be held civilly or criminally liable or be discriminated against for refusing to recommend, counsel, perform, assist, or accommodate an abortion for any reason.
- A hospital or medical facility may not be denied government assistance, be discriminated against, or be pressured in any way for refusing to permit its facilities, staff, or employees to be used in any way for the purpose of performing an abortion.

Participation in Research Harmful to Human Life:

- Louisiana currently provides no protection for the rights of healthcare providers who conscientiously object to participation in human cloning, destructive embryo research, or other forms of immoral medical research.

WHAT HAPPENED IN 2009:

- Louisiana enacted legislation banning the creation of human-animal hybrids. It is the first ban of its kind in the nation.
- The state also enacted comprehensive healthcare rights of conscience legislation allowing a person, employer, or public or private entity to elect not to provide any healthcare service that violates his/her/its conscience.
- Louisiana enacted measures providing $1.5 million to groups providing abortion alternatives and establishing the "Louisiana Right To Life Education Committee" to review grant applications for organizations seeking revenue raised by the state's "Choose Life" license plates.

- Finally, the state passed resolutions for two end-of-life studies. The first study requests the State Department of Health and Hospitals to study the use of living wills among Medicaid recipients, while the second creates a study committee to look at physician orders for life-sustaining care.

RECOMMENDATIONS FOR LOUISIANA		
	Short-term Priorities	**Additional Goals**
	ABORTION	
Informed Consent	Coerced abortion prevention	
Parental Involvement		
State Rights & Policies	Resolution opposing federal FOCA	
Abortion Funding		
Abortion Provider Requirements		
Abortion Bans	Sex-selective abortion ban	
Regulation of Abortifacients	Regulation of RU-486	
PCCs Support		
Abortion Reporting		
	LEGAL RECOGNITION AND PROTECTION FOR UNBORN & NEWLY BORN	
Fetal Homicide		
Assault on Unborn		
Prohibitions on Wrongful Birth & Wrongful Life Lawsuits		Prohibitions on wrongful birth and wrongful life lawsuits
Permit Wrongful Death Lawsuits		

Born-Alive Infant Protection		
Abandoned Infant Protection		
BIOETHICS		
Human Cloning		Ban on human cloning
DER		Ban on DER
State Funding of DER		
ART & IVF		Any medically-appropriate regulation of ART
END OF LIFE		
Assisted Suicide		
Pain Management Education		
RIGHTS OF CONSCIENCE		
Protection for Individual Providers		
Protection for Institutions		
Protection for Payers	Comprehensive ROC protection	

MAINE

RANKING: 29

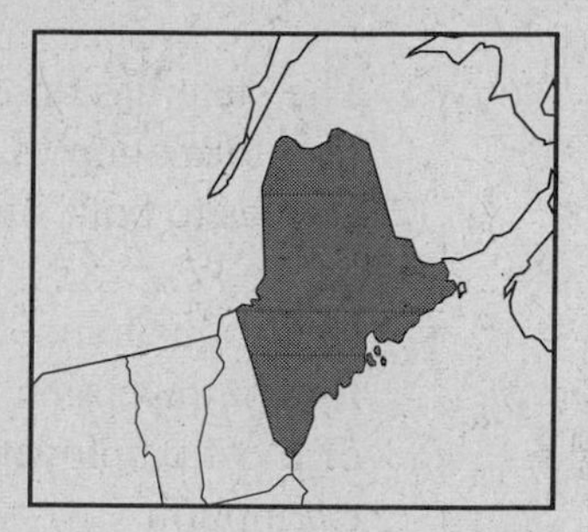

Maine provides limited protection to women seeking abortion and has taken a lead in banning fetal experimentation. Conversely, Maine is in the minority of states failing to provide any protection to unborn victims of violence, providing instead that an assault on a pregnant woman has only one victim: the woman.

ABORTION:

- A physician may not perform an abortion on a woman until after advising her of the probable gestational age of the unborn child; the risks associated with continued pregnancy and the proposed abortion procedure; and, at the woman's request, alternatives to abortion and information about and a list of public and private agencies that will provide assistance if the woman chooses to carry the pregnancy to term.

- A physician may not perform an abortion on a minor under the age of 18 until after advising her about the alternatives to abortion, prenatal care, agencies providing assistance, and the possibility of involving her parents or other adult family members in her decision. Moreover, the physician must have the written consent of one parent or adult family member unless the minor is mentally and physically competent to give consent or has secured a court order.

- The state maintains a "Freedom of Choice Act." The Act mandates the right to abortion even if *Roe v. Wade* is eventually overturned, specifically providing that it is the public policy of Maine not to restrict access to abortion before viability.

- Maine taxpayers are not required to fund abortions unless the abortion is necessary to preserve the woman's life or the pregnancy is the result of rape or incest.

- Only physicians licensed to practice medicine or osteopathy by the state of Maine may perform abortions.

- Prior to the FDA's August 2006 decision allowing over-the-counter distribution of Plan B, Maine allowed licensed pharmacists who had completed special training and developed a standardized protocol in consultation with a physician or licensed prescriber to dispense "emergency contraception" without a prescription and without the direct involvement of a physician.

- The state has an enforceable abortion reporting law, but does not require the reporting of information to the Centers for Disease Control and Prevention (CDC). The measure applies to both surgical and nonsurgical abortions.

- Health insurance plans that provide prescription coverage must also provide coverage for contraception. The provision includes an exemption so narrow it excludes the ability of most employers and insurers with moral or religious objections from exercising the exemption.

LEGAL RECOGNITION OF UNBORN AND NEWLY BORN:

- Maine does not currently recognize an unborn child as a potential victim of homicide or assault.

- Instead, Maine provides for an enhanced sentence for the homicide of a pregnant woman and has created a new crime of "elevated aggravated assault" on a pregnant woman.

- The state allows wrongful death (civil) actions only when an unborn child is born alive following a negligent or criminal act and dies thereafter.

- Maine has created a specific affirmative duty of physicians to provide medical care and treatment to born-alive infants at any stage of development.

- Maine also has a "Baby Moses" law, establishing a safe haven for mothers to legally leave their infants at designated places and ensuring that the infants receive appropriate care and protection.

- Maine provides for the issuance of a certificate of birth resulting in stillbirth when requested by the parents.

BIOETHICS LAWS:

- Maine does not maintain laws regarding human cloning or assisted reproductive technologies, but bans live fetal experimentation. A "fetus" is defined as being either intrauterine or extra-uterine. Thus, its fetal experimentation statute could be read to prohibit harmful experimentation on cloned human embryos.

END OF LIFE LAWS:

- In Maine, assisting a suicide is a felony.

HEALTHCARE RIGHTS OF CONSCIENCE LAWS:

Participation in Abortion:

- The conscientious objection of a physician, nurse, or other healthcare worker to perform or assist in the performance of an abortion may not be the basis for civil liability, discrimination in employment or education, or other recriminatory action. This includes protection for medical and nursing students.

- The conscientious objection of a hospital or other healthcare facility to permit an abortion on its premises may not be the basis for civil liability or recriminatory action.

- Private institutions, physicians, or their agents may refuse to provide family planning services based upon religious or conscientious objection.

- The state provides some protection for the civil rights of pharmacists and pharmacies.

Participation in Research Harmful to Human Life:

- Maine currently provides no protection for the rights of healthcare providers who conscientiously object to participation in human cloning, destructive embryo research, or other forms of immoral medical research.

WHAT HAPPENED IN 2009:

- Maine did not consider any measures related to abortion, but did enact a law providing for the issuance of a certificate of birth resulting in stillbirth when requested by the parents. The state also considered a measure requiring the State Department of Health and Human Services to receive reports on infants who may be affected by illegal substance abuse or suffering withdrawal symptoms from prenatal drug exposure.

- Maine enacted two end-of-life measures, with the first developing two education programs about end-of-life directives for the public and the legal community, and the second creating a "Uniform Power of Attorney Act" relating to durable healthcare powers of attorney.

- Maine considered a measure supporting adult stem cell research and establishing an umbilical cord blood bank.

- Maine did not consider any measures related to healthcare rights of conscience.

RECOMMENDATIONS FOR MAINE		
	Short-term Priorities	**Additional Goals**
ABORTION		
Informed Consent	Comprehensive informed consent law with reflection period	
Parental Involvement		
State Rights & Policies	Repeal of state FOCA	
Abortion Funding	Limitations on use of state funding for abortion counseling and referrals	Limits on using state facilities for abortions
Abortion Provider Requirements		Abortion clinic regulations
Abortion Bans		
Regulation of Abortifacients		Regulation of administration of RU-486 and abortifacients
PCCs Support		Funding of PCCs
Abortion Reporting		
LEGAL RECOGNITION AND PROTECTION FOR UNBORN & NEWLY BORN		
Fetal Homicide	Law protecting unborn child at any stage of development	
Assault on Unborn		
Prohibitions on Wrongful Birth & Wrongful Life Lawsuits		

Permit Wrongful Death Lawsuits	Law permitting wrongful death causes of action for the death of unborn children	
Born-Alive Infant Protection		
Abandoned Infant Protection		
BIOETHICS		
Human Cloning		Ban on human cloning
DER		Ban on DER
State Funding of DER	Ban on state funding of DER	
ART & IVF		Any medically-appropriate regulation of ART
END OF LIFE		
Assisted Suicide		
Pain Management Education		
RIGHTS OF CONSCIENCE		
Protection for Individual Providers	Comprehensive ROC protection	
Protection for Institutions	Comprehensive ROC protection	
Protection for Payers	Comprehensive ROC protection	

MARYLAND

RANKING: 40

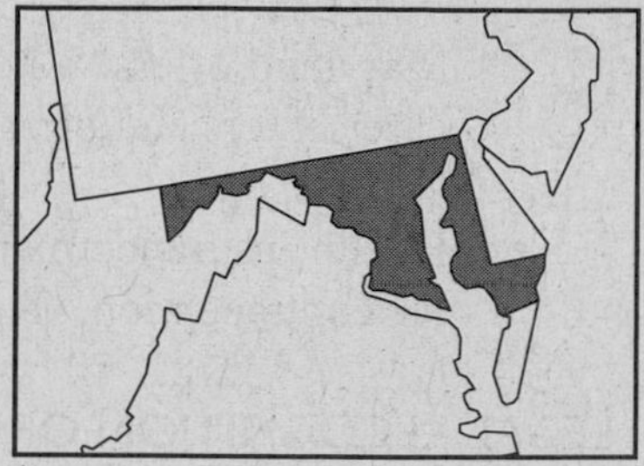

Maryland provides virtually no protection for women and minors seeking abortion. It does not have an informed consent law or abortion clinic regulations, and its parental notice law contains a loophole that eviscerates the protection this requirement typically provides. The state also allows and funds destructive embryo research.

ABORTION:

- Maryland does not have an informed consent law, a meaningful parental notice law, or abortion clinic regulations ensuring the health and safety of women undergoing abortions.

- Under current Maryland law, an unmarried minor under the age of 18 who lives with a parent may not undergo an abortion unless one parent has been notified by the physician. However, the law contains a significant loophole: A minor may obtain an abortion without parental notification if, in the professional judgment of the physician, notice to the parent may lead to physical or emotional abuse of the minor; the minor is mature and capable of giving informed consent to an abortion; or notice would not be in the "best interests" of the minor.

- The state maintains a "Freedom of Choice Act." The Act mandates the right to abortion even if *Roe v. Wade* is eventually overturned, specifically providing the state may not "interfere with the decision of a woman to terminate a pregnancy" before the fetus is viable, or if the procedure is necessary to protect the life or health of the woman, or if the unborn child is afflicted by a genetic defect or serious deformity.

- Maryland taxpayers are required to pay for "medically necessary" abortions when the continuation of the pregnancy is likely to result in the woman's death; the woman is a victim of rape, incest, or another sexual offense reported to a law enforcement, public health, or social agency; the unborn child is affected by a genetic defect or serious deformity or abnormality; there is a substantial risk that the continuation of the pregnancy could have serious and adverse affects on the woman's present or future health; or there is a substantial risk that continuation of the pregnancy is creating a serious issue for the woman's present mental health and, if carried to term, there is a substantial risk of serious or long-lasting effects on the woman's future mental health.

- Only physicians licensed in the state may perform abortions.

- Maryland offers "Choose Life" license plates, the proceeds of which benefit pregnancy care centers and/or other organizations providing abortion alternatives.

- Health insurance plans that provide prescription coverage must also provide coverage for contraception. There is an exemption for religious employers.

LEGAL RECOGNITION OF UNBORN AND NEWLY BORN:

- Maryland recognizes a "viable fetus" as a distinct victim of murder, manslaughter, or unlawful homicide. However, the law explicitly states its enactment should not be construed as conferring "personhood" on the fetus.

- The state allows wrongful death (civil) actions when a viable unborn child is killed through a negligent or criminal act.

- Maryland law does not require physicians to provide appropriate medical care to an infant who survives an abortion.

- Maryland has a "Baby Moses" law, establishing a safe haven for mothers to legally leave their infants up to 10 days of age at designated places and ensuring the infants receive appropriate care and protection.

- Maryland law provides that a child is not receiving proper care if he or she is born exposed to methamphetamine or if the mother tests positive for methamphetamine upon admission to the hospital for delivery of the infant. The state funds drug treatment programs for pregnant women and newborns.

BIOETHICS LAWS:

- Maryland maintains a "Stem Cell Research Fund" and allows and funds destructive embryonic research, but prohibits research leading to human cloning.

- Educational materials on umbilical cord blood donation are to be distributed to all pregnant patients.

- Maryland regulates insurance coverage of assisted reproductive technologies.

END OF LIFE LAWS:

- In Maryland, assisting a suicide is considered a felony.

HEALTHCARE RIGHTS OF CONSCIENCE LAWS:

Participation in Abortion:

- Under Maryland law, no person may be required to participate in or refer to any source for medical procedures that result in an abortion.

- A hospital is not required to permit the performance of abortions within its facilities or to provide referrals for abortions.

Participation in Research Harmful to Human Life:

- Maryland currently provides no protection for the rights of healthcare providers who conscientiously object to participation in human cloning, destructive embryo research, or other forms of immoral medical research.

WHAT HAPPENED IN 2009:

- Maryland enacted a provision continuing the state's policy of funding "medically necessary" abortions.

- The state also enacted an end-of-life provision altering the membership of the state Advisory Council on Quality Care at the End of Life to include a representative from the nursing home industry.

- Maryland considered a measure amending the state constitution to grant a right to unborn children "not to be deprived of life." It also considered a measure requiring ultrasound before abortion in certain facilities.

- Maryland also considered measures related to destructive embryo research and insurance coverage for infertility.

- The state did not consider any measures related to healthcare rights of conscience.

RECOMMENDATIONS FOR MARYLAND		
	Short-term Priorities	**Additional Goals**
	ABORTION	
Informed Consent	Comprehensive informed consent law with reflection period	
Parental Involvement	Parental notice (without existing loophole)	
State Rights & Policies	Repeal of state FOCA	
Abortion Funding	Limitations on state funding consistent with Hyde Amendment	
Abortion Provider Requirements		Abortion clinic regulations
Abortion Bans		
Regulation of Abortifacients		Regulation of RU-486
PCCs Support		
Abortion Reporting		Mandatory reporting on abortion including complications
	LEGAL RECOGNITION AND PROTECTION FOR UNBORN & NEWLY BORN	
Fetal Homicide	Law protecting unborn child at any stage of development	
Assault on Unborn		
Prohibitions on Wrongful Birth & Wrongful Life Lawsuits		
Permit Wrongful Death Lawsuits		

Born-Alive Infant Protection	Law requiring care for infant who survives abortion	
Abandoned Infant Protection		
BIOETHICS		
Human Cloning		Ban on human cloning
DER		Ban on DER
State Funding of DER	Ban on state funding of DER	
ART & IVF		Any medically-appropriate regulation of ART
END OF LIFE		
Assisted Suicide		
Pain Management Education		
RIGHTS OF CONSCIENCE		
Protection for Individual Providers	Comprehensive ROC protection	
Protection for Institutions	Comprehensive ROC protection	
Protection for Payers	Comprehensive ROC protection	

MASSACHUSETTS
RANKING: 38

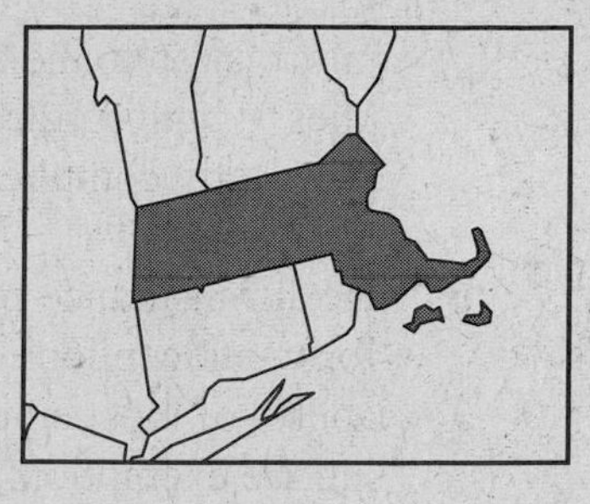

Massachusetts continues to lack enforceable abortion clinic regulations and fails to protect unborn victims of violence. Further, the state allows both human cloning-for-biomedical-research and destructive embryo research. Healthcare providers who conscientiously object to such research also remain unprotected.

ABORTION:

- A court has enjoined the enforcement of Massachusetts' informed consent law.
- A physician may not perform an abortion on an unmarried minor under the age of 18 without the written consent of one parent or a court order.
- The Massachusetts Constitution has been interpreted as providing a broader right to abortion than that provided by the U.S. Constitution.
- Massachusetts taxpayers are required to pay for "medically necessary" abortions and for abortions which result from rape or incest reported to a law enforcement agency or public health service within 60 days of the incident.
- State employee health insurance provides coverage of abortion only when a woman's life or health is endangered or in cases of rape, incest, or fetal abnormality, and may not cover partial-birth abortions. Further, health maintenance organizations (HMOs) may not be required to provide payment or referrals for an abortion unless necessary to preserve the woman's life.
- Massachusetts' requirement that abortions after the 12th week of pregnancy be performed in hospitals is, under current U.S. Supreme Court precedent, unenforceable.
- Only physicians authorized to practice medicine in the state of Massachusetts may perform abortions.
- Massachusetts requires that sexual assault victims receive information about and access to "emergency contraception" in hospital emergency rooms. The state also allows pharmacists to dispense "emergency contraception" directly and without a prescription.
- The state has an enforceable abortion reporting law, but does not require the reporting of

information to the Centers for Disease Control and Prevention (CDC). The measure applies to both surgical and nonsurgical abortions and requires abortion providers to report short-term complications.

- Health insurance plans that provide prescription coverage must also provide coverage for contraception. The provision includes an exemption so narrow that it excludes the ability of most employers and insurers with moral or religious objections from exercising the exemption.

LEGAL RECOGNITION OF UNBORN AND NEWLY BORN:

- The Massachusetts Supreme Court has determined the state's homicide law applies to the killing of an unborn child after viability.
- The state allows wrongful death (civil) actions when a viable unborn child is killed through negligent or criminal action.
- The state requires healthcare professionals to report suspected prenatal drug exposure.

BIOETHICS LAWS:

- While Massachusetts prohibits cloning-to-produce-children, it permits both cloning-for-biomedical-research and destructive embryo research (DER).
- The Massachusetts Public Health Council has reversed a rule put in place during the gubernatorial administration of Mitt Romney that prohibited scientists from creating human embryos for the purpose of destroying them for research.
- However, Massachusetts bans live fetal experimentation. Moreover, Massachusetts' fetal experimentation statute may be interpreted to prohibit harmful experimentation on cloned human embryos.
- Massachusetts has also created an umbilical cord bank.
- In 2008, Massachusetts appropriated $475 million to a life sciences fund for human cloning and stem cell research. The state had previously allocated $100 million to fund DER.
- The state regulates insurance coverage of assisted reproductive technologies.

END OF LIFE LAWS:

- In Massachusetts, assisting a suicide is a common law crime.

HEALTHCARE RIGHTS OF CONSCIENCE LAWS:

Participation in Abortion:

- A physician or person associated with, employed by, or on the medical staff of a hospital or health facility who objects in writing and on religious or moral grounds is not required to participate in abortions. Medical and nursing students are also protected.

- A private hospital or health facility is not required to admit a woman for an abortion.

Participation in Research Harmful to Human Life:

- Massachusetts currently provides no protection for the rights of healthcare providers who conscientiously object to participation in human cloning, destructive embryo research, or other forms of immoral medical research.

WHAT HAPPENED IN 2009:

- Massachusetts considered a measure requiring informed consent for abortion, but it also considered a measure that would have weakened its existing parental consent law. The state also considered a bill repealing the state's pre-*Roe* abortion ban as well as regulation of abortion providers.

- The state considered measures allowing for the adoption of human embryos and insurance coverage for infertility treatment.

- Massachusetts also considered measures promoting proper pain management for patients. Conversely, it also considered legislation allowing physician-assisted suicide.

- Massachusetts did not consider any measures related to healthcare rights of conscience.

RECOMMENDATIONS FOR MASSACHUSETTS		
	Short-term Priorities	**Additional Goals**
ABORTION		
Informed Consent	Comprehensive informed consent law with reflection period	
Parental Involvement		
State Rights & Policies	Amendment declaring no state constitutional right to abortion	
Abortion Funding		Limitations consistent with Hyde Amendment
Abortion Provider Requirements		Abortion clinic regulations
Abortion Bans		
Regulation of Abortifacients		Regulation of RU-486
PCCs Support		Funding of PCCs
Abortion Reporting		
LEGAL RECOGNITION AND PROTECTION FOR UNBORN & NEWLY BORN		
Fetal Homicide		
Assault on Unborn		
Prohibitions on Wrongful Birth & Wrongful Life Lawsuits		
Permit Wrongful Death Lawsuits		

Born-Alive Infant Protection	Law requiring care for infant who survives an abortion	
Abandoned Infant Protection		
BIOETHICS		
Human Cloning		Ban on human cloning
DER		Ban on DER
State Funding of DER	Ban on state funding of DER	
ART & IVF		Any medically-appropriate regulation of ART
END OF LIFE		
Assisted Suicide	Statutory prohibition on assisted suicide	
Pain Management Education		
RIGHTS OF CONSCIENCE		
Protection for Individual Providers	Comprehensive ROC protection	
Protection for Institutions	Comprehensive ROC protection	
Protection for Payers	Comprehensive ROC protection	

MICHIGAN

RANK: 15

Michigan protects women and the unborn in a number of ways, including requiring informed consent and parental consent before abortion. It also criminalizes assaults on unborn children. Unfortunately, Michigan reversed course in 2008 on destructive embryo research; while at one time it banned the practice, it now allows and funds such research. It also fails to protect healthcare providers who conscientiously object to participation in such research.

ABORTION:

- A physician may not perform an abortion on a woman until at least 24 hours after the woman receives information on the probable gestational age of her unborn child, along with state-prepared information or other material on prenatal care and parenting, the development of the unborn child, a description of abortion procedures and their inherent complications, and assistance and services available through public agencies.

- Women must be informed of the availability of ultrasounds and be given the opportunity to view the results of an ultrasound prior to abortion.

- A physician may not perform an abortion on an unemancipated minor under the age of 18 without the written consent of one parent or a court order.

- The Michigan Attorney General has issued opinions that the informed consent and parental consent statutes apply to both surgical abortions as well as the use of mifepristone (RU-486).

- Michigan taxpayers are not required to fund abortions except when the abortion is necessary to preserve the woman's life or the pregnancy is the result of rape or incest.

- Michigan prohibits organizations that receive state funds from using those funds to provide abortion counseling or to make referrals for abortion.

- State funds appropriated to community colleges may not be used to provide abortion coverage to employees or their dependents unless an abortion is necessary to preserve a woman's life.

- Michigan possesses an enforceable abortion prohibition should the U.S. Constitution be amended or certain U.S. Supreme Court decisions be reversed or modified.

- Under Michigan law, abortion clinics (where more than 50 percent of the patients served undergo abortions) are regulated as "freestanding surgical outpatient facilities." The regulations provide for minimum health and safety standards in such areas as clinic administration, professional qualifications, and physical plant.

- Michigan limits the performance of abortions to licensed physicians.

- Michigan has an enforceable abortion reporting law, but does not require the reporting of information to the Centers for Disease Control and Prevention (CDC). The measure applies to both surgical and nonsurgical abortions and requires abortion providers to report short-term complications.

- The Michigan Civil Rights Commission has issued a declaratory order that certain companies (with 15 or fewer employees) that offer prescription coverage must cover birth control. The state requires health maintenance organizations (HMOs) to cover prescription contraception or family planning services.

LEGAL RECOGNITION OF UNBORN AND NEWLY BORN:

- Under Michigan law, the killing of an unborn child at any stage of gestation is defined as a form of homicide.

- Michigan defines criminal assaults on a pregnant woman that result in miscarriage, stillbirth, or "damage to pregnancy" as an enhanced offense for sentencing purposes.

- Michigan defines a nonfatal assault on an unborn child as a crime.

- Michigan has applied the affirmative defense of "defense of others" to cases where a woman uses force (including deadly force) to protect her unborn child.

- The state allows wrongful death (civil) actions when an unborn child at any stage of development is killed through a negligent or criminal act.

- The state has created a specific affirmative duty of physicians to provide medical care and treatment to born-alive infants at any stage of development.

- Michigan requires healthcare professionals to report suspected prenatal drug exposure.

BIOETHICS LAWS:

- The voters in Michigan passed a "Stem Cell Initiative" in 2008, amending the state constitution to legalize destructive embryo research and to allow the funding of research on human embryos produced in fertility clinics.

- While Michigan bans both cloning-to-produce-children and cloning-for-biomedical-research, the effect of the "Stem Cell Initiative" passed in 2008 unknown. The Initiative contained no prohibition on human cloning.

- Michigan bans fetal experimentation.

- Michigan regulates the use and treatment of gametes, neonates, embryos, and/or fetuses. The state also regulates insurance coverage for assisted reproductive technologies.

END OF LIFE LAWS:

- In Michigan, assisting a suicide is a felony.

HEALTHCARE RIGHTS OF CONSCIENCE LAWS:

Participation in Abortion:

- A physician, nurse, medical student, nursing student, or individual who is a member of, associated with, or employed by a hospital, institution, teaching institution, or healthcare facility who objects on religious, moral, ethical, or professional grounds is not required to participate in abortions.

- A hospital, institution, teaching institution, or healthcare facility is not required to participate in abortion, permit an abortion on its premises, or admit a woman for the purposes of performing an abortion.

Participation in Research Harmful to Human Life:

- Michigan currently provides no protection for the rights of healthcare providers who conscientiously object to participation in human cloning, destructive embryo research, or other forms of immoral medical research.

WHAT HAPPENED IN 2009:

- The state enacted a measure condemning recent moves by the Obama Administration to rescind rules promulgated under President George W. Bush protecting the conscience rights of healthcare providers.

- Michigan considered measures banning partial-birth abortion, amending reporting requirements, criminalizing coercion, including "fetus" in the definition of an "individual" in the criminal code, banning sex-selective abortions, and creating "Choose Life" license plates.

- However, the state also considered measures that would have imposed draconian regulations on pregnancy care centers. In addition, the state considered measures expanding prescription coverage to include contraception and requiring emergency rooms to offer "emergency contraception" to assault victims.

- Michigan also considered measures regarding destructive embryo research and human cloning, supporting adult stem cell research, regulating assisted reproductive technologies, prohibiting the creation of human-animal hybrids (chimeras), and involving insurance coverage for infertility.

RECOMMENDATIONS FOR MICHIGAN		
	Short-term Priorities	**Additional Goals**
	ABORTION	
Informed Consent	Coerced abortion prevention	
Parental Involvement	Enhancements like notarized consent or identification requirements	
State Rights & Policies		
Abortion Funding		
Abortion Provider Requirements		
Abortion Bans		Sex-selective abortion ban
Regulation of Abortifacients	Regulation of RU-486	
PCCs Support	Funding of PCCs	
Abortion Reporting		
	LEGAL RECOGNITION AND PROTECTION FOR UNBORN & NEWLY BORN	
Fetal Homicide		
Assault on Unborn		
Prohibitions on Wrongful Birth & Wrongful Life Lawsuits		
Permit Wrongful Death Lawsuits		

Born-Alive Infant Protection		
Abandoned Infant Protection		
BIOETHICS		
Human Cloning		
DER		
State Funding of DER	Funding of ethical forms of stem cell research	
ART & IVF		Any medically-appropriate regulation of ART
END OF LIFE		
Assisted Suicide		
Pain Management Education		
RIGHTS OF CONSCIENCE		
Protection for Individual Providers	Comprehensive ROC protection	
Protection for Institutions	Comprehensive ROC protection	
Protection for Payers	Comprehensive ROC protection	

MINNESOTA

RANKING: 20

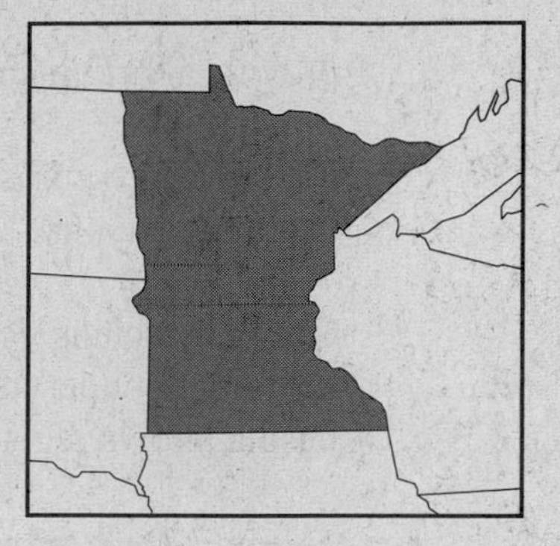

Minnesota provides comprehensive protection to unborn victims of violence and, over the past several years, has made significant strides in protecting women from the negative consequences of abortion. Minnesota has also warded off efforts to promote destructive embryo research and human cloning in the state. For example, in 2008, Governor Tim Pawlenty vetoed legislation that would have explicitly allowed destructive embryo research on cloned human embryos, and, in 2009, the state enacted legislation prohibiting taxpayer funding of human cloning.

ABORTION:

- Minnesota's informed consent law requires women be given information on the risks of and alternatives to abortion at least 24 hours prior to undergoing an abortion.

- Minnesota requires that a physician or his/her agent advise a woman seeking an abortion after 20 weeks gestation of the possibility that anesthesia would alleviate fetal pain.

- The state also explicitly requires a physician to inform a woman seeking an abortion of the link between abortion and breast cancer.

- Minnesota maintains a law prohibiting coerced abortions, defining "coercion" as "restraining or dominating the choice of a minor female by force, threat of force, or deprivation of food and shelter." The provision only applies to employees in government-run social programs and prohibits threatening to disqualify eligible recipients for their financial assistance if they do not obtain an abortion. The provision applies to older women as well as minors.

- Minnesota law provides that a physician may not perform an abortion on an unemancipated minor under the age of 18 until at least 48 hours after written notice has been delivered to both parents.

- The Minnesota constitution protects the "right to an abortion" as a fundamental right and to a broader extent than the U.S. Constitution.

- Minnesota taxpayers are required to fund "medically necessary" abortions.

- Minnesota prohibits organizations that receive state funds from using those funds to

provide abortion counseling or to make referrals for abortion.

- Minnesota requires that abortions after the first trimester be performed in a hospital or "abortion facility."

- Only physicians licensed to practice medicine by the state of Minnesota or physicians-in-training supervised by licensed physicians may perform abortions. However, Minnesota allows registered nurses to dispense all contraceptives.

- Hospitals must provide information about and access to "emergency contraception" to sexual assault victims. However, hospitals are not required to provide "emergency contraception" if it is contraindicated or if there is a positive pregnancy test.

- In 2005, Minnesota created the "Positive Alternatives Act." The law appropriates $5 million over four years to organizations that encourage women to carry their pregnancies to term.

- The state has an enforceable abortion reporting law, but does not require the reporting of information to the Centers for Disease Control and Prevention (CDC). The measure applies to both surgical and nonsurgical abortions and requires abortion providers to report short-term complications.

- The state requires health maintenance organizations (HMOs) to cover prescription contraception or family planning services.

LEGAL RECOGNITION OF UNBORN AND NEWLY BORN:

- Under Minnesota law, the killing of an unborn child at any stage of gestation is defined as a form of homicide.

- Minnesota defines a nonfatal assault on an unborn child as a criminal offense.

- Minnesota allows wrongful death (civil) actions when a viable unborn child is killed through a negligent or criminal act.

- The state has created a specific affirmative duty of physicians to provide medical care and treatment to born-alive infants but only after viability.

- A court may order a pregnant woman into an early intervention treatment program for substance abuse. Professionals, such as healthcare providers and law enforcement officers, must report the suspected abuse of a controlled substance by a pregnant woman.

In addition, healthcare professionals must test newborns for drug exposure when there is suspicion of prenatal drug use. The state funds drug treatment programs for pregnant women and newborns.

BIOETHICS LAWS:

- Minnesota has not enacted laws banning or regulating human cloning or assisted reproductive technologies.
- Minnesota bans live fetal experimentation. The statute may be interpreted to prohibit harmful experimentation on cloned human embryos.
- Minnesota prohibits the taxpayer funding of human cloning.

END OF LIFE LAWS:

- In Minnesota, assisting a suicide is a felony.

HEALTHCARE RIGHTS OF CONSCIENCE LAWS:

Participation in Abortion:

- Minnesota law provides that no person, hospital, or institution may be coerced, held liable for, or discriminated against in any way for refusing to perform, accommodate, or assist in an abortion.
- However, this rights of conscience provision has been held unconstitutional as applied to public hospitals and institutions. Thus, public hospitals may be required to perform, accommodate, or assist in abortions.
- State employees may refuse to provide family planning services if contrary to their personal beliefs.
- Health plan companies and healthcare cooperatives are not required to provide abortions or coverage of abortions.

Participation in Research Harmful to Human Life:

- Minnesota currently provides no protection for the rights of healthcare providers who conscientiously object to participation in human cloning, destructive embryo research,

or other forms of immoral medical research.

WHAT HAPPENED IN 2009:

- The state enacted legislation continuing the state's policy of funding "medically necessary" abortions.

- Minnesota enacted legislation prohibiting taxpayer funding of human cloning.

- Minnesota amended applicable statutes to permit the release of medical records to healthcare agents.

- Minnesota considered a number of life-affirming measures, including bills requiring abortion clinics to maintain medical records, mandating that only physicians with clinical privileges in the state can perform abortions, funding abortion alternatives, banning sex-selective abortions, and adding information on coercion to the existing informed consent statute. The state also considered a measure banning saline abortions.

- Conversely, the state also considered a state "Freedom of Choice Act."

- Minnesota considered measures banning all human cloning and discouraging destructive embryo research; supporting adult stem cell research; regulating assisted reproductive technologies; and requiring certain information be provided to patients seeking *in vitro* fertilization procedures or donating gametes.

- The state did not consider any measures related to healthcare rights of conscience.

RECOMMENDATIONS FOR MINNESOTA		
	Short-term Priorities	**Additional Goals**
	ABORTION	
Informed Consent	Ultrasound requirement	
Parental Involvement		
State Rights & Policies	Amendment declaring no state constitutional right to state funding for abortions	
Abortion Funding		
Abortion Provider Requirements		Comprehensive abortion clinic regulations
Abortion Bans		
Regulation of Abortifacients		Regulation of RU-486
PCCs Support		Funding of PCCs
Abortion Reporting		
	LEGAL RECOGNITION AND PROTECTION FOR UNBORN & NEWLY BORN	
Fetal Homicide		
Assault on Unborn		
Prohibitions on Wrongful Birth & Wrongful Life Lawsuits		
Permit Wrongful Death Lawsuits	Remove viability requirement from wrongful death actions	

Born-Alive Infant Protection		
Abandoned Infant Protection		
BIOETHICS		
Human Cloning		Ban on human cloning
DER	Ban on DER	
State Funding of DER		
ART & IVF		Any medically-appropriate regulation of ART
END OF LIFE		
Assisted Suicide		
Pain Management Education		
RIGHTS OF CONSCIENCE		
Protection for Individual Providers	Comprehensive ROC protection	
Protection for Institutions	Comprehensive ROC protection	
Protection for Payers	Comprehensive ROC protection	

MISSISSIPPI

RANKING: 10

Over the last several years, Americans United for Life has worked with Mississippi to enact numerous life-affirming laws, such as Mississippi's informed consent law and comprehensive protection for healthcare rights of conscience. As a result, only one abortion clinic remains in the entire state, and the state's abortion rate has dropped by more than 60 percent. However, the state still does not ban or even regulate human cloning or destructive embryo research.

ABORTION:

- A physician may not perform an abortion on a woman until at least 24 hours after the woman receives counseling on the medical risks of abortion, including the link between abortion and breast cancer, the medical risks of carrying the pregnancy to term, the probable gestational age of the unborn child, medical assistance benefits, and the legal obligations of the child's father. Mississippi also provides written material describing the development of the unborn child, the medical risks of abortion, available state benefits, and public and private agencies offering alternatives to abortion.

- In addition, an abortion provider is required to perform an ultrasound on a woman seeking abortion. The woman must be offered the opportunity to view the ultrasound image, receive a copy of the image, and listen to the unborn child's heartbeat. Abortion facilities must purchase ultrasound equipment.

- A physician may not perform an abortion on an unemancipated minor under the age of 18 without the written consent of both parents. The two-parent consent requirement has been upheld by both a federal appellate court and the Mississippi Supreme Court.

- In *Pro-Choice Mississippi v. Fordice*, the Mississippi Supreme Court found that the state constitution's right of privacy includes "an implicit right to have an abortion." However, the court still upheld the state's informed consent law, 24-hour reflection period before an abortion, and two-parent consent requirement before a minor may obtain an abortion.

- Mississippi funds abortions when necessary to preserve the woman's life, the pregnancy is the result of rape or incest, or in cases involving fetal abnormalities.
- Mississippi prohibits organizations receiving state funds from using those funds to provide abortion counseling or to make referrals for abortion. The state also restricts the use of some or all state facilities for the performance of abortion.

- Health insurance funds for state employees may not be used for insurance coverage of abortion unless an abortion is necessary to preserve the life of the mother, the pregnancy is the result of rape or incest, or the unborn child has an anomaly incompatible with live birth.

- Mississippi mandates minimum health and safety regulations for abortion clinics performing more than 10 abortions per month and/or more than 100 abortions per year. The regulations prescribe minimum health and safety standards for the building or facility, clinic administration, staffing, and pre-procedure medical evaluations. Abortion providers must maintain hospital admitting privileges.

- Further, Mississippi requires second-trimester abortions be performed in hospitals, ambulatory surgical facilities, or a licensed Level I abortion facility (as defined by statute).

- Only practicing physicians licensed by the state of Mississippi may perform abortions.

- Mississippi has enacted legislation banning abortion, except in cases of life endangerment, should *Roe v. Wade* be overturned.

- Mississippi prohibits partial-birth abortion.

- The "Abortion Complication Reporting Act" requires abortion providers to report any incident where a woman dies or needs further medical treatment as a result of an abortion. The measure applies to both surgical and nonsurgical abortions and requires hospitals to report the number of patients treated for complications resulting from abortions.

- Mississippi offers "Choose Life" license plates, the proceeds of which benefit pregnancy care centers and/or other organizations providing abortion alternatives.

LEGAL RECOGNITION OF UNBORN AND NEWLY BORN:

- The killing of an unborn child at any stage of gestation is a form of homicide.

- Further, Mississippi law also provides that an attack on a pregnant woman resulting in a stillbirth or miscarriage is a criminal assault.

- Mississippi defines a nonfatal assault on an unborn child as a criminal offense.

- Mississippi authorizes wrongful death (civil) actions for families who lose viable unborn children through violence or negligence.

- The state has created a specific affirmative duty of physicians to provide medical care and treatment to born-alive infants at any stage of development.

BIOETHICS LAWS:

- Mississippi maintains no laws regarding human cloning, destructive embryo research, or assisted reproductive technologies.

- Mississippi prohibits the "sale" of unborn children.

END OF LIFE LAWS:

- In Mississippi, assisting a suicide is a felony.

HEALTHCARE RIGHTS OF CONSCIENCE LAWS:

Participation in Abortion:

- The Mississippi "Healthcare Rights of Conscience Act" provides comprehensive rights of conscience protection for healthcare providers (including pharmacists), institutions, and insurance companies who conscientiously object to participating in any healthcare service, including abortion.

Participation in Research Harmful to Human Life:

- Mississippi protects the civil rights of all healthcare providers who conscientiously object to participating in any healthcare services, including destructive embryo research and human cloning.

WHAT HAPPENED IN 2009:

- Mississippi enacted a measure prohibiting the "sale" of unborn children.

- Mississippi considered measures requiring abortion providers to be board certified in obstetrics and gynecology and carry malpractice insurance; prohibiting sex-selective abortions; and requiring the reporting of emotional trauma following abortion. The state also considered a constitutional amendment stating, "nothing . . . shall be construed as to grant to any person the right to have an abortion under this Constitution."

- The state also considered the AUL-developed "Child Protection Act," a comprehensive measure requiring the reporting of all suspicions of sexual abuse by designated individuals, including all employees of and volunteers in abortion clinics, mandating the retention of evidentiary samples, and creating a civil cause of action against anyone who takes a minor across state lines to circumvent the home state's parental involvement laws.

- Conversely, the state considered legislation expanding insurance coverage for contraception for minors.

- The state considered measures banning destructive embryo research, providing for embryo adoption, and relating to health insurance coverage of infertility.

- Mississippi also considered end-of-life legislation establishing the state's official position is to sustain life if there is decisional conflict among a patient's family members.

- The state also considered a measure promoting proper pain management for patients.

RECOMMENDATIONS FOR MISSISSIPPI		
	Short-term Priorities	**Additional Goals**
	ABORTION	
Informed Consent	Penalties for failing to comply with informed consent law	
Parental Involvement	Penalties for failing to comply with parental consent law	
State Rights & Policies	Amendment declaring no state constitutional right to abortion	
Abortion Funding		
Abortion Provider Requirements		
Abortion Bans		
Regulation of Abortifacients		Regulation of RU-486
PCCs Support		Funding of PCCs
Abortion Reporting		
	LEGAL RECOGNITION AND PROTECTION FOR UNBORN & NEWLY BORN	
Fetal Homicide		
Assault on Unborn		
Prohibitions on Wrongful Birth & Wrongful Life Lawsuits		
Permit Wrongful Death Lawsuits	Remove viability requirement from wrongful death actions	

Born-Alive Infant Protection		
Abandoned Infant Protection		
BIOETHICS		
Human Cloning		Ban on human cloning
DER		Ban on DER
State Funding of DER	Ban on state funding of DER	
ART & IVF		Any medically-appropriate regulation of ART
END OF LIFE		
Assisted Suicide		
Pain Management Education		
RIGHTS OF CONSCIENCE		
Protection for Individual Providers		
Protection for Institutions		
Protection for Payers		

MISSOURI

RANKING: 11

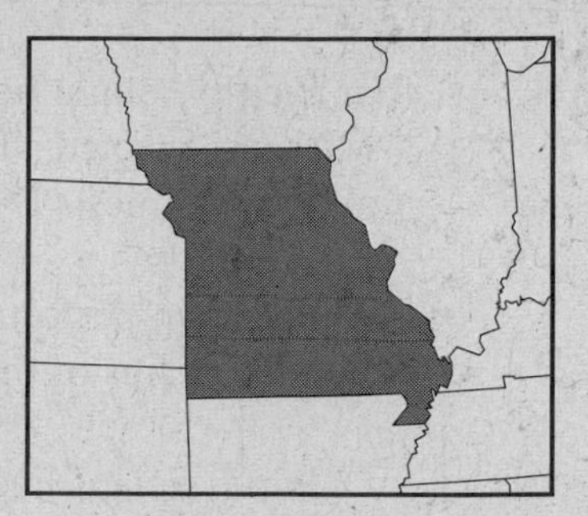

In 2009, the Missouri House of Representatives passed an AUL-developed resolution urging the U.S. Congress to summarily reject the enactment of the federal "Freedom of Choice Act"—sending a clear message that the state of Missouri remains committed to protecting women and the unborn.

ABORTION:

- Missouri requires that 24 hours prior to an abortion a woman be informed of risks of the proposed abortion procedure. The law applies to both surgical and mifepristone (RU-486) abortions.

- A physician may not perform an abortion on an unemancipated minor under the age of 18 without the informed, written consent of one parent or a court order. Further, only a parent or guardian can transport a minor across state lines for an abortion.

- The legislature has found that the life of each human being begins at conception.

- Missouri has narrowed its definition of "medical emergency" to apply only in situations where the woman's life or a "major bodily function" is at risk.

- Missouri prohibits public funds from being used for abortions unless the procedure is necessary to preserve the life of the woman or the pregnancy is the result of rape or incest.

- Public facilities may not be used for performing, assisting in, or counseling a woman on abortion unless it is necessary to preserve the woman's life. Likewise, a state employee may not participate in an abortion.

- Health insurance policies are prohibited from including coverage for abortion unless an abortion is necessary to preserve the life of the woman or an optional rider is purchased.

- Missouri mandates minimum health and safety standards for clinics and facilities where abortions are performed on more than 50 percent of total patients treated or where more than 50 percent of the clinic or facility's revenue comes from the performance of abortions. The regulations prescribe minimum health and safety standards for the building

or facility, clinic administration, staffing, and patient medical evaluations. Recently, Missouri enacted a law imposing more stringent ambulatory surgical center standards on abortion clinics. This law is currently in litigation.

- A physician performing abortions must have admitting privileges at a hospital within a 30-mile radius of the facility where the abortion is performed.

- Only physicians licensed by the State, practicing in Missouri, and having surgical privileges at a hospital that offers obstetrical or gynecological care may perform abortions. The Eighth Circuit Court of Appeals has upheld this law as constitutional.

- Missouri prohibits partial-birth abortion.

- Missouri has appropriated federal and state funds for women "at or below 200 percent of the Federal Poverty Level" to be used to encourage women to carry their pregnancies to term, to pay for adoption expenses, and/or to assist with caring for dependent children. In 2009, the state allocated $2 million to these programs.

- Missouri provides direct taxpayer funding of pregnancy care centers and prohibits organizations that receive state funds from using those funds to provide abortion counseling or to make referrals for abortion. Missouri also provides tax credits for donations to pregnancy care centers that do not perform or refer women for abortions. The state is authorized to issue tax credits for six years, worth half the value of donations between $100 and $50,000.

- The state has an enforceable abortion reporting law, but does not require the reporting of information to the Centers for Disease Control and Prevention (CDC). The measure applies to both surgical and nonsurgical abortions and requires abortion providers to report short-term complications.

- Health plans that provide prescription coverage must also cover contraception, but certain exceptions apply.

LEGAL RECOGNITION OF UNBORN AND NEWLY BORN:

- Under Missouri law, the killing of an unborn child at any stage of gestation is defined as a form of homicide.

- The state allows wrongful death (civil) actions when an unborn child at any stage of development is killed through a negligent or criminal act.

- The state has created a specific affirmative duty for physicians to provide medical care and treatment to born-alive infants at any stage of development.

- Missouri has a "Baby Moses" law, establishing a safe haven for mothers to legally leave their infants at designated places and ensuring the infants receive appropriate care and protection.

- The state funds drug treatment programs for pregnant women and newborns.

BIOETHICS LAWS:

- In November 2006, voters in Missouri approved a ballot initiative amending the state constitution to allow cloning-for-biomedical research (while banning cloning-to-produce children) and to prevent any (future) bans on stem cell research.

- Missouri has created an umbilical cord blood bank.

- Missouri has created the "Life Sciences Research Trust Fund," which prohibits public funds from being "expended, paid, or granted to or on behalf of an existing or proposed research project that involves abortion services, human cloning, or prohibited human research." However, funds may be used for adult stem-cell research.

- Missouri maintains no laws regarding assisted reproductive technologies.

END OF LIFE LAWS:

- In Missouri, assisting a suicide constitutes manslaughter.

HEALTHCARE RIGHTS OF CONSCIENCE LAWS:

Refusal to Participate in Abortion:

- A physician, nurse, midwife, or hospital is not required to admit or treat a woman for the purpose of abortion if such admission or treatment is contrary to religious, moral, or ethical beliefs or established policy. Protection is also provided to medical and nursing students.

- A law requiring insurance coverage for obstetrical and gynecological care provides: "Nothing in this chapter shall be construed to require a health carrier to perform, induce, pay for, reimburse, guarantee, arrange, provide any resources for, or refer a patient for an abortion."

Refusal to Participate in Research Harmful to Human Life:

- Missouri currently provides no protection for the rights of healthcare providers who conscientiously object to participation in human cloning, destructive embryo research, or other forms of immoral medical research.

WHAT HAPPENED IN 2009:

- The House of Representatives enacted a resolution urging the U.S. Congress to summarily reject the enactment of the federal "Freedom of Choice Act."

- Missouri allocated $2 million to organizations providing abortion alternatives.

- Missouri considered legislation supporting abortion reporting and strengthening the state's informed consent law, requiring women receive information about ultrasound services and fetal pain, and criminalizing coercion. The state also considered measures allowing for criminal prosecution of a mother who harms her unborn child by the intentional and unlawful use of controlled substances. While the state considered a bill banning abortion coverage under a new state health plan, that same measure required coverage for contraception.

- Missouri considered measures proposing a constitutional amendment prohibiting the expenditure of public funds for abortion services, human cloning, or certain human research.

- Conversely, the state considered a number of measures requiring hospitals to provide information about and access to "emergency contraception," as well as measures requiring pharmacists or pharmacies to dispense contraception.

- On the bioethics front, Missouri considered measures banning the funding of destructive embryo research and human cloning; regulating assisted reproductive technologies; limiting the number of embryos that can be transferred during a single *in vitro* fertilization cycle; and relating to insurance coverage of infertility.

- While Missouri considered legislation providing some protection to healthcare providers in regard to dispensing abortifacients, it also considered several measures forcing pharmacists to dispense contraceptives "without delay."

- The Eighth Circuit Court of Appeals upheld a lower court's ruling that the state acted unconstitutionally in failing to honor a petition for "Choose Life" license plates.

RECOMMENDATIONS FOR MISSOURI		
	Short-term Priorities	**Additional Goals**
	ABORTION	
Informed Consent	Enhancements such as ultrasound requirement,counseling on fetal pain, and/or coerced abortion prevention	
Parental Involvement		
State Rights & Policies		
Abortion Funding		
Abortion Provider Requirements		
Abortion Bans		Sex-selective abortion ban
Regulation of Abortifacients	Regulation of RU-486	
PCCs Support	Continued funding of PCCs	
Abortion Reporting		
	LEGAL RECOGNITION AND PROTECTION FOR UNBORN & NEWLY BORN	
Fetal Homicide		
Assault on Unborn	Law specifically criminalizing nonfatal assaults on unborn	
Prohibitions on Wrongful Birth & Wrongful Life Lawsuits		

Permit Wrongful Death Lawsuits		
Born-Alive Infant Protection		
Abandoned Infant Protection		
BIOETHICS		
Human Cloning		
DER		
State Funding of DER	Continued funding of ethical forms of research	
ART & IVF		Any medically-appropriate regulation of ART
END OF LIFE		
Assisted Suicide		
Pain Management Education		
RIGHTS OF CONSCIENCE		
Protection for Individual Providers	Comprehensive ROC protection	
Protection for Institutions	Comprehensive ROC protection	
Protection for Payers	Comprehensive ROC protection	

MONTANA

RANKING: 45

Montana lags far behind many other states in protecting life. It does not have an informed consent law, parental involvement law, or abortion clinic regulations. Montana does not recognize an unborn child as a potential victim of criminal violence. It has not taken any initiative to stem immoral uses of biotechnology, such as destructive embryo research or human cloning. Moreover, in late 2008, a single Montana judge ruled that the state's Constitution sanctions assisted suicide.

ABORTION:

- State court decisions have held that the Montana Constitution provides a greater right to abortion than does the U.S. Constitution. Under the auspices of these decisions, several Montana laws have been declared unconstitutional, including those limiting taxpayer funding for abortions; requiring parental notice prior to a minor undergoing an abortion; requiring a 24-hour reflection period prior to an abortion; mandating that state-prepared, informed consent information be offered to a woman prior to an abortion; and requiring that only a licensed physician perform an abortion.

- Montana taxpayers are required to fund "medically necessary" abortions.

- Montana is the only state that specifically allows physician assistants to perform abortions. Other states typically only allow a licensed physician to perform an abortion. Further, nurses are allowed to dispense all contraceptives, but may not dispense mifepristone (RU-486).

- Montana prohibits partial-birth abortion, but only after viability.

- The state offers "Choose Life" license plates, the proceeds of which benefit pregnancy care centers and/or other organizations providing abortion alternatives.

- The state has an enforceable abortion reporting law, but does not require the reporting of information to the Centers for Disease Control and Prevention (CDC). The measure applies to both surgical and nonsurgical abortions.

- Montana has a "contraceptive equity" requirement, meaning that health insurance coverage must include coverage for contraception. The requirement is derived from a state Attorney General opinion. The state does not provide an exemption to employers or insurers with a religious or moral objection to contraception.

- Montana maintains a Freedom of Clinic Access (FACE) law, making it a crime to block access to an abortion business and restricting how close sidewalk counselors and demonstrators can be to the abortion facility.

LEGAL RECOGNITION OF UNBORN AND NEWLY BORN:

- Montana law does not currently recognize an unborn child as a potential victim of homicide or assault.

- Under Montana law, a person commits an offense if he/she "purposefully, knowingly, or negligently causes the death of a premature infant born alive, if such infant is viable."

- The state allows wrongful death (civil) actions when a viable unborn child is killed through a negligent or criminal act.

- The state has created a specific affirmative duty of physicians to provide medical care and treatment to born-alive infants at any stage of development.

- Montana has a "Baby Moses" law, establishing a safe haven for mothers to legally leave their infants at designated places and ensuring the infants receive appropriate care and protection.

- Specific professionals are required to report any infant affected by drug exposure to the state health department.

- Montana maintains a measure allowing a woman who loses a child after 20 weeks gestation to obtain a certificate of birth resulting in stillbirth.

BIOETHICS LAWS:

- Montana bans cloning-to-produce-children, but not cloning for all purposes—making it a clone-and-kill state.

- Montana also bans fetal experimentation.

END OF LIFE LAWS:

- Under Montana statutes, assisted suicide remains a felony. However, a district court judge has declared the Montana Constitution encompasses a right to suicide and a right to assistance in suicide, negating the statutory prohibitions. This ruling is on appeal to the Montana Supreme Court.

HEALTHCARE RIGHTS OF CONSCIENCE LAWS: OVERALL ASSESSMENT:

Participation in Abortion:

- An individual, partnership, association, or corporation on the basis of religious or moral beliefs may refuse to participate in an abortion or to provide advice concerning abortion.

- A private hospital or healthcare facility is not required, contrary to religious or moral tenets or stated religious beliefs or moral convictions, to admit a woman for an abortion or permit the use of its facilities for an abortion.

Participation in Research Harmful to Human Life:

- Montana currently provides no protection for the rights of healthcare providers who conscientiously object to participation in human cloning, destructive embryo research, or other forms of immoral medical research.

WHAT HAPPENED IN 2009:

- Montana enacted legislation banning cloning-to-produce-children, but not cloning for all purposes.

- Montana revised its guardianship law to prohibit a guardian from giving a "do-not-resuscitate order" if it conflicts with an incapacitated person's wishes.

- Montana considered abortion clinic regulations, mandating that clinics meet certain minimum health and safety standards. The state also considered measures opposing a federal "Freedom of Choice Act," providing for parental notification, and protecting unborn victims of violence.

- Notably, in response to the district court's assisted suicide ruling, it considered a number of measures regulating physician-assisted suicide.

- Montana considered comprehensive rights of conscience legislation protecting all healthcare providers and institutions and measures specifically protecting pharmacists.

- In *Baxter v. State*, a Montana district court ruled the state constitution provides a right to suicide and a right to assistance in suicide. The case was appealed to the Montana Supreme Court, which heard oral argument in September 2009.

RECOMMENDATIONS FOR MONTANA

	Short-term Priorities	**Additional Goals**
	ABORTION	
Informed Consent		Comprehensive informed consent law with reflection period
Parental Involvement		Parental notice or consent
State Rights & Policies	Amendment declaring no state constitutional right to abortion	
Abortion Funding		
Abortion Provider Requirements		Comprehensive abortion clinic regulations
Abortion Bans		
Regulation of Abortifacients		
PCCs Support		Direct funding of PCCs
Abortion Reporting		
	LEGAL RECOGNITION AND PROTECTION FOR UNBORN & NEWLY BORN	
Fetal Homicide	Comprehensive unborn victims of violence law	
Assault on Unborn		
Prohibitions on Wrongful Birth & Wrongful Life Lawsuits		
Permit Wrongful Death Lawsuits		

Born-Alive Infant Protection		
Abandoned Infant Protection		
BIOETHICS		
Human Cloning		Ban on human cloning
DER Destructive Embryo Research		Ban on DER
State Funding of DER	Ban on state funding of DER	
ART & IVF		Any medically-appropriate regulation of ART
END OF LIFE		
Assisted Suicide		
Pain Management Education		
RIGHTS OF CONSCIENCE		
Protection for Individual Providers	Comprehensive ROC protection	
Protection for Institutions	Comprehensive ROC protection	
Protection for Payers	Comprehensive ROC protection	

NEBRASKA

RANKING: 9

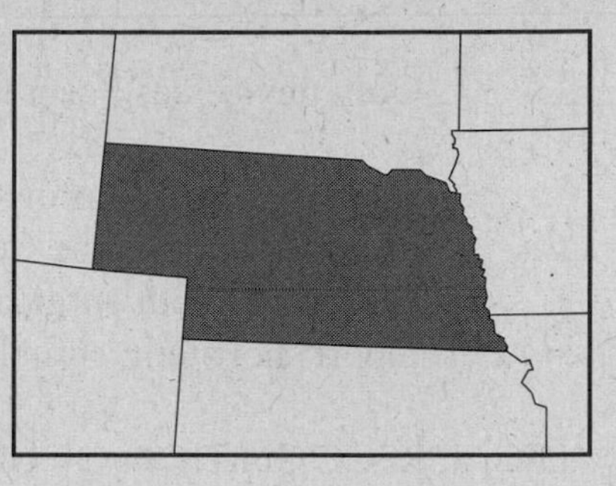

Nebraska provides basic protections for women seeking abortions, for the unborn, and for healthcare rights of conscience. It also prohibits the funding of and use of state facilities for human cloning or destructive embryo research. In 2009, Nebraska provided funding for a law supporting ethical forms of stem cell research.

ABORTION:

- Under Nebraska law, a physician may not perform an abortion on a woman until at least 24 hours after counseling the woman on the risks of abortion, the risks of continued pregnancy, and the probable gestational age of the unborn child. Nebraska also provides materials describing the development of the unborn child, the medical and psychological risks of abortion, available state benefits, and public and private agencies offering alternatives to abortion.

- An abortion provider who conducts an ultrasound prior to performing an abortion must display the ultrasound image of the unborn child so the woman may see it.

- A physician may not perform an abortion on an unemancipated minor until at least 48 hours after providing written notice to one parent or a court order is secured.

- Nebraska taxpayers are not required to pay for abortions except when the abortion is necessary to preserve the woman's life or the pregnancy is the result of rape or incest.

- Nebraska prohibits organizations that receive public funds from using those funds to provide abortion counseling or to make referrals for abortion.

- Group health insurance contracts or health maintenance agreements paid for with public funds may not include abortion coverage unless an abortion is necessary to preserve the life of a woman.

- Nebraska mandates minimum health and safety standards for abortion clinics which, at any point during a calendar year, perform 10 or more abortions during one calendar week. The regulations prescribe minimum health and safety standards for the building or facility, staffing, and medical testing of clinic employees.

- Only physicians licensed by the state of Nebraska may perform abortions.

- The state has an enforceable abortion reporting law, but does not require the reporting of information to the Centers for Disease Control and Prevention (CDC). The measure pertains to both surgical and nonsurgical abortions and requires abortion providers to report short-term complications.

LEGAL RECOGNITION OF UNBORN AND NEWLY BORN:

- Under Nebraska law, the killing of an unborn child at any stage of gestation is defined as a form of homicide. Nebraska law also provides penalties for the vehicular homicide of an unborn child.

- Nebraska criminalizes a nonfatal assault on an unborn child.

- The state allows wrongful death (civil) actions when an unborn child at any stage of development is killed through a third party's negligent or criminal act.

- Nebraska law requires "all reasonable steps, in accordance with the sound medical judgment of the attending physician, shall be employed to preserve the life of a child" who is born alive following an attempted abortion at any stage of development.

- Nebraska has a "Baby Moses" law, prohibiting the criminal prosecution of someone who relinquishes a child to an on-duty hospital employee.

- The state funds drug treatment programs for pregnant women and newborns.

BIOETHICS LAWS:

- Nebraska prohibits state facilities from performing human cloning or destructive embryo research.

- The state also bans fetal experimentation and prohibits monies from a state-supported biomedical research fund from being used for research on fetal tissues obtained from induced abortions.

- The state provides funding for ethical forms of stem cell research and prohibits the state funding of human cloning or destructive embryo research.

END OF LIFE LAWS:

- In Nebraska, assisting a suicide is a felony.

HEALTHCARE RIGHTS OF CONSCIENCE LAWS:

Participation in Abortion:

- A person is not required to participate in an abortion.
- A hospital, institution, or other facility is not required to admit a woman for an abortion or to allow the performance of an abortion within its premises.

Participation in Research Harmful to Human Life:

- Nebraska currently provides no protection for the rights of healthcare providers who conscientiously object to participation in human cloning, destructive embryo research, and other forms of immoral medical research.

WHAT HAPPENED IN 2009:

- Nebraska enacted legislation requiring an abortion provider who conducts an ultrasound prior to performing an abortion display the ultrasound image of the unborn child so the woman may view it.
- Nebraska enacted a measure that funds legislation passed in 2008 supporting ethical alternatives to stem cell research.
- The state also considered legislation opposing a federal "Freedom of Choice Act," as well as a bill requiring that abortion providers prescreen women considering abortion for potential risk factors.
- Nebraska introduced a bill seeking to ensure the poor, the working poor, and the disabled will be enrolled in government-sponsored healthcare plans that respect the beliefs and values of the enrollees, particularly as they relate to matters of abortion, abortifacients, contraception, sterilization, infanticide, and euthanasia.

RECOMMENDATIONS FOR NEBRASKA		
	Short-term Priorities	**Additional Goals**
	ABORTION	
Informed Consent	Informed consent enhancements such as counseling on fetal pain or coerced abortion prevention	
Parental Involvement	Amend parental notice law to require parental consent	
State Rights & Policies		
Abortion Funding		
Abortion Provider Requirements	Requiring admitting privileges for abortion providers	
Abortion Bans		Sex-selective abortion ban or "delayed enforcement" ban
Regulation of Abortifacients		
PCCs Support	Direct funding of PCCs	
Abortion Reporting		
LEGAL RECOGNITION AND PROTECTION FOR UNBORN & NEWLY BORN		
Fetal Homicide		
Assault on Unborn		
Prohibitions on Wrongful Birth & Wrongful Life Lawsuits		Prohibitions on wrongful birth and wrongful life lawsuits
Permit Wrongful Death Lawsuits		

Born-Alive Infant Protection		
Abandoned Infant Protection		
BIOETHICS		
Human Cloning		Ban on human cloning
DER		Ban on DER
State Funding of DER	Continued funding of ethical alternatives	
ART & IVF		Any medically-appropriate regulation of ART
END OF LIFE		
Assisted Suicide		
Pain Management Education		
RIGHTS OF CONSCIENCE		
Protection for Individual Providers	Comprehensive ROC protection	
Protection for Institutions	Comprehensive ROC protection	
Protection for Payers	Comprehensive ROC protection	

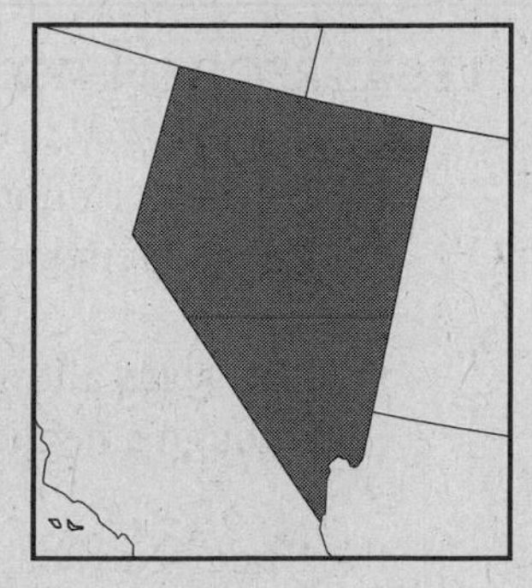

NEVADA

RANKING: 43

Nevada does not adequately protect minors from the harms of abortion. Moreover, the state provides no effective protection to patients at the end of life. Specifically, Nevada does not prohibit assisted suicide by statute, common law, or judicial decree.

ABORTION:

- A physician may not perform an abortion on a woman until after the physician or other qualified person informs her of the probable gestational age of the unborn child, describes the abortion procedure to be used and its risks, and explains the physical and emotional consequences of abortion.

- Nevada's parental notification law has been declared unconstitutional. The law sought to prohibit a physician from performing an abortion on an unemancipated minor under the age of 18 until notice had been given to one parent or a court order had been secured.

- The state maintains a "Freedom of Choice Act." The Act mandates the right to abortion even if *Roe v. Wade* is eventually overturned, specifically providing that abortions may be performed within 24 weeks after the commencement of a pregnancy. Because Nevada voters passed a ballot initiative approving this law, the statute will remain in effect and cannot be amended, repealed, or otherwise changed except by a direct vote of the people.

- Nevada taxpayers are required to pay for an abortion when the procedure is necessary to preserve the woman's life or the pregnancy is the result of rape or incest, and the woman has signed a notarized affidavit or witness declaration attesting to the rape or incest.

- Only physicians licensed by the state of Nevada or employed by the United States and using accepted medical practices and procedures may perform abortions. Chiropractic physicians and osteopathic medical professionals are explicitly prohibited from performing abortions.

- The state has an enforceable abortion reporting law, but does not require the reporting of information to the Centers for Disease Control and Prevention (CDC).

- Health plans providing prescription coverage must provide coverage for contraception. An exemption applies to certain insurers affiliated with religious organizations.

LEGAL RECOGNITION OF UNBORN AND NEWLY BORN:

- Nevada criminal law defines the killing of an unborn child after "quickening" (discernible movement in the womb) as a form of homicide.

- The state allows wrongful death (civil) actions when a viable unborn child is killed through a negligent or criminal act.

- Under Nevada law, all reasonable steps must be taken to preserve the life and health of an infant "whenever an abortion results in the birth of an infant capable of sustained survival by natural or artificial supportive systems."

- The state defines substance abuse during pregnancy as "child abuse" under civil child-welfare statutes.

BIOETHICS LAWS:

- Nevada does not ban human cloning or destructive embryo research and does not regulate assisted reproductive technologies.

END OF LIFE LAWS:

- The legal status of assisted suicide in Nevada remains undetermined. The state has not enacted a specific statute prohibiting assisted suicide and does not recognize common law crimes (including assisted suicide). Further, there is no judicial decision stating whether assisted suicide is a form of homicide under Nevada's general homicide laws.

HEALTHCARE RIGHTS OF CONSCIENCE LAWS:

Participation in Abortion:

- Except in a medical emergency, an employer may not require a nurse, nursing assistant, or other employee to participate directly in the performance of an abortion if that person has previously signed and provided a written statement indicating a religious, moral, or ethical basis for conscientiously objecting to participation in abortions.

- Except in a medical emergency, a private hospital or licensed medical facility is not required to permit the use of its facilities for the performance of an abortion.

Participation in Research Harmful to Human Life:

- Nevada currently provides no protection for the rights of healthcare providers who conscientiously object to participation in human cloning, destructive embryo research, and other forms of immoral medical research.

WHAT HAPPENED IN 2009:

- Nevada enacted legislation defining "unprofessional conduct" to include instances where chiropractic physicians procure or aid in procuring a criminal abortion. A separately enacted bill provides for licensing of osteopathic medical professionals and prohibits them from performing or assisting in performance of abortion.

- Nevada did not consider any measures relating to bioethics or healthcare rights of conscience.

RECOMMENDATIONS FOR NEVADA		
	Short-term Priorities	**Additional Goals**
ABORTION		
Informed Consent	Comprehensive informed consent law with reflection period	
Parental Involvement	Parental notice or consent	
State Rights & Policies	Repeal of state FOCA	
Abortion Funding	Limits on use of state funding for abortions	
Abortion Provider Requirements		
Abortion Bans		
Regulation of Abortifacients		Regulation of RU-486
PCCs Support		Direct funding of PCCs
Abortion Reporting		
LEGAL RECOGNITION AND PROTECTION FOR UNBORN & NEWLY BORN		
Fetal Homicide	Protection for unborn from conception	
Assault on Unborn		
Prohibitions on Wrongful Birth & Wrongful Life Lawsuits		
Permit Wrongful Death Lawsuits		

Born-Alive Infant Protection		
Abandoned Infant Protection		
BIOETHICS		
Human Cloning		Ban on human cloning
DER		Ban on DER
State Funding of DER	Ban on state funding of DER	
ART & IVF		Any medically-appropriate regulation of ART
END OF LIFE		
Assisted Suicide	Statutory prohibition on assisted suicide	
Pain Management Education		
RIGHTS OF CONSCIENCE		
Protection for Individual Providers	Comprehensive ROC protection	
Protection for Institutions	Comprehensive ROC protection	
Protection for Payers	Comprehensive ROC protection	

NEW HAMPSHIRE

RANKING: 35

New Hampshire's failure to protect human life is abysmal. The state provides no meaningful protection for women or the unborn—even its litigated parental notice law has been repealed. Further, New Hampshire allows post-viability abortion-on-demand and offers no protection to unborn victims of violence. On the bioethics front, the state does not prohibit or regulate either human cloning or destructive embryo research.

ABORTION:

- New Hampshire does not provide even rudimentary protection for women considering abortions. The state does not have an informed consent law, parental involvement law, ultrasound requirement, abortion clinic regulations, or a prohibition on anyone other than a licensed physician performing an abortion.

- New Hampshire taxpayers are not required to pay for abortions unless the abortion is necessary to preserve the woman's health or the pregnancy is the result of rape or incest.

- New Hampshire law allows abortions after viability, even in cases where the mother's life or health is not endangered.

- Prior to the FDA's decision in 2006, New Hampshire enacted a "collaborative practice" bill which allowed "emergency contraception" to be sold without a physician's prescription.

- New Hampshire law requires group or blanket health insurance policies issued or renewed by insurers, health service corporations, and health maintenance organizations to provide coverage for contraceptives if they otherwise provide coverage for outpatient services or other prescription drugs. The law contains no exemptions for religious or other employers with ethical or moral objections.

LEGAL RECOGNITION OF UNBORN AND NEWLY BORN:

- New Hampshire does not criminalize the killing of an unborn child outside the context of abortion. However, it does provide that an attack on a pregnant woman which results in a stillbirth or miscarriage is a criminal assault.

- The state allows wrongful death (civil) actions when a viable unborn child is killed through a negligent or criminal act.

- New Hampshire has a "Baby Moses" law, establishing a safe haven for mothers to legally leave their infants at designated places and ensuring the infants receive appropriate care and protection.

- New Hampshire has approved stillbirth certificates.

BIOETHICS LAWS:

- New Hampshire does not ban human cloning or destructive embryo research.

- New Hampshire has enacted limited regulation of practitioners and participants in assisted reproductive technologies.

END OF LIFE LAWS:

- In New Hampshire, assisting suicide is a felony.

HEALTHCARE RIGHTS OF CONSCIENCE LAWS:

Participation in Abortion:

- New Hampshire currently provides no protection for the rights of conscience of healthcare providers.

Participation in Research Harmful to Human Life:

- New Hampshire currently provides no protection for the rights of healthcare providers who conscientiously object to participation in human cloning, destructive embryo research, and other forms of immoral medical research.

WHAT HAPPENED IN 2009:

- New Hampshire considered measures related to informed consent and parental notification for abortion, as well as a measure prohibiting the State Department of Health and Human Services from entering into a contract with Planned Parenthood or any abortion provider.

- The state considered a measure allowing physician-assisted suicide.
- New Hampshire did not consider any measures relating to bioethics or healthcare rights of conscience.

RECOMMENDATIONS FOR NEW HAMPSHIRE		
	Short-term Priorities	**Additional Goals**
	ABORTION	
Informed Consent	Comprehensive informed consent law with reflection period	
Parental Involvement	Parental notice or consent	
State Rights & Policies		
Abortion Funding	Additional limits on use of state funding for abortions	
Abortion Provider Requirements		Abortion clinic regulations
Abortion Bans		
Regulation of Abortifacients		Regulation of RU-486
PCCs Support		Direct funding of PCCs
Abortion Reporting		Mandatory reporting on abortions
	LEGAL RECOGNITION AND PROTECTION FOR UNBORN & NEWLY BORN	
Fetal Homicide	Comprehensive protection for unborn from conception	
Assault on Unborn		
Prohibitions on Wrongful Birth & Wrongful Life Lawsuits		
Permit Wrongful Death Lawsuits		

Born-Alive Infant Protection	Law requiring care for infant who survives an abortion	
Abandoned Infant Protection		
BIOETHICS		
Human Cloning		Ban on human cloning
DER		Ban on DER
State Funding of DER	Ban on state funding of DER	
ART & IVF		Any medically-appropriate regulation of ART
END OF LIFE		
Assisted Suicide		
Pain Management Education		
RIGHTS OF CONSCIENCE		
Protection for Individual Providers	Comprehensive ROC protection	
Protection for Institutions	Comprehensive ROC protection	
Protection for Payers	Comprehensive ROC protection	

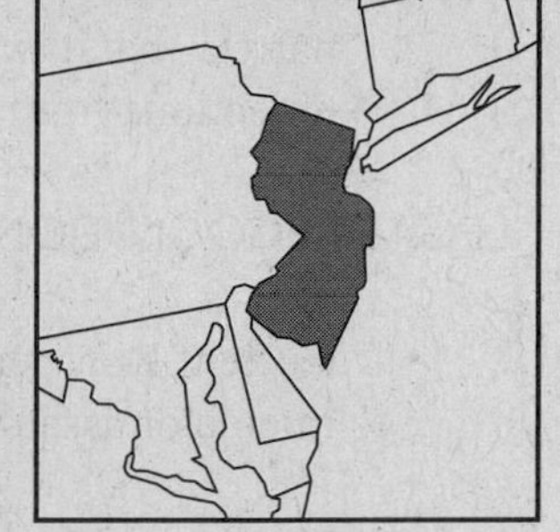

NEW JERSEY

RANKING: 47

New Jersey directly supports the destruction of human life by allowing and funding destructive experimentation on cloned human embryos and cloned human fetuses. Tragically, New Jersey permits maintaining a cloned human up to the threshold of live birth and then destroying him or her for research. Moreover, the state does not protect women from the negative consequences of abortion, lacking common-sense laws such as informed consent and parental involvement.

ABORTION:

- New Jersey does not have an informed consent law or an enforceable parental involvement law for abortion.

- The New Jersey Supreme Court has ruled the state constitution provides a broader right to abortion than the U.S. Constitution. Pursuant to this ruling, the New Jersey Supreme Court has struck down the state's parental notification requirement and restrictions on the use of taxpayer funds to pay for abortions.

- New Jersey provides court-ordered Medicaid coverage for all "medically necessary" abortions.

- Under the State Health Benefits plan, any contracts entered into by the State Health Benefits Commission must include coverage of abortion.

- New Jersey requires abortions after the first trimester be performed in licensed ambulatory care facilities or hospitals.

- Only physicians licensed to practice medicine and surgery in New Jersey may perform abortions.

- Hospitals providing emergency care for sexual assault victims must provide "emergency contraception."

- New Jersey requires individual, group, and small-employer health insurance policies, medical or hospital service agreements, health maintenance organizations, and prepaid prescription service organizations to provide coverage for contraceptives if they also provide coverage for other prescription drugs. The provision includes an exemption so narrow that it excludes the ability of most employers and insurers with moral or religious objections from exercising the exemption.

LEGAL RECOGNITION OF UNBORN AND NEWLY BORN:

- Current New Jersey law does not recognize an unborn child as a potential victim of homicide or assault.
- The state allows wrongful death (civil) actions only when an unborn child is born alive following a negligent or criminal act and dies thereafter.
- New Jersey does not require infants who survive an abortion be given appropriate, potentially life-saving medical care.
- New Jersey has a "Baby Moses" law, establishing a safe haven for mothers to legally leave their infants at designated places and ensuring the infants receive appropriate care and protection.

BIOETHICS LAWS:

- New Jersey permits and funds destructive experimentation on both cloned human embryos and cloned human fetuses up to the time of live birth.
- State statutes contain no language that could be interpreted as discouraging the initiation of pregnancies using cloned embryos (*i.e.*, cloning-to-produce-children).
- State funding earmarked for stem cell research may also be available for adult stem cell research.
- The state regulates insurance coverage of assisted reproductive technologies.

END OF LIFE LAWS:

- In New Jersey, assisting a suicide is a felony.

HEALTHCARE RIGHTS OF CONSCIENCE LAWS:

Participation in Abortion:

- A person is not required to perform or assist in the performance of an abortion.

- A hospital or healthcare facility is not required to provide abortions. The New Jersey Supreme Court has determined that this prohibition is unconstitutional as applied to nonsectarian or nonprofit hospitals.

Participation in Research Harmful to Human Life:

- New Jersey currently provides no protection for the rights of healthcare providers who conscientiously object to participation in human cloning, destructive embryo research, and other forms of immoral medical research.

WHAT HAPPENED IN 2009:

- New Jersey considered a measure requiring a woman be offered the opportunity to see an ultrasound image before abortion, as well as a measure amending the constitution to prohibit the use of state funds for abortion. The state also considered a measure prohibiting wrongful life and wrongful birth lawsuits.

- New Jersey considered an end-of-life measure requiring healthcare representatives to make healthcare decisions for incapacitated patients in accordance with patient's religious beliefs.

- New Jersey did not consider any measures related to bioethics or healthcare rights of conscience.

RECOMMENDATIONS FOR NEW JERSEY		
	Short-term Priorities	**Additional Goals**
	ABORTION	
Informed Consent	Comprehensive informed consent law with reflection period	
Parental Involvement	Parental notice or consent	
State Rights & Policies	Amendment declaring no state constitutional right to abortion	
Abortion Funding	Limits on use of state funding for abortion	
Abortion Provider Requirements		Comprehensive regulation of any facility performing abortions
Abortion Bans		
Regulation of Abortifacients		Regulation of RU-486
PCCs Support		Direct funding of PCCs
Abortion Reporting		
LEGAL RECOGNITION AND PROTECTION FOR UNBORN & NEWLY BORN		
Fetal Homicide	Comprehensive unborn victims of violence protection	
Assault on Unborn		
Prohibitions on Wrongful Birth & Wrongful Life Lawsuits		
Permit Wrongful Death Lawsuits		

Born-Alive Infant Protection	Law requiring care of infant who survives an abortion	
Abandoned Infant Protection		
BIOETHICS		
Human Cloning		Ban on human cloning
DER		Ban on DER
State Funding of DER	Ban on state funding of DER	
ART & IVF		Any medically-appropriate regulation of ART
END OF LIFE		
Assisted Suicide		
Pain Management Education		
RIGHTS OF CONSCIENCE		
Protection for Individual Providers	Comprehensive ROC protection	
Protection for Institutions	Comprehensive ROC protection	
Protection for Payers	Comprehensive ROC protection	

NEW MEXICO

RANKING: 37

New Mexico lacks many common sense laws and protective regulations. For example, New Mexico does not adequately protect the health and safety of women seeking abortions because it lacks an informed consent law, an enforceable parental involvement law, or comprehensive regulations of facilities performing abortions. In addition, New Mexico has not addressed potential abuses of biotechnology, including human cloning, destructive embryo research, or assisted reproductive technologies.

ABORTION:

- New Mexico does not have an informed consent law for abortion.

- New Mexico has enacted a parental notice law that is constitutionally problematic. The state Attorney General has issued an opinion that the law does not provide the constitutionally-required judicial bypass procedure and is unenforceable.

- The New Mexico Supreme Court has held that the Equal Rights Amendment to the state constitution provides a broader right to abortion than the U.S. Constitution. Under this ruling, the court has struck down restrictions on the use of taxpayer funds to pay for abortions.

- New Mexico provides court-ordered Medicaid coverage for all "medically necessary" abortions.

- New Mexico maintains no regulations mandating that abortion clinics meet minimum health and safety standards, but only physicians licensed in New Mexico may perform abortions.

- New Mexico prohibits partial-birth abortion, but only after viability.

- New Mexico mandates the provision of "emergency contraception" in hospital emergency rooms. In addition, "emergency contraception" is available directly from pharmacists without a prescription.

- The state has an enforceable abortion reporting law, but does not require the reporting of information to the Centers for Disease Control and Prevention (CDC). The measure applies to both surgical and nonsurgical abortions.

- Health insurance plans that provide prescription coverage must also provide coverage for contraception. An exemption applies to religious employers.

LEGAL RECOGNITION OF UNBORN AND NEWLY BORN:

- Current New Mexico law does not recognize an unborn child as a potential victim of homicide or assault.

- New Mexico defines criminal assaults on a pregnant woman that result in miscarriage, stillbirth, or "damage to pregnancy" as enhanced offenses for sentencing purposes.

- The state allows a wrongful death (civil) action when a viable unborn child is killed through a negligent or criminal act.

- New Mexico does not require that an infant who survives an abortion be given appropriate medical care.

- New Mexico has a "Baby Moses" law, establishing a safe haven for mothers to legally leave their infants at designated places and ensuring the infants receive appropriate care and protection.

BIOETHICS LAWS:

- New Mexico bans live fetal experimentation. A "fetus" is defined as "the product of conception from the time of conception until the expulsion or extraction from the opening of the uterine cavity." Thus, it is unclear whether the statute applies to cloned human embryos.

- New Mexico has enacted the "Umbilical Cord Blood Banking Act," which requires physicians and hospitals to inform new mothers of the option to donate their children's umbilical cord blood for research.

- New Mexico maintains no laws regarding assisted reproductive technologies.

END OF LIFE LAWS:

- In New Mexico, assisting a suicide is a felony.

HEALTHCARE RIGHTS OF CONSCIENCE LAWS:

Participation in Abortion:

- A person associated with, employed by, or on the staff of a hospital who objects on religious or moral grounds is not required to participate in an abortion.

- A hospital is not required to admit a woman for the purpose of performing an abortion.

Participation in Research Harmful to Human Life:

- New Mexico currently provides no protection for the rights of healthcare providers who conscientiously object to participation in human cloning, destructive embryo research, and other forms of immoral medical research.

WHAT HAPPENED IN 2009:

- New Mexico considered multiple measures that would have enacted a state "Freedom of Choice Act."

- On the other hand, the state considered a measure that would have required parental notification before a minor could obtain an abortion.

- New Mexico considered measures requesting the creation of a statewide task force to assess and improve access to substance abuse treatment and prenatal care for pregnant women with substance abuse problems, as well as a bill providing for certificates of stillbirth.

- New Mexico considered measures allowing destructive embryo research and prohibiting cloning-to-produce-children.

- New Mexico considered legislation allowing physician-assisted suicide. It also considered a constitutional amendment providing the right to make decisions about health care and banning mandatory healthcare coverage.

- The state also considered legislation protecting the rights of conscience of researchers. The bill provided that an employee shall not be required to conduct scientific research, experimentation, or study that involves the creation or use of pre-implantation embryos in relation to human embryonic stem cell research to the extent that such research conflicts with the sincerely-held religious practices or beliefs of the employee.

RECOMMENDATIONS FOR NEW MEXICO		
	Short-term Priorities	**Additional Goals**
	ABORTION	
Informed Consent	Comprehensive informed consent law with reflection period	
Parental Involvement	Parental notice or consent	
State Rights & Policies	Amendment declaring no state constitutional right to abortion	
Abortion Funding	Limits on use of state funding for abortions	
Abortion Provider Requirements		Abortion clinic regulations
Abortion Bans		
Regulation of Abortifacients		Regulation of RU-486
PCCs Support		Direct funding of PCCs
Abortion Reporting		
LEGAL RECOGNITION AND PROTECTION FOR UNBORN & NEWLY BORN		
Fetal Homicide	Comprehensive unborn victims of violence protection	
Assault on Unborn		
Prohibitions on Wrongful Birth & Wrongful Life Lawsuits		
Permit Wrongful Death Lawsuits		

Born-Alive Infant Protection	Law requiring care for infant who survives an abortion	
Abandoned Infant Protection		
BIOETHICS		
Human Cloning		Ban on human cloning
DER		Ban on DER
State Funding of DER	Ban on state funding of DER and continued funding of ethical alternatives	
ART & IVF		Any medically-appropriate regulation of ART
END OF LIFE		
Assisted Suicide		
Pain Management Education		
RIGHTS OF CONSCIENCE		
Protection for Individual Providers	Comprehensive ROC protection	
Protection for Institutions	Comprehensive ROC protection	
Protection for Payers	Comprehensive ROC protection	

NEW YORK

RANKING: 41

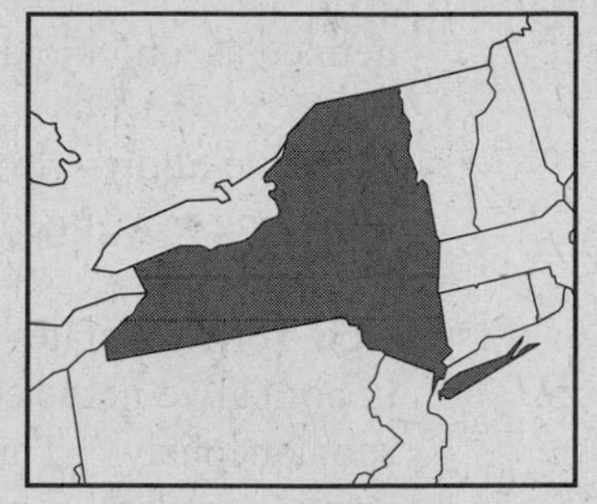

New York lags far behind other states in enacting laws that adequately protect the health and safety of a woman considering or seeking an abortion. It does not have either an informed consent or parental involvement law, nor does it provide effective limits on the public funding of abortion.

ABORTION:

- New York does not have an informed consent law for abortion and does not protect the right of parents to be involved in the abortion decisions of their minor daughters.
- In *Hope v. Perales,* the due process provision of the New York Constitution was interpreted as protecting a woman's right to abortion.
- New York taxpayers are required to fund "medically necessary" abortions for women receiving public assistance.
- New York's requirement that abortions after the first trimester be performed in hospitals is, under current federal precedent, unenforceable. However, the state limits the performance of abortions to licensed physicians.
- Hospitals providing emergency care for sexual assault victims must provide "emergency contraception."
- New York provides funding to pregnancy care centers and other abortion alternatives.
- The state has an enforceable abortion reporting law, but does not require the reporting of information to the Centers for Disease Control and Prevention (CDC). The measure applies to both surgical and nonsurgical abortions.
- Health plans that provide prescription coverage must provide coverage for contraception. The provision includes an exemption so narrow that it excludes the ability of most employers and insurers with moral or religious objections from exercising the exemption.

LEGAL RECOGNITION OF UNBORN AND NEWLY BORN:

- Under New York law, the killing of an unborn child after the 24th week of pregnancy is defined as a homicide.

- The state allows wrongful death (civil) actions only when an unborn child is born alive following a negligent or criminal act and dies thereafter.

- New York law states the "opportunity to obtain medical treatment of an infant prematurely born alive in the course of an abortion shall be the same as the rights of an infant born spontaneously." Thus, the state has created a specific affirmative duty of physicians to provide medical care and treatment to born-alive infants at any stage of development.

- New York has a "Baby Moses" law, establishing a safe haven for mothers to legally leave their infants at designated places and ensuring the infants receive appropriate care and protection.

- The state funds drug treatment programs for pregnant women and newborns.

BIOETHICS LAWS:

- New York maintains no laws related to human cloning.

- New York maintains an institute to disburse state monies for destructive embryo research.

- However, the state does facilitate the donation of umbilical cord blood for stem cell collection, preservation, and storage for public or private use.

- New York regulates commercial surrogacy, screening of semen donors, gamete donation, and insurance coverage for infertility.

END OF LIFE LAWS:

- New York expressly prohibits assisted suicide. Under a criminal statute, assisted suicide is defined as a form of manslaughter. This prohibition has been upheld by the U.S. Supreme Court.

HEALTHCARE RIGHTS OF CONSCIENCE LAWS:

Participation in Abortion:

- A person who objects in writing and on the basis of religious beliefs or conscience is not required to perform or assist in an abortion.

- Staff members of the State Department of Social Services may refuse to provide family planning services if in conflict with their cultural values, conscience, or religious convictions.

Participation in Research Harmful to Human Life:

- New York currently provides no protection for the rights of healthcare providers who conscientiously object to participation in human cloning, destructive embryo research, and other forms of immoral medical research.

WHAT HAPPENED IN 2009:

- New York enacted legislation making technical corrections to provisions designating surrogate decision-making committees as guardians of mentally-retarded persons for the purposes of healthcare decisions.

- New York considered measures requiring informed consent before abortion; requiring women receive information about fetal pain; and requiring parental involvement. The state also considered a range of measures relating to the unborn and newly born, from unborn victims of violence measures, to the availability of stillbirth certificates, to expansion of the state's "Baby Moses" law.

- Conversely, the state considered measures mandating insurance coverage for abortion; requiring residents receive medical training in contraception and abortion, without exception; and imposing burdensome regulations on pregnancy care centers. Notably, it also debated a state "Freedom of Choice Act."

- New York considered measures promoting the accessibility of "emergency contraception," mandating insurance coverage of contraception, allowing nurses and pharmacists to dispense "emergency contraception," and promoting "emergency contraception" on New York college campuses.

- On the bioethics front, the state considered legislation promoting destructive embryo research, banning cloning for all purposes, and regulating assisted reproductive technologies.

- The state considered measures promoting proper palliative care and pain management and education.

- New York considered amending its existing healthcare rights of conscience laws to prohibit discrimination based on objections to certain end-of-life care, life-sustaining treatment, or contraception. Conversely, the state considered legislation requiring pharmacists and pharmacies to fill prescriptions without regard to religious or moral beliefs.

- In *Tummino v. Torti*, the Eastern District of New York ruled that Plan B ("emergency contraception") should be made available to 17-year-olds and directed the FDA to reconsider its policies regarding minors' access. The Obama Administration did not appeal and the FDA plans to comply.

RECOMMENDATIONS FOR NEW YORK

	Short-term Priorities	Additional Goals
ABORTION		
Informed Consent	Comprehensive informed consent law with reflection period	
Parental Involvement	Parental notice or consent	
State Rights & Policies	Amendment declaring no state constitutional right to abortion; continue to defend against state FOCA	
Abortion Funding	Limits on use of state funding for abortions	
Abortion Provider Requirements		Abortion clinic regulations
Abortion Bans		
Regulation of Abortifacients		Regulation of RU-486
PCCs Support		Direct funding of PCCs
Abortion Reporting		
LEGAL RECOGNITION AND PROTECTION FOR UNBORN & NEWLY BORN		
Fetal Homicide	Comprehensive unborn victims of violence protection	
Assault on Unborn		
Prohibitions on Wrongful Birth & Wrongful Life Lawsuits		

Permit Wrongful Death Lawsuits		
Born-Alive Infant Protection		
Abandoned Infant Protection		
BIOETHICS		
Human Cloning		Ban on human cloning
DER		Ban on DER
State Funding of DER	Ban on state funding of DER	
ART & IVF		Any medically-appropriate regulation of ART
END OF LIFE		
Assisted Suicide		
Pain Management Education		
RIGHTS OF CONSCIENCE		
Protection for Individual Providers	Comprehensive ROC protection	
Protection for Institutions	Comprehensive ROC protection	
Protection for Payers	Comprehensive ROC protection	

NORTH CAROLINA

RANKING: 27

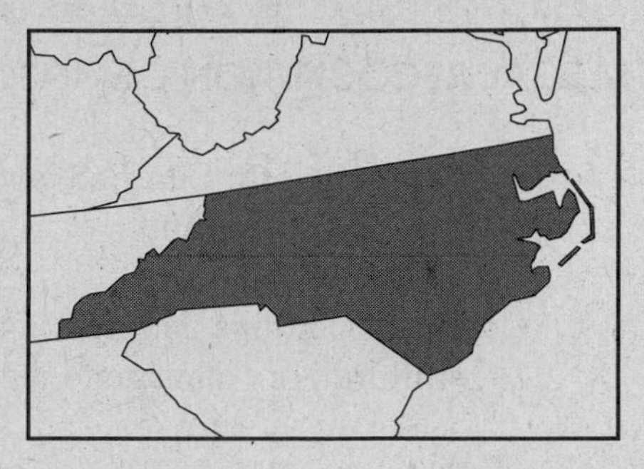

North Carolina lacks many common sense and life-affirming laws. For example, North Carolina does not require informed consent for abortion and does not protect unborn victims of violence. Moreover, despite the significant threats of abuse inherent in some biotechnologies, North Carolina does not regulate destructive embryo research, human cloning, or assisted reproductive technologies. Finally, North Carolina is one of a small number of states that does not expressly prohibit assisted suicide.

ABORTION:

- A physician may not perform an abortion on an unemancipated minor under the age of 18 without the written consent of one parent or a grandparent with whom the minor has lived for at least six months. A court order may be issued foregoing the consent requirement if the judge finds the minor "is mature and well informed enough to make her own decision, that parental consent is not in her best interest, or that she is the victim of rape or felonious incest."

- North Carolina prohibits public funding of abortion unless the pregnancy is the result of rape or incest or the woman's life is at risk.

- North Carolina has enacted comprehensive regulations establishing minimum health and safety standards for abortion clinics. Among the areas regulated are clinic administration, staffing, patient medical evaluations, and post-operative care.

- Only physicians licensed to practice medicine in North Carolina may perform abortions.

- The state has an enforceable abortion reporting law, but does not require the reporting of information to the Centers for Disease Control and Prevention (CDC). The measure applies to both surgical and nonsurgical abortions.

- Health insurance plans that provide prescription coverage must also provide coverage for contraception. The provision includes an exemption so narrow that it excludes the ability of most employers and insurers with moral or religious objections from exercising the exemption.

LEGAL RECOGNITION OF UNBORN AND NEWLY BORN:

- Current North Carolina law does not recognize an unborn child as a potential victim of homicide or assault.
- North Carolina defines criminal assaults on a pregnant woman that result in miscarriage, stillbirth, or "damage to pregnancy" as an enhanced offense for sentencing purposes.
- The state allows for wrongful death (civil) actions when a viable unborn child is killed through a negligent or criminal act.
- North Carolina does not require that infants who survive an abortion be given appropriate medical care.
- North Carolina has a "Baby Moses" law, establishing a safe haven for mothers to legally leave their infants at designated places and ensuring the infants receive appropriate care and protection.
- The state funds drug treatment programs for pregnant women and newborns.

BIOETHICS LAWS:

- North Carolina maintains no laws regarding human cloning, destructive embryo research, or assisted reproductive technologies.
- North Carolina requires the State Department of Health and Human Services to make publicly available publications on umbilical cord stem cells and umbilical cord blood banking. The Department also encourages healthcare professionals to provide the publications to their pregnant patients.

END OF LIFE LAWS:

- North Carolina's treatment of assisted suicide is unclear. While the state has statutorily adopted the common law of crimes, it has also abolished the common law crime of suicide. Assisted suicide may still be a common law crime.

HEALTHCARE RIGHTS OF CONSCIENCE LAWS:

Participation in Abortion:

- A licensed physician or nurse who objects on religious, moral, or ethical grounds is not required to participate in abortions.
- A hospital or other healthcare institution is not required to provide abortions.
- The state provides some protection for the civil rights of pharmacists and pharmacies.

Participation in Research Harmful to Human Life:

- North Carolina currently provides no protection for the rights of healthcare providers who conscientiously object to participation in human cloning, destructive embryo research, or other forms of immoral medical research.

WHAT HAPPENED IN 2009:

- North Carolina enacted a law requiring the State Department of Health and Human Services to make publicly available publications on umbilical cord stem cells and umbilical cord blood banking.
- North Carolina considered measures requiring informed consent with a 24 hour reflection period, requiring notarized parental consent, requiring abortion providers to perform ultrasounds, prohibiting coverage of abortion under the state health plan, and authorizing "Choose Life" license plates.
- The state also considered a measure defining a child born alive as a result of abortion as a "person," as well as a number of measures protecting unborn victims of violence.
- North Carolina considered a measure providing protection to persons who conscientiously object to the provision of drugs or devices that result in abortion.

RECOMMENDATIONS FOR NORTH CAROLINA

	Short-term Priorities	Additional Goals
ABORTION		
Informed Consent	Comprehensive informed consent law with reflection period	
Parental Involvement		Parental consent enhancements like notarized consent or identification requirements
State Rights & Policies		
Abortion Funding	Ban on use of state funding for abortion counseling or referrals	Ban on use of state facilities for abortion
Abortion Provider Requirements		
Abortion Bans		
Regulation of Abortifacients		Regulation of RU-486
PCCs Support	Direct funding of PCCs	
Abortion Reporting		
LEGAL RECOGNITION AND PROTECTION FOR UNBORN & NEWLY BORN		
Fetal Homicide	Comprehensive unborn victims of violence protection	
Assault on Unborn		
Prohibitions on Wrongful Birth & Wrongful Life Lawsuits		
Permit Wrongful Death Lawsuits		

Born-Alive Infant Protection		
Abandoned Infant Protection		
BIOETHICS		
Human Cloning		Ban on human cloning
DER		Ban on DER
State Funding of DER	Ban on state funding of DER	
ART & IVF		Any medically-appropriate regulation of ART
END OF LIFE		
Assisted Suicide	Statutory prohibition on assisted suicide	
Pain Management Education		
RIGHTS OF CONSCIENCE		
Protection for Individual Providers	Comprehensive ROC protection	
Protection for Institutions	Comprehensive ROC protection	
Protection for Payers	Comprehensive ROC protection	

NORTH DAKOTA
RANKING: 7

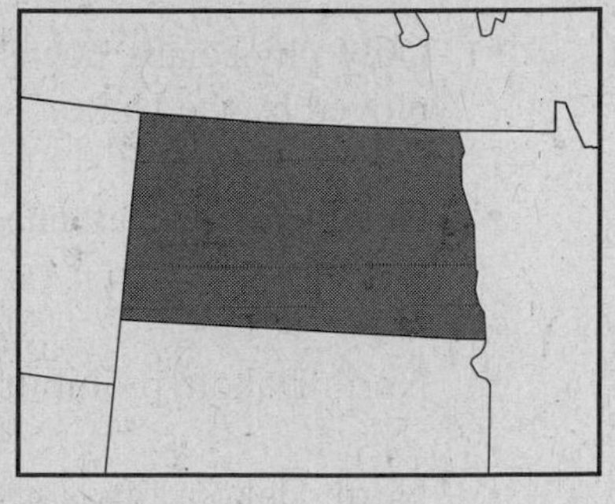

North Dakota has taken the lead in two important and emerging areas: public funding for abortion alternatives and meaningful regulation of biotechnologies. North Dakota has allocated hundreds of thousands of dollars in state funds to organizations promoting alternatives to abortion. It is also one of only a handful of states that bans both human cloning and destructive embryo research.

ABORTION:

- A physician may not perform an abortion on a woman until at least 24 hours after the woman has been informed of the medical risks associated with abortion; the medical risks of carrying the pregnancy to term; the probable gestational age of the unborn child; state assistance benefits; the father's legal obligations; the availability of state-prepared information on the development of the unborn child; and a list of agencies that offer alternatives to abortion. Women must be also be informed that "the abortion will terminate the life of a whole, separate, unique, living human being."

- Abortion providers must offer a woman the opportunity to view an ultrasound image of her unborn child.

- North Dakota prohibits anyone from coercing a woman into abortion. Further, notice must be posted at all abortion facilities stating that no one can force a woman to have an abortion.

- A physician may not perform an abortion on an unmarried minor under the age of 18 without the written consent of one parent or a court order.

- North Dakota prohibits organizations receiving state funds from using those funds to provide abortion counseling or to make referrals for abortion.

- An abortion may not be performed in hospitals owned or operated by the state, unless the abortion is necessary to preserve the life of the woman.

- State health insurance contracts, policies, and plans must exclude coverage for abortion unless the abortion is necessary to preserve the woman's life. Private insurance companies are also prohibited from covering abortion except in cases of life endangerment.

- Only physicians licensed by North Dakota to practice medicine or osteopathy or employed by the United States may perform abortions.

- North Dakota has enacted a measure banning abortion should *Roe v. Wade* be overturned.

- North Dakota prohibits partial-birth abortion.

- North Dakota funds organizations that promote abortion alternatives.

- The state has an enforceable abortion reporting law, but does not require the reporting of information to the Centers for Disease Control and Prevention (CDC). The measure applies to both surgical and nonsurgical abortions.

- The state requires that health maintenance organizations cover prescription contraception or family planning services.

LEGAL RECOGNITION OF UNBORN AND NEWLY BORN:

- Under North Dakota criminal law, the killing of an unborn child at any stage of gestation is defined as homicide.

- North Dakota defines a nonfatal assault on an unborn child as a criminal offense.

- The state has created a specific affirmative duty of physicians to provide medical care and treatment to born-alive infants only after viability.

- North Dakota requires healthcare professionals to report suspected prenatal drug exposure. In addition, healthcare professionals must test newborns for prenatal drug exposure when there is adequate suspicion of prenatal use by the mother.

BIOETHICS LAWS:

- North Dakota bans both cloning-to-produce-children and cloning-for-biomedical-research.

- North Dakota bans fetal experimentation.

- North Dakota has enacted a measure relating to the inheritance rights of children created through assisted reproductive technologies.

END OF LIFE LAWS:

- In North Dakota, assisting a suicide is a felony.

HEALTHCARE RIGHTS OF CONSCIENCE LAWS:

Participation in Abortion:

- A hospital, physician, nurse, hospital employee, or any other person is not under a legal duty or contractual obligation to participate in abortions.

Participation in Research Harmful to Human Life:

- North Dakota currently provides no protection for the rights of healthcare providers who conscientiously object to participation in human cloning, destructive embryo research, and other forms of immoral medical research.

WHAT HAPPENED IN 2009:

- North Dakota enacted a measure requiring that an abortion provider offer a woman the opportunity to view an ultrasound image of her unborn child.

- The state also enacted a measure aimed at preventing coerced abortions, requiring that notice be posted at all abortion facilities stating that no one can force a woman to have an abortion.

- The state amended its informed consent requirements to include a statement that an "abortion will terminate the life of a whole, separate, unique, living human being."

- North Dakota also enacted legislation providing direct funding to abortion alternatives.

- North Dakota enacted a measure related to inheritance rights of children created through assisted reproductive technologies.

- The state also enacted a measure creating a registry for advance directives for healthcare.

- North Dakota did not consider any measures related to healthcare rights of conscience.

RECOMMENDATIONS FOR NORTH DAKOTA		
	Short-term Priorities	**Additional Goals**
	ABORTION	
Informed Consent	Counseling on fetal pain	
Parental Involvement	Parental consent enhancements like notarized consent or identification requirements	
State Rights & Policies	Resolution opposing federal FOCA	
Abortion Funding		
Abortion Provider Requirements	Comprehensive abortion clinic regulations	
Abortion Bans		
Regulation of Abortifacients		Regulation of RU-486
PCCs Support		
Abortion Reporting		
	LEGAL RECOGNITION AND PROTECTION FOR UNBORN & NEWLY BORN	
Fetal Homicide		
Assault on Unborn		
Prohibitions on Wrongful Birth & Wrongful Life Lawsuits		
Permit Wrongful Death Lawsuits		

Born-Alive Infant Protection		
Abandoned Infant Protection		
BIOETHICS		
Human Cloning		
DER		
State Funding of DER	Funding of ethical alternatives	
ART & IVF		Any medically-appropriate regulation of ART
END OF LIFE		
Assisted Suicide		
Pain Management Education		
RIGHTS OF CONSCIENCE		
Protection for Individual Providers	Comprehensive ROC protection	
Protection for Institutions	Comprehensive ROC protection	
Protection for Payers	Comprehensive ROC protection	

OHIO
RANKING: 17

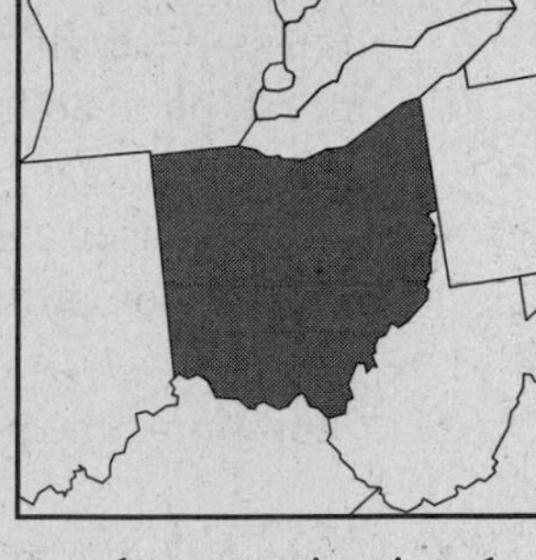

Ohio maintains fairly comprehensive protections for women and the unborn, including a regulation requiring abortion providers to abide by the FDA-approved protocol when administering the dangerous abortion drug, RU-486. However, the state has fallen behind in regulating biotechnologies, failing to ban or even regulate destructive embryo research or human cloning. Ohio also fails to protect healthcare providers who conscientiously object to participating in such immoral research.

ABORTION:

- A physician may not perform an abortion on a woman until at least 24 hours after the physician informs her of the nature of the proposed abortion procedure and its risks; the probable gestational age of the unborn child; and the medical risks of carrying the pregnancy to term. The physician must also provide state-prepared materials describing the development of the unborn child; public and private agencies providing assistance; state medical assistance benefits; and the father's legal obligations.

- Ohio requires abortion providers to offer a woman the opportunity to view an ultrasound and to obtain a copy of the image when an ultrasound is performed as part of the preparation for an abortion.

- Abortion facilities must post signs informing women that no one can force them to have abortions. The law also increases the penalty for domestic violence if the offender knew the woman was pregnant, and permits recovery of compensatory and exemplary damages when mandatory reporters fail to report suspected abuse.

- A physician may not perform an abortion on an unemancipated minor under the age of 18 until receiving the consent of one parent or guardian.

- Ohio prohibits public funds from being used for abortions unless the procedure is necessary to preserve the life of the woman or the pregnancy is the result of rape or incest.

- Ohio prohibits insurance coverage of abortion for government employees, the use of public funds for abortion counseling, and the use of public facilities to perform abortions.

- State employee health insurance may not provide coverage for abortion unless the abor-

tion is necessary to preserve the woman's life, the pregnancy is the result of rape or incest, or an additional premium is paid for an optional rider.

- Ohio licenses and regulates abortion clinics as a subset of ambulatory surgical centers. All abortion providers must maintain admitting privileges.

- Ohio limits the performance of abortions to licensed physicians.

- Ohio prohibits partial-birth abortion throughout pregnancy under a law which has been litigated and upheld in federal court.

- In 2004, Ohio enacted a law regulating the provision of RU-486 and creating criminal penalties for providing the drug without following FDA-approved guidelines. The law also requires abortion providers to inform the state medical board whenever RU-486 leads to "serious complications." In July 2009, the Sixth Circuit Court of Appeals vacated a lower court injunction against the law, allowing the law to be enforced.

- Ohio permits motorists to pay a $30 fee for "Choose Life" specialty license plates, with $20 from the proceeds of each plate designated for non-profit groups that encourage adoption. In 2007, the state also allocated $150,000 over two years to a "Choose Life" fund.

- The state has an enforceable abortion reporting law, but does not require the reporting of information to the Centers for Disease Control and Prevention (CDC). The measure applies to both surgical and nonsurgical abortions and requires abortion providers to report short-term complications.

- The state requires health maintenance organizations to cover prescription contraception and family planning services.

LEGAL RECOGNITION OF UNBORN AND NEWLY BORN:

- Under Ohio criminal law, the killing of an unborn child at any stage of gestation is homicide.

- Ohio defines a nonfatal assault on an unborn child as a crime.

- Ohio allows wrongful death (civil) actions when a viable unborn child is killed through negligent or criminal act.

- Ohio has a "Baby Moses" law, establishing a safe haven for mothers to legally leave their infants at designated places and ensuring the infants receive appropriate care and protection.

- The state funds drug treatment programs for pregnant women and newborns.

- Under the "Grieving Parents Act," the state requires a fetal death certificate and burial for the death of an unborn child.

BIOETHICS LAWS:

- Ohio maintains no laws regarding human cloning or destructive embryo research, but bans fetal experimentation.

- Ohio maintains minimal guidance relating to assisted reproductive technologies (ART) and regulates insurance coverage of ART services.

END OF LIFE LAWS:

- Ohio has declared that assisted suicide is against public policy. However, current Ohio law does not specifically criminalize assisted suicide. Under existing Ohio laws, an injunction may be issued to prevent a healthcare professional from participating in a suicide, and assisting a suicide is grounds for professional discipline.

HEALTHCARE RIGHTS OF CONSCIENCE LAWS:

Participation in Abortion:

- No person is required to participate in medical procedures that result in abortion.

- A hospital is not required to permit its facilities to be used for abortions.

Participation in Research Harmful to Human Life:

- Ohio currently provides no protection for the rights of healthcare providers who conscientiously object to participation in human cloning, destructive embryo research, or other forms of immoral medical research.

WHAT HAPPENED IN 2009:

- Ohio enacted legislation requiring abortion facilities to post signs informing women that no one can force them to have abortions. The measure also increases the penalty for domestic violence if the offender knew the woman was pregnant, and permits recovery of compensatory and exemplary damages when mandatory reporters fail to report suspected abuse.

- The state also considered measures opposing a federal "Freedom of Choice Act," as well as legislation related to parental consent.

- Ohio considered legislation supporting umbilical cord blood banking and donation.

- The state did not consider any measures related to healthcare rights of conscience.

- The Ohio Supreme Court ruled that its 2004 RU-486 law requires abortion providers to dispense the drug according to the drug label and that it can only be dispensed to women through 49 days gestation. With that clarification in hand, the Sixth Circuit Court of Appeals vacated a broad injunction entered by a lower court in a federal challenge to the law, allowing the law to finally be enforced.

RECOMMENDATIONS FOR OHIO		
	Short-term Priorities	**Additional Goals**
ABORTION		
Informed Consent	Fetal pain counseling	
Parental Involvement	Enhancements such as notarized consent or identification requirements	
State Rights & Policies		
Abortion Funding		
Abortion Provider Requirements		
Abortion Bans		Sex-selective ban or "delayed enforcement" law
Regulation of Abortifacients		
PCCs Support	Continued funding of PCCs	
Abortion Reporting		Mandatory reporting of abortion complications
LEGAL RECOGNITION AND PROTECTION FOR UNBORN & NEWLY BORN		
Fetal Homicide		
Assault on Unborn		
Prohibitions on Wrongful Birth & Wrongful Life Lawsuits		
Permit Wrongful Death Lawsuits		

Born-Alive Infant Protection		
Abandoned Infant Protection		
BIOETHICS		
Human Cloning		Ban on human cloning
DER		Ban on DER
State Funding of DER	Ban on state funding of DER	
ART & IVF		Any medically-appropriate regulation of ART
END OF LIFE		
Assisted Suicide	Statutory prohibition on assisted suicide	
Pain Management Education		
RIGHTS OF CONSCIENCE		
Protection for Individual Providers	Comprehensive ROC protection	
Protection for Institutions	Comprehensive ROC protection	
Protection for Payers	Comprehensive ROC protection	

OKLAHOMA

RANKING: 2

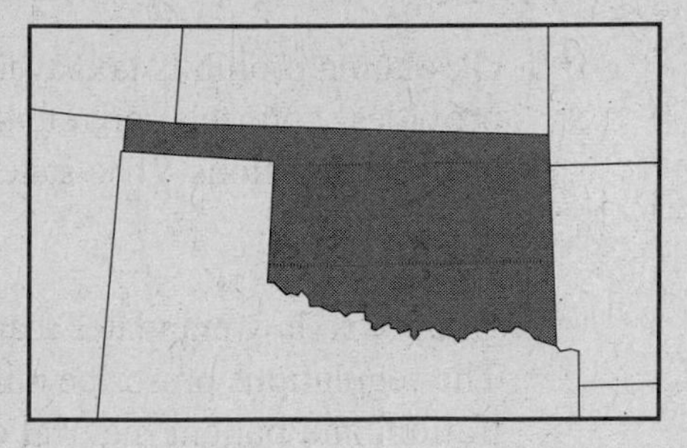

In recent years, Oklahoma has made great strides in protecting both women and the unborn. Among several life-affirming measures passed in 2009, both houses of the Oklahoma legislature enacted an AUL-drafted resolution declaring their opposition to the federal "Freedom of Choice Act."

ABORTION:

- Oklahoma requires that, 24 hours before an abortion, a woman receive counseling on the medical risks of abortion and pregnancy, the name of the physician performing the abortion, and the gestational age of the unborn child. The woman must also receive information on anatomical and physiological characteristics of unborn children at different stages of development and her right to receive state-prepared materials on potential government benefits, child support, and a list of support agencies and their services.

- Oklahoma has supplemented its informed consent requirements, mandating that women seeking abortions at 20 weeks gestation or later receive information about fetal pain and requiring that women be given the opportunity to review an ultrasound prior to undergoing abortions.

- A physician may not perform an abortion on an unemancipated minor without the consent of a parent or guardian. A parent or guardian must sign a consent form and provide photo identification, and the abortion provider must also sign a document attesting to the quality of the identification provided. In a medical emergency, an abortion provider must notify a parent or guardian of the minor's abortion no less than 24 hours after the procedure, unless the minor obtains a judicial waiver.

- Oklahoma has amended its definition of "abortion" to include the use of abortifacients (such as RU-486). It has also amended the definition of "medical emergency" as applied to all of its abortion laws, narrowing the exception to exclude "mental health" and applying it only to cases where a physical condition could cause major impairment of a bodily function or death.

- Oklahoma taxpayers are not required to fund abortions except when the abortion is necessary to preserve the woman's life or the pregnancy is the result of rape or incest that has been reported to the police or a counselor.

- Oklahoma prohibits taxpayer funding of any entity associated with another entity that provides, counsels, or refers for abortion and prohibits health insurance coverage for elective abortions. The state also restricts the use of state facilities for the performance of abortion.

- Oklahoma law mandates that abortion clinics meet minimal health and safety standards. The regulations prescribe minimum standards for the building or facility, clinic administration, and patient medical evaluations. An additional requirement that abortions after the first trimester be performed in a hospital has been ruled unconstitutional.

- Only physicians licensed to practice medicine in Oklahoma may perform abortions.

- Oklahoma possesses an enforceable abortion prohibition should the U.S. Constitution be amended or certain U.S. Supreme Court decisions be reversed or modified.

- Oklahoma prohibits partial-birth abortions and sex-selective abortions.

- Oklahoma has directed the State Department of Health to "facilitate funding to nongovernmental entities that provide alternatives to abortion services." The State has allocated direct taxpayer funding to abortion alternatives.

- The state also offers "Choose Life" license plates, the proceeds of which benefit pregnancy care centers and/or other organizations providing abortion alternatives.

- Abortion providers must report specific and detailed information, including information on the number of women receiving state abortion counseling materials and the number of abortions exempted from the counseling requirement because of a "medical emergency." In addition, abortion providers must report specific and detailed information regarding minors' abortions, including whether physicians received the mandatory parental consent, whether minors sought judicial bypass, and whether or not such bypass was granted. The measure applies to both surgical and nonsurgical abortions, but it is not required that any of this information be reported to the Centers for Disease Control and Prevention (CDC).

- The state requires health maintenance organizations to cover prescription contraception or family planning services.

LEGAL RECOGNITION OF UNBORN AND NEWLY BORN:

- Oklahoma criminalizes the unlawful killing of an unborn child from "the moment of conception."

- Oklahoma also criminalizes a nonfatal assault on an unborn child.

- The state's newly-enacted "Pregnant Woman's Protection Act" provides an affirmative defense to women who use force to protect their unborn children from criminal assaults.

- Oklahoma allows wrongful death (civil) actions when a viable unborn child is killed through a negligent or criminal act.

- Under Oklahoma law, "the rights to medical treatment of an infant prematurely born alive in the course of an abortion shall be the same as the rights of an infant of similar medical status prematurely born." Thus, the state has created a specific affirmative duty of physicians to provide medical care and treatment to born-alive infants at any stage of development.

- Oklahoma has a "Baby Moses" law, establishing a safe haven for mothers to legally leave their infants at designated places and ensuring the infants receive appropriate care and protection.

- Oklahoma requires healthcare professionals to report suspected prenatal drug exposure.

BIOETHICS LAWS:

- Oklahoma bans destructive embryo research and human cloning for all purposes. The state also bans fetal experimentation.

- Oklahoma has created an Advisory Council on Cord Blood/Stem Cell Donations and has allocated funding for a state trust fund to ethical forms of stem cell research.

- Oklahoma regulates the donation and transfer of human embryos used in assisted reproductive technologies and establishes that donors of embryos relinquish all parental rights with respect to the donation of any resulting children.

END OF LIFE LAWS:

- In Oklahoma, assisting a suicide is a felony.

HEALTHCARE RIGHTS OF CONSCIENCE LAWS:

Participation in Abortion:

- No person is required to participate in medical procedures that result in or are in preparation for an abortion except when necessary to preserve a woman's life.
- A private hospital is not required to permit abortions within its facilities.

Participation in Research Harmful to Human Life:

- Oklahoma currently provides no protection for the rights of healthcare providers who conscientiously object to participation in human cloning, destructive embryo research, and other forms of immoral medical research. A 2008 law providing such protection is currently in litigation.

WHAT HAPPENED IN 2009:

- In a very busy legislative session, Oklahoma enacted legislation declaring the legislature's opposition to a federal "Freedom of Choice Act."
- The state enacted the AUL-drafted "Pregnant Woman's Protection Act," which provides an affirmative defense to women who use force to protect their unborn children from criminal assaults.
- Oklahoma enacted a measure prohibiting sex-selective abortions. The measure also requires abortion providers to report certain information about women's and minors' abortions for statistical purposes. This measure is in litigation.
- The state enacted legislation that funds abortion alternatives.
- On the bioethics front, Oklahoma enacted legislation banning destructive embryo research and cloning for all purposes. The state also considered measures funding ethical alternatives, regulating assisted reproductive technologies, and regulating embryo donation and adoption.
- Oklahoma enacted a measure creating a registry for advance directives for healthcare. The state also considered a measure making it unlawful to practice interventional pain management without licensing.

- The state considered a draconian measure requiring that prescriptions for contraceptives be filled "without delay," as well as legislation requiring insurance coverage of contraceptives.

- In August 2009, a state court judge invalidated a 2008 omnibus provision requiring a woman to undergo an ultrasound prior to abortion; regulating the provision of RU-486; requiring abortion clinic personnel have a private session with minors to ensure decisions are not the result of coercion; prohibiting coerced abortions; and allowing individual healthcare providers and individual medical facilities to decline to participate in abortions, destructive biotechnologies, and assisted suicide based on moral or religious beliefs. However, the state officials intend to appeal the ruling to the Oklahoma Supreme Court.

RECOMMENDATIONS FOR OKLAHOMA

	Short-term Priorities	Additional Goals
ABORTION		
Informed Consent		
Parental Involvement	Coerced abortion prevention	
State Rights & Policies		
Abortion Funding		
Abortion Provider Requirements		
Abortion Bans		
Regulation of Abortifacients		
PCCs Support	Continued funding of PCCs	
Abortion Reporting		
LEGAL RECOGNITION AND PROTECTION FOR UNBORN & NEWLY BORN		
Fetal Homicide		
Assault on Unborn		
Prohibitions on Wrongful Birth & Wrongful Life Lawsuits		
Permit Wrongful Death Lawsuits	Remove viability requirement from wrongful death actions	

Born-Alive Infant Protection		
Abandoned Infant Protection		
BIOETHICS		
Human Cloning		Ban on human cloning
DER		Ban on DER
State Funding of DER	Continued funding of ethical alternatives	
ART & IVF		Any medically-appropriate regulation of ART
END OF LIFE		
Assisted Suicide		
Pain Management Education		
RIGHTS OF CONSCIENCE		
Protection for Individual Providers	Comprehensive ROC protection	
Protection for Institutions	Comprehensive ROC protection	
Protection for Payers	Comprehensive ROC protection	

OREGON
RANKING: 42

Oregon has a dismal record of failing to protect women, the unborn, the sick, and the dying. For example, Oregon does not mandate informed consent or parental involvement for abortion, does not recognize an unborn child as a potential victim of homicide or assault, and does not limit destructive embryo research or human cloning. Most disturbing is Oregon's law permitting physician-assisted suicide.

ABORTION:

- Oregon does not provide even rudimentary protection for women considering abortions. The state does not have an informed consent law, a parental involvement law for minors seeking abortions, abortion clinic regulations, ultrasound requirements, or a prohibition on anyone other than a licensed physician performing an abortion.

- Oregon taxpayers fund "medically necessary" abortions for women eligible for state medical assistance for general care.

- Oregon has established the "Sexual Assault Victims' Emergency Medical Response Fund," which pays for medical assessments and the provision of "emergency contraception" to victims of sexual assault—including the provision of and prescription for "emergency contraception" to minors.

- Hospitals must provide sexual assault victims with information about and access to "emergency contraception."

- The state has an enforceable abortion reporting law, but does not require the reporting of information to the Centers for Disease Control and Prevention (CDC). The measure applies to both surgical and nonsurgical abortions and requires abortion providers to report short-term complications.

- Health plans that provide prescription coverage must also cover prescription contraceptives. Religious employers may refuse coverage if their primary purpose is the inculcation of religious values, primarily employ and serve people with the same values, and are nonprofit entities under federal law.

LEGAL RECOGNITION OF UNBORN AND NEWLY BORN:

- Current Oregon law does not recognize an unborn child as a potential victim of homicide or assault.

- The state allows wrongful death (civil) actions when a viable unborn child is killed through a negligent or criminal act.

- Oregon does not require that an infant who survives an abortion be given appropriate, potentially life-saving medical care.

- Oregon has a "Baby Moses" law, establishing a safe haven for mothers to legally leave their infants at designated places and ensuring the infants receive appropriate care and protection.

- The state funds drug treatment programs for pregnant women and newborns.

BIOETHICS LAWS:

- Oregon maintains no laws regarding human cloning or destructive embryo research.

- Oregon mandates that only physicians perform artificial insemination procedures.

END OF LIFE LAWS:

- Oregon permits physician-assisted suicide under statutorily-specified circumstances.

HEALTHCARE RIGHTS OF CONSCIENCE LAWS:

Participation in Abortion:

- A physician is not required to participate in or give advice about abortion if he or she discloses this election to the patient.

- A hospital employee or medical staff member is not required to participate in abortions if he or she has notified the hospital of this election.

- A private hospital is not required to admit a woman for an abortion.

- Department of Human Services employees who object in writing may refuse to offer family planning and birth control services.

Participation in Research Harmful to Human Life:

- Oregon currently provides no protection for the rights of healthcare providers who conscientiously object to participation in human cloning, destructive embryo research, or other forms of immoral medical research.

WHAT HAPPENED IN 2009:

- Oregon amended its laws for advance directives, giving the healthcare representative the authority to approve short-term hospitalization for dementia patients.

- Oregon considered legislation expanding its homicide laws to include the killing of an unborn child.

- Oregon considered legislation promoting and funding destructive embryo research. The state also considered legislation that discouraged cloning-to-produce-children, as well as a measure requiring health coverage for treatment of infertility.

- The state did not consider any legislation related to healthcare rights of conscience.

RECOMMENDATIONS FOR OREGON

	Short-term Priorities	Additional Goals
ABORTION		
Informed Consent	Comprehensive informed consent with reflection period	
Parental Involvement	Parental notice or consent	
State Rights & Policies		
Abortion Funding	Limits on state funding of abortion	
Abortion Provider Requirements		Abortion clinic regulations
Abortion Bans		
Regulation of Abortifacients		Regulation of RU-486
PCCs Support		
Abortion Reporting		
LEGAL RECOGNITION AND PROTECTION FOR UNBORN & NEWLY BORN		
Fetal Homicide	Comprehensive unborn victims of violence protection	
Assault on Unborn		
Prohibitions on Wrongful Birth & Wrongful Life Lawsuits		
Permit Wrongful Death Lawsuits		

Born-Alive Infant Protection		
Abandoned Infant Protection		
BIOETHICS		
Human Cloning		Ban on human cloning
DER		Ban on DER
State Funding of DER	Ban on state funding of DER	
ART & IVF		Any medically-appropriate regulation of ART
END OF LIFE		
Assisted Suicide	Repeal of law permitting assisted suicide	
Pain Management Education		
RIGHTS OF CONSCIENCE		
Protection for Individual Providers	Comprehensive ROC protection	
Protection for Institutions	Comprehensive ROC protection	
Protection for Payers	Comprehensive ROC protection	

PENNSYLVANIA

RANKING: 3

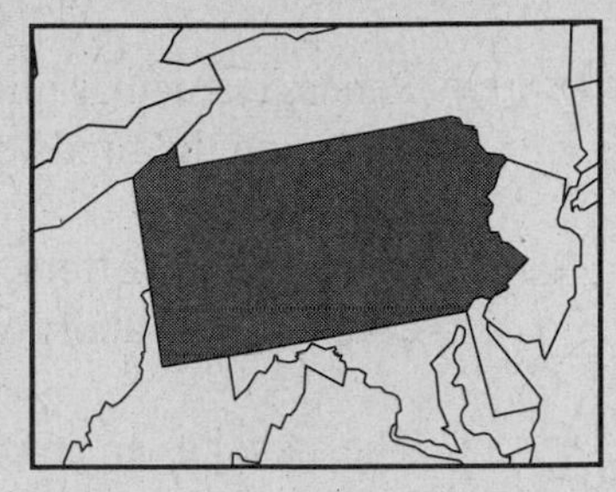

Pennsylvania's efforts to protect women from the negative consequences of abortion have been ground-breaking, as memorialized in the landmark case *Planned Parenthood v. Casey*. Pennsylvania has led the way for other states by enacting such measures as informed consent, parental consent, and state funding of abortion alternatives. However, there has been little effort to regulate human cloning.

ABORTION:

- In the landmark case, *Planned Parenthood v. Casey*, Pennsylvania's informed consent requirements, mandated 24-hour reflection period prior to an abortion, and parental consent requirement for a minor seeking an abortion were upheld as constitutional by the U.S. Supreme Court.

- The state requires abortion providers to state in their printed materials that it is illegal for someone to coerce a woman into having an abortion.

- Pennsylvania does not provide public funding or public facilities for an abortion unless the abortion is necessary to preserve the woman's life or the pregnancy is the result of rape or incest.

- Health plans funded by the state may not include coverage for abortions unless an abortion is necessary to preserve a woman's life, the pregnancy is the result of rape or incest reported by the woman to a law enforcement agency, or there is a fetal abnormality.

- Pennsylvania prohibits organizations that receive state funds from using those funds to provide abortion counseling or to make referrals for abortion. The state also restricts the use of some or all state facilities for the performance of abortion.

- Pennsylvania mandates minimum health and safety standards for abortion clinics. The regulations prescribe minimum requirements for the building or facility, staffing, clinic administration, patient medical evaluations, and post-operative care. These standards require a patient safety plan and the reporting of "serious" incidents (as defined in the enabling legislation). Abortion providers must also maintain hospital admitting privileges.

- Only physicians or doctors of osteopathy licensed to practice medicine in Pennsylvania may perform abortions.

- Pennsylvania has allocated millions of dollars to abortion alternative programs. Entities receiving the funds cannot perform abortions or provide abortion counseling.

- Pennsylvania offers "Choose Life" license plates, the proceeds of which are used to fund adoption and abortion alternatives services.

- The state has an enforceable abortion reporting law, but does not require the reporting of information to the Centers for Disease Control and Prevention (CDC). The measure applies to both surgical and nonsurgical abortions and requires abortion providers to report short-term complications.

LEGAL RECOGNITION OF UNBORN AND NEWLY BORN:

- Under Pennsylvania criminal law, the killing of an unborn child at any stage of gestation is defined as homicide.

- Pennsylvania defines a nonfatal assault on an unborn child as a criminal offense.

- The state allows wrongful death (civil) actions when a viable unborn child is killed through a negligent or criminal act.

- The state has created a specific affirmative duty for physicians to provide medical care and treatment to born-alive infants at any stage of development.

- Pennsylvania funds drug treatment programs for pregnant women and newborns.

- Pennsylvania law provides for "fetal death registrations."

BIOETHICS LAWS:

- Pennsylvania prohibits harmful experimentation on any "unborn child," which is defined as "an individual organism of the species *homo sapiens* from fertilization until live birth." The law may be interpreted to also prohibit harmful experimentation on cloned human embryos.

- Pennsylvania maintains fairly comprehensive regulations for assisted reproductive technologies (ART), including who may practice and participate in the services, record keeping, and standards for maintenance of clinical facilities involved in ART. It also requires quarterly reports of ART data, including number of eggs fertilized, destroyed, or discarded and the number of women implanted.

END OF LIFE LAWS:

- In Pennsylvania, assisting a suicide is a felony.

HEALTHCARE RIGHTS OF CONSCIENCE LAWS:

Participation in Abortion:

- If an objection is made in writing and is based on religious, moral, or professional grounds, a physician, nurse, staff member, or other employee of a hospital or healthcare facility is not required to participate in abortions and cannot be held liable for refusing to participate. Medical and nursing students are also protected.

- Except for facilities that perform abortions exclusively, each facility that performs abortions must prominently post a notice of the right not to participate in abortions.

- A private hospital or other healthcare facility is not required to perform abortions and may not be held liable for this refusal.

- Pennsylvania also protects healthcare providers who object to providing abortifacients.

Participation in Research Harmful to Human Life:

- Pennsylvania currently provides no protection for the rights of healthcare providers who conscientiously object to participation in human cloning, destructive embryo research, or other forms of immoral medical research.

WHAT HAPPENED IN 2009:

- Pennsylvania enacted legislation funding abortion alternatives and providing for stillbirth certificates.

- Pennsylvania considered legislation requiring healthcare providers to report treatment of a minor who is pregnant or has a sexually transmitted disease to preserve evidence against sexual offenders. The state also considered legislation requiring parental involvement for minors seeking contraception and measures protecting unborn victims of violence.

- Conversely, the state considered legislation requiring hospitals and healthcare facilities provide information about and access to "emergency contraception," as well as measures requiring insurance coverage of abortion.

- Pennsylvania considered legislation allowing physician-assisted suicide, but it also considered measures aimed at improving the quality of care for patients suffering pain.

- Pennsylvania did not consider any measures related to bioethics or healthcare rights of conscience.

RECOMMENDATIONS FOR PENNSYLVANIA		
	Short-term Priorities	**Additional Goals**
	ABORTION	
Informed Consent	Enhancements such as ultrasound requirement, counseling on fetal pain, and/or coerced abortion prevention	
Parental Involvement	Enhancements such as notarized consent or identification requirements	
State Rights & Policies		
Abortion Funding		
Abortion Provider Requirements		
Abortion Bans		
Regulation of Abortifacients		Regulation of RU-486
PCCs Support	Continued funding of PCCs	
Abortion Reporting		
LEGAL RECOGNITION AND PROTECTION FOR UNBORN & NEWLY BORN		
Fetal Homicide		
Assault on Unborn		
Prohibitions on Wrongful Birth & Wrongful Life Lawsuits		

Permit Wrongful Death Lawsuits		
Born-Alive Infant Protection		
Abandoned Infant Protection		
BIOETHICS		
Human Cloning		Ban on human cloning
DER		Ban on DER
State Funding of DER	Ban on state funding of DER	
ART & IVF		Any medically-appropriate regulation of ART
END OF LIFE		
Assisted Suicide		
Pain Management Education		
RIGHTS OF CONSCIENCE		
Protection for Individual Providers	Comprehensive ROC protection	
Protection for Institutions	Comprehensive ROC protection	
Protection for Payers	Comprehensive ROC protection	

RHODE ISLAND

RANKING: 28

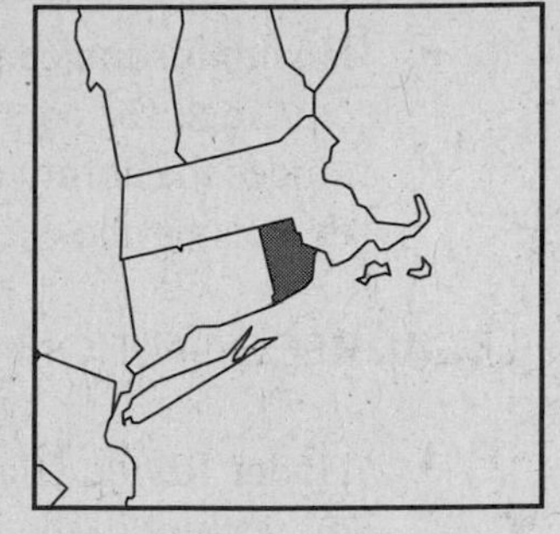

While Rhode Island maintains some basic protection for women and minors, in 2009, the state considered legislation that would have endangered that protection. For example, the state considered a state "Freedom of Choice Act," which would have invalidated all existing abortion-related laws, and a measure that would have allowed a physician or psychiatrist to unilaterally conclude a minor should not be required to obtain parental consent before abortion, thus thwarting current state law.

ABORTION:

- A physician may not perform an abortion on a woman until the physician or the physician's agent has informed her of the probable gestational age of her unborn child and the nature and risks of the proposed abortion procedure. The woman must also sign a statement indicating she was informed that, if she decides to carry her child to term, she may "be able to place the child with either a relative, or with another family through foster care or adoption."

- A physician may not perform an abortion on an unemancipated minor under the age of 18 without the consent of one parent or a court order.

- Rhode Island taxpayers are not required to fund abortions except when necessary to preserve the woman's life or the pregnancy is the result of rape or incest.

- The state health insurance plan provides abortion coverage when a woman's life or health is endangered or in cases of rape, incest, or fetal abnormality.

- Rhode Island has a complex system of abortion clinic regulations under which different standards apply at different stages of pregnancy, and different facilities may be used to perform abortions at different stages of gestation.

- Rhode Island possesses an enforceable abortion prohibition should the U.S. Constitution be amended or certain U.S. Supreme Court decisions be reversed or modified.

- The state has an enforceable abortion reporting law, but does not require the reporting of information to the Centers for Disease Control and Prevention (CDC). The measure applies to both surgical and nonsurgical abortions.

- Health insurance plans which provide prescription coverage are also required to provide coverage for contraception. The provision includes an exemption so narrow that it excludes the ability of most employers and insurers with moral or religious objections from exercising the exemption.

LEGAL RECOGNITION OF UNBORN AND NEWLY BORN:

- Under Rhode Island law, the killing of an unborn child after "quickening" (discernible movement in the womb) is homicide.

- The state allows wrongful death (civil) actions when a viable unborn child is killed through a negligent or criminal act.

- Any physician, nurse, or other licensed medical person who knowingly and intentionally fails to provide reasonable medical care and treatment to an infant born alive in the course of an abortion, and as a result the infant dies, shall be guilty of the crime of manslaughter. Thus, the state has created a specific affirmative duty to provide medical care and treatment to born-alive infants at any stage of development.

- The state defines substance abuse during pregnancy as "child abuse" under civil child-welfare statutes. Rhode Island also requires healthcare professionals to report suspected prenatal drug exposure.

- Rhode Island maintains a measure allowing a woman who loses a child after 20 weeks gestation to obtain a certificate of birth resulting in still birth. The certificate is also filed with the state registrar.

BIOETHICS LAWS:

- Rhode Island bans cloning-to-produce-children, thus making it a clone-and-kill state.

- Rhode Island bans harmful experimentation on a human fetus "whether before or after expulsion from its mother's womb." "Fetus" is defined to include an embryo.

- The state regulates insurance coverage of assisted reproductive technologies.

END OF LIFE LAWS:

- Under Rhode Island law, assisting a suicide is a felony.

HEALTHCARE RIGHTS OF CONSCIENCE LAWS:

Participation in Abortion:

- A physician or other person associated with, employed by, or on the staff of a healthcare facility who objects in writing and on religious and/or moral grounds is not required to participate in abortions.

Participation in Research Harmful to Human Life:

- Rhode Island provides no protection for the rights of healthcare providers who conscientiously object to participation in human cloning, destructive embryo research, and other forms of immoral medical research.

WHAT HAPPENED IN 2009:

- Rhode Island considered legislation requiring informed consent before abortion; prohibiting coercion; requiring an ultrasound before abortion; and prohibiting the use of public facilities, public employees, and public funds for the purpose of performing, assisting in, or encouraging an abortion. The state also considered measures protecting unborn victims of violence.

- Conversely, the state considered a state "Freedom of Choice Act" and a measure modifying the state's parental involvement statute to allow a physician or psychiatrist to conclude a minor should obtain an abortion without parental consent or judicial authorization.

- The state considered healthcare rights of conscience legislation providing comprehensive protection for providers, institutions, and payers, but it also considered a measure requiring pharmacies to dispense prescription and over-the-counter contraceptives without regard to moral or religious objection.

RECOMMENDATIONS FOR RHODE ISLAND		
	Short-term Priorities	**Additional Goals**
ABORTION		
Informed Consent	Comprehensive informed consent law with reflection period	
Parental Involvement		
State Rights & Policies		
Abortion Funding	Ban on use of state funding for abortion counseling or referrals	Ban on use of state facilities for abortion
Abortion Provider Requirements		
Abortion Bans		
Regulation of Abortifacients		Regulation of RU-486
PCCs Support		Direct funding of PCCs
Abortion Reporting		
LEGAL RECOGNITION AND PROTECTION FOR UNBORN & NEWLY BORN		
Fetal Homicide	Protection for unborn from conception	
Assault on Unborn		
Prohibitions on Wrongful Birth & Wrongful Life Lawsuits		
Permit Wrongful Death Lawsuits		

Born-Alive Infant Protection		
Abandoned Infant Protection		
BIOETHICS		
Human Cloning		Ban on human cloning
DER		Ban on DER
State Funding of DER	Ban on state funding of DER	
ART & IVF		Any medically-appropriate regulation of ART
END OF LIFE		
Assisted Suicide		
Pain Management Education		
RIGHTS OF CONSCIENCE		
Protection for Individual Providers	Comprehensive ROC protection	
Protection for Institutions	Comprehensive ROC protection	
Protection for Payers	Comprehensive ROC protection	

SOUTH CAROLINA

RANKING: 18

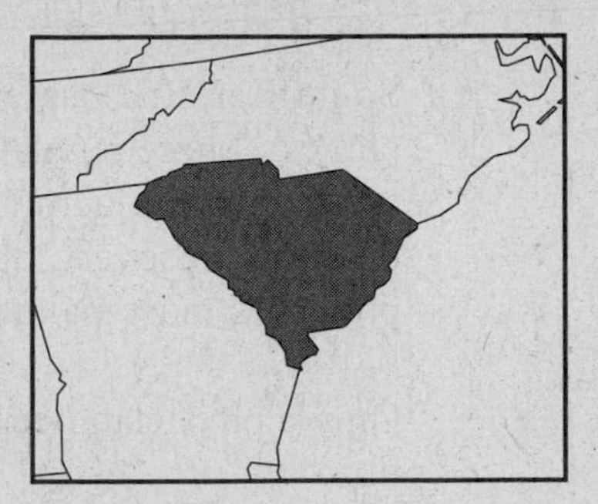

South Carolina maintains a number of life-affirming laws, including comprehensive abortion clinic regulations. While South Carolina has enacted common sense regulations to protect women from the negative consequences of abortion, it has failed to discourage immoral and destructive research on human embryos.

ABORTION:

- A physician may not perform an abortion on a woman until after she is informed of the probable gestational age of her unborn child; the abortion procedure to be used; and the availability of state-prepared, written materials describing fetal development, listing agencies offering alternatives to abortion, and describing available medical assistance benefits.

- If a woman chooses to review the state-prepared, written materials, she must be given at least a one-hour reflection period before an abortion can be performed.

- South Carolina requires a woman be offered an ultrasound and the opportunity to view the image prior to abortion.

- Unless the pregnancy is the result of incest, a physician may not perform an abortion on an unemancipated minor under the age of 17 without the informed, written consent of one parent or grandparent or a court order.

- South Carolina permits Medicaid funding only for abortions necessary to preserve the life of a woman or when the pregnancy is the result of rape or incest reported to the police (unless the woman is unable to report for physiological or psychological reasons).

- State taxpayer funds appropriated to the State Health Insurance Plan may not be used to pay for an abortion except in cases of rape, incest, fetal abnormality, or to preserve a woman's life or health.

- The South Carolina Department of Health and Environmental Control and its employees may not provide referral services or counseling for abortion.

- South Carolina also prohibits any funds appropriated under the South Carolina Birth Defects Program from being used to counsel or refer women for abortions.

- South Carolina has enacted comprehensive health and safety regulations for abortion clinics. These regulations are based on national abortion care standards and cover such areas as clinic administration, physical plant, sanitation standards, patient care, post-operative recovery, and proper maintenance of patient records. Additionally, abortion providers must maintain admitting privileges.

- Only a physician licensed to practice medicine in South Carolina may perform an abortion.

- South Carolina prohibits abortions after 24 weeks gestation unless the attending physician and another independent physician certify in writing that the abortion is necessary to preserve the woman's life or health. If both physicians certify the abortion is necessary to preserve the woman's mental health, an independent psychiatrist must also certify the abortion is necessary.

- South Carolina prohibits partial-birth abortion.

- A South Carolina law requires medical treatment for sexual assault victims include "medication for pregnancy prevention (*i.e.*, "emergency contraception") if indicated and if desired."

- The state has an enforceable abortion reporting law, but does not require the reporting of information to the Centers for Disease Control and Prevention (CDC). The measure applies to both surgical and nonsurgical abortions.

LEGAL RECOGNITION OF UNBORN AND NEWLY BORN:

- The "Unborn Victims of Violence Act" provides that the killing of an unborn child at any stage of gestation may be prosecuted as homicide. The Act also criminalizes a nonfatal assault on an unborn child.

- The state allows wrongful death (civil) actions when a viable unborn child is killed through a negligent or criminal act.

- South Carolina does not require infants who survive an abortion be given appropriate medical care.

- South Carolina has a "Baby Moses" law, establishing a safe haven for mothers to legally leave their infants at designated places and ensuring the infants receive appropriate care and protection.

- The state defines substance abuse during pregnancy as "child abuse" under civil child-welfare statutes.

BIOETHICS LAWS:

- South Carolina does not prohibit human cloning or destructive embryo research.
- South Carolina does not regulate the provision of assisted reproductive technologies or the facilities that provide it.

END OF LIFE LAWS:

- Assisted suicide is a felony in South Carolina.

HEALTHCARE RIGHTS OF CONSCIENCE LAWS:

Participation in Abortions:

- A physician, nurse, technician, or other employee of a hospital, clinic, or physician who objects in writing is not required to recommend, perform, or assist in the performance of an abortion.
- A healthcare provider's conscientious objection to performing or assisting in abortions may not be the basis for liability or discrimination. A person discriminated against in employment may bring a civil action for damages and reinstatement.
- Except in an emergency, a private or nongovernmental hospital or clinic is not required to permit the use of its facilities for the performance of abortions or to admit a woman for an abortion.
- A hospital's refusal to perform or to permit the performance of abortions within its facility may not be the basis for civil liability.

Participation in Research Harmful to Human Life

- South Carolina currently provides no protection for the rights of healthcare providers who conscientiously object to participation in human cloning, destructive embryo research, and other forms of immoral medical research.

WHAT HAPPENED IN 2009:

- South Carolina considered strengthening its informed consent requirement by amending the one-hour waiting period to 24 hours and providing for a state "Born Alive Infant Protection Act."

- South Carolina considered legislation providing that the State Department of Health and Environmental Control may not remove a resident from a community residential care facility if the resident, the resident's family or the resident's healthcare power of attorney, the resident's physician, and the facility agree to the resident's continued stay, and the facility is capable of providing or obtaining necessary services for the resident.

- South Carolina did not consider any measures related to bioethics or healthcare rights of conscience.

RECOMMENDATIONS FOR SOUTH CAROLINA

	Short-term Priorities	Additional Goals
ABORTION		
Informed Consent	Enhancements such as counseling on fetal pain or coercion	
Parental Involvement	Enhancements such as notarized consent or identification requirements	
State Rights & Policies		
Abortion Funding	Ban on use of state funding for abortion counseling or referrals	Ban on use of state facilities for abortion
Abortion Provider Requirements		
Abortion Bans		
Regulation of Abortifacients	Regulation of RU-486	
PCCs Support		Direct funding of PCCs
Abortion Reporting		
LEGAL RECOGNITION AND PROTECTION FOR UNBORN & NEWLY BORN		
Fetal Homicide		
Assault on Unborn		
Prohibitions on Wrongful Birth & Wrongful Life Lawsuits		
Permit Wrongful Death Lawsuits		

Born-Alive Infant Protection	Protection for unborn who survive abortion	
Abandoned Infant Protection		
BIOETHICS		
Human Cloning		Ban on human cloning
DER		Ban on DER
State Funding of DER	Ban on state funding of DER	
ART & IVF		Any medically-appropriate regulation of ART
END OF LIFE		
Assisted Suicide		
Palliative Care & Pain Management Education		
RIGHTS OF CONSCIENCE		
Protection for Individual Providers	Comprehensive ROC protection	
Protection for Institutions	Comprehensive ROC protection	
Protection for Payers	Comprehensive ROC protection	

SOUTH DAKOTA

RANKING: 6

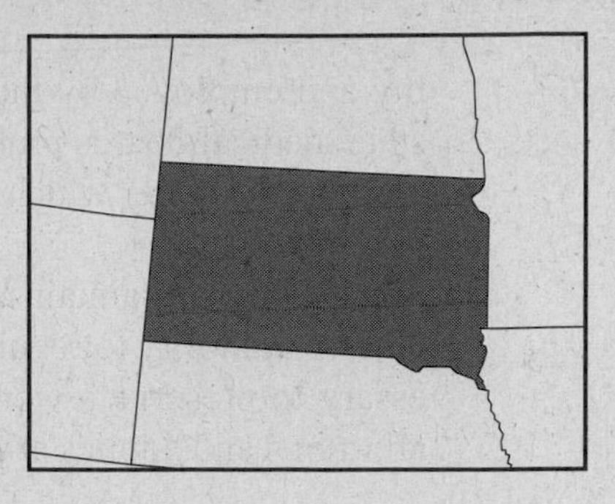

South Dakota has enacted some of the most protective, abortion-related laws in the nation. In addition, the state bans human cloning and destructive embryo research. However, South Dakota has yet to provide comprehensive protection for healthcare providers who conscientiously object to participating in or facilitating procedures and treatments other than abortion.

ABORTION:

- A physician may not perform an abortion on a woman until at least 24 hours after she has been informed of the probable gestational age of her unborn child; the medical risks of abortion; the medical risks of carrying the pregnancy to term; and the name of the physician who will perform the abortion. She must also be informed about available medical assistance benefits; the father's legal responsibilities; and her right to review additional information prepared by state health department officials.

- In addition, South Dakota requires a woman be offered an ultrasound and the opportunity to view the image prior to undergoing an abortion. The law also requires abortion providers report the number of women who undergo abortions after choosing to view an ultrasound.

- A physician may not perform an abortion on an unemancipated minor under the age of 18 until at least 48 hours after providing written notice to one parent or after obtaining a court order. South Dakota also requires parental notification within 24 hours after the performance of an "emergency abortion" on a minor and an exception to the requirement is permitted if a minor indicates that she will seek a judicial bypass.

- South Dakota prohibits public funding for abortion unless the procedure is necessary to preserve the woman's life.

- South Dakota requires that all abortion clinics in the state meet minimum health and safety standards. An earlier law requires second-trimester abortions (beginning at 14 weeks and 6 days gestation) "be performed in a hospital, or if one is not available, in a licensed physician's medical clinic or office of practice subject to the requirements of §34-23A-6 [blood supply requirements]."

- Only a physician licensed by the state or a physician practicing medicine or osteopathy and employed by the state or the United States may perform an abortion. Further, state medical boards prohibit physician assistants and nurses from entering into practice agreements under which they may perform abortions.

- South Dakota maintains a law that would "on the date that the states are given the exclusive authority to regulate abortion" ban abortion throughout pregnancy except if necessary to preserve a woman's life. It specifically applies both to surgical and chemical abortions and applies at all stages of pregnancy.

- South Dakota prohibits partial-birth abortion.

- South Dakota provides that no abortion may be performed after the 24th week of pregnancy unless the procedure is necessary to preserve the woman's life or health.

- The state offers "Choose Life" license plates, the proceeds of which benefit pregnancy care centers and/or other organizations providing abortion alternatives.

- For each abortion performed, an abortion provider must complete a reporting form mandated and provided by the South Dakota Department of Health. The information that must be reported includes: (1) the method of abortion; (2) the approximate gestational age of the fetus; (3) the specific reason for the abortion; (4) the entity, if any, that paid for the abortion; (5) a description of any complications from the abortion; (6) the method used to dispose of fetal tissue; (7) the specialty area of the attending physician; (8) whether the attending physician has been subject to license revocation, suspension, or other professional sanction; (9) the number of previous abortions the woman has had; (10) the number of previous live births of the woman; (11) whether the woman received the RH test and tested positive for the RH-negative factor; and (12) the marital and educational status and race of the woman. The provision applies to both surgical and non-surgical abortions, but does not require that any information be reported to the Centers for Disease Control and Prevention (CDC).

LEGAL RECOGNITION OF UNBORN AND NEWLY BORN:

- Under South Dakota law, the killing of an unborn child at any stage of gestation is defined as a form of homicide.

- South Dakota defines a nonfatal assault on an unborn child as a crime.

- The state allows wrongful death (civil) actions when an unborn child at any stage of development is killed through a negligent or criminal act.

- The state has created a specific affirmative duty for physicians to provide medical care and treatment to a born-alive infant at any stage of development.

- The state defines substance abuse during pregnancy as "child abuse" under civil child-welfare statutes.

- South Dakota maintains a measure allowing a woman who loses a child after 20 weeks gestation to obtain a certificate of birth resulting in a stillbirth.

BIOETHICS LAWS:

- South Dakota bans human cloning for any purpose, as well as research on cloned embryos or on embryos produced through *in vitro* fertilization.

- South Dakota provides minimal regulation of facilities offering assisted reproductive technologies. Specifically, the state regulates the use and treatment of gametes, neonates, embryos, and fetuses.

END OF LIFE LAWS:

- Assisting a suicide is a felony in South Dakota.

HEALTHCARE
RIGHTS OF CONSCIENCE LAWS:

Participation in Abortions:

- South Dakota law protects the rights of physicians, nurses, counselors, social workers, and other persons to refuse to perform, assist in, provide referrals for, or counsel on abortions.

- A healthcare provider's conscientious objection to performing or assisting in an abortion may not be a basis for liability, dismissal, or other prejudicial actions by a hospital or medical facility with which the person is affiliated or employed.

- A counselor, social worker, or other person in a position to address "the abortion question . . . as part of [the] workday routine" who objects to providing abortion advice or assistance may not be held liable to any person or subject to retaliation by an institution with which the person is affiliated or employed.

- No hospital is required to admit a woman for the purpose of abortion. The refusal of a hospital to participate in abortions may not be a basis for liability.

- A pharmacist is not required to dispense medication if there is reason to believe the medication would be used to cause an abortion.

Participation in Research Harmful to Human Life

- South Dakota currently provides no specific protection for the rights of healthcare providers who conscientiously object to participation in human cloning, destructive embryo research, or other forms of immoral medical research.

WHAT HAPPENED IN 2009:

- In response to abortion providers traveling into the state from neighboring states to perform abortions, South Dakota considered a bill requiring the physical presence of an abortion provider in the clinic at least one day prior to performing abortions. It also considered legislation requiring insurance coverage of contraception.

- South Dakota did not consider any measures related to bioethics, end-of-life issues, or healthcare rights of conscience.

- In August 2009, a federal district court upheld a provision of South Dakota law requiring, prior to an abortion, a woman be informed that an abortion ends the life of a "whole, separate, unique, living human being." However, the court simultaneously struck down requirements the woman be informed that abortion increases the likelihood she will later commit suicide and that she has an "existing relationship" with her unborn child. These rulings are on appeal to the Eighth Circuit Court of Appeals.

RECOMMENDATIONS FOR SOUTH DAKOTA		
	Short-term Priorities	**Additional Goals**
	ABORTION	
Informed Consent	Enhancements such as counseling on fetal pain or coerced abortion prevention	
Parental Involvement	Amend parental notice law to require parental consent	
State Rights & Policies		
Abortion Funding	Ban on use of state funding for abortion counseling or referrals	Ban on use of state facilities for abortion
Abortion Provider Requirements		
Abortion Bans		
Regulation of Abortifacients	Regulation of RU-486	
PCCs Support		Direct funding of PCCs
Abortion Reporting		
	LEGAL RECOGNITION AND PROTECTION FOR UNBORN & NEWLY BORN	
Fetal Homicide		
Assault on Unborn		
Prohibitions on Wrongful Birth & Wrongful Life Lawsuits		
Permit Wrongful Death Lawsuits		

Born-Alive Infant Protection		
Abandoned Infant Protection		
BIOETHICS		
Human Cloning		
DER		
State Funding of DER		
ART & IVF		Any medically-appropriate regulation of ART
END OF LIFE		
Assisted Suicide		
Pain Management Education		
RIGHTS OF CONSCIENCE		
Protection for Individual Providers	Comprehensive ROC protection	
Protection for Institutions	Comprehensive ROC protection	
Protection for Payers	Comprehensive ROC protection	

TENNESSEE

RANKING: 30

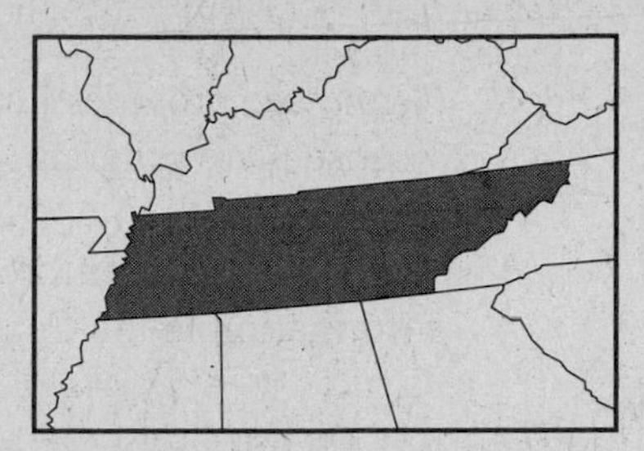

Tennessee is one of 16 states with a court-created state constitutional right to abortion; in fact, Tennessee's court-declared right is one of the broadest in the nation. This decision has been used to nullify the state's informed consent law and mandatory reflection period before an abortion.

ABORTION:

- A court has enjoined the enforcement of Tennessee's informed consent law.
- A physician may not perform an abortion on an unemancipated minor under the age of 18 without the written consent of one parent or a court order. In 2001, the Tennessee Attorney General issued an opinion that this requirement also applies to the use of mifepristone (RU-486).
- The Tennessee Supreme Court has manufactured a state constitutional right to abortion into the state constitution. This right is deemed to be broader than that provided under the federal constitution. Under the auspices of this state constitutional right to abortion, the Tennessee Supreme Court has invalidated a law requiring a three-day reflection period and informed consent prior to an abortion.
- Tennessee provides public funding for abortions when the procedure is necessary to preserve the woman's life or when the pregnancy is a result of rape or incest.
- A federal district court has declared Tennessee's abortion clinic regulations unconstitutional (as applied to the particular abortion provider who challenged the law).
- Only a physician licensed or certified by the state may perform an abortion. Tennessee law provides that no nurse practitioner or physician's assistant may write or sign a prescription, or dispense any drug or medication, or perform any procedure involving a drug or medication whose sole purpose is to cause an abortion.
- Tennessee prohibits partial-birth abortion.
- No abortion may be performed after viability unless necessary to preserve the woman's life or health.

- Tennessee provides funding to pregnancy care centers through a "Choose Life" specialty license plate program.

- The state has an enforceable abortion reporting law, but does not require the reporting of information to the Centers for Disease Control and Prevention (CDC).

LEGAL RECOGNITION OF UNBORN AND NEWLY BORN:

- Under Tennessee law, the killing of a viable fetus is a form of homicide.

- The state allows wrongful death (civil) actions only when an unborn child is born alive following a negligent or criminal act and dies thereafter.

- The state has created a specific affirmative duty for physicians to provide medical care and treatment to a born-alive infant at any stage of development.

- Tennessee has a "Baby Moses" law, establishing a safe haven for mothers to legally leave their infants at designated places and ensuring the infants receive appropriate care and protection.

BIOETHICS LAWS:

- Tennessee does not specifically prohibit human cloning or destructive embryo research, but it does ban fetal experimentation.

- Tennessee does not regulate assisted reproductive technologies.

END OF LIFE LAWS:

- Assisting a suicide is a felony in Tennessee.

HEALTHCARE RIGHTS OF CONSCIENCE LAWS:

Participation in Abortions:

- A physician is not required to perform an abortion and no person may be required to participate in the performance of an abortion.

- A hospital is not required to permit the performance of an abortion within its facilities.

Participation in Research Harmful to Human Life

- Tennessee currently provides no protection for the rights of healthcare providers who conscientiously object to participation in human cloning, destructive embryo research, or other forms of immoral medical research.

WHAT HAPPENED IN 2009:

- Tennessee amended its "Baby Moses" law to include police and fire stations, as well as "emergency medical services facilities," as permitted locations to relinquish custody of an infant.

- Tennessee considered measures amending its abortion clinic regulations, requiring informed consent before abortion, requiring parental notification, providing abortion funding limitations, requiring abortion reporting, and promoting abortion alternatives

- Notably, a measure initiating a constitutional amendment declaring that a right to abortion is not provided for in the state's constitution and effectively countering the Tennessee Supreme Court decision declaring abortion to be a fundamental right will carry over to 2010.

- The state also considered measures providing for stillborn death certificates, criminalizing fetal assault, and requiring a pregnant woman testing positive for alcohol or drugs be referred for substance abuse treatment.

- On the bioethics front, Tennessee considered measures relating to embryo adoption.

- The state did not consider any measures related to end-of-life issues.

- Tennessee considered healthcare rights of conscience legislation providing comprehensive protection for all healthcare providers, institutions, and payers.

RECOMMENDATIONS FOR TENNESSEE

	Short-term Priorities	Additional Goals
ABORTION		
Informed Consent	Comprehensive informed consent with reflection period	
Parental Involvement		
State Rights & Policies	Amendment declaring no state constitutional right to abortion	
Abortion Funding	Ban on use of state funds for abortion counseling or referrals	Ban on use of state facilities for abortion
Abortion Provider Requirements		Abortion clinic regulations
Abortion Bans		
Regulation of Abortifacients		
PCCs Support		Direct funding of PCCs
Abortion Reporting		
LEGAL RECOGNITION AND PROTECTION FOR UNBORN & NEWLY BORN		
Fetal Homicide	Comprehensive unborn victims of violence protection	
Assault on Unborn		
Prohibitions on Wrongful Birth & Wrongful Life Lawsuits		
Permit Wrongful Death Lawsuits		

Born-Alive Infant Protection		
Abandoned Infant Protection		
BIOETHICS		
Human Cloning		Ban on human cloning
DER		Ban on DER
State Funding of DER	Ban on state funding of DER; funding of ethical alternatives	
ART & IVF		Any medically-appropriate regulation of ART
END OF LIFE		
Assisted Suicide		
Pain Management Education		
RIGHTS OF CONSCIENCE		
Protection for Individual Providers	Comprehensive ROC protection	
Protection for Institutions	Comprehensive ROC protection	
Protection for Payers	Comprehensive ROC protection	

TEXAS

RANKING: 4

As a result of aggressive legislative action over the past several years, Texas has become one of the most protective states in the nation. It maintains fairly comprehensive protections for women and the unborn and has appropriated millions of dollars to supporting abortion alternatives. However, the state has yet to act to ban human cloning and destructive embryo research.

ABORTION:

- A physician may not perform an abortion on a woman until at least 24 hours after obtaining her informed consent and after informing her of the nature and risks of the proposed abortion procedure, including the gestational development of the unborn child and available assistance from both public and private agencies.

- The state also explicitly requires a physician to inform a woman seeking abortion of the abortion-breast cancer link.

- Texas prohibits insurance companies from restraining or dominating a woman's abortion decision through force or by threatening adverse alteration to an insurance plan.

- A physician may not perform an abortion on an unemancipated minor under the age of 18 without the consent of one parent or a guardian or securing a court order. In addition, agencies that receive state funding must obtain parental consent before providing minors with contraception.

- The Texas Supreme Court has upheld a law limiting taxpayer assistance for abortion to cases where the abortion is necessary to preserve a woman's life or when the pregnancy is the result of rape or incest.

- Texas prohibits organizations that perform or counsel on behalf of abortion from receiving state funds, and organizations receiving state family planning funds must maintain strict separation from abortion providers. In addition, agencies that receive state funding must obtain parental consent before providing minors with contraception.

- Texas has enacted comprehensive health and safety regulations for abortion clinics. These regulations are based on national abortion care standards and cover such areas as clinic administration, sanitation standards, patient care, post-operative recovery, and proper maintenance of patient records. Further, abortion providers must maintain admitting privileges.

- Only a physician licensed in Texas may perform an abortion.

- Texas possesses an enforceable abortion prohibition should the U.S. Constitution be amended or certain U.S. Supreme Court decisions be reversed or modified.

- A third-trimester abortion may not be performed on a viable fetus unless necessary to preserve the woman's life or prevent a "substantial risk of serious impairment" to her physical or mental health, or if the fetus has a severe and irreversible abnormality. Additionally, a second law provides that a third-trimester abortion may not be performed on a viable fetus unless necessary to prevent "severe, irreversible brain damage" to the woman, paralysis, or if the fetus has a severe and irreversible "brain impairment."

- Texas continues to allocate millions of dollars to the mission of pregnancy care centers and others providing abortion alternatives.

- The state has an enforceable abortion reporting law, but does not require the reporting of information to the Centers for Disease Control and Prevention (CDC). The measure applies to both surgical and nonsurgical abortions and requires abortion providers to report deaths that occur in their facilities as a result of abortion as well as short-term complications.

LEGAL RECOGNITION OF UNBORN AND NEWLY BORN:

- Under Texas law, the killing of an unborn child at any stage of gestation is defined as a form of homicide.

- Texas defines a nonfatal assault on an unborn child as a criminal offense.

- Texas allows parents and other relatives to bring a wrongful death (civil) lawsuit when an unborn child at any stage of development is killed through the negligence or criminal act of another.

- Under Texas law, a "living human child born alive after an abortion or premature birth is entitled to the same rights, powers and privileges as are granted by the laws of [Texas] to any other child born alive after the normal gestational period." Thus, the state has created a specific affirmative duty of physicians to provide medical care and treatment to born-alive infants at any stage of development.

- The state defines substance abuse during pregnancy as "child abuse" under civil child-welfare statutes. The state has also created a task force charged, in part, with advising on potential criminal liability for a woman who exposes her unborn child to controlled substances.

BIOETHICS LAWS:

- Texas does not prohibit human cloning or destructive embryo research, but it does ban fetal experimentation.

- Texas recently appropriated $5 million in state funding for adult stem cell research and also encourages research using umbilical cord blood.

- Texas requires facilities performing *in vitro* fertilization meet minimum standards and regulates insurance coverage of assisted reproductive technologies. The state includes embryo donation in its definition of assisted reproductive technology.

END OF LIFE LAWS:

- Assisting a suicide is a felony in Texas.

HEALTHCARE RIGHTS OF CONSCIENCE LAWS:

Participation in Abortions:

- A physician, nurse, staff member, or employee of a hospital who objects to participating directly or indirectly in an abortion may not be required to participate in an abortion.

- A healthcare provider's conscientious objection to participating in abortions may not be a basis for discrimination in employment or education. A person whose rights are violated may bring an action for relief, including back pay and reinstatement.

- A private hospital or healthcare facility is not required to make its facilities available for the performance of an abortion unless a physician determines that the woman's life is immediately endangered.

Participation in Research Harmful to Human Life

- Texas currently provides no protection for the rights of healthcare providers who conscientiously object to participation in human cloning, destructive embryo research, or other forms of immoral medical research.

WHAT HAPPENED IN 2009:

- Texas renewed funding for pregnancy care centers and other abortion alternatives and a budgetary rider that requires that recipients of state family planning funding segregate their family planning services from abortion services.

- Texas enacted a measure creating a task force charged, in part, with advising on potential criminal liability for women who expose their unborn children to controlled substances.

- The state amended its Health and Safety Code to allow for electronic signatures on advance directives and to permit notarization of "do-not-resuscitate" orders (as an alternative to two witnesses). Texas also mandated licensing and regulation for pain management clinics.

- Texas considered measures requiring an ultrasound before an abortion; strengthening its informed consent law by adding information on coercion; requiring cost information to be posted in abortion clinics; creating "Choose Life" license plates; and, in a unique measure, requiring informed consent for women obtaining "emergency contraception."

- In February 2009, Texas Governor Rick Perry announced the state would provide $5 million in funding for adult stem cell research.

- Conversely, the state considered legislation broadening existing exceptions to the informed consent law, as well as regulations which would have required pregnancy care centers be licensed by the state in order to receive any funding. The state also considered legislation requiring assault victims receive information about and access to "emergency contraception."

- While Texas considered legislation requiring parental involvement for minors seeking contraception, it also considered legislation expanding insurance coverage of contraception for minors.

- Texas considered several measures which would have prohibited cloning-to-produce-children, but not cloning for all purposes. On the other hand, the state also considered measures promoting adult stem cell research and prohibiting the use of state money or facilities for destructive embryo research.

- The state considered a broad constitutional amendment protecting freedom of conscience, including that of healthcare providers.

RECOMMENDATIONS FOR TEXAS		
	Short-term Priorities	**Additional Goals**
	ABORTION	
Informed Consent	Enhancements such as ultrasound requirement or counseling on fetal pain	
Parental Involvement	Enhancements such as judicial bypass standards	
State Rights & Policies		
Abortion Funding		
Abortion Provider Requirements		
Abortion Bans		Sex-selective abortion ban
Regulation of Abortifacients		
PCCs Support	Continued funding of PCCs including "Choose Life" license plates	
Abortion Reporting		
	LEGAL RECOGNITION AND PROTECTION FOR UNBORN & NEWLY BORN	
Fetal Homicide		
Assault on Unborn		
Prohibitions on Wrongful Birth & Wrongful Life Lawsuits		
Permit Wrongful Death Lawsuits		

Born-Alive Infant Protection		
Abandoned Infant Protection		
BIOETHICS		
Human Cloning		Ban on human cloning
DER		Ban on DER
State Funding of DER	Ban on state funding of DER; funding of ethical alternatives	
ART & IVF		Any medically-appropriate regulation of ART
END OF LIFE		
Assisted Suicide		
Pain Management Education		
RIGHTS OF CONSCIENCE		
Protection for Individual Providers	Comprehensive ROC protection	
Protection for Institutions	Comprehensive ROC protection	
Protection for Payers	Comprehensive ROC protection	

UTAH

RANKING: 25

Utah provides a reasonable degree of protection for women, the unborn, and newly born. However, it does not prohibit destructive embryo research, human cloning, or assisted suicide.

ABORTION:

- A physician may not perform an abortion on a woman until at least 24 hours after informing her of the probable gestational age of her unborn child; fetal development; the nature of, risks of, and alternatives to the proposed abortion procedure; that adoptive parents may legally pay the costs of prenatal care; and the medical risks of carrying the pregnancy to term.

- Additionally, Utah requires that a woman receive information on ultrasound services and that a woman seeking abortion at 20 weeks gestation or later must be offered anesthesia for the unborn child.

- Utah prohibits and criminalizes acts intended to coerce a woman into undergoing an abortion. The state also requires abortion providers to state in printed materials that it is illegal for someone to coerce a woman into having an abortion.

- A physician may not perform an abortion on a minor until the physician obtains the consent of one parent or guardian or a court order.

- The Utah legislature has resolved "it is the finding and policy of the Legislature … that unborn children have inherent and inalienable rights that are entitled to protection by the state of Utah pursuant to the provisions of the Utah Constitution. … The state of Utah has a compelling interest in the protection of the lives of unborn children. … It is the intent of the Legislature to protect and guarantee to unborn children their inherent and inalienable right to life…."

- Moreover, the legislature has found and declared "it is the public policy of this state to encourage all persons to respect the right to life of all other persons, regardless of age, development, condition or dependency, including all … unborn persons."

- Utah funds abortions when necessary to preserve the woman's life, the woman's physical health is threatened by a continued pregnancy, the pregnancy is the result of rape or incest, or in the case of fetal abnormalities.

- Utah mandates minimum health and safety requirements for facilities performing abortions after the first trimester. The regulations prescribe minimum standards for the building or facility, staffing, clinic administration, and patient medical evaluations. Further, abortion providers must maintain admitting privileges.

- Only a physician or osteopathic physician licensed by the state to practice medicine may perform an abortion.

- Utah prohibits post-viability abortions except in cases of life endangerment, "serious risk of substantial and irreversible impairment of a major bodily function," severe fetal abnormality as certified by two physicians, or rape or incest reported to the police. Performing a prohibited abortion is a felony.

- Utah prohibits partial-birth abortion under a law which has been litigated and upheld in federal court. Although modeling the federal ban, Utah's law provides harsher penalties.

- The state has an enforceable abortion reporting law, but does not require the reporting of information to the Centers for Disease Control and Prevention (CDC). The measure applies to both surgical and nonsurgical abortions.

- Utah requires healthcare facilities provide information about and access to "emergency contraception" to assault victims.

LEGAL RECOGNITION OF UNBORN AND NEWLY BORN:

- Under Utah law, the killing of an unborn child at any stage of gestation is defined as a form of homicide.

- The state allows wrongful death (civil) actions only when an unborn child is born alive following a negligent or criminal act and dies thereafter.

- Utah has a "Baby Moses" law, establishing a safe haven for mothers to legally leave their infants at designated places and ensuring the infants receive appropriate care and protection.

- Utah requires substance abuse treatment programs receiving public funds to give priority admission to pregnant women and teenagers. The state also requires healthcare professionals to report suspected prenatal drug exposure.

BIOETHICS LAWS:

- Utah does not prohibit human cloning or destructive embryo research, but it does ban fetal experimentation.

- Utah does not regulate assisted reproductive technologies.

END OF LIFE LAWS:

- Utah does not have a specific statute criminalizing assisted suicide. Thus, the legal status of assisted suicide in Utah is currently indeterminable.

HEALTHCARE RIGHTS OF CONSCIENCE LAWS:

Participation in Abortions:

- A physician or other person associated with, employed by, or on staff with a hospital that objects on religious or moral grounds is not required to participate in abortions.

- A healthcare provider's conscientious objection to participating in abortion may not be a basis for damages, disciplinary action, or other recriminatory action.

- Moral or religious objections to abortion may not be a basis for discrimination in hiring.

- A private or denominational hospital is not required to admit a woman for the performance of an abortion.

Participation in Research Harmful to Human Life

- Utah currently provides no protection for the rights of healthcare providers who conscientiously object to participation in human cloning, destructive embryo research, or other forms of immoral medical research.

WHAT HAPPENED IN 2009:

- Utah enacted legislation banning post-viability abortions. It also created a trust account for funds to be used in defending pro-life statutes when challenges arise.

- The state also enacted legislation requiring a woman seeking an abortion at 20 weeks gestation or later be offered anesthesia for the unborn child.

- Conversely, the state enacted legislation requiring healthcare facilities provide information about and access to "emergency contraception."

- Utah amended its "Advance Health Care Directive Act" to expand the list of healthcare professionals authorized to determine a patient's decision-making capacity and effectuate a patient's healthcare directive.

- Utah did not consider any measures related to bioethics or healthcare rights of conscience.

RECOMMENDATIONS FOR UTAH		
	Short-term Priorities	**Additional Goals**
ABORTION		
Informed Consent		
Parental Involvement	Enhancements such as notarized consent or identification requirements	
State Rights & Policies		
Abortion Funding	Limits on use of state funding for abortion counseling or referrals	
Abortion Provider Requirements		
Abortion Bans		Sex-selective abortion ban and "delayed enforcement" law
Regulation of Abortifacients		
PCCs Support		Direct funding of PCCs
Abortion Reporting		
LEGAL RECOGNITION AND PROTECTION FOR UNBORN & NEWLY BORN		
Fetal Homicide		
Assault on Unborn		
Prohibitions on Wrongful Birth & Wrongful Life Lawsuits		
Permit Wrongful Death Lawsuits		

Born-Alive Infant Protection	Law requiring care for infant who survives an abortion	
Abandoned Infant Protection		
BIOETHICS		
Human Cloning		Ban on human cloning
DER		Ban on DER
State Funding of DER	Ban on state funding of DER and funding of ethical alternatives	
ART & IVF		Any medically-appropriate regulation of ART
END OF LIFE		
Assisted Suicide	Statutory ban on assisted suicide	
Pain Management Education		
RIGHTS OF CONSCIENCE		
Protection for Individual Providers	Comprehensive ROC protection	
Protection for Institutions	Comprehensive ROC protection	
Protection for Payers	Comprehensive ROC protection	

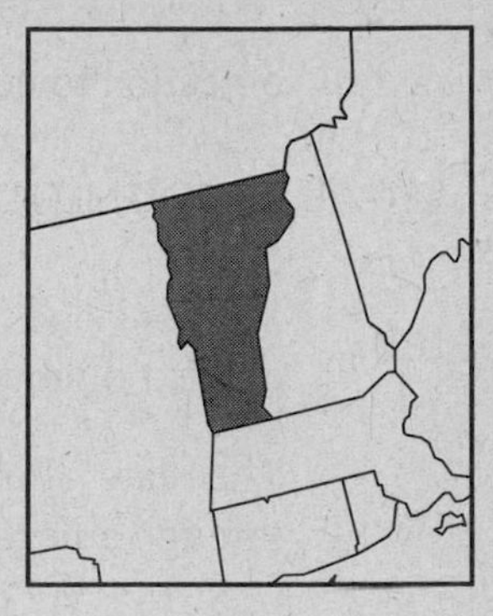

VERMONT
RANKING: 46

Vermont utterly lacks the most basic protections for women considering abortion; for unborn victims from criminal violence; and for human life at its earliest stage from immoral and destructive research. Moreover, Vermont is one of only a few states that does not protect the civil rights of healthcare providers who conscientiously object to participating in any healthcare procedure, including abortion, human cloning, and assisted suicide.

ABORTION:

- Vermont does not provide even rudimentary protection for women considering abortions. The state does not have an informed consent law, parental involvement law for minors seeking abortions, ultrasound requirement, abortion clinic regulations, or a prohibition on anyone other than a licensed physician performing an abortion.
- The Vermont Constitution has been construed to provide a broader right to abortion than the U.S. Constitution.
- Further, the Vermont Legislature has resolved "it is critical for the … personal health and happiness of American women, that the right of women … to make their own personal medical decisions about reproductive and gynecological issues be vigilantly preserved and protected. … This legislative body reaffirms the right of every Vermont woman to privacy, autonomy, and safety in making personal decisions regarding reproduction and family planning…"
- Vermont taxpayers fund "medically necessary" abortions for women receiving public assistance.
- Vermont allows abortions after viability, even in cases where the mother's life or health is not endangered.
- Prior to the FDA's 2006 decision, Vermont enacted a measure allowing pharmacists to dispense "emergency contraception" without a valid prescription.
- The state has an enforceable abortion reporting law, but does not require the reporting of information to the Centers for Disease Control and Prevention (CDC). The measure applies to both surgical and nonsurgical abortions.
- Vermont has a "contraceptive equity" law, requiring health insurance coverage for contraception. No exemption is provided for employers or insurers with a moral or religious

objection to contraception.

LEGAL RECOGNITION OF UNBORN AND NEWLY BORN:

- Vermont does not criminalize the killing of or assault on an unborn child outside the context of abortion.
- The state allows wrongful death (civil) actions when a viable unborn child is killed through a negligent or criminal act.
- Vermont does not require infants who survive abortions be given appropriate, potentially life-saving medical care.
- The "Baby Safe Haven Law" allows mothers to legally leave their infants at designated places and ensures the infants receive appropriate care and protection. The state permits a person or facility receiving an infant to not reveal the identity of the person relinquishing the child unless there is suspected abuse.

BIOETHICS LAWS:

- Vermont does not prohibit human cloning or destructive embryo research.
- Vermont does not regulate assisted reproductive technologies, including *in vitro* fertilization.

END OF LIFE LAWS:

- Vermont does not have a specific statute criminalizing assisted suicide. However, under Vermont law, assisted suicide remains a common law crime.
- Vermont requires the state department of health to provide an annual report on end-of-life care and pain management. The state also has a "Patient's Bill of Rights for Palliative Care and Pain Management" to ensure that healthcare providers inform patients of all of their treatment options.

HEALTHCARE
RIGHTS OF CONSCIENCE LAWS:

Participation in Abortions:

- Vermont currently provides no protection for the rights of conscience of healthcare providers who conscientiously object to participating or assisting in abortions or any other healthcare procedure.

Participation in Research Harmful to Human Life

- Vermont currently provides no protection for the rights of healthcare providers who conscientiously object to participation in human cloning, destructive embryo research, or other forms of immoral medical research.

WHAT HAPPENED IN 2009:

- Vermont enacted a "Patient's Bill of Rights for Palliative Care and Pain Management" to ensure healthcare providers inform patients of all of their treatment options.

- The state considered measures allowing physician-assisted suicide.

- Vermont did not consider any measures related to abortion, protection of the unborn or newly born, bioethics, or healthcare rights of conscience.

RECOMMENDATIONS FOR VERMONT		
	Short-term Priorities	**Additional Goals**
	ABORTION	
Informed Consent	Comprehensive informed consent with reflection period	
Parental Involvement	Parental notice or consent	
State Rights & Policies	Amendment declaring no state constitutional right to abortion	
Abortion Funding	Limits on state funding of abortion	
Abortion Provider Requirements		Comprehensive abortion clinic regulations
Abortion Bans		
Regulation of Abortifacients		Regulation of RU-486
PCCs Support		Direct funding of PCCs
Abortion Reporting		
LEGAL RECOGNITION AND PROTECTION FOR UNBORN & NEWLY BORN		
Fetal Homicide	Comprehensive unborn victims of violence protection	
Assault on Unborn		
Prohibitions on Wrongful Birth & Wrongful Life Lawsuits		
Permit Wrongful Death Lawsuits		

Born-Alive Infant Protection	Law requiring care for infants who survive an abortion	
Abandoned Infant Protection		
BIOETHICS		
Human Cloning		Ban on human cloning
DER		Ban on DER
State Funding of DER	Ban on state funding of DER	
ART & IVF		Any medically-appropriate regulation of ART
END OF LIFE		
Assisted Suicide	Statutory ban on assisted suicide	
Pain Management Education		
RIGHTS OF CONSCIENCE		
Protection for Individual Providers	Comprehensive ROC protection	
Protection for Institutions	Comprehensive ROC protection	
Protection for Payers	Comprehensive ROC protection	

VIRGINIA

RANKING: 16

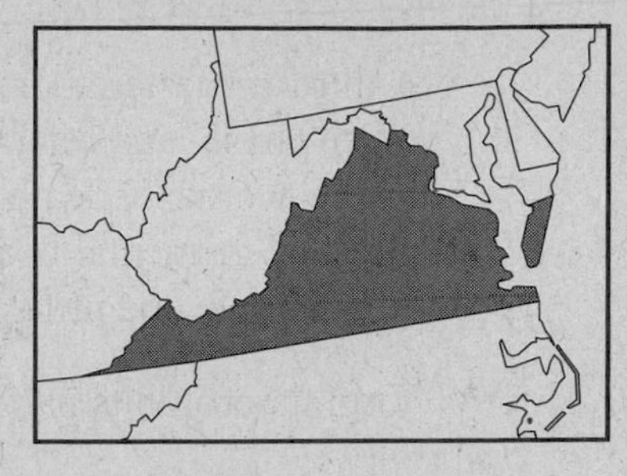

Virginia is one of only a small number of states that has enacted meaningful, protective regulation of emerging biotechnologies. Importantly, Virginia bans all forms of human cloning and prohibits the use of state funds for destructive embryo research. Further, it also regulates *in vitro* fertilization, requiring informed consent for the procedure. In addition, Virginia provides fairly comprehensive protection for women, the unborn, and newly born. In 2009, the Fourth Circuit Court of Appeals reversed a lower court's decision enjoining the state's constitutional ban on partial-birth infanticide.

ABORTION:

- A physician may not perform an abortion on a woman until at least 24 hours after the woman is provided with "a full, reasonable, and comprehensible medical explanation of the nature, benefits, risks of and alternatives to abortion"; the probable gestational age of her unborn child; and a description of available assistance, benefits, agencies, and organizations providing alternatives to abortion and the father's legal responsibilities.

- A physician may not perform an abortion on an unemancipated minor under the age of 18 until he or she secures written consent from one parent or the minor secures a court order.

- Virginia taxpayers are not required to pay for abortions for women receiving state Medicaid assistance unless the woman's life or health would be substantially endangered if the unborn child were carried to term; the pregnancy is a result of rape or incest that has been reported to a law enforcement or public health agency; or a physician certifies that the unborn child will be born with a gross and totally incapacitating physical deformity or mental deficiency.

- No post-partum family planning funds provided to women under the state's Medicaid program may be used to make direct referrals for abortion.

- Benefits provided to state employees through the Commonwealth of Virginia Health Benefits Plan may not provide coverage for abortion unless the procedure is necessary to preserve the woman's life or health; the pregnancy is the result of rape or incest that has been reported to a law enforcement or public health agency; or a physician certifies the unborn child is believed to have an incapacitating physical deformity or mental deficiency.

- Virginia requires that second-trimester abortions be performed in a hospital or ambulatory surgical center. The U.S. Supreme Court has upheld the constitutionality of this requirement.

- A third-trimester abortion may not be performed unless the attending physician and two other physicians certify in writing that continuation of the pregnancy is likely to result in the woman's death or would "substantially and irremediably impair" the woman's physical or mental health. Further, measures for life support for the unborn child "must be available and utilized if there is any clearly visible evidence of viability."

- Virginia prohibits partial-birth infanticide (*i.e.* partial-birth abortion).

- Only a physician licensed by the state to practice medicine and surgery may perform an abortion.

- Virginia offers "Choose Life" license plates, the proceeds of which benefit abortion alternatives.

- The state has an enforceable abortion reporting law, but does not require the reporting of information to the Centers for Disease Control and Prevention (CDC). The measure pertains to both surgical and nonsurgical abortions.

- The state permits a certified sexual assault nurse examiner to provide "emergency contraception" to assault victims.

LEGAL RECOGNITION OF UNBORN AND NEWLY BORN:

- Under Virginia law, the killing of an unborn child at any stage of gestation is defined as a form of homicide.

- The state allows wrongful death (civil) actions only when an unborn child is born alive following a negligent or criminal act and dies thereafter.

- Virginia protects born-alive infants at any stage of development from "deliberate acts" undertaken by a physician that result in the death of the infant.

- Virginia has enacted a "Baby Moses" law, establishing a safe haven for mothers to legally leave their infants at designated places and ensuring the infants receive appropriate care and protection.

- Virginia requires emergency personnel to report child abuse, including cases of *in utero* exposure to controlled substances. The state also funds drug treatment programs for pregnant women and newborns.

BIOETHICS LAWS:

- Virginia prohibits human cloning for any purpose.

- Virginia maintains the "Virginia Cord Blood Bank Initiative" as a nonprofit legal entity.

- Virginia has restricted the use of state funds for destructive embryo research. The Biotechnology Commercialization Loan Fund provides: "No loan shall be made to any entity which conducts human stem-cell research from human embryos, or for any loan to conduct such research; however, research conducted using adult stem cells may be funded."

- However, Virginia allows tax incentives for destructive embryo research by providing that research equipment is not taxed.

- Virginia is one of only a small number of states that prescribes some regulation of assisted reproductive technologies, requiring that informed consent include information on the success rate for *in vitro* fertilization.

END OF LIFE LAWS:

- Virginia does not have a specific statute criminalizing assisted suicide. However, Virginia has adopted the common law of crimes, including the crime of assisted suicide.

HEALTHCARE RIGHTS OF CONSCIENCE LAWS:

Participation in Abortions:

- Any person who objects in writing and on personal, ethical, moral, and/or religious grounds is not required to participate in abortions.
- A physician, hospital, or medical facility is not required to admit a woman for the purposes of performing an abortion.
- The conscientious objection of an individual healthcare provider, hospital, or medical facility to participating in an abortion may not be a basis for a claim for damages, denial of employment, disciplinary action, or any other recriminatory action.

Participation in Research Harmful to Human Life

- Virginia currently provides no protection for the rights of healthcare providers who conscientiously object to participation in human cloning, destructive embryo research, or other forms of immoral medical research.

WHAT HAPPENED IN 2009:

- Virginia approved "Choose Life" license plates.

- Unfortunately, the state also enacted legislation allowing certified sexual assault nurse examiners to provide emergency contraception to assault victims.

- Virginia enacted measures creating a "Uniform Power of Attorney Act," clarifying the process for determining whether a patient lacks decision-making capacity, and specifying how a patient's do-not-resuscitate orders may be effectively revoked.

- The state considered legislation requiring ultrasound and fetal pain information before abortion; relating to parental consent; regulating abortion clinics and requiring abortion providers have admitting privileges at local hospitals; prohibiting schools from providing abortion services and prohibiting abortion providers from dispensing information in schools; and amending the state constitution to provide that "the right to enjoyment of life" vests in born and unborn human beings.

- Conversely, the state considered legislation seeking to compel individual pharmacists and pharmacies to violate their consciences and dispense contraceptives and abortifacients.

- Virginia did not consider any measures related to bioethics or healthcare rights of conscience.

- The Fourth Circuit Court of Appeals reversed a lower court decision which had declared the state's partial-birth infanticide statute unconstitutional.

RECOMMENDATIONS FOR VIRGINIA		
	Short-term Priorities	**Additional Goals**
	ABORTION	
Informed Consent	Enhancements such as ultrasound requirement, counseling on fetal pain, and/or coerced abortion prevention	
Parental Involvement	Enhancements such as notarized consent or identification requirements	
State Rights & Policies		
Abortion Funding		
Abortion Provider Requirements		Abortion clinic regulations applicable to first-trimester abortions
Abortion Bans		
Regulation of Abortifacients	Regulation of RU-486	
PCCs Support		Direct funding of PCCs
Abortion Reporting		
	LEGAL RECOGNITION AND PROTECTION FOR UNBORN & NEWLY BORN	
Fetal Homicide		
Assault on Unborn		
Prohibitions on Wrongful Birth & Wrongful Life Lawsuits		

Permit Wrongful Death Lawsuits		
Born-Alive Infant Protection		
Abandoned Infant Protection		
BIOETHICS		
Human Cloning		
DER		
State Funding of DER	Continued funding of ethical alternatives	
ART & IVF		
END OF LIFE		
Assisted Suicide		
Pain Management Education		
RIGHTS OF CONSCIENCE		
Protection for Individual Providers	Comprehensive ROC protection	
Protection for Institutions	Comprehensive ROC protection	
Protection for Payers	Comprehensive ROC protection	

WASHINGTON

RANKING: 50

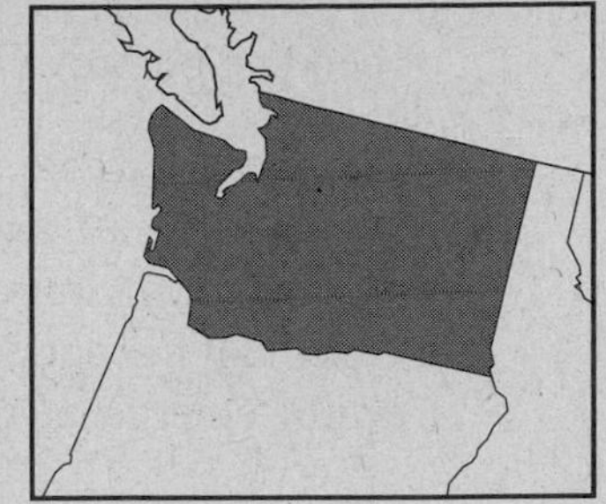

Washington does not adequately protect women from the negative consequences of abortion and to protect the unborn from criminal violence. Washington has failed to enacted common sense, publicly-supported laws such as informed consent, parental involvement, and abortion clinic regulations. The state also has the stigma of failing to protect citizens at the end of life—explicitly allowing physician-assisted suicide.

ABORTION:

- Washington does not have an informed consent law for abortion, parental involvement law for minors seeking abortion, or abortion clinic regulations.
- The state maintains a "Freedom of Choice Act." The Act mandates the right to abortion even if *Roe v. Wade* is eventually overturned, specifically providing: "The sovereign people hereby declare that every individual possesses a fundamental right of privacy with respect to personal reproductive decisions. Accordingly, it is the public policy of the state of Washington that: (1) Every individual has the fundamental right to choose or refuse birth control; (2) Every woman has the fundamental right to choose or refuse to have an abortion . . . ; (3) . . . the state shall not deny or interfere with a woman's fundamental right to choose or refuse to have an abortion; and (4) The state shall not discriminate against the exercise of these rights in the regulation or provision of benefits, facilities, services, or information."
- Further, a state voter initiative declared: "The state may not deny or interfere with a woman's right to choose to have an abortion prior to viability of the fetus, or to protect her life or health."
- Washington taxpayers are required to fund "medically necessary" abortions for women receiving state Medicaid assistance.
- Only a physician licensed in Washington may perform an abortion.
- No abortion may be performed after viability unless necessary to protect the woman's life or health.
- Washington allows pharmacists to provide "emergency contraception" without a prescription. A pharmacist may dispense the abortifacient under written guidelines or protocols established and approved by a practitioner authorized to prescribe drugs. A law requiring pharmacists to dispense "emergency contraception" and life-ending drugs is

pending before a federal district court.

- Hospitals providing emergency care for sexual assault victims must provide victims with "medically and factually accurate and unbiased written and oral information" about "emergency contraception." In addition, hospitals must orally inform a sexual assault victim of her option to be provided with "emergency contraception" and provide a victim with "emergency contraception" upon request.

- The state has an enforceable abortion reporting law, but does not require the reporting of information to the Centers for Disease Control and Prevention (CDC). The measure applies to both surgical and nonsurgical abortions and requires abortion providers to report short-term complications.

- Washington has a "contraceptive equity" law, requiring health insurance coverage for contraception. No exemption is provided for employers or insurers with a moral or religious objection to contraception.

- Washington protects physical access to abortion clinics and limits the First Amendment rights of sidewalk counselors and demonstrators.

LEGAL RECOGNITION OF UNBORN AND NEWLY BORN:

- Under Washington criminal law, the killing of an unborn child after "quickening" (discernible movement in the womb) is defined as a form of homicide.

- The state allows wrongful death (civil) actions when a viable unborn child is killed through a negligence or criminal act.

- Under Washington law, "the right of medical treatment of an infant born alive in the course of an abortion procedure shall be the same as the right of an infant born prematurely of equal gestational age." Thus, the state has created a specific affirmative duty of physicians to provide medical care and treatment to born-alive infants at any stage of development.

- Washington has enacted a "Baby Moses" law, establishing a safe haven for mothers to legally leave their infants at designated places and ensuring the infants receive appropriate care and protection.

- The state funds drug treatment programs for pregnant women and newborns.

BIOETHICS LAWS:

- Washington law does not prohibit human cloning or destructive embryo research.
- Washington does not regulate assisted reproductive technologies.

END OF LIFE LAWS:

- Washington has legalized physician-assisted suicide (PAS) by voter initiative. The initiative creates financial incentives for healthcare insurance companies to deny coverage for life-saving treatment and to pressure vulnerable patients to choose PAS—a practice already occurring in Oregon. Moreover, the initiative does not provide safeguards for those suffering from treatable mental illness, such as depression, and requires physicians participating in patient suicides to falsify death certificates.
- The initiative superseded a prior law which made assisted suicide a felony. That law had been upheld in the landmark case of *Washington v. Glucksberg*, where the U.S. Supreme Court refused to recognize a federal constitutional right to assisted suicide.

HEALTHCARE RIGHTS OF CONSCIENCE LAWS:

Participation in Abortions:

- An individual healthcare worker or private medical facility cannot be required by law or contract to participate in the performance of abortions.
- No person may be discriminated against in employment or professional privileges because of participating or refusing to participate in an abortion.
- Overall, Washington protects individual healthcare providers, as well as private hospitals and medical facilities, who conscientiously object to participating in any healthcare procedure. However, this protection does not extend to public hospitals and medical facilities.

Participation in Research Harmful to Human Life

- Washington currently provides no protection for the rights of healthcare providers who conscientiously object to participation in human cloning, destructive embryo research, or other forms of immoral medical research.

WHAT HAPPENED IN 2009:

- Washington enacted legislation adding medical clinics (during their hours of operation) as an acceptable location to legally relinquish an infant.

- Washington considered legislation requiring parental consent before abortion and mandating that a woman be given the right to undergo and view an ultrasound prior to an abortion. Conversely, the state considered legislation expanding access to contraception, including emergency contraception, and promoting its use.

- Washington did not consider any measures related to bioethics or end-of-life issues.

- The state did consider healthcare rights of conscience legislation providing comprehensive protection for all healthcare providers and institutions.

- The Ninth Circuit Court of Appeals reversed a lower court decision enjoining Washington's draconian rule requiring pharmacists to dispense all drugs, despite their moral or ethical concerns. The case, *Stormans v. Selecky*, continues, and has implications for both emergency contraception and lethal drugs used in physician-assisted suicide.

RECOMMENDATIONS FOR WASHINGTON		
	Short-term Priorities	**Additional Goals**
	ABORTION	
Informed Consent	Comprehensive informed consent with reflection period	
Parental Involvement	Parental notice or consent	
State Rights & Policies	Repeal of state FOCA	
Abortion Funding	Limits on state funding of abortion	
Abortion Provider Requirements		Comprehensive abortion clinic regulations
Abortion Bans		
Regulation of Abortifacients		Regulation of RU-486
PCCs Support		Direct funding of PCCs
Abortion Reporting		
	LEGAL RECOGNITION AND PROTECTION FOR UNBORN & NEWLY BORN	
Fetal Homicide	Protection for the unborn from conception	
Assault on Unborn		
Prohibitions on Wrongful Birth & Wrongful Life Lawsuits		
Permit Wrongful Death Lawsuits		

Born-Alive Infant Protection		
Abandoned Infant Protection		
BIOETHICS		
Human Cloning		Ban on human cloning
DER		Ban on DER
State Funding of DER	Ban on state funding of DER	
ART & IVF		Any medically-appropriate regulation of ART/IVF
END OF LIFE		
Assisted Suicide	Laws limiting provision of assisted suicide such as family member notification and mental health evaluations	
Pain Management Education		
RIGHTS OF CONSCIENCE		
Protection for Individual Providers	Comprehensive ROC protection	
Protection for Institutions	Comprehensive ROC protection	
Protection for Payers	Comprehensive ROC protection	

WEST VIRGINIA

RANKING: 33

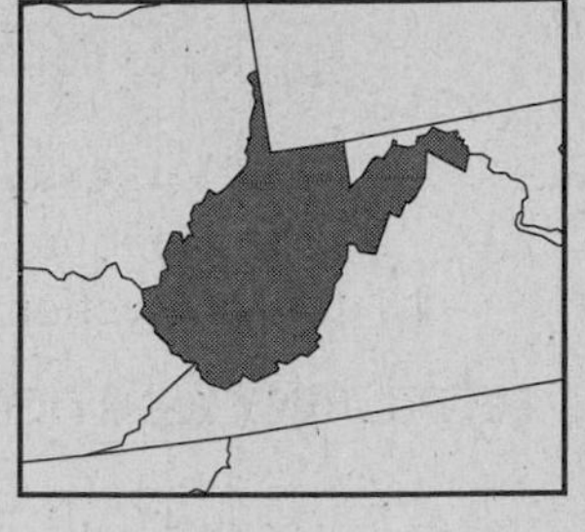

Over the past several years, West Virginia has made significant strides toward protecting women and the unborn, enacting an informed consent law for abortion and protections for unborn victims of violence. However, West Virginia still lacks important protections for women, does not protect the lives of infants born alive following abortion, and does not prohibit human cloning or destructive embryo research.

ABORTION:

- A physician may not perform an abortion on a woman until at least 24 hours after obtaining her informed consent and after informing her of the nature and risks of the proposed abortion procedure; the risks of carrying the pregnancy to term; and the probable gestational age of the unborn child.
- At least 24 hours prior to an abortion, the woman must also receive information about medical assistance benefits that may be available for prenatal care, childbirth, and neonatal care; the father's liability for child support; and her right to review state-prepared materials in print or on the state website that describe the development of the unborn child, describe common methods of abortion, discuss the medical risks of abortion, and list agencies that offer alternatives to abortion.
- The state includes information about the abortion-breast cancer link in the educational materials that a woman must receive prior to abortion.
- A physician may not perform an abortion on an unemancipated minor under the age of 18 until at least 24 hours after actual notice has been provided to one parent or the minor secures a court order. The law also allows an abortion to be performed without parental notice if a physician who is not performing the abortion determines that the minor is "mature enough to make the abortion decision independently or that parental notice is not in the minor's best interest."
- The West Virginia Supreme Court has ruled the state constitution provides for a broader right to abortion than the U.S. Constitution.
- West Virginia taxpayers are required to fund "medically necessary" abortions for women receiving state medical assistance.
- The state has an enforceable abortion reporting law, but does not require the reporting of information to the Centers for Disease Control and Prevention (CDC). The measure

applies to both surgical and nonsurgical abortions.

- West Virginia has a "contraceptive equity" law, requiring health insurance coverage for contraception. The law provides an exemption to employers or insurers with a conscientious objection to contraceptives.

LEGAL RECOGNITION OF UNBORN AND NEWLY BORN:

- West Virginia law recognizes an unborn child at any stage of gestation as a potential victim of homicide.
- The state also criminalizes nonfatal assaults on the unborn.
- The state allows wrongful death (civil) actions when an unborn child at any stage of development is killed through a negligent or criminal act.
- West Virginia does not require physicians or hospitals to provide appropriate, potentially life-saving care to infants who survive attempted abortions.
- West Virginia has enacted a "Baby Moses" law, establishing a safe haven for mothers to legally leave their infants at designated places and ensuring the infants receive appropriate care and protection.

BIOETHICS LAWS:

- West Virginia does not prohibit human cloning or destructive embryonic research.
- West Virginia does not regulate assisted reproductive technologies.

END OF LIFE LAWS:

- West Virginia does not have a specific statute criminalizing assisted suicide. However, assisted suicide remains a common law crime.

HEALTHCARE RIGHTS OF CONSCIENCE LAWS:

Participation in Abortions:

- West Virginia protects the civil rights of healthcare providers, including individuals, hospitals, and other medical facilities, who conscientiously object to participating in abortions.

Participation in Research Harmful to Human Life:

- West Virginia currently provides no protection for the rights of healthcare providers who conscientiously object to participation in human cloning, destructive embryo research, or other forms of immoral medical research.

WHAT HAPPENED IN 2009:

- West Virginia amended its "Management of Pain Act," eliminating the definition of "intractable pain," defining the word "pain," and expanding the definition of "pain-relieving controlled substance."
- West Virginia considered a number of life-affirming measures, including legislation requiring an ultrasound and anesthesia for fetal pain prior to abortion; requiring parental consent or notification before abortion; criminalizing the transportation of minors across state lines for abortion without parental involvement; regulating abortion clinics and who may perform abortions; prohibiting partial-birth and sex-selective abortions; banning post-viability abortions; defining abortion reporting requirements; and creating "Choose Life" license plates.
- Conversely, the state also considered legislation regulating pregnancy care centers and requiring that assault victims receive information about and access to "emergency contraception." It also considered legislation expanding insurance coverage of contraception for minors.
- West Virginia considered a human cloning ban that did not define human cloning—so it is unclear whether it would have prohibited human cloning for all purposes. The state also considered a measure banning fetal experimentation.
- The state also considered measures protecting healthcare rights of conscience.

RECOMMENDATIONS FOR WEST VIRGINIA

	Short-term Priorities	Additional Goals
	ABORTION	
Informed Consent	Ultrasound requirement; counseling on fetal pain	
Parental Involvement		Amend parental notice to require parental consent
State Rights & Policies	Amendment declaring no state constitutional right to abortion	
Abortion Funding	Limits on use of state funding for abortion	
Abortion Provider Requirements		Comprehensive abortion clinic regulations
Abortion Bans		
Regulation of Abortifacients		Regulation of RU-486
PCCs Support		Direct funding of PCCs
Abortion Reporting		
	LEGAL RECOGNITION AND PROTECTION FOR UNBORN & NEWLY BORN	
Fetal Homicide		
Assault on Unborn		
Prohibitions on Wrongful Birth & Wrongful Life Lawsuits		
Permit Wrongful Death Lawsuits		

Born-Alive Infant Protection	Law protecting an infant who survives an abortion	
Abandoned Infant Protection		
BIOETHICS		
Human Cloning		Ban on human cloning
DER		Ban on DER
State Funding of DER	Ban on state funding of DER	
ART & IVF		Any medically-appropriate regulation of ART/IVF
END OF LIFE		
Assisted Suicide	Statutory prohibition on assisted suicide	
Pain Management Education		
RIGHTS OF CONSCIENCE		
Protection for Individual Providers	Comprehensive ROC protection	
Protection for Institutions	Comprehensive ROC protection	
Protection for Payers	Comprehensive ROC protection	

WISCONSIN
RANKING: 21

Wisconsin maintains several common sense laws protecting the health and welfare of women, the unborn, and newly born. However, the state does not prohibit human cloning, and even funds destructive embryo research. Moreover, in 2009, Wisconsin targeted healthcare providers' rights of conscience, compelling pharmacies to dispense "emergency contraception."

ABORTION:

- A physician may not perform an abortion on a woman until at least 24 hours after the woman is informed of the probable gestational age of her unborn child; the details of the proposed abortion procedure and its inherent risks; the particular medical risks of her pregnancy; her right to view an ultrasound prior to an abortion; available medical assistance benefits; the father's legal responsibilities; and alternatives to abortion.
- In addition, Wisconsin requires women receive information about ultrasound services.
- The state also requires abortion providers to state in their printed materials that it is illegal for someone to coerce a woman into having an abortion.
- A physician may not perform an abortion on an unemancipated minor without the informed, written consent of one parent, grandparent, aunt, uncle, or sibling who is at least 25 years of age.
- Wisconsin provides state Medicaid funding for abortions that are directly and medically necessary to preserve the woman's life; directly and medically necessary because of an existing medical condition to prevent grave, long-lasting physical health damage to the woman; or when the pregnancy is the result of sexual assault or incest reported to law enforcement authorities.
- Generally, no state, local, or federal funds passing through the state's pregnancy programs, projects, or services may be used to refer or counsel for abortion. However, referrals may be made if the abortion is necessary to preserve the woman's life.
- Wisconsin's Private Employer Health Care Purchasing Alliance, a voluntary program for private employers, may not include coverage for abortion unless the abortion is needed to preserve the woman's life. However, coverage for abortions that are "medically necessary" may be obtained only by an optional rider or supplemental coverage provision that is offered and provided on an individual basis and for which an additional premium is

paid. Under no circumstances is an employer required to provide coverage for abortion.

- Wisconsin imposes minimal health and safety requirements on abortion clinics.
- Physicians may only perform first-trimester abortions within 30 minutes travel time of a hospital.
- Only a licensed physician may perform an abortion.
- Wisconsin possesses an enforceable abortion prohibition should the U.S. Constitution be amended or certain U.S. Supreme Court decisions be reversed or modified.
- Wisconsin's Attorney General has issued a statement declaring the state's partial-birth abortion law unenforceable, finding it broad and possibly restrictive of other forms of abortion.
- No abortion may be performed after viability unless necessary to preserve the woman's life or health. Moreover, a physician must use the abortion method most likely to preserve the life and health of the unborn child unless that method would increase the risk to the woman.
- Wisconsin requires sexual assault victims receive information about and access to "emergency contraception." A hospital is not required to provide "emergency contraception" if a woman has a positive pregnancy test.
- The state has an enforceable abortion reporting law, but does not require the reporting of information to the Centers for Disease Control and Prevention (CDC). The measure applies to both surgical and nonsurgical abortions and requires abortion providers to report short-term complications.
- Wisconsin has a "contraceptive equity" requirement, meaning health insurance coverage must include coverage for contraception. No exemption is provided for employers or insurers with a moral or religious objection to contraception.

LEGAL RECOGNITION OF UNBORN AND NEWLY BORN:

- Under Wisconsin law, the killing of an unborn child at any stage of gestation is defined as a form of homicide.
- Wisconsin defines a nonfatal assault on an unborn child as a crime.
- The state allows wrongful death (civil) actions when a viable unborn child is killed through a negligent or criminal act.
- The state has created a specific affirmative duty of physicians to provide medical care

and treatment to born-alive infants at any stage of development.

- Wisconsin has enacted a "Baby Moses" law, establishing a safe haven for mothers to legally leave their infants at designated places and ensuring the infants receive appropriate care and protection.

- The state defines substance abuse during pregnancy as "child abuse" under civil child-welfare statutes.

BIOETHICS LAWS:

- Wisconsin does not ban human cloning. Importantly, the governor has twice vetoed a comprehensive ban on human cloning.

- Wisconsin provides funding for destructive embryo research.

- Wisconsin maintains no comprehensive measures regulating assisted reproductive technologies.

END OF LIFE LAWS:

- Under Wisconsin law, assisting in a suicide is a felony.

HEALTHCARE RIGHTS OF CONSCIENCE LAWS:

Participation in Abortions:

- A physician or other person associated with, employed by, or on staff with a hospital who objects in writing and on moral or religious grounds is not required to participate in abortions.

- A healthcare provider's conscientious objection to participating in abortion may not be a basis for damages, discrimination in employment or education, disciplinary action, or other recriminatory action.

- An individual or entity is not required, because of the receipt of any grant, contract, or loan under state or federal law, to participate in or make its facilities available for the performance of an abortion if such action is contrary to stated religious or moral beliefs.

- A hospital's conscientious objection, based on moral or religious grounds, to permitting or performing an abortion may not be a basis for civil damages.

- No individual or entity may be required to participate in or make its facilities available for abortion contrary to religious beliefs or moral convictions because of the receipt of any grant, contract, or loan under state or federal law.

- However, the state's 2009 budget provides that a pharmacy, when presented with a valid prescription, must dispense contraceptives, including "emergency contraception," within "the same time frame" as they would dispense other drugs.

Participation in Research Harmful to Human Life

- Wisconsin currently provides no protection for the rights of healthcare providers who conscientiously object to participation in human cloning, destructive embryo research, or other forms of immoral medical research.

WHAT HAPPENED IN 2009:

- Wisconsin appropriated $154,000 for abortion alternatives.

- Conversely, the state enacted a budget provision mandating contraceptive coverage in health insurance policies. This budget provision also requires a pharmacy, when presented with a valid prescription, must dispense contraceptives, including "emergency contraception," within "the same time frame" as they would dispense other drugs.

- The state also considered a budget provision providing millions of dollars in state funding to Planned Parenthood.

- Wisconsin did not consider any measures related to bioethics or healthcare rights of conscience.

RECOMMENDATIONS FOR WISCONSIN		
	Short-term Priorities	**Additional Goals**
	ABORTION	
Informed Consent		
Parental Involvement	Enhancements such as notarized consent or identification requirements	
State Rights & Policies		
Abortion Funding		
Abortion Provider Requirements		Admitting privileges requirement for abortion providers
Abortion Bans	Enforceable ban on partial-birth abortion	
Regulation of Abortifacients	Regulation of RU-486	
PCCs Support		
Abortion Reporting		
	LEGAL RECOGNITION AND PROTECTION FOR UNBORN & NEWLY BORN	
Fetal Homicide		
Assault on Unborn		
Prohibitions on Wrongful Birth & Wrongful Life Lawsuits		
Permit Wrongful Death Lawsuits		

Born-Alive Infant Protection		
Abandoned Infant Protection		
BIOETHICS		
Human Cloning		Ban on human cloning
DER		Ban on DER
State Funding of DER	Ban on state funding of DER	
ART & IVF		Any medically-appropriate regulation of ART/IVF
END OF LIFE		
Assisted Suicide		
Pain Management Education		
RIGHTS OF CONSCIENCE		
Protection for Individual Providers	Comprehensive ROC protection and repeal of pharmacist compulsion rule	
Protection for Institutions	Comprehensive ROC protection	
Protection for Payers	Comprehensive ROC protection	

WYOMING

RANKING: 32

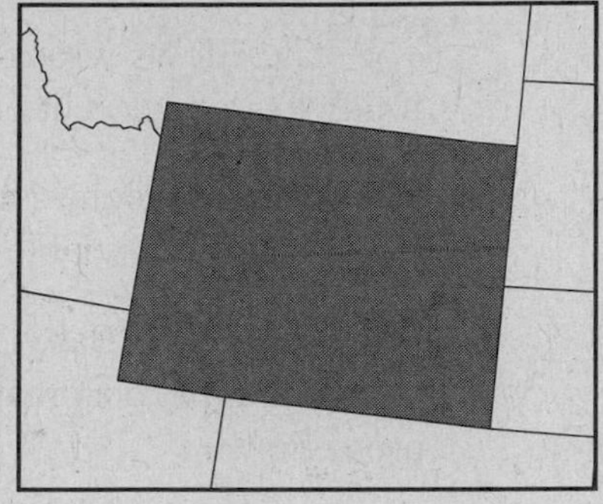

Wyoming lacks basic protections for human life. For example, Wyoming does not require informed consent for abortion; does not mandate minimum health and safety standards for abortion clinics; does not protect unborn victims of violence; does not ban human cloning or destructive embryo research; and does not criminalize assisted suicide. Unfortunately, it considered very few life-affirming measures in 2009.

ABORTION:

- Wyoming does not have an informed consent law for abortion.
- A physician may not perform an abortion on an unemancipated minor under the age of 18 who is not in active military service or who has not lived independently and apart from her parents for more than six months without receiving the consent of one parent or a court order.
- Wyoming taxpayers are not required to fund abortions except when necessary to preserve the woman's life, or the pregnancy is the result of rape or incest.
- Only a physician licensed to practice medicine in the state using accepted medical procedures may perform an abortion.
- No abortion may be performed after viability unless necessary to protect the woman from "imminent peril that substantially endangers her life or health."
- The state has an enforceable abortion reporting law, but does not require the reporting of information to the Centers for Disease Control and Prevention (CDC). The measure pertains to both surgical and nonsurgical abortions and requires abortion providers to report short-term complications.
- The state requires health maintenance organizations to cover prescription contraception or family planning services.

LEGAL RECOGNITION OF UNBORN AND NEWLY BORN:

- Wyoming law does not recognize the unborn child as a potential victim of homicide or assault. However, Wyoming law does define attacks on a pregnant woman resulting in a miscarriage or stillbirth as a criminal assault.

- The state allows wrongful death (civil) actions only when an unborn child is born alive following a negligent or criminal act and dies thereafter.

- Wyoming law requires the "commonly accepted means of care shall be employed in the treatment of any viable infant aborted alive with any chance of survival."

- Wyoming has a "Baby Moses" law, establishing a safe haven for mothers to legally leave their infants at designated places and ensuring the infants receive appropriate care and protection.

BIOETHICS LAWS:

- Wyoming has not banned human cloning or destructive embryo research, but it does ban fetal experimentation.

- Wyoming maintains no comprehensive measures regulating assisted reproductive technologies.

END OF LIFE LAWS:

- Wyoming has not enacted a statutory prohibition against assisted suicide. Moreover, since the state does not recognize common law crimes (including assisting in suicide), the legal status of assisted suicide in Wyoming is unclear.

HEALTHCARE RIGHTS OF CONSCIENCE LAWS:

Participation in Abortions:

- A person is not required to participate in an abortion or in any act that assists in the performance of an abortion.

- A healthcare provider's conscientious objection to participation in abortions may not be the basis for civil liability, discrimination in employment, or the imposition of other sanctions by a hospital, person, firm, association, or group. Moreover, a healthcare provider injured because of a violation of his or her right of conscience may bring a civil action for damages or injunctive relief.

- A private hospital, institution, or facility is not required to perform or to admit a woman for the purposes of performing an abortion.

- A private hospital, institution, or facility's conscientious objection to permitting an abortion within its facility or admitting a patient for an abortion may not be a basis for civil liability.

Participation in Research Harmful to Human Life

- Wyoming currently provides no protection for the rights of healthcare providers who conscientiously object to participation in human cloning, destructive embryo research, or other forms of immoral medical research.

WHAT HAPPENED IN 2009:

- Wyoming considered legislation requiring abortion providers to perform an ultrasound prior to abortion and to report the use of abortifacient drugs. The state also considered legislation relating to unborn victims of violence.
- Wyoming considered a measure criminalizing assisted suicide.
- The state did not consider any measures related to bioethics or healthcare rights of conscience.

RECOMMENDATIONS FOR WYOMING		
	Short-term Priorities	**Additional Goals**
ABORTION		
Informed Consent	Comprehensive informed consent with reflection period	
Parental Involvement		
State Rights & Policies		
Abortion Funding	Ban on use of state funds for abortion counseling or referrals	
Abortion Provider Requirements		Comprehensive abortion clinic regulations
Abortion Bans		
Regulation of Abortifacients	Regulation of RU-486	
PCCs Support		Direct funding of PCCs
Abortion Reporting		
LEGAL RECOGNITION AND PROTECTION FOR UNBORN & NEWLY BORN		
Fetal Homicide	Comprehensive protection for unborn victims of violence	
Assault on Unborn		
Prohibitions on Wrongful Birth & Wrongful Life Lawsuits		
Permit Wrongful Death Lawsuits		

Born-Alive Infant Protection		
Abandoned Infant Protection		
BIOETHICS		
Human Cloning		Ban on human cloning
DER		Ban on DER
State Funding of DER	Ban on state funding of DER	
ART & IVF		Any medically-appropriate regulation of ART/IVF
END OF LIFE		
Assisted Suicide	Statutory prohibition on assisted suicide	
Pain Management Education		
RIGHTS OF CONSCIENCE		
Protection for Individual Providers	Comprehensive ROC protection	
Protection for Institutions	Comprehensive ROC protection	
Protection for Payers	Comprehensive ROC protection	

Appendix

ABOUT AMERICANS UNITED FOR LIFE

Americans United for Life (AUL) is the nation's foremost public interest law and policy organization working to pass pro-life laws in state legislatures and defend those laws in court.

AUL's experts work hand in hand every day with state legislators, policy makers, and activists, helping pass laws that:

- Reduce abortion.
- Address current and emerging bioethical issues.
- Defend those people at the end-of-life.
- Protect the right of conscience of all healthcare providers.

Once a state passes a new pro-life law, AUL works with the state's Attorney General to defend the law in court.

Founded in 1971, Americans United for Life is the oldest national pro-life organization in the country. Over the past 39 years, AUL has been a leader in the fight to overturn *Roe v. Wade* and restore to the people the right of self-government on the issue of abortion. AUL has been involved in every United States Supreme Court case on abortion since *Roe* was decided in 1973.

AUL's work promotes a culture of life through the law. For assistance on legislation, questions about litigation, or to have AUL host a briefing for legislators and policy makers in your state, please contact:

AMERICANS UNITED FOR LIFE

Washington DC
655 15th St NW, Suite 410
Washington, DC 20005
(202) 289-1478

Chicago
310 South Peoria Street, Suite 500
Chicago, IL 60607
(312) 568-4700

Info@AUL.org
www.AUL.org

DEFENDING LIFE ONLINE

AUL's annual publication, *Defending Life: Proven Strategies for a Pro-Life America*, is the definitive legal guide to abortion, bioethics, healthcare rights of conscience, and the end of life. Cutting through the murky cloud of media chatter and controversy, *Defending Life* provides comprehensive, timely, and thought-provoking information to anyone who wants to understand key pro-life issues and utilize proven strategies to address them.

For convenient online access, *Defending Life 2010* is available at **DL.AUL.org**. In addition to the entirety of the contents in the volume edition, the online version includes supplementary material and resources, as well as periodic updates.

THE AUL STATE SUPREME COURT PROJECT

When *Roe v. Wade* is ultimately overturned, the abortion issue will change from being a significantly federal issue to a largely state issue, and state supreme courts will have the final say in challenges to abortion-related laws. Instead of focusing on one national President, one Senate, and one Supreme Court, the pro-life movement will need to focus on 50 state governors, 50 state legislatures, and 50 state supreme courts.

Detailed information of state supreme courts and their judges/justices will provide the insight necessary for pro-life forces to write life-affirming laws tailored to meet the needs of a particular state. Information on state supreme courts will also provide the guidance necessary to formulate the most effective plans for enacting life-affirming laws that will be upheld by specific state supreme courts.

In addition, retention elections for state supreme court judges/justices take place every year. As such, voters need to be as informed as possible about the ideology, judicial demeanor, and voting record of every judge/justice who stands for retention. Unlike federal judges with lifetime appointments, state supreme court members are subject to regular retention elections and are accountable to the voters in their states/districts. Thus, state supreme court judges/justices face the possibility of being voted off the bench for their records while on the bench. As voters become more informed about their state's judiciary, more activist judges would likely see their tenures cut short by the voters.

To that end, Americans United for Life initiated the State Supreme Court Project, an in-depth look at the 50 state supreme courts' treatment of life issues and an examination of judicial restraint and/or activism at the state level. We commissioned 50 white papers, covering the status of each state's supreme court, examining their record on life issues, and examining judicial restraint and/or activism within that state.

AUL's State Supreme Court Project website has compiled all 50 state supreme court white papers into an online pro-life reference on the status of state supreme courts around the country. Summaries of all white papers are also available in PDF format.

All white papers and summaries, as well as analyses and other resources, can be accessed at: **www.AULStateSupremeCourtProject.org**.

The AUL State Supreme Court Project is just one way that Americans United for Life is preparing for the day after *Roe*. We invite you to explore our main website, **www.AUL.org**, for more information on our work.

FIGHTFOCA.COM

The time to Fight FOCA is now.

The Freedom of Choice Act (FOCA) would eliminate every restriction on abortion nationwide.

- FOCA will do away with state laws on parental involvement, on partial birth abortion, and on all other protections for women and the unborn.
- FOCA will compel taxpayer funding of abortions.
- FOCA will force faith-based hospitals and healthcare facilities to perform abortions.

FOCA would erase these laws and prevent states from enacting similar protective measures in the future.

FightFOCA.com is a project of AUL Action. In addition to providing resources and analyses on the threat of FOCA, **www.FightFOCA.com** enables concerned pro-life citizens with the means to make their voices heard and stand against the threat of FOCA.

AUL ACTION

Washington DC
655 15th St NW, Suite 410
Washington, DC 20005
(202) 289-1478

Chicago
310 South Peoria Street, Suite 500
Chicago, IL 60607
(312) 568-4700

AUL Action, 501(c)(4) organization, is the legislative arm of Americans United for Life (AUL).

REALHEALTHCARERESPECTSLIFE.COM

With several competing bills in Congress aiming to reform America's health care system, it is imperative that those who value life from conception to natural death make their voices heard in Washington.

RealHealthCareRespectsLife.com features the AUL legal team's expert analysis on the health care reform plans currently in the House and Senate. Learn how these plans would mandate taxpayer-funded abortions, deprive medical providers of their rights of conscience, and possibly result in denial of care for the elderly and the disabled. In addition to providing resources and analyses on health care reform, **www.RealHealthCareRespectsLife.com** enables concerned pro-life citizens with the means to make their voices heard.

RealHealthCareRespectsLife.com is a project of AUL Action.

AUL ACTION

Washington DC
655 15th St NW, Suite 410
Washington, DC 20005
(202) 289-1478

Chicago
310 South Peoria Street, Suite 500
Chicago, IL 60607
(312) 568-4700

AUL Action, 501(c)(4) organization, is the legislative arm of Americans United for Life (AUL).

ABOUT THE AUL FELLOWS PROGRAM

Every summer, students from across the country apply for a limited number of openings in the Americans United for Life Fellows Program. Law students and undergraduate students with an interest in pro-life law come to Washington, D.C., for a summer internship that is unparalleled.

LAW STUDENTS

AUL accepts select 1L and 2L students for up to eight weeks each summer at the AUL headquarters in Washington, D.C. Mentored by an AUL attorney, each fellow is tasked with a special legal project. During their summer, they meet regularly with AUL staff in conjunction with their work. All law student fellows receive a salary.

UNDERGRADUATE STUDENTS

AUL accepts select undergraduate students for work in the communications and research departments. Areas assigned depend upon each fellow's talents, interests, and specific organization needs.

Qualifications for becoming an AUL Fellow include a firm commitment to life issues and demonstrated excellence both inside and outside the classroom. Additionally, we look for individuals who stand out to the faculty of their school.

For more information, contact Americans United for Life at **(312) 568-4700**, by email at **fellows@AUL.org**, or by visiting **www.AUL.org**.

ABOUT THE AUL EXTERNSHIP PROGRAM

Each year, AUL accepts highly-qualified and motivated law students to serve as legal externs during the Fall and Spring semesters.

Externs work closely with AUL attorneys in researching, drafting, and editing scholarly articles. These articles are published in a variety of resources and venues, including AUL's *Defending Life*, law reviews, national magazines, and websites. Externs also undertake legal research and drafting of amicus briefs, model legislation and public policy educational material on life issues including abortion, bioethics, healthcare rights of conscience, and the end of life.

Candidates are not required to be in the Washington, D.C., or Chicago areas, but must be available by telephone and email. The externships are unpaid and may be undertaken for credit (as approved by the extern's law school) or to fulfill other graduation requirements.

Qualifications include excellent legal research and writing skills, demonstrated initiative and attention to detail, and an ability to work with minimal direct supervision.

For more information, contact Americans United for Life at **(312) 568-4700**, by email at **Resumes@AUL.org**, or by visiting **www.AUL.org**.